Modern Metalworking

by

JOHN R. WALKER

South Holland, Illinois
THE GOODHEART-WILLCOX COMPANY, INC.
Publishers

INTRODUCTION

MODERN METALWORKING emphasizes the important place metals occupy in our everyday lives; it explores the numerous metalworking career opportunities. It is designed to provide a broad experience in metalworking through the use of tools, machines, and materials that are basic to this important area.

MODERN METALWORKING supplies basic information on tools, materials, and procedures used in metalworking occupations. It covers both hand and machine-tool operations, and supplies background knowledge on industrial equipment and processes.

Metal is used for many different purposes. It is used to manufacture such items as jet and rocket engines, where the material must withstand terrific heat. It is used to make buckets for mammoth earth movers, where toughness is a must. And it is used to make modern aircraft, where light weight and great strength are required.

Metals are used to make things of beauty such as jewelry, tableware, furniture, and works of art. Fuel that powers nuclear submarines is a metal. It needs only a few pounds to generate enough power to propel a submarine around the world. Still another combination of metals has the unique ability to convert sunlight to electrical energy. A thin layer of metal only a microinch (1/1,000,000 in.) thick makes it possible for a computer to make split-second computations.

Metal has been used in some way during the production of almost everything we eat, see, feel, hear, smell, and touch.

With so much of our daily living depending upon metals, it is essential that we learn something about them, how they are worked, and the industry that uses them. The following paragraphs may answer your question, "Why study about metals?"

1. The metalworking industries in the United States employ more workers than any other industries. There is a great possibility that you will be employed in this area of our economy. This course will increase your understanding of the occupational requirements and opportunities in this field.

2. By studying and participating in the metalworking areas, you have the opportunity to develop and practice basic skills necessary for vocation competence. These basic skills will also enable

Library of Congress Catalog Card Number 84-27891
International Standard Book Number 0-87006-509-2
23456789-85-9876

Library of Congress Cataloging in Publication Data

Walker, John R., 1924-
Modern metalworking.

Includes index.
1. Metal-work.
I. Title.
TS205.W35   1985   671   84-27891
ISBN 0-87006-509-2

you to plan and complete the operations necessary to turn out high quality, and professional-looking metal products.

3. If you are a potential engineering student, you will have the opportunity to acquire information and develop skills that are considered basic to many engineering programs. These same skills may enable you to secure a better than average paying job during your summer vacation.

4. The technical knowledge you acquire may help you to advance more rapidly in the Armed Forces, should you decide to make this your career.

5. The basic metalworking skills you learn are applicable to many areas of industrial endeavor. You will be able to readily adapt to new technologies when they are introduced to industry in the future.

6. Many of the major items you will purchase during your lifetime (automobiles, hand and power tools, appliances, etc.) will be made from metal. This course will help you develop an appreciation for well-designed products. It will also help you expand your ability to select, care for, and use home and industrial quality products wisely.

7. You will learn and practice safe work habits.

8. The problem-solving situations you encounter will give you opportunities to make practical applications of the math and science you have studied.

9. Metalworking is a very interesting and challenging area of study. You will find many opportunities to develop leadership skills.

10. Perhaps you just like to work with your hands. If so, this will give you a chance to satisfy this desire.

John R. Walker

CONTENTS

The launch of the Space Shuttle is a direct result of constant and rapid technological growth.

Unit 1

TECHNOLOGY AND CAREERS

Technology has done more to shape the world we live in than all other forces. As technical advances continue at an ever increasing tempo, Fig. 1-1, "technology" has become the catchphrase of an era. And because of these continued advances, careers in technological fields are constantly growing.

In this chapter, the evolution, current status, and types of technology will be discussed, along with careers made possible by advances in technology.

Fig. 1-1. Astronaut Bruce McCandless II on an extravehicular activity (EVA) using a nitrogen propelled, hand controlled device called the Manned Maneuvering Unit (MMU). This device will make possible the construction of a large space station. This photo was taken from the Space Shuttle Challenger.   (NASA)

AN INTRODUCTION TO TECHNOLOGY

Technology started more than a million years ago when people first learned to make and use tools. The first tools, Fig. 1-2, crude though they were, made human survival possible.

From the stone age until about two hundred years ago, technical advances such as hollowing a log to make a boat, weaving, printing, making sails, wheels, and plows, were important contributions to the growth of civilization. However, farming was the most important occupation of almost all people. Unless a town or city was nearby, only enough food was grown to meet the needs of the immediate family. Most other necessities—cloth, and clothing, furniture, tools—were made from wool, leather, and wood from the farm.

Slightly more than two hundred years ago, changes started to occur that completely altered the way people lived. It eventually became known as the INDUSTRIAL REVOLUTION (1760s to 1790s). Industry was taken out of the home and handwork was replaced by machinery. Mechanical power sources (the water wheel then the steam engine)

Fig. 1-2. Technology started more than a million years ago when people first learned to make and use tools of stone.

started to be used in manufacturing and transportation.

Industrialization spread rapidly, Fig. 1-3. Scientific knowledge was applied to problems of production. Automatic machinery was invented and perfected. Mass-production techniques were developed and put into use.

Since the Industrial Revolution, technological development has become even more influential in our lives. It would require many hours to list the technical advances of the past two hundred years and how they affect what we do every day. One basic effect is that technology enables people to do more work in less time, thus increasing leisure time. Technology has also provided people with objects and gadgets to use and enjoy in their free time.

THE TECHNOLOGICAL REVOLUTION

There is every indication that we are experiencing a technological revolution. Consider these recently developed and developing innovations:

1. Landing on the moon and returning safely was the first step to the stars.
2. Space shuttle flights are now routine, Fig. 1-4.
3. Research continues into artificial intelligence (AI) which enables computers to simulate certain human thought processes.
4. Computer aided processes that speed and improve engineering and design are being used with increased frequency in automated manufacturing (the latest techniques used are called flexible manufacturing systems, FMS), Fig. 1-5. FMS can be programmed to produce several different parts simultaneously, or can be quickly reprogrammed to accommodate design changes.

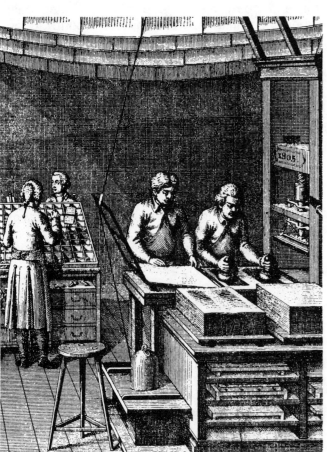

Fig. 1-3. The invention of printing from movable type made printed matter, and the ideas it contained, available to everyone. Until this time, only a few people could read because there were few books. Those that were available had been laboriously lettered by hand.
(Gutenberg Museum, Mainz, W. Germany)

Fig. 1-4. Space shuttle flights are now routine. With experience gained by these flights, humans will land on Mars in your lifetime. Just think, the Wright Brothers first flew in 1903! (NASA)

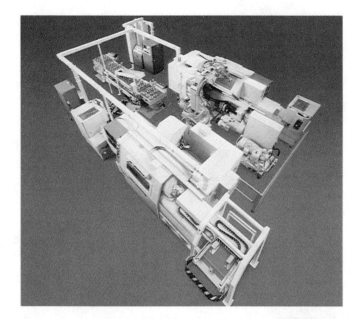

Fig. 1-5. A flexible manufacturing system, the latest in automated manufacturing. Computer controlled, it manufacturers quality parts while virtually unattended. However, highly skilled and educated technicians are required for its manufacture and maintenance. (Cincinnati Milacron)

5. New metals and materials that are superior to existing substances are being developed continually, Fig. 1-6.
6. Robotics research is producing robots capable of performing complex tasks to ever more demanding specifications, Fig. 1-7. They can work in environments that would be unsafe for humans.

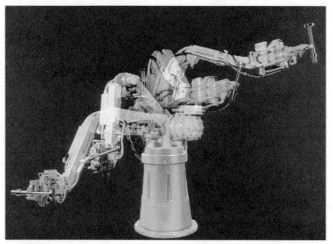

Fig. 1-7. Robots are capable of performing work in environments that would be unsafe for humans. (Cincinnati Milacron)

While the preceding are some positive effects of technology, technology also has many negative effects. For example, with advanced technology, Fig. 1-8, there will be little need for uneducated and unskilled workers.

The careless use of technology has also caused environmental problems and damage. For example, acid rain is destroying our lakes and forests.

Fig. 1-6. New metals and materials are available today to build this gigantic flying wing freight aircraft. You can get some idea of its size from the people and trailer truck in the foreground. (NASA)

Fig. 1-8. This master computer control station continually monitors 58 robots on the robogate welding line at this Chrysler assembly plant. The high technology system applied spot welds to 97 percent of the weld locations on each van. Plants like this have little need for uneducated and unskilled workers. (Chrysler Corporation)

Highly radioactive spent fuel elements from atomic generating plants are a constant source of environmental problems. Likewise, generating plants that have exceeded their usefulness (most are designed with an operating life of 25 years) cause great concern.

Toxic wastes from some manufacturing processes are difficult to dispose of, and the affect of dangerous chemicals and substances already stored in special dumps is difficult to determine.

Automobiles are responsible for the death and injury of thousands of people each year.

Ironically, only innovative technology (new ideas and approaches to problems) can solve and/or correct the problems that have been created, Fig. 1-9.

TYPES OF TECHNOLOGY

TECHNOLOGY is the know-how linking science and the industrial arts. Its purpose is to solve problems and enhance (improve in value and/or quality) the natural and human-made environment. In the process of doing this, creativity (inventiveness), human skills, tools, machines, and resources are employed, Fig. 1-10.

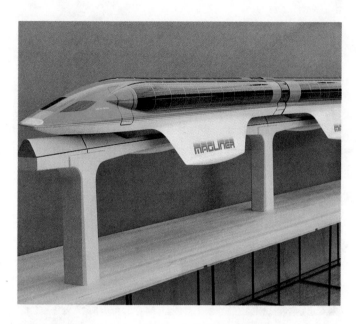

Fig. 1-10. Model of a proposed train of the future called Mag-Lev. Fast, quiet and resistant to derailing, the magnetically levitated train will travel at over 300 miles per hour. It will use super-conductors (transmits huge currents without electrical resistance, and thus sustains intense, steady magnetic fields) to levitate, guide, and propel the train.
(Electromotive Division, General Motors Corp.)

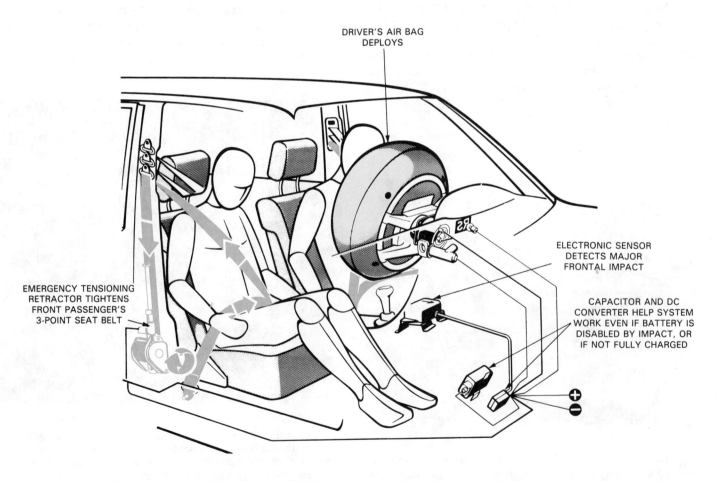

Fig. 1-9. Innovative technology like this automatic air bag system would save thousands of lives yearly if placed in each car. (Mercedes-Benz of North America, Inc.)

HIGH TECHNOLOGY and STATE-OF-THE-ART TECHNOLOGY are terms mentioned often in the media. They simply are areas of technology that employ the very latest ideas, techniques, research, tools, and machines available, Fig. 1-11.

There are many facets (sides) to technology. When applied to special areas, they receive designations such as AGRICULTURAL TECHNOLOGY, MEDICAL TECHNOLOGY, INDUSTRIAL TECHNOLOGY, and METALWORKING TECHNOLOGY.

AGRICULTURAL TECHNOLOGY pertains to our food and related products. MEDICAL TECHNOLOGY is concerned with our health and well-being. INDUSTRIAL TECHNOLOGY deals with the design, research, development, and production techniques that convert raw materials into finished products. METALWORKING TECHNOLOGY is an area of industrial technology that is involved with the fields of machining, forging, casting, and the like.

This book will be concerned with the many aspects of metalworking technology and related areas.

Can YOU name any other areas of technology?

Fig. 1-11. Another view of a computer controlled robotic welding system. Lasers are employed to gauge position and fit of body panels. (Chrysler Corporation)

METALWORKING TECHNOLOGY

Through metalworking technology, it is possible to process raw materials into finished products, Fig. 1-12. This, however, is not always an easy task—financially or technically.

Fig. 1-12. This die for molding plastic model cars started as a block of metal. Metalworking technology, along with human skills and creativity, have converted the metal block into a precisely made tool to produce a product for the hobbyist. (MRC/Tamiya)

Technically, metalworking is the process of shaping things out of metal. This requires a vast amount of time and people, working toward a finished product.

Financially, a PROFIT must be made if the company is to remain in business. Profit is the income of a business AFTER all expenses—salaries, raw material purchases, utilities—have been paid. Furthermore, a profit is necessary if people are to risk their time, ability, and money in a business venture.

Profit can be a long time coming. Large projects like aircraft, cars, computers, and robots, for example, take several years from the original concept to the first finished product, Fig. 1-13. Many millions (often billions) of dollars will be invested in tools, machines, raw materials, and plants before anything is produced. In addition, the talents of thousands of highly skilled people contribute to the design, development, and manufacture of a product and they subsequently must be paid.

Many of the people have spent several years getting advanced training and/or education to perform their jobs. They oftentimes possess highly technical skills, which are necessary for successful completion of a job. A great deal of thought and effort have gone into their career decisions.

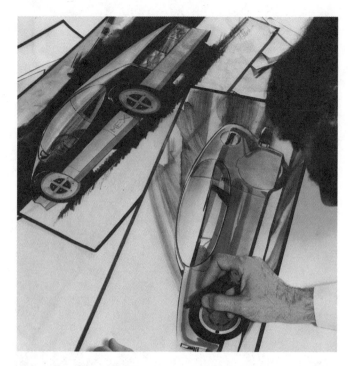

Fig. 1-13. It takes many years from the original concept of a car until the first production model is ready for sale. The talents of thousands of skilled people contribute to the design, development, and production of such a product. Many millions (often billions) of dollars will be invested in tools, machines, materials, and plants before the first dollar of profit is made. (General Motors Corp.)

Fig. 1-14. Shipbuilding is a direct use of metals. The 31 ft. diameter bronze propeller of this 265,000 dwt tanker dwarfs a shipyard employee as the ship is ready to be floated out of the basin at Bethlehem Steel Corporation's Sparrows Point, Maryland shipyard. The rudder behind the propeller has the cubic capacity of a normal, modern house. (Bethlehem Steel Corp.)

Have you ever given any thought to the choice of a career? Like the people mentioned in the previous paragraph, your choice may be one of the most important you can make. Your choice will affect the quality of your life for many years to come.

CAREERS IN THE METALWORKING INDUSTRIES

Many people want a career with challenges and activities they enjoy. Their philosophy is, ''You only work when you dislike what you are doing.'' Others are satisfied with whatever job comes along. In which category are YOU?

If you are looking for a career that is both interesting and challenging, the field of metalworking might be your choice. It can provide many opportunities. You may not realize it, but chances are you will be employed in an occupation that is made possible, either directly, Fig. 1-14, or indirectly, Fig. 1-15, by the metalworking industries. The scope of the industries is that great.

Your choice of employment in metalworking may be classed as SEMISKILLED, SKILLED, TECHNI—CAL, or PROFESSIONAL. One of the basic requirements, if you want to advance in your chosen field, is a continuing educational program. As jobs become more competitive and complex, persons

Fig. 1-15. Even though metal is not used directly in developing the aerodynamic shape of this new car model, the designers must know metal characteristics—how it can be formed, welded, etc. Otherwise, the vehicle might never get into production. (Ford Motor Company)

with a higher level of education and up-to-date specialized training will have a better opportunity for securing and retaining employment, Fig. 1-16.

There is little need for unskilled workers (those people in jobs that require little or no training) in a modern technical world, Fig. 1-17. The school dropout, and those students who do not plan their continuing educational program carefully, find it very difficult to locate satisfying employment with any sort of future. Employers prefer workers who have completed high school and acquired salable skills.

Fig. 1-17. Modern technology, like these robot welders, is eliminating many unskilled and semiskilled jobs. They do the job faster and better, and are not affected by the welding fumes. (Pontiac Motor Division, GMC)

Fig. 1-16. As jobs become more competitive and complex, men and women with a higher level of education and up-to-date specialized training will have a better opportunity for securing and retaining employment. These specialists are modifying the design of a part, using a computer-aided design (CAD) system. (Information Displays, Inc.)

Jobs in metalworking industries fall into the four general categories previously mentioned:
1. SEMISKILLED.
2. SKILLED.
3. TECHNICAL.
4. PROFESSIONAL.

SEMISKILLED WORKERS

SEMISKILLED WORKERS are those who perform operations that do not require a high degree of skill or training. Most of the work is routine and may be classified as follows:
1. Those who serve as helpers to skilled workers.
2. Machine tenders who perform simple, repetitive operations that can be learned relatively quickly.
3. Those who do a limited number of assembly operations in manufacturing a product, Fig. 1-18.

Fig. 1-18. Semiskilled workers perform a limited number of assembly or forming operations, such as shaping aluminum skin fuselage sections for the F-16. They will perform these operations over and over, as long as the aircraft is in production. (General Dynamics)

4. Those who inspect and test manufactured products to insure they are properly made and operate satisfactorily.

In general, semiskilled workers are told what and how work is to be done. There is little opportunity for advancement out of semiskilled jobs, without additional study and training. Most semiskilled work is found in production shops where there are great numbers of repeat operations.

SKILLED WORKERS

Skilled workers are found in all areas of metalworking. A few of the specialty fields are welding, Fig. 1-19, music instrument manufacturing, Fig. 1-20, shipbuilding, sheet metal work, and steel erection, Fig. 1-21, and in the manufacture of aircraft, automobiles, and other forms of transportation, Fig. 1-22.

Fig. 1-20. Musical instrument makers are highly skilled artisans and usually spend several years learning their trade. (King Musical Instruments)

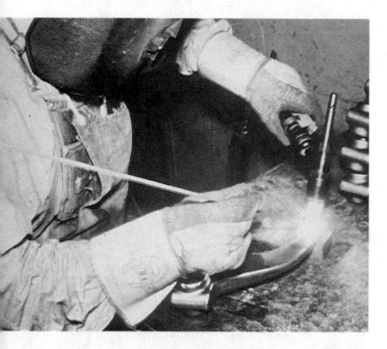

Fig. 1-19. Welders are classified as skilled craftworkers. They must be familiar with metal characteristics and able to read and understand drawings. They work indoors and outdoors, in all kinds of weather. (Lincoln Electric Co.)

Fig. 1-21.Steel erectors fabricated these buildings. Both of the buildings are framed with steel. (Bethlehem Steel Corp.)

Many of today's skilled workers received their training in APPRENTICE PROGRAMS, Fig. 1-23. The period of instruction usually required four or more years of study with experienced craftworkers. In addition to working in the shop, an apprentice studied related subjects such as math, science, English, print reading, metallurgy, safety, and production techniques. Upon successful completion of

an apprentice program, the worker was capable of performing the exacting work and skills of the trade, Fig. 1-24.

Today, however, the number of apprentice programs being offered is on the decline. Most workers

Fig. 1-22. Aircraft machinists and sheet metal workers must be skilled in their trade in order to work to the close tolerances required. A mistake can be dangerous and risky for the pilot and means the loss of a very expensive aircraft. (General Dynamics)

Fig. 1-23. An apprentice studies under an experienced craftworker in a carefully planned program. The training also includes the study of manufacturing processes, math, English, science, and other related subjects.

Fig. 1-24. After completing an apprentice program workers are capable of performing the exacting work and skills of their trade. This tool and die maker is checking the dies for molding a plastic pattern used to cast a complex jet engine component. This process must meet exacting quality control standards. (Precision Castparts Corp.)

now entering the metalworking trades receive their training in the ARMED FORCES, Fig. 1-25, or in vocational/technical programs offered in high schools and community colleges. Many community college programs are offered in conjunction with local industries.

TECHNICIANS

Modern technology has brought about a demand for persons capable of doing complex work of a highly technical nature. These men and women are called TECHNICIANS. Many colleges and community colleges offer two year technical programs. The course of study stresses math, science, English, computer science, manufacturing, and production techniques, Fig. 1-26.

The technician assists the engineer by constructing and testing experimental devices and equipment. He or she aids in compiling statistical information, making cost estimates, and preparing technical reports. In some manufacturing plants, the person who programs parts for production by numerical control (automatic machine control us-

Fig. 1-26. New metalworking technology has brought about a demand for persons to do complex work of a highly technical nature. These men and women are called TECHNICIANS. This young woman is training in and studying machine tool operations.

ing numerical instructions coded on perforated tape, punch cards, or magnetic tape) is classified as a technician. In the same category are the specialists who repair and maintain numerically controlled machines and robotic equipment.

THE PROFESSIONS

The professions offer many excellent opportunities in the field of metalworking.

TEACHING, Fig. 1-27, is one of the most satisfying of the professions and is a field students too often overlook. The teacher of industrial arts, industrial, vocational, and technical education is in a most fortunate position. It is a challenging profession that offers freedom not found in most other professions.

Four years of training at the college level is required, and while industrial experience is not a prerequisite, it will prove helpful.

ENGINEERING is a fast growing and challenging profession. Engineers use mathematics and science to develop new products and processes in industry, Fig. 1-28.

Fig. 1-25. The Army, and other branches of the Armed Forces, offer excellent opportunities for learning a trade and getting paid while you study.   (U.S. Army)

Fig. 1-27. Teaching is a very satisfying profession. Statistics show that there will be a steady demand for teachers of industrial education for many years.

A bachelor's degree in engineering is usually the minimum requirement for entering the engineering profession. However, some men and women have been able to enter the profession (without a degree) after several years of experience as drafters or engineering technicians. They were required, however, to take some college-level training.

Fig. 1-28. Engineers, with the aid of mathematics and science, use their knowledge to develop new products and processes for industry. One of the newest techniques they use is CAD/CAM (computer aided design/computer aided manufacturing). The computer permits complex design studies to be made in much less time than was previously required. (California Computer Products, CALCOMP)

There are many types of engineers. INDUSTRIAL ENGINEERS are primarily concerned with the safest and most efficient ways to utilize machines, materials, and personnel. In some cases, they design special machinery and equipment, Fig. 1-29.

MECHANICAL ENGINEERS, Fig. 1-30, are normally responsible for the design and development of new machines, devices, and ideas. They are also involved with the redesign and improvement of existing equipment. Some mechanical engineers specialize in the various areas of transportation (ships, transit vehicles, etc.).

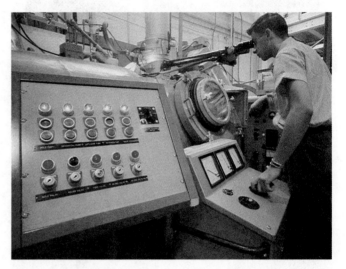

Fig. 1-29. Industrial engineers were responsible for the design and development of this electron beam welder.

Fig. 1-30. Some mechanical engineers specialize in various areas of transportation. This monorail is under serious study by several large cities that are searching for dependable high speed transportation systems.

The TOOL AND MANUFACTURING ENGINEER devises the methods and means to manufacture the products designed by mechanical engineers.

CIVIL ENGINEERS, Fig. 1-31, design and construct buildings, bridges, ports, and the like. These structures use vast quantities of metal in their construction.

AEROSPACE ENGINEERS, Fig. 1-32, design and develop aircraft and aerospace vehicles.

METALLURGICAL ENGINEERS, Fig. 1-33, are responsible for the development and testing of metals that are used in products or manufacturing processes.

Fig. 1-33. An experimental melt is poured from a 300-pound induction furnace at Bethlehem Steel Corporation's Homer Research Laboratory. Metallurgical engineers are responsible for testing and developing metals that eventually will be used in manufactured products.   (Bethlehem Steel Corp.)

Fig. 1-31. The bridge deck, which is supported by a fixed arch span, of the Lewiston-Queenston Bridge nears completion. The bridge is located on the Niagara River, only a few miles from the Falls. Its 1000-foot long span is the longest of its type and was designed by civil engineers.   (Bethlehem Steel Corp.)

Fig. 1-32. The space shuttle was designed by aerospace engineers. Support systems like the launch tower and crawler-transporter were the responsibility of civil, mechanical, and industrial engineers.   (NASA)

MANAGEMENT

MANAGEMENT consists of the people who plan, direct, and supervise the operation of an industrial organization, Fig. 1-34. They bring together and coordinate natural resources, capital, labor, and other factors needed to reach a carefully chosen goal.

LEADERSHIP IN AMERICAN TECHNOLOGY

Modern metalworking technology requires a highly skilled and educated workforce. However, the nature of American technology is such that strong and dynamic LEADERSHIP is also required at ALL LEVELS if it is to be competitive with other technologically-oriented countries.

LEADERSHIP is the ability to be a leader. A LEADER is a person who is in charge or in command. The quality of leadership usually determines whether an organization will be a success or failure, Fig. 1-35.

Fig. 1-34. Management must make the decisions to manufacture a new product. These decisions may end up costing millions (even billions) of dollars. The design and construction of this huge mill/drill machine was one such decision. It automatically positions and clamps the sports car body in place, pierces four slots, drills 39 vertical holes, machines 39 horizontal surfaces, verifies that the operations are complete, and unloads the body onto a conveyor line. Tolerances are held to within 0.05 mm in location, size, and height.
(Pontiac Motor Division, GMC)

PLANT CLOSED

Fig. 1-35. The quality of leadership usually determines whether an organization will be a success or a failure.

WHAT MAKES A GOOD LEADER?

No one is quite sure what motivates people to work enthusiastically for one leader yet accomplish little (and be very unhappy) under another leader in the same situation. Strange as it may seem, this motivation is seldom based on standard rewards such as increased salaries and improved working conditions.

There are no tests that will determine whether a person will be a strong leader. However, studies have shown that strong, dynamic leaders seem to have the following traits (qualities) in common:

VISION. Knows what must be done. Has short and long range goals with well defined plans, and a schedule to achieve these goals. Is never satisfied with the status quo (existing conditions or situations). Is always looking for ways to improve things. Enjoys the challenge of leadership and can inspire others.

COMMUNICATION. Can communicate in such a way that will engage the assistance and cooperation of others. Has the ability to create situations where the energies and ideas of others can be harnessed to achieve desired goals and/or results.

PERSISTENCE. Has the ability to stay on course regardless of the obstacles met. However, is flexible and will make changes when new ideas emerge. Will work long hours to achieve goals.

ORGANIZATIONAL ABILITIES. Knows how to organize and direct the activities of the group. Learns from mistakes and uses the resulting knowledge to improve efficiency and performance. Is tactful but can be autocratic (cooperation demanded of others within the group) when necessary.

RESPONSIBILITY. Will accept responsibility for actions, but readily gives credit and recognition to others when deserved or warranted.

DELEGATES AUTHORITY. Not reluctant or afraid to make assignments that provide opportunities for others in the group to take on leadership roles. Helps others develop leadership skills.

GETTING LEADERSHIP EXPERIENCE

How can you get experience in leadership? The Industrial Arts/Industrial Education program, and other areas in your school and clubs offer leadership training to students willing to take advantage of the opportunities.

Many programs provide leadership experience through student industrial arts/industrial education organizations such as the AMERICAN INDUSTRIAL ARTS STUDENT ASSOCIATION (AIASA) AND THE VOCATIONAL INDUSTRIAL CLUBS OF AMERICA (VICA). They are designed to develop leadership and personal abilities as they relate to the industrial-technical world, Fig. 1-36.

WHAT TO EXPECT AS A LEADER

As a leader you will be expected to set a good example. The responsibility of leadership also means that you must get all members of the group involved in activities. This requires encouragement and tact.

A good leader is not expected to have answers for every problem the group encounters. Members should be motivated to recommend possible solutions. It is up to the leader to decide which to use.

Fig. 1-36. Student organizations like the American Industrial Arts Student Association (AIASA) offers many opportunities for developing leadership.

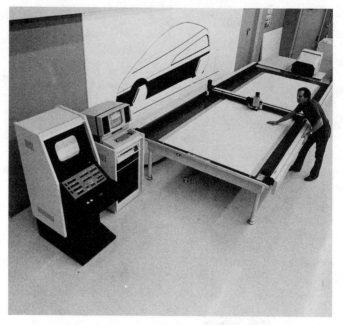

Fig. 1-37. Advanced technology is continually creating occupations that did not previously exist. This photo shows an engineer at General Motors Advanced Concept Center developing a concept vehicle for a future product, programmed on a computer-controlled flat-bed plotter.
(General Motors Corp.)

Leadership is not easy, or without difficulties. Decisions must be made that some group members may not like. People (even friends) may have to be reprimanded or dismissed for being imcompetent or for trying to take advantage of the group.

If you think you have the traits of a strong leader (or believe you can develop them) and can handle the unpleasant tasks that are part of leadership, by all means, look into joining groups where it will be possible for you to become a leader.

WHAT TO EXPECT WHEN YOU ENTER THE WORLD OF WORK

You will be very disappointed if you think that graduation means the end of training and study. Advanced technology, Fig. 1-37, means constantly developing new ideas, materials, processes, and manufacturing techniques that in turn are creating occupations that did not previously exist. It has been said that young graduates will be employed in—on the average—five different jobs during their lifetime, and three of them do not now exist!

To hold your job and advance in it, you will have to study to keep up-to-date with the knowledge and new skills needed by modern technology.

You will be expected to start work on time, and be in attendance every work day. Sick leave was originated to help workers and, therefore, should not be abused.

Industry also expect a fair day's work for a fair day's pay. High manufacturing costs and competition with foreign made products have made this a real necessity.

Do your assigned work, and never knowingly turn out a piece of substandard or faulty work. Take

pride in what you do. YOU must assume the responsibility for your actions. Industry is always on the lookout for bright young people who are not afraid to work or assume responsibility.

WHERE TO GET INFORMATION ABOUT METALWORKING OCCUPATIONS

Information on metalworking oriented occupations can be secured from many sources. The guidance office and industrial arts/industrial education department in your school are the closest.

Almost all community colleges have CAREER INFORMATION CENTERS. They can furnish any needed occupational information.

Most metalworking occupations are described in the OCCUPATIONAL OUTLOOK HANDBOOK published by the United States Department of Labor and available through the Government Printing Office. The Department of Labor also publishes the DICTIONARY OF OCCUPATIONAL TITLES. This book has job descriptions of most metalworking occupations. Both books can usually be found in the library or guidance office.

The local STATE EMPLOYMENT SERVICE is another excellent source of information. They can inform you about local and state opportunities in metalworking, as well as the names and addresses of trade unions concerned with metalworking trades.

HOW TO GO ABOUT GETTING A JOB

After graduation, securing your first full-time job will be a very important task. To be successful, you will have to spend as much time looking for this position as you would working at a regular job. In addition, there are several other things that you can do to make this task easier.

You will have to decide what type of work you would like to do. Most schools and state employment services will administer tests that will help you determine the area(s) of employment where you will have a good chance of succeeding.

Answering the following questions will give you additional help:
1. What can I do with some degree of success?
2. What have I done that others have commended me for doing well?
3. What are the things I really like to do?
4. What are the things I DO NOT like to do?
5. What jobs have I held? Why did I leave them?
6. What skills have I acquired while in school?

You will probably have two or more areas of interest. After listing them, you should start gathering information on your areas of interest. Use as many different sources as time permits. This may include reading, talking with persons doing this type of work, and visiting industry.

If time permits, plan your school program to prepare for entry into the job, or for advanced schooling if you are near graduation.

The next problem is how do you go about getting that job? Jobs are always available. Workers get promoted, they retire, some quit, die, or get fired. Technological progress creates new jobs. HOWEVER, YOU MUST TRACK THEM DOWN. There is no easy way to get a challenging job.

Concentrate on getting the job. MAKE YOUR JOB APPLICATION IN PERSON. Always be specific on the type of job you are after. (However, you must be qualified for that job.) Never, under any circumstances, just ask for a job or inquire of the employment office, ''What openings do you have?''

To speed the tedious task of filling out job applications, prepare a JOB RESUME in advance. (A resume is a summary of your education and employment, submitted when applying for a job.) It will assure uniform information with little chance for confusing responses. Your resume should include:
1. Your FULL name.
2. FULL address and phone number. Do not forget the zip code.
3. Place and date of birth. For some jobs, it may be necessary to include a CERTIFIED copy of your birth certificate. Have a copy available in advance.
4. Your social security number.
5. The places you have worked. Start with the most recent place of employment. Include the following items under each place of employment:
   a. Name and address.
   b. Dates employed.
   c. Immediate supervisor's name.
   d. Salary.
   e. Reason for leaving.
6. Schooling and special training. Include the dates attending.
7. The equipment you can safely operate.
8. Names and addresses of references. Do not include relatives unless you have worked for them. SECURE PERMISSION BEFORE USING A PERSON FOR A REFERENCE.

Last, but not least, know where to look for a job. Look over the classified section of local newspapers each day. Talk with friends and relatives who are employed. They may be aware of job openings at their place of employment before the jobs become official and are advertised.

New offices and factories usually indicate possible job openings. It would also be to your advantage to prepare a list of desirable employers in your community and visit their employment offices. Plan these visits on a routine basis when jobs are not readily available. The employment office will then know you are interested in working for their firm and may give you preference.

One thing you MUST remember. The job will not come to you. YOU must search for it.

TEST YOUR KNOWLEDGE, Unit 1

Please do not write in the text. Place your answers on a separate sheet of paper.
1. The catchphrase of today is_____.
2. Technology started when _____.
3. Until the time of the Industrial Revolution, _____ was the occupation of most people.
4. Where did these people get their clothing, furniture, and other needs?
5. What occurred during the period we now know as the Industrial Revolution?
6. List three problems you think have been caused by technology.
   a. _____.
   b. _____.
   c. _____.
7. How will these problems be solved? (Check the correct answer or answers.)
   a. By the government.
   b. By themselves.
   c. By innovative technology.
   d. All of the above.
   e. None of the above.
8. Briefly explain what you think technology is.

9. Define high technology and state-of-the-art technology.
10. To remain in business, a company must make a _____ on the products it sells.
11. The above is also necesary if people are to _____ in a business venture.
12. List the four categories of metalworking occupations.
    a. _____.
    b. _____.
    c. _____.
    d. _____.
13. Employers prefer workers who _____ _____.
14. Semiskilled workers: (List the correct answer or answers.)
    a. Are those who perform operations that do not require a high degree of skill or training.
    b. Serve as helpers to skilled workers.
    c. Are told what and how work is to be done.
    d. All of the above.
    e. None of the above.
15. Many present day skilled workers started as _____ which required four or more years of study with experienced craftworkers.
16. Today, most skilled workers entering the metalworking trades received their training in the _____ or in _____ _____.
17. The _____ assists the engineer by constructing and testing experimental devices and equipment.
18. List two of the metalworking professions.
    a. _____.
    b. _____.
19. What are two ways a person can become an engineer?
20. Management plays an important role in metalworking. It consists of the men and women who _____ the operation of an industrial organization.

Match each word or phrase in the left column with the correct sentence in the right column.
21. ____ Leadership.   a. One of the difficulties
22. ____ Leader.   of leadership.
23. ____ Quality of   b. Determines whether
         leadership.   an organization will
24. ____ Good example.   be a success or a
25. ____ Unpopular   failure.
         decisions.   c. The ability to be a
                           leader.
                        d. A person who is in
                           charge or in com-
                           mand.
                        e. A leader must be
                           this.

26. What are two things industry will expect from you when you start work?
27. Name three sources of information about metalworking occupations.

RESEARCH AND DEVELOPMENT

1. Start a notebook of articles relating to metalworking technology. Clip the material from magazines and newspapers.
2. Prepare a term paper on the Industrial Revolution. What were some of the positive effects and some of the negative effects of the Industrial Revolution?
3. Research early methods of transportation. Present your findings to the class.
4. Research one of the latest areas of technology (space shuttles, high-speed transportation, lasers, robots, etc.). Present your findings to the class.
5. Visit a museum that has displays of tools used in earlier times. Write a report on how you think they were made and used. (Do not forget to view the other exhibits on display.)
6. Prepare a list of occupations that have been made possible directly or indirectly by the metalworking industries.
7. Invite a speaker from the state employment office to talk with your shop class about employment opportunities in local and statewide metalworking industries.
8. Study the help wanted columns in the daily papers for a period of two weeks. Prepare a list of the metalworking positions available, the salaries offered (if given), the minimum requirements for securing the jobs, and whether the company advertising is an Equal Opportunity Employer. How often are additional benefits like insurance and hospitalization mentioned?
9. Secure job applications from several nearby companies. (They do not have to be metalworking companies.) Summarize the information they request. Prepare a bulletin board display around these applications. Invite the personnel director from one of the companies to discuss with the class what is expected of their employees.
10. Summarize the information on several metalworking occupations described in the Occupational Outlook Handbook. Make it available to the class.
11. Contact the local office of the International Association of Machinists for information on machinist trades apprentice programs.
12. Contact several engineering societies and make arrangements to borrow a few of their films on the engineering profession.

13. Prepare a job resume for yourself. Use the outline suggested in the text.
14. With your teacher's permission, contact the AMERICAN INDUSTRIAL ARTS STUDENT ASSOCIATION* and VOCATIONAL IN-DUSTRIAL CLUBS OF AMERICA** for information on how to organize an Industrial Arts/Industrial Education club in your school. (Conduct a student survey to determine whether there is interest in forming such a club.)

*American Industrial Arts Association, 1908 Association Drive, Reston, VA 22091. **Vocational Industrial Clubs of America, Inc., P.O. Box 3000, Leesburg, VA 22075.

A high degree of advanced technical knowledge is necessary for the successful completion of this design project.

Most steel products will rust if left out in the elements long enough, destroying the metal's usefulness. Steel can be protected by paint and other types of coatings but these protective coverings must be replaced from time to time. U.S. Steel has developed a "weathering steel" for buildings and sculptures like the one shown. No protective coating is required. The steel, called COR-TEN, weathers to a deep rust-like color in four or five years. This oxide coating halts any additional corrosion and the steel becomes maintenance-free.

Unit 2

METALS WE USE

Just about everything we eat, see, feel, hear, smell, and touch has used metal somewhere in its manufacture. Since metal plays such a prominent role in our everyday life, it would appear that everyone knows about metal. But do we know as much about it as we think we know? Can YOU define what metal is?

Chances are that in your description of metal you mentioned a material that is hard, strong, tough, and withstands heat without melting. However, while many metals have these characteristerics, there are others that DO NOT have these features. For example: MERCURY is fluid at room temperature; body heat will melt GALLIUM in the palm of your hand; LITHIUM is so soft it is easily scratched with a fingernail; SILVER makes photography possible (the picture you see is formed by minute particles of the metal); MP (metal particle) tape or the higher grade ME (metal evaporated) tape records sight and sound on the tapes used in tape decks and video equipment, Fig. 2-1.

One thing we do know, metals are available in a large range of standard shapes and sizes, Fig. 2-2.

Can YOU tell by looking at a piece of metal whether it is a FERROUS metal—a metal containing iron—or a NONFERROUS metal—a metal containing no iron? Is it an ALLOY—a mixture of two or more metals? Could it be a BASE metal like tin, copper, or zinc? Then again, might it be a PRECIOUS metal such as gold, silver, or platinum?

When you consider it from a practical point of view, it is almost impossible to tell much about a piece of metal by just looking at it. To help us better understand the properties of metals, industry has developed the science of METALLURGY. The person who does this job is called a METALLURGIST. One of their most important duties is to develop metals with special properties that will do a specific job better, and do it more economically. To accomplish this, the metallurgist must make many tests, Fig. 2-3.

When making products in industry, or projects in the school shop, it is important to know which metal, or metals, are best suited for a particular job. Must the metal be tough and hold an edge? Does it have to resist corrosion? Is weight an important factor? Does the metal have to be polished, or will its natural finish be satisfactory? These are only a

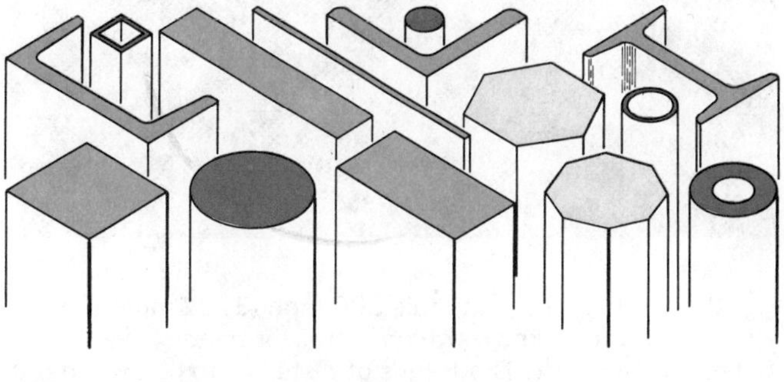

Fig. 2-1. Video recording equipment utilizes metallic coated tape to record sight and sound. A 8mm tape cassette can record up to 90 minutes of information. (Eastman Kodak Company)

Fig. 2-2. Metal is available in innumerable shapes and sizes. Only a few of the stock shapes are shown here.

Fig. 2-3. As molten steel fills this ladel, some of the lighter slag containing impurities rises to the top and flows into an adjacent slag pot. (Bethlehem Steel Corp.)

few of the many questions that must be considered when designing a product, Fig. 2-4.

Metals are usually classified as follows:

  a. Ferrous metals.
  b. Nonferrous metals.
  c. Precious metals.
  d. High temperature metals.
  e. Rare metals.

Many of these metals can be found in the school shop.

FERROUS METALS

Iron is the basic ingredient of all ferrous metals. They are the most useful metals known to the human race.

CAST IRON

CAST IRON is a widely used metal. It is a hard, brittle metal that has excellent wear resistance. This is especially true where there are borderline lubrication conditions. Cast iron contains 3.0 to 4.0 percent carbon. WHITE CAST IRON is extremely hard and used primarily in applications requiring wear and abrasion resistance. Its cost is relatively low. White cast iron is converted into MALLEABLE IRON by an annealing process that involves heating white cast iron, then slowly cooling it under carefully controlled temperature and time conditions. This annealing process may take several days.

Malleable iron is a great deal stronger and tougher, but more expensive than GRAY IRON, another form of cast iron. Gray iron castings are used in considerable quantities. Generally, this is because of the ability of gray iron to readily flow into intricate mold passages and form complex shapes for cylinder blocks of gasoline engines and diesel engines, Fig. 2-5.

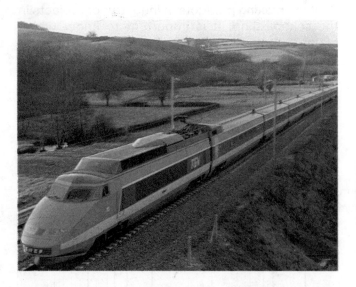

Fig. 2-4. When designing this 200 mph (320 kmph) train, it was important to know which metal, or metals, were best suited for each part. Thousands of tests had to be carried out to be sure the metals selected met design specifications. (French National Railroads)

Fig. 2-5. The main engine castings in this racing stock car are made from cast iron alloys. They are capable of operating at speeds up to 200 mph (320 kmph) for hours at a time, without failing. (Champion Spark Plug Company)

WROUGHT IRON

WROUGHT IRON is an iron that has most of the carbon removed. It is tough and bends easily whether it is cold or heated. Wrought iron rusts very slowly and is readily welded. Ornamental iron work, Fig. 2-6, furnace smoke stacks, and oil pipelines are made from wrought iron.

Fig. 2-6. Wrought iron is used for ornamental ironwork because of its resistance to rust. It can be shaped and welded easily. This is a section of the wrought iron railing from Federal Hall where George Washington stood during his inauguration in 1789. (Courtesy of the New York Historical Society, New York City)

STEEL

STEEL is an ALLOY (mixture) of iron and other chemical elements. (Iron is seldom used in a pure state.) The alloying elements impart certain desirable characteristics to the iron that are necessary if the metal is to be used for specific applications.

CARBON STEELS

When carbon is the alloying element, the steel is called CARBON STEEL. Carbon steels are classified by the percentage of carbon in ''points'' or hundredths of one percent they contain.

LOW CARBON STEELS contain less than 0.30 percent carbon. These steels are easy to work, can be welded, but cannot be hardened. Low carbon steel is available as band iron, black iron sheet, and in many different shapes and sizes of bars and rods.

MEDIUM CARBON STEELS contain 0.30 to 0.60 percent carbon. Hammer heads, clamps, and many other tools are made from medium carbon steels.

HIGH CARBON STEELS contain 0.60 to 1.50 percent carbon. Many products that must be heat-treated are manufactured from high carbon steels.

ALLOY STEELS

When alloying elements other than carbon, such as CHROMIUM, MANGANESE, MOLYBDENUM, NICKEL, TUNGSTEN, and VANADIUM are used to make steel harder, tougher, and stronger, the resulting metals are called ALLOY STEELS, Fig. 2-7.

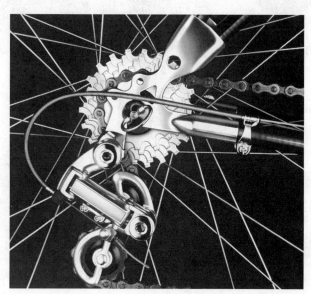

Fig. 2-7. Derailleur on this bicycle has been made with alloy steel. Alloy steel makes possible a strong, lightweight assembly. (O.F. Mossberg & Sons, Inc.)

CHROMIUM is added when toughness, hardness, and wear resistance are desired. It is the basis of STAINLESS STEEL. Chromium steel is used extensively for automobile and aircraft parts, Fig. 2-8.

MANGANESE purifies steel and adds strength and toughness. Manganese steel is used for parts that must withstand shock and hard wear.

MOLYBDENUM is the alloying element added when steel must remain tough at high temperatures.

NICKEL imparts toughness and strength to steel. Nickel steel does not rust easily. It also enables the metal to withstand shock. Much armor plate is nickel steel.

TUNGSTEN, added in the proper amount, makes steel that is self-hardening. Tools made from tungsten steel need no special hardening treatment and will withstand heat. It is used extensively for making cutting tools.

VANADIUM, as an alloying element, makes steel that has a fine grain structure and is very tough. Vanadium steel is used when a tough, strong, but

Fig. 2-8. Chromium steel is used extensively in the landing gear assembly of this F-16 used by the USAF Thunderbirds Demonstration Team.

Fig. 2-9. Vanadium steel is very tough, making it ideal for this huge truck body. (Euclid)

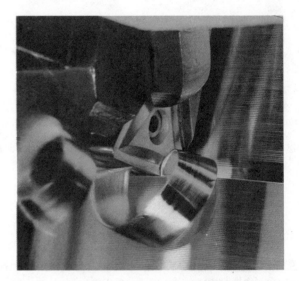

Fig. 2-10. Carbide cutting tools are available in tungsten carbide, titanium carbide, and titanium carbide coated (a thin coating of titanium carbide, metallurgically bonded to a carbide core). Shown in a Kennametal Kenloc insert cutting AISI 4340 steel at 500 sfm speed (500 feet of metal passes the cutter each minute). The cut is 0.250 in. deep. Note that the metal is almost red hot as it leaves the cutting tool.

not brittle, metal is needed, Fig. 2-9.

TOOL STEELS

TOOL STEELS, by their nature, are dense steels containing either a high percentage of carbon or a high alloy content, or a combination of both. These steels are tough and are made into tools that must hold a cutting edge.

HIGH SPEED STEELS (HSS)

Some alloy steels are also classified as HIGH SPEED STEELS. They are capable of making deeper cuts at higher machine speeds than regular tool steels because they possess the characteristic known as RED HARDNESS. Red hardness is the ability of the metal to retain its hardness (cutting edges do not dull) at high temperatures. They also retain high abrasion resistance (cutting edges do not dull easily).

TUNGSTEN CARBIDE

TUNGSTEN CARBIDE is the hardest human-made metal. It is almost as hard as a diamond. The metal is shaped by molding tungsten, carbon, and cobalt powders under heat and pressure in a process called SINTERING. The metals fuse together without melting. Tungsten carbide, while not a true steel, is usually classified with the steels. Tools made from this family of materials can cut many times faster than high speed cutting steel tools, Fig. 2-10.

STAINLESS STEELS

There are more than a hundred different stainless steels. They all have one characteristic in common: each contains enough chromium to make the metal corrosion resistant, Fig. 2-11.

There are three basic groups of stainless steel:
1. AUSTENITIC. These chromium-nickel and chromium-nickel-manganese stainless steels are nonmagnetic.
2. MARTENSITIC. Alloys of iron, carbon, and chromium that are magnetic in nature.
3. FERRITIC. Magnetic stainless steels with more than 18 percent chromium.

Stainless steels can be machined using techniques similar to those required on mild steel. Tools must be kept sharp. Tool and work vibration (called CHATTER) must be kept to a minimum.

Fig. 2-11. Many fittings on this racing boat are made from stainless steel because of the corrosion resistance of the metal. (Champion Spark Plug Company)

STEEL TERMINOLOGY

Rods, bars, plates, sheets, and structural shapes are produced by passing steel (and other metals) through a series of forming rolls. Rolling gradually reduces an INGOT (unfinished steel mass from the steel mill) into a BLOOM (semifinished steel bar with a cross-sectional area of more than 36 square inches), BILLET (longer and smaller in cross section than a bloom), or a SLAB (generally several times wider than a bloom or billet), and finally to the desired shape and size, Fig. 2-12.

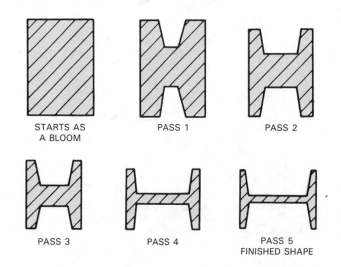

STARTS AS A BLOOM   PASS 1   PASS 2

PASS 3   PASS 4   PASS 5 FINISHED SHAPE

Fig. 2-12. Sequence for rolling steel I-beams.

When metal is shaped while "red hot," it is called HOT-ROLLED STEEL. Hot-rolled steel is characterized by the blue-black oxide that forms during the rolling process, Fig. 2-13.

Some hot-rolled steel shapes are PICKLED (passed through a dilute acid) to remove the oxide coating. The metal is then rolled cold into final shape and size. The steel that is shaped cold is known as COLD-FINISHED STEEL. Cold-finished steels are used where a fine finish is required; where a uniformity of temper (degree of hardness) is essential for the best machinability; and where accuracy of shape and size are necessary, without the extra expense of additional machining.

Hot-rolled and cold-finished steels sometimes receive additional treatment to shape them to final size and configuration (form, shape, or profile). Steel finished in this manner has a smooth bright finish and is very accurate in size and shape. This steel is called COLD DRAWN STEEL because it is pulled, or "drawn," through a series of smooth holes that are in a hardened steel block called a DIE, Fig. 2-14.

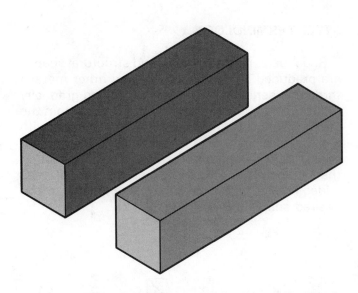

Fig. 2-13. Hot-rolled steel has a black oxide coating that is formed during the rolling process. Cold finished steel does not have such a coating.

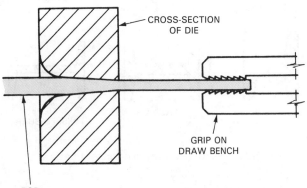

CROSS-SECTION OF DIE

GRIP ON DRAW BENCH

ROD

Fig. 2-14. How wire is cold drawn to size.

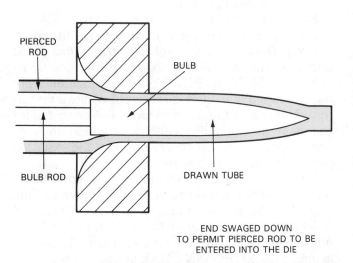

PIERCED ROD

BULB

BULB ROD

DRAWN TUBE

END SWAGED DOWN TO PERMIT PIERCED ROD TO BE ENTERED INTO THE DIE

Fig. 2-15. Seamless tubing is also made by drawing it through dies.

This gradually reduces the bar or rod until it is the desired size. Hot-rolled steel must be cooled and pickled before it can be drawn. Wire and some seamless tubing, Fig. 2-15, are made by this technique.

Sheet steel (and other metals) can be made more rigid by embossing designs into its surface, Fig. 2-16. Economy is gained in some applications by slitting and expanding the metal sheet, until it is many times its original width, Fig. 2-17.

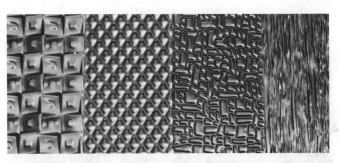

Fig. 2-16. A few of the many embossed surface finishes available on metal sheet. These finishes enhance the appearance of the metal, make it more rigid, and make scratches and abrasion marks more difficult to see.

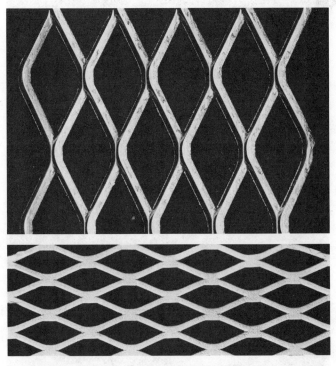

Fig. 2-17. Expanded metal is made by piercing, or cutting, slits in a section of sheet metal. The edges of the sheet are gripped in a special machine, and pressure is applied to pull or expand the sheet to many times its original width. There is not lost or waste metal when manufacturing this kind of metal sheet. (Wheeling Corrugating Co.)

IDENTIFYING STEELS

Because the different kinds of steels look alike, several methods of identification have been devised. They include identification by chemical composition, mechanical properties, their ability to meet a standard specification or industry accepted practice, or their ability to be fabricated into an identified part. The shape of the mill form (rod, bar, structural shape, etc.), and the intended use for the metal, can also determine the method of identification.

The American Iron and Steel Institute (AISI) and the Society of Automotive Engineers (SAE) have devised almost identical standards that are widely used for identifying steel. Both systems make use of an identical FOUR-NUMBER CODE (some steels require a fifth digit) that describe the physical characteristics of the various steels.

The AISI system also makes use of a PREFIX LETTER (A, B, C, etc.) that indicates the steel manufacturing process.

The four-numeral code works as follows. The first digit classifies the steel. (See the table on page 514.) The second digit indicates the approximate percentage of the alloying element in the steel. The last two digits show the approximate carbon content of the steel in points of hundredths of one percent. For example, steel designated as SAE 1020 is a carbon steel with approximately 20 points or 0.20 percent carbon.

The AISI and SAE four-digit code applies primarily to bar, rod, and wire products.

COLOR CODING

COLOR CODING, Fig. 2-18, is another method of identifying the many kinds of steel. Each commonly used steel is designated by a specific color. (See the table on page 514.) The color coding is painted on the end of bars 1 in. or larger. On bars less than 1 in., the color code may be applied to the end of the bar or on an attached tag.

SPARK TEST

The SPARK TEST, Fig. 2-19, is also employed at times to determine grades of steel. The metal should touch the grinding wheel lightly and the sparks carefully observed. SAFETY NOTE: Wear approved eye protection, have the grinder eye shield cleaned and in place, and have the tool rest properly adjusted.

NONFERROUS METALS

There are many metals that do not have iron as their basic ingredient. These metals, known as NONFERROUS METALS, offer specific properties, or combination of properties, that make them ideal for tasks where ferrous metals are not suitable, Fig. 2-20.

Many nonferrous metals are found in the school shop.

ALUMINUM

ALUMINUM has come to mean a large family of aluminum alloys, not just a single metal. As first produced, aluminum is 99.5 to 99.76 percent pure. It is somewhat soft and not very strong. However, its strength can be greatly increased by adding small amounts of alloying elements, heat-treating, or cold working. A combination of the three techniques has produced aluminum alloys that, pound for pound, are stronger than structural steel. In addition to increasing strength, alloying elements can be selected that will improve welding characteristics, corrosion resistance, machinability, etc.

Many new aluminum alloys are being developed. ALCOA (Aluminum Company of America) is now producing ALITHALITE® , aluminum-lithium alloys. If used on commercial aircraft such as the Boeing 767, it would reduce the weight of the aircraft by seven tons. No new tools or manufacturing techniques are needed to work these alloys.

Another material becoming available is a composite reinforced aluminum laminate that will provide most of the benefits of aluminum alloys and composite materials, while offering a weight reduction of 30-40 percent compared with conventional aluminum alloys.

There are two main classes of aluminum alloys—wrought alloys and cast alloys. The shape of wrought alloys is changed by mechanically working them—forging, rolling, extruding, hammering,

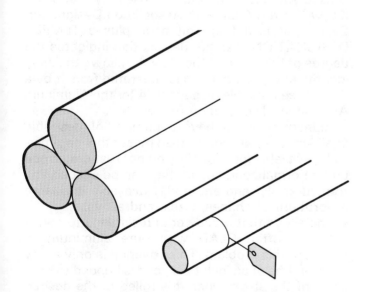

Fig. 2-18. Color coding steel rods.

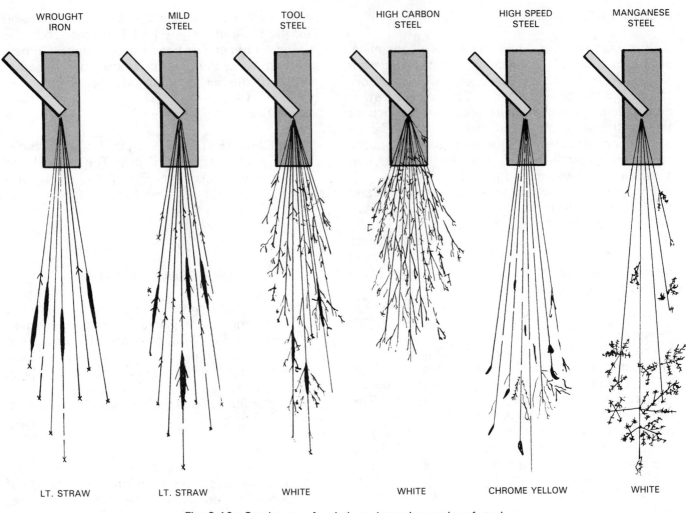

WROUGHT IRON	MILD STEEL	TOOL STEEL	HIGH CARBON STEEL	HIGH SPEED STEEL	MANGANESE STEEL
LT. STRAW	LT. STRAW	WHITE	WHITE	CHROME YELLOW	WHITE

Fig. 2-19. Spark tests often help to determine grades of steel.

Fig. 2-20. This camera has many parts made from steel and nonferrous metals like aluminum, brass, copper, titanium, etc.

etc. Cast alloys are shaped by pouring molten metal into a mold and allowing it to solidify.

Each alloy is given an identifying number which is used when it is important to use only that alloy. Known as the Aluminum Association Designation System, it is a four-digit code plus a TEMPER DESIGNATION. Temper designation indicates the degree of hardness of the alloy. It follows the alloy identification number and is separated from it by a dash. (See the table on page 514 for the Aluminum Association Designation System.)

Aluminum alloys have a number of desirable qualities. They are lighter than most other commercially available metals. They do not rust or corrode under normal conditions. They can be shaped and formed easily, and are readily available in a large assortment of shapes, sizes, and alloys.

The alloys that are lower in resistance to corrosion are often CLAD with pure aluminum to eliminate this problem. This covering is only a few thousandths of an inch thick, and is bonded to both sides of the sheet when it is rolled to the desired thickness.

Fig. 2-21. Typical perforated metal sheet patterns.

Like other metals in sheet form, aluminum can be secured with hundreds of different surface patterns, finishes, and perforations, Fig. 2-21.

MAGNESIUM

MAGNESIUM, Fig. 2-22, is the lightest of our structural metals. It is obtained from the inexhaustible waters of the oceans and is silvery-white in color. Magnesium has many desirable characteristics—high strength to weight, excellent machinability, and the ability to be worked by all common metal-working techniques.

For higher strength, magnesium is alloyed with aluminum, zinc, manganese, zirconium, thorium (this alloy is slightly radioactive), or combinations of these elements.

SAFETY NOTE: Extreme care must be taken when machining magnesium because the chips (not the solid metal) are highly flammable. Burning magnesium chips are so intensely hot they cannot be extinguished by conventional fire-fighting techniques. Water actually intensifies the fire!

TITANIUM

TITANIUM is one of the space age metals. As strong as steel but only half as heavy, it bridges the gap between steel and aluminum, Fig. 2-23. It is silvery and attractive in appearance, and extremely resistant to corrosion. Most titanium alloys are capable of continuous operation at temperatures of about 800°F (427°C), making them ideal for use in high speed aircraft components. Aluminum fails rapidly at temperatures above 250°F (121°C).

Titanium can be machined with conventional equipment if the tools are kept sharp, and the tool and work setups are rigid. Since titanium can be easily contaminated, the cutting tools used in its machining should be used exclusively for that purpose. They should not be used to machine other metals. Gold plating the cutting edges of tools greatly improves machining results on titanium.

BERYLLIUM

BERYLLIUM is a metal originally developed for highly specialized applications, but has since evolved into a material of broad utility. Its many uses include nuclear applications and fabrication of lightweight aerospace structures, Fig. 2-24.

Fig. 2-22. Light weight with high power enables a race car to be competitive. Magnesium wheels and other parts permit a considerable weight reduction without a loss of strength. (Champion Spark Plug Company)

Fig. 2-23. Titanium is as strong as steel, but only half as heavy. This, plus being extremely resistant to corrosion, make it an ideal metal for constructing this advanced design helicopter that will be used by the Navy. (Sikorsky Aircraft Div., United Technologies)

Fig. 2-24. The strength and weight of beryllium (stronger than steel on a weight-to-strength ratio and lighter than aluminum) made it an ideal choice for many parts of the Space Shuttle. (NASA)

Beryllium has a high strength-to-weight ratio, similar to that of high strength steel or titanium, but is about one-third lighter than many aluminum alloys. However, it has low impact strength and is quite expensive.

BERYLLIUM COPPER is another copper base alloy that has excellent resistance to corrosion. For this reason many ship and boat propellers are made from this material.

SAFETY NOTE: Machining beryllium copper can pose a definite health hazard if precautions are not observed by those working with it. The fine dust generated by machining and filing can cause severe respiratory damage and a respirator-type face mask should be worn.

COPPER

COPPER, Fig. 2-25, is a base metal that is the oldest metal known. It is easily identified by its rich reddish-brown color. The metal is a good conductor of electricity, second only to silver. Much copper is used for art metalwork because of its easy-to-work qualities. It can be shaped easily but becomes hard when worked and must be softened or annealed. This is done by heating the metal to a cherry-red color and quenching or cooling it in water. Copper can be readily joined with rivets, and both soft and hard solders.

When copper is exposed to the atmosphere for a period of time a greenish tinge called PATINA develops on its surface(s). This can be removed by polishing. However, on certain copper articles, a fine natural patina is desirable.

Copper can be purchased in a large variety of shapes and sizes. Copper sheet is measured by one of two methods:

THICKNESS BY GAUGE (Brown & Sharpe and American Standard).

WEIGHT IN OUNCES PER SQUARE FOOT.

BRASS

BRASS is an alloy of copper and zinc. It is bright yellow and one of the more important alloys of copper. The proportion of copper varies according to

Fig. 2-25. Much copper and copper alloy is needed in the generation of electric power.

the use of the metal. Commercial brass contains about 90 percent copper and 10 percent zinc. The working characteristics are almost identical to those of copper, Fig. 2-26.

BRONZE

BRONZE is another alloy with copper as the chief ingredient. It is composed of copper and tin, and is a reddish-gold in color. Bronze is harder than brass and is also more expensive.

ZINC

ZINC alloys resist many forms of corrosion. They are available in wire, sheet, strip, foil, and rods. Zinc is most familiar as a protective coating on steel and iron. This coating is called GALVANIZING, and is done by dipping the steel and iron into molten zinc or by electroplating.

Zinc is a relatively inexpensive metal but only has moderate strength and toughness. The low melting point of zinc makes it an excellent die casting metal. The automotive and home appliance industries use large quantities of zinc alloys.

TIN

TIN is a soft, shiny, silvery metal that is rarely used except as an alloying agent. Tin is familiar as the shiny exterior surface of "tin cans" because it provides excellent protection against corrosion and is nontoxic. When alloyed with copper it forms bronze. Tin is also the chief ingredient of pewter.

PEWTER

Modern PEWTER or BRITANNIA METAL is an alloy of tin (91 percent), copper (1.5 percent), and antimony (7.5 percent). When polished, it has a fine silvery sheen. Modern pewter DOES NOT CONTAIN LEAD and food and drink can be served in it, Fig. 2-27. However, old pewter MAY contain lead and should not be used to serve food or drink. Pewter is a pleasant metal to work, but requires skill to join it properly. Because a soldered joint will oxidize and become noticeable (solder contains lead), all joints must be fused.

GAR-ALLOY

GAR-ALLOY is a zinc-base alloy. Small amounts of copper and silver have been added to impart strength. For some applications (no food or drink to be served in it), gar-alloy can be substituted for pewter. It is not as costly as pewter and has several qualities of pewter. It is a bluish-gray metal that works well cold, and can be buffed to a high polish. The polished surfaces must be protected with a thin coat of lacquer. Otherwise, they will quickly tarnish.

GERMAN SILVER

GERMAN or NICKEL SILVER is a substitute for silver in the manufacture of many kinds of jewelry. It is another copper-base alloy with varying quantities of nickel and zinc. It has working characteristics that are very similar to those of brass, with the exception that it is rather brittle and

Fig. 2-26. Reproduction of a colonial chandelier is made from brass.

Fig. 2-27. Modern pewter contains no lead; food and drink can be safely served in it.

cannot be hammered into shape. Nickel silver, with a composition of 64 percent copper, 18 percent nickel, and 18 percent zinc, is usually the base for most silver plated tableware.

PRECIOUS METALS

Used at one time only to manufacture tableware and jewelry, precious metals are finding many uses in industry.

SILVER

SILVER when combined with a small amount of copper (7.6 percent) is known as STERLING. When polished, it has a very shiny silvery-white color. Sterling silver has outstanding working characteristics. It can be readily shaped, cast and formed, and hard solders well.

Silver is an excellent conductor of electricity and can be found in many electrical/electronic devices. Its resistance to many chemicals makes it a good choice for use in corrosion resistant equipment. Silver is also being used in the manufacture of long shelf life, powerful batteries.

GOLD

GOLD is highly malleable (can be easily shaped by hammering or rolling) metal that has many uses in industry, as well as in manufacturing jewelry and coinage. Because it resists attack from many chemicals and acids, gold is employed as the lining of chemical equipment, for making high melting point solders, and in medical and dental applications. Many electronic devices also require gold in their manufacture, Fig. 2-28.

PLATINUM

PLATINUM is a heavy grayish-white metal that is resistant to most chemicals. While some platinum is used for making fine jewelry, most of the metal is utilized to coat the pellets found in automotive engine catalytic converters, Fig. 2-29. Platinum reacts with the hot exhaust gases and significantly lowers the harmful exhaust emissions.

Platinum can also be found in the manufacture of electrical/electronic devices used in space, chemical, and laboratory equipment.

HIGH TEMPERATURE METALS

This category includes metals that have the unique property of maintaining high strength when operated for extended periods at elevated temperatures. They are sometimes called

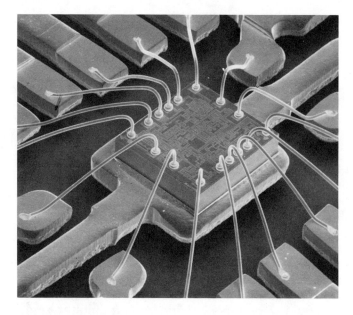

Fig. 2-28. Gold is used in the manufacture of microcircuitry because it does not tarnish and is readily soldered. To give you some idea how small this fuel injection computer for an automobile is, the wires are less than one-half the thickness of a human hair.
(Delco Electronics Div., General Motors Corporation)

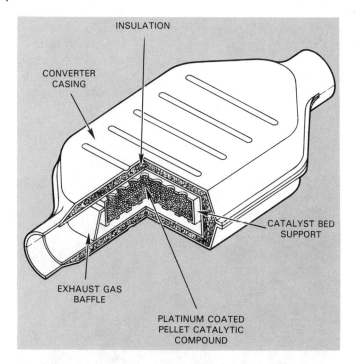

Fig. 2-29. A large percentage of platinum mined today is used to coat the ceramic pellets found in automotive engine catalytic converters. The metal reacts with the exhaust gases and significantly lowers the harmful exhaust emissions.

SUPERALLOYS and have been developed for nuclear and aerospace applications.

COLUMBIUM

COLUMBIUM is of interest to the aerospace industry. It has a high melting point—4380°F (2403°C).

Columbium is also resistant to radiation damage, making it acceptable for nuclear reactor applications.

Columbium can be fabricated by most conventional techniques and machining can be accomplished with high speed tools. The material, however, must be flooded with coolant at all times.

NICKEL BASE ALLOYS

These metals are known commercially by such names as Iconel-X, Hastealloy-X, Rene 41, etc. They have many uses in jet engines, rocket engines, and electric heat-treating furnaces. These applications require metals that can operate at temperatures of 1200 to 1900°F (1023 to 1356°C). One such metal, molybdenum, is highly resistant to corrosion by acids, molten glass, and metals, and is machined in much the same manner as cast iron.

TANTALUM

TANTALUM is not a new metal. It has been used since the turn of the century as filament in light bulbs. Tantalum alloys are now being utilized for rocket nozzles, heat exchangers in nuclear reactors, and other applications where dependability at temperatures above 2000°F (1097°C) is required.

Tantalum can be worked at room temperatures. Machining can be done with cemented carbide tools at high cutting speeds if the work is kept flooded with coolant. The metal can be welded easily by the electron beam technique.

TUNGSTEN

TUNGSTEN melts at a higher temperature, 6200°F (3412°C), than any known metal. However, it is not resistant to oxidation at high temperatures and must be protected with a suitable coating.

Because of its high melting point, tungsten has found considerable use in spark plug electrodes and in the field of welding. High abrasion resistance of the metal, combined with its good resistance to electrical spark erosion, makes it an ideal material for breaker points on gasoline engines.

The high melting temperature of tungsten makes the production by the melting and casting process very expensive. Shaping is done almost exclusively by powder metallurgy (see Unit 30).

RARE METALS

Most metals in this category are available in small quantities for experimental purposes. Most of them, at this time, cost more than gold which limits their use for serious study. Included in this group are such metals as YTTRIUM (pronounced itream), CERIUM, and EUROPIUM.

It has not been too long since the metals titanium, uranium, and beryllium were classified as rare metals. Less than a hundred years ago aluminum was also in this category.

Who knows what new metals will be developed in YOUR lifetime? Perhaps YOU will be the person who discovers and develops an economical way to produce an anti-gravity metal (cancels the effect of gravity); or a metal that can fuel a device used to replace the internal combustion engine, without doing environmental damage.

OTHER MATERIALS

Many ways have been deviced to give existing metals greater strength and rigidity while reducing weight. HONEYCOMB SANDWICH STRUCTURES, Fig. 2-30, is one such material. Sections of thin metal (aluminum, stainless steel, titanium, etc.) are bonded together in such a manner that when expanded, a structure is formed that is similar in appearance to the wax comb honeybees use to store honey.

The honeycomb structure is joined with an adhesive, or fused by brazing or resistance welding, to form a sandwich like panel. It becomes a structure that has very high strength-to-weight and rigidity-to-weight ratios.

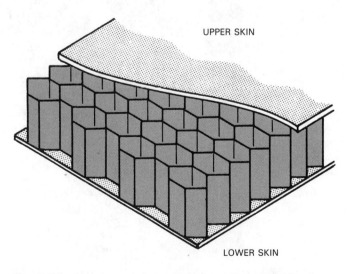

UPPER SKIN

LOWER SKIN

Fig. 2-30. Honeycomb has great strength and rigidity for a given weight. It has many applications in the aerospace industries.

The space shuttle utilizes large quantities of aluminum, stainless steel, and titanium honeycomb in its structure.

Also in this special category is a fairly new development that utilizes fibers of conventional metals (and some not so common metals), in both pure and alloy forms. They are bonded together with special plastic matrixes (binding substances) in much the same manner as fiberglass auto bodies and boat hulls are made. This material is called a COMPOSITE and is generally lighter and stronger than many conventional metals.

Present usage of composites is mainly concerned with aerospace applications, Fig. 2-31. However, some are finding limited usage in lightweight (and expensive) bicycle frames, Fig. 2-32, golf clubs, tennis racquets, and fishing poles. Much research is being done to reduce the cost of composites so they can be employed to make lighter and safer automobile bodies.

MEASUREMENT AND SHAPES OF METALS

The chart, Fig. 2-33, lists several metals commonly found in the school shop and how they are measured and purchased. The standard shapes in which a number of metals are manufactured, measured, and purchased are shown in Fig. 2-34.

Fig. 2-31. Until the advent of composites, it was not possible to take advantage of the aerodynamic characteristics of the forward swept aircraft wing in high-speed flight. Metal was not rigid enough. The X-29 is the first of many such aircraft that will explore the use of this type of wing.   (Grumman Aerospace Corp.)

Fig. 2-32. One of the first commercial uses of a composite. This bicycle frame is fabricated from a graphite composite called MAGNAMITE* which is stiffer than steel and lighter than titanium. (O.F. Mossberg & Sons, Inc.)

*Registered trademark of Hercules, Inc.

MATERIAL Sheet (less than 1/4'' thick)	HOW MEASURED	HOW PURCHASED	CHARACTERISTICS
Copper	Gauge number (Brown & Sharpe & Amer. Std.)	24 x 96'' sheet or 12 or 18'' by lineal feet on roll	Pure metal
Brass	Gauge number (B & S and Amer. Std.)	24 x 76'' sheet or 12 or 18'' by lineal feet on roll	Alloy of copper & zinc
Aluminum	Decimal	24 x 72'' sheet or 12 or 18'' by lineal feet on roll	Available as commercially pure metal or alloyed for strength, hardness, & ductility
Galvanized steel	Gauge number (U.S. Std.)	24 x 96'' sheet	Mild steel sheet with zinc plating, also available with zinc coating that is part of sheet
Black annealed steel sheet	Gauge number (U.S. Std.)	24 x 96'' sheet	Mild steel with oxide coating-hot rolled
Cold rolled steel sheet	Gauge number (U.S. Std.)	24 x 96'' sheet	Oxide removed and cold rolled to final thickness
Tin plate	Gauge number (U.S. Std.)	20 x 28'' sheet 56 or 112 to pkg	Mild steel with tin coating
Nickel silver	Gauge number (Brown & Sharp)	6 or 12'' wide by lineal sheet	Copper 50%, Zinc 30%, nickel 20%
Expanded	Gauge number (U.S. Std.)	36 x 96''	Metal is pierced and expanded (stretched) to diamond shape; also available rolled to thickness after it has been expanded
Perforated	Gauge number (U.S. Std.)	30 x 36'' 36 x 48''	Design is cut in sheet; many designs available

Fig. 2-33. Metals we use . . . how they are purchased and measured, and their characteristics.

SHAPES		LENGTH	HOW MEASURED	*HOW PURCHASED	OTHER
	 Sheet less than 1/4'' thick	to 144''	Thickness x width widths to 72''	Weight, foot, or piece	Available in coils of much longer lengths
	 Plate more than 1/4'' thick	to 20'	Thickness x width	Weight, foot, or piece	
	 Band	to 20'	Thickness x width	Weight, foot, or piece	Mild steel with oxide coating
	 Rod	12 to 20'	Diameter	Weight, foot, or piece	Hot rolled steel to 20' length—cold finished steel to 12' length— steel drill rod 36''
	 Square	12 to 20'	Width	Weight, foot, or piece	
	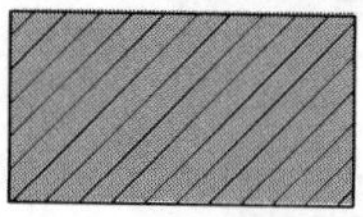 Flats	Hot rolled 20-22' Cold finished	Thickness x width	Weight, foot, or piece	
	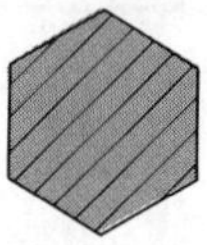 Hexagon	12 to 20'	Distance across flats	Weight, foot, or piece	
	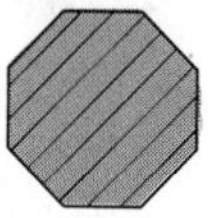 Octagon	12 to 20'	Distance across flats	Weight, foot, or piece	
	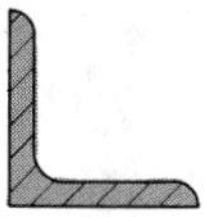 Angle	Lengths to 40'	Leg length x leg length x thickness of legs	Weight, foot, or piece	
	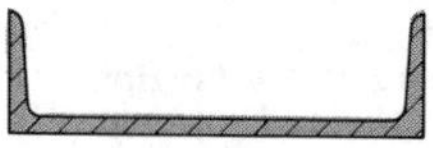 Channel	Lengths to 60'	Depth x web thickness x flange width	Weight, foot, or piece	
	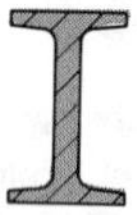 I-beam	Lengths to 60'	Height x web thickness x flange width	Weight, foot, or piece	

*Charge made for cutting to other than standard lengths.

Fig. 2-34. Metals we use . . . the shapes available, how they are measured and purchased, and their characteristics.

TEST YOUR KNOWLEDGE, Unit 2

Please do not write in the text. Place your answers on a separate sheet of paper.
1. In your own words, define metal.
2. Metals are usually classified under one of five groups. List them.
   a. _____.
   b. _____.
   c. _____.
   d. _____.
   e. _____.
3. A metal is considered a ferrous metal when it:
   a. Contains a large portion of iron.
   b. Contains no iron.
   c. Is a mixture of two or more metals.
   d. All of the above.
   e. None of the above.

4. A metal is called an alloy when it:
   a. Contains a large portion of iron.
   b. Contains no iron.
   c. Is a mixture of two or more metals.
   d. All of the above.
   e. None of the above.
5. A nonferrous metal:
   a. Contains a large portion of iron.
   b. Contains no iron.
   c. Is a mixture of two or more metals.
   d. All of the above.
   e. None of the above.
6. Carefully examine the following list of metals. Which does not belong?
   a. Copper.
   b. Aluminum.
   c. Bronze.
   d. Brass.
7. Which metal does not belong on this list?
   a. Copper.
   b. Tin.
   c. Zinc.
   d. Steel.
8. Chromium, manganese, molybdenum, nickel, tungsten, and vanadium are used to make steel _____, _____, and _____.
9. Hot rolled steel is characterized by the _____ that forms during the rolling process.
10. Steel that is rolled cold is known as _____ steel.
11. The _____ test is sometimes used to determine types of steel.
12. Sheet steel that has been coated with zinc is known as _____ steel sheet.
13. Name the three groups of stainless steel.
    a. _____.
    b. _____.
    c. _____.
14. What do all stainless steels have in common?
15. Aluminum is a _____ metal.
16. List three ways to increase the strength of aluminum.
    a. _____.
    b. _____.
    c. _____.
17. What is unique about magnesium?
18. Why must extreme care be taken when machining magnesium?
19. Care must also be taken when machining _____ because the dust generated by the machining operation is a health hazard.
20. What metal is as strong as steel, but only half the weight?
21. The oldest metal known to the human race is _____.
22. Brass is an alloy of _____ and _____.
23. When copper and tin are alloyed, _____

is formed.
24. The metal used as a substitute for silver in the manufacture of many kinds of jewelry is known as _____ or _____.
25. High temperature metals were developed primarily for _____ and _____ applications..
26. Describe the material known as the honeycomb sandwich structure.

RESEARCH AND DEVELOPMENT

1. Prepare a display panel with an automobile or aircraft as the central theme, and list around it the many metals needed for its manufacture. Run a piece of cord or yarn from the metal to the approximate place on the vehicle where the material is used. Secure samples of the various metals and alloys, and fasten them on the panel beside the name plates.
2. In your study of metals you must become familiar with many of their properties. The following terms are used to describe the properties. Research their meanings as they pertain to metals.
   a. Malleability.
   b. Ductility.
   c. Elasticity.
   d. Machinability.
   e. Fusibility.
   f. Hardness.
   g. Brittleness.
   h. Resistance to corrosion.
3. Design a display panel using samples of the following metals:
   a. Aluminum (soft).
   b. Aluminum (hard).
   c. Brass.
   d. Bronze.
   e. Tin.
   f. Cold-finished steel.
   g. Hot-finished steel.
   h. Copper.
   i. Tin plate.
   j. Galvanized steel.
   k. Pewter.
   l. Magnesium.
4. Contact industries in your community to obtain samples of their products that make use of one or more of the above metals. Mount product samples on a display panel, along with samples of the metals used in manufacturing the product.
5. Secure samples of honeycomb in both compressed and expanded forms. Demonstrate its strength by epoxing thin aluminum to the expanded honeycomb.
6. Prepare a notebook on space age and high

temperature metals from articles that appear in technical and trade magazines.

7. Secure samples of titanium and demonstrate forming and machining techniques on it. Prepare experiments comparing its working chacteristics with those of steel and aluminum

8. Make a list of industries in your community. Separate them according to whether they use metal directly, indirectly, or use no metal at all.

9. Select a simple product like a pencil sharpener, automatic pencil, ball point pen, etc., and determine the various kinds of metals and their forms (sheet, tubing, etc.) that went into their manufacture.

Aerospace engineers test feasibility of using various metals in new supersonic aircraft designs.

Unit 3

UNDERSTANDING DRAWINGS

Drawings tell the metalworker how a part is to be made, or how the product is assembled. Lines, symbols, and special figures are employed to give the drawing meaning. See Fig. 3-1. They have been standardized to mean the same wherever drawings are made and used. Frequently these lines and symbols are called THE LANGUAGE OF INDUSTRY.

DRAWINGS INCLUDE THE NECESSARY DIMENSIONS

A properly made drawing includes ALL dimensions, in proper relation to one another, that are needed to produce the part.

Until recently, drawings were only dimensioned

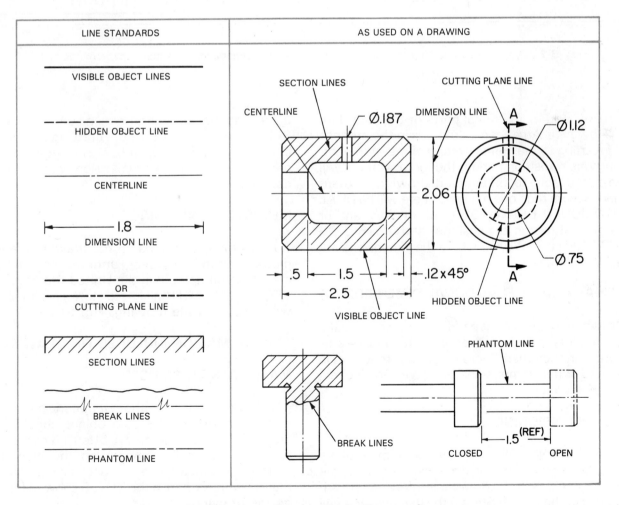

Fig. 3-1. Lines that give the drawing meaning.

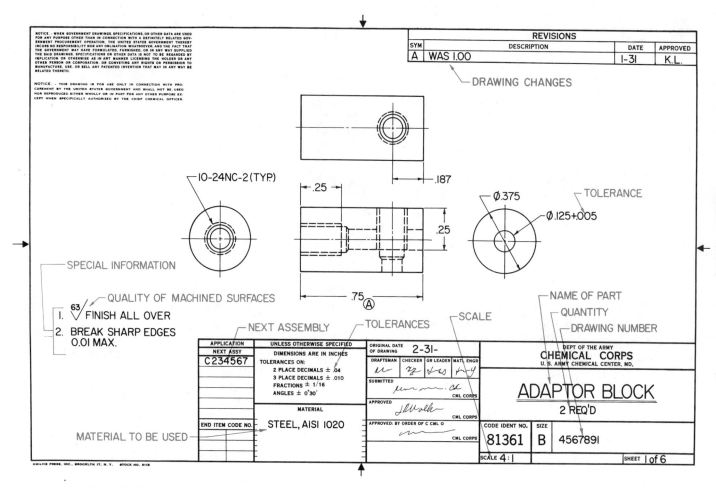

Fig. 3-2. Typical detail drawing that is dimensioned using decimal and/or fractional parts of the inch.

in decimal and/or fractional parts of the inch, Fig. 3-2. However, American industry is in the process of converting to the metric system of measurement. During this transition period, the metalworkers will have to be able to understand drawings dimensioned in more than one manner. There will be DUAL DIMENSIONED DRAWINGS (both decimal and/or fraction and metric dimensions) and METRIC DIMENSIONED DRAWINGS where the dimensions are usually millimeters.

DECIMAL AND/OR FRACTIONAL DIMENSIONING

Drawings using fractional dimensioning usually show objects that do not require a high degree of accuracy in their manufacture. Greater precision is indicated when dimensions are given in decimal parts of the inch.

DUAL DIMENSIONING

DUAL DIMENSIONING is a system that employs the English inch and metric dimensions on the same drawing, Fig. 3-3. If the drawing is intended primarily for use in the United States, the decimal inch will

appear above the metric dimension, as in A, Fig. 3-4. The reverse is true if the drawing is to be used in a metric country, as in B. Some American companies place the metric dimension within brackets, as in C.

METRIC DIMENSIONING

All of the dimensions on the drawing are in the metric system. However, until the conversion to metrics is completed in the United States, a CONVERSION CHART (millimeter to inch dimensions) will appear on the drawing, Fig. 3-5.

INFORMATION INCLUDED ON DRAWINGS

MATERIALS TO BE USED

The general classification of materials to be used in the manufacture of the object should be indicated. The classification is often indicated by the type of section line shown on the plan. Exact material specification is included in a section of the title block. It is often in the NOTES shown elsewhere on the drawing.

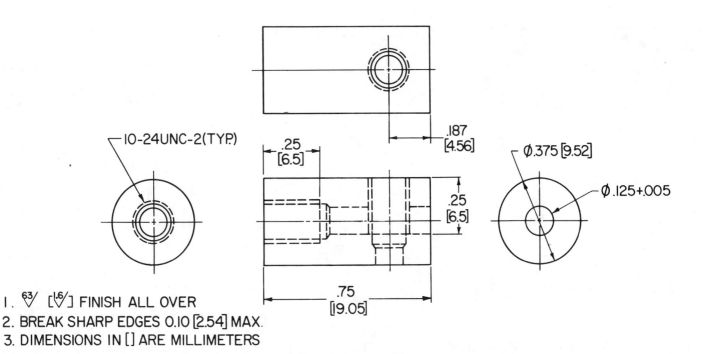

1. ⁶³∀ [¹⁶∀] FINISH ALL OVER
2. BREAK SHARP EDGES 0.10 [2.54] MAX.
3. DIMENSIONS IN [ ] ARE MILLIMETERS

Fig. 3-3. Dual dimensioned drawing. Note that the hole size and thread specifications are not dual dimensioned because there is no metric drill or tap of equivalent size. This drawing was dual dimensioned for use in the United States.

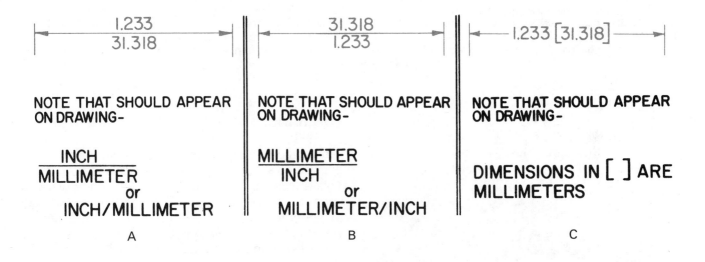

Fig. 3-4. How the inch and metric dimensions are indicated on a dual dimensioned drawing. A—When drawing is to be used in the United States. B—When drawing is to be used primarily in a metric country and the United States. C—Brackets are sometimes used to indicate the metric equivalent on a drawing to be used in the United States.

SURFACE FINISHES REQUIRED

In the past, symbols were used to indicate how the surfaces of the part were to be finished (machined). With so many machining techniques now in use, the symbol cannot be used because it does not indicate the quality of the surface finish required. A technique has been developed that gives more complete surface finish information. Numbers indicate surface roughness in MICROINCHES (a microinch is one-millionth of an inch—0.000001 in.), or MICROMETERS (one-millionth of a meter). The machinist can compare the work surface to required standards by using a set of SURFACE ROUGHNESS COMPARISON STANDARDS, Fig. 3-6, as a guide. If the surface finish is critical, as in instrument components, it is measured electronically with a PROFILOMETER.

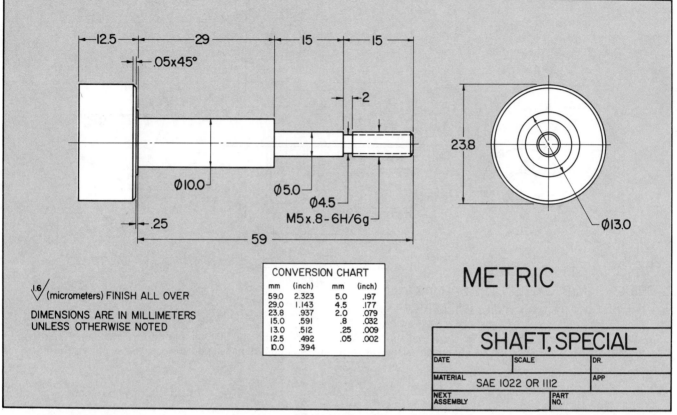

CONVERSION CHART			
mm	(inch)	mm	(inch)
59.0	2.323	5.0	.197
29.0	1.143	4.5	.177
23.8	.937	2.0	.079
15.0	.591	.8	.032
13.0	.512	.25	.009
12.5	.492	.05	.002
10.0	.394		

METRIC

SHAFT, SPECIAL

DATE		SCALE		DR.
MATERIAL	SAE 1022 OR 1112			APP
NEXT ASSEMBLY			PART NO.	

Fig. 3-5. Metric detail drawing. Several things should be noted on this drawing: A—To avoid possible misunderstanding, metric is shown on the drawing in large lettering. B—The conversion chart. C—Metric thread sizes are specified differently from the familiar NC and NF threads. The M denotes the thread system symbol for the standard metric screw thread. The 5 denotes the nominal thread diameter in millimeters, the 0.8 indicates the thread pitch in millimeters, and the 6H and 6g indicate tolerance class designation.

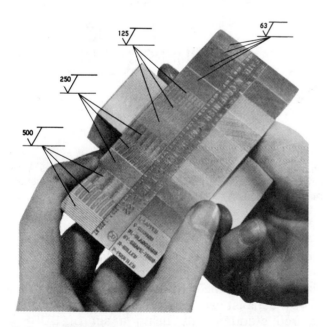

Fig. 3-6. A surface roughness gauge being used to check the finish on a milled aluminum block. As it is often difficult to check machined surfaces visually, a test by feel is also used. The more obvious roughness standards are identified by the appropriate symbols.

TOLERANCES TO BE ALLOWED

It would be very costly to make everything to exact size so acceptable TOLERANCES are permitted. Tolerances are allowances. They tell you how much larger or smaller the part can be made and still work to specifications. Acceptable tolerances may be shown on the drawing in several different ways.

English units of measurement will be shown in the examples (metric tolerancing uses the same techniques).

When the dimension is given in inches and fractions of an inch, UNLESS OTHERWISE INDICATED ON THE DRAWING, permissible tolerances can be assumed to be ± 1/64 in. The symbol ± means that surface can be PLUS (larger) or MINUS (smaller) by 1/64 in. The dimension can be larger or smaller by 1/64 in. and still meet specifications. When the tolerance is plus AND minus, it is called BILATERAL TOLERANCE.

If it is permissible to make the dimension larger, but not smaller, the dimension on the plan would read 2 1/2 + 1/64. If only a minus tolerance is permitted, the dimension would read 2 1/2 − 1/64. When the tolerance is plus OR minus (one direction), it is called a UNILATERAL DIMENSION.

Dimensions shown as inches and decimals indicate the work must be made more accurately. Two methods of showing these tolerances are in general use. Under normal conditions, UNLESS OTHERWISE INDICATED, the tolerances can be assumed to be ± 0.010 in. A PLUS tolerance would be shown as $2.500 + .010$ or $\frac{2.510}{2.500}$, while a MINUS tolerance would be shown as $2.500 - .010$ or $\frac{2.500}{2.490}$. The dimensions show that the part could be used as long as the machined dimensions measure within these limits.

QUANTITY OF UNITS

The drawing may also show the number of units required for each assembly. This aids in ordering the needed material, and will help to determine the most economical method for manufacturing the part.

SCALE OF DRAWING

When drawings are made other than actual size they are called SCALE DRAWINGS. This occurs when the part drawn is too large or too small, and it would not be practical to draw it full size. A drawing made one-half size would be shown by the figures 1:2, while 2:1 would mean that the drawing is twice actual size.

NAME OF THE OBJECT AND ON WHAT IT IS TO BE USED

A portion of the title block is designed especially for this information. It tells the mechanic the correct name of the piece, and the name of the major unit on which it is to be used.

Very seldom are the original drawings found in the shop because they might be lost, damaged, or destroyed. On many jobs several sets of drawings are needed.

Several methods of duplicating original drawings have been developed. OZALID prints are almost universally used. These have black, blue, green, or maroon lines on a white background. Prints enlarged photographically from microfilm, Fig. 3-7, are starting to be used in greater numbers. The principal reason for this is because the original can be stored easier and can be located in storage. They can be reproduced very rapidly in print form by data processing equipment.

TYPES OF DRAWINGS

Most products made by industry require numerous drawings to give a complete description of the object. Each piece, even the smallest rivet,

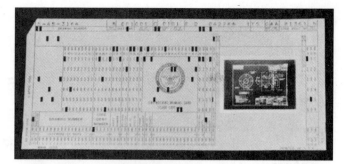

Fig. 3-7. The small negative on the microfilm aperture card is enlarged by a photographic process to the desired print size on a microfilm reader/printer. The enlarged print can be verified on the view screen and then enlarged to the required size in print form.   (RECORDAK)

requires a drawing. Such drawings are called WORKING DRAWINGS. They supply the craftworker with the information necessary to make and assemble the many pieces that make up the product. There are two kinds of working drawings. One is the DETAIL DRAWING. It includes a drawing of the part, usually a multiview drawing, with dimensions and other information needed to make the part. See Figs. 3-2, 3-3, and 3-5. The other type of working drawing is called an ASSEMBLY DRAWING, Fig. 3-8. It shows where, and how, the part described on detail drawings fit into the complete assembly of the unit. On large or complicated products, SUBASSEMBLY DRAWINGS, Figs. 3-9 and 3-10, are frequently used. Such drawings show the assembly of a portion of the complete product.

The detail drawing, in most instances, gives information on only one item. However, if the mechanism is small in size, or if it is composed of only a few parts, details and assembly may appear on the same sheet.

The parts are identified by name and/or number on the assembly drawings. Also shown on the drawing will be NOTES indicating changes, if any, that have have been made on the original part.

The number of pieces required in the assembly (but not on entire production run) will be included

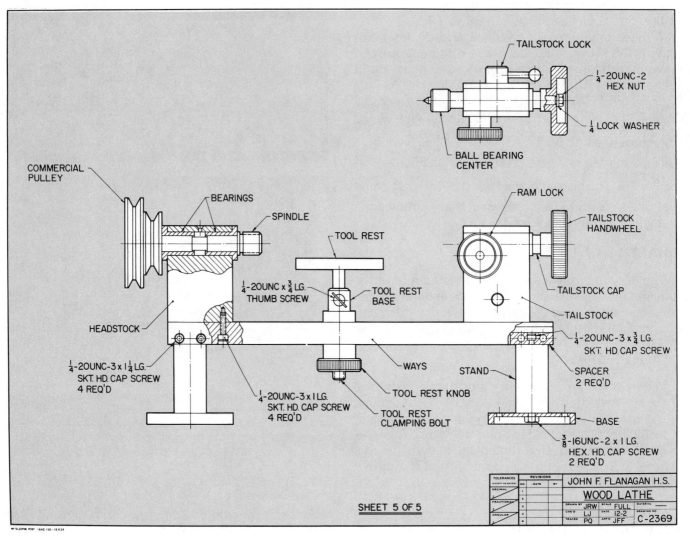

Fig. 3-8. An assembly drawing of a wood lathe.

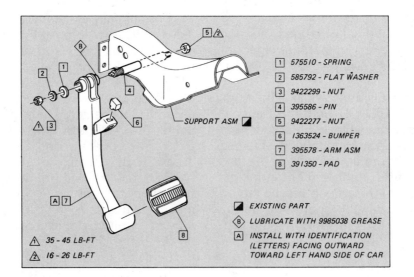

1	575510 - SPRING
2	585792 - FLAT WASHER
3	9422299 - NUT
4	395586 - PIN
5	9422277 - NUT
6	1363524 - BUMPER
7	395578 - ARM ASM
8	391350 - PAD

SUPPORT ASM

▰ EXISTING PART

B LUBRICATE WITH 9985038 GREASE

A INSTALL WITH IDENTIFICATION (LETTERS) FACING OUTWARD TOWARD LEFT HAND SIDE OF CAR

△1 35 - 45 LB-FT

△2 16 - 26 LB-FT

Fig. 3-9. A pictorial type subassembly drawing. This kind of drawing is often used with semiskilled workers who have received a minimum of training in print reading. (General Motors Corp.)

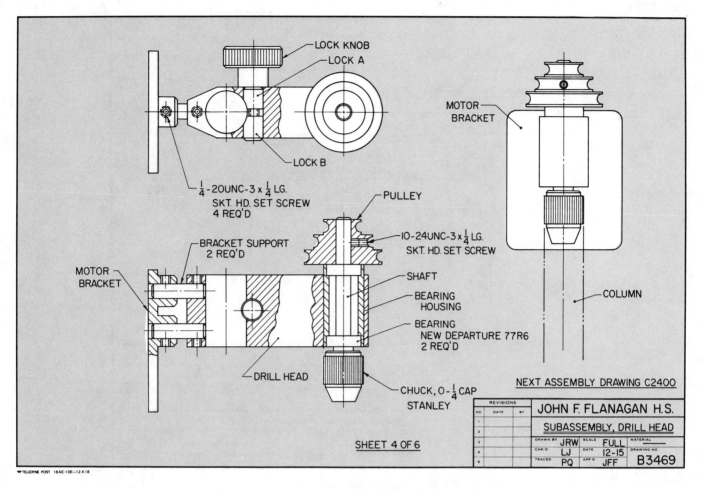

LOCK KNOB
LOCK A

MOTOR
BRACKET

$\frac{1}{4}$ - 20UNC - 3 x $\frac{1}{4}$ LG.
SKT. HD. SET SCREW
4 REQ'D

LOCK B

PULLEY

IO - 24UNC - 3 x $\frac{1}{4}$ LG.
SKT. HD. SET SCREW

BRACKET SUPPORT
2 REQ'D

MOTOR
BRACKET

SHAFT

BEARING
HOUSING

BEARING
NEW DEPARTURE 77R6
2 REQ'D

COLUMN

DRILL HEAD

CHUCK, O - $\frac{1}{4}$ CAP
STANLEY

NEXT ASSEMBLY DRAWING C2400

SHEET 4 OF 6

REVISIONS			JOHN F. FLANAGAN H.S.
NO	DATE	BY	SUBASSEMBLY, DRILL HEAD

DRAWN BY JRW	SCALE FULL	MATERIAL
CHK'D LJ	DATE 12-15	DRAWING NO
TRACED PQ	APP'D JFF	B3469

TELEDYNE POST 18AE-10E—12 X 18

Fig. 3-10. A conventional type subassembly drawing. It
shows the assembly of drill press head.

on the drawing in the form of a PARTS LIST or BILL OF MATERIAL.

DRAWING SIZES AND IDENTIFICATION INFORMATION

Most firms have standardized the sizes of the sheets on which drawings are made. This simplifies storage of completed drawings.

For convenience in filing and locating drawings, each plate or drawing is given an IDENTIFYING NUMBER. See Fig. 3-2.

PLANNING YOUR WORK

It is to YOUR advantage to carefully plan your work. Time will be saved and waste kept to a minimum. Problem areas can usually be noted in advance and solutions to them devised. You can also get some idea on how much time will be needed to do the work.

The first step in planning should be to study the prints or drawings for the job. From information they contain, a BILL OF MATERIAL can be prepared. This should include all of the items (metal, fasteners, finishes, etc.) that will be necessary to complete the job.

After the bill of material is completed, list the machines, tools, and equipment that will be required. Be sure to use their correct names. If you are not sure of the names, look them up in this text or in tool catalogs.

Finally, a PLAN OF PROCEDURE will have to be developed. This is an outline, in sequential order, of the operations that should be followed to complete the job or project.

A PROJECT PLAN SHEET used in many shops is shown in Fig. 3-11. It includes a BILL OF MATERIAL, TOOL AND EQUIPMENT LISTING, and a PLAN OF PROCEDURE. It may be used as presented or another type may be designed.

PLAN YOUR WORK, FOLLOW YOUR PLAN . . . a good habit to develop.

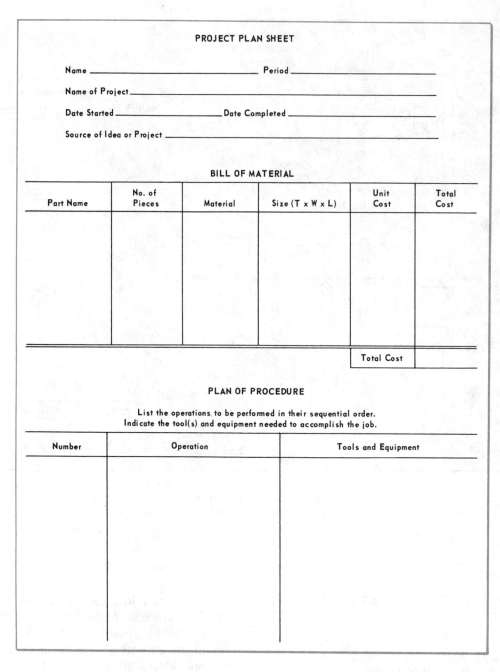

PROJECT PLAN SHEET

Name _____ Period _____

Name of Project _____

Date Started _____ Date Completed _____

Source of Idea or Project _____

BILL OF MATERIAL

Part Name	No. of Pieces	Material	Size (T x W x L)	Unit Cost	Total Cost
				Total Cost	

PLAN OF PROCEDURE

List the operations to be performed in their sequential order.
Indicate the tool(s) and equipment needed to accomplish the job.

Number	Operation	Tools and Equipment

Fig. 3-11. Typical planning sheet that includes a bill of material
and a plan of procedure.

TEST YOUR KNOWLEDGE, Unit 3

Please do not write in the text. Place your answers on a separate sheet of paper.
1. Drawings are used to:
   a. Standardize parts.
   b. Protect the original sketches.
   c. Show what to make or how the product is to be assembled.
   d. Show in multiview what an object looks like before it is made.
2. The symbols and lines used to make drawings are often called _____.
3. A drawing, if properly made, includes _____ that are needed to make the part.
4. A _____ drawing employs the English inch and metric dimensions on the same drawing.
5. Show how the dimensioning system described above would show the dimensions on a drawing that would be used primarily in the United States.
6. A subassembly drawing differs from an assembly drawing by:

a. Showing only a small portion of the completed object.
b. Making it easier to use smaller drawings.
c. Showing the object without all needed dimensions.
d. None of the above.
7. Prints are used instead of the actual drawing because:
   a. The actual drawing does not show all of the details.
   b. They might be lost, damaged, or destroyed.
   c. They are easier to read.
   d. None of the above.
8. What kind of drawings give the metalworker all of the information needed to make the part?
9. _____ drawings show where and how the parts described on other drawings fit into the complete assembly of the unit.
10. Standard size drawings have been developed to:
    a. Make them easier to store.
    b. Cause less confusion.
    c. Make them easier to handle.
    d. None of the above.
11. Why plan your work?
12. A bill of material lists _____.
13. What is a plan of procedure?

RESEARCH AND DEVELOPMENT

1. Secure sample drawings from a local industry. Develop a bulletin board display around them.
2. Make a tracing and reproduce it in print form.
3. Secure samples of the various kinds of drawings.
4. Prepare a display panel showing a simple project from drawing to completed product.
5. Prepare transparencies for the overhead projector that show the title block, parts list, and materials list of an actual industrial drawing. Use these to explain or describe an industrial drawing to the class. If possible, secure a sample of the product shown on the drawing.
6. Make a display panel showing how six metals are identified by section lines. If possible, obtain and attach a sample of the actual metal under each drawing.
7. Contact a local industry and secure the drawings of a simple assembly. If possible, also secure samples of the piece that was manufactured from each print. Develop a display panel around the drawings and pieces made from them.
8. Design a planning sheet for use in your school shop.

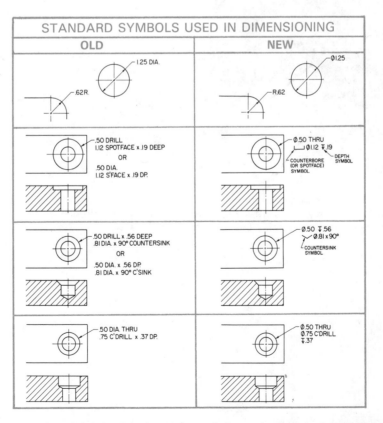

Recently ANSI (American National Standards Institute) recommended certain changes in specifying circles and holes. Study and compare the examples shown above.

Note how these workers are dressed as they pour molten stainless steel into a mold. Their clothing is aluminized to reflect the high temperatures; leg guards, and heavy shoes are worn to protect them from molten metal that might splash; heavy, fireproof insulated gloves guard their hands, and a full face shield is worn.   (Precision Castparts Corp.)

Unit 4

SHOP SAFETY

SAFETY COMES FIRST and is everyone's concern. The development of safe work habits cannot be overemphasized. YOUR safety and well-being are of paramount importance to your instructors. Please remember this when they insist on safe work practices. If you are diligent and follow instructions with care, safe work practices will be observed by force of habit.

It is a mark of intelligence to wear eye protection, use machine guards, and observe the thousand-and-one safe work practices of metalworking. Eyesight that is destroyed cannot be replaced. Most accidents occur because simple safety rules were not observed.

The safety practices presented in this unit are general in nature. Safety precautions for specific machines, tools, and operations are explained in the text along with the description of the equipment and techniques. Study them carefully and apply as necessary. Do not take chances—IT HURTS TO GET HURT.

FOR THE SHOP

ALWAYS protect your eyes. Wear safety glasses, goggles, or a face shield, Fig. 4-1. It is good practice to have personal safety glasses or goggles. Their cost is reasonable. Your instructor can help you determine what kind and style is best suited to your needs.

The shop is a place to work. It is not for "horseplay" or joke playing which frequently ends up tragically. Daydreaming increases your chance of injury.

Keep the shop clean. Metal scraps should be placed in a scrap box rather than letting them drop on the floor. When they are in the scrap box, the metal pieces cannot cause you or a fellow student to trip or fall. Some of your scrap may then be available for reuse by other students.

Avoid using compressed air to remove chips and cutting fluids from a machine. The flying chips can

Fig. 4-1. This student is properly dressed for the job he is doing. He is wearing a T-shirt, approved safety glasses, and a snug fitting apron. He has carefully lubricated and checked his machine before attempting to operate it.

cause painful eye injuries, and vaporized oil may be ignited and cause serious burns.

Oily rags must be placed in a closed safety container. Rags used to clean machines become embedded with metal slivers. Place them where they will not be used again.

Keep hand tools in good condition. Store them in such a way that a person will not be injured when the tool is taken from the tool panel or storage rack. Report broken, dull, or damaged tools to your instructor.

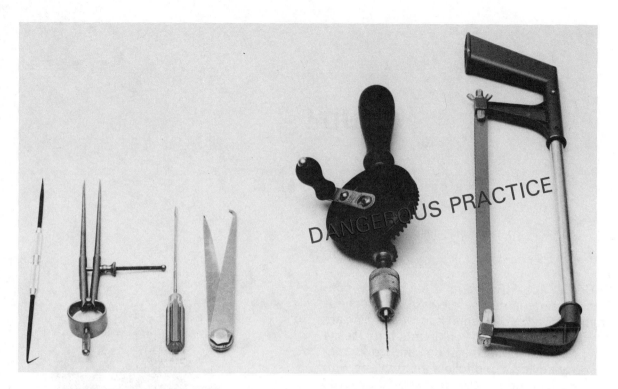

PREFERRED WAY TO PLACE SHARP OR POINTED
TOOLS ON WORK AREA.

AVOID PLACING TOOLS IN THIS MANNER.
CHANCES ARE YOU WILL REACH INTO THE SMALL
DRILL OR PICK UP THE SAW BY THE CUTTING EDGE
OF THE BLADE.

Fig. 4-2. Place sharp and pointed tools on the bench in such a manner that they will not injure you when you pick them up.

When working with tools like scribers, dividers, and other pointed or sharp-edged tools, place them on the bench with the points and cutting edges facing away from you, Fig. 4-2. There will be less chance of them puncturing or cutting your hand when you reach to pick them up to use.

Avoid carrying tools in your pocket, Fig. 4-3.

Get help when moving heavy machine accessories or large pieces of metal stock.

Have adequate ventilation for jobs where dust and fumes are a hazard. Return oils and solvents to proper storage. Wipe up any fluid that has been spilled. DO NOT pour used fluids in the sink drain. Dispose of them as directed by your instructor.

Carefully read instructions when using the new synthetic oils, solvents, and adhesives. The fumes from many of them are dangerous. Some of the fluids can also cause serious skin irritations if they get on your hands.

Dress properly. Avoid wearing loose fitting clothes. Rings and other jewelry that might get caught in moving machinery should be removed. (Store them where they will not get stolen.) Keep your sleeves rolled up. If you wear a tie, remove it or wear a bow tie.

Should your shop be extremely noisy, wear hearing protectors, Fig. 4-4. Take no chances. Protect

Fig. 4-3. It is a dangerous practice to carry tools in your pocket.

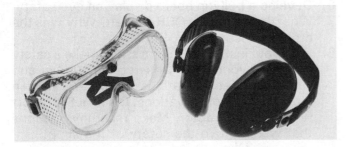

Fig. 4-4. Some shop areas produce both noise and flying chips. Protect sight and hearing when working in such places.

your sight and hearing at all times you are in the shop.

Know your job. It is foolish to attempt to operate a machine or use a tool without receiving instructions. Get help if you are not sure what and/or how a job is to be done.

Be sure all of the tools you use are sharp, in good condition, and fitted with suitable handles.

When operating machines:

1. Do not operate a machine unless ALL guards are in place.
2. Stop the machine to make measurements and/or adjustments. Avoid using your hands to stop a rotating machine part. Let it stop of its own accord, or use the brake if it has one.
3. Resist the urge to touch the surfaces of machined work while the machine is running.
4. Keep the floor around the machine clear of chips and scrap.
5. Do not talk to classmates while operating a machine. It is easy to become distracted and in-

jure yourself, damage the machine, or ruin the work.

6. Chips and cuttings should never be removed with your hands, or while the machine is running. Stop the machine and use a brush, Fig. 4-5. Long stringy chips are best removed with pliers. Better still, grind a chip breaker into the cutting tool and prevent long chips from forming.
7. Get prompt medical attention for any cut, bruise, scratch, or burn, no matter how minor it may appear.
8. Above all, never attempt to operate a machine while your senses are impaired by medication or other substances.

THINK BEFORE ACTING. It costs nothing and may save you from painful injury that could result in permanent disability!

TEST YOUR KNOWLEDGE, Unit 4

Please do not write in the text. Place your answers on a separate sheet of paper.

1. Safety goggles, glasses, or face shields must be worn in the shop to:
   a. Help you see better.
   b. Prevent eye injury.
   c. Prevent sweat from running into your eyes.
   d. Keep fumes from entering the eyes.
   e. All of the above.
   f. None of the above.
2. Always stop machines when making _____ and _____.
3. Most accidents are caused because _____ _____.
4. Compressed air should not be used to clean chips from machines because:
   a. It does the job too quickly.
   b. It may damage the machine.
   c. Flying chips may cause serious eye injuries.
   d. All of the above.
   e. None of the above.
5. Oily rags should be placed in _____.
6. What precautions should be observed before starting to use a machine?
7. Remove chips from the machine with a ____, never with _____.

RESEARCH AND DEVELOPMENT

1. Invite a safety expert from a local industry, or a supplier of safety equipment, to evaluate your present shop safety program and make recommendations, if necessary, to improve it.
2. Work with school officials to see that necessary protective eyewear is available for each student.

Fig. 4-5. Use a brush to remove metal chips, never use your hand. Do not remove the chips until the machine has stopped.

3. Develop and produce a series of safety posters suitable for your school shop.
4. Contact the NATIONAL SOCIETY FOR THE PREVENTION OF BLINDNESS, 1790 Broadway, New York City, for information on the WISE OWL CLUB OF AMERICA, sponsored by that organization.
5. Produce a series of 35mm slides on safe work habits to be observed when using hand tools.
6. Develop a bulletin board display on eye safety.
7. What do the initials OSHA mean? Why was the program instituted?
8. With your instructor's permission, make a safety survey of your shop. Observe the number and kinds of safety violations. Prepare a written report of your observations. Discuss the report with your instructor. Make recommendations that will improve the safety of the shop.

Many thousands of safety requirements were included in the manufacture of the Space Shuttle Challenger. This overhead view was taken from a camera placed onboard a satellite launched from the shuttle itself.

Unit 5

MEASUREMENT

Industry regularly makes measurements to a millionth (0.000001) part of an inch. A distance this small is called a MICROINCH. If the microinch were enlarged to the thickness of a dime, an inch would be high as four Empire State Buildings!

In addition to using the English units of measure (inch, foot, etc.), American industry has been gradually changing to metric units of measure (millimeters, meter, etc.). The United States has adopted the modern form of the metric system known as the INTERNATIONAL SYSTEM OF UNITS (abbreviated SI).

Metric based measuring tools will offer no problems. As a matter of fact, many think they are easier to read than inch based measuring tools.

Regardless of how fine industry can measure, the job at hand is to learn to read a rule to 1/64 in. and

0.50 millimeter; progress through 1/1000 (0.001) in. and 0.01 millimeter by micrometer and 0.02 by Vernier type measuring tools; and finally progress to 1/10000 (0.0001) in. and 0.002 millimeter by the Vernier scale on the sleeve of some micrometers.

THE RULE

The STEEL RULE, often incorrectly referred to as a scale, is the simplest of the measuring tools found in the shop. See Fig. 5-1 for the three basic types of rule graduations. A few of the many rule styles are shown in Figs. 5-2 through 5-8.

READING THE RULE (ENGLISH UNITS)

A careful study of the enlarged section of the rule, Fig. 5-9, will show the different fractional divisions of the inch from 1/8 to 1/64 in. The lines representing the divisions are called GRADUATIONS. On many rules, every fourth graduation is numbered on the 1/32 edge, and every eighth graduation on the 1/64 edge.

The best way to learn to read the rule is to:
1. Become thoroughly familiar with making 1/8 and 1/16 measurements.
2. Do the same with the 1/32 and 1/64 measurements.
3. Practice until you become proficient enough to read the measurements accurately and quickly.

Some steel rules (inch based) are graduated in 10ths, 20ths, 50ths, and 100ths. Additional practice will be necessary to read these rules accurately and quickly.

Fractional measurements are ALWAYS reduced to the lowest terms. A measurement of 14/16 is 7/8; 2/8 is 1/4; etc.

READING THE RULE (METRIC UNITS)

Most metric rules are divided into millimeters or

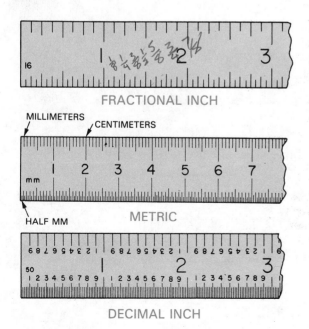

Fig. 5-1. A comparison of the metric (millimeter) graduated rule with the familiar fractional and decimal inch rules.

Fig. 5-2. Pocket rule (6 in.).

Fig. 5-3. Narrow rule.

Fig. 5-4. Flexible rule.

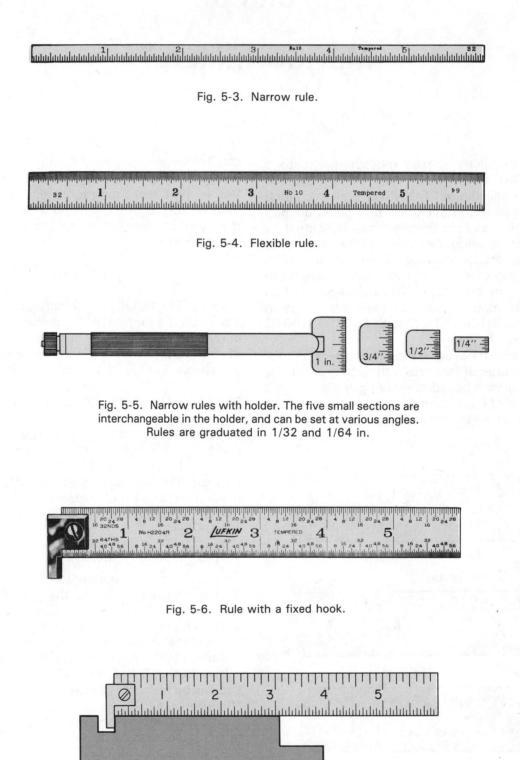

Fig. 5-5. Narrow rules with holder. The five small sections are interchangeable in the holder, and can be set at various angles. Rules are graduated in 1/32 and 1/64 in.

Fig. 5-6. Rule with a fixed hook.

Fig. 5-7. How the hooked rule is used.

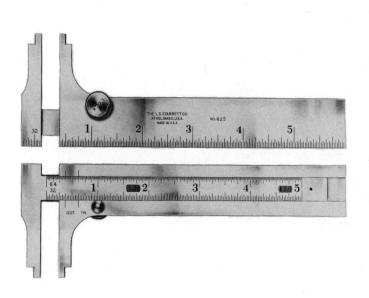

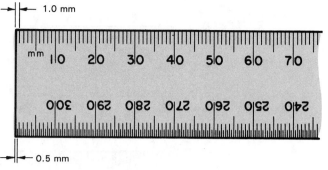

Fig. 5-10. Most metric rules are graduated in millimeters and 0.5 millimeters. They are available in 150 mm, 300 mm, 450 mm, 600 mm, 900 mm, and 1200 mm lengths.

Fig.5-8. A slide caliper rule is fitted to the work and locked. Outside dimensions are read at the point marked ''out.'' Inside dimensions at the point marked ''in.''

CARE OF THE RULE

The steel rule is precision made and, like all tools, the quality of service depends upon the care it receives. Here are a few suggestions:

1. Use a screwdriver to loosen and tighten screws and to open paint cans. The rule was not designed to do this sort of work.
2. Keep the rule clear of moving machinery. Using it to clean metal chips as they form on the cutting tool will not only ruin the rule, but will prove extremely dangerous to the person attempting it.
3. Avoid laying other tools on the rule.
4. Steel rules will not rust if they are wiped with an oily cloth before being returned to storage.
5. An occasional cleaning with fine steel wool will keep the graduations legible.
6. Make it a practice to make measurements and tool settings from the 1 in. line (10 mm line on metric rules), or other major graduations, rather than from the end of the rule.
7. Store rules separately. Do not throw them in a drawer with other tools.
8. Use the rule with care so the ends do not become nicked or worn.
9. Use the correct rule for the job being done.
10. Coat the tool with wax or a rust preventative if the rule is to be stored for a prolonged period.

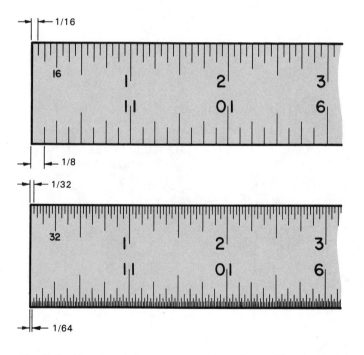

Fig. 5-9. Fractional measurements found on a No. 4 rule.

THE MICROMETER CALIPER

A Frenchman, Jean Palmer, devised and patented a measuring tool that made use of a screw thread, making it possible to read measurements quickly and accurately without calculations. It incorporated a series of engraved lines on the sleeve and around the thimble. The device, Fig. 5-12, called ''Systeme Palmer,'' is the basis of the modern MICROMETER CALIPER.

0.5 millimeters (abbreviated mm). They are numbered every 10 mm. See Fig. 5-10. The distance of the measurement is determined by counting the number of millimeters. A measurement of 11 millimeters is written 11.0 mm. A measurement of 15 1/2 millimeters is written 15.5 mm.

How many measurements in Fig. 5-11 can you read?

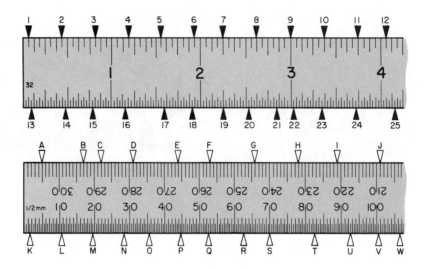

Fig. 5-11. Study and determine the measurements shown on each rule.

The micrometer caliper, known as a ''mike,'' is a precision measuring tool capable of measuring to 1/1000 (0.001) in. or 1/100 (0.01) mm and when fitted with Vernier scale to 1/10000 (0.0001) in. or 2/1000 (0.002) mm.

While manufactured in sizes up to 60 in. and 1500 mm, the spindle movement is limited to 1 in. and 25 mm. Only the frame of the tool is enlarged.

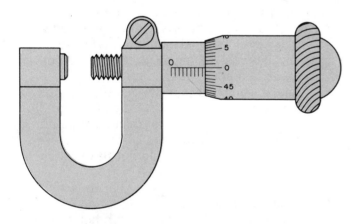

Fig. 5-12. A drawing of Systeme Palmer. The modern micrometer caliper works on the same principle as this 1848 measuring tool.

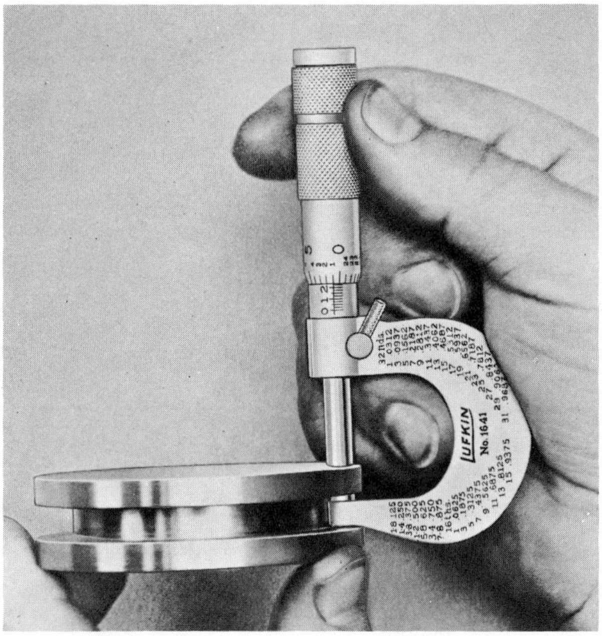

TYPES OF MICROMETERS

Micrometers are made in a large variety of models. A few of the more commonly used are:
OUTSIDE MICROMETER, Fig. 5-13. Measures diameters and thicknesses.
INSIDE MICROMETER. Measures inside diameters of cylinders and rings, widths of slots, setting

Fig. 5-13. The 0 to 1 in. outside micrometer caliper. Note how the machinist is holding it to make the measurement.

Fig. 5-14. Conventional inside micrometer.

gauges, etc. There are two generally used styles: The CONVENTIONAL INSIDE MICROMETER, Fig. 5-14, whose range is extended by fitting longer rods to the micrometer head, and the JAW-TYPE INSIDE MICROMETER, Fig. 5-15. Its range is

Fig. 5-15. Jaw-type inside micrometer. (Scherr-Tumico)

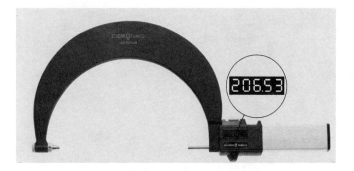

Fig. 5-17. A digital readout micrometer. This electronic measuring tool can make measurements in inches or millimeters. (Scherr-Tumico)

limited to 1 in. or 25 mm. Note that the scale on the sleeve of the jaw-type is graduated from right to left.

DIRECT READING MICROMETER, Fig. 5-16. Measurement is read directly from the numbers appearing in the opening in the frame. An ELECTRONIC DIGITAL READOUT MICROMETER, Fig. 5-17, senses the spindle position on the work and indicates the measurement on the digital display.

MICROMETER DEPTH GAUGE, Fig. 5-18. Depths of holes, slots, projections, etc., can be measured with this tool. The measuring range can be increased by changing to spindles of longer lengths. Note that measurements are read from RIGHT TO LEFT.

SCREW THREAD MICROMETER, Fig. 5-19. This micrometer has a pointed spindle and a double ''V'' anvil, both correctly shaped to contact the screw thread. It measures the pitch diameter of the thread, which equals the outside diameter of the screw minus the depth of one thread.

SPECIAL MICROMETERS, Fig. 5-20. Many cutting tools have cutting edges that are uneven in number. This makes it impossible to measure their diameter with a conventional ''mike.'' Special micrometers have been devised to handle this and other measurement problems.

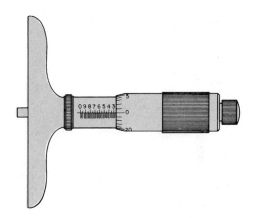

Fig. 5-18. Micrometer depth gauge.

READING AN INCH BASED MICROMETER

The principle of the micrometer—a sectional view is shown in Fig. 5-21—is based on a very accurately made screw thread that rotates in a fixed nut. The screw thread is ground on the SPINDLE and is attached to the THIMBLE. The spindle advances or recedes from the ANVIL by rotating the thimble. The

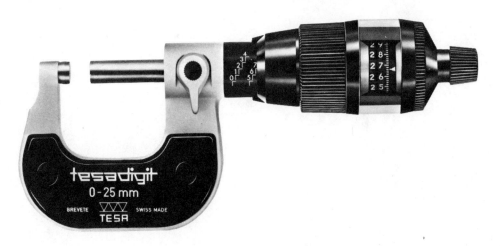

Fig. 5-16. A direct reading metric micrometer. (Brown and Sharpe Mfg. Co.)

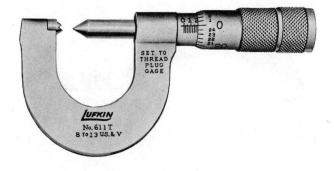

Fig. 5-19. The screw thread micrometer caliper.

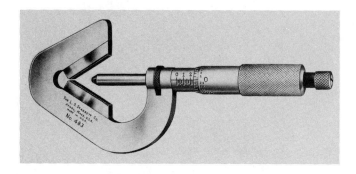

Fig. 5-20. One of many specially designed micrometer-type measuring tools. This tool can also be used to check whether a diameter is out-of-round.

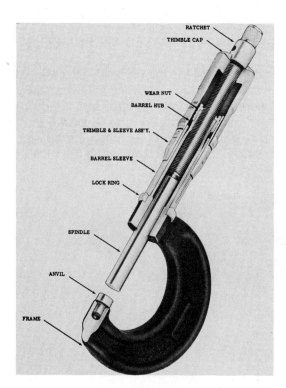

Fig. 5-21. A sectional view of a micrometer caliper. (Scherr-Tumico)

threaded section has 40 threads per inch; therefore, each revolution of the thimble moves the spindle 1/40 (0.025) in.

The line engraved lengthwise on the sleeve is divided into 40 equal parts per inch which corresponds to the number of threads on the spindle. Each vertical line represents 1/40 or 0.025 in. Every fourth division is numbered 1, 2, 3, etc., representing 0.100 in., 0.200 in., etc.

The beveled edge of the thimble is divided into 25 equal parts around its circumference. Each division equals 1/1000 (0.001) in. On some micrometers every division is numbered, while every fifth division is numbered on others.

The "mike" is read by recording the highest number on the sleeve, 1 = 0.100, 2 = 0.200, etc. To this number is added the number of vertical lines visible between the number and thimble edge, 1 = 0.025, 2 = 0.050, etc. To this total is added

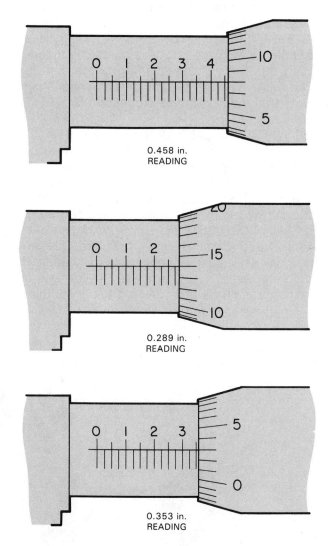

0.458 in.
READING

0.289 in.
READING

0.353 in.
READING

Fig. 5-22. Micrometer caliper readings, Examples 1, 2, and 3.

the number of thousandths indicated by the line on the thimble that coincides with the horizontal line on the sleeve. See Fig. 5-22.

EXAMPLE 1

The reading is composed of:

4 large graduations or 4 × 0.100	= 0.400
2 small graduations or 2 × 0.025	= 0.050
and 8 graduations on the thimble or 8 × 0.001	= 0.008
Total reading	= 0.458 in.

EXAMPLE 2

The reading is composed of:

2 large graduations or 2 × 0.100	= 0.200
3 small graduations or 3 × 0.025	= 0.075
and 14 graduations on the thimble or 14 × 0.001	= 0.014
Total reading	= 0.289 in.

EXAMPLE 3

The reading is composed of:

3 large graduations or 3 × 0.100	= 0.300
2 small graduations or 2 × 0.025	= 0.050
and 3 graduations on the thimble or 3 × 0.001	= 0.003
Total reading	= 0.353 in.

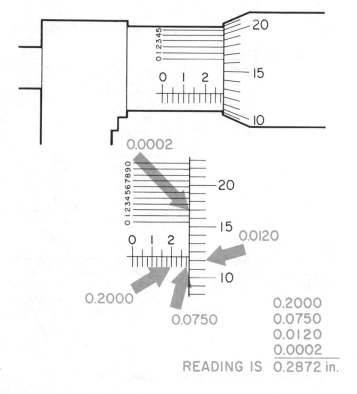

Fig. 5-23. How to read an inch based Vernier micrometer caliper. Add the total reading in thousandths, then observe which of the lines on the Vernier scale coincide with a line on the thimble. Only one of them can. In this case it is line 2, so 0.0002 will be added to the reading.

READING A VERNIER MICROMETER

On occasion, it is necessary to measure finer than 1/1000 (0.001) in. When this situation is encountered, the Vernier micrometer caliper is employed. This micrometer has a third scale AROUND THE SLEEVE, Fig. 5-23, that will furnish the 1/10000 (0.0001) in. reading without estimating or guessing.

The Vernier has 11 parallel lines that occupy the same space as 10 lines on the thimble. The lines around the thimble are numbered 1 to 10. The difference between the spaces on the sleeve and those on the thimble is one-tenth of a thousandth (0.001) of an inch. To read, first obtain the thousandths reading, then observe which of the lines of the Vernier scale coincides with a line on the thimble. Only one of them can. If it is line 1, add 0.0001 to the reading, if line 2, add 0.0002 to the reading, etc. See Fig. 5-23.

READING A METRIC BASED MICROMETER

The metric based micrometer, Fig. 5-24, is read as shown in Fig. 5-25. If you are able to read the conventional based micrometer, the change over to reading the metric based tool will offer no difficulties.

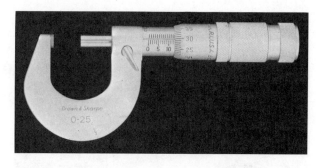

Fig. 5-24. Metric based micrometer.

READING A METRIC VERNIER MICROMETER

Metric Vernier micrometers, Fig. 5-26, are used like those graduated in hundredths of a millimeter (0.01 mm). However, using the Vernier scale on the sleeve, an additional reading of two-thousandths of a millimeter (0.002 mm) can be obtained. This is illustrated in Fig. 5-27.

USING THE MICROMETER

The proper way to hold a micrometer when making a measurement is shown in Fig. 5-28. The work

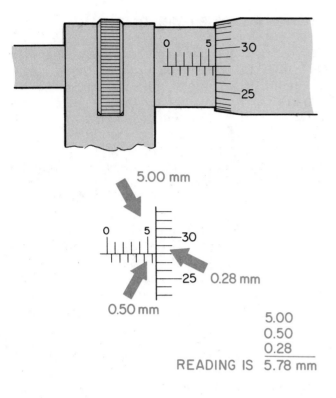

5.00 mm

0.28 mm

0.50 mm

```
          5.00
          0.50
          0.28
READING IS 5.78 mm
```

Fig. 5-25. To read metric micrometer, add the total reading in millimeters visible on the sleeve to the reading on hundredths of a millimeter, indicated by the graduation on the thimble, which coincides with the longitudinal line on the micrometer sleeve.

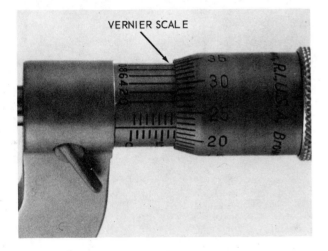

Fig. 5-26. Vernier scale on a metric based micrometer.

device is used to rotate the spindle. When the pressure reaches a predetermined amount, the ratchet stop slips and prevents further turning of the spindle. Uniform contact pressure with the work is assured even if different people use the same micrometer.

Some micrometers are fitted with a FRICTION THIMBLE, Fig. 5-13. It is a friction control mechanism built into the upper section of the thimble. It produces the same results as the ratchet stop but permits one hand use of the micrometer.

When several identical parts are to be gauged, lock the spindle in place with the LOCK RING, Fig. 5-21. Gauging parts with a micrometer locked at the proper setting is an easy way to determine whether the pieces are oversize, correct size, or undersize.

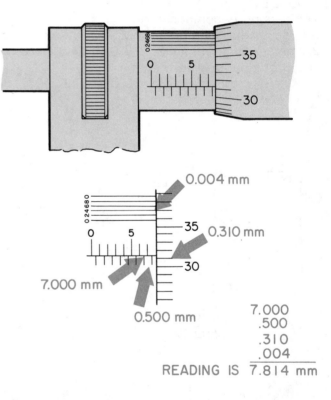

0.004 mm

0.310 mm

7.000 mm

0.500 mm

```
          7.000
           .500
           .310
           .004
READING IS 7.814 mm
```

Fig. 5-27. Reading a metric based Vernier micrometer caliper. To the regular reading in hundredths of a millimeter (0.01 mm), add the reading from the Vernier scale that coincides with a line on the thimble. Each line on the Vernier scale is equal to two thousandths of a millimeter (0.002 mm).

READING AN INSIDE MICROMETER

To get a correct reading with an INSIDE MICROMETER, it is important that the tool be held square across the diameter and positioned so it will measure the diameter on exact center, Fig. 5-30.

is placed into position, and the thimble rotated until the part is clamped LIGHTLY between the anvil and spindle. Guard against excessive pressure. It will cause an erroneous reading.

The correct contact pressure will be applied if a mike with a RATCHET STOP is used, Fig. 5-29. This

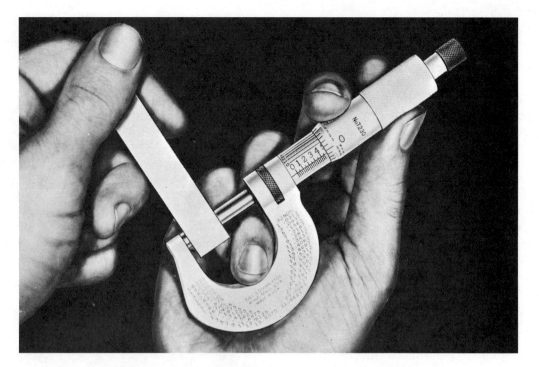

Fig. 5-28. The correct way to hold 0 to 1 in. micrometer when making a measurement on work.

Measurement is made by holding one end of the tool in place and then "feeling" for the maximum possible setting by moving the other end from left to right, and then in and out of the opening. The measurement is taken when no left or right movement is felt, and a slight drag is noticeable on the in and out swing. It may be necessary to take several readings and average them.

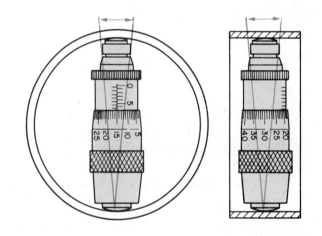

Fig. 5-30. Inside micrometer and how it is used. Extension rods can be added for measuring larger openings.

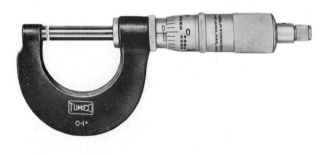

Fig. 5-29. Micrometer with a ratchet stop.

READING A MICROMETER DEPTH GAUGE

Be sure to read a MICROMETER DEPTH GAUGE, Fig. 5-31, correctly. Unlike an outside micrometer, the graduations on this measuring tool are in REVERSE ORDER. That is they read 0, 9, 8, 7, 6, etc. The graduations UNDER the thimble must be read rather than those that are exposed.

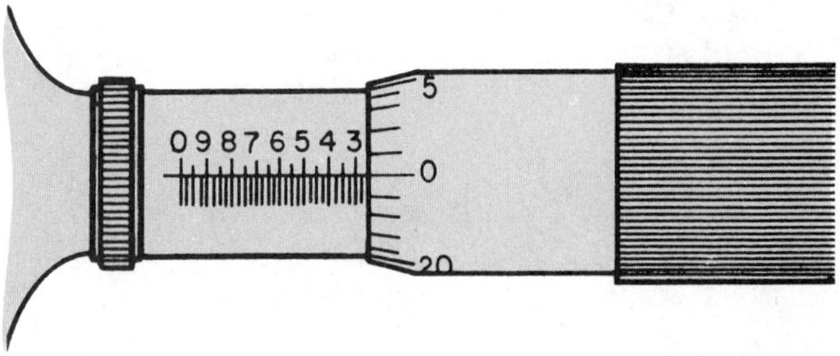

Fig. 5-31. Micrometer depth gauge. Remember, when making measurements with a depth micrometer, the graduations are in reverse order.

CARE OF A MICROMETER

Micrometers must be handled with care or their accuracy will be destroyed. The following techniques are recommended:

1. Place the micrometer on the work carefully so the faces of the anvil and spindle will not be damaged. The same applies when removing the tool after the measurement has been made.
2. Keep the micrometer clean. Wipe it with a slightly oiled cloth to prevent rust and tarnish. A drop of light oil on the screw thread will keep it operating smoothly.
3. Avoid springing micrometers not fitted with a ratchet stop or friction thimble by applying too much pressure when making a measurement.
4. Clean the spindle and anvil faces before use. This can be done with a soft cloth or by LIGHTLY closing the jaws on a clean piece of paper and drawing the paper out.
5. Check for accuracy by closing the spindle gently on the anvil and note whether the zero line on the thimble coincides with the zero on the sleeve. If they are not aligned, make adjustments by following the manufacturer's recommendations for this operation.
6. Avoid placing a micrometer where it may fall on the floor, or have other tools be placed on it.
7. If the micrometer must be opened or closed a considerable distance to make a measurement, roll the thimble on the palm of your hand. Avoid "twirling" the frame as this can damage the tool.
8. Clean and oil a micrometer if it is to be stored for some time. If possible, place the tool in a small box for protection.

VERNIER MEASURING TOOLS

The Vernier principle of measuring was named for its inventor, Pierre Vernier (1580-1637), a French mathematician.

The VERNIER CALIPER, Fig. 5-32, unlike the micrometer caliper, can make both inside and outside measurements, Fig. 5-33. The design of the tool permits measurements to be made over a large range of sizes. It is manufactured as a standard item

Fig. 5-32. Vernier caliper.   (Scherr-Tumico)

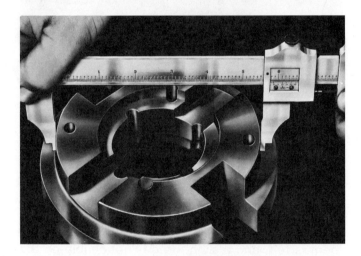

Fig. 5-33. Top. Making an inside measurement with a Vernier caliper. Bottom. Making an outside measurement with a Vernier caliper. Note how the machinist is making the final adjustment with the adjusting nut.   (L.S. Starrett Co.)

in 6 in., 12 in., 24 in., 36 in., and 48 in. lengths. Metric Vernier calipers are available in 150 mm, 300 mm, and 600 mm lengths. The 6 in. and 12 in. and 150 mm and 300 mm sizes are most commonly used.

A Vernier caliper can make accurate measurements to 0.001 (1/1000) in. Metric measurements are made to 0.02 (1/50) mm.

The following measuring tools utilize the Vernier principle.

VERNIER HEIGHT GAUGES, Fig. 5-34 and 5-35, are designed for use in toolrooms and inspection departments for layout work, checking hole and/or pin location, jig and fixture work, etc.

VERNIER DEPTH GAUGE, Fig. 5-36. Used to measure the depth of holes, slots, and recesses. It is ordinarily fitted with a 6 in. or 12 in. blade.

GEAR TOOTH VERNIER CALIPER, Fig. 5-37, is needed to measure gear teeth, form, and threading tools.

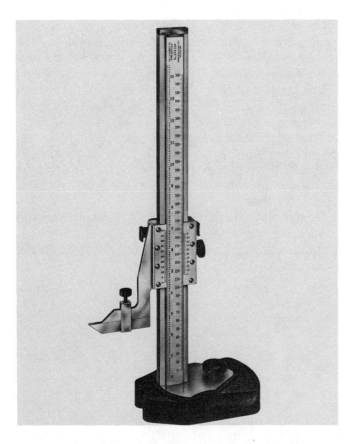

Fig. 5-34. A conventional Vernier height gauge.
(L.S. Starrett Co.)

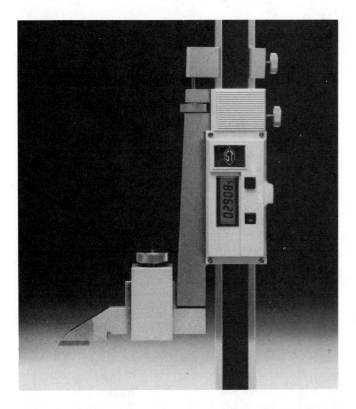

Fig. 5-35. An electronic digital readout Vernier height gauge, capable of making inch and millimeter measurements.
(Scherr—Tumico)

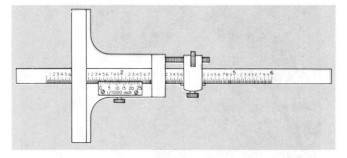

Fig. 5-36. Vernier depth gauge.

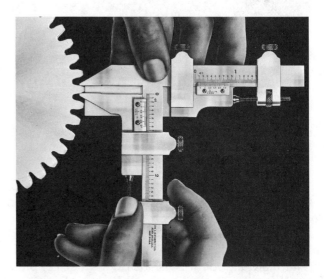

Fig. 5-37. Measuring with a gear tooth Vernier caliper. It is read in the same manner as a Vernier caliper or Vernier height gauge.   (L.S. Starrett Co.)

UNIVERSAL VERNIER BEVEL PROTRACTOR, Fig. 5-38. Designed for the precision layout and accurate measurement of angles. Angles are measured in degrees, minutes, and seconds.

Vernier measuring tools (with the exception of the Vernier bevel protractor) consist of a graduated beam with a fixed jaw or base, and a Vernier slide assembly. The Vernier slide assembly is composed of a movable jaw (or scribe), Vernier plate, and clamping screws. The slide moves as a unit along the beam.

Unlike other Vernier measuring tools, the beam of the Vernier caliper is graduated on both sides. One side is for making OUTSIDE measurements, the other for INSIDE measurements.

Many of the newer Vernier measuring tools are graduated to make both inch and millimeter measurements.

READING AN INCH BASED VERNIER SCALE

These measuring tools are available with either 25 or 50 division Vernier plates.

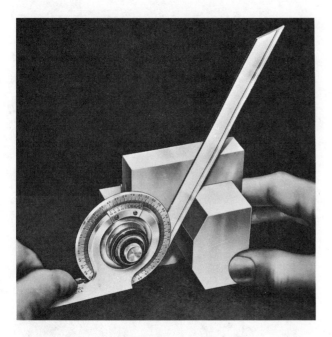

Fig. 5-38. Universal Vernier bevel protractor.
(L.S. Starrett Co.)

Every inch section on the beam of measuring tools using the 25 division Vernier plate is graduated into forty equal parts. Each graduation is 1/40 or 0.025 in. Every fourth division, representing 1/10 or 0.100 in., is numbered.

There are 25 equal divisions on the Vernier plate. Every fifth line is numbered—0, 5, 10, 15, 20, and 25. The 25 divisions occupy the same space as 24 divisions on the beam. This slight difference, equal to 0.001 (1/1000) in. per division, is the basis of the Vernier principle of measuring.

To read a 25 division Vernier plate measuring tool, note how many inches (1, 2, 3, etc.), tenths (0.100, 0.200, etc.), and fortieths (0.025, 0.050, or 0.075) there are between the "O" line on the Vernier scale and the "O" line on the beam, then add them.

Then count the number of graduations (each graduation equals 0.001 or 1/1000 in.) that lie between the "O" line on the Vernier plate and the line that coincides with a line on the beam. Only one line will coincide. Add this to the above total for the reading.

EXAMPLE (Illustrated in Fig. 5-39.)
  The reading is composed of:
  The "O" line on the Vernier plate
    is between 2 and 3 on the beam = 2.000
  Plus three 0.1000 (1/10)
    graduations   = 0.300
  Plus two 0.025 (1/40)
    graduations   = 0.050
  Plus eighteen 0.001 (1/1000)
    graduations   = 0.018
              Total reading   = 2.368 in.

On the 50 division Vernier plate, every second graduation between the inch lines is numbered, and equals 1/10 or 0.100 in. The unnumbered graduations equal 1/20 or 0.050 in.

The Vernier plate is graduated into 50 parts, each representing 0.001 (1/1000) in. Every fifth line is numbered—5, 10, 15, 20 . . . 40, 45, and 50.

To read a 50 division Vernier measuring tool, first count how many inches, tenths (0.100), and twentieths (0.050) there are between the "O" line on the beam, and the "O" line on the Vernier plate. Then add them.

Next, count the number of 0.001 graduations on the Vernier plate from its "O" line to the line that coincides with a line on the beam. Add this to the above total. This is the reading.

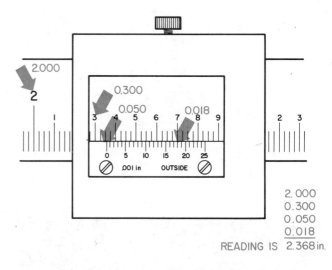

2.000
0.300
0.050
0.018
READING IS 2.368 in.

Fig. 5-39. How to read a 25 division Vernier scale.

EXAMPLE (Illustrated in Fig. 5-40.)
  The reading is composed of:
  The "O" line on the Vernier plate
    is between 2 and 3 on the beam = 2.000
  Plus two 0.100 (1/10)
    graduations   = 0.200
  Plus one 0.050 (1/20)
    graduations   = 0.050
  Plus fifteen 0.001 (1/1000)
    graduations   = 0.015
              Total reading   = 2.265 in.

READING A METRIC BASED VERNIER SCALE

The same principles are used in reading metric Vernier measuring tools as those for English measure. However, the readings on the Vernier scale are obtained in 0.02 mm. A 25 division Vernier scale is explained in Fig. 5-41, while a 50 division scale is described in Fig. 5-42.

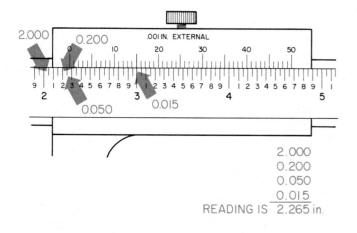

	2.000
	0.200
	0.050
	0.015
READING IS	2.265 in.

Fig. 5-40. How to read a 50 division Vernier scale.

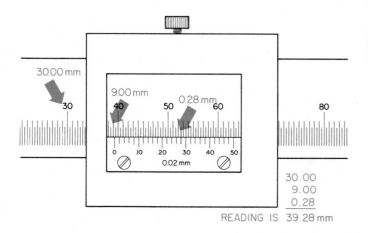

	30.00
	9.00
	0.28
READING IS	39.28 mm

Fig. 5-41. How to read a 25 division metric based Vernier scale. The readings on the scale are obtained in two hundredths of a millimeter (0.02 mm).

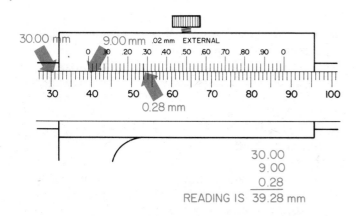

	30.00
	9.00
	0.28
READING IS	39.28 mm

Fig. 5-42. How to read a 50 division metric based Vernier scale. Each division also equals two hundredths of a millimeter (0.02 mm).

USING THE VERNIER CALIPER

As with any precision tool, the Vernier caliper must not be forced on the work. Slide the Vernier

assembly until the jaws almost contact the section being measured. Lock the clamping screw. Make the tool adjustment with the fine adjusting nut. The jaws must contact the work firmly but not tightly. Lock the slide to the beam. Carefully remove the tool from the work and make your reading.

Points permitting accurate divider and trammel point settings, for precise layout work, are located on the outside measuring scale and on the slide assembly.

ELECTRONIC DIGITAL READOUT CALIPERS, Fig. 5-43, are direct reading, and are switchable to give inch or metric measurement. They are used in the same manner as the Vernier caliper.

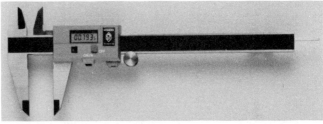

Fig. 5-43. Electronic digital readout caliper.   (Scherr-Tumico)

THE UNIVERSAL VERNIER BEVEL PROTRACTOR

There are many times when angles must be measured with great accuracy. The UNIVERSAL VERNIER BEVEL PROTRACTOR, Fig. 5-44, can measure angles accurately to 1/12 degree or 5 minutes. A quick review of the circle, angles, and units of measurement associated with them will help in understanding how to read this instrument.

DEGREE—A circle, no matter what size, contains 360 degrees. This is normally written 360°. Angles are also measured by degrees.

MINUTE—If a degree were divided into 60 equal parts, each part would be 1 minute. The minute is used to represent a fractional part of a degree. It would be written like this: 0°0'.

SECOND—Very accurate work requires that the minute be divided into smaller units known as seconds. There are 60 seconds in one minute. An angular measurement written in degrees, minutes, and seconds would be 36°18'22''. This would read 36 degrees, 18 minutes, and 22 seconds.

The Universal bevel protractor is a finely made tool with a dial graduated into degrees, a base or stock, and a sliding blade that can be extended in either direction or set at any angle to the stock. The blade can be locked against the dial by tightening the blade clamp nut. The blade and dial can be

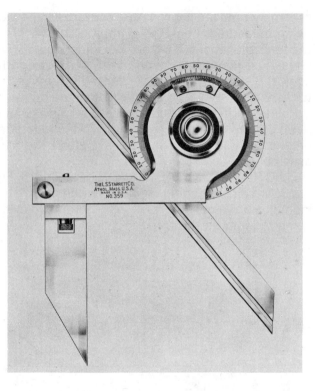

Fig. 5-44. Universal Vernier bevel protractor.

of the tool.

2. Store the tool in the case designed to hold it.
3. Never force the tool when making measurements.
4. Use a magnifying glass or jeweler's lope to make Vernier readings. Hold the tool so the light is reflected on the scale.
5. Hold the tool as little as possible. Sweat and body acids cause rapid rusting and staining.
6. Periodically check for accuracy. Use a measuring standard, Jo block, or ground parallel.
7. Wipe the tool with a lightly oiled, soft cloth after use and before storage. Return the tool to the manufacturer for adjustments and repairs.

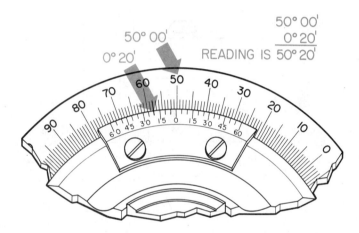

Fig. 5-45. How to read a universal Vernier bevel protractor.

rotated as a unit to any desired position, and locked by tightening the dial clamp nut.

The protractor dial, graduated into 360 degrees, reads 0-90 degrees and 90-0 degrees. Every ten degrees is numbered, and each 5 degrees is indicated by a line longer than those on either side. The Vernier scale is divided into twelve equal parts on each side of the "0." Every third graduation is numbered 0, 15, 30, 45, and 60, representing minutes. Each division equals 5 minutes. Since each degree is divided into 60 minutes, each division is equal to 5/60 of a degree.

To read the protractor, note the number of degrees that can be read up to the "0" on the Vernier plate. To this, add the number of minutes indicated by the line beyond the "0" on the Vernier plate that aligns exactly with a line on the dial. EXAMPLE (Illustrated in Fig. 5-45.)

The reading is composed of:

The "0" is slightly beyond 50	= 50°00'
The line indicating 20 minutes is aligned with a line on the dial	= 20'
Total reading	= 50°20'

CARE OF VERNIER TOOLS

Reasonable care in handling these expensive tools will ensure their accuracy.

1. Wipe with a soft lint-free cloth before using. This will prevent dirt and grit from being "ground in," which would eventually destroy the accuracy

GAUGES

It is obviously impractical, considering the large number of individual parts manufactured each year, to check every dimension on every part with conventional measuring tools. To facilitate rapid checking, PLUG, RING, and SNAP GAUGES, PRECISION GAUGE BLOCKS, DIAL INDICATORS, and other ELECTRONIC, OPTICAL, and AIR-TYPE GAUGES are employed. These gauging devices can quickly determine whether the dimensions of the manufactured part are within specified limits or tolerances.

Gauging, which is the term used when checking parts with various gauges, differs somewhat from measuring. Measuring requires the skillful use of precision measuring tools to determine the exact size of the piece. Gauging, on the other hand, simply shows whether the piece is made within the specified tolerances.

When great numbers of an item, with several critical dimensions, are manufactured, it may not be possible to check each piece. It therefore becomes necessary to decide how many pieces, picked at random, must be checked to assure satisfactory quality and adherence to specifications. This technique is called STATISTICAL QUALITY CONTROL.

Several types of gauges have been developed. Each has been devised to do a specific job.

PLUG GAUGE

PLUG GAUGES are used to check whether hole diameters are within specified tolerances. The DOUBLE END CYLINDRICAL PLUG GAUGE, Fig. 5-46, has two gauging members known as GO and NO GO plugs. The GO plug should enter the hole with little or no interference. The NO GO plug should not enter if the opening is made to specifications.

The GO plug is made longer to distinguish it from the NO GO plug. The PROGRESSIVE or STEP PLUG GAUGE, Fig. 5-46, is able to check the GO and NO GO dimensions in one motion.

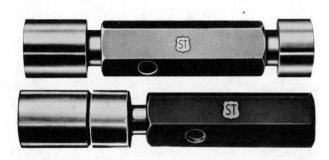

Fig. 5-46. Top. Double end cylindrical plug gauge. Bottom. Progressive or step plug gauge. (Standard Tool Co.)

RING GAUGE

External diameters are checked with RING GAUGES. The GO and NO GO RING GAUGE, Fig. 5-47, are separate units, and can be distinguished from each other by a groove cut on the knurled outer surface of the NO GO gauge. On ring gauges the gauge tolerance is opposite to that applied to the plug gauge. The opening of the GO gauge is larger than that of the NO GO gauge.

Fig. 5-47. Ring gauges. The larger sizes are cut away to reduce weight. (Standard Tool Co.)

SNAP GAUGE

A SNAP GAUGE functions much the same as a ring gauge. It is made in two general types, the ADJUSTABLE SNAP GAUGE, Fig. 4-48, which can be adjusted through a range of sizes, and the NON-ADJUSTABLE SNAP GAUGE, Fig. 5-49, which is made for one specific size.

Fig. 5-48. Adjustable type snap gauge. Gauge size is stamped on aluminum disc attached to side of gauge. (Taft-Pierce Mfg. Co.)

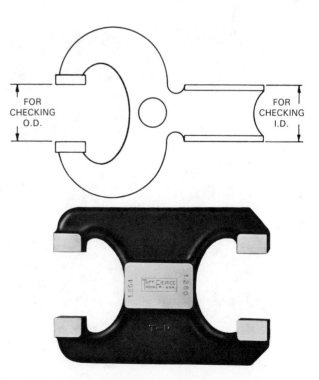

FOR CHECKING O.D.

FOR CHECKING I.D.

Fig. 5-49. Top. Combination internal and external non-adjustable gauge. Bottom. Non-adjustable type snap gauge.

THREAD GAUGES

Gauges similar to those just described are used to check screw thread fits and tolerances. They are the THREAD PLUG GAUGE, Fig. 5-50, THREAD RING GAUGE, Fig. 5-51, and THREAD SNAP GAUGE, Fig. 5-52.

GAUGE BLOCKS

GAUGE BLOCKS, Fig. 5-53, are extremely accurate steel measuring standards commonly known as JO BLOCKS. They are accepted by major world powers as standards of accuracy for all types of manufacturing.

The accuracy of master gauges is checked and verified with gauge blocks. They are also employed as working gauges for toolroom work; and for laying out and setting up work for machining where extreme accuracy is required.

Gauge blocks can be purchased in various combinations or sets ranging from a few carefully

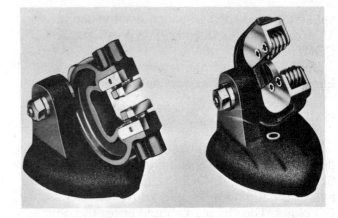

Fig. 5-52. A Go—No Go thread snap gauge. (Taft-Pierce Mfg. Co.)

selected blocks that meet conditions found in most shops, to a complete set of 121 blocks. The blocks are available in both inch based and metric based sizes.

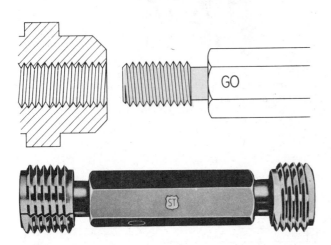

Fig. 5-50. Top. Using a thread plug gauge to check thread size. Bottom. Thread plug gauge.   (Standard Tool Co.)

Fig. 5-51. Thread ring gauge.   (Standard Tool Co.)

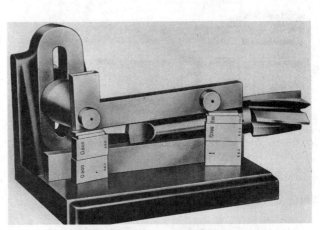

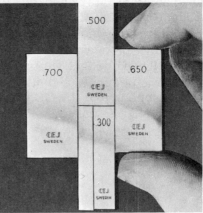

Fig. 5-53. Top. Measuring a taper with Johannson sine bar and precision gauge blocks. Bottom. Gauge blocks are so accurately made that clean blocks will adhere to one another with considerable pressure when they are "wrung" together. Two or more smaller blocks can be assembled into a larger unit and still maintain the accuracy of a single unit.
(C.E. Johannson & Co.)

DIAL INDICATORS

Industry is constantly searching for ways to reduce costs, yet maintain or improve quality. Inspection has always been a costly part of manufacturing. To speed up this phase of production, without sacrificing accuracy, the dial indicator is widely used. It is used for centering work on machines, Fig. 5-54; checking for eccentricity, Fig. 5-55; and for visual inspection, Fig. 5-56.

Dial indicators are made like fine watches, with

Fig. 5-56. Checking the spacing of bored holes in a drill press casting with a dial indicator fitted to a Vernier height gauge. (Clausing)

Fig. 5-54. Centering work on a vertical milling machine. (L.S. Starrett Co.)

shockproof movements and jeweled bearings. They are either of the BALANCED TYPE, where the figures read in both directions from ''0;'' or the CONTINUOUS TYPE, that reads from ''0'' in a clockwise direction. See Fig. 5-57.

Dial faces are available in a wide range of graduations. They usually read in 1/1000 (0.001), 1/10000 (0.0001) in. increments, or 0.01, 0.002 mm increments. The device must be mounted to a rigid holding attachment.

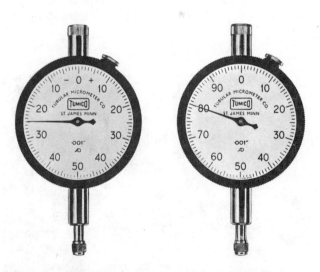

Fig. 5-57. Left. Balanced type dial indicator face. Right, continuous type dial indicator face. (Scherr-Tumico)

USING A DIAL INDICATOR

The hand of a dial indicator is actuated by a plunger or lever that is in contact with the work.

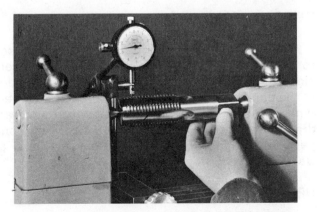

Fig. 5-55. Checking run-out of a tap with a dial indicator. Bench center aids the inspector with his job. (DoAll Co.)

Place the contact lightly against the work until the hand moves. Rotate the dial face until the "0" line coincides with the hand. As the work is moved under the contact, the indicator will show the difference between the high and low points, or the total run-out of the piece. Adjustments are made to the work position until there is little or no indicator movement.

OTHER GAUGING TOOLS

Industry employs a wide range of other types of gauging tools. Most of them are for special purposes and not found in school shops.

LASER GAUGING

The LASER is a device that produces a very narrow beam of extremely intense light that can be used for communication, medical, and industrial purposes. Laser is the abbreviation of L(ight) A(mplification by) S(timulated) E(mission of) R(adiation).

The laser is another area of technology that has moved from the laboratory into the shop. When used for inspection purposes, it can be used for checking the accuracy of critical parts in machined parts, Fig. 5-58.

AIR GAUGE

The AIR GAUGE, Fig. 5-59, is especially useful for measuring deep internal bores. There is no ac-

Fig. 5-59. Checking the diameter of a bored hole in a drill press casting with an air gauge. As long as the indicators in the gauge fall within preset limits, the holes are bored to specified sizes. (Clausing)

tual contact between the measuring plug on the instrument and the walls of the bore.

In operation, air is forced under pressure into the bore. The gauge measures the air leakage past the measuring plug. Measurement of the back pressure gives an accurate measurement on the hole's diameter.

Pressure change is indicated on a dial, a cork floating on the air stream, a manometer type U-tube, or in the form of an electronic digital readout. The scale on the tool shows how bore diameter compares with the required tolerances.

ELECTRONIC GAUGE

The ELECTRONIC GAUGE, Fig. 5-60, is another tool that is capable of making extremely close measurements. It is a comparison type gauge and must be set by means of master gauge blocks.

OPTICAL COMPARATOR

An OPTICAL COMPARATOR, Fig. 5-61, is used for production inspection in operations where very close tolerances must be met. An enlarged image of the part being inspected is projected on a screen, where it is then superimposed upon an accurate drawing of the correct shape and size. The comparison is made visually. Variations as small as 0.0005 can be noted by a skilled operator.

OPTICAL FLATS

OPTICAL FLATS, Fig. 5-62, are precise measuring instruments. They utilize light waves as a

Fig. 5-58. Laser being used to inspect a part used in an automatic transmission. Manually, one person could inspect no more than four an hour. The laser can inspect the part as fast as it is turned out—120 or more an hour. (Ford Motor Company)

Fig. 5-60. An electronic comparator checking the pitch diameter of a tap by means of the thread wire method. (DoAll Co.)

measuring standard. The flats are made of quartz, with one or both faces ground and polished to extreme accuracy. They provide a simple, accurate measurement of flatness.

The surface of the flat is both transparent and reflective. Monochromatic light (light of one color) passed through the flat is split in two longitudinally (in lengths). One part is reflected back by the flat. The other part passes through the flat and is reflected back by the surface being inspected. The split light appear as interference bands, Fig. 5-63. The shape of these bands indicates the accuracy of the part in millionths (0.000001) of an inch.

MISCELLANEOUS MEASURING AND GAUGING TOOLS

There are some measuring and gauging tools that do not fall into a specific category, yet they are frequently used.

THICKNESS (FEELER) GAUGE

THICKNESS or FEELER GAUGES, Fig. 5-64, are usually arranged in leaf form. However, individual

Fig. 5-61. A 50-power optical comparator permits a fast check on the size and profile of these threads.

thicknesses (0.001 to 0.030 in. and 0.03 to 0.50 mm) are available in 12 in. lengths and 25 ft. rolls. For convenience the thickness is marked at regular intervals. Thickness gauges are made from tempered steel and are 1/2 in. or 12.7 mm in width.

Fig. 5-62. Optical flats.

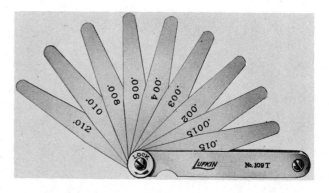

Fig. 5-64. Thickness or feeler gauge.

Thickness gauges are ideal for measuring narrow slots, setting small gaps and clearances, determining fit between mating surfaces, and checking flatness of parts in straightening operations.

SCREW PITCH GAUGE

SCREW PITCH GAUGES, Fig. 5-65, aid in determining the pitch, or number, of threads per inch on a threaded section. Metric screw pitch gauges are similar, but indicate only the pitch of the thread. Each blade is marked with the number of threads per inch, or thread pitch.

FILLET AND RADIUS GAUGE

The thin steel blades of the FILLET AND RADIUS GAUGE, Fig. 5-66, are useful in checking convex and concave radii on corners, or against shoulders,

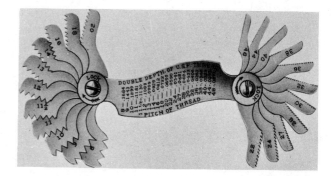

Fig. 5-65. The screw pitch gauge. It can only be used to determine the number of threads per inch on a threaded section. Metric screw pitch gauges are also available.

DRILL ROD

DRILL ROD is steel rod manufactured to close tolerances in sizes equivalent to twist drill diameters. The rods are helpful for inspecting hole alignment and location and, when used like a plug gauge, for checking the sizes of drilled holes. Drill rod can be heat-treated.

TELESCOPING GAUGE

A TELESCOPING GAUGE, Fig. 5-68, is used with a micrometer to determine internal dimensions. To use the tool, compress the contact points (they telescope within one another under spring pressure). Insert the tool into the opening at a very slight angle and on exact center. Lock the contact in position. Straighten the gauge. When properly fitted in the opening, a slight drag should be felt on the contact points, Fig. 5-69. No up-and-down or side-to-side movement will be felt. Remove the gauge and make your reading with a micrometer.

Six telescoping gauges with a measuring capacity of 5/16 in. (7.9 mm) to 6 in. (152 mm) comprise a set.

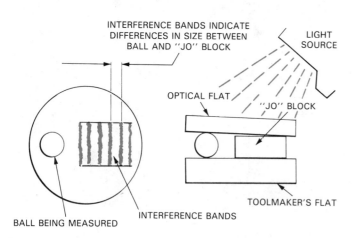

Fig. 5-63. The principle of how optical flats measure.

for layout work, inspection, as a template when grinding form cutting tools, etc. A HOLDER, Fig. 5-67, is especially helpful for checking radii in hard to reach locations. The gauges increase in radius by 1/64 in. or 0.05 mm increments.

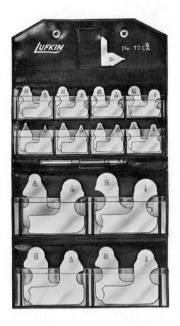

Fig. 5-66. A set of radius and fillet gauges.

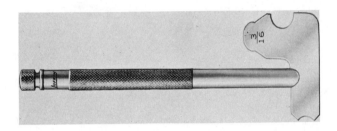

Fig. 5-67. A radius gauge and holder. The holder is made in such a manner that it permits the gauge to be set at different angles.

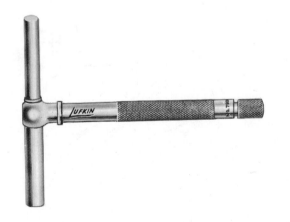

Fig. 5-68. A telescoping gauge. They are available in a number of sizes.

SMALL HOLE GAUGE

The SMALL HOLE GAUGE, Fig. 5-70, permits measuring smaller openings than is possible with a telescoping gauge. The contacts are designed to allow accurate measurement of shallow grooves, slots, etc., and are adjusted to size by the knurled knob at the end of the handle. Measurement is made over the contacts with a micrometer, Fig. 5-71.

A set consists of four gauges with a range of 1/8 in. (3.2 mm) to 1/2 in. (12.7 mm).

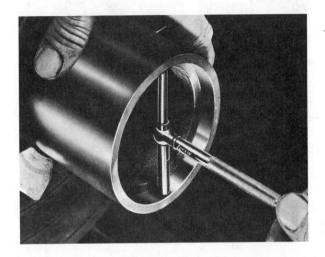

Fig. 5-69. Fitting a telescoping gauge into a hole. A micrometer will then be used to determine the hole diameter by measuring across the contacts of the gauge.

Fig. 5-70. Measuring a shallow groove with a small hole gauge. (L.S. Starrett Co.)

OUTSIDE CALIPER

The OUTSIDE CALIPER, Fig. 5-72, is sometimes employed to make external measurements where a 1/64 in. (0.4 mm) tolerance is permitted. A caliper does not have a dial or gauge which shows a measurement, and must be used with a rule.

Measurement 77

Fig. 5-71. Correct way to measure a small hole gauge with a micrometer. (L.S. Starrett Co.)

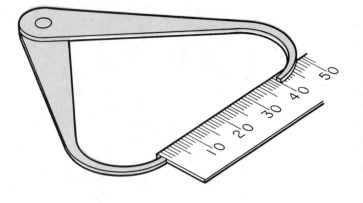

Fig. 5-73. Setting outside caliper.

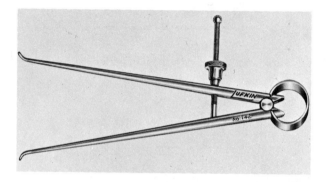

Fig. 5-74. A spring-joint inside caliper.

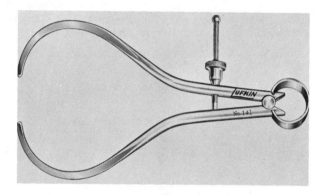

Fig. 5-72. A spring-joint outside caliper.

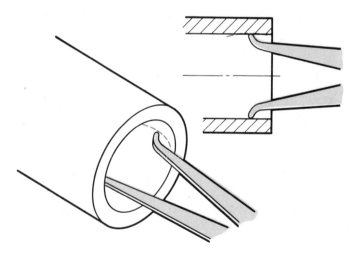

Fig. 5-75. Measuring with an inside caliper.

Round stock is measured by setting the caliper to the approximate diameter of the material. Then, holding the caliper square with the work, move the caliper legs down on the stock. Rotate the adjusting screw until the caliper points bear lightly on the centerline of the material. The weight of the caliper should cause the tool to pass over the diameter. Hold the caliper to the rule, Fig. 5-73, to read the size.

An INSIDE CALIPER, Fig. 5-74, is used for making internal measurements where 1/64 in. (0.4 mm) accuracy is acceptable.

Hole diameter can be measured, Fig. 5-75, by setting the tool to the approximate size of the hole, and inserting the legs into the opening. Hold one leg firmly against the wall of the opening, and rotate

the adjusting screw until the other leg lightly touches the wall exactly opposite the first leg. The legs should "drag" slightly when moved in-and-out, or from side-to-side. Read the hole or opening size by holding the caliper to a steel rule, Fig. 5-76.

Considerable skill is required to make accurate

measurements with calipers. Much depends upon the machinist's sense of touch. With practice, measurements to within 0.003 to 0.005 in. and 0.08 to 0.13 mm can be made. A micrometer or Vernier caliper should be used if greater accuracy is specified.

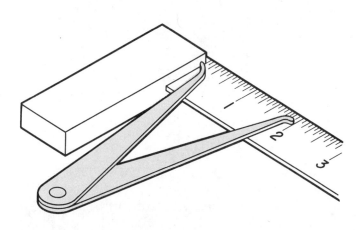

Fig. 5-76. Reading the measurement made by the caliper.

TEST YOUR KNOWLEDGE, Unit 5

Please do not write in the text. Place your answers on a separate sheet of paper.

1. Measure and record readings from the rule shown.

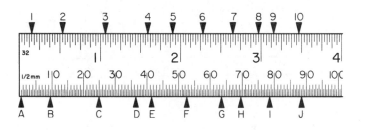

2. Measure and record readings from the micrometers shown.

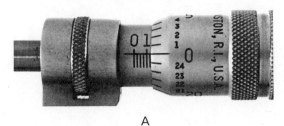

A

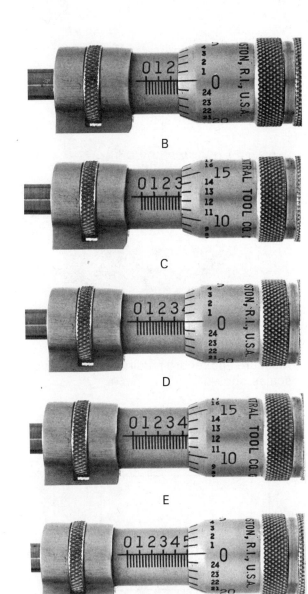

B

C

D

E

F

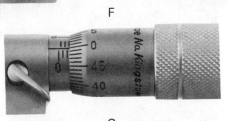

G

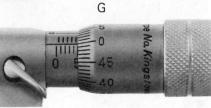

H

I

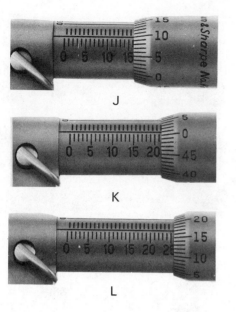

J

K

L

3. Measure and record readings from the Vernier scales shown.

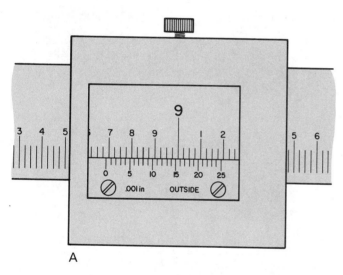

A

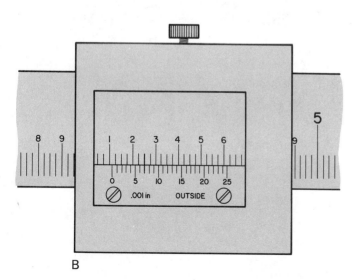

B

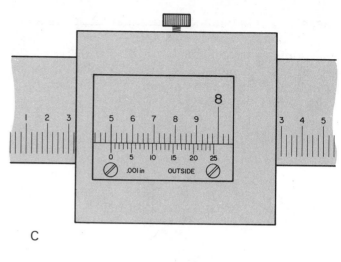

C

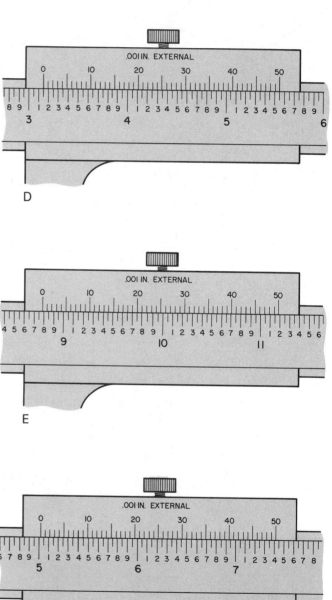

D

E

F

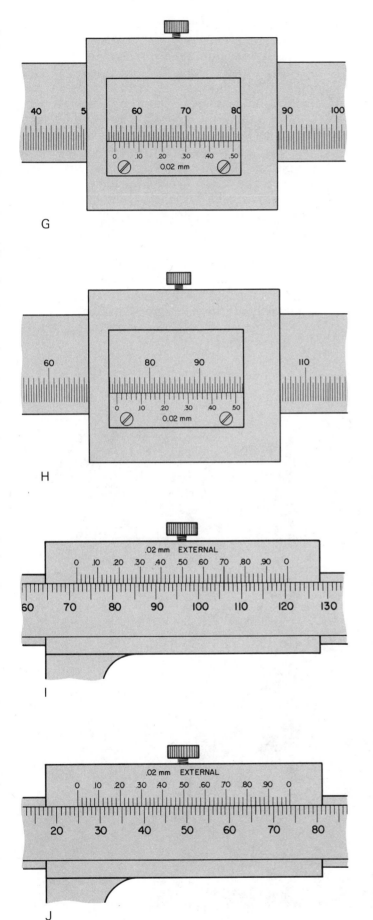

G

H

I

J

4. The Vernier caliper has an advantage over the micrometer in that it:
   a. Is more accurate.
   b. Is easier and quicker to use.
   c. Can be used to make both inside and outside measurements over a number of sizes.
   d. All of the above.
   e. None of the above.
5. The micrometer has been nicknamed _____.
6. A _____ is a tool that can be used to make accurate measurements but must be used with a micrometer or Vernier caliper.
   a. Rule.
   b. Dial indicator.
   c. Telescoping gauge.
   d. Inside micrometer.
   e. Ring gauge.
7. The one-millionth part of a standard inch is known as a _____.
8. The micrometer can measure _____ and _____ part of the inch and metric versions to _____ and _____ mm.
9. The Vernier caliper can measure to the _____ part of the inch and the metric version to _____ mm.
10. The plug gauge is employed to check _____ size to determine whether it is within specified tolerances.
11. The ring gauge is used to check _____ size to determine whether it is within specified tolerances.
12. Precision gauge blocks are usually referred to as _____ blocks.
13. Dial indicators are _____ measuring tools.
14. An air gauge measures by _____ _____.
15. Of what use are fillet and radius gauges?
16. What is a screw pitch gauge?
17. The _____ gauge permits measuring openings that are too small to be measured with a telescoping gauge.
18. How is an optical comparator used to determine whether a part is within prescribed tolerances?
19. External measurements are made with an _____ caliper.
20. The outside caliper is used to make _____ measurements.
21. Internal measurements are made with the _____ caliper.
22. Calipers are used where _____ in. or _____ mm accuracy is acceptable.
23. When an accuracy closer than 0.003 to 0.005 in. or 0.08 to 0.13 mm is required, a _____ or _____ caliper should be used.

RESEARCH AND DEVELOPMENT

1. Early humans used parts of the body for measuring. Prepare drawings of the parts of the body that represented the cubit, inch, yard (2 methods), and foot. If your school has the facilities, use these drawings to prepare transparencies for use with the overhead projector.
2. Make a large working model of the hub and thimble of the micrometer. Use different size cardboard mailing tubes.
3. Develop a working model of the Vernier scale and a section of the Vernier caliper. Make the model at least six times actual size.
4. Arrange for an inspector employed by one of the local industries to describe his or her job and the specialized measuring tools used. Use a tape recorder to transcribe your conversation. Do not go to the meeting cold. Have several questions ready to ask in case the interview starts to drag.
5. Demonstrate how optical flats are used. Use a film or film strip if the actual tools cannot be borrowed.
6. Prepare a research paper on how temperature changes affect measuring accuracy. Prepare one-inch long pieces of aluminum, brass, steel, plastic, and cast iron. Record their exact length at room temperature with a micrometer. Place the pieces in a freezer for 24 hours and quickly measure them again. Record your findings. Place the pieces in boiling water for 15 minutes. Measure and record your findings.

    Prepare a table to show how the lengths varied from one extreme to the other, and how they differed at each extreme, from room temperature.
7. Make an enlarged section of #4 rule 10 times actual size. Use plywood or hardboard.
8. Prepare a transparency (use several overlays if necessary) that can be used with an overhead projector to teach beginners how to read a rule or a micrometer.

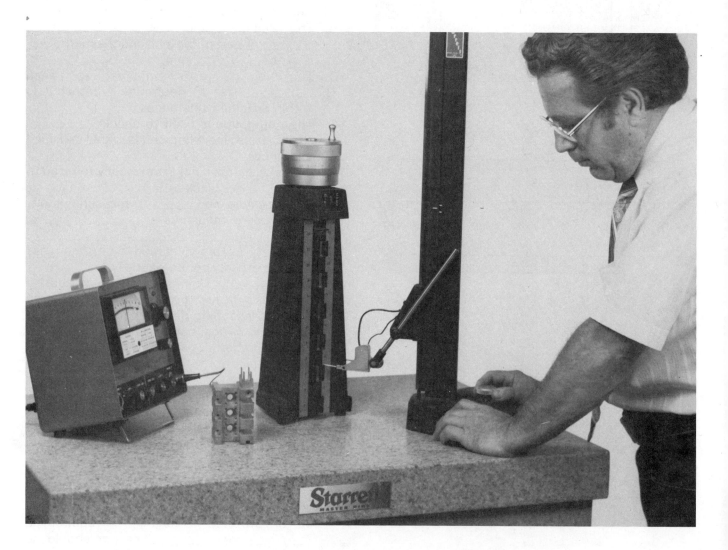

A few of the many tools you may need to know how to use if you work in the industry.

Unit 6

LAYOUT WORK

LAYING OUT is the term used to describe the locating and marking out of lines, circles, arcs, and points for drilling holes. These lines and reference points on the metal show the machinist where to machine.

The tools used for this work are known as LAYOUT TOOLS. Many common hand tools fall into this category. The accuracy of the job will depend upon the proper and careful use of these tools.

MAKING LINES ON METAL

The shiny finish of metal makes it difficult to distinguish the layout lines from the metal. LAYOUT DYE, Fig. 6-1, is probably the easiest to use of the many coatings devised to make the lines stand out better. This blue colored fluid, when applied to the metal, offers an excellent contrast between the metal and the layout lines. All grease and oil must be removed before applying the dye, otherwise it

will not adhere properly. In a pinch, layout fluid can be made by dissolving the coating on spirit duplicator carbons on alcohol. Chalk can be used on hot rolled metal as a layout background.

A layout, to be accurate, requires fine lines that must be scribed or scratched in the metal. A SCRIBER, Fig. 6-2, is used to produce these lines. The point is made of hardened steel, and is kept needle sharp by frequent honing on a fine oilstone. Many styles of scribers are available, 6-3. CAUTION: NEVER CARRY AN OPEN SCRIBER IN YOUR POCKET.

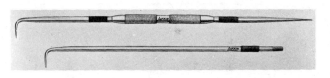

Fig. 6-2. Scriber.

Fig. 6-3. Pocket scriber. The point is reversed and stored in handle when the tool is not being used.

Where the scriber is used to draw straight and gradually curved lines, circles and arcs are made with the DIVIDER, Fig. 6-4. It is essential that both legs of the tool be equal in length and kept pointed. The divider can be used to lay off and measure distances, Fig. 6-5. To set the tool to the correct dimension, place one point on an inch mark of a steel rule, and open the divider until the other leg

Fig. 6-1. Applying layout fluid prior to making the layout.

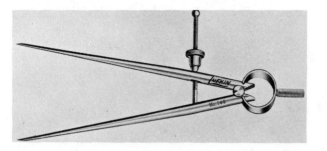

Fig. 6-4. The divider.

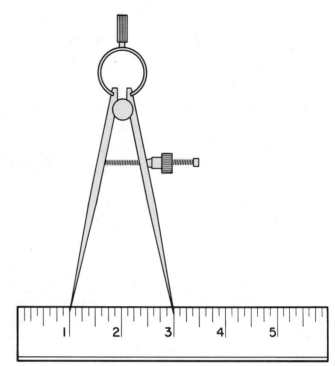

Fig. 6-6. Setting a divider to the correct dimension.

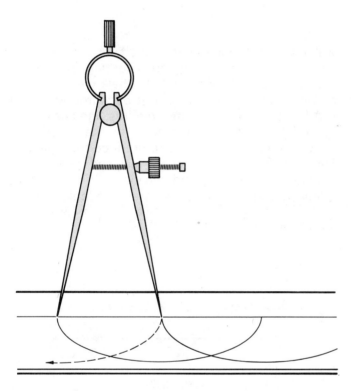

Fig. 6-5. Laying out equal spaces with a divider.

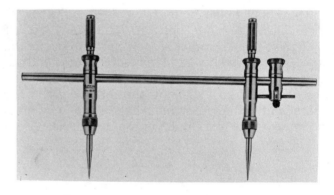

Fig. 6-7. The trammel.

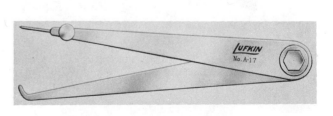

Fig. 6-8. Hermaphrodite caliper.

is set to the proper distance, Fig. 6-6.

Circles and arcs that are too large to be made with the divider are drawn with a TRAMMEL, Fig. 6-7. This consists of a long thin rod, called a BEAM, on which two SLIDING HEADS with scriber points are mounted. One head is fitted with an ADJUSTING SCREW. EXTENSION RODS can be added to the beam to increase the capacity of the tools.

The HERMAPHRODITE CALIPER, Fig. 6-8, is a layout tool which has one leg shaped like a caliper, and the other pointed like a divider. The tool is used to lay out lines parallel to the edge of the material, Fig. 6-9, and to locate the center of irregularly shaped stock.

A SURFACE GAUGE, Fig. 6-10, is used for many purposes, but is most frequently used for layout work. It consists of a BASE, SPINDLE, and SCRIBER. An ADJUSTING SCREW is fitted for mak-

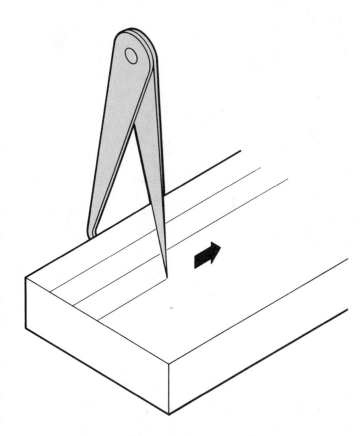

Fig. 6-9. Laying out lines parallel to edge with hermaphrodite caliper.

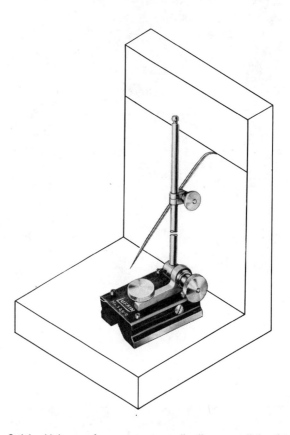

Fig. 6-11. Using surface gauge to scribe lines parallel to base.

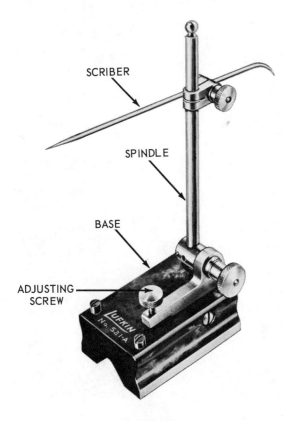

Fig. 6-10. Surface gauge.

ing fine adjustments. The scriber is mounted in such a manner that it can be pivoted into any position. The surface gauge can be used for scribing lines, at a given height, and parallel to the surface, Fig. 6-11. A V-slot in the base permits the tool to be used on a curved surface.

Parallelism of a part can be checked when the tool is fitted with a dial indicator. The indicator is set to the required dimension by using gauge blocks, and it is then moved back and forth along the work, Fig. 6-12. PRECISION LAYOUT TOOLS, Figs. 6-13 through 6-15, are used when the drawings call for positions to be located to within 0.001 in. (0.025 mm).

An extremely precise surface is needed if accurate layout work is to be done. A SURFACE PLATE, Fig. 6-16, is most frequently used.

The surface plate can be purchased in sizes up to 72 by 144 in. and in semi-steel or granite. A TOOLMAKER'S BENCH, Fig. 6-17, is ideal for many operations that require a smooth, accurate, work surface.

Surface plates are used primarily for layout and inspection work, and should never be used for any job that would mar or nick the surface.

When square reference surfaces are needed, the RIGHT ANGLE PLATE, Fig. 6-18, is used. The blocks can be placed in about any position, with the

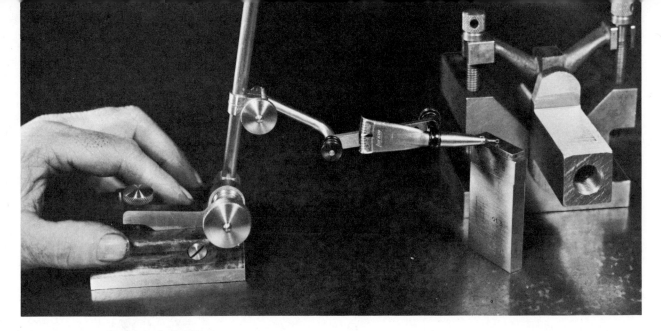

Fig. 6-12. Setting indicator mounted on surface gauge, using gauge blocks.
(Lufkin Rule Co.)

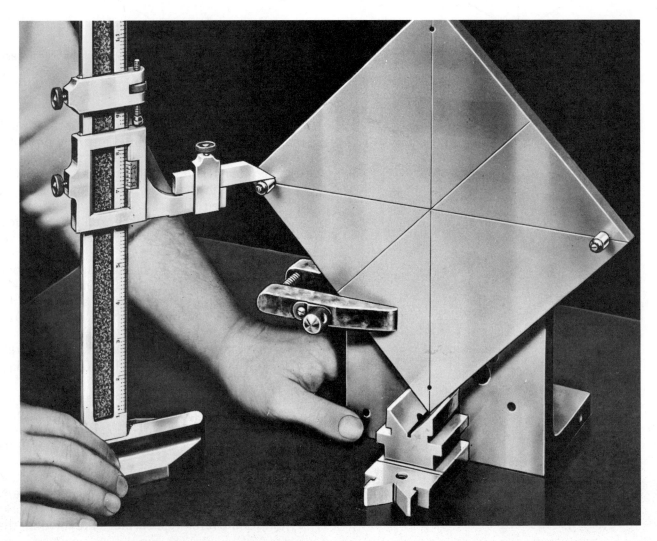

Fig. 6-13. Vernier height gauge. Note that a V-block and angle plate are used
to support the job. (L.S. Starrett Co.)

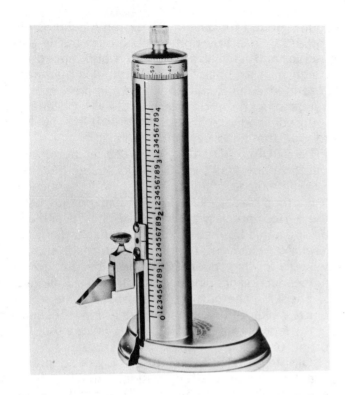

Fig. 6-14. A micrometer type height gauge. (H.B. Tools)

Fig. 6-17. Toolmaker's and machinist's workbench. (Challenge Machinery Co.)

Fig. 6-18. The right angle plate. (Challenge Machinery Co.)

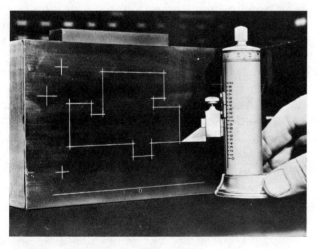

Fig. 6-15. Height gauge in use.

Fig. 6-19. Box parallels. (Challenge Machinery Co.)

Fig. 6-16. A semi-steel surface plate.

work clamped to the face for layout and measurement.

Accurate working surfaces parallel to the surface plate can be obtained by using BOX PARALLELS, Fig. 6-19. All surfaces are precision ground to close tolerances.

V-BLOCKS, Fig. 6-20, are used to support round work for layout and inspection. They are furnished in matched pairs, with surfaces that are ground square to close tolerances. Ribs are cast into the

Fig. 6-20. V-blocks.

body of the block for strength and weight reduction, and to provide clamping surfaces.

Long flat surfaces are checked for accuracy with a steel STRAIGHTEDGE, Fig. 6-21. This tool is also used for laying out long straight lines.

SQUARES

The square is used to check the accuracy of 90 degree (square) angles. The tool is also used for laying out lines that must be at right angles to a given edge, or parallel with one another. Some simple machine setups can be made quickly and easily with the square.

Many different types of squares are available. A few of the most commonly used are:

The HARDENED STEEL SQUARE, Fig. 6-22, is recommended for use where extreme accuracy is required. It has true right angles, both inside and outside, and is accurately ground and lapped for straightness and parallelism. The tool is manufactured in sizes up to 36 in. Extreme care must be exercised in handling these tools. The blade is mounted solidly to the beam and if the tool is dropped the blade can be ''sprung.''

The DOUBLE SQUARE, Fig. 6-23, is more practical for many jobs than the solid square because the sliding blade is adjustable and interchangeable with other blades. The tool should not be used where great precision is required. The bevel blade has one angle for measuring octagons, and one for checking hexagons. A drill grinding blade is also available for this square. One end is beveled to 59 degrees for drill grinding and the other at 41 degrees for checking the cutting angle of machine screw countersinks. Both ends are graduated for measuring the length of the cutting lips, to assure that the cutting tool is sharpened on center.

COMBINATION SETS, Fig. 6-24, are adaptable to a large variety of operations, making them especially valuable in the shop. The complete combination set consists of a HARDENED BLADE (#4 graduated rule), SQUARE HEAD, CENTER HEAD, and a BEVEL PROTRACTOR. The blade fits all three heads.

The square head, having one 45 degree edge, makes it possible for the tool to serve as both a try and miter square. By projecting the blade the desired distance below the edge, it serves as a depth gauge, Fig. 6-25. The spirit level built into one edge makes it possible to use it as a simple level.

With the rule properly inserted, the center head can be used to quickly locate the center of round stock, Fig. 6-26.

The protractor head can be rotated through 180 degrees and is graduated accordingly. The head can

Fig. 6-21. Steel straightedge. (Challenge Machinery Co.)

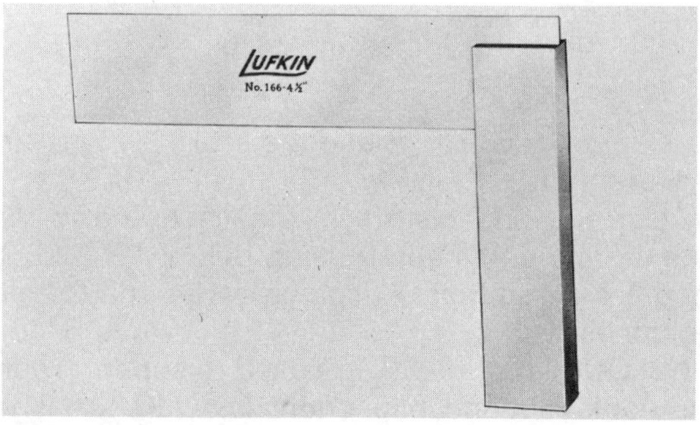

Fig. 6-22. Hardened steel square.

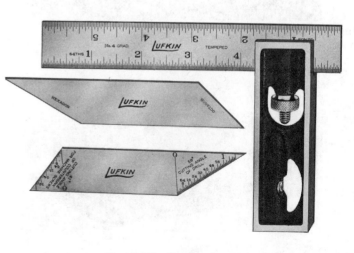

Fig. 6-23. Double square.

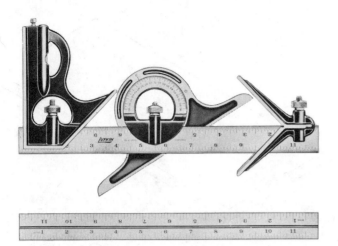

Fig. 6-24. The combination set.

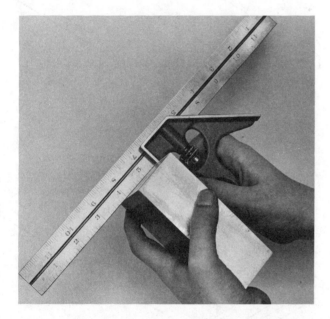

Fig. 6-25. Using the combination set as a square.

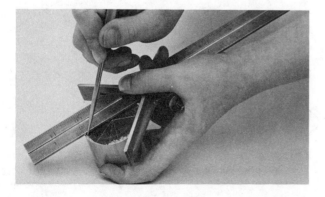

Fig. 6-26. Using center head to locate the center of a piece of round stock.

be locked with a locking nut, making it possible to accurately determine, or lay out, angles. The head with a level built in, makes it possible to use as a level.

MEASURING ANGLES

Other angle measuring tools are used in layout work in addition to the protractor head of the combination set. The accuracy required by the job will determine which tool must be used.

When angles do not have to be checked or laid out to extreme accuracy, a PLAIN PROTRACTOR, Fig. 6-27, will prove satisfactory. The head is graduated from 0 to 180 degrees in both directions for easy reading. The PROTRACTOR DEPTH GAUGE, Fig. 6-28, can be used to check angles and measure slot depths.

The UNIVERSAL BEVEL, Fig. 6-29, is useful for checking, laying out, and transferring angles. Both the blade and stock are slotted, making it possible to adjust the blade into the desired position. A thumbscrew locks it tightly.

When the job requires extreme accuracy, the machinist uses the VERNIER PROTRACTOR, Fig. 6-30. With this tool it is possible to accurately measure angles of 1/12 of a degree (5 minutes).

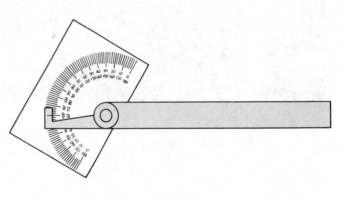

Fig. 6-27. Plain steel protractor.

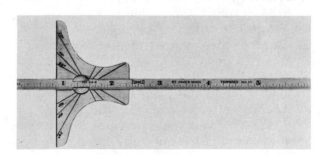

Fig. 6-28. A protractor depth gauge.
(Scherr-Tumico)

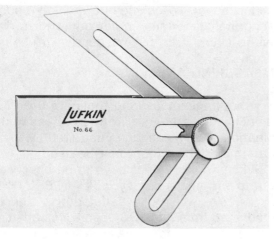

Fig. 6-29. A universal bevel.

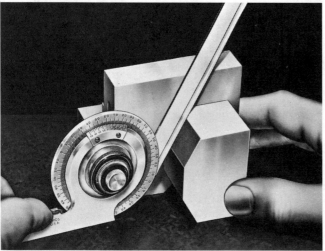

Fig. 6-30. The Vernier protractor.
(L.S. Starrett Co.)

STEPS IN MAKING A LAYOUT

Each layout job has its pecularities and requires some planning before the operation can be started. Fig. 6-31 shows a typical job.

1. Study the drawings carefully.
2. Cut the stock to size and remove all burrs and sharp edges.
3. Clean the work surface of all oil and grease, and apply layout dye.
4. Locate and scribe a REFERENCE or BASE LINE. Make all of your measurements from this line. If the material has one true edge, it can be used in place of the reference line.
5. Locate the center points of all circles and arcs.
6. Use the PRICK PUNCH, Fig. 6-32, to mark the

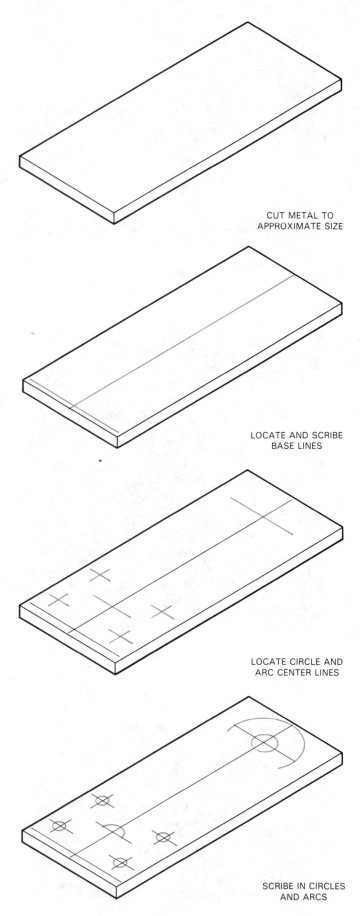

CUT METAL TO
APPROXIMATE SIZE

LOCATE AND SCRIBE
BASE LINES

LOCATE CIRCLE AND
ARC CENTER LINES

SCRIBE IN CIRCLES
AND ARCS

Fig. 6-31. Steps in laying out a job.

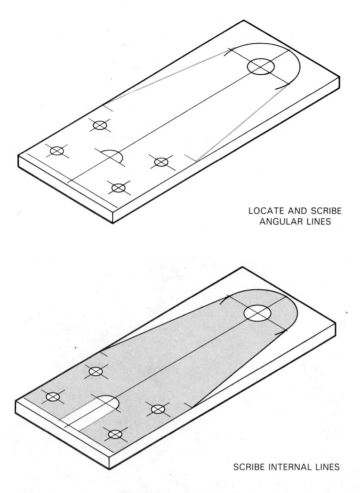

LOCATE AND SCRIBE
ANGULAR LINES

SCRIBE INTERNAL LINES

Fig. 6-31. *Continued.*

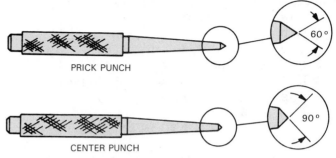

PRICK PUNCH

CENTER PUNCH

Fig. 6-32. Differences between a prick punch and a center punch.

point where the centerlines intersect. The sharp point (30 to 60 degrees) of this punch makes it easy to locate this position. After the prick punch mark has been checked and found on center, it is enlarged with the CENTER PUNCH, Fig. 6-32.

7. Using the divider or trammel, scribe in all circles and arcs.
8. If angular lines are necessary, use the proper protractor type tool, or locate the correct points by measuring, and connect them by using a rule or straightedge.
9. Scribe in all other internal openings.
10. Use only clean sharp lines. Any double lines or sloppy line work should be removed by cleaning, or by applying another coat of dye and then rescribing the line.

SAFETY

1. Never carry an open scriber, divider, trammel, or hermaphrodite caliper in your pocket.
2. Always cover all sharp points with a cork when the tool is not being used.

3. Wear goggles when grinding the points of scriber type tools.
4. Get help when you must move heavy angle plates, large V-blocks, etc.
5. Remove all burrs and sharp edges from stock before starting to work on the job.

TEST YOUR KNOWLEDGE, Unit 6

Please do not write in the text. Place your answers on a separate sheet of paper.
1. Layout lines are used to:
   a. Take the place of blueprints.
   b. Tell the machinist where to machine.
   c. Give the machinist practice in measuring.
   d. None of the above.
2. _____ is used to make the layout lines easier to see.
3. A _____ is used to draw circles and arcs on metal.
4. The _____ is used to draw circles and arcs that are too large for the above tool to draw.
5. A _____ is used to draw lines on metal.
6. A surface plate is a _____
   _____.
7. The combination set CANNOT be used to:
   a. Draw angular lines.
   b. Measure shoulders.
   c. Draw circles and arcs.
   d. Level angular surfaces.
8. A good layout job is determined by:
   a. Its neatness.
   b. Its accuracy.
   c. The time it took to make it.
   d. None of the above.
9. _____ are frequently used to support round stock layout and inspection.
10. Long flat surfaces can be checked with a _____.
11. The _____ of the combination set is used to quickly locate the center of a round piece.

12. Angular lines may be laid out with a:
    a. Straightedge.
    b. Rule.
    c. Square.
    d. Bevel protractor.
13. The _____ punch has a sharper point than a _____ punch.

RESEARCH AND DEVELOPMENT

1. Write a term paper on how surface plates are made. Why are they made of cast iron and granite, and not of other materials?
2. Prepare a transparency for the overhead projector (use several overlays if needed) that will show the proper layout sequence. Then tape record your narration for presentation, along with the transparency, to the class.
3. Make a display panel that shows the different layout fluids used. Protect your samples with clear plastic spray to prevent the scribed lines from rusting.

Layout work was necessary at some point in the assembly of these now completed automobiles.

Unit 7

HAND TOOLS

Hand tools are required in all areas of metalworking. How you use them makes it easy to tell whether you are an artisan or a "metal hacker."

When used incorrectly, a hand tool will sometimes be damaged, but more importantly the user may be injured. It is to your advantage to learn to work safely with hand tools. When in doubt about how to safely use a tool, ask your instructor.

CLAMPING DEVICES

Clamping devices are employed to hold and/or position material while it is being worked.

VISES

The MACHINIST'S or BENCH VISE is mounted far enough out on the bench edge to permit clamping long work in a vertical position. It may be a SOLID BASE VISE, Fig. 7-1, or of the SWIVEL BASE type, Fig. 7-2, which allows the vise to be rotated. A SMALL BENCH VISE, Fig. 7-3, is used to hold small precision parts.

Fig. 7-2. A swivel base vise. Base is made in two parts so the vise body can be rotated to any desired position. This cut-away shows the interior structure of the vise.
(Columbian Vise and Mfg. Co.)

Fig. 7-1. A solid base machinist's or bench vise.
(Wilton Tool Mfg. Co., Inc.)

Fig. 7-3. A small vise used by the toolmaker. It can be rotated and pivoted to secure the desired working position.
(Wilton Tool Mfg. Co., Inc.)

Vise size is determined by the width of the jaws, Fig. 7-4.

Clamping action of the vise is obtained from a heavy screw turned by the handle. The handle is long enough to apply ample pressure for all work that will fit the vise. Under no circumstance should the handle be hammered tight, nor should additional pressure be applied using a section of pipe for leverage.

Vise jaws are hardened and unless they are covered by CAPS, Fig. 7-5, should not be used to clamp work that may be damaged or marred by the jaw serrations. SAFETY NOTE: When clamping work, avoid projecting work or vise handle into the aisle. See Fig. 7-6.

CLAMPS

The C-CLAMP, Fig. 7-7, and the PARALLEL CLAMP, Fig. 7-8, are used to hold parts together while they are being worked on. The C-clamp is made in many sizes. The jaw opening determines the size.

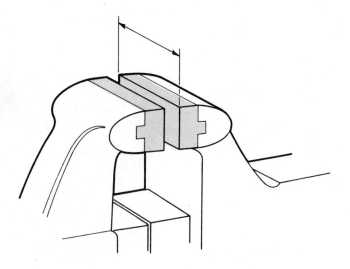

Fig. 7-4. The size of a vise is determined by the width of the vise jaws.

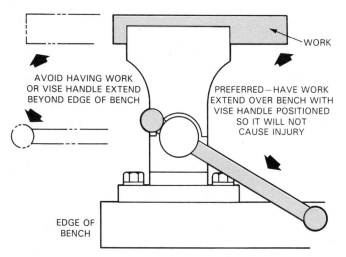

Fig. 7-6. Caution: To prevent injury, avoid letting the vise handle project into the aisle.

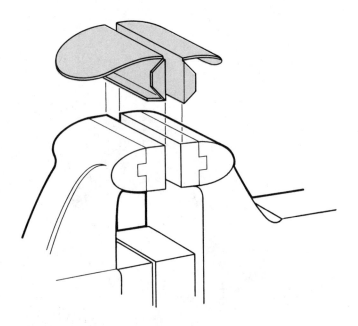

Fig. 7-5. Caps made of copper, lead, or aluminum are slipped over the hardened vise jaws to protect the work from becoming marred or damaged by the jaw serrations.

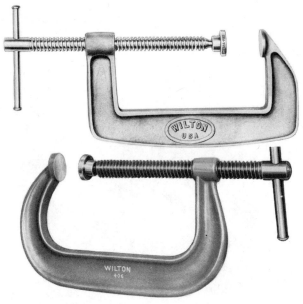

Fig. 7-7. The C-clamp is widely used in the metalworking industry.

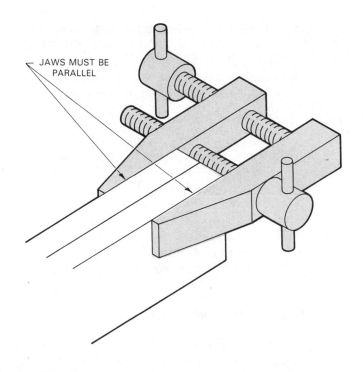

Fig. 7-8. For maximum clamping action with a parallel clamp, the jaws must be parallel.

The parallel clamp is ideal for holding small work. For maximum clamping action, the jaw faces must be parallel. A strip of paper the width of the clamp jaw placed between the work and clamp jaws will improve clamping action.

PLIERS

The COMBINATION or SLIP-JOINT PLIERS, Fig. 7-9, are widely used. The slip-joint permits the pliers to be opened wider at the hinge pin to grip larger size work. It is made in 5, 6, 8, and 10 in. sizes. The size indicates the overall length of the tool. Some combination pliers are made with cutting edges for clipping wire and small metal sections to needed lengths. The better grade pliers are forged.

DIAGONAL PLIERS, Fig. 7-10, are another widely used tool. The cutting edges are at an angle to permit the pliers to cut flush with the work surface. Diagonal pliers are made in 4, 5, 6, and 7 in. lengths.

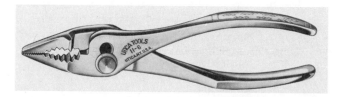

Fig. 7-9. Combination or slip-joint pliers.

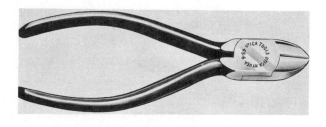

Fig. 7-10. Diagonal pliers.

SIDE-CUTTING PLIERS, Fig. 7-11, are useful for cutting heavier wire and pins. Some side-cutting pliers have a wire stripping groove and insulated handles. They are made in 6, 7, and 8 in. lengths.

ROUND-NOSE PLIERS, Fig. 7-12, are helpful when forming wire and light metal. Their jaws are smooth and will not mar the metal being worked. Round-nose pliers are available in 4, 4 1/2, 5, and 6 in. sizes.

NEEDLE-NOSE PLIERS, both straight, Fig. 7-13, and curved-nose, Fig. 7-14, are handy when work space is limited, and for holding small work.

TONGUE AND GROOVE PLIERS, Fig. 7-15, have aligned teeth for flexibility in gripping different size

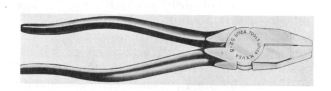

Fig. 7-11. Side-cutting pliers.

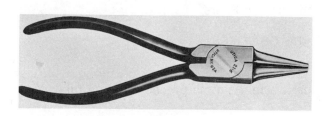

Fig. 7-12. Round-nose pliers.

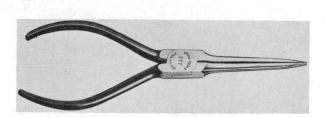

Fig. 7-13. Straight needle-nose pliers.

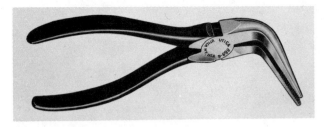

Fig. 7-14. Curved needle-nose pliers.

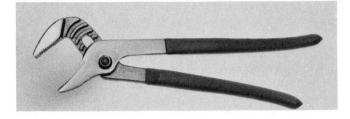

Fig. 7-15. Tongue and groove pliers.

work. Jaw opening size can be adjusted easily. The 6 in. size had five adjustments while the larger 16 in. size has 11 adjustments. They are made in many different sizes.

ADJUSTABLE CLAMPING PLIERS, Fig. 7-16, are a relatively new addition to the plier family. Jaw opening can be adjusted through a range of sizes. After fitting on the work, a squeeze of the hand locks the jaws onto the work with more than 2000 lbs. of pressure. Jaw pressure can be relieved by opening the quick release on the handle. These pliers are made in many sizes with straight, curved, or long-nose jaws. They are known by several names, including Vise Grips®, Tog-L-Lock Pliers®, and Locking Pliers.

CARE OF PLIERS

Like other tools, pliers will give long, useful service if a few simple precautions are taken:

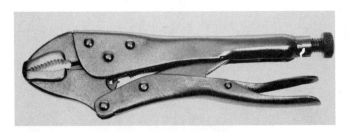

Fig. 7-16. Adjustable clamping pliers that can be locked on work are known by many names: Vise Grip pliers®, adjustable locking pliers, etc.

1. Avoid using pliers as a substitute for a wrench.
2. Pliers with cutters will deform or break if the tool is used to cut metal sizes that are too large, or work that has been heat-treated. Breakage will also occur if additional leverage is applied to the handles.
3. Clean and oil pliers occasionally.
4. Store pliers in a clean, dry place. Avoid throwing them in a drawer or tool box with other tools.

WRENCHES

WRENCHES comprise a family of tools used for assembling and disassembling threaded fasteners. They are made in a vast number of types and sizes. Only the most commonly used wrenches will be covered.

TORQUE LIMITING WRENCHES

TORQUE is the amount of turning or twisting force applied to a threaded fastener or part. It is measured in force units of FOOT-POUNDS (ft.-lbs.) or in NEWTON-METERS (N·m) for metrics. Torque is the product of the force applied, times the length of the lever arm. See Figs. 7-17 and 7-18.

A TORQUE LIMITING WRENCH permits tightening a threaded fastener or part for maximum holding power, without danger of the fastener or part failing, or causing the work to warp or spring out of shape, Fig. 7-19.

There are many types of torque limiting wrenches, Fig. 7-20. It is possible to obtain torque wrenches that are direct reading, or that feature a sensory signaling mechanism (clicking sound or momentarily releases) when the preset torque is reached.

The right and wrong methods of gripping the wrench handle are shown in Fig. 7-21. Under NO condition should the handle be lengthened for ad-

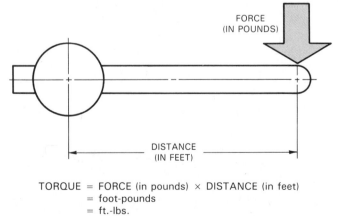

TORQUE = FORCE (in pounds) × DISTANCE (in feet)
= foot-pounds
= ft.-lbs.

Fig. 7-17. How torque is measured using standard inch-foot-pound measurement.

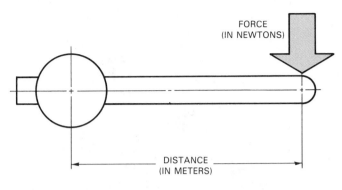

FORCE
(IN NEWTONS)

DISTANCE
(IN METERS)

TORQUE = FORCE (in newtons) × DISTANCE (in meters)
       = newton-meters
       = N·m

(The newton (N) is that force which applied to a mass of 1 kilogram, gives it an acceleration of 1 meter per second squared.)

Fig. 7-18. Torque values in SI metric measure are given in newton-meters (N·m).

RIGHT   RIGHT

WRONG   WRONG

Fig. 7-21. Right and wrong ways to apply pressure to a torque limiting wrench handle.

Fig. 7-19. Torque limiting wrenches are employed when fasteners must be tightened to within certain limits in order to prevent undue stresses and strains from developing in the part.

ditional leverage. These tools are designed to take a specific maximum force load. Any over this amount will destroy the accuracy of the wrench.

Torque limiting wrenches will give accurate measurement whether they are pushed or pulled. For safety, the preferred method is to pull on the wrench handle.

ADJUSTABLE WRENCHES

The term ADJUSTABLE WRENCH is a misnomer (not named properly). Other wrenches, such as the

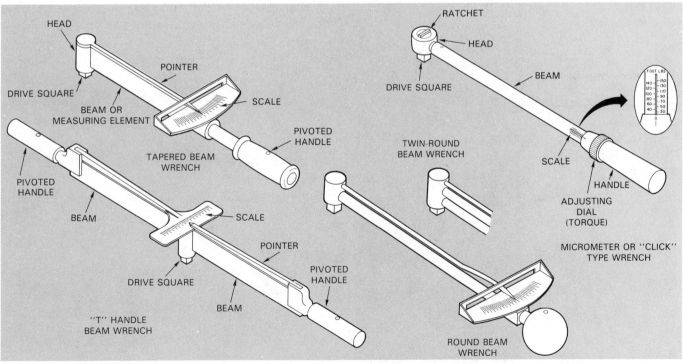

Fig. 7-20. Several kinds of torque limiting wrenches.

monkey wrench and pipe wrench, are also adjustable. However, the wrench which is somewhat like an open-end wrench, but with an adjustable jaw, is commonly referred to as an ''adjustable wrench,'' Fig. 7-22.

As the name implies, the wrench can be adjusted to fit a range of bolt head and nut sizes. Although convenient to use at times, the adjustable wrench is not intended to take the place of open-end, box, or socket wrenches.

Three important points must be remembered when using the adjustable wrench:
1. The wrench should be placed on the bolt head or nut so the movable jaw FACES THE DIRECTION the fastener is to be rotated, Fig. 7-23.
2. Adjust the thumbscrew so the jaws fit the bolt head or nut snugly, Fig. 7-24.
3. Avoid placing an extension on the wrench handle for additional leverage. Never hammer on the handle to loosen a stubborn fastener. Do use the SMALLEST adjustable wrench that will fit the fastener on which you are working to minimize

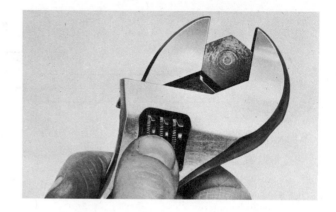

Fig. 7-24. The wrench must be adjusted to fit the fastener snugly.

the possibility of twisting the fastener off.

SAFETY NOTE: Pushing on any wrench is normally considered dangerous. When the fastener loosens unexpectedly, or fails, you will almost invariably strike and injure your knuckles on the work. This operation is commonly known as ''knuckle dusting.'' ALWAYS PULL ON A WRENCH—DO NOT PUSH!

The PIPE WRENCH, Fig. 7-25, is a wrench that will grip round stock. However, the jaws always leave marks on the work. Avoid using a pipe wrench on bolt heads or nuts unless they cannot be turned with another type of wrench (for instance, if the corners have been rounded).

OPEN-END WRENCHES

OPEN-END WRENCHES, Fig. 7-26, are usually double ended with two different size openings. They

Fig. 7-22. Adjustable wrench. Use the smallest adjustable wrench that will fit the fastener you are loosening and tightening. (Snap-On Tool Corp.)

Fig. 7-25. The pipe wrench. Avoid using it to loosen or tighten a nut or bolt.

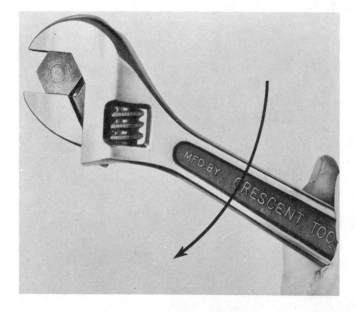

Fig. 7-23. The movable jaw should always face the direction of rotation. (Crescent Tool Co.)

Fig. 7-26. Open-end wrench.

are made about 0.005 in. oversize to permit them to easily slip on bolt heads and nuts of the wrench size. Openings are angled with the wrench body so they can be used in close quarters. Standard and metric size open-end wrenches are available.

BOX WRENCHES

BOX WRENCHES, Fig. 7-27, are so called because the wrench opening completely surrounds the bolt head or nut. It is usually preferred over other wrenches because it will not slip. Box wrenches are available in the same sizes as open-end wrenches, and with straight or offset handles.

COMBINATION OPEN AND BOX WRENCHES

A COMBINATION OPEN AND BOX WRENCH, Fig. 7-28, has an open end on one side and a box wrench on the other side of the handle. They are made in standard and metric sizes.

SOCKET WRENCHES

SOCKET WRENCHES, Fig. 7-29, are box-like and are made with a detachable tool that fits many types

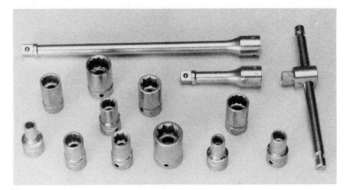

Fig. 7-29. Portion of a socket wrench set.

of handles. A typical socket wrench set contains various handles and a wide range of socket sizes. Many sets include both standard and metric sockets.

The various types of socket openings are shown in Fig. 7-30.

SPANNER WRENCHES

SPANNER WRENCHES are special wrenches usually furnished with machine tools and attachments. They are used to turn flush and recessed type threaded fittings. The fittings have slots or holes to receive the wrench end.

A HOOK SPANNER, Fig. 7-31, is equipped with a single lug that is placed in a notch cut in the fitting. The handle points towards the direction the fitting is to be turned.

The END SPANNER, Fig. 7-32, has lugs on both faces of the wrench for better access to the fitting. The lugs fit notches machined into the face of the fitting.

On PIN SPANNER WRENCHES, Fig. 7-33, the lugs are replaced with pins. The pins fit into holes rather than into notches.

ALLEN WRENCHES

The wrench used with socket head threaded fasteners is more commonly known as a ALLEN

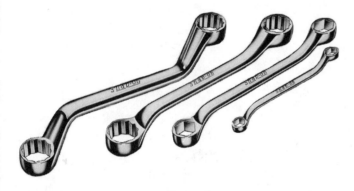

Fig. 7-27. Box wrenches.

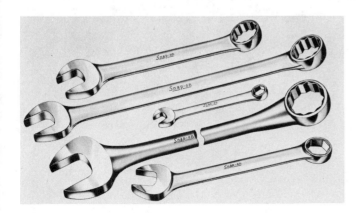

Fig. 7-28. Combination wrenches.

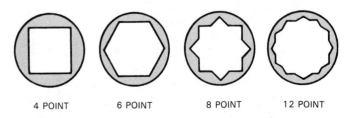

4 POINT   6 POINT   8 POINT   12 POINT

Fig. 7-30. Types of socket openings available. Which socket opening can be used with both square and hex head fasteners?

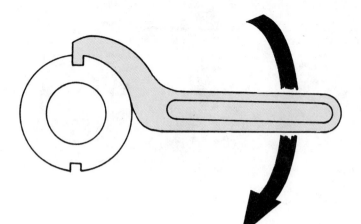

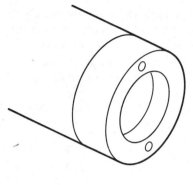

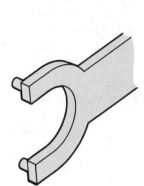

Fig. 7-31. A hook spanner wrench. Some can be adjusted to fit different size fasteners.

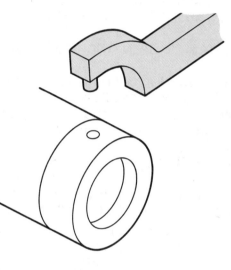

Fig. 7-33. Pin spanner wrenches.

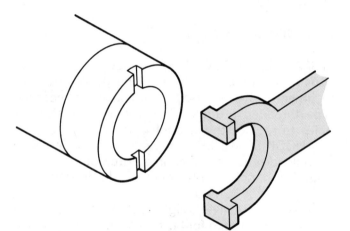

Fig. 7-32. End spanner wrench.

WRENCH, Fig. 7-34. It is manufactured in many sizes to fit fasteners of various standard and metric dimensions.

GENERAL SAFETY RULES FOR WRENCH USE

1. Always pull on a wrench. You have more control over the tool and there is less chance of injury.
2. Select a wrench that fits properly. A loose fitting wrench may slip and round off the corners of the bolt head or nut.
3. Never hammer on a wrench to loosen a stubborn fastener, unless the tool has been designed for this type of work.
4. It is a dangerous practice to lengthen a wrench handle for additional leverage. Use a larger

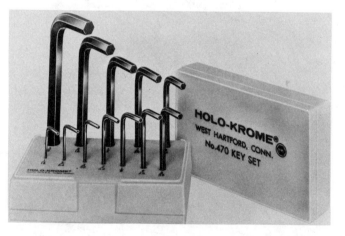

Fig. 7-34. Allen wrenches are used with socket head fasteners, and are made in both inch and metric sizes. (Holo-Krome)

wrench.

5. When using a wrench, clean grease and oil from the tool handle and the floor in the work area. This will reduce the possibility of your hands or

feet slipping.

6. Do not use a wrench on moving machinery.

SCREWDRIVERS

SCREWDRIVERS are manufactured with several different tip shapes, Fig. 7-35. Each shape has been designed for a particular type of fastener. The STANDARD and PHILLIPS type screwdrivers are familiar to all shop workers. The other shapes are not as well known.

The STANDARD screwdriver has a flattened wedge shaped tip that fits into the slot in the screw head. This tool is made in 3 to 12 in. lengths with the shank diameter, and the width and thickness of the tip being proportional with the length. Length is measured from blade tip to the handle. The blade is heat-treated to give it the necessary hardness and toughness to withstand the pressures put upon it.

Well-known and used for most work is the conventional straight shank screwdriver, Fig. 7-36, A. The ELECTRICIAN'S screwdriver, Fig. 7-36, B, has a long, thin shank and an insulated handle. It is very useful when handling small screws. A HEAVY-DUTY type, Fig. 7-36, C, has a heavy, square shank that permits a wrench to be applied for driving or removing large or stubborn screws. The DOUBLE-END OFFSET screwdriver, Fig. 7-36, D, is used where there is not enough space to use the conventional straight shank screwdriver. STUBBY or CLOSE QUARTER screwdrivers, Fig. 7-36, E, are designed for use where work space is limited.

Both the standard and Phillips type screwdrivers are made with ratchet devices. This moves the screw on the power stroke but not on the return stroke. It can be adjusted for right- or left-hand operation. See Figs. 7-37 and 7-38.

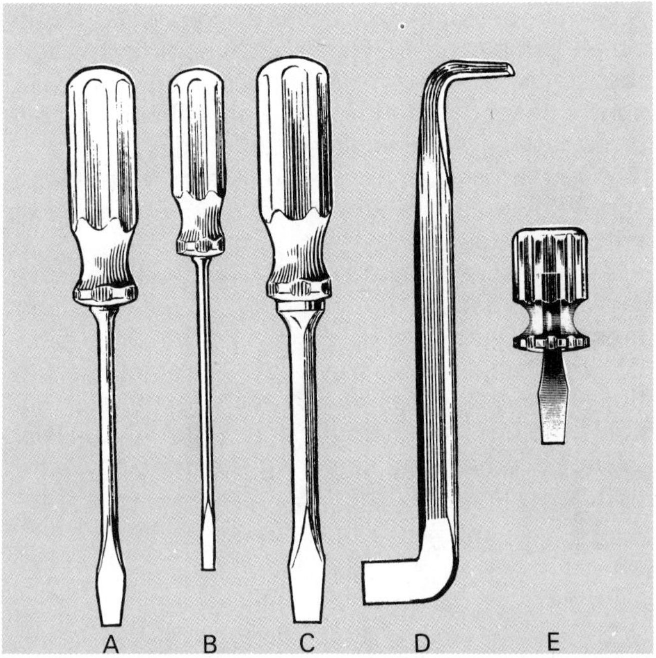

Fig. 7-36. Styles and types of standard screwdrivers: A—Conventional straight shank. B—Electrician's C—Heavy-duty. D—Double-end offset. E—Stubby or close quarter.

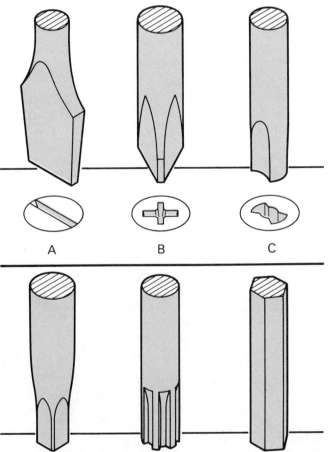

Fig. 7-35. Screwdrivers. A—Standard. B—Phillips. C—Clutch. D—Square. E—Torx. F—Hex.

Fig. 7-37. Ratchet type offset screwdriver.

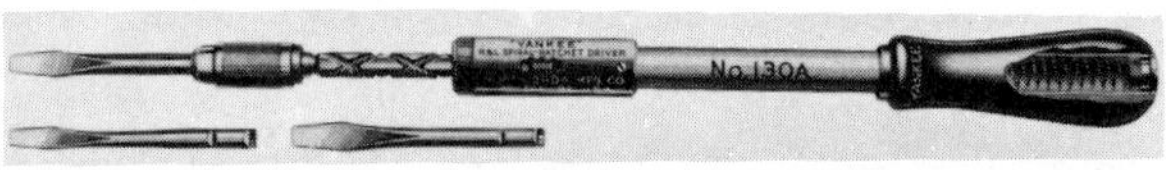

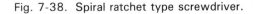

Fig. 7-38. Spiral ratchet type screwdriver.

The Phillips type screwdriver has an X-shaped point for use with Phillips recessed head screws. Four sizes (#1, #2, #3, and #4) handle the full range of this type screw. They are manufactured in the same styles as the standard screwdriver.

The POZIDRIV® screwdriver tip is similar in appearance to the Phillips type tip. However, it has been designed for POZIDRIV® screws used extensively in the aircraft, automotive, electronic, and appliance industries. The tip of this screwdriver has a black oxide finish to distinguish it from a Phillips type tool. A Phillips tip will damage the opening in the head of the POZIDRIV® screw.

The CLUTCH HEAD, ROBERTSON, TORX®, and HEX TYPE screwdrivers are used for special industrial and security applications.

USING THE SCREWDRIVER

Always select the correct size screwdriver for the screw being handled, Fig. 7-39. A poor fit damages the screw slot and frequently the tip. Damaged screw heads are dangerous, and difficult to drive or remove. They should be replaced.

When driving or removing a screw, hold the screwdriver square with the screw. Guide the tip with your free hand.

A worn screwdriver tip, Fig. 7-40, left, must be reground. Use a fine grinding wheel and light pressure. Check the tip during the grinding operation by fitting it to a screw slot. A properly ground tip, Fig. 7-40, right, fits snugly into the slot and holds the head firmly in the screw slot. CAUTION: Do not overheat the tip during the grinding operation. It will destroy the tool.

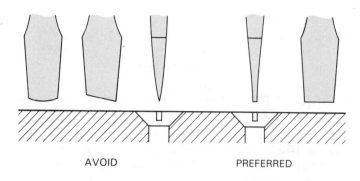

AVOID   PREFERRED

Fig. 7-40. The tips on the left should be avoided. They are worn or improperly sharpened. The tip to the right is ground correctly. Note that the concave sides hold the tip more firmly in the slot when pressure is applied.

The screwdriver is not a substitute for a chisel, nor is it made to be hammered on, or used as a pry.

SAFETY PRECAUTIONS FOR SCREWDRIVER USE

1. Wear goggles when resharpening screwdriver tips.
2. Screws with burred heads are dangerous and should be replaced or the burrs removed with a file or abrasive cloth.
3. Always turn electric power off when working on electrical equipment. The screwdriver should also have an insulated handle specifically designed for electrical work.
4. Avoid carrying a screwdriver in your pocket. It is a dangerous practice that can cause you or someone else injury. It can also damage your clothes, Fig. 7-41.

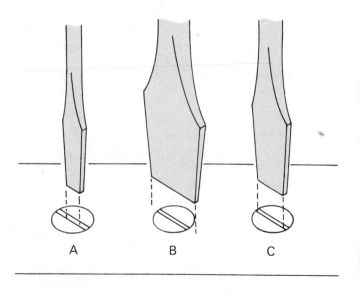

A   B   C

Fig. 7-39. Use the correct tip for the job being done. Tip A is too narrow and will damage the screw head. Tip B is too wide and will damage the work. Tip C is the correct size.

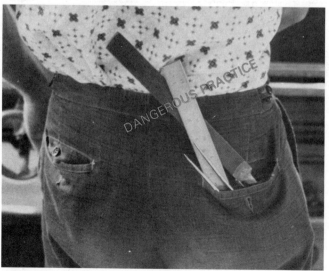

Fig. 7-41. Caution: Do not carry tools, like screwdrivers, in your pocket.

STRIKING TOOLS

The MACHINIST'S BALL-PEEN HAMMER, Fig. 7-42, is the most commonly used shop hammer. It has a hardened striking face and is employed for all general purpose work that requires a hammer.

Ball-peen hammers are classified according to the weight of the head, without the handle. They are available in weights of 2, 4, 8, or 12 ounces, and 1, 1 1/2, 2, or 3 pounds.

SOFT-FACE HAMMERS or MALLETS, Fig. 7-43, permit heavy blows to be struck where a steel face hammer would damage or mar the work surface. They are especially useful for setting work tightly on parallels (steel bars) when mounting the material in a vise for machining.

Soft-face hammers are made of many different materials: copper, lead, rawhide, and plastic, and range in weight from a few ounces to several pounds.

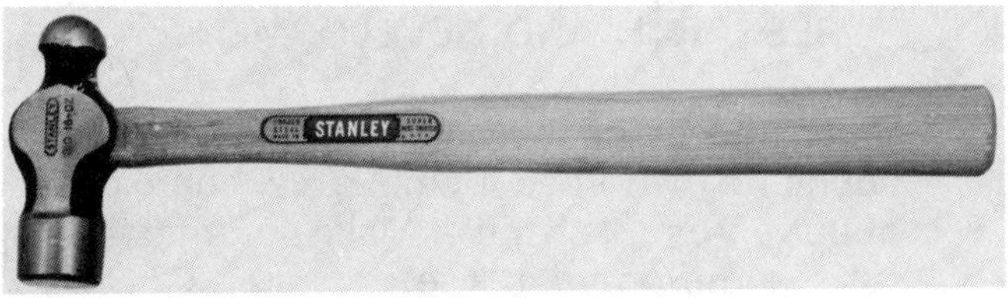

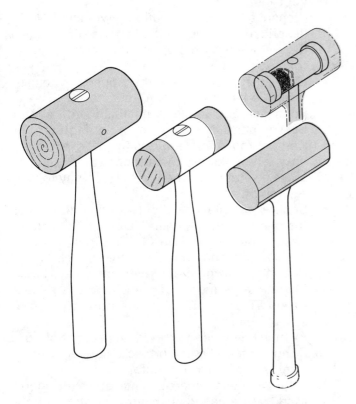

Fig. 7-42. Ball-peen hammer.

Fig. 7-43. There are many types of non-marring soft face hammers and mallets available for shop use. Shown are the rawhide mallet, plastic face hammer, and "dead blow" hammer. The latter, encased in urethane plastic with tiny steel shots to provide the striking power, will not rebound as will other mallets and soft face hammers.

SAFETY PRECAUTIONS FOR STRIKING TOOL USE

1. NEVER strike two hammers together. The faces are very hard and the blow might cause a chip to break off and fly out at high speed.
2. Avoid using a hammer unless the head is on tightly and the handle is solid.
3. Knuckles can be injured if you "choke up" too far on the handle when striking a blow.
4. Unless the blow is struck squarely, the hammer may glance off of the work and injure you, or someone working nearby.
5. Place a hammer on the bench carefully. A falling hammer can cause painful foot injuries, or damage precision tools on the bench.

TEST YOUR KNOWLEDGE, Unit 7

Please do not write in the text. Place your answers on a separate sheet of paper.

1. The bench vise is mounted on the edge of the bench to: (List the correct answer or answers.)
   a. Make the vise easier to use.
   b. Permit clamping long work in a vertical position.
   c. Hold small parts without damage.
   d. All of the above.
   e. None of the above.
2. Vise jaws are hardened and can damage or mar the work. Protect the work by placing soft metal _____ caps over the jaw serrations.
3. Vise size is determined by _____.
4. Make a sketch of a C-clamp and a parallel clamp.
5. How is C-clamp size determined?
6. Combination pliers are also known as _____ pliers.
7. Combination plier size indicates their _____.
8. The cutting edge of a diagonal pliers is at an angle to: (List the correct answer or answers.)
   a. Permit work to be cut close to the surface.
   b. Permit work to be cut flush to the surface.
   c. Permit work to be cut on a diagonal.
   d. All of the above.
   e. None of the above.
9. Wire and small metal pieces can be formed with _____ pliers.
10. Heavy wire and pins should be cut with _____ pliers.

11. When work is confined to small or restricted places, _____ pliers are usually used.
12. Never use pliers as a substitute for a _____.
13. The jaws on _____ pliers can be adjusted to fit the work and then locked in place.
14. Wrenches comprise a family of tools used for _____ and _____ of _____.
15. When a threaded fastener or part must be tightened for maximum holding power without danger of the fastener failing or work warping or springing out of shape, a _____ wrench should be used.
16. The jaws of an _____ wrench can be moved to fit a range of bolt head and nut sizes.
17. The _____ wrench and _____ wrench also fit this description.
18. List three important points that must be remembered when using adjustable wrenches.
19. To prevent skinned knuckles, always _____ on a wrench.
20. The box wrench is preferred over the open-end wrench because: (List the correct answer or answers.)
    a. It is cheaper.
    b. It works on several sizes of fasteners.
    c. It completely surrounds the fastener and cannot slip.
    d. All of the above.
    e. None of the above.
21. What are spanner wrenches?
22. The wrench used with socket head threaded fasteners is commonly known as a _____ wrench.
23. The _____ screwdriver has an X-shaped tip.
24. The _____ or _____ screwdrivers are used when there is not enough room to use a conventional straight shank screwdriver.

Match each phrase in the left column with the correct term in the right column.

25. ____ Has a flattened wedge shaped tip.
26. ____ Is short and used when space is limited.
27. ____ Has a square shank to to permit additional force to be applied with a wrench.
28. ____ Useful when handling small screws.
29. ____ Tip is similar in appearance to the tip of a Phillips head screwdriver.
30. The screwdriver is not a substitute for a

a. Stubby.
b. Offset.
c. Electrician's.
d. Ratchet.
e. Standard
f. Heavy-duty.
g. POZIDRIV®.
h. Automatic.
i. Hex type.

_____, nor should it be used as a _____.
31. The most commonly used hammer in the metal shop is a _____ hammer.
32. The ball-peen hammer is classed according to its: (List the correct answer or answers.)
    a. Length.
    b. Size.
    c. Weight.
    d. Handle length.
33. A mallet, or soft face hammer, is used as a striking tool when a regular hammer would _____ or _____ the work.
34. Why is it dangerous to strike two hammer heads together?
35. Never use a hammer with a _____ head or a handle that is not _____.

RESEARCH AND DEVELOPMENT

1. Clean and check the vise at your work station. Lubricate the thread. Remove any sharp edges or burrs from the handle. Make soft metal caps if none are on your vise.
2. Clean and check the shop pliers. Lubricate and wipe them with a light coating of oil. Bring broken and damaged pliers to the attention of your instructor.
3. Prepare a term paper featuring wrenches NOT described in this unit. Include drawings. Reproduce it by the spirit duplicator process for distribution to the class.
4. Give a demonstration on the proper way to use a torque limiting wrench.
5. Repair all adjustable wrenches in the shop. Secure parts lists from the manufacturer.
6. Contact tool manufacturers for information on how wrenches are manufactured.
7. Make a safety poster on the proper way to use a wrench.
8. Secure samples of the following threaded fasteners—slotted, Allen, POZIDRIV®, clutch head, Robertson, TORX®, and hex. Mount and identify them on a suitable panel.
9. Regrind a worn screwdriver tip.
10. Make a large model of a properly sharpened screwdriver tip and illustrate how it fits in a screw head.
11. Examine and clean screwdrivers in the shop. Bring damaged and worn screwdrivers to the attention of your instructor.
12. Examine the hammers and mallets in the shop. Mark all damaged hammers, or those with loose handles, as unsafe and not usable. Bring them to the attention of your instructor so repairs can be made.

Unit 8

HAND TOOLS THAT CUT

Not all cutting in metalworking is done by machine. There are several basic hand tools that are used for cutting. These tools, when in good condition, sharp, and properly handled, are safe in use.

CHISELS

Chisels are tools used to cut cold metal and for this reason are called "cold" chisels. The four chisels illustrated in Fig. 8-1, are the most widely used types. The general term COLD CHISEL is used when referring to these chisels. Other chisels in this category are variations or combinations of these four chisels.

The work to be cut will determine how the chisel should be sharpened. A chisel with a slightly curved cutting edge, Fig. 8-2, A, will work better when cutting on a flat plate. If it is to be used to shear metal

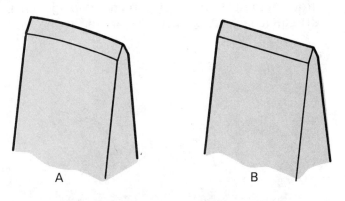

Fig. 8-2. The work to be done determines how the chisel should be sharpened. A—Slightly rounded for cutting on flat plates. B—Flat for shearing.

held in a vise, it will work best if the cutting edge is straight, Fig. 8-2, B. The curved edge will help

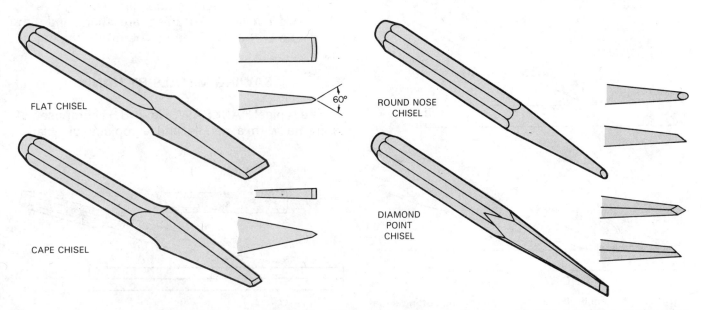

Fig. 8-1. Cold chisels. The flat chisel is used for general cutting and chipping work. The cape chisel has a narrower cutting edge than the flat chisel and is used to cut grooves. The round nose chisel can cut radii and round grooves. A diamond point chisel is principally used for squaring corners.

prevent the chisel from cutting unwanted grooves in the surrounding metal when shearing rivet heads.

The chisel is frequently used to chip castings. Chipping is started by holding the chisel at an angle as shown in Fig. 8-3, A. The angle must be great enough to cause the cutting edge to enter the metal. After the cut has been started and the proper depth reached, the chisel angle can be decreased enough to hold the cutting action at the proper depth, Fig. 8-3, B. The cut depth can be reduced by decreasing the chisel angle. Decrease the angle too much and the chisel will ride on the cutting edge heel, Fig. 8-3, C, and lift out of the cut.

Grip the metal so the layout line is just below the vise jaws when shearing it to a line. This will leave sufficient metal to finish by filing or grinding. When cutting, it is best to hold the metal in the vise without using vise jaw caps. This provides a better shearing action between the vise jaw and the chisel. Advance the chisel after each blow so that the cutting is done by the center of the cutting edge.

The chisel is an ideal tool for removing rivets. The head is sheared off and the rivet punched out. A variation of the conventional cold chisel used to remove rivet heads is called a "rivet buster," Fig. 8-4.

When there is not enough room to swing a hammer with sufficient force to cut the rivet, drill a hole about the size of the rivet body and almost through the head, Fig. 8-5, A. The head can then be removed with the chisel.

If the rivet head is so large that the entire head cannot be removed in one piece, saw the head almost through and cut away half of the head at a time. Fig. 8-5, B and C, shows how this may be done. A cape chisel can also be used to remove rivets, Fig. 8-6.

There are few things more dangerous than metal knocked off a chisel head that has become mushroomed, Fig. 8-7, A. Remove this dangerous condition by grinding, Fig. 8-7, B, before a painful injury results.

CHISEL SAFETY

1. Flying chips are dangerous. Wear safety goggles and erect a shield when using a chisel, to protect yourself and the people working near you.
2. Hold the chisel in such a manner that should you miss a stroke with the hammer it will not strike and injure your hand.
3. Remove any chisel head mushrooming by grinding, before it becomes dangerous.
4. Edges cut with the chisel are sharp and can cause bad cuts. Remove them by grinding or filing.

SAWING METALS BY HAND

The typical HACKSAW, Fig. 8-8, is composed of a frame with a handle and a replaceable blade.

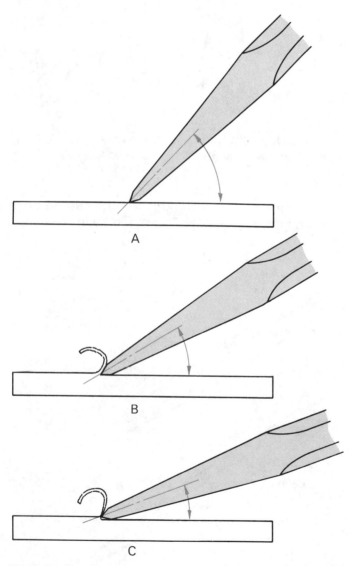

Fig. 8-3. The proper chisel angles for various cutting situations. A—Starting the cut. B—Maintaining the cut at the desired depth. C—Reducing the cutting angle too much will cause the chisel to lift out of the cut.

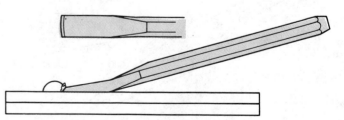

Fig. 8-4. This chisel (a variation of the flat chisel) is often referred to as a "rivet buster." Note drawing in color that shows how it is sharpened.

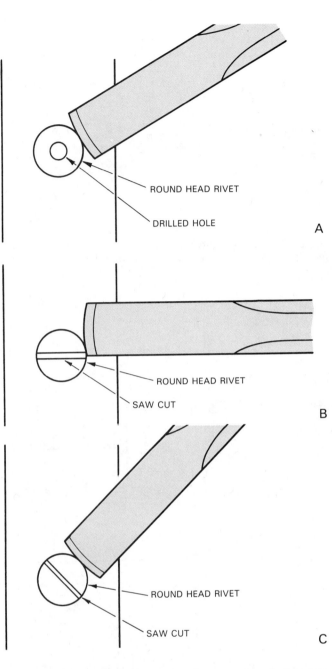

ROUND HEAD RIVET

DRILLED HOLE

A

ROUND HEAD RIVET

SAW CUT

B

ROUND HEAD RIVET

SAW CUT

C

Fig. 8-5. Recommended practice for removing rivet heads. A—When there is not enough room to swing the hammer with sufficient force. B and C—When the rivet heads are too large to be removed at one time.

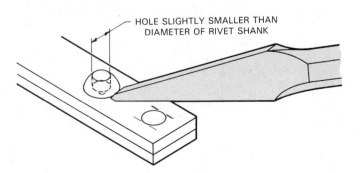

HOLE SLIGHTLY SMALLER THAN DIAMETER OF RIVET SHANK

Fig. 8-6. The cape chisel may also be used to remove rivets.

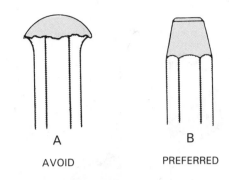

A
AVOID

B
PREFERRED

Fig. 8-7. A—Chisel with a dangerous mushroom head. B— This should be ground to a safe condition, before a chip flying from it injures someone.

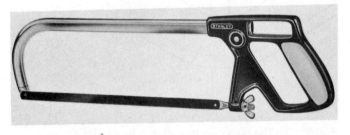

Fig. 8-8. A typical hacksaw. It is adjustable to fit several different blade lengths. (Stanley Tool Co.)

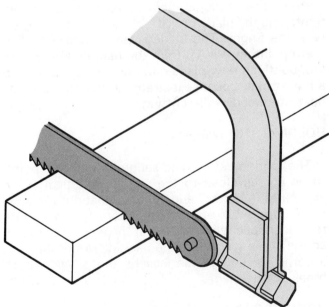

Fig. 8-9. The blade set in the conventional vertical position.

Almost all hacksaws made today are adjustable to accommodate several different blade lengths, and are made so that the blade can be installed in either a vertical or horizontal position, Figs. 8-9 and 8-10.

Hand Tools That Cut 107

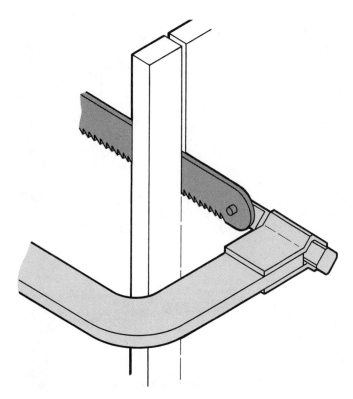

Fig. 8-10. The blade positioned in a horizontal position.

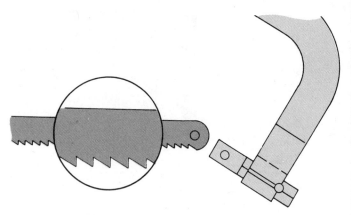

Fig. 8-11. Inserting the blade. It must be inserted with the teeth positioned to cut on the forward stroke of the hack saw.

When placing a blade in the saw frame, make sure the frame is adjusted for the blade length to be used, with sufficient adjustment remaining to permit tightening the blade until it "pings" when snapped with the finger. The blade is positioned with the teeth pointing AWAY from the handle, Fig. 8-11. Frequently, a new blade must be retightened after a few strokes because it stretched slightly from the heat produced while cutting.

HOLDING THE WORK

The work must be held securely, with the point to be cut as close to the vise as practical. This eliminates "chatter" and vibration that dull the saw teeth. Fig. 8-12, offers suggestions for holding irregular shaped work. Note that the work is clamped so the cut is started on the flat side rather than on a corner or edge. This lessens the possibility of breaking the blade.

HOW TO START THE CUT

When starting to cut to a marked line, it is best to notch the work with a file, Fig. 8-13, or to use the thumb of the left hand to guide the blade until it starts to cut. Some blades are manufactured with very fine teeth at the front to make starting the cut easier. Use enough pressure so the blade will begin to cut immediately.

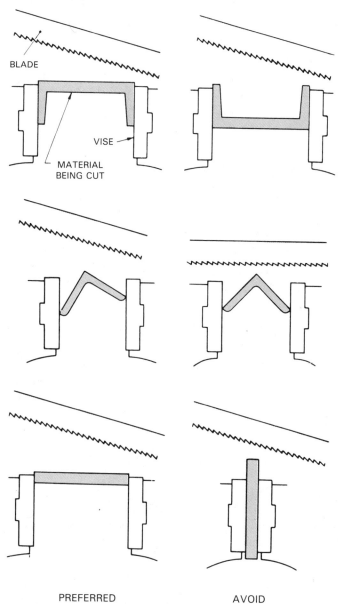

Fig. 8-12. Holding irregular shaped work for sawing.

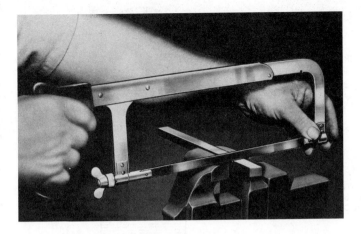

Fig. 8-13. Starting the cut. A file was used to notch the work to permit easier starting.   (L.S. Starrett Co.)

CUTTING METAL

Grasp the saw firmly by the handle and the front of the frame. Apply enough pressure on the forward stroke to make the teeth cut. Insufficient pressure will permit the teeth to slide over the material and become dull. Also, lift the saw slightly on the return stroke, as the blade cuts only on the forward stroke.

Use the complete length of the blade and make about 40 to 50 strokes per minute. More strokes per minute may generate enough heat to draw the blade temper and dull the teeth. Keep the blade moving in a straight line. Avoid any twisting or binding which can break the blade.

DULLING OR BREAKING A BLADE BEFORE COMPLETING THE CUT

If the cut is started with an old blade and it becomes necessary to replace it with a new blade because of breakage or dullness, do not continue in the same cut with the new blade. As the blade becomes dull, the KERF, the term given to the slot made by the blade, becomes narrower and to continue the cut in the slot will cause the new blade to bind and stick and be ruined in the first few strokes. Start a new cut by rotating the work, if possible, or by starting a new cut.

FINISHING THE CUT

Saw carefully when the blade has cut almost through the material, and support the stock being cut off with your left hand, so it will not drop when the cut is completed.

SAW BLADES

All hacksaws are heat treated to provide hardness and toughness needed to cut. The FLEXIBLE BACK BLADE has only the teeth hardened. The ALL-HARD BLADE is hardened throughout except that the hardness is reduced near the holes to reduce the possibility of breakage at this point. Flexible back blades are used for sawing soft materials or materials with thin cross-sections. The all-hard blade does not buckle when heavy pressure is applied. It is best for cutting hard metals.

The number of teeth per inch of blade has an important bearing on the shape and kind of material to be cut, and upon the blade life. Two or three teeth should be cutting at all times, otherwise, the teeth will straddle the section being cut and snap off when cutting pressure is applied, Fig. 8-14.

The SET of the blade provides the necessary clearance, and prevents the blade from binding in the cut. The blade may have one of three sets: RAKER, ALTERNATE, or UNDULATING, Fig. 8-15.

UNUSUAL CUTTING SITUATIONS

Cutting soft metal tubing can be a problem. The blade may bind and tear the tubing or the tubing may flatten. This can be eliminated by inserting a wooden dowel of the proper size into the tubing, and cutting through the tubing and dowel, Fig. 8-16 and 8-17.

Cutting a narrow strip of considerable length can be accomplished by setting the blade at right angles to the frame and making the cut in the usual way, Fig. 8-18. Strips of any width up to the capacity of the saw frame can be made in this manner.

Thin metal can be cut by putting it between two pieces of wood, and cutting through both of them, Fig. 8-19.

HACKSAW SAFETY

1. Do not test the sharpness of the blade by running your fingers across the teeth.
2. Store the saw so you will not accidentally reach into the teeth when you pick it up.
3. The burr formed on the cut surface is sharp and can cause a serious cut. Do not brush away the chips with your hand.
4. All-hard blades can shatter and produce flying chips. Wear your goggles!
5. Be sure the blade is properly tensioned. If the blade should break while you are on the cutting stroke, your hand may strike the work and cause a painful injury.

FILES

Until about 1860, all files were laboriously made by hand. Steel blanks were forged to shape, and the teeth were cut by hammer and chisel, one row at a time.

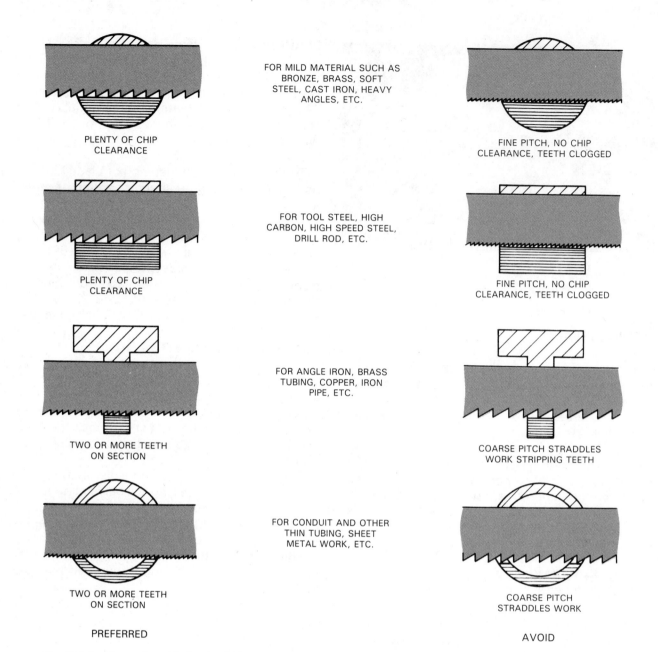

FOR MILD MATERIAL SUCH AS BRONZE, BRASS, SOFT STEEL, CAST IRON, HEAVY ANGLES, ETC.

PLENTY OF CHIP CLEARANCE

FINE PITCH, NO CHIP CLEARANCE, TEETH CLOGGED

FOR TOOL STEEL, HIGH CARBON, HIGH SPEED STEEL, DRILL ROD, ETC.

PLENTY OF CHIP CLEARANCE

FINE PITCH, NO CHIP CLEARANCE, TEETH CLOGGED

FOR ANGLE IRON, BRASS TUBING, COPPER, IRON PIPE, ETC.

TWO OR MORE TEETH ON SECTION

COARSE PITCH STRADDLES WORK STRIPPING TEETH

FOR CONDUIT AND OTHER THIN TUBING, SHEET METAL WORK, ETC.

TWO OR MORE TEETH ON SECTION

COARSE PITCH STRADDLES WORK

PREFERRED

AVOID

Fig. 8-14. The proper blade should be used for each job to assure long blade life and rapid cutting action.

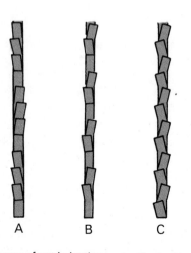

Fig. 8-15. Types of set in hack saw teeth. A—Undulated. B—Raker. C—Alternate.

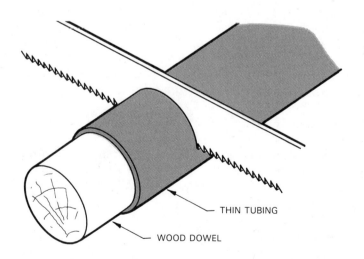

Fig. 8-16. Insert a snug fitting dowel into thin wall tubing before attempting to make a cut.

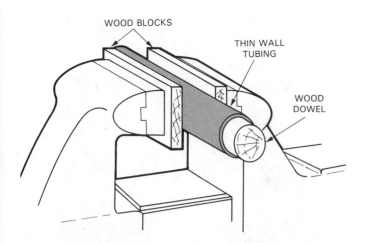

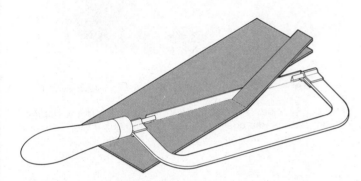

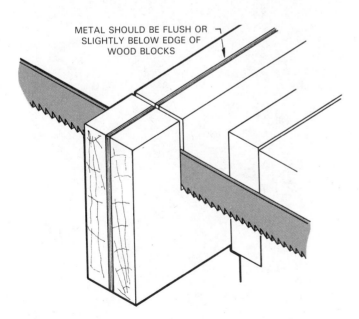

Fig. 8-17. Soft wood blocks placed between the vise jaws and the work will prevent marring and damaging the exterior surfaces of the metal. Caution: Avoid using too much pressure to hold thin wall tubing when it is being cut.

Fig. 8-18. The blade is pivoted to the horizontal position for cutting long narrow strips. Best results can be obtained if the strip is bent up slightly (as shown) during the sawing operation.

Fig. 8-19. Thin metal can be cut easily by sandwiching it between two pieces of wood.

Today, files are made from high grade carbon steel and are heat treated for hardness and toughness. In the first production step, the blank is cut to approximate shape and size. The tang and point are formed next after which the blank is annealed and straightened. The point and tang are trimmed after the sides and faces have been ground and the teeth cut. After another straightening, they are heat treated, cleaned, and oiled. Tests are made continually to assure a quality tool. Fig. 8-20 shows the steps in the manufacture of a modern file.

HOW FILES ARE CLASSIFIED

Files are classified by their shape. The shape of the file is its general outline and cross section. The outline, Fig. 8-21, is either tapered or blunt.

Files are also classified according to the cut of the teeth—SINGLE-CUT, DOUBLE-CUT, RASP, and CURVED-TOOTH, Fig. 8-22, and to the coarseness of the teeth—ROUGH, COARSE, BASTARD, SECOND-CUT, SMOOTH, and DEAD SMOOTH.

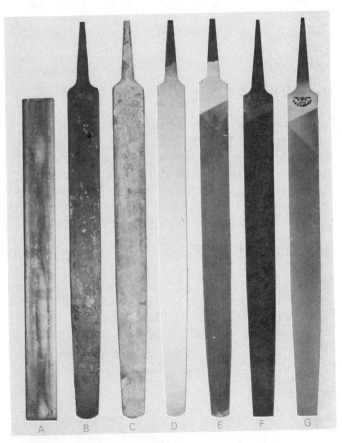

Fig. 8-20. How a file is manufactured: A—Steel bar cut to the correct length. B—The bar forged to shape. C—The blank after it has been annealed. D—The annealed blank straightened and ground smooth to remove any scale. E—The teeth cut on the blank. F—The blank trimmed and coated for heat treatment. G—The completed file, cleaned and inspected.
(Nicholson File Co.)

Fig. 8-21. Blunt and tapered files.

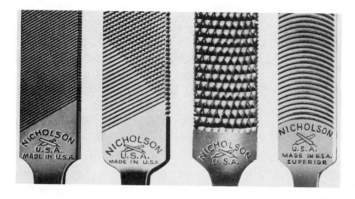

Fig. 8-22. Single-cut, double-cut, rasp, and curved tooth files.

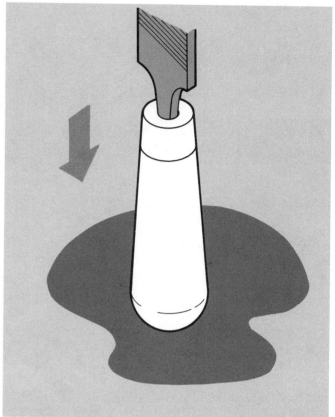

Fig. 8-24. Insert the tang into the hole drilled in the handle, then strike handle against the bench top as shown. This will seat the file tang in the handle.

HANDLING A FILE

A file should never be used without a handle. It is too easy to drive the unprotected tang into your hand. Fit the handle to the file by drilling a hole in the handle equal in diameter to the tang at its midpoint, Fig. 8-23. Mate the file and handle by placing the tang into the hole then sharply striking the handle on a solid surface, Fig. 8-24.

FILE CARE

Files should be stored in such a manner that they are always separated. NEVER THROW FILES IN A DRAWER OR STORE THEM IN A DAMP PLACE.

Clean files frequently with a FILE CARD or BRUSH, Fig. 8-25. Some soft metals cause PIN-

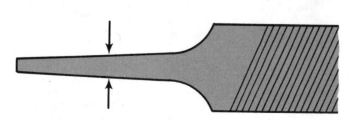

Fig. 8-23. The hole in the file handle should be equal in diameter to the width of the file tang at the point indicated.

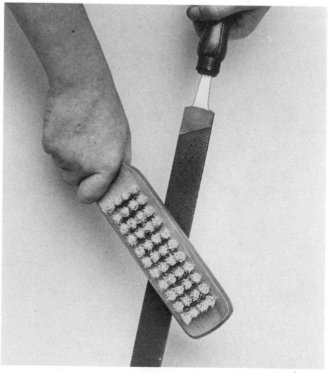

Fig. 8-25. Using a combination file card and brush to clean a file.

NING, that is, the teeth become loaded with some of the material the file has removed. Pinning causes gouging and scratching on the work surface. The particles can be removed from the file by using a PICK or SCORER (the point of a scriber will do nicely). A file card combines the card, brush, and pick.

FILE SELECTION

There is almost no limit to the number of different kinds, shapes, and cuts of files that are manufactured, Fig. 8-26. We will confine this material to the general classification of files.

Files have three distinct characteristics: LENGTH, KIND, and CUT. The length is always measured from the heel to the point, Fig. 8-27. The tang is not included in this measurement.

The kind of a file refers to its shape or style, such as FLAT, MILL, HALF-ROUND, or SQUARE.

The cut of a file indicates the relative coarseness of the teeth. SINGLE-CUT files are usually used to produce a smooth surface finish. Their use requires light pressure. DOUBLE-CUT files remove metal much faster than single-cut files. They require heavier pressure and they produce a rougher surface finish. RASPS are used for working wood and soft materials. The CURVED-TOOTH file is used to file flat surfaces of aluminum and steel sheet.

Some files have SAFE EDGES, Fig. 8-28. The term safe edge denotes that the file has one or both edges without teeth. This permits filing corners without danger to the portion of the work that is not to be filed.

Many factors must be considered in selecting the file to obtain maximum cutting efficiency:
1. The nature of the work—flat, concave, convex, notched, grooved, etc.
2. The kind of material.
3. The amount of material to be removed.
4. The surface finish and accuracy demanded.

Of the many file shapes available, the most commonly used shapes are FLAT, PILLAR, SQUARE, 3-SQUARE, KNIFE, HALF-ROUND, ROUND, and CROSSING, Fig. 8-29.

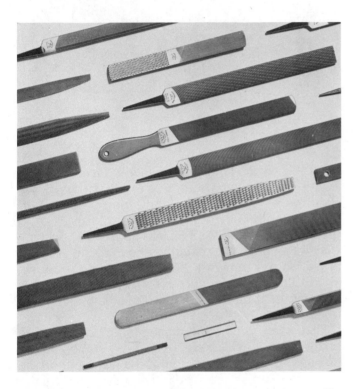

Fig. 8-26. A photo showing a few of the many hundred different kinds of files that are manufactured.
(Nicholson File Co.)

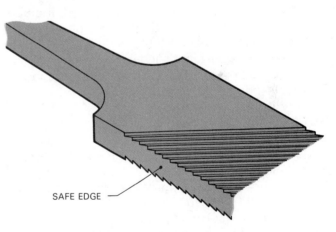

SAFE EDGE

Fig. 8-28. The safe edge of a file does not have teeth.

Fig. 8-27. How a file is measured. (Nicholson File Co.)

FLAT   PILLAR   SQUARE   3-SQUARE

KNIFE   HALF-ROUND   CROSSING   RAT TAIL

Fig. 8-29. Cross-sectional views of the most widely used file shapes.

Each shape is available in many sizes and degrees of coarseness: ROUGH, COARSE, BASTARD, SECOND-CUT, SMOOTH, and DEAD SMOOTH, Fig. 8-30. A rough cut small file (4 in.) may be as fine as a large (16 in.) second-cut file.

KINDS OF FILES

The vast variety of files fall into five general groups:

1. The MACHINIST FILE is used whenever metal must be removed rapidly, and the finish is of secondary importance. It is made in a large range of shapes and sizes, and is double-cut.
2. The MILL FILE is a single-cut file and tapers the last third of the length toward the point. It is used for general filing when a smooth finish is required. A mill file is used for draw filing, lathe work, and working on brass and bronze.
3. SWISS PATTERN and JEWELERS' FILES are manufactured in over a hundred different shapes. They are used primarily by tool and diemakers, jewelers, and others who do precision filing.
4. The RASP has teeth that are individually formed and disconnected from each other. It is used for woodworking and for working relatively soft metals when quantities of material must be removed rapidly.
5. The group of SPECIAL PURPOSE FILES include those specifically designed to cut one type of metal. The long-angle lathe file, Fig. 8-31, that does a more efficient filing job on the lathe, and the curved-tooth file used by the auto body repair industry, fall into this category.

HOW TO USE THE FILE

Much consideration has been given to the proper technique of using the file, the correct way to grasp it, how to hold the work, and the proper height to hold the work.

The vise is most frequently used to hold work for filing. Cover the vise jaws with CAPS made of soft copper sheet if there is any danger of the vise jaw serrations damaging the work.

Hold the work at about elbow height for general

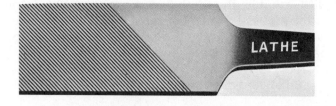

Fig. 8-31. Long angle file.

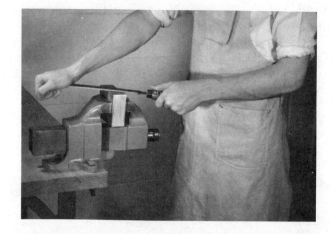

Fig. 8-32. Mount the work at elbow height for general filing.

filing, Fig. 8-32, and slightly lower if a large quantity of material must be removed by heavy filing. Hold the work solidly or "chattering" may occur, making it difficult to get a smooth finish.

STRAIGHT or CROSS FILING consists of pushing the file lengthwise, straight ahead, or at a slight angle, across the work. Grasp the file as shown in Fig. 8-33. Heavy-duty filing requires heavy pressure and can best be done if the file is held as shown in Fig. 8-34.

Files can be ruined by using too much pressure or too little pressure on the cutting stroke. Apply just enough pressure to permit the file to cut on the entire forward stroke. Too little pressure allows the file to slide over the work and it becomes dull. Too much pressure "overloads" the file and causes the teeth to clog and chip. Lift the file from the work on the reverse stroke except when filing soft metal.

Fig. 8-30. The range in coarseness of a typical machinist flat bastard file. File sizes range from 4 in. (102.0 mm) to 16 in. (406.0 mm).

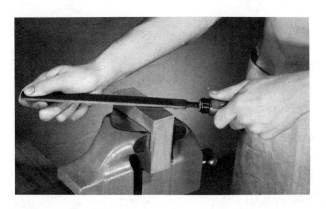

Fig. 8-33. The proper way to hold a file for straight or cross filing.

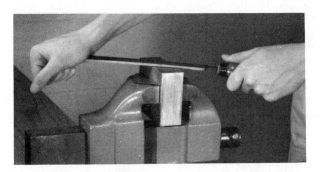

Fig. 8-34. Additional pressure is required when a considerable quantity of material must be removed.

Then the pressure on the return stroke should be no more than the weight of the file.

DRAW FILING, when properly done, produces a finer finish than straight filing. Hold the file as shown in Fig. 8-35. Do not use a short angle file for draw filing, as there is the likelihood of scoring or scratching instead of shaving and shearing, as the file should while being pushed and pulled across the metal. Use a double-cut file to ''rough down'' the surface and a single-cut file to produce the final finish.

FILE SAFETY

1. Never use a file without a handle. Painful injuries may result.
2. Use a file card to clean the file, not your hand. The chips can penetrate your hand and cause a painful infection.
3. Files are very brittle and should never be used as a pry.
4. Use a piece of cloth to wipe the surface being filed. Short burrs are formed in filing and can cause serious cuts.
5. Never hammer with a file. It may shatter and chips will fly in all directions.

Fig. 8-35. Draw filing improves the surface finish when done properly.

HAND REAMING

A drill does not produce a smooth or accurate enough hole for a precision fit. Reaming is the operation that is used to produce smoothness and accuracy. Ordinarily, only final sizing is done by hand reaming.

HAND REAMER

The hand reamer, Fig. 8-36, has a square on the shank end that is suitable for holding it in a tap wrench. The reamer may be made of high speed steel or carbon steel, and is available in sizes from 1/8 to 1 1/2 in. (3.175 to 38.1 mm). The cutting end is ground with a slight taper to provide easy starting in the hole. Straight fluted reamers are suitable for most work; however, when reaming a hole with a keyway or other interruption, it is better to use a reamer with spiral flutes. When preparing a piece to be reamed by hand, 0.005 to 0.010 in. (0.13 to 0.25 mm) of stock should be left in the hole for removal by the tool.

The EXPANSION HAND REAMER, Fig. 8-37, is used when the hole must be cut a few thousandths over nominal size for fitting purposes. Slots are cut into the hollow center of the tool, and the center opening is machined on a slight taper. The reamer is expanded by tightening a taper screw into this opening. The amount of expansion is limited and the reamer may be broken if expanded too much. It is not recommended that the expansion reamer be used in place of a solid reamer because of the

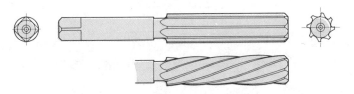

Fig. 8-36. The hand reamer. Top. Straight flutes. Bottom. Spiral flutes.

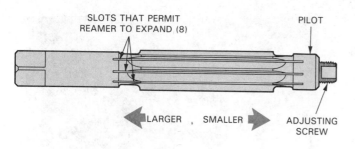

Fig. 8-37. The expansion hand reamer.

danger of producing oversize holes.

The ADJUSTABLE HAND REAMER, Fig. 8-38, is threaded its entire length and fitted with tapered slots to receive the adjustable blades. The blades are tapered along one edge to correspond with the taper slots in the reamer body, so that when they are in position, the cutting edges of the blade are parallel. The diameter of the reamer is set by loosening one adjusting nut and tightening the other. The blade can be moved in either direction. This type reamer is manufactured in sizes ranging from 3/8 to 3 1/2 in. (9.525 to 86.2 mm) and each reamer has sufficient adjustment to increase the diameter to the size of the next larger reamer.

The TAPER REAMER, Fig. 8-39, is used to finish a taper hole accurately and with a smooth finish. Because of the long cutting edges, taper reamers are somewhat difficult to operate. To provide for easier removal of the surplus metal, a roughing reamer is run into the hole first. This reamer is slightly smaller (0.010 in. or 0.25 mm) than the

finish reamer, and has a left hand spiral groove cut along the cutting edges to break up the chips.

USING THE HAND REAMER

A two-handle tap wrench is used as a handle because it permits an even application of pressure. It is virtually impossible to secure a satisfactory hole using a single end wrench. To start, rotate the reamer slowly to allow it to align with the hole. It is desirable to check whether the reamer has started square at several points around its circumference, Fig. 8-40. Feed should be steady and rapid. Keep the reamer cutting, or it will start to ''chatter,'' producing a series of tool marks in the surface of the hole, and causing it to be out-of-round. Turning pressure is applied evenly with both hands, and ALWAYS in a clockwise direction, Fig. 8-41. NEVER TURN A REAMER IN A COUNTERCLOCKWISE DIRECTION, as the cutting edges will be dulled. Feed the reamer deeply enough into the hole to take care of the starting taper. Cutting fluid to be applied will depend upon the metal being reamed.

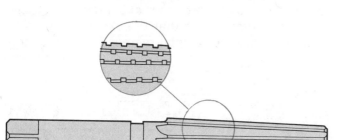

Fig. 8-38. The adjustable hand reamer.

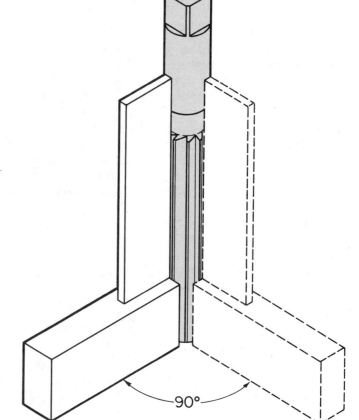

Fig. 8-40. Checking reamer for squareness with work.

Fig. 8-39. A taper hand reamer. Inset shows how the cutting edges are notched on the roughing taper reamer.

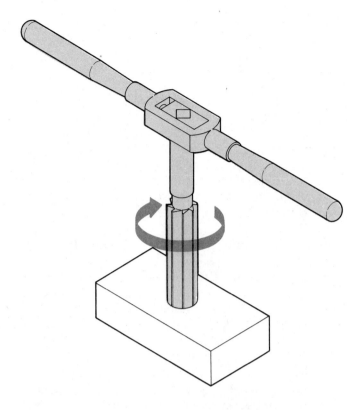

Fig. 8-41. A hand reamer is always turned in a clockwise direction.

HAND REAMING SAFETY

1. Remove all burrs from reamed holes.
2. Never use your hands to remove chips and cutting fluid from the reamer. Use a piece of cotton waste.
3. Store reamers carefully so they do not touch one another. Reamers should never be thrown in a drawer.
4. Clamp the work solidly before starting to ream.
5. Never clean a reamed hole with an air hose.

TEST YOUR KNOWLEDGE, Unit 8

Please do not write in the text. Place your answers on a separate sheet of paper.

1. List the four basic types of chisels.
   a. _____.
   b. _____.
   c. _____.
   d. _____.
2. The cutting edge of the chisel should be ground _____ if it is to shear metal held in a vise.
3. The chisel designed to remove rivets is called a _____.
4. A _____ chisel head should be ground away before use to prevent _____.
5. List three safety precautions that should be observed when cutting metal with a chisel.
6. A typical hacksaw is composed of a _____ and a _____.
7. The hacksaw blade is fitted in the frame correctly when it cuts on the _____ stroke.
8. If the work is not mounted solidly and close to the vise: (List the correct answer or answers.)
   a. The blade will break.
   b. The work will vibrate or "chatter" causing the teeth to snap off.
   c. The blade will slide over the work and not cut.
   d. All of the above.
   e. None of the above.
9. The _____ of the teeth keeps the blade from binding in the cut.
10. A new blade started in a cut made by a dull blade will: (List the correct answer or answers.)
    a. Cut faster and cleaner than the old blade.
    b. Stick and bind, ruining the new blade.
    c. Require care in restarting the cut.
    d. All of the above.
    e. None of the above.
11. Only the teeth are hardened on a _____ blade.
12. The _____ _____ blade is hardened throughout. It is used to cut _____ metal.
13. Modern files are made from _____.
14. Files are classified according to the cut of their teeth. List the four cuts.
15. Files are also classified by their shape. The shape of a file is its: (List the correct answer or answers.)
    a. General outline and cross section.
    b. Length and width.
    c. Taper and thickness.
    d. All of the above.
    e. None of the above.
16. Files are manufactured in six degrees of coarseness. Name them.
17. Sketch the cross section shape of the following files:
    a. Three-square.
    b. Half-round.
    c. Knife.
    d. Rat tail.
    e. Mill.
18. Files are cleaned with a _____.
19. A single-cut file does not remove metal as fast as a _____ file.
20. The edge that does not have teeth cut on it is called a _____.
21. The _____ file should be used when metal must be removed rapidly with little regard for the quality of the finish.
22. The _____ and _____ files are made

in over a hundred different shapes.

23. Work should be mounted at _____ height for general filing.
24. When a file is pushed and pulled across the work the operation is called: (List the correct answer or answers.)
    a. Push-pull filing.
    b. Straight filing.
    c. Draw filing.
    d. None of the above.
25. When a file is pushed lengthwise, straight ahead, or at a slight angle, across the work, the operation is called: (List the correct answer or answers.)
    a. Push-pull filing.
    b. Straight filing.
    c. Draw filing.
    d. All of the above.
26. Reaming will produce a hole that is _____
    _____.
27. Why does a hand reamer have a square shank?
28. When preparing a piece to be reamed by hand, _____ to _____ inch of stock should be left in the hole for removal by the tool.
29. When is an expansion reamer used?
30. Turning a hand reamer _____ will ruin the cutting edges.
31. Why are the cutting edges notched on the tapered roughing reamer?
32. It is virtually impossible to produce an accurately and smoothly reamed hole using an adjustable wrench to apply the turning action because: (List the correct answer or answers.)
    a. It applies too much pressure.
    b. It applies pressure unevenly causing "chatter."
    c. It prevents the reamer from starting square with the hole.
    d. All of the above.
    e. None of the above.
33. List four safety precautions that should be

observed when hand reaming.

RESEARCH AND DEVELOPMENT

1. The pneumatic chisel is often used in industry. Secure information on this tool for a bulletin board display and, if possible, borrow a sample of the actual tool for examination.
2. Make a small panel with two chisels—one that has a mushroomed head, and the other that is safe to use. Develop it into a safety display.
3. Design a safety poster showing the correct way to use a chisel.
4. Demonstrate the proper way to sharpen a chisel.
5. Demonstrate the proper way to use a hacksaw.
6. Prepare a display panel that shows the various types of hacksaw blades. Label each blade for recommended use.
7. Design a safety poster on the hacksaw.
8. Make a display panel of drawings which show the cross sections of the most commonly used file shapes. Make it large enough to be used in class discussion.
9. Design and produce safety posters around the following unsafe practices:
    a. Using the file as a pry.
    b. The file without a handle.
    c. Using the file as a hammer.
10. Inspect the files in your school shop. Clean them, repair, or replace missing handles, and make a new file rack if the present rack is not suitable.
11. Prepare a sample block of metal to illustrate the difference between a drilled hole and a reamed hole.
12. Make a large drawing of a reamer to post in the shop. Write in the names of the various parts.

Unit 9

HAND THREADING

Threaded sections have many applications in our everyday life (a thread is that spiral or helical ridge found on nuts and bolts). When required on a job, threads are indicated on plans and drawings in a special way, Fig. 9-1. They are specified by diameter and number of threads per inch. The suffix indicates the thread series.

The AMERICAN NATIONAL THREAD SYSTEM was adopted in 1911. It is the common thread form used in the United States and is characterized by the 60° angle formed by the sides of the thread and the small flat at the thread crest and root, Fig. 9-2.

The NATIONAL COARSE (NC), used for general purpose work, and the NATIONAL FINE (NF), used for precision assemblies, are the most widely used thread groups in the American National Thread Series. The NF group has more threads per inch for a given diameter than the NC group.

A considerable amount of confusion resulted during World War II from the many different forms and kinds of threads used by the Allies. As a result, the powers that make up NATO (North Atlantic Treaty

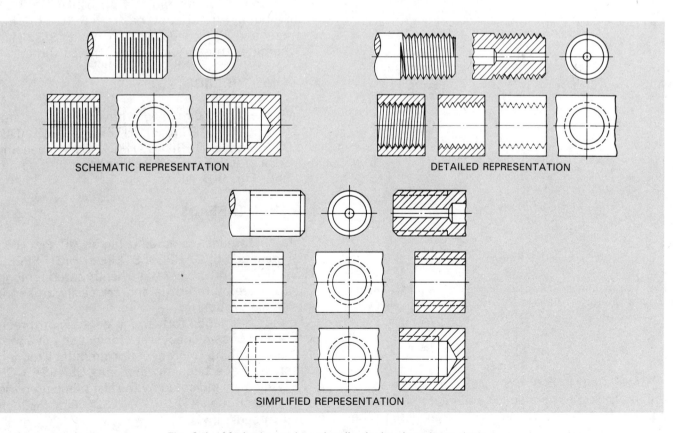

SCHEMATIC REPRESENTATION

DETAILED REPRESENTATION

SIMPLIFIED REPRESENTATION

Fig. 9-1. Methods used to visually depict threads on drawings. Only one type will be used on a drawing.

Organization) adopted a standard thread form. It is referred to as the UNIFIED SYSTEM, Figs. 9-2 and 9-3. It is very similar to the American National Thread System. It differs only in the shape of the root, which is rounded, and the crest, which may be flat or rounded. The threads are identified by UNF and UNC. Fasteners using this thread series are interchangeable with fasteners using the American National thread.

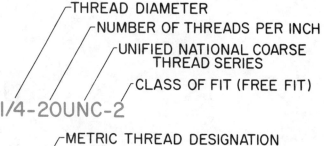

Fig. 9-4. How inch and metric based thread sizes are indicated on a drawing.

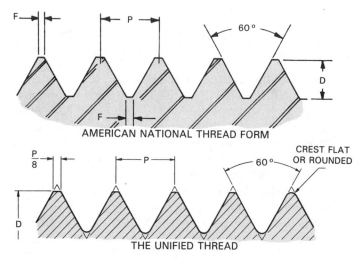

Fig. 9-2. The drawings illustrate the difference between the American National Thread form, and the Unified Thread form.

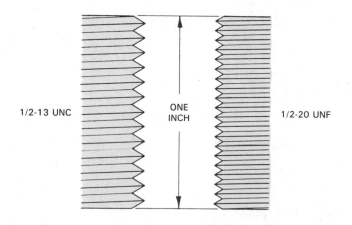

Fig. 9-3. A comparison of the Unified Coarse (UNC), and the Unified Fine (UNF) threads. Both have the same geometric shape.

Metric unit threads have the same shape as the unified thread but are specified in a different manner, Fig. 9-4. Metric thread sizes, in general, fall between the inch coarse and fine series for a comparable diameter.

THREAD SIZE

Thread sizes smaller than 1/4 in. diameter are not measured as fractional sizes but by NUMBER SIZES that range, for most shop purposes, from #0 (approximately 1/16 or 0.060 in. in diameter) to #12 (just under 1/4 or 0.216 in. in diameter). UNC and UNF series are available. Care must be taken so that the numbers of threads per inch are not mistaken for a fraction. For example: a #8-32 UNC thread would be a thread that has a #8 (0.164 in.) diameter and 32 threads per inch, not an 8/32 (1/4 in.) diameter thread with a UNC series thread.

CUTTING THREADS

Because thread dimensions have been standardized, the use of TAPS to cut INTERNAL THREADS, and DIES to cut EXTERNAL THREADS have become universal practice whenever threads are to be cut by hand, Fig. 9-5.

INTERNAL THREADS

Internal threads are made using a TAP, Fig. 9-5. Taps are made of CARBON STEEL or HIGH SPEED STEEL (HSS) and are carefully heat treated for long life. Taps are quite brittle and are easily broken if not handled properly.

To meet demands for varying degrees of thread accuracy, it became necessary for industry to adopt standard working tolerances for threads. Working tolerances have been divided into CLASSES OF FITS, which are indicated by the last number on the thread description (1/2-13 UNC-2). Fits for inch based threads are:

Class 1 . . . . Loose Fit
Class 2 . . . . Free Fit

Class 3 . . . . Medium Fit
Class 4 . . . . Close Fit

The class of fits for metric based threads are different but too extensive to list in a text of this limited nature.

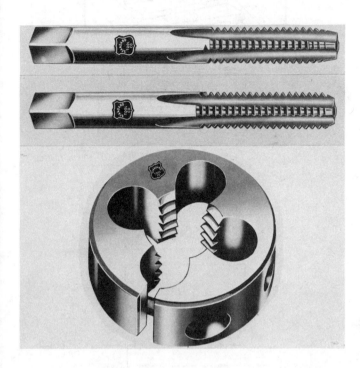

Fig. 9-5. Top. Taps used for cutting internal threads. Bottom. Die used for cutting external threads. (Standard Tool Co.)

TAPS

Standard hand taps are made in sets of three known as TAPER, PLUG, and BOTTOMING TAPS, Fig. 9-6. Threads are started with the TAPER TAP

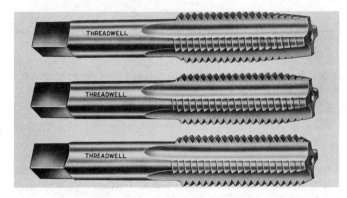

Fig. 9-6. Standard hand taps are manufactured in sets of three. Top. Taper—for starting the thread. Center. Plug—for continuing the thread after the taper tap has cut as far into the hole as possible. Below. Bottoming—for continuing the threads to the bottom of the hole.
(Threadwell Manufacturing Co.)

which is tapered back from the end 6 to 10 threads before full thread diameter is reached. The PLUG TAP is used after the taper tap has cut threads as far into the hole as possible. It tapers back 3 or 4 threads before the full thread diameter is reached. Threads are cut to the bottom of a blind hole (the hole does not go through the part) with a BOTTOMING TAP. It is only necessary to use the full set of taps when a blind hole is to be tapped, Fig. 9-7.

The PIPE TAP, Fig. 9-8, is another type that is used in the shop. There is a "straight" pipe tap and a "tapered" pipe tap. The tapered pipe tap cuts a tapered thread so that a "wedging" action is set up to make a leaktight joint. The fraction that indicates the tap size may be confusing at first because it indicates the pipe size AND NOT the thread diameter. A pipe thread is indicated by NPT (National Pipe Thread) and the threads taper 3/4 in. per foot of length.

Fig. 9-7. Openings in this metal block illustrate the three types of threaded holes. Left. Open or through hole. Center. Blind hole that has been drilled deeper than the desired threads. Right. Blind hole with threads tapped to the bottom.

CUTTING INTERNAL THREADS

Threads going all of the way through the part are made with a TAPER TAP. See Fig. 9-7. The long taper permits easier and straighter starting. However, it cannot be used to thread to the bottom of a blind hole as the end of the tap will strike the bottom of the hole before a full thread can be cut.

The PLUG TAP can be used in much the same manner as the taper tap if soft material is being threaded. It can be used to thread a blind hole, if the hole has been drilled deeper than the required thread, Fig. 9-7.

Threads that must be cut to the bottom of a blind hole are made with a BOTTOMING TAP, Fig. 9-7. Normally, the thread is started with a taper tap, cut further with a plug tap, and finished with a bottoming tap.

Fig. 9-8. Photo which shows 1/8 standard thread, and 1/8 pipe thread.

TAP DRILL SIZES

The drill used to make the hole prior to tapping is called the TAP DRILL. Theoretically, it should be equal in diameter to the minor diameter of the screw that is to be fitted into the completed thread, Fig. 9-9. To accomplish this, the tap must cut a full depth thread which would require too much pressure to drive the tap, and cause excessive tap breakage to occur. However, full depth threads are not necessary. With three-quarter depth threads, the fastener usually breaks before the threads strip.

Drill sizes can be secured from a TAP DRILL CHART, Fig. 9-10.

TAP HOLDERS

Two types of tap holders are available. The type to be employed will depend upon the tap size. A T-HANDLE TAP WRENCH, Fig. 9-11, should be used with all small taps as it allows a more sensitive "feel" when tapping. The HAND TAP WRENCH, Fig. 9-12, is best suited for large taps when more leverage is required.

When tapping by hand, the chief requirement is to see that the tap is started straight, and remains square during the entire threading operation, Fig. 9-13. The tap should be backed off a half turn every one or two cutting turns to break the chips free and allow them to drop through the tap flutes. This prevents them from jamming the tap and damaging the threads. Some machinists, when tapping blind holes, will insert a piece of grease pencil, wax

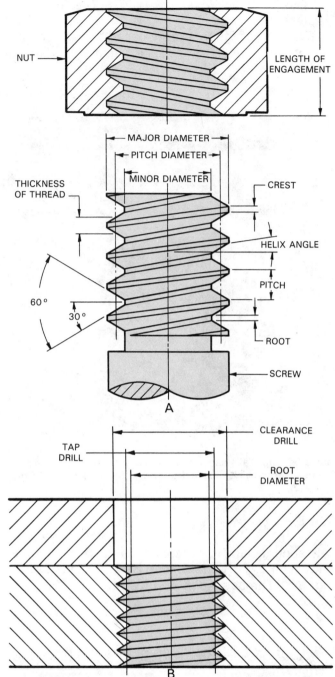

Fig. 9-9. A—Nomenclature of a thread. B—Cross section of a typical piece at a point where a bolt will be used to clamp the two pieces together. The clearance drill permits the bolt or threaded section to enter without binding.

crayon, or a dab of grease in the holes. As the tap cuts the threads, the grease is forced up and out of the hole carrying the chips along.

CARE IN TAPPING

Considerable care must be exercised when tapping:

UNIFIED COARSE, AND UNIFIED FINE THREADS AND TAP DRILLS

Size	Threads Per Inch	Major Dia.	Minor Dia.	Pitch Dia.	Tap Drill 75% Thread	Decimal Equiv- alent	Clearance Drill	Decimal Equiv- alent
2	56	.0860	.0628	.0744	50	.0700	42	.0935
	64	.0860	.0657	.0759	50	.0700	42	.0935
3	48	.099	.0719	.0855	47	.0785	36	.1065
	56	.099	.0758	.0874	45	.0820	36	.1065
4	40	.112	.0795	.0958	43	.0890	31	.1200
	48	.112	.0849	.0985	42	.0935	31	.1200
6	32	.138	.0974	.1177	36	.1065	26	.1470
	40	.138	.1055	.1218	33	.1130	26	.1470
8	32	.164	.1234	.1437	29	.1360	17	.1730
	36	.164	.1279	.1460	29	.1360	17	.1730
10	24	.190	.1359	.1629	25	.1495	8	.1990
	32	.190	.1494	.1697	21	.1590	8	.1990
12	24	.216	.1619	.1889	16	.1770	1	.2280
	28	.216	.1696	.1928	14	.1820	2	.2210
1/4	20	.250	.1850	.2175	7	.2010	G	.2610
	28	.250	.2036	.2268	3	.2130	G	.2610
5/16	18	.3125	.2403	.2764	F	.2570	21/64	.3281
	24	.3125	.2584	.2854	I	.2720	21/64	.3281
3/8	16	.3750	.2938	.3344	5/16	.3125	25/64	.3906
	24	.3750	.3209	.3479	Q	.3320	25/64	.3906
7/16	14	.4375	.3447	.3911	U	.3680	15/32	.4687
	20	.4375	.3725	.4050	25/64	.3906	29/64	.4531
1/2	13	.5000	.4001	.4500	27/64	.4219	17/32	.5312
	20	.5000	.4350	.4675	29/64	.4531	33/64	.5156
9/16	12	.5625	.4542	.5084	31/64	.4844	19/32	.5937
	18	.5625	.4903	.5264	33/64	.5156	37/64	.5781
5/8	11	.6250	.5069	.5660	17/32	.5312	21/32	.6562
	18	.6250	.5528	.5889	37/64	.5781	41/64	.6406
3/4	10	.7500	.6201	.6850	21/32	.6562	25/32	.7812
	16	.7500	.6688	.7094	11/16	.6875	49/64	.7656
7/8	9	.8750	.7307	.8028	49/64	.7656	29/32	.9062
	14	.8750	.7822	.8286	13/16	.8125	57/64	.8906
1	8	1.0000	.8376	.9188	7/8	.8750	1- 1/32	1.0312
	14	1.0000	.9072	.9536	15/16	.9375	1- 1/64	1.0156
1-1/8	7	1.1250	.9394	1.0322	63/64	.9844	1- 5/32	1.1562
	12	1.1250	1.0167	1.0709	1- 3/64	1.0469	1- 5/32	1.1562
1-1/4	7	1.2500	1.0644	1.1572	1- 7/64	1.1094	1- 9/32	1.2812
	12	1.2500	1.1417	1.1959	1-11/64	1.1719	1- 9/32	1.2812
1-1/2	6	1.5000	1.2835	1.3917	1-11/32	1.3437	1-17/32	1.5312
	12	1.5000	1.3917	1.4459	1-27/64	1.4219	1-17/32	1.5312

Fig. 9-10. Thread and tap drill sizes.

1. Use the correct size tap drill. Secure this information from a tap drill chart or consult your instructor.
2. Use a sharp tap and apply sufficient quantities of a good cutting oil. Special tapping fluids are available.
3. Start the taper tap square.
4. Do not force the tap to cut. Remove the chips as necessary.
5. Avoid running a tap to the bottom of a blind hole while continuing to apply pressure. Do not allow the hole to fill with chips and jam the tap.
6. Remove burrs on the tapped hole with a smooth file. Use a rag, not your fingers, to wipe away excess cutting oil and chips.

BROKEN TAPS

Taps sometimes break off in a hole. Several tools and techniques have been developed for removing

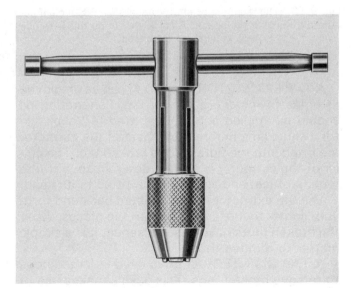

Fig. 9-11. T-Handle tap wrench. (Threadwell Mfg. Co.)

broken taps. THEY DO NOT ALWAYS WORK and the part may have to be discarded.

Many times the tap will shatter in the hole and it is possible to remove the fragments with a pointed tool such as a scribe. Broken carbon steel taps can be annealed and drilled out. This CANNOT be done with high speed taps. If they are large enough, HSS taps can be ground out with a hand grinder.

Fig. 9-12. The hand tap wrench. (Threadwell Mfg. Co.)

Fig. 9-13. The tap must be started square with the hole if accurate threads are to be cut. A quick way to do this is to use a square, as illustrated.

A TAP EXTRACTOR, Fig. 9-14, can be employed at times to remove a broken tap. Penetrating oil should be applied and be permitted to "soak" in for a short time before the fingers of the extractor are fitted into the flutes of the broken tap. The collar of the extractor is slipped down flush with the work surface, and a tap wrench fitted to its head.

The tap extractor is then twisted back and forth very lightly to loosen the broken tap pieces. After the broken parts have been loosened, it is a simple matter to remove them.

A TAP DISINTEGRATOR is used in large shops to remove broken taps. This device makes use of an electric arc to cause the tap to disintegrate without affecting the metal surrounding the tap.

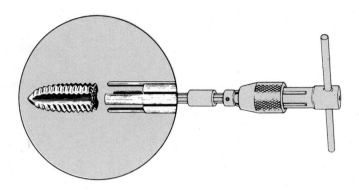

Fig. 9-14. A tap extractor can be used to remove a broken tap. The circled area shows the fingers of the extractor, and how they fit into the flutes of the broken tap.

CUTTING EXTERNAL THREADS

DIES are employed to cut external threads by hand. SOLID DIES, Fig. 9-15, are not adjustable and for that reason are not often used. The ADJUSTABLE ROUND DIE, Fig. 9-15, and the TWO PART ADJUSTABLE DIE, Fig. 9-16, are the most widely used dies for hand use.

The latter has a wide range of adjustment and is fitted with guides to keep it true on the work. Dies are available for cutting most standard threads.

DIE STOCKS

A DIE STOCK, Fig. 9-17, holds the die and provides leverage for turning the die on the work.

When cutting external threads, it is necessary to remember:
1. Stock diameter is the SAME SIZE as the DESIRED THREAD DIAMETER. That is, 1/2-13 UNC threads are cut on a 1/2 in. diameter shaft. What diameter shaft would be needed to cut 1/2-20 UNF threads?
2. Hold the work securely.
3. Set the die to the proper size. Make trial cuts on a piece of scrap until the proper adjustment is made.
4. Grind a small chamfer on the shaft end, Fig. 9-18. This permits the die to start easy.
5. Start the cut with the tapered end of the die.
6. Back off the die every one or two turns to break the chips.
7. Use liberal quantities of cutting oil. Place a paper towel down over the work to absorb excess cutting oil. The towel will also prevent the oil from getting on the floor.

THREADING TO A SHOULDER

When a thread must be cut down to a shoulder, start and run the the threads as far as possible in

Fig. 9-15. Left and Center. A hexagonal rethreading die and a square bolt die. These solid dies are not adjustable and, therefore, not often used. Right. An adjustable round die, one of the most widely used dies for hand use.

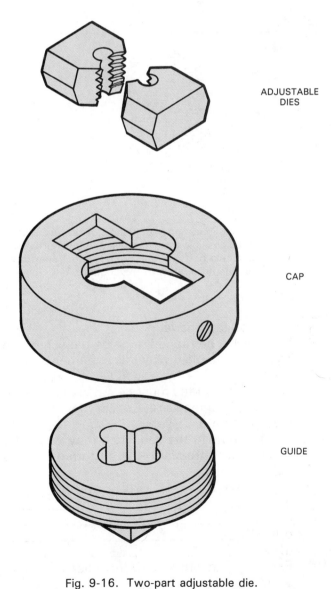

ADJUSTABLE DIES

CAP

GUIDE

Fig. 9-16. Two-part adjustable die.

Fig. 9-17. The die stock holds the die and serves as the means for applying pressure to make the die cut.
(Threadwell Mfg. Co.)

the usual manner, Fig. 9-19. Remove the die. Turn it over with the guides up. Run the threads down to the shoulder. Never try this operation without first starting the threads in the usual manner.

PROBLEMS IN CUTTING EXTERNAL THREADS

Ragged threads are the most common problem encountered when cutting external threads with a die. They are caused by:
1. Little or no cutting oil.
2. Dull die cutters.
3. Stock too large for threads being cut.
4. Die not started square.
5. One set of cutters could be upside down when using a two part die.

HAND THREADING SAFETY

1. If the tap, die, or threaded piece is to be cleaned of chips with compressed air, protect your eyes from flying chips by wearing goggles. Take care not to endanger persons working in the area near you.
2. Chips produced by threading are sharp. Use a

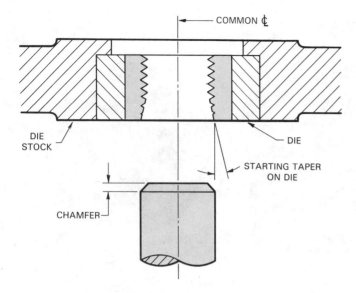

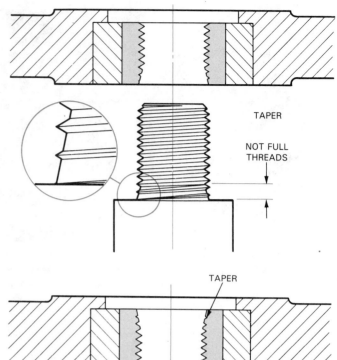

Fig. 9-18. The die will start easier if a small chamfer is cut or ground on the end of the shaft to be threaded. Section through die in the die stock showing the proper way to start the threads.

brush or a piece of cloth, not your hand, to remove them.

3. Newly cut external threads are also sharp. Again, use a brush or cloth to clean them.

4. Wash your hands after using cutting fluids. Some cutting fluids cause skin rash. This can develop into a serious skin disorder if the oils are left on the hands for extended periods.

5. Have cuts treated by a qualified person. Infections occur when injuries are not properly treated.

6. Be sure that the die is clamped firmly in the die stock. It may fall from the holder and cause a painful foot injury.

7. Broken taps have sharp edges and are very dangerous. Handle them as you would broken glass.

Fig. 9-19. Cutting a thread up to a shoulder. After die has been run down as far as possible the die is reversed, the cutters are reversed if it is a two-part die, and run down the shaft until threads are cut up to the shoulder.

TEST YOUR KNOWLEDGE, Unit 9

Please do not write in the text. Place your answers on a separate sheet of paper.

1. The _____ is used to cut internal threads.

2. A _____ is used to cut external threads.

3. The UNF thread series differs from the UNC series in that it:
   a. Has fewer threads per inch for a given diameter.
   b. Has more threads per inch for a given diameter.
   c. Is an external thread while the UNC is only used for internal threads.
   d. None of the above.

   e. All of the above.

4. The hole to be tapped must be the same size as the tap. Explain why this statement is true or false.

5. An external thread must be cut on a diameter equal to the thread size. Explain why this statement is true or false.

6. List the taps in the sequence they would be used to cut threads to the bottom of a blind hole.

7. Explain what 1/2-13 UNC-2 means.
   a. 1/2_____.
   b. 13 _____.
   c. UNC _____.
   d. 2 _____.

8. Explain what M5 x .8-6H/6g means.
   a. M5_____.

b. .8 _____.
c. 6H/6g _____.

9. The drill used to make a hole prior to tapping is called a _____.

10. The _____ tap wrench is used with small taps because_____.

11. It has been established that the hole to be threaded must be smaller than the thread. For example, a 5/16 in. diameter hole must be drilled for a 3/8-16UNC thread. How much larger must a shaft be machined to receive a 3/8-16 UNC thread?

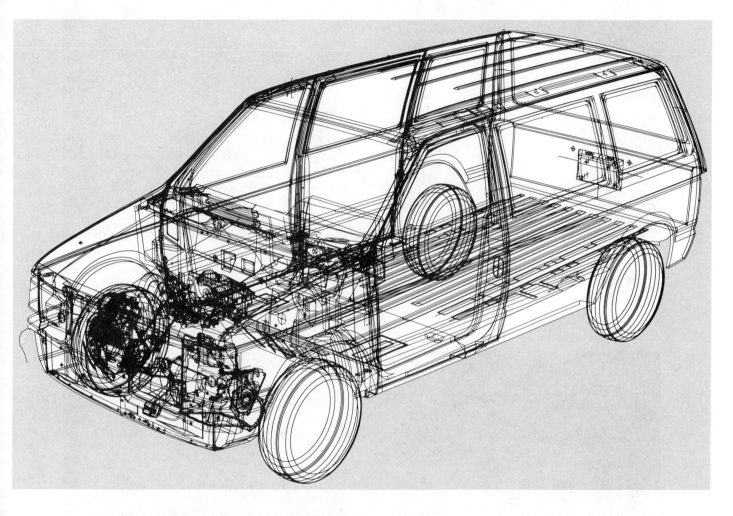

Computer drawing of Dodge Caravan wagon. Many metric threaded fasteners were utilized in the assembly to permit damaged components to be replaced quickly and easily. (Dodge Div., Chrysler Corp.)

Aircraft like this F-14 require tens of thousands of fasteners, each carefully designed for a specific job. Every type of fastener described in this text, plus several adhesives, were used in the manufacture of the aircraft. (Grumman Aerospace Corp.)

While many types of metal fasteners were available when this old mill was built, wooden fasteners were used in its construction. Even the tools needed to operate the mill (shovels, buckets, etc.) were made of wood. Do you have any idea why so little metal was used?

Unit 10

FASTENERS

Manufactured products, Fig. 10-1, are assembled by many different methods: screws, nuts and bolts, pins, staples, and adhesives. Several fastening techniques are frequently employed on the same assembly.

Selecting the proper fasteners for a job can often result in considerable savings in labor costs while still providing an assembly that meets approved standards.

Designers, engineers, and skilled workers must be familiar with many different kinds of fasteners (one auto manufacturer uses more than 11,000 kinds and sizes of fasteners).

THREADED FASTENERS

Threaded fasteners utilize the wedging action of the screw thread to clamp parts together. These fasteners vary in cost from several thousand dollars each for special bolts that attach the wings to the fuselage of large aircraft, to the small machine screw that costs a fraction of a penny, Fig. 10-2.

Fig. 10-1. Almost every type of fastener used by industry was needed to fabricate this Navy ship.   (U.S. Navy)

Fig. 10-2. There is a wide range of threaded fasteners available to industry. Do you notice anything different about the head of the large threaded fastener?

Most threaded fasteners are available in metric sizes and, since many American manufacturers have started to use metric fasteners in their products, some problems have arisen. Metric threads, while having the same basic profile (shape) as unified threads, are not interchangeable, Fig. 10-3. Until a full changeover to metrication is made, and products already made with unified threads wear out or are discarded, some method will have to be devised to easily identify metric threaded fasteners from inch threaded fasteners. While no foolproof method has yet been contrived, Figs. 10-4 and 10-5 illustrate two possible solutions.

MACHINE SCREWS

Machine screws are widely used in general assembly. They may have slotted or recessed heads. They are made in a number of head styles, Fig. 10-6. Machine screws are available in body diameters from #0 (0.060 in.) to 1/2 (0.500 in.) and in lengths from 1/8 to 3 in. Metric sizes are also manufactured. Nuts (square or hexagonal) are sold separately.

MACHINE BOLTS

Machine bolts, Fig. 10-7, are used to assemble parts that do not require close tolerances. They are

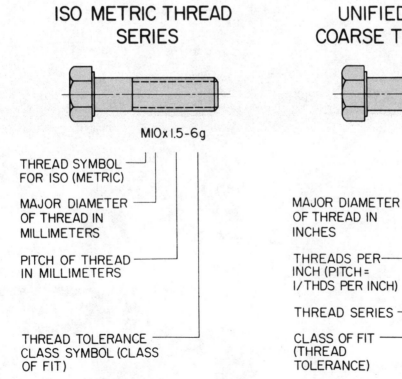

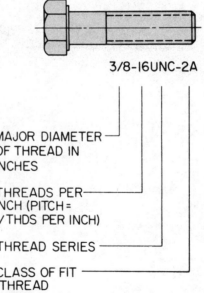

Fig. 10-3. Metric threads have same basic profile (shape) as unified thread series; however, unified and metric threaded fasteners are not interchangeable.

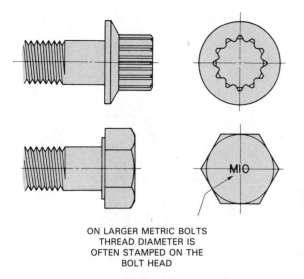

ON LARGER METRIC BOLTS
THREAD DIAMETER IS
OFTEN STAMPED ON THE
BOLT HEAD

Fig. 10-4. Metric fasteners are manufactured in same variety of head shapes. During changeover to full metrication, a major problem is finding a way to easily identify metric threaded fasteners from inch threaded fasteners. Some larger size hex headed fasteners have the size stamped on the head. A twelve-spline flange head is under consideration for eight sizes of metric threads—5, 6.3, 8, 10, 13, 14, 16, and 20 mm.

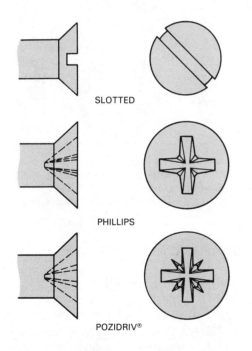

SLOTTED

PHILLIPS

POZIDRIV®

Fig. 10-5. The Pozidriv® cross-recessed head has been suggested as a means of identifying metric screws. It would be used in place of Phillips cross-recessed head, which would only be used with inch size screws.

manufactured with square and hexagonal heads, in a range of diameters from 1/4 in. to 3 in., and in lengths from 1/2 in. to 30 in. The nuts are similar

in shape to the bolt head. They are usually furnished along with the machine bolts.

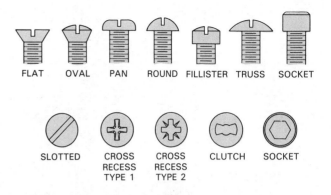

FLAT   OVAL   PAN   ROUND   FILLISTER   TRUSS   SOCKET

SLOTTED   CROSS RECESS TYPE 1   CROSS RECESS TYPE 2   CLUTCH   SOCKET

Fig. 10-6. A sampling of the many types of machine screws manufactured.

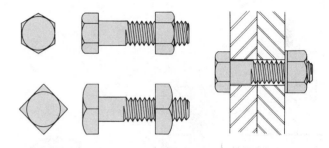

Fig. 10-7. Machine bolts.

CAP SCREWS

Cap screws, Fig. 10-8, are found in assemblies requiring higher quality and a more finished appearance. Instead of tightening a nut to develop clamping action as with the machine bolt, the cap screw passes through a clearance hole in one of the pieces and screws into a threaded hole in the other. Clamping action is accomplished by tightening the bolt.

Cap screws are held to much closer tolerances in their manufacture, and are provided with a machined or semifinished bearing surface under the head. They are stocked in coarse and fine thread series and in diameters from 1/4 to 2 in. Lengths from 3/8 to 10 in. are available. Metric size cap screws can also be supplied.

SETSCREWS

Setscrews, Fig. 10-9, are usually made of heat-treated steels. They are semipermanent fasteners that are used to prevent pulleys from slipping on

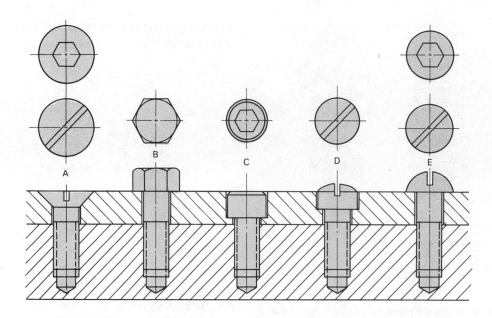

Fig. 10-8. Many types of cap screws are available. A—Flat head. B-Hexagonal head. C-Socket head. D—Fillister head. E—Button or round head.

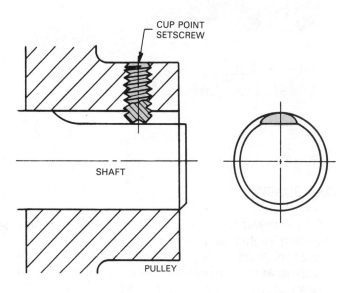

Fig. 10-9. Typical application of a setscrew.

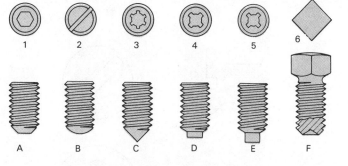

Fig. 10-10. Setscrew head and point designs. A—Flat point. B—Oval point. C—Cone point. D—Half dog point. E—Full dog point. F—Cup point. 1—Socket head. 2—Slotted head. 3, 4, and 5—Fluted head. 6—Square head.

shafts, holding collars in place on shafts, and holding shafts in place on assemblies. Setscrews are classified in two ways—by their head style, and by their point style, Fig. 10-10.

STUD BOLTS

Stud bolts, Fig. 10-11, are headless bolts that are threaded the entire length, or on both ends. One end is screwed into a tapped hole, the part to be clamped is fitted over the stud, and a nut is screwed on to clamp the two pieces together. Automobile engine heads are held to the block with stud bolts.

THREAD FORMING SCREWS

Thread forming screws, Fig. 10-12, form a thread as they are driven. A costly tapping operation is eliminated. A variation of the thread forming screw, Fig. 10-13, eliminates expensive drilling, punching, and aligning operations because the screw drills its own hole as it is driven into place.

THREAD CUTTING SCREWS

Thread cutting screws, Fig. 10-14, differ from the thread forming screws in that they actually cut threads into the metal as they are driven into the material. They are hardened and are used to join heavy gauge sheet metal, and in nonferrous metal assemblies.

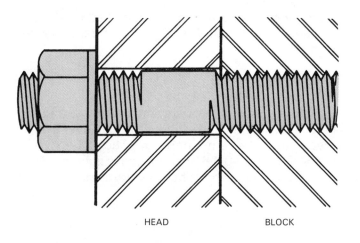

HEAD   BLOCK

Fig. 10-11. Stud bolt.

Fig. 10-12. Thread forming screw.

Fig. 10-13. Self-drilling screw. They are known as TEKS® . (USM Corp., Fastener Group)

DRIVE SCREWS

Drive screws, Fig. 10-15, are simply hammered into a drilled or punched hole of the proper size. A permanent assembly is made.

NUTS

Nuts for most threaded fasteners have external hexagonal or square shapes, and are used with bolts having the same shaped head. The standard hex nut, Fig. 10-16, is available in various degrees of

finish: REGULAR is not machined on any surface except the threads; REGULAR SEMI-FINISHED is machined on the bearing face to provide a truer surface for the washer; FINISHED, which is the same as the regular semi-finished nut, but is made to closer tolerances. The standard machine screw nut is regular.

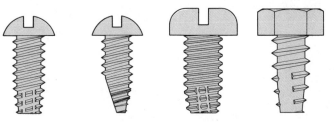

Fig. 10-14. Thread cutting screws.

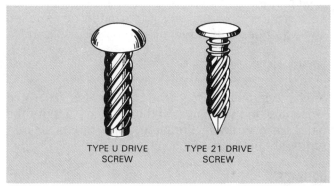

TYPE U DRIVE SCREW   TYPE 21 DRIVE SCREW

Fig. 10-15. Drive screws.

JAM NUT

Thinner than the standard nut, the jam nut, Fig. 10-16, is frequently used to lock a full size nut in place.

CASTELLATED AND SLOTTED NUTS

Castellated and slotted nuts, Fig. 10-16, are slotted across their flats. After the nut has been tightened, a cotter pin is fitted in one set of slots and through a hole in the bolt. The cotter pin prevents the nut from turning loose under working conditions that include vibration.

These nut types are being replaced on many applications by self-locking nuts, Fig. 10-16. These nuts have nylon inserts, or are slightly deformed, so that they cannot vibrate loose. No hole is required when self-locking nuts are employed in an assembly.

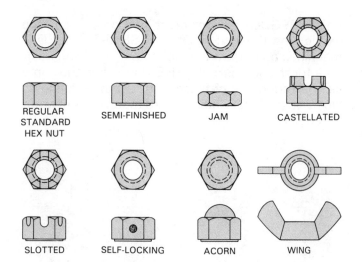

REGULAR STANDARD HEX NUT

SEMI-FINISHED

JAM

CASTELLATED

SLOTTED

SELF-LOCKING

ACORN

WING

Fig. 10-16. A few of the many nut designs available.

CAP OR ACORN NUT

Cap or acorn nuts, Fig. 10-16, are applied when appearance is of primary importance or exposed sharp edges on the fastener must be avoided.

WING NUT

The wing nut, Fig. 10-16, provides for rapid loosening and tightening of the fastener without the need for a wrench. Frequent adjustments or part removal can be made quickly.

INSERTS

Inserts are a special form of nut. They are designed to provide higher strength threads in soft metals and plastics. The type shown in Fig. 10-17

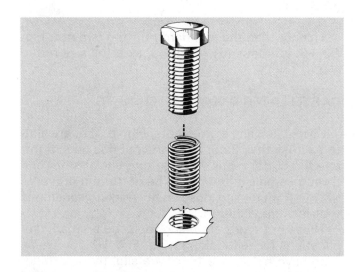

Fig. 10-17. Insert for threaded hole. Frequently used to replace damaged or stripped threads in a part. (Heli-Coil Corp.)

is frequently used to replace damaged or stripped threads. Its internal thread is of standard size and form.

WASHERS

Washers provide an increased bearing surface for bolt heads and nuts, distribute the load over a larger area, and prevent marring. The STANDARD WASHER, Fig. 10-18, is produced in light, medium, heavy-duty, and extra heavy-duty series.

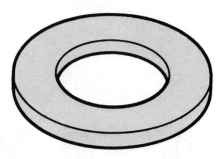

Fig. 10-18. Standard flat washer.

LOCK WASHERS

The application of a lock washer will prevent a bolt or nut from loosening under vibration.

The SPLIT-RING LOCK WASHER, Fig. 10-19, A, is rapidly being replaced by the TOOTH-TYPE LOCK WASHER, Fig. 10-19, B, to 10-19, E, which have greater holding power on most applications. PRE-ASSEMBLED LOCK WASHER AND SCREW NUTS and LOCK WASHER AND NUT UNITS, Fig. 10-20, are employed to lower assembly time and reduce waste in the mass-assembly market.

NON-THREADED FASTENING DEVICES

Permanent assemblies are made with RIVETS, Fig. 10-21. Solid rivets can be set by hand or machine. Hand setting techniques are shown on page 156.

BLIND RIVETS are mechanical fasteners that have been developed for applications where the joint is accessible from one side only. They require special tools to put them in place, Fig. 10-22. Blind rivet types are shown in Fig. 10-23.

DOWEL PINS

Dowel pins, Fig. 10-24, are used to position mating parts. They often support a major portion of the load placed upon the components.

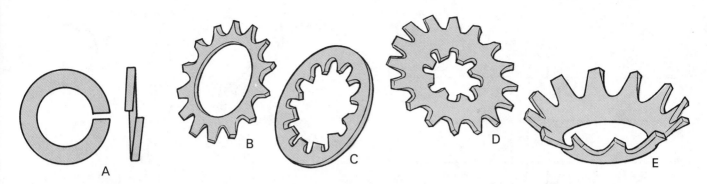

Fig. 10-19. Lock washer variations. A—Split-ring type. B—External type; should be used whenever possible as it provides the greatest resistance. C—Internal type; used with small head screws and where it is desirable to hide the teeth either for appearance or to prevent snagging. D—Internal-external type; used when the mounting holes are oversize. E—Countersunk type; for use with flat or oval-head screws.

Fig. 10-20. Lock washer and screw units, and lock washer and nut units. (Shakeproof Division, Illinois Tool Works, Inc.)

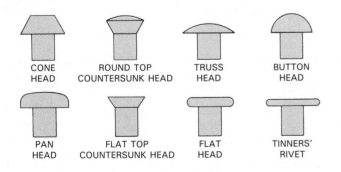

Fig. 10-21. Rivet head styles.

Pins are available in a number of sizes and types, Fig. 10-25.

COTTER PIN

The cotter pin is fitted into a hole drilled crosswise in a shaft to prevent parts from slipping on, or falling off of, a shaft.

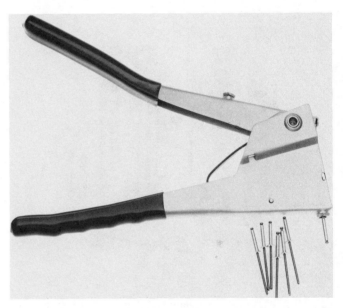

Fig. 10-22. Tool used to insert one type of blind rivet.

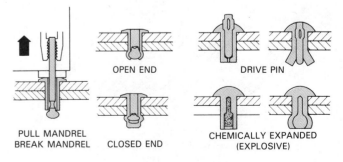

Fig. 10-23. Types of blind rivets.

Many sizes and types of cotter pins are manufactured, Fig. 10-26.

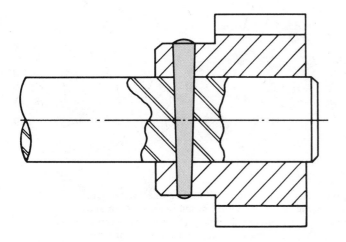

Fig. 10-24. Taper dowel pin positions and holds gear on shaft.

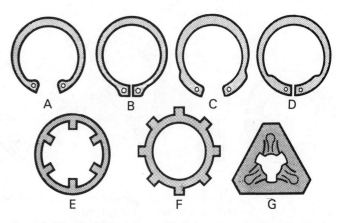

Fig. 10-27. Retaining rings. A—Basic internal ring. B—Basic external ring. C—Inverted internal ring. D—Inverted external. E—External self-locking ring. F—Internal self-locking ring. G—Triangular self-locking ring.

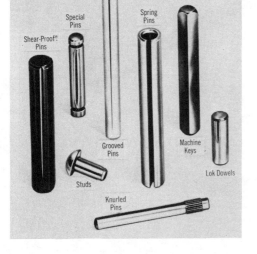

Fig. 10-25. Types of dowel pins. They are made in a wide range of sizes. (Driv-Lok Inc.)

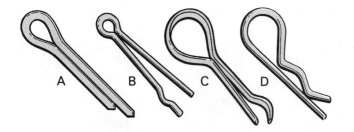

Fig. 10-26. Cotter pins. A—Standard. B—Humped. C—Clinch. D—Hitch.

RETAINING RINGS

The retaining ring, Fig. 10-27, has been developed for both internal and external applica-tions. While most retaining rings are seated in grooves, a self-locking type does not require the recess. Special pliers, Fig. 10-28, are needed to facilitate assembly and removal of the rings.

Retaining rings reduce both cost and weight of the product on which they are used.

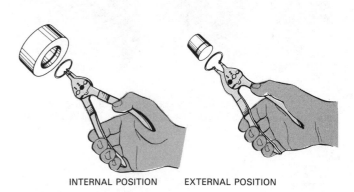

INTERNAL POSITION   EXTERNAL POSITION

Fig. 10-28. Special pliers are used to install Truarc (trademark) rings. (Waldes Kohinoor Inc.)

KEYS

A key is a section of metal that is employed to prevent a gear or pulley from rotating on a shaft. One-half of the key fits into a KEYSEAT on the shaft while the remainder of the key fits into a KEYWAY in the hub of the gear or pulley, Fig. 10-29. See Fig. 10-30 for several types of keys.

A SQUARE KEY is usually one-fourth the shaft diameter. It may be slightly tapered on the top to make it easier to fit into place.

The PRATT AND WHITNEY KEY is similar to the square key except that it is rounded at both ends. It fits into a keyseat of the same shape.

The GIB HEAD KEY is interchangeable with the square key. The head design permits easy removal from the assembly.

A WOODRUFF KEY is semicircular in shape and fits into a keyseat of the same shape. The top of the key fits into the keyway of the mating part.

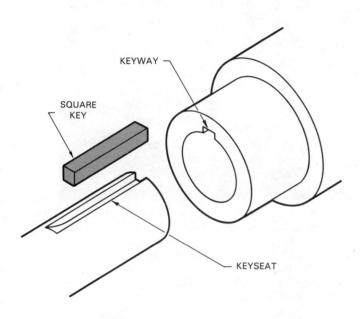

Fig. 10-29. This square key is used to prevent a pulley or gear from rotating on a shaft.

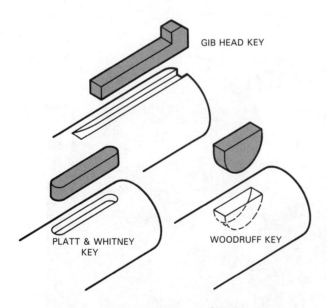

Fig. 10-30. Three types of keys.

ADHESIVES

One of the newest ways to joint metals and to keep threaded fasteners from vibrating loose is by the use of adhesives. In some applications, the resulting joints are stronger than the metals joined. Adhesive bonded joints do not require costly and time consuming operations such as drilling, countersinking, riveting, etc., Figs. 10-31 and 10-32. Their major drawback is heat. While some adhesives retain their strength at temperatures as high as 700 °F (371 °C), most of them should not be used above temperatures of 150-200 °F (66-93 °C).

Adhesives for locking threaded fasteners in place are made in a number of formulations. The permanence of the threaded joint will determine the type of adhesive to use.

Many commercial adhesives are sold in small quantities that are suitable for school and home uses, Fig. 10-33.

CAUTION: The chemicals that make up adhesives suitable for joining metal to metal, or metal to some other material, can cause severe irritation of the skin. ALL OF THEM can impair or cause loss of your sight. Fumes can also be dangerous. Handle adhesives with care. To be safe, wear safety glasses and disposable plastic gloves when preparing and using the adhesives. Work in a well-ventilated area. Above all, follow the instructions on the container when mixing and using these adhesives. Mix only the amount you will need.

Adhesives are available in liquid, paste, or solid form. Many can be applied directly from the container. Others may be mixed with a catalyst or hardener. A few pressure sensitive adhesives are manufactured in sheet form.

Most adhesives require the following five steps to produce solid bonded joints:
1. SURFACE PREPARATION. ALL adhesives require CLEAN surfaces to produce full strength bonds. Preparation may range from simply wiping surfaces with a solvent to multistage cleaning and chemical treatment.
2. ADHESIVE PREPARATION. Mixing, delivery to work area, setting up equipment, etc.
3. ADHESIVE APPLICATION. Brush, roller, spray, dipping, etc.
4. ASSEMBLY. Positioning of materials to be joined, using jigs to align material, etc.
5. BOND DEVELOPMENT. Curing of adhesives, evaporation of solvents, application of pressure and/or heat, etc.

SAFETY

1. Wear goggles when making openings, drilling, punching, countersinking, etc., to receive fasteners.
2. Do not use your hands to remove metal chips from holes that are to receive fasteners. Use a brush. Burrs are usually raised around the opening and can cause nasty cuts.

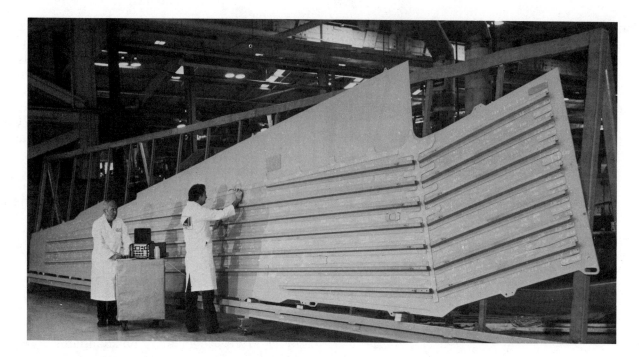

Fig. 10-31. This wing section for British Aerospace BA 146 feeder liner aircraft is the largest and longest adhesively bonded panel ever produced. It is 96 in. (2 438.4 mm) wide and 533 in. (13 538 mm) long. Bonding integrity is being inspected with ultrasonic test equipment. Bonded assembly is made up of 30 individual parts. Complete bonding cycle was 2 1/2 hours at 150 psi (1 034 kPa) and a maximum temperature of 302 °F (150 °C).
(AVCO Aerostructures Division, AVCO Corp.)

Fig. 10-32. The British Aerospace BA 146 Feeder Jet. This four turbofan aircraft is assembled at Hatfield, Hertfordshire, England from assemblies manufactured in the United States, Sweden, and England. The engines are American made. (Pacific Southwest Airlines, PSA)

3. If air is used to blow clean drilled or tapped holes, wear goggles and protect the piece in such a manner that there is no danger of flying chips injuring nearby workers.
4. Remove all burrs. Do not check whether burrs have been removed with your fingers.
5. Some adhesives use solvents that are highly flammable. Do not apply such adhesives near areas where there are open flames. Apply only in a well-ventilated area.
6. Follow the instructions on the container. Remove any adhesive from your skin by promptly washing with water. CYANOACRYLATE ADHESIVES cure in a very short time (10-15 seconds). Do not allow any of this adhesive on your fingers as it will cause them to adhere and will require a rather painful operation to separate the joined fingers. It is known by such names as ''funny glue,'' Permabond, Zip Grip, Eastman 910, etc. Use this adhesive with care.

Fig. 10-33. Adhesives available for use in the school metals lab or shop. They are the same types used by industry.

TEST YOUR KNOWLEDGE, Unit 10

Please do not write in the text. Place your answers on a separate sheet of paper.
1. List four fastening devices that can be used to join materials.
2. Name the four threaded fasteners.
   a. _____ - used for general assembly work.
   b. _____ - prevents pulley from slipping on shafts.
   c. _____ - forms threads as it is driven.
   d. _____ - cuts threads as it is driven.
3. Permanent assemblies are made with _____.
4. _____ washers are often used to prevent bolts or nuts from loosening under vibration.
5. The shape of the _____ permits it to be loosened and tightened without a wrench.

Match each word in the left column with the correct sentence in the right column.
6. ____ Cotter pin.
7. ____ Jam nut.
8. ____ Machine screw.
9. ____ Machine bolt.
10. ____ Threaded fasteners.
11. ____ Drive screws.
12. ____ Thread forming screw.
13. ____ Acorn nut.
14. ____ Key.
15. ____ Keyseat.
16. ____ Keyway.
17. ____ Retaining ring.
18. ____ Standard washer.
19. ____ Blind rivet.
20. ____ Dowel pins.

a. Used when appearance is of primary importance.
b. Used in general assembly work.
c. Often used to lock regular nut in place.
d. Used when assemblies do not require close tolerance fasteners.
e. Hammered into drilled or punched holes.
f. Provides an increased bearing surface for bolt heads and nuts.
g. Fitted in reamed holes to align mating parts.
h. Utilizes wedging action of screw thread to clamp assemblies.
i. Must be seated into a groove.
j. Developed for applications where it is not possible to set regular rivets.
k. Forms threads as they are driven.
l. Fitted into a hole drilled crosswise in a shaft.
m. Prevents pulley or gear from rotating on shaft.
n. Slot cut in gear or pulley to receive ''m.''
o. Slot cut in shaft to receive ''m.''

RESEARCH AND DEVELOPMENT

1. Prepare a panel that displays samples of the fasteners described in this unit.
2. Secure or make samples of threaded and non-threaded fasteners applied to an actual job. Mount them on a display panel.
3. Demonstrate the correct and safe way to set solid rivets and blind rivets.
4. Research the manufacture of early screw type fasteners. Prepare a paper on the subject.
5. Secure samples of several adhesives suitable for joining metal to metal. Demonstrate the proper and safe way to use these materials.
6. Devise a test method that will determine the strength of the various adhesives.
7. Organize the storage of fasteners in your school shop or lab. Count them and determine which fasteners will have to be reordered.

Making tin plate.   (Blaw-Knox)

Unit 11

SHEET METAL

Metal sheet is made by passing a metal slab between rolls until the desired thickness is attained, Fig. 11-1. Metal thickness is continually monitored and the rolls are adjusted automatically to maintain the required tolerances.

Many methods have been devised to work and shape sheet metal. Production applications are

Fig. 11-1. As the metal becomes thinner, its length increases. The spread of the sheet through the mill also increases, often reaching more than 60 miles per hour.
(Aluminum Company of America.)

covered in Unit 28, COLD FORMING METAL SHEET. This unit will be concerned with the techniques applicable to the tools and equipment normally found in a school shop.

PATTERNS

Sheet metal is given three-dimensional shape and rigidity by bending and forming it to a predetermined pattern. The pattern is a full-size drawing of the surface of the object stretched out on a single plane, Fig. 11-2. For this reason a pattern is often referred to as a STRETCHOUT.

Sheet metal pattern development falls into two basic classifications: PARALLEL-LINE DEVELOPMENTS, and RADIAL-LINE DEVELOPMENTS. Combinations and variations of the basic developments are used to develop the patterns for more complex geometric shapes.

Parallel-line developments are those like the prism, Fig. 11-3, and the cylinder, Fig. 11-4, that unfold into rectangular patterns. Radial-line developments, like the pyramid, Fig. 11-5, and cone, Fig. 11-6, unfold into a triangular pattern. TRUNCATED GEOMETRICAL SHAPES, those cut off at an angle, are developed as shown in Fig. 11-7. The TRANSITION PIECE is used to connect

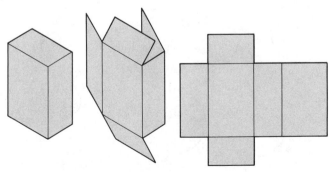

Fig. 11-2. A simple pattern, or stretchout.

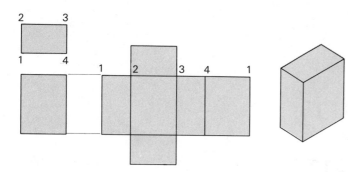

Fig. 11-3. Stretchout of prism.

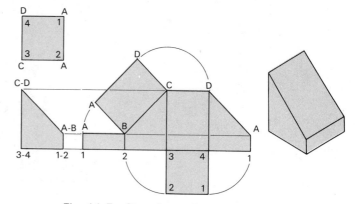

Fig. 11-7. Stretchout of a truncated prism.

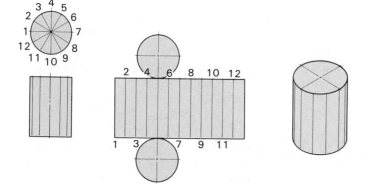

Fig. 11-4. Stretchout of cylinder.

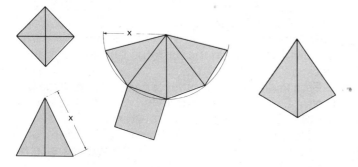

Fig. 11-5. Stretchout of a pyramid.

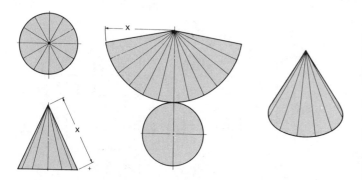
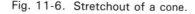

Fig. 11-6. Stretchout of a cone.

two different shaped openings like a circular opening to a square opening, Fig. 11-8.

HEMS, EDGES, AND SEAMS

When developing a pattern or stretchout, allow additional metal for hems, edges, and seams.

HEMS, Fig. 11-9, are used to strengthen the lips of sheet metal objects. They are made in standard fractional sizes, 3/16, 1/4, 3/8 inch, etc.

The WIRED EDGE, Fig. 11-10, gives additional strength and rigidity to sheet metal edges.

SEAMS, Fig. 11-11, make it possible to join sheet metal sections. They are usually finished by soldering and/or riveting.

The pattern may be developed directly on the sheet metal, Figs. 11-12 and 11-13, or on paper and transferred to the metal. A metal template should be made if a number of identical pieces must be fabricated.

CUTTING SHEET METAL

SNIPS or HAND SHEARS, used when cutting the layout from the metal sheet, are made in a number of sizes and styles. Large sheet metal sections are cut on SQUARING SHEARS.

CUTTING STRAIGHT AND CURVED SECTIONS

Circular work is cut with CIRCULAR SNIPS, Fig. 11-14. Straight and circular work can be cut with COMBINATION SNIPS, Fig. 11-15. AVIATION SNIPS, Fig. 11-16, find wide use for cutting compound curves and intricate designs in sheet metal. They are usually color coded in keeping with industry standards—green cuts right, red cuts left, yellow cuts straight. Internal openings are cut with HAWK-BILLED SNIPS, Fig. 11-17.

Modern snips are designed to cut freely with a minimum curling of the metal. The snips are generally held in the right hand, at right angles to the work, Fig. 11-18. Open the blades widely for maximum

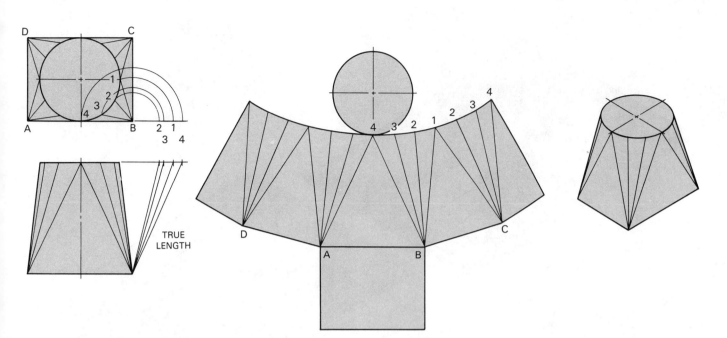

Fig. 11-8. Transition piece.

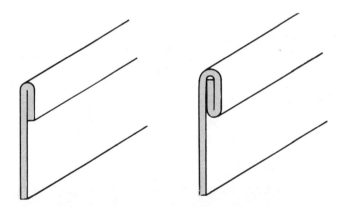

Fig. 11-9. Single and double hems.

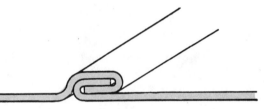

Fig. 11-11. Grooved seam.

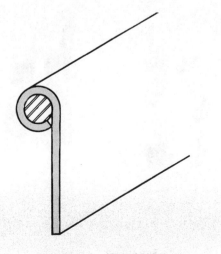

Fig. 11-10. Wired edge.

Fig. 11-12. Developing a pattern directly on sheet metal.

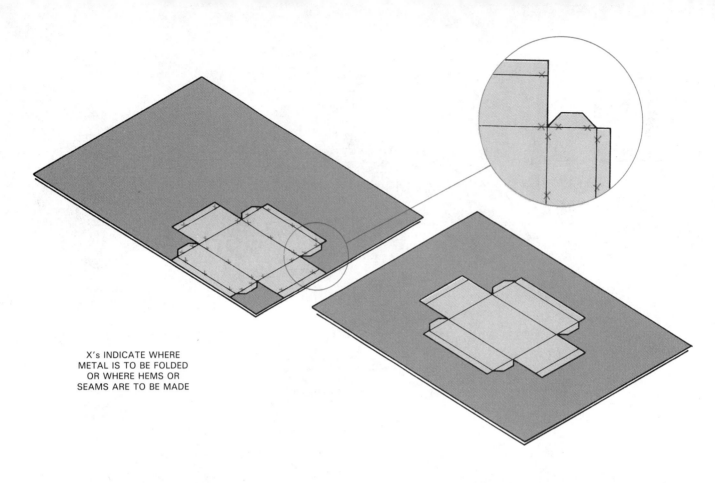

X's INDICATE WHERE
METAL IS TO BE FOLDED
OR WHERE HEMS OR
SEAMS ARE TO BE MADE

PREFERRED LAYOUT
VERY LITTLE WASTE

AVOID THIS KIND
OF LAYOUT
TOO MUCH WASTE

Fig. 11-13. Sheet metal layout.

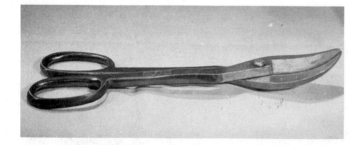

Fig. 11-14. Circular snips.

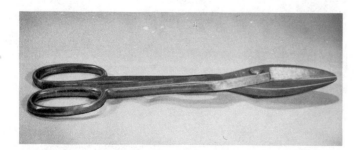

Fig. 11-15. Combination snips.

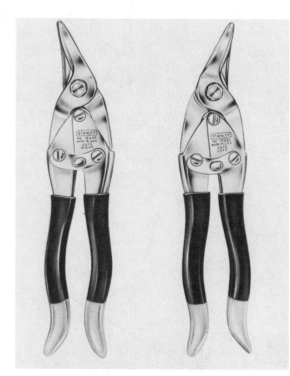

Fig. 11-16. Aviation snips. (Stanley Tools)

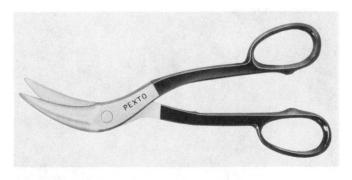

Fig. 11-17. Hawk-billed snips.

Fig. 11-19. Making a circular cut.

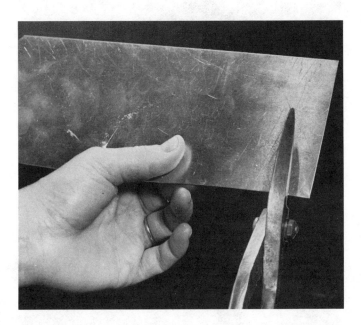

Fig. 11-18. Proper method for cutting a straight edge.

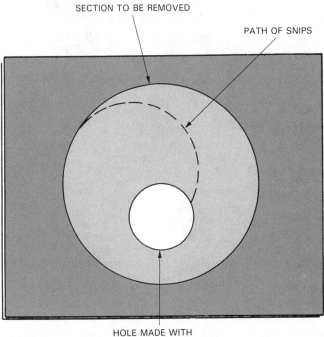

SECTION TO BE REMOVED

PATH OF SNIPS

HOLE MADE WITH
HOLLOW PUNCH

Fig. 11-20. Cutting a circular opening in a sheet metal section.

leverage. Do not permit them to close completely at the end of a cut or a rough edge will result. Cut circular sections from the right wide, Fig. 11-19.

When making internal circular cuts, make a small opening near the center of the opening, insert the snips and cut from the upper side, gradually increasing the radius of the cut until the opening is completed, Fig. 11-20.

The COMBINATION NOTCHER, COPER, AND SHEAR, Fig. 11-21, is ideal for notching corners or the edge of sheet metal. The blades are adjustable for conventional notching or for piercing, starting inside the blank.

PORTABLE POWER SHEARS, Fig. 11-22, are used for production work. They are designed to do straight or circular cutting, Figs. 11-23 and 11-24.

Small diameter openings can be made with a SOLID PUNCH, Fig. 11-25, or a HOLLOW PUNCH, Fig. 11-26. Locate the position of the hole. Select the correct size punch and hammer, then place the

metal section on a lead cake or on the end grain of a block of hard wood, Fig. 11-27. Strike the punch sharply with the hammer. Turn the punched section over so the burred section is up, then smooth it with a mallet.

FOOT OPERATED SQUARING SHEARS, Fig. 11-28, make it possible to square and trim large sheets. Do not attempt to cut metal thicker than the designed capacity of the shears. The maximum capacity of the machine is stamped on the manufacturer's specification plate on the front of the shears.

Fig. 11-21. Top. Combination notcher, coper, and shear.
Bottom. It is ideal for notching corners or edges of sheet metal.

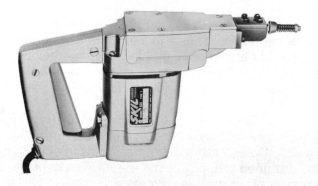

Fig. 11-22. Portable power shears.

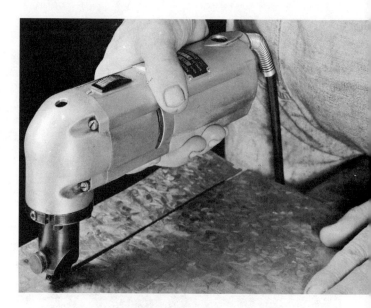

Fig. 11-23. Cutting a straight section with power shears.
(Skil Corp.)

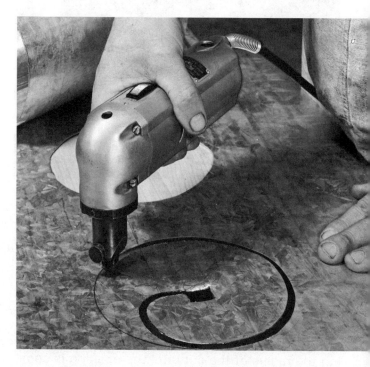

Fig. 11-24. Cutting a circular section with power shears.

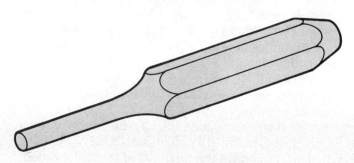

Fig. 11-25. Solid punch.

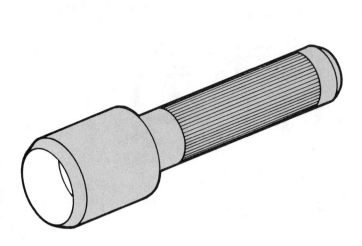

Fig. 11-26. Hollow punch.

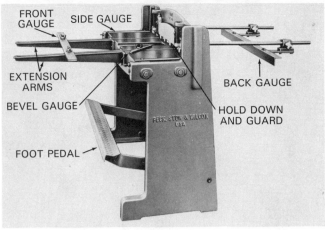

Fig. 11-28. Squaring shears.

Check the thickness of the metal against this size, with a SHEET METAL GAUGE, Fig. 11-29.

DO NOT cut wire, band iron, or steel rods on the squaring shears.

The length of the cut is determined by the position of the BACK GAUGE when the metal is inserted from the front of the shears. The FRONT GAUGE controls the length of the cut when the metal sheet is inserted from the rear. The front gauge is seldom used and is usually removed from the shears. A BEVEL GAUGE permits angular cuts to be made.

To make a cut, set the back gauge to the required dimension by using the graduated scale on the top

Fig. 11-29. Using a sheet metal gauge to check sheet thickness.

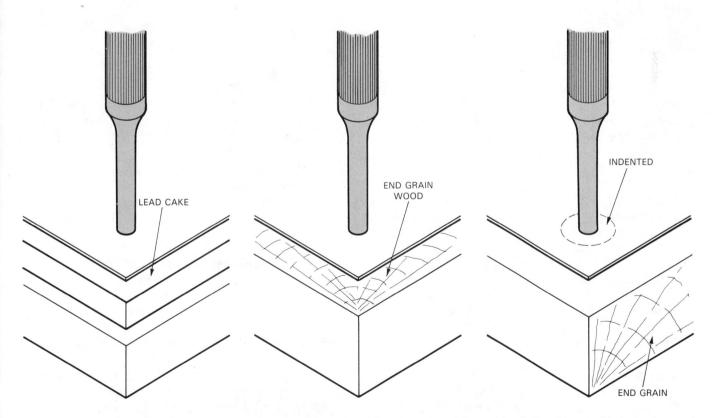

Fig. 11-27. Correct and incorrect method of backing sheet metal for making hole with punch.

Fig. 11-30. Ring and circular shears.

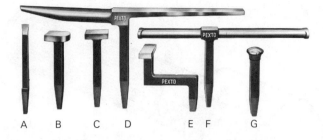

Fig. 11-31. Stakes. A—Bottom stake. B—Coppersmith's square stake. C—Common square stake. D—Beakhorn stake. E—Bevel edge square stake. F—Double seaming stake. G—Round head stake.

Fig. 11-32. Bench plate.

of the extension arms or on the graduated section on the bed top. Hold the piece firmly against the SIDE GAUGE with both hands until the HOLD DOWN comes into position and apply pressure to the FOOT PEDAL.

RING AND CIRCULAR SHEARS, Fig. 11-30, are intended for cutting inside and outside circles in sheet metal. The CLAMPING HEAD is positioned for the desired diameter and the blank inserted. Lower the CUTTING DISC and make the cut.

KEEP THE HANDS CLEAR OF THE BLADE AND THE FOOT FROM BENEATH THE FOOT PEDAL.

BENDING SHEET METAL

Metal sheet is given three-dimensional shape and rigidity by bending. Both hand and machine bending techniques have been developed. Several of the methods are described in the following section.

BENDING SHEET METAL BY HAND

METAL STAKES, Fig. 11-31, enable the sheet metal crafter to make a variety of bends by hand. Stakes, available in a number of shapes and sizes, are designed to fit in a BENCH PLATE, Fig. 11-32, or a UNIVERSAL STAKE HOLDER, Fig. 11-33, that clamps to the bench.

Narrow sections can be formed with the HAND SEAMER, Fig. 11-34. Its main use is for bending an edge or folding a seam.

The SETTING-DOWN HAMMER and the MALLET, Fig. 11-35, provide the necessary force when using wooden or angle iron forming blocks to make angular bends in sheet metal, Fig. 11-36.

Curbed sections are formed over a stake or metal rod of a suitable shape and size, Fig. 11-37.

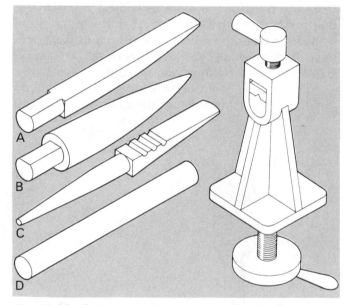

Fig. 11-33. Stakes and universal stake holder. A—Rectangular end of beakhorn stake. B—Beakhorn stake. C—Creasing stake with horn. D—Conductor stake.

BENDING SHEET METAL BY MACHINE

Many machines have been devised to perform specific sheet metal bending operations.

THE BAR FOLDER AND BRAKE

The BAR FOLDER, Fig. 11-38, is designed to bend sheet metal to form edges and prepare the metal for a wire edge. Seams can also be formed on this machine.

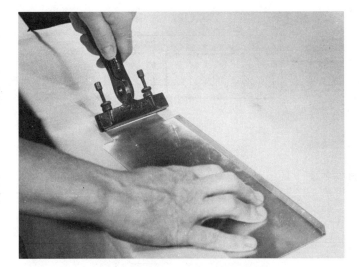

Fig. 11-34. Forming an edge with a hand seamer.

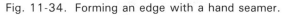

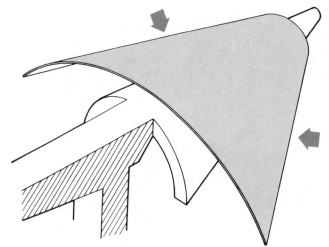

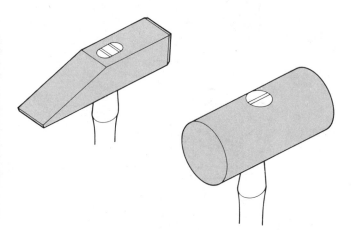

Fig. 11-35. Left. Setting-down hammer. Right. Wood mallet.

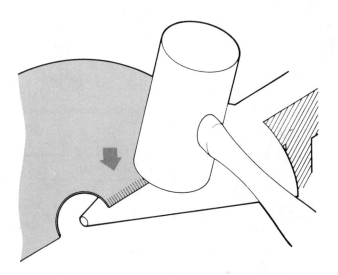

Fig. 11-37. Bending a conical section over a blowhorn stake.

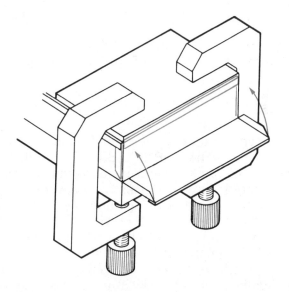

Fig. 11-36. Using a wood block to make an angular bend.

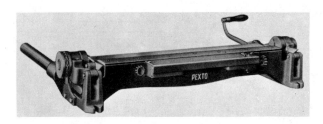

Fig. 11-38. Bar folder.

The width of the folder edge is determined by the setting of the DEPTH GAUGE, Fig. 11-39. The sharpness of the folded edge, whether it is to be sharp for a hem or seam or rounded to make a wire edge, is determined by the position of the WING, Fig. 11-40. Right angle (90 degree) and 45 degree bends can be made by using the 90 degree and 45 degree ANGLE STOP.

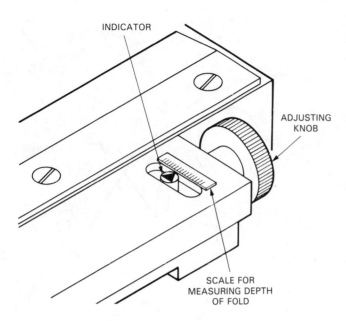

Fig. 11-39. Fold size is determined by setting of depth gauge.

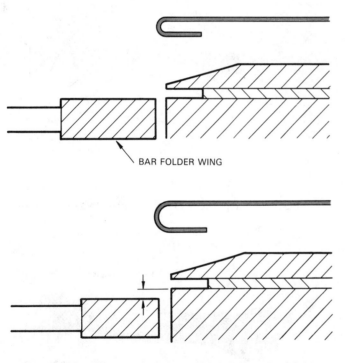

Fig. 11-40. Wing setting determines tightness of fold.

Hemmed edges are made in the following manner, Fig. 11-41.
1. Adjust the depth gauge for the required size, and position the wing for the desired fold sharpness.
2. Set the metal in place, resting it lightly against the gauge fingers.
3. With the left hand holding the metal, pull the handle as far forward as it will go. Return the handle to its original position.
4. Place the folded section on the beveled section

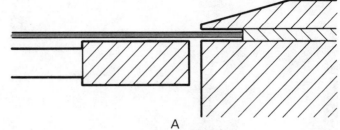

A

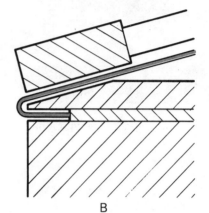

B

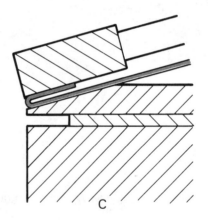

C

Fig. 11-41. Making a hemmed edge. A—Adjust depth gauge to size. B—Make the fold. C—Flatten the fold.

of the blade, as close to the wing as possible. Flatten the fold by pulling the handle forward rapidly.

BRAKES

Large sheet metal sections are formed on BENDING BRAKES. The CORNICE BRAKE, Fig. 11-42, is capable of bending metal sections that are many feet in length. Fig. 11-43 illustrates several shapes that can be formed by using various shaped forming blocks on the BENDING LEAF BAR, Fig. 11-44.

It is often impossible to bend all four sides of a box on a conventional brake. The BOX AND PAN BRAKE, Fig. 11-45, has been designed to handle this situation. The upper jaw is made up of a number of blocks of varied widths that can be positioned

Fig. 11-42. Cornice brake. (Dreis and Krump)

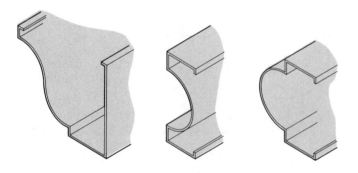

Fig. 11-43. Typical sections that can be formed on a cornice brake.

or removed easily to permit all four sides of a box to be formed.

FORMING ROLLS

When forming cylinders and conical shapes, no sharp bends are necessary; rather, a gradual curve must be put into the metal until the ends meet. The easiest method of forming these shapes is on the SLIP ROLL FORMING MACHINE, Fig. 11-46. Three rolls do the forming, Fig. 11-47. The two front rolls are the feed rolls and can be adjusted to accommodate various thicknesses of metal. The rear roll, also adjustable, gives the section the desired curvature. The top roll pivots up to permit the cylinder to be removed without danger of distortion. Grooves are machined in the two bottom rolls for the purpose of accommodating a wired edge when forming a section with this type edge, or for rolling wire into a ring.

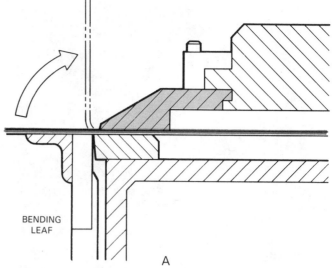

BENDING LEAF

A

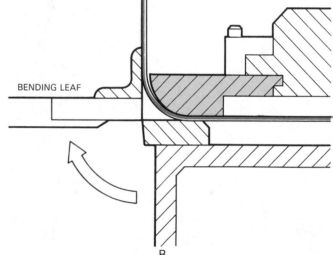

BENDING LEAF

B

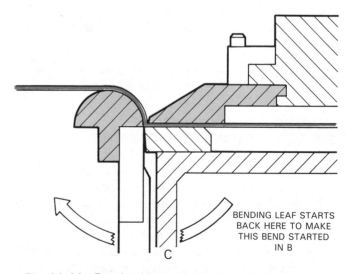

BENDING LEAF STARTS BACK HERE TO MAKE THIS BEND STARTED IN B

C

Fig. 11-44. Forming blocks in place on cornice brake.

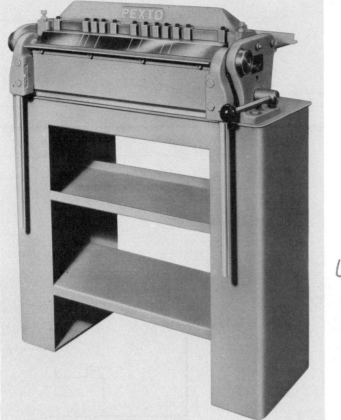

Fig. 11-45. Box and pan brake.

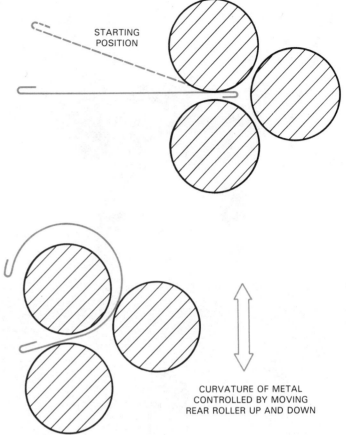

Fig. 11-47. Forming cylinders on forming rolls.

Fig. 11-46. Slip roll forming machine.

Fig. 11-48. Combination rotary machine with extra forming rolls.

TURNING FOR A WIRED EDGE, BURRING, BEADING, AND CRIMPING

Preparing sheet metal for a wired edge, turning a burr, beading, and crimping are probably the most difficult of the sheet metal forming operations to perform. When production warrants, large shops have a machine for each operation. However, a COMBINATION ROTARY MACHINE, Fig. 11-48, with a selection of rolls, will prove satisfactory for school shop applications.

WIRING AN EDGE

There are many methods of preparing an edge for wiring. Cylindrical shapes should be wired before forming to shape. In this case, the wire edge is constructed by using the bar folder to make the initial bend, Fig. 11-49, and, after the wire is inserted,

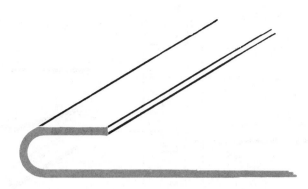

Fig. 11-49. Initial bend for a wire edge.

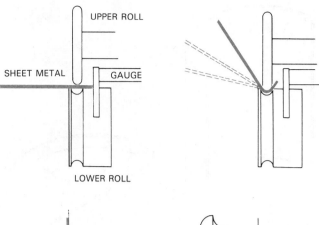

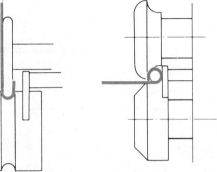

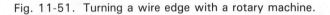

Fig. 11-51. Turning a wire edge with a rotary machine.

by turning the edge down on the rotary machine. An allowance of two and one half times the wire diameter must be added to the basic size of the pattern for a wired edge, Fig. 11-50.

The wire edge must be applied to tapered shapes after they are formed. This is accomplished by turning the edge on the rotary machine, Fig. 11-51. Gradually lower the upper roll until the groove is large enough for the wire. The edge is pressed around the wire with the rotary machine in the same manner as illustrated in Fig. 11-49.

The wire edge can be finished by hand if a rotary machine is not available. The edge is formed on the bar folder and forced in place around the wire with a setting-down hammer or pliers, Fig. 11-52.

TURNING A BURR

A BURR, in sheet metal terminology, is a narrow flange turned on the circular section to be attached

2 1/2 × WIRE DIA.

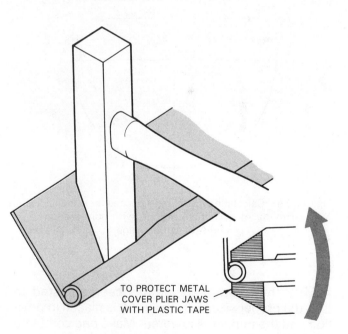

Fig. 11-52. Setting wire edge with setting-down hammer or pliers.

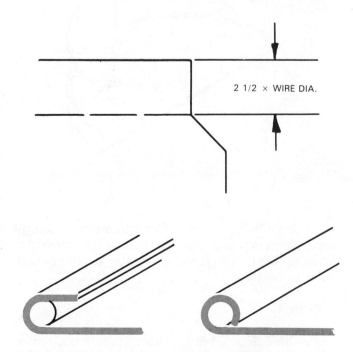

Fig. 11-50. Allowance for making wire edge.

to the end of a cylinder, Fig. 11-53.

Before cutting the section, remember that additional material must be added to the basic dimensions of the object for the burr. Fig. 11-54 shows how to calculate this additional material.

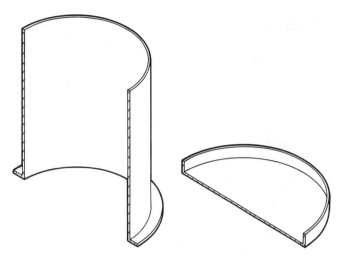

Fig. 11-53. Burrs turned on cylindrical section.

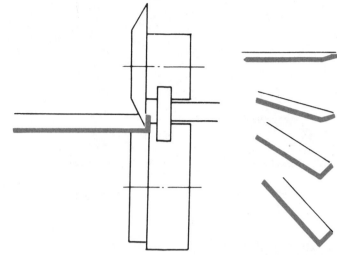

Fig. 11-55. Turning a burred edge with a rotary machine.

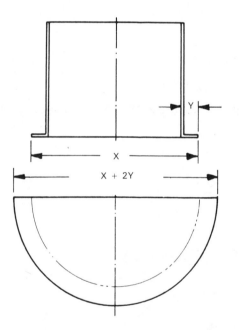

Fig. 11-54. Calculating the material needed for a double seam. X = Diameter of cylindrical section with burred edge. Y = Width of burred edge.

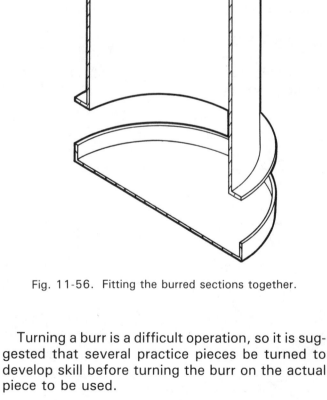

Fig. 11-56. Fitting the burred sections together.

After the rotary machine has been adjusted to turn the proper size burr, the work is placed in position and the upper roll lowered. Make one complete revolution of the piece, scoring the edge slightly. Lower the upper roll a bit further and make another revolution. Continue this operation, raising the disc slightly after each turn until the burr is turned to the desired angle, Fig. 11-55.

This technique is also used to turn the burr on the bottom of the cylinder for a double seam, Fig. 11-56. The two pieces are snapped together, the burr set down, and the seam completed, Fig. 11-57.

Turning a burr is a difficult operation, so it is suggested that several practice pieces be turned to develop skill before turning the burr on the actual piece to be used.

BEADING

BEADING, Fig. 11-58, is used to give additional rigidity to cylindrical sheet metal objects and/or for

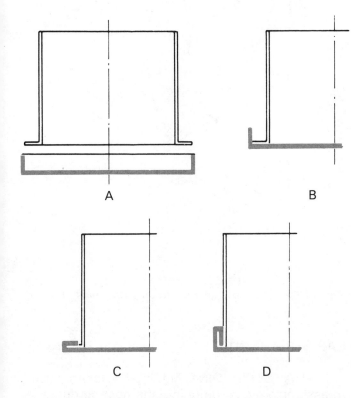

Fig. 11-57. Making a double seam on a cylindrical section. A—Check the sections for size. B—Snap the two sections together. C—Set the burr down. D—Complete the seam.

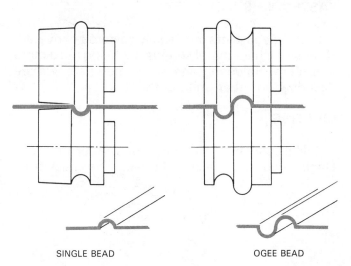

SINGLE BEAD   OGEE BEAD

Fig. 11-58. Turning a bead with a rotary machine.

decorative purposes. It can be a simple bead or an ogee (S-shape) bead. They are made on the rotary machine using beading rolls.

CRIMPING

CRIMPING, Fig. 11-59, reduces the diameter of a cylindrical shape permitting it to be slipped into the next section, eliminating the costly process of making each cylinder on a slight taper.

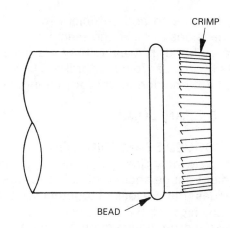

CRIMP

BEAD

Fig. 11-59. A crimped section.

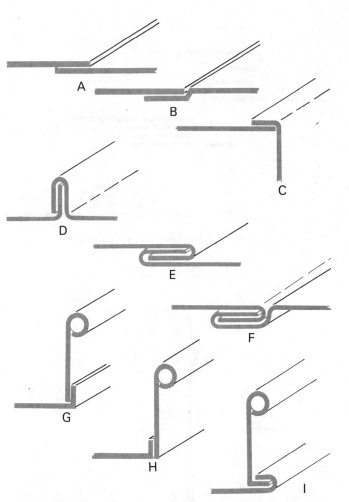

Fig. 11-60. Typical sheet metal seams. A—Lap seam. B—Countersunk lap seam. C—Outside lap seam. D—Standing seam. E—Flat lock seam. F—Grooved flat lock seam. G—Lap bottom seam. H—Insert bottom seam. I—Single bottom seam.

MAKING COMMON SHEET METAL JOINTS

Many kinds of seams are used to join sheet metal sections. Several of the more widely used seams are shown in Fig. 11-60. When developing the pattern, be sure to add sufficient material to the basic dimensions to make the seams. The folds can be made by hand; however, they are made much more easily on a bar folder or brake. The joints can be finished by soldering and/or riveting.

GROOVED SEAM JOINT

The GROOVED SEAM JOINT, Fig. 11-61, is one of the most widely used methods for joining light and medium gauge sheet metal. It consists of two folded edges that are locked together with a HAND GROOVER, Fig. 11-62.

To make a grooved seam on a cylinder, fit piece over a stake and then lock it as shown in Fig. 11-63.

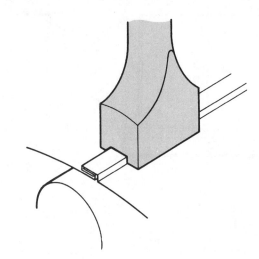

Fig. 11-63. Locking a grooved seam with a hand groover.

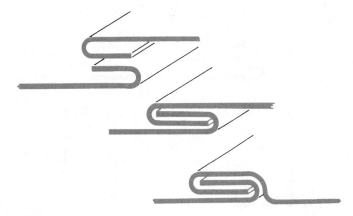

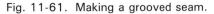

Fig. 11-61. Making a grooved seam.

CAP STRIP JOINT

The CAP STRIP JOINT, Fig. 11-64, is often used to assemble air conditioning and heating ducts. A variation of the joint, the LOCKED CORNER SEAM, Fig. 11-65, is widely accepted for the assembly of rectangular shapes.

FASTENING SHEET METAL

Sheet metal joints are usually soldered or riveted. However, sheet metal screws are being used more and more. Soldering and sheet metal screws are described in other units in this text.

RIVETING

Drill or punch a hole of proper size for the rivet. Observe correct spacing of rivets. The space from

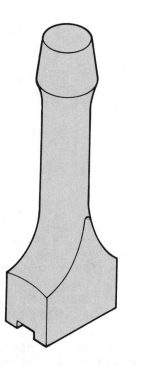

Fig. 11-62. Hand groover.

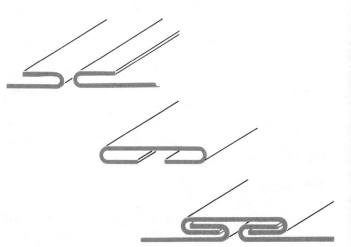

Fig. 11-64. Cap strip seam.

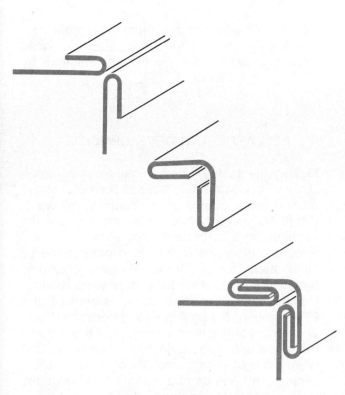

Fig. 11-65. Locked corner seam.

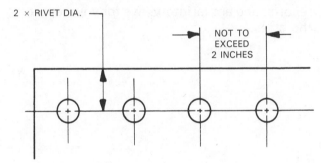

Fig. 11-66. Spacing rivets.

the edge of the metal should be at least twice the rivet diameter, Fig. 11-66.

With practice, a good job of riveting can be done with minimum hammer blows, Fig. 11-67.
1. Seat rivet and draw sheets together.
2. Flatten rivet.
3. Form rivet head with a RIVET SET.

SHEET METAL SAFETY

1. Sheet metal can cause serious cuts. Handle it with care. Wear steel-reinforced gloves whenever possible.
2. Treat every cut immediately, no matter how minor.
3. Remove all burrs from the metal sheet before attempting further work on it.
4. Use a brush to clean the work area. NEVER

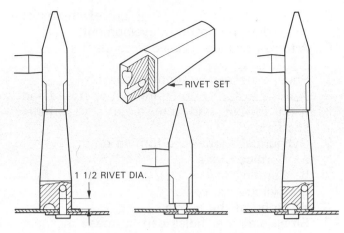

Fig. 11-67. Setting a rivet.

brush metal with your hands.
5. Use tools that are sharp.
6. Keep your hands clear of the blade on the squaring shears.
7. A serious and painful foot injury will result if your foot is under the foot pedal of the squaring shears when a cut is made.
8. Do not run your hands over the surface of sheet metal that has just been cut or drilled. Painful cuts can be received from the burrs.
9. Get help when cutting large pieces of sheet metal. Keep your helper well clear of the shears when you are making the cut.
10. Keep your hands and fingers clear of the rotating parts on forming machines.
11. Place scrap pieces of sheet metal in the scrap box.
12. Do not use tools that are not in first-class condition—hammer heads loose on the handle, chisels with mushroomed heads, power tools with guards removed, etc.
13. Wear goggles when in the shop.

TEST YOUR KNOWLEDGE, Unit 11

Please do not write in the text. Place your answers on a separate sheet of paper.
1. A sheet metal pattern is:
   a. A three-dimensional drawing of the object.
   b. A full-size drawing of the object.
   c. An isometric drawing of the object.
   d. None of the above.
2. Sheet metal patterns are also known as _____.
3. Pattern developments fall into two basic classifications. _____ developments unfold into rectangular patterns. _____ developments unfold into triangular patterns.
4. _____ and _____ are examples of the parallel-line pattern developments.

5. _____ and _____ are examples of the radial-line pattern development.
6. A transition piece is used to connect _____ _____.
7. Sheet metal can be cut by hand with _____.
8. _____ _____ are foot operated and used to cut and trim large sheet metal sections.
9. Cylindrical shapes are formed on a:
   a. Cornice brake.
   b. Forming roll.
   c. Cylinder maker.
   d. None of the above.
10. Small diameter holes can be made in sheet metal with a _____ punch or a _____ punch.
11. The bar folder and brake permit _____ and _____ to be folded quickly and accurately.
12. The wired edge is added to the lip of a sheet metal object for _____.
13. A burr is:
   a. A narrow flange turned on the edge of a circular sheet metal section to form part of a joint.
   b. A rounded edge on the lip of a sheet metal object.
   c. An edge formed on the bar folder.
   d. None of the above.
14. Beading is added to the sheet metal object for added rigidity and for _____ purposes.
15. Most sheet metal joints are finished by _____ and/or _____.
16. Seams are used to _____ _____ _____.

RESEARCH AND DEVELOPMENT

1. Make large scale models of the most common sheet metal joints. If suitable sheet metal equipment is not available, make sectional views of the joints using heavy cardboard. Mount the samples on a suitable display panel.
2. Secure samples of sheet metal work made by local sheet metal shops. Prepare a display around them. Explain how they were made.
3. Demonstrate how sheet metal is worked at a PTA meeting, during American Education Week, or during your school's open house program.
4. Prepare a list of the objects in your home that were made of sheet metal. How many different joining methods can be identified? How many different metals are used?
5. Prepare a report on the job opportunities for sheet metal work in your community. Use classified advertisements, employment service reports, and actual interviews for your report to the class.

Unit 12

ART METAL

There is no clear dividing point where sheet metal ceases and art metal begins, as many of the shaping and forming operations are common to both areas.

Art metal falls into many categories. Examples of a few types are shown in Figs. 12-1 through 12-6. Regardless of the area of interest, art metal offers the individual an opportunity to develop true craft skills since most work is hand crafted, with machines playing only a minor role.

Fig. 12-2. Jewelry is a favorite form of art metal. The bracelet shown can be made from sterling silver or nickel silver. The ornament (it may be made of a contrasting metal) is silver soldered to the bracelet.

Fig. 12-1. This bud vase is an example of hollowware. It permits a single flower to be displayed without distracting from the beauty of the blossom.

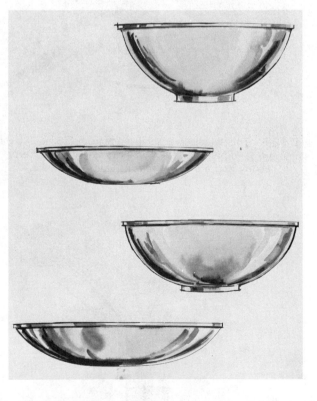

Fig. 12-3. Bowls can be made in a vast variety of shapes and sizes. Pewter, aluminum, copper, and brass are ideal metals. They are finished with a highly polished exterior and a matt finished interior.

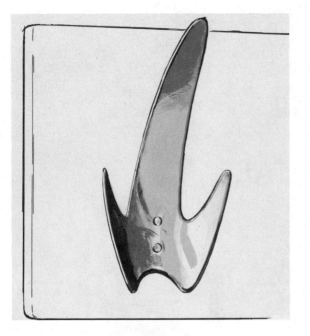

Fig. 12-4. Hat and coat hanger made from 1/8 in. (3.0 mm) aluminum or brass. It is formed on a stake and then, after all burrs and sharp edges are removed, it is highly polished.

Fig. 12-5. This salad server set is made from 1/8 in. (3.0 mm) aluminum. The handles are of walnut, mahogany, cherry, or ebony and are attached with epoxy or rivets.

INDUSTRIAL TECHNIQUES

While hand crafted pieces as in Fig. 12-7 are highly cherished, demand has reached such proportions that production techniques have been incorporated to produce pieces in sufficient quantities. Many well-designed quality pieces available have been produced, in large part, by mechanical processes, Fig. 12-8. A portion of the sequence followed in manufacturing quality tableware is shown in Figs. 12-9 to 12-17 inclusive.

AN INTRODUCTION TO ART METAL

ANNEALING AND PICKLING

ANNEALING is a process of softening metal by carefully heating and controlling the cooling sequence.

Metal becomes hard and brittle as it is worked and must be annealed from time to time before further shaping can be done. Reworking without annealing may cause the metal to fracture.

Closely related to annealing is the PICKLING operation. During annealing an oxide forms on the metal. If not removed before reworking, the oxide scale will be forced into the surface, marring its appearance. It can be removed with abrasives but this is a time consuming process. The scale can be removed rapidly by submerging the piece in a dilute solution of sulphuric acid.

Copper and sterling silver are annealed by heating to a dull red, and quenching in water or pickling solution.

Alloyed metals, such as brass, bronze, and nickel silver (German silver), are heated to a dull red and allowed to cool slightly before plunging into water or pickling solution.

Aluminum may be difficult to anneal because it is not easy to determine when the metal has reached the required temperature. Two methods for

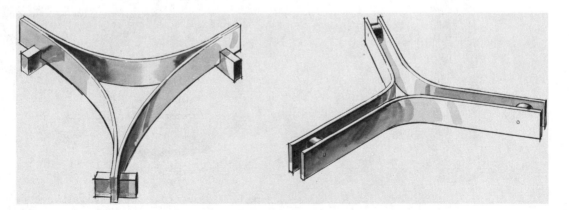

Fig. 12-6. A trivet is a device used to prevent hot dishes and pans from damaging the surface of the table. These were made from brass and were highly polished on the outside while the interior had a matt finish.

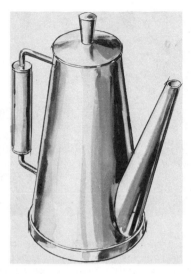

Fig. 12-7. Hand crafted art metal objects are in great demand. This is a drawing of a coffee server that was made from pewter.

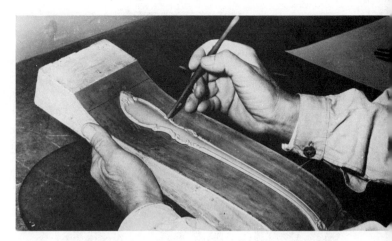

Fig. 12-10. A model of the design is fashioned in red wax, about twice the size of a tablespoon, to permit every detail of the design to be brought out and perfected.

Fig. 12-8. Sterling bowl, enamel lined. (Towle Silversmiths)

Fig. 12-11. Sheet metal—the proper proportions of copper, zinc, and nickel are melted together in an electric furnace. The molten metal is then poured into molds where it hardens gradually, forming bars of nickel silver.

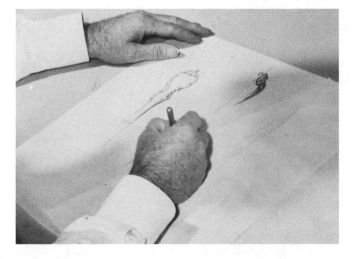

Fig. 12-9. A flatware pattern begins with the artist who sketches the design.　(International Silver Co.)

Fig. 12-12. Rolling—bars of nickel silver are rolled down in a series of passes between steel rollers, annealed (heated), and rolled again until required gauge of metal is attained.

Fig. 12-13. Cross rolling—blanks are passed between heavy rollers to distribute the metal in correct proportions for length, width, and thickness.

Fig. 12-14. Bowl forming—bowl forming is accomplished by stamping the bowl, or tine, portion of article in contour die designed especially for each piece.

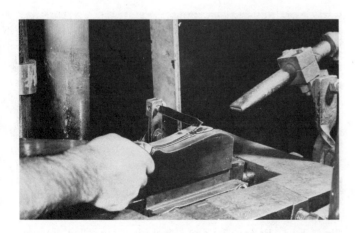

Fig. 12-15. Stamping—striking the design on front and back of handle.

Fig. 12-16. Spot plating—backs of forks are placed on rack so the most used sections to be overlaid with pure silver are in a silver cyanide solution, giving the wear points overlaid reinforcing.

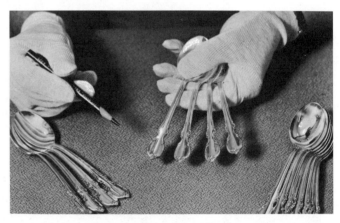

Fig. 12-17. Final inspection—each item is individually checked by experienced inspectors to rigid standards of quality.

determining when the correct annealing temperature of aluminum has been reached are:

1. Heat carefully, occasionally touching the surface of the metal with a piece of white pine. When the surface is hot enough to cause the pine to char and leave a mark, withdraw the heat and permit the aluminum to cool at room temperature.
2. Rub cutting oil on the piece and heat until the oil burns. This indicates that annealing temperature has been reached. Allow to cool at room temperature.

As no oxide forms on aluminum during annealing, it is not necessary to clean the surface in a pickling solution.

The pickling solution for copper, brass, and silver is made by slowly adding 8 oz. of sulphuric acid to a gallon of cold water contained in a glass or earthenware jar. Stir the mixture with a stick of wood.

(NEVER ADD THE WATER TO THE ACID.) Use only in a well-ventilated area and cover the container with a wooden top when not in use. Avoid breathing the fumes.

The annealing and pickling operations are usually part of the same work sequence. The heated metal is held by tongs at arm's length and dropped into the pickling solution. WEAR GOGGLES. When the oxide has dissolved, remove the piece from the solution with wooden tongs, rinse thoroughly in running water, and dry it in clean sawdust or with paper towels.

When shaping is complete and it is not necessary to anneal the piece again, place it in the solution without heating. Permit it to remain in the bath until it is clean. Remove, rinse, and dry as previously described.

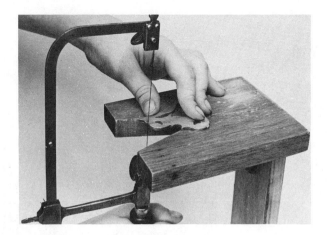

Fig. 12-19. A solid work support is needed when using a jeweler's saw.

DECORATING METAL

SAWING AND PIERCING

Internal designs are cut into metal with a JEWELER'S SAW, Fig. 12-18. This operation, called PIERCING, is performed by drilling a small hole to permit the blade to be inserted. Use a solid support when sawing, Fig. 12-19.

Blades for the jeweler's saw are designated by numbers, Fig. 12-20. Note that the smaller the number, the finer the blade. The #2 blade is well suited for general work.

Piercing weakens the metal, so it is advisable to allow sufficient metal in the surrounding area for rigidity and strength.

REPOUSSÉ (CHASING)

Repoussé is a French word meaning "to thrust back." It might better be called "sculpturing in

Size No.	Thickness	Width	Blades
8/0	.006	.013	*Saws Finer Than 4/0*
7/0	.007	.014	*Not Illustrated*
6/0	.007	.014	
5/0	.008	.015	
4/0	.008	.017	
3/0	.010	.019	
2/0	.010	.020	
0	.011	.023	
1	.012	.025	
1½	.012	.025	

Size No.	Thickness	Width	Blades
2	.014	.027	
3	.014	.029	
4	.015	.031	
5	.016	.034	
6	.019	.041	
8	.020	.048	
10	.020	.058	
12	.023	.064	
14	.024	.068	

Fig. 12-20. Jeweler's saw blade schedule.

metal." The actual tooling, done with punches and a light hammer, Fig. 12-21, is called CHASING, Fig. 12-22.

Often hollowware, Fig. 12-23, is decorated with raised designs. Obviously, it is impossible to get the punches and hammer inside the object. A device known as a SNARLING IRON, Fig. 12-24, is used to raise or push up the necessary metal. It works by vibration. One end is fastened in a vise, the work is positioned, and the snarling iron is struck with a hammer, Fig. 12-25.

RAISING METAL

Raising is the process of giving three-dimensional shape to flat sheet metal by using hammers, mallets, stakes, and sandbags.

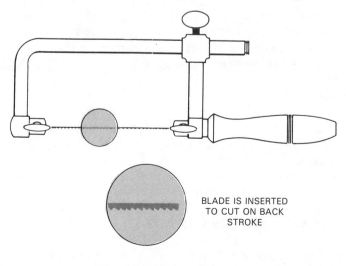

BLADE IS INSERTED TO CUT ON BACK STROKE

Fig. 12-18. Jeweler's saw.

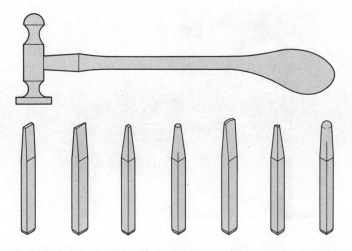

Fig. 12-21. Chasing hammer and assortment of punch shapes.

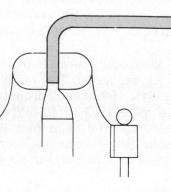

Fig. 12-24. A snarling iron mounted in a vise.

Fig. 12-22. A handmade fork in sterling silver is hand chased by a craftworker who is a talented artist. The height and depth of the design bring out the shadows and highlights. (International Silver Co.)

Fig. 12-25. A snarling iron in use.

Fig. 12-23. Copper mug, silver plated interior. (Bernard B. Gavula)

HAMMERS

Several different types of hammers are used in art metalwork, Fig. 12-26. These hammers are made of steel, with faces clear of nicks and rough spots. The faces of planishing hammers should be polished to a mirror finish.

MALLETS

Like hammers, many styles of mallets, Fig. 12-27, are used. They are made of wood, rawhide, plastic, or live rubber, and are used for forming softer metals. After forming with a mallet, the piece is finished with a hammer.

STAKES AND ANVIL HEADS

Stakes and anvil heads are used to support the metal while it is being worked. They have a smooth,

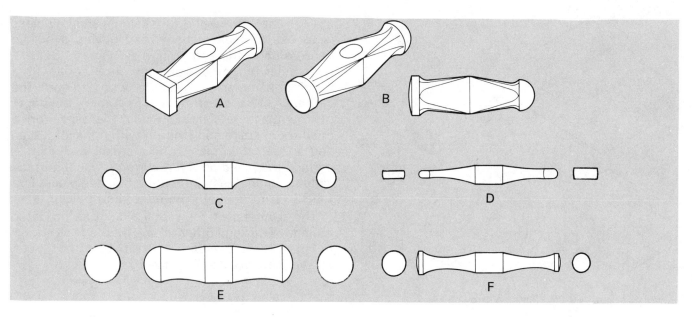

Fig. 12-26. Art metal hammers. A—Planishing. B—Forming. C—Forming. D—Raising. E—Forming. F—Planishing.

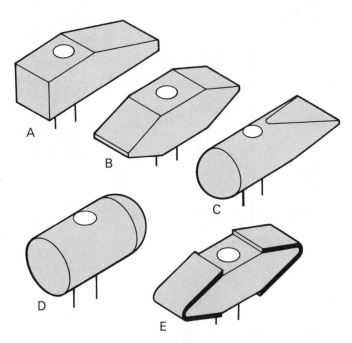

Fig. 12-27. Mallets. A—Hardwood forming mallet. B—Double wedge forming mallet. C—Round forming mallet. D—Round end forming mallet. E—Leather-faced forming matter.

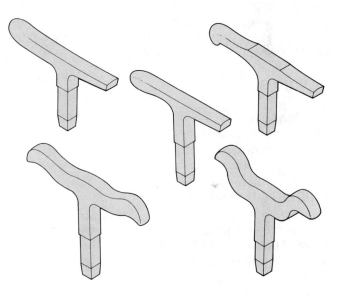

Fig. 12-28. Stakes.

hard surface which should be free from nicks and scratches. Avoid striking the surface of the stake with a hammer, and never cut metal on it with a cold chisel. The more commonly used stakes and anvil heads are shown in Figs. 12-28 and 12-29.

PLATE AND TRAY STAKES

Plate and tray stakes, Fig. 12-30, are often helpful in forming edges and corners in shallow art

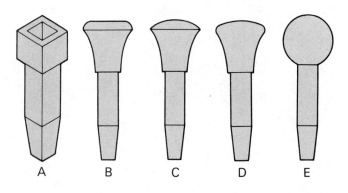

Fig. 12-29. Anvils. A—Extension arm. B—Mushroom. C—Mushroom. D—Mushroom. E—Mushroom.

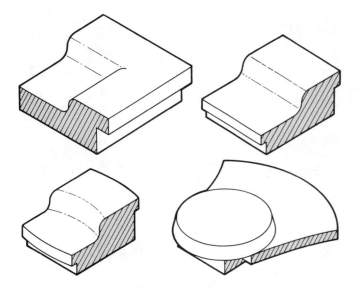

Fig. 12-30. Plate and tray stakes.

metal objects. The stakes are made of wood or metal. Keep them free of nicks and scratches and avoid striking them directly with a hammer. When not being used, protect metal stakes with a light coating of oil or wax.

SANDBAG

A sandbag, Fig. 12-31, is made of several layers of heavy canvas and is partially filled with fine, clean sand. It is only partially filled with sand so it can be adjusted easily to fit many different shapes.

RAISING AN OBJECT

Several methods may be employed to raise a bowl. The design of the object and the equipment available will determine the method to use.

The simplest method for raising a shallow piece is to use a block of hardwood having a hollow depression in the end grain side, Fig. 12-32.

Hammer the metal along the outer edge with a forming hammer and slowly work toward the center. As this is a stretching operation, the depth of the piece is limited. Place the piece on a mushroom stake and smooth with a mallet. Clean and anneal, then planish on a stake.

Place the piece on a flat surface. Use a surface gauge to mark the height of the finished piece, Fig. 12-33. Trim, smooth the edge, and polish.

The diameter of the metal blank can be determined for this and other raising methods as shown in Fig. 12-34. Use care when making the layout, to eliminate waste, Fig. 12-35.

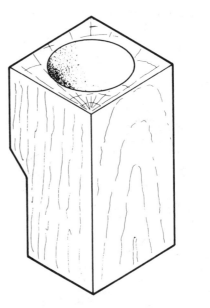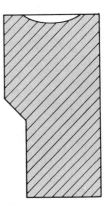

Fig. 12-32. Hardwood block with depression.

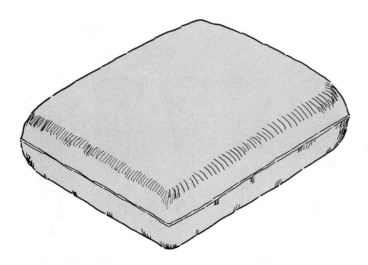

Fig. 12-31. Sandbag.

Fig. 12-33. Surface gauge being used to mark desired height.

The sandbag and mallet can also be used to raise a bowl. Cut a disc of the required size and scribe concentric circles, Fig. 12-36. Place the disc on the sandbag and elevate the edge opposite the one to be struck with the mallet, Fig. 12-37. Strike the disc around circle #1 until it has been completely rotated, Fig. 12-38. Continue working on circle #2 and #3 until the desired depth is obtained. Planish on a stake, trim to height, and polish.

Trays and boxes, Fig. 12-39, can be raised by a unique method. Two blocks of hardwood are cut

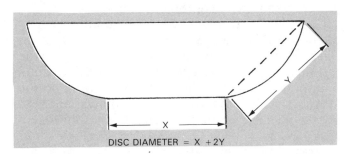

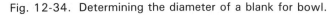

Fig. 12-34. Determining the diameter of a blank for bowl.

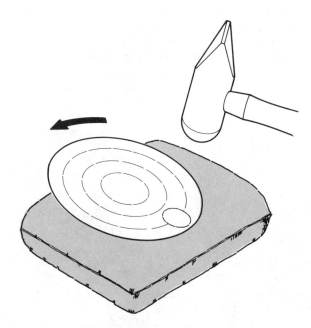

Fig. 12-37. Raising a bowl on a sandbag.

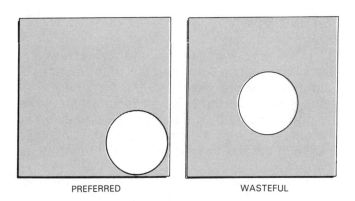

PREFERRED   WASTEFUL

Fig. 12-35. Use care when making layout.

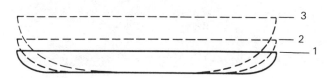

Fig. 12-38. Sequence in raising a bowl.

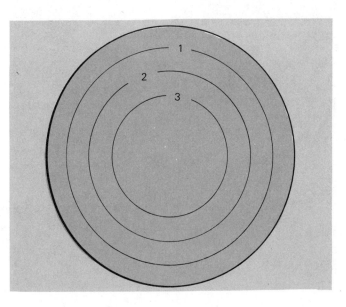

Fig. 12-36. Disc with concentric circles.

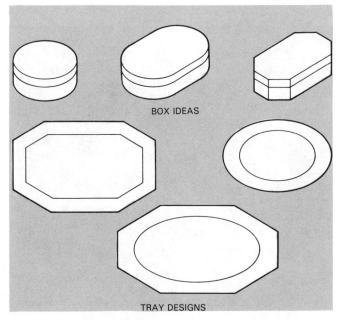

BOX IDEAS

TRAY DESIGNS

Fig. 12-39. Box and tray ideas.

to size and shape. A metal blank of suitable size and shape is placed between the blocks and the unit is mounted in a vise, Fig. 12-40. Then strike the metal near the block with a forming hammer (a leather-faced mallet is used with pewter), Fig. 12-41. Make a complete rotation around the blocks. Anneal if necessary, and continue working until the desired depth has been obtained. Remove the piece from between the blocks, trim, and finish.

Fig. 12-40. Forming blocks and metal disc.

Fig. 12-41. Strike near the block.

Avoid sharp corners when designing pieces to be made by this technique, as wrinkles may form at these points. Should folds and wrinkles start to develop in spite of careful planning, they can be hammered out on a stake.

The final method involves raising a form over a stake, Fig. 12-42. Objects of considerable height can be obtained by using this technique if one is careful, and does not try to do too much hammering between annealing operations.

Cut a disc of the required size and draw the series of concentric circles. Start the raising operation on the sandbag. After annealing, place the work on the raising stake and begin hammering by going round and round. It is important to hold the work on the stake in such a manner that the blows land just above the point where the metal touches the stake, Fig. 12-43.

From this point, the above operations are repeated until the desired height is reached. After annealing and pickling, the piece is trimmed, planished, and polished.

BEATING DOWN

A rather simple way of sinking shallow trays and plates is by beating down portions of the metal over a hardwood stake, Fig. 12-44.

Develop the pattern. Use guide lines to indicate the portion to be beat down. Allow an additional one-quarter inch of material outside the rim guide lines to offset the drawing-in effect of this method of forming.

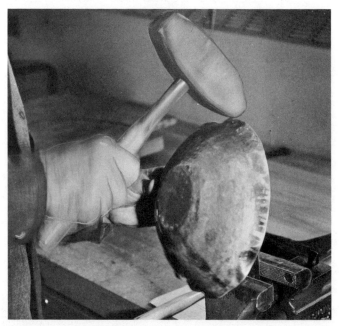

Fig. 12-42. Raising a form on a stake.   (Henry J. Kauffman)

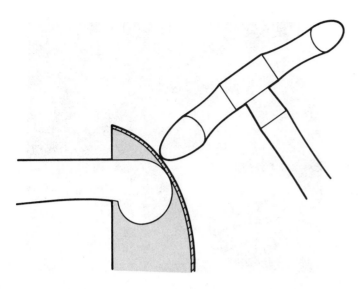

Fig. 12-43. Strike the bowl at a point just above where it touches the stake.

A clean sharp edge at the point where the depression meets the rim is made by the alternate use of a planishing hammer and forming hammer, Fig. 12-45, on a plate and tray stake, or a hardwood block.

Trim, planish, and polish.

As work done by this method has a tendency to warp slightly, it must be flattened by placing on a flat, clean surface, and using a wooden block and mallet to hammer the surface true, Fig. 12-46.

PLANISHING

Planishing is the process of making the surface of the metal smooth by hammering with planishing hammer, Fig. 12-47. Only a hammer with a mirror smooth face should be used. Planishing does not change the shape of the piece appreciably, but rather, should true it and remove any irregularities from the surface.

The hammer blows should be laid on evenly, with

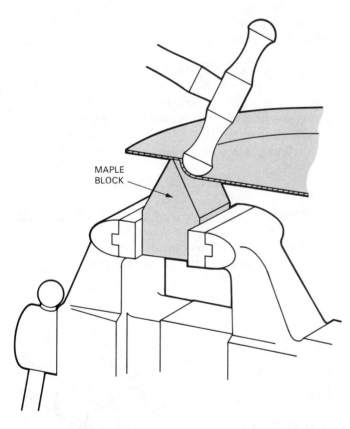

Fig. 12-44. Beating down on tray on a maple block.

Hold the metal blank over the wood block with the inner guide line about one-eighth inch back from the edge of the block. Hammering is done with a forming hammer. Rotate the blank slightly after each series of blows until the desired depth is reached. Use a cardboard or metal template to check the progress.

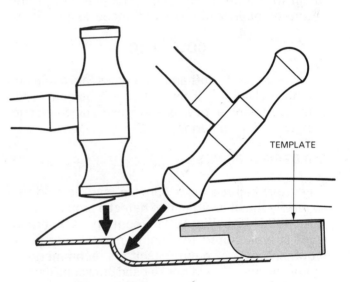

Fig. 12-45. Working edge to clean sharp corner.

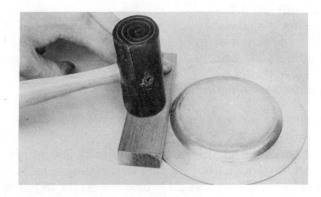

Fig. 12-46. Leveling unevenness with wood block and mallet.

Fig. 12-47. Planishing on a stake.

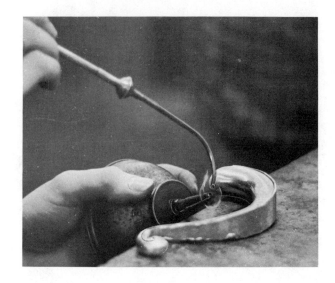

Fig. 12-48. Soldering pewter with a blowpipe and alcohol lamp.

the work being rotated slowly so that no two blows fall in the same place. Select a stake with a curvature as near to the desired shape as possible.

SOLDERING

Soldering, both soft and hard types, are explained in detail in Unit 17. This section will be concerned with how to solder pewter and how to bind and support work for soldering.

SOLDERING PEWTER

Pewter, being almost pure tin, can be soldered so readily that it is difficult to detect a properly made joint. A 60-40 solder (60 percent tin—40 percent lead) is well suited for joining pewter. For some work, snippets of pewter itself are recommended. However, they should not be used until considerable soldering experience has been gained. In soldering pewter, it is important that the flame be moving constantly. A blowpipe and alcohol lamp are commonly used, Fig. 12-48. A soldering copper is NEVER used.

Flux is also necessary when soldering pewter. A suitable flux may be made by adding 10 drops of hydrochloric acid to one ounce of glycerine. Commercial fluxes are available. Wash excess flux from joint after soldering.

BINDING WORK FOR SOLDERING

In order to secure satisfactory joints and to prevent the pieces from slipping while being soldered, it is frequently necessary to bind the pieces together with wire. Soft iron wire in sizes 18 and 24 are commonly used.

Considerable ingenuity must sometimes be employed to bind the various pieces together for soldering. Three ideas are shown in Fig. 12-49.

POLISHING

Polishing actually starts when the joints and edges are first filed. The care taken from this point on will determine the final polish. Full details on metal finishes are included in Unit 20.

ART METAL SAFETY

1. Remove all burrs and sharp edges from metal before attempting to work it.
2. Use caution when handling hot metal. Do not place it where it could start a fire.

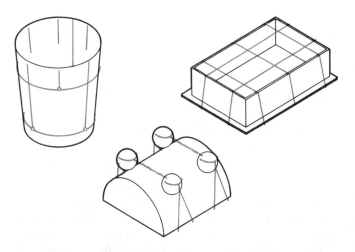

Fig. 12-49. Typical wire binding setups, as used to prevent movement of the pieces during soldering.

3. Pour acid into water, NEVER water into acid.
4. Wear goggles when working with pickling solutions.
5. Use pickling solution in well-ventilated areas. Do not breathe fumes.
6. Do not stand over the pickling solution when plunging hot metal into it.
7. Clear the soldering area of solvents and other flammable material before soldering.
8. Secure medical attention for any cut, bruise, or burn.

TEST YOUR KNOWLEDGE, Unit 12

Please do not write in the text. Place your answers on a separate sheet of paper.

1. Annealing is the process of _____ metal by heating and allowing it to cool under controlled conditions.
2. _____ is the operation that is used to remove the oxide scale that forms on most metals during annealing.
3. _____ does not need to be pickled because no oxide scale forms during annealing.
4. When mixing the pickling solution NEVER add acid to the water. True or False?
5. Always wear _____ when plunging hot metal into the pickling solution.
6. When is a surface gauge used in art metal work?
7. Internal designs are cut into metal by a technique called _____.
8. Repoussé is a French word meaning:
   a. To thrust back.
   b. Sculpturing in metal.
   c. Chasing.
   d. None of the above.
9. Raising is the process of_____

_____.
10. _____ are used to support metal while it is being worked.

RESEARCH AND DEVELOPMENT

1. Visit a nearby museum and study samples of art metalwork made by well-known craftsworkers.
2. Secure catalogs from sources that sell pieces which are recognized as being of good design and quality. Use the photos and drawings as design ideas for your work.
3. Invite a local crafter to demonstrate how art metalwork is produced.
4. Design and craft a pewter or sterling silver chalice of traditional colonial style.
5. Many early pieces that fall into the art metal category were stamped with a touch mark. What was its purpose?
6. Design and craft an award to be presented to the outstanding student art metal worker.

A portable disc grinder fitted with a flexible abrasive disc being employed to smooth and polish a ship's propeller. The propeller was cast in a bronze alloy developed especially for use in salt water.
(Black & Decker Co.)

Unit 13

SAND CASTING

The technique of making a sand mold casting in the school shop is similar to the technique used by industry. The major differences concern casting size and precision, and quantity of castings produced.

The manufacture of castings is a two-step operation. The first step is to convert the raw materials into molten metal, Fig. 13-1. This molten metal must be heated to the correct temperature, Fig. 13-2, and properly alloyed.

The second step is to prepare a MOLD, Fig. 13-3. A mold is a cavity or opening the size and shape of the article to be cast, made of a medium suitable for holding the molten metal.

Sand was perhaps the earliest material used for mold making. It is still the most widely used mold making material. However, other materials, de-

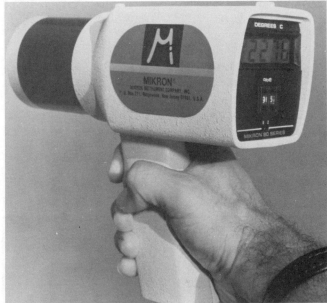

Fig. 13-2. The molten metal must be heated to the proper temperature if quality castings are to be made. Often a hand held infrared pyrometer is used to check metal temperature. (Mikron Instrument Co., Inc.)

scribed in a later unit, are being employed to produce an increasingly larger percentage of castings.

The sand may be used in a moist state. A mold made with moist sand is called a GREEN SAND MOLD. Or the sand may be held together with an oily binder. Plastic binders are also used. When baked dry they form a DRY SAND MOLD. A dry sand mold is more costly to use but produces a more accurate casting, Fig. 13-4. However, green sand molding is the most widely used method in the production of castings.

Sand molds can be used only once as they must be destroyed to remove the casting.

Molding sand is a mixture of sand and other materials that serve as binders. In industry the ingredients are blended together in MULLING

Fig. 13-1. The first step in making a casting is to convert raw materials into molten metal. Shown is molten metal pouring from an induction furnace. It will be transported to the holding furnace shown in Fig. 13-12. (Central Foundry Div., General Motors)

MACHINES, Fig. 13-5.

A sand mold is made by packing the sand in a box called a FLASK, around a PATTERN of the shape to be cast. Hand ramming of sand around a pattern

Fig. 13-3. The second step in making a casting is the preparation of the mold. The mold is carefully engineered to produce a casting with uniform metal properties and minimum distortion. (Aluminum Company of America)

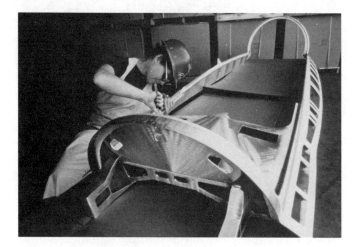

Fig. 13-4. Precision casting of a 12 foot long Navy/Grumman F-14 fighter canopy frame. The thin-walled unit is cast by simultaneously pouring molten aluminum into each end of a 10,000 pound sand mold. Only a small amount of finish machining is required. (Aluminum Company of America)

Fig. 13-5. Modern mulling equipment for producing molding sands.
(Reading Gray Iron Castings, Inc.)

Fig. 13-6. Modern motive sand slinger for floor work. The machine moves from mold to mold packing sand around the patterns. (Reading Gray Iron Castings, Inc.)

Fig. 13-7. An overhead sand unit and molding station for light squeezer work. The squeezer packs small molds that were at one time rammed up by hand.

is rarely employed today except under special circumstances. A SAND SLINGER, Fig. 13-6, or a JOLT SQUEEZE MACHINE, Fig. 13-7, are generally used to pack sand in a mold. To allow for easy removal of the pattern, the flask is made to separate horizontally at a point called the PARTING LINE. When the pattern is DRAWN (removed) from the

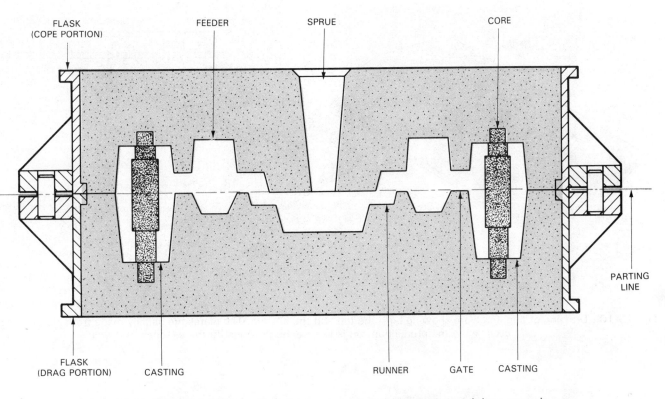

FLASK (COPE PORTION)   FEEDER   SPRUE   CORE

PARTING LINE

FLASK (DRAG PORTION)   CASTING   RUNNER   GATE   CASTING

Fig. 13-8. Sectional view of a typical two-part mold, showing cope and drag, cores in place, casting cavity, sprue, runners, and gates.

mold and the two mold halves, called the COPE and DRAG, are reassembled, a cavity remains in the sand. The molten metal reaches the cavity through a GATING SYSTEM, which consists of vertical openings called SPRUES, through horizontal distribution channels, RUNNERS, and finally through the gates to the cavity itself, Fig. 13-8.

Because metals shrink as they cool, provisions must be made to supply additional metal to those parts of the casting that freeze last, or voids and hollows will occur in the finished casting. These reservoirs of molten metal are called FEEDERS or RISERS.

Holes and cavities are often required in castings. They are made by inserts of sand called CORES, Fig. 13-9. The cores are fitted into position in the mold cavity before the mold is closed. They are knocked out of the finished casting.

The PATTERNS that shape the mold cavities are usually made from wood, if production is of a limited nature. For longer production runs, MATCH PLATES, Fig. 13-10, are used. A match plate is a plate of metal on which the pattern and gating system is split along the parting line and mounted back to back to form a single piece.

After the mold has been prepared, the necessary cores inserted, and the mold halves closed, the mold is moved to the pouring area, Fig. 13-11, and is

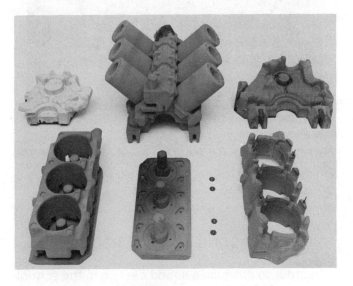

Fig. 13-9. Typical coring for a V-6 gasoline engine block.

poured by the foundry worker, Fig. 13-12.

When the mold has solidified, it is taken to the "shake-out" area where the sand is broken from around the casting and cleaned, Fig. 13-13. From here it is inspected, passed through chipping and grinding, and is then ready for shipment to the customer.

Sand Casting   175

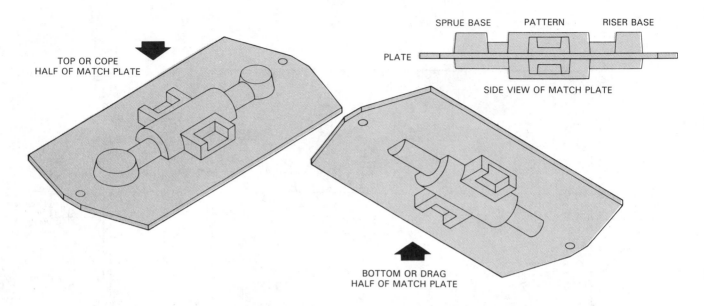

SIDE VIEW OF MATCH PLATE

SPRUE BASE   PATTERN   RISER BASE

PLATE

TOP OR COPE
HALF OF MATCH PLATE

BOTTOM OR DRAG
HALF OF MATCH PLATE

Fig. 13-10. Drawing of a match plate showing both the top and the bottom. The plates are usually made from metal and are used when the production run is large enough to justify the expense.

Fig. 13-11. A view of a foundry. The photo shows squeezer machine in the background, completed molds awaiting pouring, and molds being poured in the foreground.
(Steel Founders Society of America)

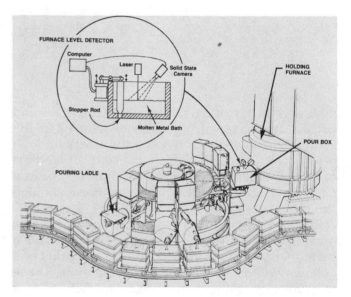

Fig. 13-12. The laser-based furnace level detector helps control the amount of molten iron poured into each mold from the rotary mechanical iron pourers. A solid state camera sees the reflection of the laser beam off the surface of the molten metal bath. The computer translates the information into how long the stopper rod stays up to tap iron into the pouring ladles.
(Central Foundry Div., General Motors)

METAL CASTING IN THE SCHOOL SHOP

In order to produce a sound casting in the school shop, a similar sequence of operations must be followed.

PATTERNMAKING

A pattern is used to make a cavity in the sand mold into which the molten metal is poured. A SIMPLE PATTERN, Fig. 13-14, is made in one piece. More complex patterns, for round or irregular shaped work, are made in two or more parts and are called SPLIT PATTERNS, Fig. 13-15.

Since metal contracts when it cools, patterns must be made oversize to allow for shrinkage. A SHRINK RULE, Fig. 13-16, on which the inch measurements are slightly larger than the standard inch, is used by the PATTERNMAKER when constructing a pattern. This rule allows for dimensional changes as the casting cools.

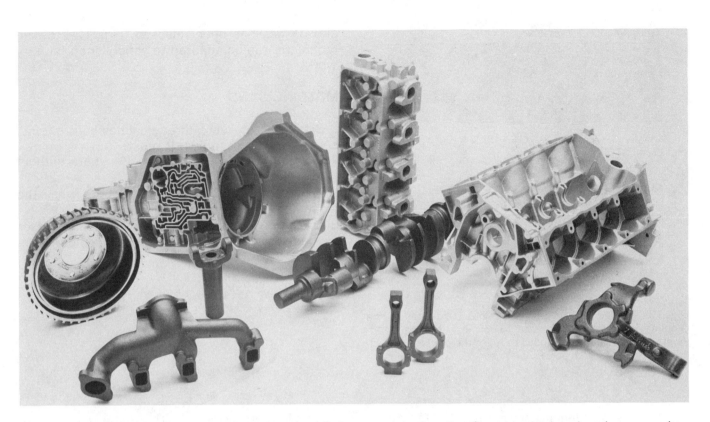

Fig. 13-13. Automotive castings made of aluminum, nodular iron, grey iron, ArmaSteel®, and an aluminum/grey iron composite.

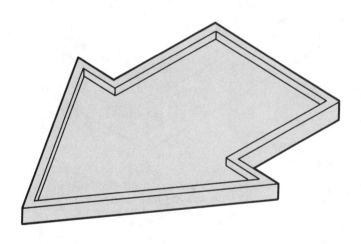

Fig. 13-14. A simple pattern.

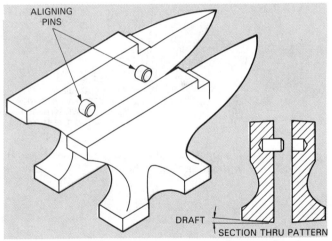

Fig. 13-15. A split pattern. The point of separation is the parting line of the mold.

A pattern must have DRAFT, Fig. 13-17, if it is to be pulled from the sand without damaging the mold. Sharp inside corners are to be avoided whenever possible. When they do occur on a pattern, they may be rounded off with FILLETS, Fig. 13-18, made of wax, leather, or wood.

SAND CORES

Sand cores are used to make openings in the casting. Special sands are mixed with binders and rammed into a CORE BOX, Fig. 13-19, that has been made to produce cores of the proper dimensions. Cores must be baked at a carefully controlled temperature to make them hard enough to withstand the pressures of casting. Cores of complex shapes may be made in several sections and cemented together.

Industry makes wide use of cores made from a mixture of sand and waterglass into which carbon

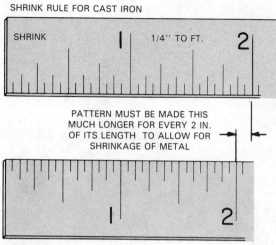

PATTERN MUST BE MADE THIS MUCH LONGER FOR EVERY 2 IN. OF ITS LENGTH TO ALLOW FOR SHRINKAGE OF METAL

STANDARD RULE

Fig. 13-16. The shrink rule takes into consideration the amount the metal will shrink as it cools after casting. A different shrink rule must be used to make the pattern for each type of metal used.

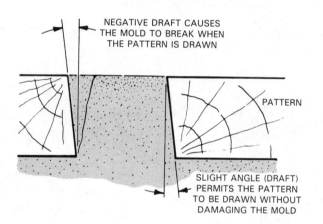

NEGATIVE DRAFT CAUSES THE MOLD TO BREAK WHEN THE PATTERN IS DRAWN

PATTERN

SLIGHT ANGLE (DRAFT) PERMITS THE PATTERN TO BE DRAWN WITHOUT DAMAGING THE MOLD

Fig. 13-17. Draft permits the pattern to be lifted from the sand without damaging the mold.

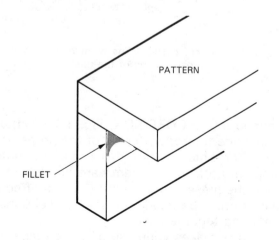

PATTERN

FILLET

Fig. 13-18. A typical fillet.

dioxide gas has been released, Fig. 13-20. The technique can be adapted to school shop foundry work.

MOLDING SAND

Sand must possess three qualities before it can be used to make molds. It must:
1. Withstand the heat of the molten metal without breaking down.
2. Hold the shape of the mold cavity while the metal is being poured.
3. Be porous enough to permit the escape of gases generated when the molten metal comes in contact with the moist sand.

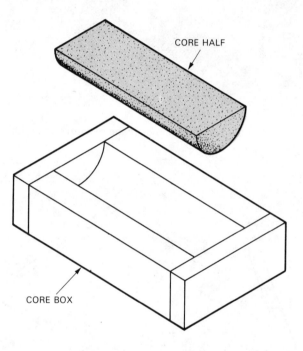

CORE HALF

CORE BOX

Fig. 13-19. The two core halves will be cemented together to form an opening in a casting.

Sand must be TEMPERED or dampened enough to be workable. After mixing water and sand thoroughly, test by squeezing a hand full of sand and breaking it in two. When properly tempered, the sand will bear the imprint of your fingers and break cleanly, Fig. 13-21. It will crumble when too dry and sand will adhere to your hands if it is too moist.

TOOLS AND EQUIPMENT

Tools and equipment needed for foundry work in the school shop are shown in Fig. 13-22. Since they are needed to make a mold, their uses will be explained and illustrated.

Fig. 13-20. Cores being solidified with CO_2. The carbon dioxide is injected into the specially prepared sand core with a long slender tube.

Fig. 13-21. Properly tempered sand.

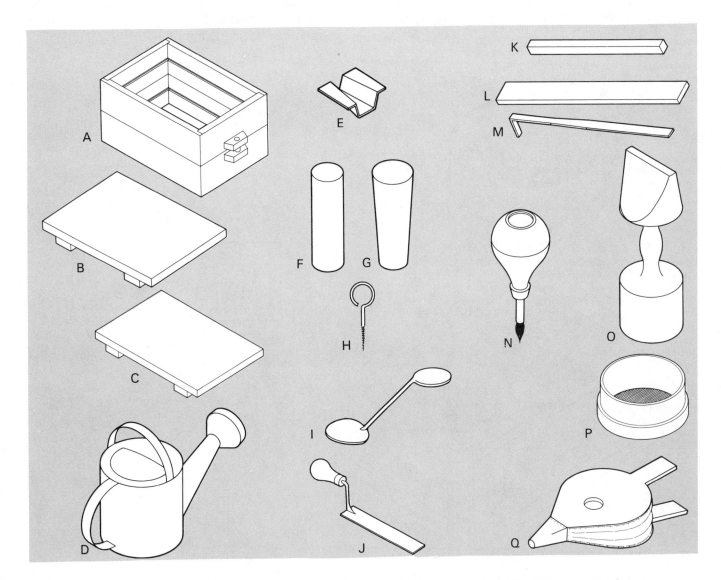

Fig. 13-22. Foundry tools. A—Flask. B—Molding board. C—Bottom board. D—Sprinkling can. E—Gate cutter. F—Riser pin. G—Sprue pin. H—Draw screw. I—Slick and oval. J—Trowel. K—Rapping bar. L—Strike-off bar. M—Lifter. N—Bulb sponge. O—Bench rammer. P—Riddle. Q—Molder's bellows.

MAKING A SIMPLE MOLD

1. Temper the molding sand.
2. Select or make the required pattern. Clean the pattern and remove any rough spots.
3. Position the DRAG on the MOLDING BOARD with the aligning pins pointed downward, Fig. 13-23.
4. Place the pattern on the molding board near the center of the flask. The flat back of the pattern should be placed on the board, Fig. 13-23.
5. Dust the pattern lightly with PARTING COMPOUND. This is a waterproof material that prevents the moist sand from adhering to the pattern and allows the sand on the parting surfaces of the cope and drag to separate without clinging.
6. Sift a 1 in. (25.4 mm) layer of molding sand over the pattern with the RIDDLE. The sand is riddled to reduce it to fine loose particles, Fig. 13-24.

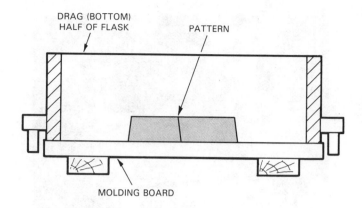

Fig. 13-23. Drag and pattern are in position on the molding board ready to receive the sand.

7. Pack the riddled sand around the pattern with your fingers. Roughen the surface of the packed sand and fill the flask with unriddled, tempered sand, Fig. 13-25.

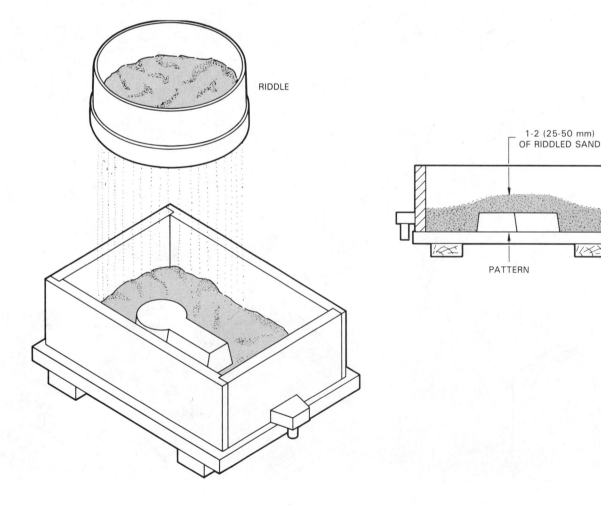

Fig. 13-24. Sand is riddled over the pattern until it is about 1 1/2 in. deep. Riddling removes debris from the sand that is packed around the pattern.

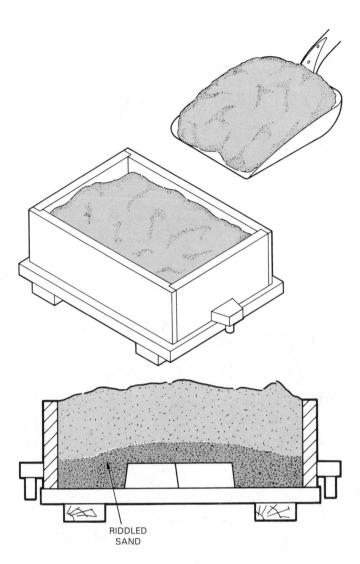

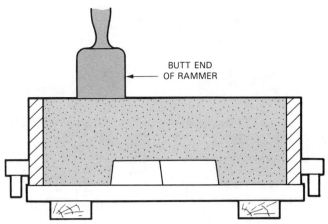

Fig. 13-27. Packing sand in the drag is completed with the butt end of the bench rammer.

10. Strike off the excess sand with the STRIKE-OFF BAR, Fig. 13-28.
11. Place the BOTTOM BOARD on the top of the drag and roll (turn) it over. The aligning pins will point upwards, Fig. 13-29.
12. Expose the pattern by removing the molding board. Examine the sand surface and, if necessary, smooth and level the sand with a TROWEL or SLICK.
13. Place the COPE on the drag and press the SPRUE and RISER PINS in the sand in the drag about 1 in. (25.4 mm) away from each end of the pattern, Fig. 13-30. The riser pin should be located near the heaviest section of the pattern.
14. Dust the entire unit with parting compound. This will prevent the surface from sticking together when the cope is separated from the drag.

Fig. 13-25. Filling of drag is completed with unriddled sand.

8. Use the PEEN end of the BENCH RAMMER and pack the loose sand firmly around the pattern and the inside edges of the flask, Fig. 13-26.
9. Add sufficient additional sand to permit the drag to be fully packed with sand. Use the BUTT end of the rammer, Fig. 13-27.

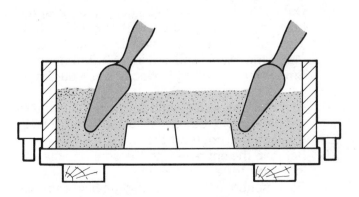

Fig. 13-26. Ramming sand around pattern with the peen end of the bench rammer.

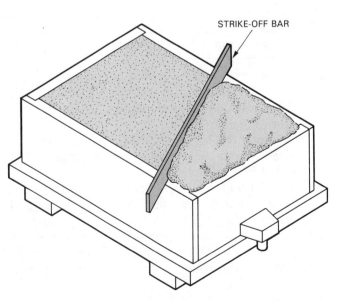

Fig. 13-28. Packed sand is leveled with the strike-off bar.

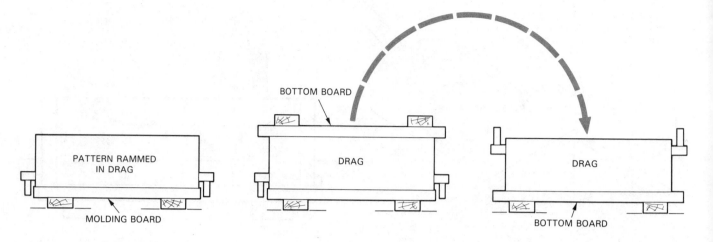

Fig. 13-29. Rolling the drag over.

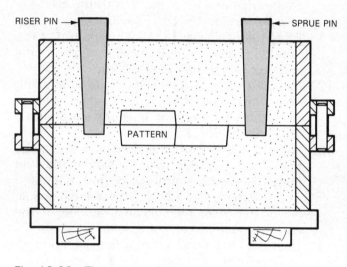

Fig. 13-30. The sprue and riser pins are placed about 1 in. away from the pattern.

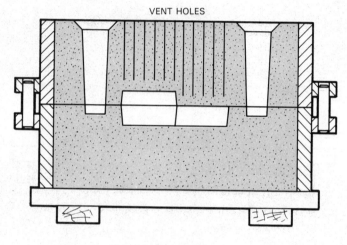

Fig. 13-31. Vent holes.

15. Riddle, ram, and strike off the sand in the cope as was done before. Take care not to pack the sand too tightly.
16. Most molds require venting to permit the gases to escape. Pierce the mold with a VENT WIRE. The vent holes should almost touch the pattern, Fig. 13-31.
17. Remove the sprue and riser pins and smooth the resulting holes into a funnel shape, Fig. 13-32, with your fingers.
18. Carefully lift the cope from the drag and place it on edge to one side where it will not be damaged.
19. Moisten the sand around the edge of the pattern with the BULB SPONGE. This prevents the sand from breaking up when the pattern is drawn, Fig. 13-33.
20. Insert a DRAW SCREW into the pattern near its center. Tap the screw lightly with the RAP-

PING BAR to loosen the pattern in the mold.
21. Carefully draw the pattern from the mold. Steady your hand on the flask to prevent the edge of the cavity from being damaged by the pattern.
22. Repair any defects in the mold with the SLICK and SPOON, Fig. 13-34.
23. Cut a GATE from the mold cavity to the sprue hole and to the riser hole with the GATE CUTTER, Fig. 13-35. This should be about 1/2 in. (12.7 mm) wide and 1/2 in. (12.7 mm) deep. Smooth the resulting surfaces with your finger or a slick.
24. Remove any loose sand particles that are in the mold cavity using a MOLDER'S BELLOWS.
25. Replace the cope on the drag.
26. Remove the entire unit to the pouring area and let it dry for a short time.
27. Pour molten metal into the sprue hole carefully and rapidly. Hold the ladle or crucible close to the surface of the mold. Large molds may have

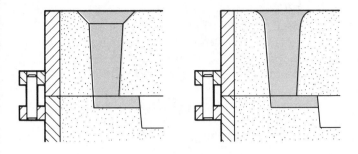

Fig. 13-32. Properly shaped sprue holes.

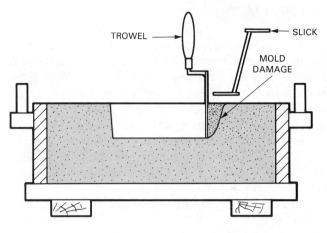

Fig. 13-34. Repairing a damaged mold.

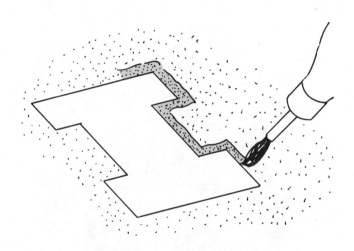

Fig. 13-33. Sand is dampened around the pattern to prevent the sand from breaking up when the pattern is removed from the mold.

to be weighted or clamped to prevent the cope from FLOATING and permitting the molten metal from flowing out of the mold at the parting line.

28. Allow the casting to cool, then break the mold from around it.

Molds that require the use of a split pattern are made in much the same manner. The major deviation involves the use of the pattern. It is made in two parts, one of which is fitted with aligning pins (dowels), the other has the holes into which the pins fit. The pattern half with the holes is rammed up in the drag. The second half, with the pins, is put on after the drag has been rolled over, Fig. 13-36.

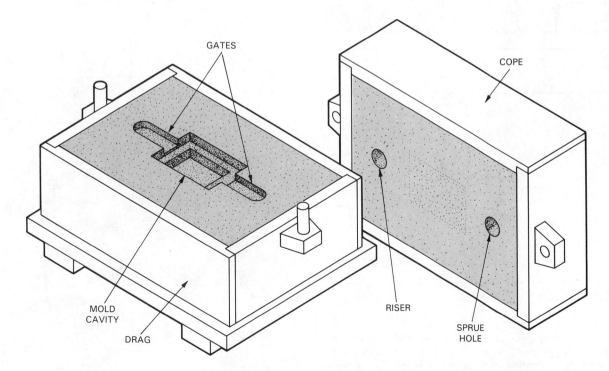

Fig. 13-35. Metal enters the mold cavity through the gates.

MELTING METAL

While almost any metal can be melted and cast, aluminum and brass are most frequently cast in the school shop. A gas fired CRUCIBLE FURNACE, as shown in Fig. 13-37, is capable of heating these metals to the correct pouring temperature. Other metals, like type metal, lead, pewter, and the zinc alloys (garalloy), are used when smaller quantities are needed. These can be melted in a SOLDERING FURNACE, Fig. 13-38, because of their lower melting temperature.

Aluminum and brass are melted in a graphite CRUCIBLE, Fig. 13-39. This type container is capable of withstanding the higher temperature. The crucible is removed from the furnace with CRUCIBLE TONGS, Fig. 13-40, and placed in a CRUCIBLE SHANK, Fig. 13-41, for pouring.

As metals are melted, they absorb impurities from many sources. A FLUX must be added to remove them. In most cases it is added while the metal is melting. However, with aluminum and its alloys, flux should be added just prior to pouring.

POURING THE METAL

Get a sufficient quantity of metal together before lighting the furnace. Take care that different metals

Fig. 13-37. Crucible furnace. (Johnson Gas Appliance)

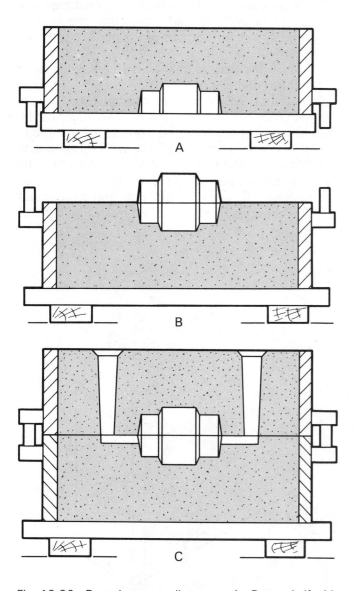
Fig. 13-36. Ramming up a split pattern. A—Pattern half with aligning holes is rammed first. B—After drag is rolled over, the pattern half with aligning pins is put in place. C—Mold is rammed up in conventional manner.

Fig. 13-38. Soldering furnace.

are not mixed in accidentally. Secure a crucible of the correct size, add the metal, and insert the crucible into the furnace. Light the furnace and allow the metal to come to pouring temperature. If additional metal must be added to the crucible, take every precaution to prevent metal with moisture from being added to the molten metal. WATER AND MOLTEN METAL REACT VIOLENTLY WHEN THEY COME IN CONTACT WITH ONE ANOTHER. KEEP THEM SEPARATE.

Check frequently as the metal approaches pour-

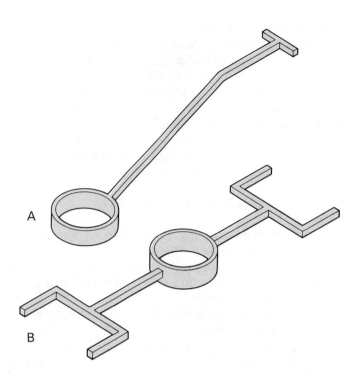

Fig. 13-41. Crucible shank. A—One-worker type. B—Two-worker type.

Fig. 13-39. Clay graphite crucible.

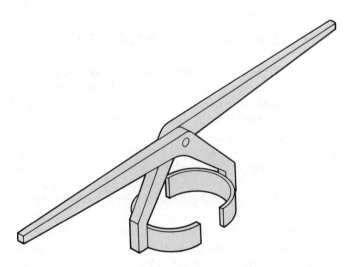

Fig. 13-40. Crucible tongs.

purities will rise to the surface as SLAG. Skim off the slag.

The high temperatures needed to melt aluminum and brass for casting makes protective clothing mandatory. Goggles, asbestos gloves (gauntlet type), leggings, and apron must be worn.

Turn off the furnace and remove the crucible of molten metal from the furnace with crucible tongs and insert it in the crucible shank for pouring. STAND TO ONE SIDE OF THE MOLD AS YOU POUR, NEVER DIRECTLY OVER IT. Steam is generated when the metal is poured into the mold and may burn you. Also, molten metal may spurt

ing temperature. This can be done visually or with a PYROMETER, Fig. 13-42. A pyrometer measures the temperature with extreme accuracy. Do not permit the metal to become overheated as this will produce defective castings. Upon reaching the proper temperature, add the flux and stir it in. The im-

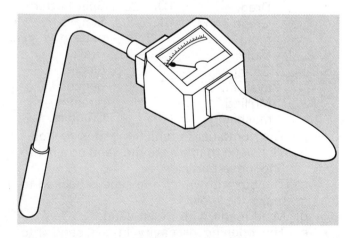

Fig. 13-42. Immersion-type pyrometer.

out if the mold is too moist.

Pour the metal as rapidly as possible. Stop when the riser and sprue holes remain full. Return the crucible to the furnace and allow it to cool slowly. Surplus metal should be poured into an ingot mold.

Allow the casting to cool, then SHAKE OUT (break up) the mold. When the casting is cool enough to handle with bare hands, cut off the metal that forms the sprues and risers. The casting is then ready for machining and finishing.

SAND CASTING SAFETY

1. Never pour a casting unless you are wearing protective clothing and goggles.
2. Moisture and molten metal react violently. Under no condition should moist or wet metal be added to molten metal.
3. Place hot castings where they will not cause accidental burns or fires.
4. Keep the foundry area clean.
5. Be sure your safety clothing is in first-class condition.
6. Do not talk with anyone while pouring a casting.
7. Stand to one side of the mold as you pour, never directly in front of it. Steam is generated during the pouring operation and may scald you. Molten metal may spurt from the mold if it is too moist.
8. Clamp or weigh down molds of large castings to prevent the mold from floating and permitting molten metal to escape from the mold at the parting line.

TEST YOUR KNOWLEDGE, Unit 13

Please do not write in the text. Place your answers on a separate sheet of paper.

Match each term with the correct sentence below.

1. _____ Flask.
2. _____ Cope.
3. _____ Drag.
4. _____ Green sand mold.
5. _____ Mold.
6. _____ Gating system.
7. _____ Mulling machine.
8. _____ Parting line.
9. _____ Core.
10. _____ Split pattern.
11. _____ Simple pattern.
12. _____ Draft.
13. _____ Riddle.
14. _____ Bench rammer.
15. _____ Crucible.

a. The container in which metal is melted.
b. The sieve that breaks the sand down into fine loose particles.
c. The box into which the sane is packed to make the mold.
d. Mold made with moist sand.
e. The opening or cavity in the sand into which the molten metal is poured to produce the require casting.
f. The bottom half of the flask.
g. The machine that mixes the sand.
h. The device used to pack sand in the flask.
i. How the molten metal reaches the mold.
j. The top half of the flask.
k. A single piece pattern.
l. Necessary if the pattern is to be removed from the sand without damaging the mold.
m. A pattern made in two or more parts.
n. Point at which the flask comes apart.
o. Inserts to make holes and cavities in castings.

16. How many times can a sand mold be used? Why?
17. In a modern production foundry a SAND SLINGER is used to _____ _____ _____.
18. What is a match plate? When is it used?
19. Why is a pattern made slightly oversize?
20. A core is used in a mold when_____ _____ _____
21. Why is draft used on a pattern? Sketch your answer.
22. Excess sand is removed from a rammed mold with a _____.
23. List the three qualities needed in a molding sand.
24. Flux is used to _____ _____.

RESEARCH AND DEVELOPMENT

1. Visit a local foundry. Use a portable tape recorder to record a description of what you see and hear as you follow the mold making sequence from start to finish. Play back the recording to the class.
2. If you do not have access to a tape recorder, secure samples of the various ingredients a foundry uses in the production of a casting. Secure plastic pill bottles from a drug store to display them.
3. Prepare a chart that will show the procedure followed in making a casting. Mount samples on the chart of ingredients used.
4. Secure a sample of a commercially made casting as it comes from the mold, and a similar casting after it has been cleaned and the sprues and gates have been removed.
5. Present a film on the casting process.
6. Prepare a sand mold with a core, and use it as the center of a display in a school exhibition case. Use colored twine to lead from the mold to the tools used to make the mold.
7. Prepare and cast a mold with a core.

These two die castings form body and lens mount of world famous Nikon F3 camera. Aluminum castings are used because they are strong, rigid, light and easy to machine.

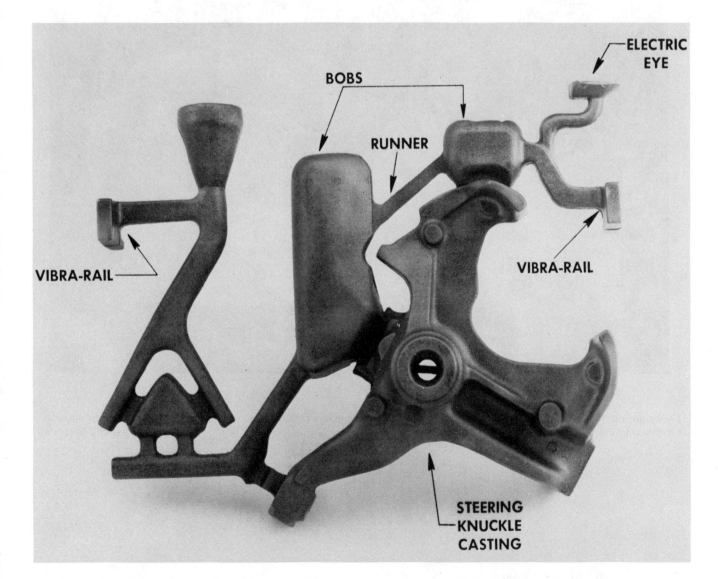

Gating for an integral ductile iron steering knuckle showing runners and shrink bobs. This casting is made in a vertically parted sand mold and shaken out on vibrating rails. Mold is filled by an automatic hot metal pouring device that stops pouring when hot metal is visible to an electic eye at top of mold.   (Central Foundry, Div. of GMC)

Quality performance of tires on the highway depends on precision in each step of the production process. The pattern maker is measuring the groove depths of this plaster tire section which will be used as the pattern for making the mold that will shape the finished tire. (The Firestone Tire & Rubber Co.)

Unit 14

OTHER CASTING TECHNIQUES

Because the sand mold process has limitations, industry must sometimes utilize other casting techniques. Not all metals can be cast in sand molds. Product specifications and metallurgical requirements can make another casting technique more cost effective. Closer tolerances and better surface finishes may be needed.

All casting techniques require the following steps to produce a finished casting:
1. Preparation of the mold.
2. Melting the metal.
3. Putting the molten metal into the mold.
4. Removing the casting from the mold.
5. Cleaning and trimming the casting.

DIE CASTING

DIE CASTING is one of the most important and versatile quantity production processes used by the metalworking industry. In this process, molten metal is forced into a DIE, or mold, under pressure. Pressure is maintained until the metal has solidified at which time the die is opened and the casting is ejected, Fig. 14-1.

Fig. 14-1. This modern die casting machine represents the latest technology. (Kelsey-Hayes)

After the casting has been removed, the die is closed and the cycle is ready to be repeated. To run this cycle at a high rate of speed a die casting machine is used. The cycle speed, or number of castings that can be produced an hour, is governed by the casting size, its complexity, and the alloy used to cast it. See Fig. 14-2.

A DIE CASTING, the term used to describe the casting made by the process just described, is

Fig. 14-2. A die cast aluminum wheel emerging from the die of the machine. This wheel is 36 percent lighter in weight than a similar wheel produced by the conventional casting method. (Kelsey-Hayes)

characterized by dimensional accuracy and a sharply defined, smooth surface, Figs. 14-3 and 14-4. When properly designed a die casting requires little finish machining.

As in other casting processes, after the casting is formed and removed from the die (mold), the sprue and runners must be cut or broken off and the flash that often forms at the die parting line must be trimmed away. This may be done by hand or by machine.

Fig. 14-3. A few of the hundreds of die cast parts used by the auto industry. They are very lightweight and require little machining. (Kelsey-Hayes)

TYPES OF DIE CASTING MACHINES

In die casting it is very important that the dies be securely locked in the machine. The greater the locking pressure the higher the metal injection pressure, which in turn means a better quality casting. All modern die casting machines have safety devices that prevent injection of the metal into the die until the machine has been locked closed. An electronic temperature sensor prevents the die from being opened until the metal has solidified.

Die casting machines are classified by the method used to inject molten metal into the die. The methods used are:
1. PLUNGER.
2. AIR INJECTION.
3. COLD CHAMBER.

PLUNGER type die casting machines, Fig. 14-5, are primarily designed for casting zinc alloys and metals of low melting temperatures. In this machine there is a main metal pot in which is immersed a

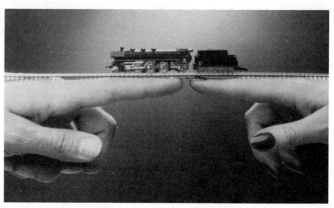

Fig. 14-4. Because the die casting process produces castings characterized by dimensional accuracy and sharply defined, smooth surfaces, the parts for this model train were specified to be made by this process. (Marklin, Inc.)

fixed cylinder with a spout firmly connected against the die. A plunger operates in the cylinder. Raising the plunger uncovers or opens a port or slot that is below the metal level, and molten metal fills the cylinder. When the plunger is forced downward,

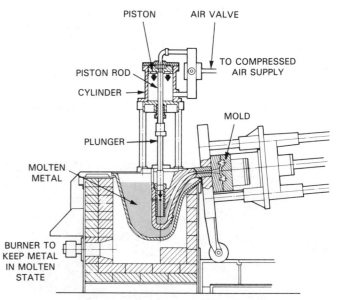

Fig. 14-5. Cross section of a portion of a plunger die casting machine for zinc alloy, showing a vertical plunger activated by compressed air. (American Die Casting Institute)

metal in the cylinder is forced out through the spout into the die. The plunger is withdrawn as soon as the metal solidifies in the die. The die is then opened and the casting ejected. Then the die is closed and securely locked into position, and the casting cycle is repeated.

An AIR INJECTION die casting machine, Fig. 14-6, has a chamber (called a "gooseneck") that contains the desired amount of molten metal. This gooseneck usually is supported above a larger metal pot and is filled by dipping the spout into the molten metal. The gooseneck spout is locked against the die. Air under high pressure forces the molten metal through the spout into the die.

Air pressure is released after the metal solidifies in the die. The gooseneck is lowered, breaking it away from the die, to be refilled. The die is opened and the die casting is ejected. Relocking the die in place and bringing the spout into position readies the machine for another casting cycle. Aluminum alloys are cast in this type of machine, but it can also be used with alloys of lower melting points.

A COLD CHAMBER die casting machine, Fig. 14-7, differs from the plunger type machine only in that the injecting plunger and cylinder are not submerged in the molten metal. Molten metal is still forced into the die by a hydraulically activated plunger. However, the metal is poured into the "cold chamber" through a port or pouring slot with a ladle that only holds enough metal for one "shot" (die filling or casting cycle). Immediately after the ladle is emptied the plunger advances, seals the

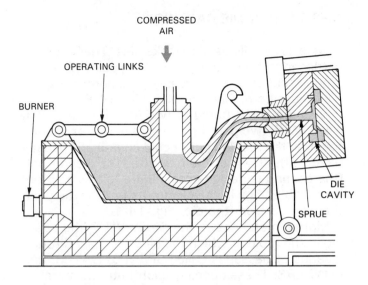

Fig. 14-6. Diagram showing the arrangement of an air injection machine having a horizontal nozzle in position for filling a die by air pressure without a plunger.

port, and forces the molten metal into the die.

As molten metal does not remain in the "cold chamber" very long, higher melting point metals, like the copper alloys, can be cast in this type machine. It operates at a much slower cycle than the other type machines. In all cases, enough metal is injected to more than fill the die. A metal slug that remains at the end of the cylinder is either sheared off, or left to be ejected with the casting.

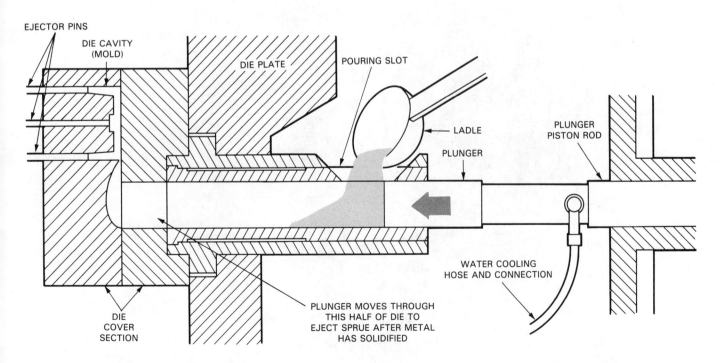

Fig. 14-7. Sectional diagram showing the die, cold chamber, and horizontal ram of plunger (in charging position) of a modern cold chamber die casting machine.

DIES USED IN DIE CASTING

Steel is usually used to make dies. They must be hardened to cast the higher melting point alloys. To produce castings with exceptional smoothness, the dies must be highly polished, Fig. 14-8.

Dies are constructed of two or more parts, Fig. 14-9. With two part dies, the cover half or section towards the melting pot or cold chamber is usually fixed to the front of the machine. The ejector half (the casting is designed to adhere to this section) is movable. Pins in the ejector half of the die push the casting from the die, Fig. 14-10.

Molten metal enters the die CAVITY (the opening in the mold in which the piece is cast) through a series of passages called SPRUES, GATES, and RUNNERS. These openings distribute the metal so that the die cavity is properly filled. When molten metal enters the mold, the air within the cavity must be expelled through vents on the PARTING LINE of the die. These are shallow passages, frequently only 0.005 in. (0.13 mm) deep. They are usually partially filled by metal which forms FLASH. The metal solidifies almost instantly which prevents the molten metal from squirting through where the die sections join.

Some dies have only a single cavity. Others have several cavities for simultaneous filling. If all of the

Fig. 14-8. To produce castings with exceptional smoothness, the dies must be highly polished. Here a reciprocating type hand grinder is polishing a die casting mold using finer and finer grades of abrasive dust. (Diamond Tool Div., Engis Corp.)

dies are identical, the dies are called MULTIPLE-CAVITY dies. If different shapes of cavities are provided, the dies are called COMBINATION dies. The latter are often used to produce several parts for the same assembly.

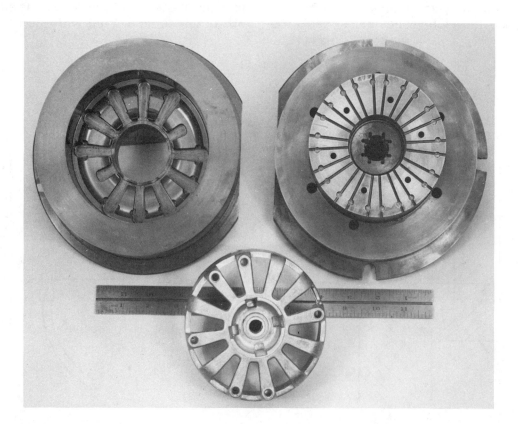

Fig. 14-9. The die and finished die casting of an electric motor bearing housing.

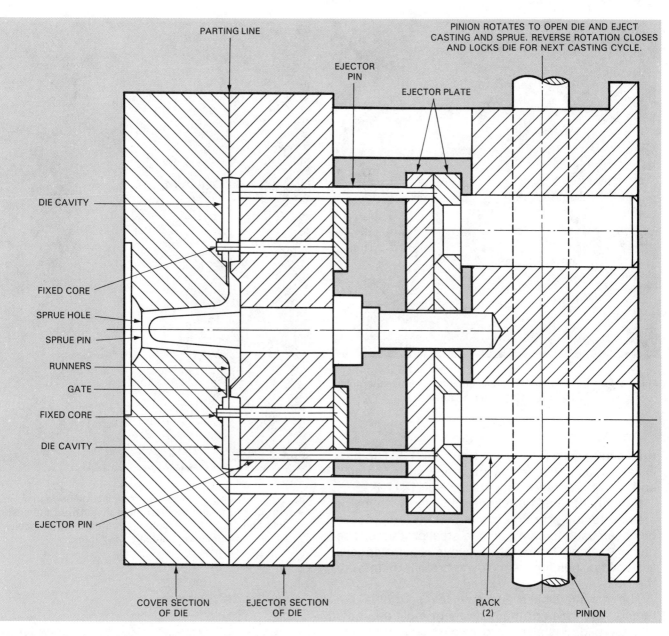

Fig. 14-10. Cross section of a typical die in which the various parts are identified.   (American Die Casting Institute)

DIE CASTING ALLOYS

Only nonferrous alloys are suitable for die castings and the range of these, though more limited than for sand castings, is adequate for most manufacturing needs. Alloys based on zinc account for most die castings. Next in approximate order come the alloys based on aluminum, copper, magnesium, lead, tin, and zinc.

PERMANENT MOLD CASTING

Some molds used for metal casting are made of metal. These molds are called PERMANENT MOLDS because they do not have to be destroyed to remove

Fig. 14-11. This piston was made in a permanent mold. Note the interior design of a similar piston that was sawed in half. Pistons in most production auto engines are made by this process.

Fig. 14-12. Pouring molten aluminum into a permanent mold. (Aluminum Company of America)

Fig. 14-13. Removing the core from a large permanent mold casting prior to taking the iron mold away from the casting. Mold and core for this lighting standard are reusable. (Aluminum Company of America)

the casting. See Figs. 14-11 and 14-12. The process produces castings with a fine surface finish and a high degree of accuracy, Fig. 14-13.

Permanent molds are generally used with lower melting temperature metals, although the process has been used to cast iron and steel products. The higher melting temperature alloys require special surface finishes for the molds to protect them from the heat.

The fishing sinker and toy soldier molds are familiar examples of the permanent mold process. The technique is also used to cast such items as automobile and truck pistons, Fig. 14-14, home appliance parts, and many other familiar items.

A variation of the permanent mold casting process is known as SLUSH MOLDING, Fig. 14-15. Molten metal, usually an alloy of zinc, lead, or tin, is poured into the mold and left long enough to form a thin shell of metal in the mold. The remaining metal is poured out leaving a hollow casting. This process is primarily used to cast inexpensive toys and the souvenirs found at most places of historical interest.

A permanent mold is also used in the CENTRIFUGAL CASTING process. The mold is rotated rapidly while the metal is poured into it. Centrifugal force presses the molten metal against the mold wall, producing a smooth finish. The casting also has a fine grain metal structure. The process is widely used to cast pipes, gun tubes, and items of cylindrical form. See Fig. 14-16.

Fig. 14-14. Most pistons used in internal combustion engines are made by the permanent mold process. Pistons in small engines, however, are machined from solid bar stock.

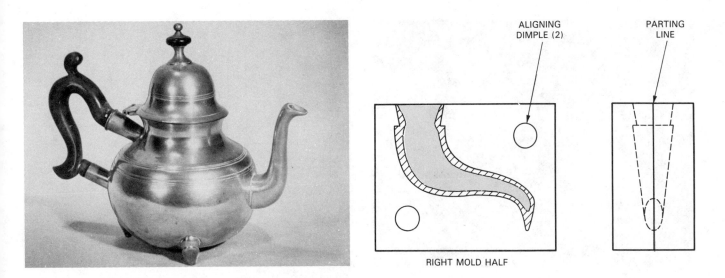

ALIGNING DIMPLE (2)

PARTING LINE

RIGHT MOLD HALF

Fig. 14-15. The spout of this pewter teapot was cast by the slush molding technique. The mold was filled with molten pewter, allowed to cool for a short time and then poured out. A hollow casting was removed from the mold.

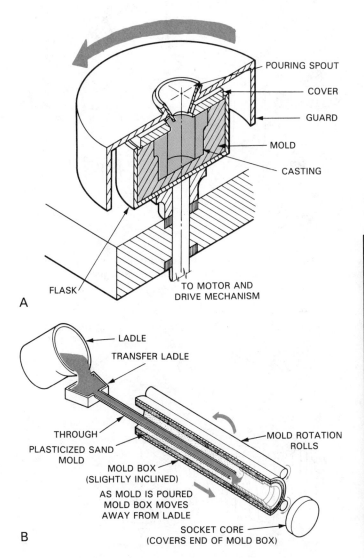

POURING SPOUT

COVER

GUARD

MOLD

CASTING

FLASK

TO MOTOR AND DRIVE MECHANISM

A

LADLE

TRANSFER LADLE

THROUGH

PLASTICIZED SAND MOLD

MOLD BOX (SLIGHTLY INCLINED)

AS MOLD IS POURED MOLD BOX MOVES AWAY FROM LADLE

MOLD ROTATION ROLLS

SOCKET CORE (COVERS END OF MOLD BOX)

B

Fig. 14-16. Two uses for centrifugal casting. A—Casting a small part by the centrifugal casting technique. B—Casting a long section of pipe by the centrifugal casting technique.

INVESTMENT CASTING

INVESTMENT or LOST WAX CASTING is primarily a precision method of casting metals that are difficult to work, and because of their complex shape or intricate design, are expensive to machine, Fig. 14-17.

In the investment casting process, patterns made of wax or plastic, Fig. 14-18, are placed in a fluid refractory ceramic material (material that will withstand great heat). After the ceramic coating has

Fig. 14-17. Many complex parts can be precision cast by the investment casting process. (Howmet Corp.)

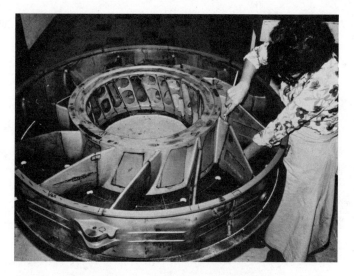

Fig. 14-18. Careful preparation and inspection of the wax pattern is one of the first steps toward a quality product. An engineered gating system, through which the molten alloy will flow to the part, must be designed for each casting in order to guarantee soundness and proper structural quality. (Precision Castparts Corp.)

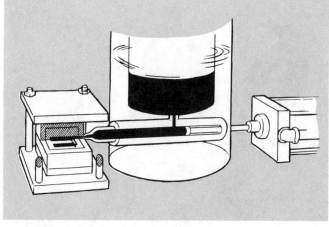

Fig. 14-20. Wax injected into mold under pressure, to insure maximum uniformity and dimensional accuracy.

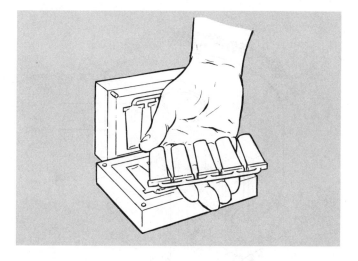

Fig. 14-21. Wax patterns removed from mold and inspected for accuracy and surface smoothness.

dried and hardened, it is placed in an oven and heated until the wax or plastic pattern is burned out. This leaves a cavity in the mold the shape of the pattern. Molten metal is forced into the mold cavity. After solidifying, the metal casting is broken from the mold and the casting is ready for finishing operations, as required. Figs. 14-19 through 14-30 illustrate the fundamentals of the investment casting process.

The dental profession makes extensive use of this process, in casting stainless steel, silver, gold, and other alloys to exact specifications for bridges and crowns. The medical profession also uses the process for items such as pins to repair fractures, and

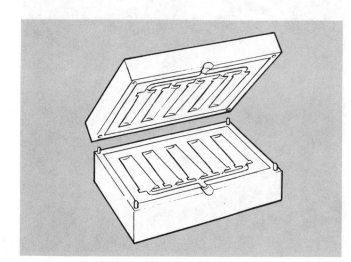

Fig. 14-19. Multiple cavity mold prepared from oversize metal master patterns, ready for injection.

Fig. 14-22. Sections of wax patterns grouped into a cluster of patterns for mass production of castings.

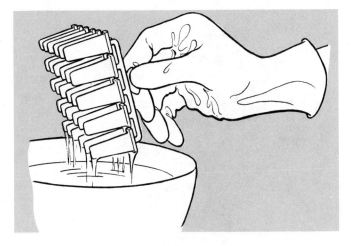

Fig. 14-23. Cluster of patterns coated with primary investment, to promote smooth castings and intricate detail.

Fig. 14-26. Mold removed from furnace, after proper drying and heating, is directly clamped to casting furnace.

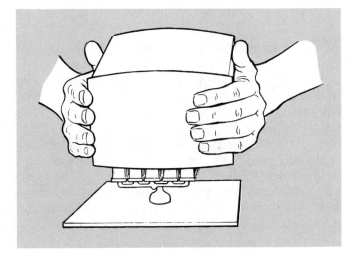

Fig. 14-24. Encased with high temperature metal rings, the cluster is made ready for secondary investment.

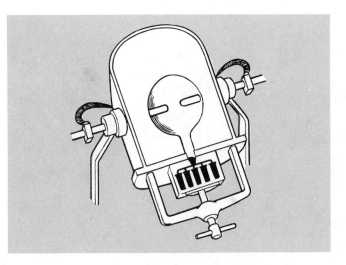

Fig. 14-27. The casting furnace is inverted and the molten metal (under pressure) is cast into final form.

Fig. 14-25. The refractory mold is filled with secondary investment; it is then vibrated, hardened, steamed, and made ready for the furnace.

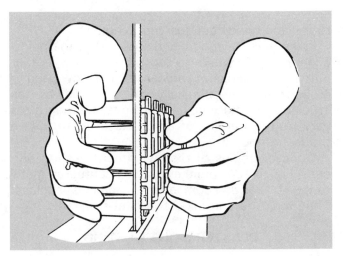

Fig. 14-28. Removing sprues and gates from the completed casting.

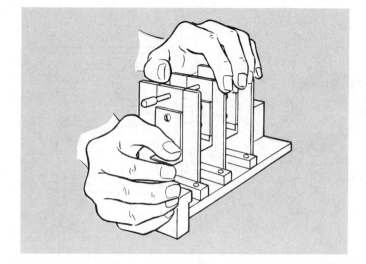

Fig. 14-29. Parts are inspected for dimensional accuracy, then X-ray and Zyglo inspected for sound structure, if required.

Fig. 14-31. Many parts on this turbo-jet engine are made by the investment casting process. This is the only way some of the high temperature alloys can be cast into intricate shapes. (Garrett Corp.)

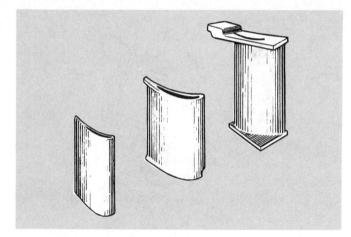

Fig. 14-30. Typical examples of Microcast parts . . . turbine blades used in most turbine engines.
(Figs. 14-19 to 14-30, Austenal Co. Div. of Howe Sound Co.)

primarily of plaster along with sand. The use of plaster molds makes it possible to produce castings of very intricate design. As a matter of fact, some of the castings are so complex, Fig. 14-32, that they must be made in sections. These sections are cast in plaster or plastic molds, Fig. 14-33, and when the plaster has "set" sufficiently they are removed, inspected, and fired in low temperature ovens to remove all traces of moisture. The mold segments are again inspected and then assembled into a single mold using a plastic resin as an adhesive, Fig. 14-34.

to replace bone sections and joints.

Investment casting has developed to the point, economically, where it can compete with other machining and casting processes. It is now used to produce parts that originally had to be made by less efficient and more costly methods. Casting sizes vary from a fraction of an ounce to more than a thousand pounds.

Good examples of the investment casting process, Fig. 14-31, are the complex contoured metal turbine blades and components used in jet engines. They must be corrosion and heat-resistant.

PLASTER MOLD CASTING

In this foundry process the mold is made either entirely of plaster or a combination consisting

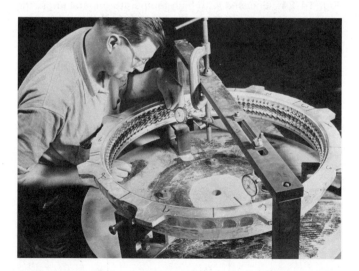

Fig. 14-32. Checking dimensional accuracy of a tire mold tread ring made by the plaster cast process. Note the intricate tread design and the smooth surface finish. These are characteristic of the process.
(Aluminum Company of America)

Fig. 14-33. Pouring plaster segment for the tire mold tread ring. Supports have been inserted in the tread mold to give additional strength to the mold.

Fig. 14-34. Assembling plaster segments into a mold for the tire mold tread ring. The pieces are cemented together. (Aluminum Company of America)

After assembly, the entire mold is fired again to set the adhesive and then is sent to the foundry for casting. Plaster molds can be used only once as they must be broken up to remove the casting.

Recent improvements have made it possible to adapt this method of shaping metal to modern production techniques. The plaster mold process combines the intricacies of sand casting with the close dimensional accuracies and smooth surface finishes usually associated with die casting.

Another advantage of this process is that the plaster mold has less chilling effect (process of moisture cooling the molten metal) on the metal being cast than a sand or metal mold. This makes it possible to cast thinner sections than with the sand or permanent mold methods.

The plaster mold process has successfully produced parts for automobile automatic transmissions on a quantity basis, Fig. 14-35. These parts, cast of aluminum, weigh about 10 lbs. and are about 14 in. in diameter. However, parts up to 40 in. in diameter and up to 300 lbs. have been cast using the plaster mold casting technique.

Fig. 14-35. Cast aluminum automatic transmission parts. The turbines contain from nineteen to thirty-three intricately formed blades.

SAFETY

1. When preparing a plaster mold, one point of safety cannot be overemphasized: DO NOT POUR MOLTEN METAL INTO A PLASTER MOLD UNTIL ALL TRACES OF MOISTURE HAVE BEEN REMOVED FROM THE MOLD.
2. Wear protective clothing and eye protection that covers your entire face.
3. Avoid placing hot castings where they might cause a serious burn.
4. Moisture and molten metal are very dangerous when they are combined. DO NOT ATTEMPT TO REMELT A PIECE OF METAL THAT HAS BEEN COOLED IN WATER OR OTHER LIQUID UNTIL ALL TRACES OF MOISTURE HAVE EVAPORATED.

SHELL MOLDING

SHELL MOLDING is a foundry process in which the molds are made in the form of thin shells. Castings produced by this process have a superior finish and improved dimensional accuracy over castings produced in green sand molds. Shell molds can be used to produce castings with thin sections and/or intricate designs because they contain very little moisture to chill the molten metal. This results in reduced machining costs. In fact, machining operations can often be eliminated completely.

The shell molding process is well adapted to mass-production techniques. Two persons operating four-station shell molding and closing machines, as in Fig. 14-36, can produce up to 240 molds per hour. The finished molds can be easily stored.

Fig. 14-37. Note metal patterns used to make molds for small engine crankshafts. The four cylindrical objects on the cope half (right) are risers, which are connected to the casting and provide liquid metal to the casting during the period the casting is solidifying. This surplus metal compensates for the internal shrinkage of the casting as the metal cools and solidifies. The patterns are inserted in the machine shown in Fig. 14-38.

Fig. 14-36. Typical shell molding operation. The four-station shell molding machine and controls are on the right. The four-station shell closing machine is on the left. Sand and resin storage is behind the shell molding machine.

Fig. 14-38. Four-station shell molding machine. Each station automatically performs a different operation: the first station loads the mold with sand and resin then rolls it over to remove excess sand. Stations two and three are the curing stations, where the desired mold hardness is obtained. The fourth station ejects the finished shell mold.

Shell molds are made in the following sequence of operations:
1. A metal pattern, Fig. 14-37, is inserted in the molding machine, Fig. 14-38. The casting produced from the mold made with this pattern will be a crankshaft for an outboard motor.
2. After the pattern has been set in the molding machine, a water-jacketed flask is fitted over the pattern, Fig. 14-39. This holds a measured volume of mix consisting of thermosetting resin and sand. This material adheres to the heated pattern, and forms a thin plastic and sand shell. Water cooling the flask prevents a buildup of the mix on the inside of the flask.
3. Excess sand is removed by a roll-over operation,

Fig. 14-40. The flask is removed and the thin soft shell on the face of the pattern moves through a curing station where the desired hardness is obtained, Fig. 14-41.
4. The finished mold is automatically ejected by the machine, Fig. 14-42. This particular shell consists of a cope half and a drag half which are easily separated by the machine operator.

Fig. 14-39. The water-jacketed flask is fitted over the heated metal pattern and holds the resin and sand mixture. The water cools the flask and prevents the buildup of sand on the inside of the flask.

Fig. 14-40. The roll-over operation dumps the excess sand and resin leaving a thin, soft shell on the face of the pattern. The surplus sand and resin are recycled back into the sand handling system.

Fig. 14-41. Mold curing stations where the desired mold hardness is obtained. These two stations are fitted with infrared heaters.

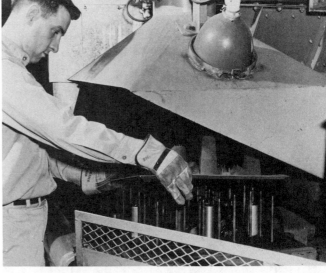

Fig. 14-42. After the shell has been cured properly it is automatically ejected by the machine.

5. The drag half and the cope half (right), Fig. 14-43, move to the closing machine.
6. At the closing machine, Fig. 14-44, the cope is placed on the drag. Cores have been set into place and adhesive applied to the two mold halves.

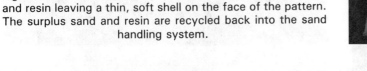

Fig. 14-43. Completed mold halves ready to have the cores inserted (if needed). This shows patterns for two crankshaft castings.

7. The mold sections are clamped until the bonding agent (adhesive) has cured, Fig. 14-45. Molds can be used immediately or stored for an indefinite period, Fig. 14-46.
8. After the molten metal has been poured, Fig. 14-47, and solidified, the molds are "shaken out," meaning the mold is broken from around the casting. The casting is cleaned by shot blasting and after heat treatment, it is machined.

Fig. 14-44. At the closing machine the cope and drag are united for bonding. The mold halves, in this case are held together with adhesives. In some instances, however, the shells are held together with clamps.

Fig. 14-46. The lightweight shell molds can be stored easily, without loss of their dimensional accuracy.
(Figs. 14-36 to 14-46, Link-Belt Co.)

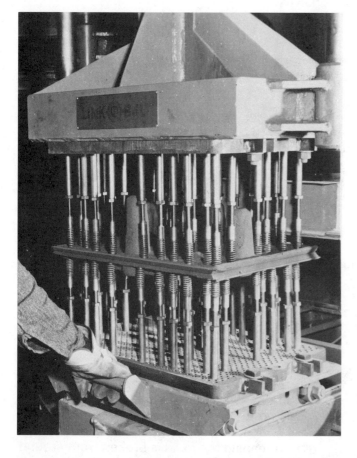

Fig. 14-45. The mold halves are clamped until the bonding agent has cured.

Fig. 14-47. After the metal has been poured and solidified, the shell mold is broken to remove the casting(s).
(Union Carbide Corp.)

The nature of the shell molding process permits it to be fitted into limited spaces. The use of shells permits an almost dustless operation from the preparation of the mold to final "shake out" of the casting. Waste sand and cores are quickly disposed of, in contrast to the large volume of hot sand that must be handled and disposed of in the conventional sand mold process.

TEST YOUR KNOWLEDGE, Unit 14

Please do not write in the text. Place your answers on a separate sheet of paper.

1. Why are casting techniques other than the sand mold process used?
2. All casting techniques require the same basic steps to produce a casting. List them.
3. In die casting, the molten metal is forced into the mold under _____.
4. The cycle of a die casting machine refers to:
   a. The sequence followed to make a casting.
   b. The speed at which the machine operates.
   c. The number of castings made per hour.
   d. All of the above.
   e. None of the above.
5. A die casting is characterized by its _____ _____.
6. The die in die casting is the same as the _____ in sand casting.
7. List the three types of die casting machines:
   a. _____.
   b. _____.
   c. _____.
8. Which of the following metals cannot be die cast?
   a. Aluminum.
   b. Cast iron.
   c. Copper-based alloys.
   d. Zinc.
9. One very important safety factor built into every modern die casting machine is:
   a. The machine will not operate if the metal supply is low.
   b. An inexperienced operator cannot operate the machine.
   c. Molten metal cannot be injected into the mold until it has been locked closed.
   d. None of the above.
10. Permanent molds refer to molds that:
    a. Do not wear out.
    b. Do not have to be destroyed to remove the casting.
    c. Are made of a special metal.
    d. None of the above.
11. The _____ and _____ are familiar examples of the permanent mold casting technique.
12. In _____ casting, molten metal is poured into the mold and left long enough to form a thin shell of metal in the mold.
13. In the _____ casting process, the mold is rotated while the molten metal is poured into it. This process is widely used to cast _____, _____, and _____.
14. Investment casting is also known as _____ _____ _____.

15. Investment casting patterns are made of _____ or _____.
16. Investment casting is a technique which makes it possible to:
    a. Lower the cost of making simple casting.
    b. Use one pattern over and over again.
    c. Cast metals that are difficult to machine.
    d. All of the above.
    e. None of the above.
17. Investment casting is also widely used by the _____ and _____ professions.
18. Describe how an investment casting is made.
19. Plaster molds are fired at low temperature in an oven to remove all traces of moisture because:
    a. The moisture will cause the molds to crumble and become unusable.
    b. The mold cannot be handled easily or safely when moist.
    c. The moisture will create steam when it comes into contact with the molten metal and literally cause the mold to explode.
    d. All of the above.
    e. None of the above.
20. Plaster molds used to make complex castings are made in several sections or pieces. These pieces must be aligned and fastened together with:
    a. Pins.
    b. Screws.
    c. Wire.
    d. All of the above.
    e. None of the above.
21. Many plaster molds are made in _____ sections because of the complex shape of the object that is to be cast.
22. When plaster molds are to be made and cast, what safety precautions should be observed?
23. Castings made by the shell molding technique have the following advantages over sand castings:
    a. Are more accurate and have a better surface finish.
    b. Castings with thin sections and intricate designs can be made.
    c. The technique is well suited for mass-production techniques.
    d. All of the above.
    e. None of the above.
24. In shell molding _____ patterns must be used.
25. The sand in a shell mold is held together with a _____ mixture.
26. Excess sand is removed from the mold by a _____ operation.
27. Shell molds can be used _____ or stored for _____.
28. The castings are cleaned by _____.

Other Casting Techniques   203

RESEARCH AND DEVELOPMENT

1. Prepare a display board showing the die casting cycle. Show the various steps with drawings and photos from booklets and advertisements prepared by die casting producers.
2. Secure several castings produced by die casting. Locate the parting lines of the mold parts. Can you determine the number of parts in the mold used to cast them?
3. Make a panel that will illustrate the differences between a die casting and a sand mold casting. Use examples of each process.
4. Arrange a visit to a plant that makes die castings. If a trip is not possible, borrow examples of die castings before the sprues and flashing are removed.
5. Secure items made by the various permanent mold processes. Prepare a display panel that shows, with a series of drawings, how they are made.
6. Prepare a series a transparencies for the overhead projector that illustrate how the various permanent mold processes work. Write a script on the processes and record it. Present the slides and recording to the class.
7. Secure or make samples of permanent molds and demonstrate them to the class. For safety reasons, you may want to record the demonstration on 35mm slides for presentation.
8. Visit your dentist or local dental supply laboratory to see how the dental profession makes use of investment castings. Give a short report to the class on what you observed.
9. Prepare a short term paper on the professional life of Benvenuto Cellini, a master artisan who developed the lost wax process. Try to secure photographs, pictures, or drawings of his more famous works. Visit museums and inquire whether any of his work is on display.
10. Give a demonstration on how investment casting is done. Mold material and pattern wax may be obtained from dental supply houses.
   CAUTION: Allow the molds to dry thoroughly. The heat used to remove the pattern from the mold often is not enough to thoroughly dry the mold. WEAR FULL FACE AND EYE PROTECTION AND PROTECTION FOR YOUR HANDS, ARMS, AND CLOTHING WHEN POURING THE MOLD.
11. Make arrangements to visit a foundry that employs the investment casting technique.
12. Simpie plaster molds can be made in the school shop. Develop several small molds to cast such objects as buttons, toy soldiers, etc. Experiment with several gate arrangements until a satisfactory casting is made. Remember to wear protective clothing.
13. Contact a nearby foundry that uses the shell molding technique and request a mold sample. If this is not possible, secure a casting made by the process. Compare it with a sand mold casting and evaluate it with respect to:
   a. Surface finish.
   b. Dimensional accuracy.
   c. Flashing at the parting line.
   Prepare a short report on your findings.
14. Shell molds can be produced in the school shop. Investigate the possibilities of introducing the process in your school shop and, if possible, prepare a few experimental molds.
15. Prepare diagrams showing the manufacturing sequence of the shell molding technique, for reproduction by the spirit duplicator process. Present copies to members of your class. Such information may be secured from companies that make shell molds, or companies that manufacture the machines to make them.

Unit 15

WROUGHT METAL

Wrought ironwork originally consisted of those metal products formed and shaped by a blacksmith, Fig. 15-1. The work was not only decorative, it was also highly functional, Fig. 15-2. Today iron hand railings, porch supports, and some forms of metal furniture, Fig. 15-3, are synonymous with wrought ironwork. Wrought ironwork is also known as ornamental ironwork and bench metal.

Wrought iron is almost pure iron with most of the carbon removed. It is easily bent, hot or cold, and may be readily welded. However, many hot rolled steel shapes can be and are frequently used for contemporary wrought ironwork because they are less costly.

BENDING AND FORMING WITH HAND TOOLS

Metal bars, flats, and rods often need to be bent to usable shapes. Metal up to 1/4 in. thick can be

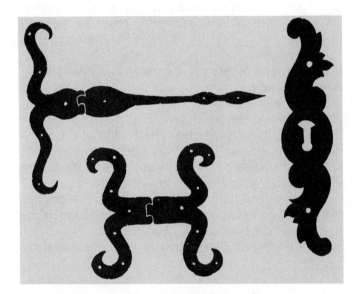

Fig. 15-2. Colonial wrought ironwork was functional as well as attractive.

Fig. 15-1. Wrought ironwork originally consisted of those metal objects made by the local blacksmith. He worked from a coal-fired forge with hammer, anvil, and tongs. (New York State Historical Association)

Fig. 15-3. Contemporary ironwork.

bent cold. Heavier sections should be heated.

While the metal rods may be cut with a hacksaw, considerable time can be saved if a ROD PARTER, Fig. 15-4, is used. The cutting head is designed to accommodate several different rod sizes. The rod is inserted into the appropriate opening and with the application of pressure the rod is sheared or cut.

BENDING ANGLES

Several factors must be considered when making a bend in metal:

1. Allowance must be made in the layout for the thickness of the metal. One-half of its thickness must be added to the length for each bend.
2. If several bends must be made in the same piece, the bending sequence must be planned beforehand, Fig. 15-5, or difficulties may be encountered.

Most metal bends can be made in a heavy vise. After making the layout, place the metal in the vise with the extra material allowed for the bend projecting above the vise jaws, Fig. 15-6. Start the bend by striking the metal with the flat of the hammer near the vise, Fig. 15-7. Square the bend, if it is a right angle bend, by placing the metal in the vise parallel with the vise jaw, Fig. 15-8.

Acute angles (angles less than 90 degrees) are made by squeezing the metal in a vise after the initial bend has been made, Fig. 15-9.

Angular bends can be made in sheet metal by

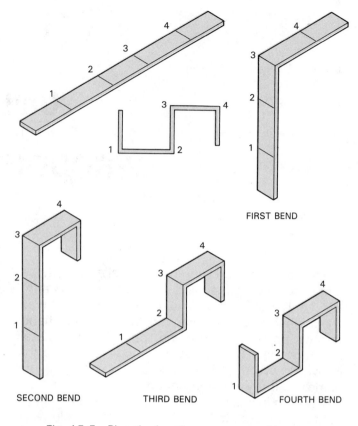

FIRST BEND

SECOND BEND   THIRD BEND   FOURTH BEND

Fig. 15-5. Plan the bending sequence with care.

Fig. 15-4. Metal rod being cut with a rod parter.

Fig. 15-6. An allowance of one-half the metal thickness must be added to the total length of the piece for each bend. The section with this additional length is placed above the vise.

Fig. 15-7. Start the bend by striking the metal close to the vise.

placing the metal between two pieces of angle iron or wooden blocks held in a vise, and using a mallet to make the bend, Fig. 15-10.

TWISTING METAL

Metal is, at times, twisted to permit it to be fastened, for additional stiffness, or to break the monotony of a long flat surface, Fig. 15-11.

Lay out the section to be twisted. As the length of the metal decreases when it is twisted, cut the piece slightly longer than the desired length of the finished piece. Short pieces should be clamped vertically in the vise; long strips should be clamped in a horizontal position. Place the lower limit mark even with the top of the vise jaw, Fig. 15-12. Place a monkey wrench at the other limit mark and rotate it to twist the metal, Fig. 15-13. A piece of pipe

Fig. 15-8. Square the bend by placing the piece in the vise parallel to the jaws.

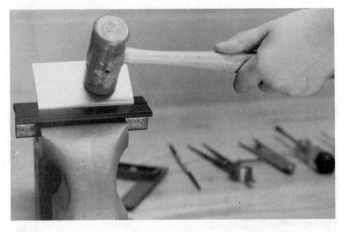

Fig. 15-10. When bending thin metal, mount it between two pieces of angle iron or blocks of hardwood.

Fig. 15-9. Acute angles are made in the vise after the initial bend has been made.

Fig. 15-11. Twisted sections.

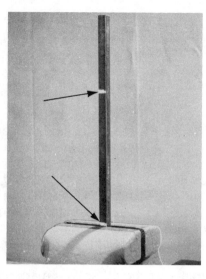

Fig. 15-12. The lower limit mark is placed flush with the vise jaws.

Fig. 15-13. The monkey wrench is placed even with the upper limit mark.

slipped over long sections will help keep them from bending out of line during the twisting operation. Rotate the wrench clockwise for a right hand twist; counterclockwise for a left hand twist.

Minor straightening of a twisted section can be done with a mallet.

BENDING CIRCULAR SHAPES

Curved sections can be made over the edge or horn of the anvil or with a bending jig or bending fork, Fig. 15-14. Whatever method is used, it is advisable to make a full-size pattern of the required

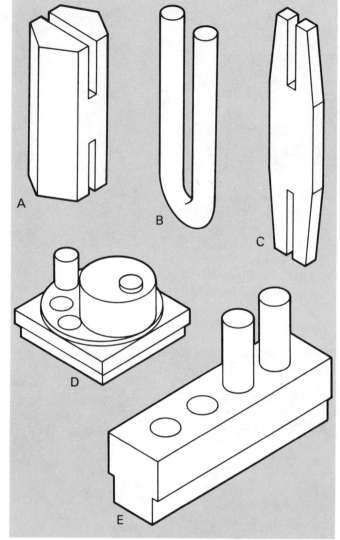

Fig. 15-14. Bending jigs. A—Hexagonal bar with slots for bending. B—Bending fork. C—Bending fork machined from flat metal stock. D—Adjustable bending device. E—Bending block with movable pins.

curved section, Fig. 15-15. This is used to check the curves during the bending operation.

The SCROLL is a curved section widely used for decorative purposes. It is not a true circle but a curve with a constantly expanding radius—something like a loose clock spring, Fig. 15-16. The scroll is made by placing the metal in a bending jig and applying pressure to start the curve, Fig. 15-17. After starting the bend, the operation is repeated to form one portion of the scroll at a time until it is completed, Fig. 15-18. Check the curve against the pattern from time to time to assure accuracy.

Some scroll applications require the starting end of the section to be flared or decorated, Fig. 15-19. This must be done before starting the bending operation.

Often a scroll is required on both ends of the

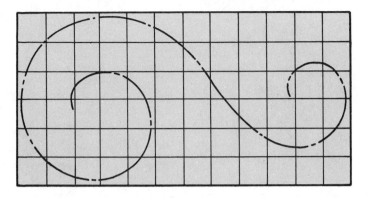

Fig. 15-15. Make a full-size pattern or layout of the desired curved section.

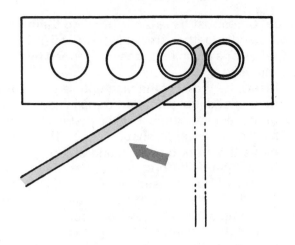

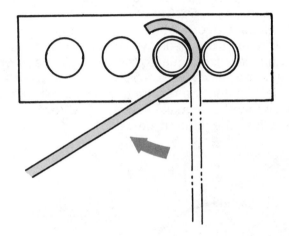

Fig. 15-18. One section of the scroll is bent at a time.

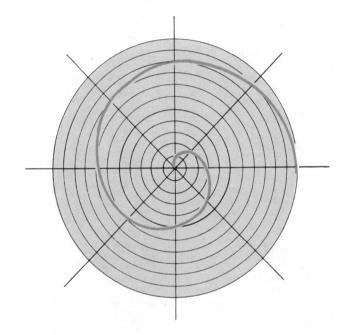

Fig. 15-16. A scroll.

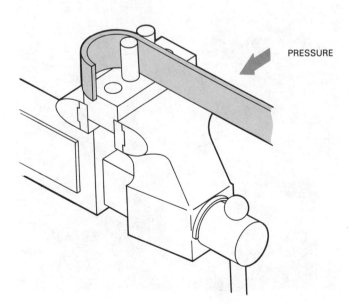

PRESSURE

Fig. 15-17. Bending a scroll.

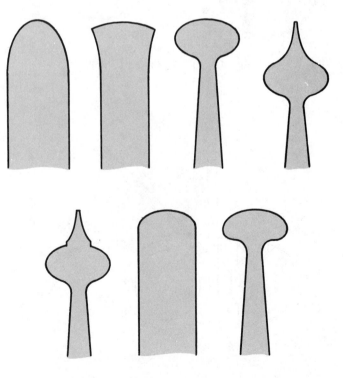

Fig. 15-19. Typical scroll ends.

piece. Care must be taken in bending them so that they blend together smoothly, Fig. 15-20.

Curves of a given radius can be formed by several techniques:

1. Place the work in the vise with a piece of rod or pipe of equal diameter to the inside diameter of the required curve. Pull the metal forward and as the curve takes shape, loosen the vise and move the work further in and around the pipe. Reclamp it as before, and repeat the operation until the curved section is completed, Fig. 15-21. The same technique can be used to shape an eye on the end of a rod, Fig. 15-22.
2. Shape the curve by bending it over a piece of pipe or rod (of the correct diameter) held in a vise, Fig. 15-23.
3. Bend it over a stake, Fig. 15-24.

Wire rings are made by bending wire around a rod with a diameter equal to the inside diameter of the ring to form a coil, Fig. 15-25. The coil is cut along its length and the resulting rings can be closed or fitted together to make a section of wire chain. Weld or solder the joints if desired.

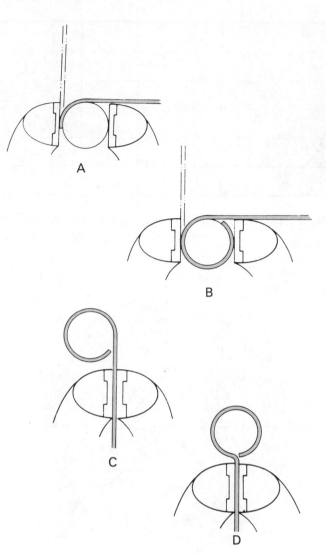

Fig. 15-22. Forming an eye.

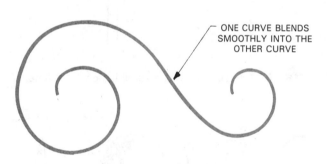

ONE CURVE BLENDS SMOOTHLY INTO THE OTHER CURVE

Fig. 15-20. Double end scroll.

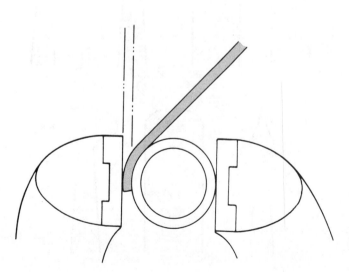

Fig. 15-21. Forming a radius in a vise.

Fig. 15-23. Bending over a metal rod.

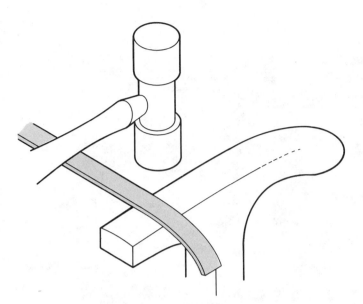

Fig. 15-24. Bending over a stake.

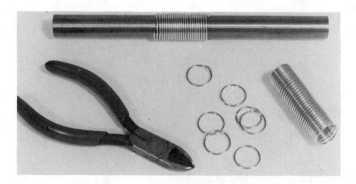

Fig. 15-25. Materials needed for forming a wire coil.

BENDING AND FORMING WITH SPECIAL TOOLS

Several bending machines have been developed that have light production and school shop applications. All of them, basically, are means of applying power either manually or mechanically to perform the bending operation.

When using bending machines, certain elementary principles must be observed:
1. Plan the bending sequence BEFORE cutting the metal. Do not fail to make allowances for the bends.
2. Select material sizes that will provide sufficient strength and rigidity and yet permit satisfactory bending.
3. Use the largest bend radius that is practical for the job. This will often produce a better bend in both strength and appearance.
4. The smallest recommended radius for bending tubing is one and one-half times its outside

diameter measured on the centerline of the tubing provided an inside mandrel is used during bending. The bend radius must be increased to two and one-half times the tubing diameter if no mandrel is used.
5. When making a bend at the end of a piece of tubing, allow sufficient metal for trimming, otherwise, the tubing will flatten.
6. Allow for metal springback when planning a bend. Use a bending form with a radius slightly smaller than the required radius. As springback varies with metal thickness, sample bends may have to be made to determine the proper size bending form needed.
7. Study instruction for machine being used.

METAL FORMER

A metal forming device, Fig. 15-26, is a modified machinist's vise to which forming rolls have been adapted. The design provides accurate control of the work. Various interchangeable accessories permit the tool to be used to bend, shape, and form tubing, rods, and sheet into intricate shapes.

HOSSFELD UNIVERSAL BENDER

The HOSSFELD BENDER, Fig. 15-27, is designed to permit bar, angle iron, rod, and pipe to be bent into many and varied shapes. No tool changes are needed to bend the various sizes and shapes.

Bender setups for making various bends are illustrated in Figs. 15-28, 15-29, and 15-30.

DI-ACRO BENDER

DI-ACRO BENDERS, both hand and power operated, have identical operating characteristics.

Fig. 15-26. This metal forming device may be fitted to existing vises. Scrolls and bends can be repeated with accuracy. (Hossfeld Mfg. Co.)

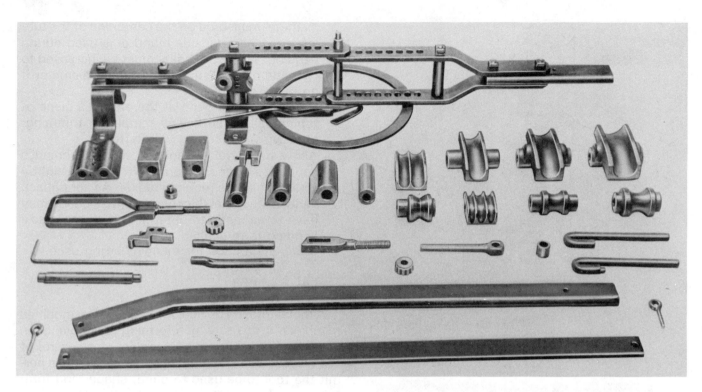

Fig. 15-27. Universal bender with a few of the attachments available. (Hossfeld Mfg. Co.)

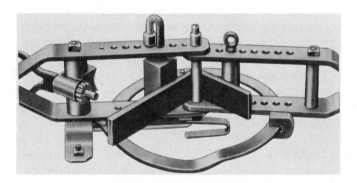

Fig. 15-28. Technique used to bend flat stock.

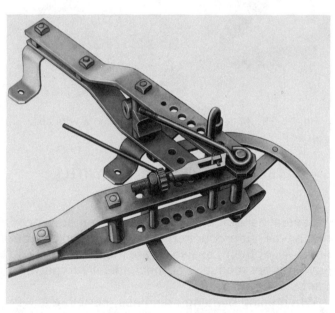

Fig. 15-30. Setup for bending an eye.

Fig. 15-29. Bending flat stock into a radius.

Fig. 15-31 illustrates the basic parts of the machine series.

These machines can be adapted to produce a variety of bends, and handle different shapes of metal by interchanging the various radius forming accessories and forming noses, Fig. 15-32. Special attachments are available for tube bending. Several

Fig. 15-31. The Di-Acro bender.

Fig. 15-32. Accessory blocks for the Di-Acro bender.

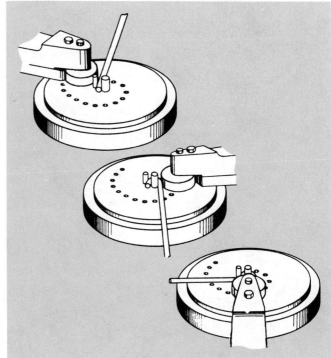

Fig. 15-33. Using Di-Acro bender for off-center eye bending.

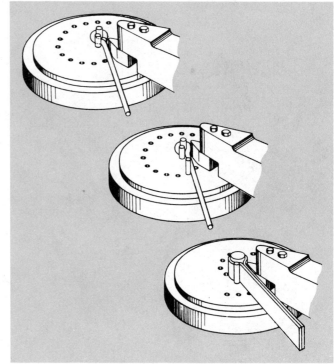

Fig. 15-34. Alternate methods of centered eye bending.

of the accessories are shown in use in Figs. 15-33 through 15-37.

ASSEMBLING WROUGHT IRONWORK

Wrought iron pieces may be assembled by various methods depending on the design of the piece and the facilities available.

RIVETING

Rivets are frequently used to assemble this kind of work. Fig. 15-38 illustrates riveting techniques. Note how the length of the rivet shank differs between the round and flat head rivet styles.

WELDING

Oxyacetylene and electric arc welding are also widely used to assemble modern wrought ironwork. Welding procedures are explained in detail in Unit 18.

FINISHING

Originally, wrought ironwork acquired a surface texture (finish) when the rough iron pieces were forged to usable sizes before shaping. With the availability of a large range of standard sizes, it was no longer necessary to forge rough stock to size

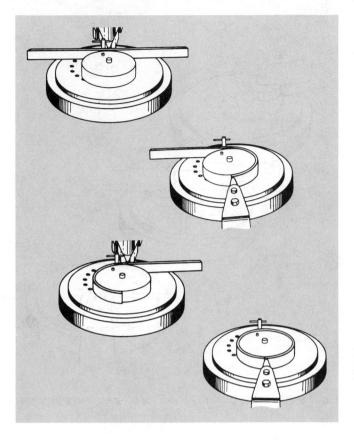

Fig. 15-35. Using Di-Acro bender for bending circles.

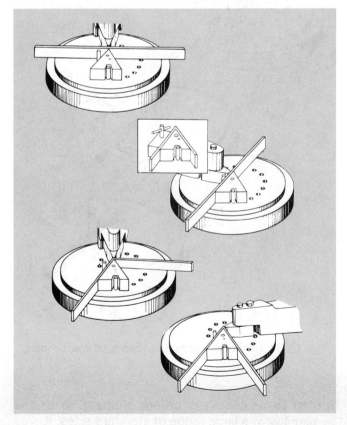

Fig. 15-36. Forming sharp zero radius bends.

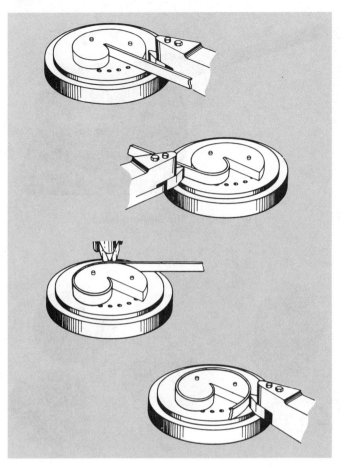

Fig. 15-37. Scrolls and other shapes of irregular radii can be formed with bender by using collar having same contour as the shape to be formed.

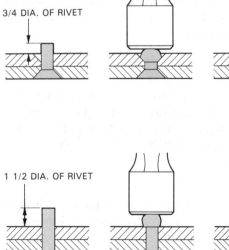

3/4 DIA. OF RIVET

1 1/2 DIA. OF RIVET

BALL PEEN HAMMER

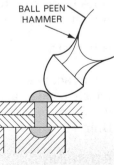

RIVET SET

Fig. 15-38. Setting rivets.

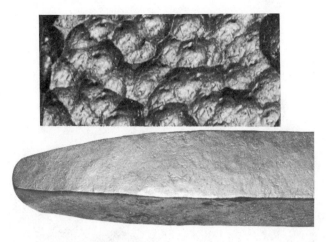

Fig. 15-39. Top. Close-up of a peened surface. Bottom. Type of finish acquired when metal is forged to size. Notice how much more pleasing it is to the eye than the peened surface.

before shaping. The resulting smooth surfaces brought about the development of peening to apply surface texture, Fig. 15-39. While peening is not an honest finish (a surface acquired during the sizing and shaping of the rough metal), it has received considerable acceptance and is widely used as the surface treatment on contemporary ironwork.

Most work of this nature is finished with a flat black lacquer or paint. These produce an acceptable effect without the trouble or mess of the older scorched oil finishes.

SAFETY

1. Remove burrs from the stock before attempting to make bends.
2. Have any cuts, bruises, and burns treated promptly.
3. Keep fingers clear of moving bender parts.
4. Do not use a bending machine without studying or receiving instructions, or checking over the machine.
5. Wear approved safety glasses when cutting metal with a chisel or when operating the grinder.
6. Use extreme care when handling long sections of small diameter rods. Carelessness can cause serious injury to nearby persons.
7. Finishing materials are never used near an open flame nor in an area that is not properly ven-

tilated. Store oily and solvent soaked rags in a closed container.

TEST YOUR KNOWLEDGE, Unit 15

Please do not write in the text. Place your answers on a separate piece of paper.
1. Wrought ironwork is also known as _____.
2. Metal up to _____ in. thick can usually be bent cold.
3. An allowance of _____ the thickness of the metal must be added to the length of the piece for each bend.
4. Wrought metal sections are twisted:
   a. To permit a suitable point of attachment.
   b. For additional stiffness.
   c. To break the monotony of a long flat section.
   d. All of the above.
   e. None of the above.
5. The scroll is widely used for _____.
6. When forming a scroll it is suggested that a _____.
7. Describe how wire rings are made. Use sketches if helpful.
8. Most wrought ironwork is finished by:
   a. Filing the rough edges smooth.
   b. Applying a flat black lacquer or paint.
   c. Hammering marks on exposed surfaces.
   d. All of the above.
   e. None of the above.

RESEARCH AND DEVELOPMENT

1. Visit a nearby museum and sketch or photograph early wrought ironwork. Develop a bulletin board display around the sketches.
2. Prepare a display panel showing the proper sequence to follow when developing and making a double end scroll.
3. Secure catalogs from historic developments (Williamsburg, Cooperstown, Greenfield Village, Old Sturbridge Village, etc.) and develop wrought-iron projects adaptable to the school shop based on the drawings and photos presented in the catalogs.
4. Investigate the use of metal benders in local industries. Secure samples of their work and devise ways to duplicate them in the school shop.

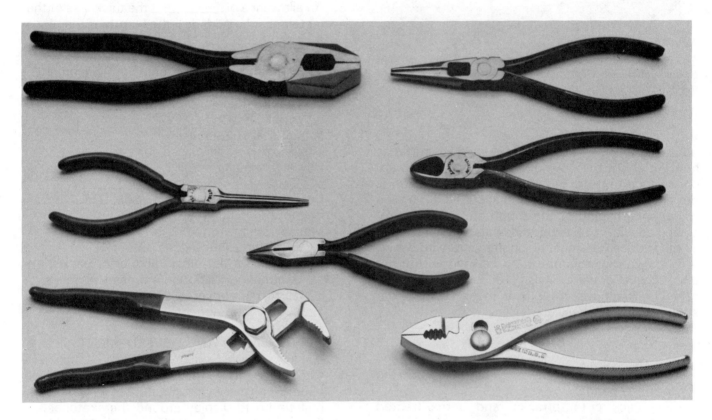

Top quality hand tools are forged to shape rather than cast. Pictured are a few of the many types and sizes of forged pliers available to the craftworker. How many of the pliers can you identify?

Unit 16

FORGING

FORGING is the process of using pressure to shape metal. The pressure may be applied with a hammering action or by squeezing or compression forces. In some forging techniques the metal is heated (but not to the melting point) to make it easier to shape. HAND FORGING is one of the many aspects of this metal shaping technique, and was in use long before written records were kept.

EQUIPMENT FOR HAND FORGING

As with other metalworking processes, special tools peculiar to hand forging have been devised.

FORGE

The FORGE, Fig. 16-1, is used to heat the metal prior to forging. It may be fired by gas or coal.

However, gas is usually used because it is a cleaner burning fuel.

ANVIL

Heated metal is shaped on an ANVIL, Fig. 16-2. Circular shapes are formed over the anvil HORN. Various tools may be mounted in the HARDY HOLE. The PRITCHEL HOLE is used for punching holes and for bending small diameter rods.

The anvil must be mounted on a solid base.

TONGS

While being shaped, the hot metal is held with TONGS. They are manufactured in many shapes and sizes. The tongs most frequently used are shown in Fig. 16-3. It is important to use tongs that fit the work, Fig. 16-4.

Fig. 16-1. A gas-fired forge is clean and temperatures can be easily controlled. (Johnson Gas Appliance Co.)

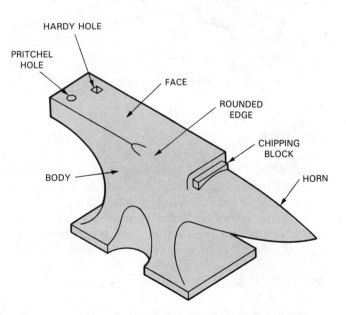

Fig. 16-2. This anvil is used for hand forging.

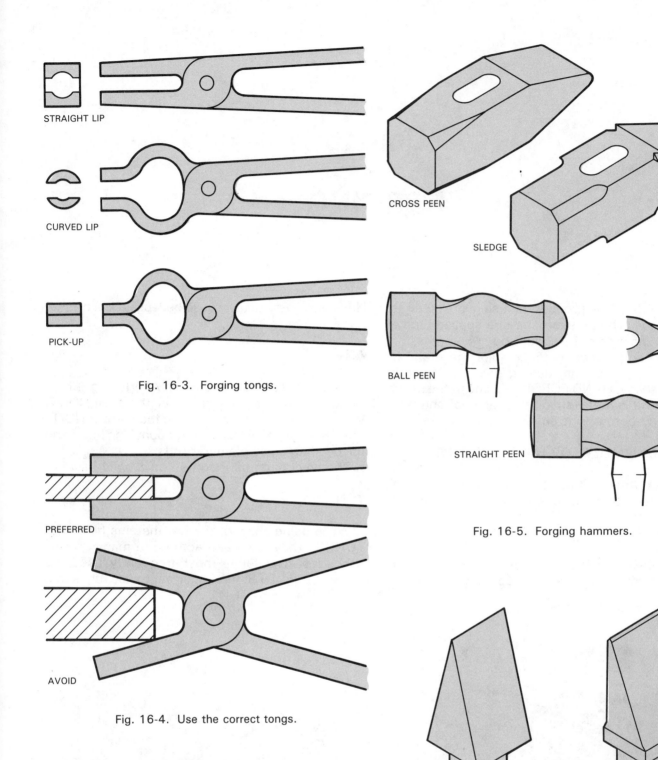

STRAIGHT LIP

CURVED LIP

PICK-UP

Fig. 16-3. Forging tongs.

PREFERRED

AVOID

Fig. 16-4. Use the correct tongs.

CROSS PEEN

SLEDGE

BALL PEEN

STRAIGHT PEEN

Fig. 16-5. Forging hammers.

Fig. 16-6. Hardies.

HAMMERS

HAMMERS of many shapes and sizes are used in hand forging, Fig. 16-5. A 1 1/2 or 2 lb. hammer is suitable for light work, while a 3 lb. hammer will be satisfactory for larger or heavier work. Avoid ''choking-up'' on the handle. Too much power is wasted when the hammer is held in this manner.

ANVIL TOOLS

Numerous anvil tools are available. Many of them have been designed to fit the hardy hole of the an-

vil. HARDIES, Fig. 16-6, are useful for cutting hot and cold metal. The square hole is placed in the hardy hole, and the metal to be cut is placed on the cutting edge and struck with a hammer. The metal is nicked on both sides, and bent back and forth until it breaks. Metal thicker than 1/2 in. (12.7 mm) should be cut hot.

CHISELS, Fig. 16-7, are used to cut metal in much the same way as the hardy. However, they have handles for safer and easier manipulation.

The HOT CHISEL is thinner than the COLD CHISEL and, as the name implies, is used to cut hot metal.

Holes can be made in hot metal with a PUNCH, Fig. 16-8. Punches are made in many sizes and shapes.

LIGHTING A GAS FORGE

The following procedure is recommended to safely light a gas forge:
1. Be sure the gas valve is closed.
2. Open the forge door if it is fitted with one.

3. Start the air blower and open the air valve slightly.
4. Apply the lighter and SLOWLY turn on the gas. CAUTION: DO NOT ATTEMPT TO LIGHT THE FORGE WITH A MATCH. Also, stand to one side and avoid looking into the forge when you start it.
5. When the gas has ignited, adjust the gas and air valves for the best combination of economy of operation and heat-up speed.

FORGING

Metal must be heated to the proper temperature before it can be forged easily. A bright red heat is needed for most mild steels. Tool steel must not be heated to more than a dull red, or it may lose many of its desirable characteristics. NEVER permit the metal to come to a white heat where sparks fly from the piece.

HOW TO DRAW OUT METAL

DRAWING OUT means the metal is stretched or lengthened by the forging operation. Round stock is drawn out as shown in the sequence in Fig. 16-9. Square stock must be rounded off as the first step in the drawing out process. If this is not done, the metal has a tendency to split or crack on the edges, or to become distorted.

Round stock can be drawn out to a point, as shown in Fig. 16-10.

HOW TO BEND METAL

A bend can be made in a piece of stock by one of several methods. In all methods the metal must

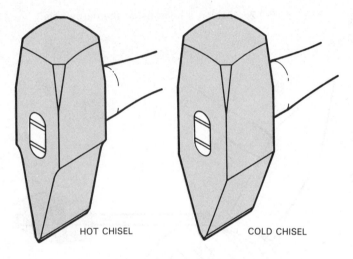

HOT CHISEL   COLD CHISEL

Fig. 16-7. Forging chisels.

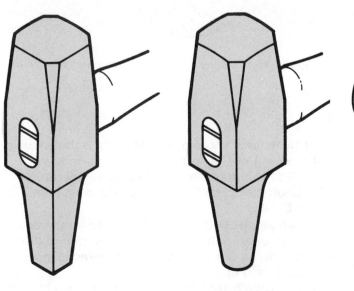

Fig. 16-8. Forging punches.

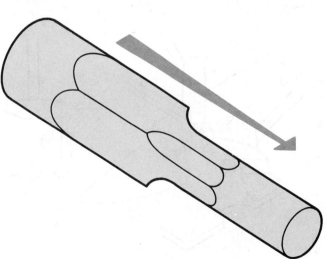

Fig. 16-9. Drawing out sequence.

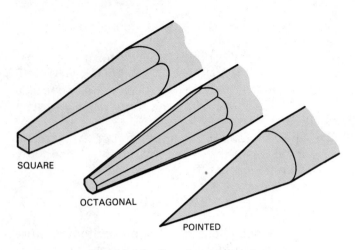

SQUARE

OCTAGONAL

POINTED

Fig. 16-10. Drawing out a point.

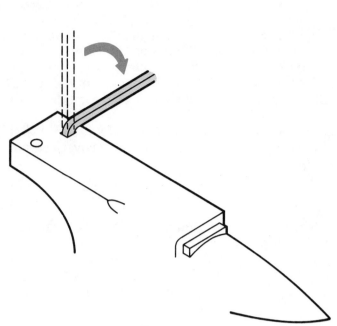

Fig. 16-12. Making a bend using the hardy hole.

be heated until red.

1. Place the work over the anvil face so that the point of the bend is located where the face edge is rounded, Fig. 16-11. Strike the extended section until it assumes the desired angle. Square off the bend over the anvil edge.

2. Place the heated metal into the hardy or pritchel hole and bend with tongs, Fig. 16-12.

3. Thin sections of metal can be bent in the vise without being heated. Heavier sections must be heated. A pipe may be fitted over the extended portion of the metal for improved leverage.

4. Curved sections are formed over the anvil horn. Place the heated metal over the horn at the most suitable point for the work being done. Shape by striking hammer blows as shown in Fig. 16-13.

HOW METAL IS UPSET

UPSET is the term used to describe the forging operation that thickens or bulges the piece and, at

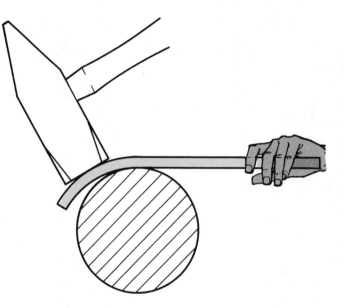

Fig. 16-13. Forming a circular section on an anvil horn.

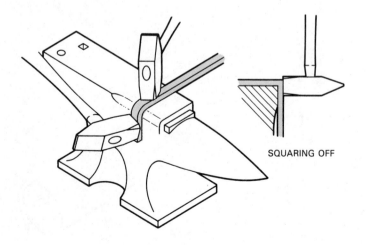

SQUARING OFF

Fig. 16-11. Bending on the anvil.

the same time, shortens it. Upsetting is the opposite of drawing out. The procedure is as follows:

1. Heat the metal to the desired temperature.

2. Short pieces can be upset on the anvil face, Fig. 16-14.

3. Longer pieces can be held in a vise for the upsetting operation. The heated section extends above the vise jaws and is hammered to increase its size, Fig. 16-15.

4. Long and heavy metal bars can be upset by ramming the heated end against the anvil face.

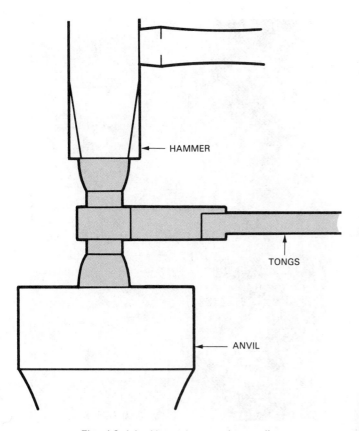

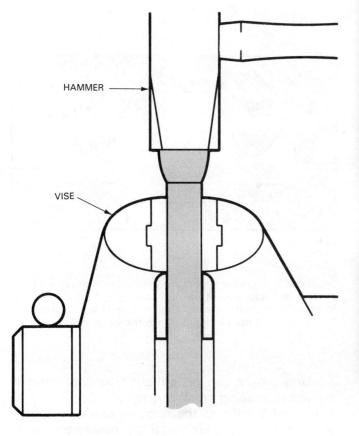

Fig. 16-14. Upsetting on the anvil.

Fig. 16-15. Upsetting in a vise.

INDUSTRIAL FORGING PROCESSES

Forging, Fig. 16-16, is one of the few metalworking processes that improves the physical characteristics of most metals. A forged piece of metal is stronger than an identical piece that has been cast or machined from a solid bar of metal, Fig. 16-17.

DROP FORGING

The flat hammer and anvil of the SMITH or OPEN DIE FORGE, are shown in Fig. 16-18. In open die forging, the work is manipulated by hand. This is used mostly for ''rough'' work that needs additional forging or machining.

The DROP FORGE, Fig. 16-19, is a refinement of the open die technique. Dies, Fig. 16-20, replace the hammer and anvil and can shape metal to much closer tolerances.

Fig. 16-16. Forging is one of the few metalworking processes that improves the physical characteristics of most metals. Shown is a 10,000 ton forging press.
(Aluminum Company of America)

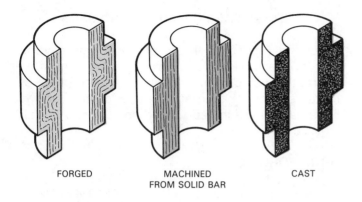

FORGED   MACHINED   CAST
FROM SOLID BAR

Fig. 16-17. A forged piece is stronger than an identical piece that has been cast or machined from a solid bar of metal.

Fig. 16-19. A drop forge and die shaping a blank of aluminum. (Mueller Brass Co.)

Fig. 16-18. A smith, or open die, forging press. (Mueller Brass Co.)

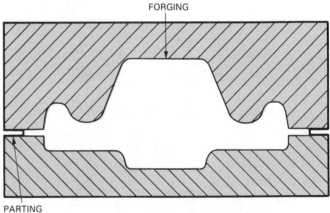

Fig. 16-20. A double impression forging die. This type die has part of the impression of the desired forging sunk (machined) in each die in such a manner that no part of one die projects past the parting line into the other die.

Several methods have been devised to apply the pressure. The simplest is gravity. This system operates by alternating lifting to a set height and dropping the hammer, or in the case of the drop forge, the upper die block. In the latter, the lower half of the die block is positioned between rails that guide the upper die block. The force of the blow is determined by the weight of the hammer, or the assembly that houses the upper die block, and the height from which it drops. This, and because only uniform blows can be obtained, gravity drop is limited to making small forgings.

A large portion of the forgings made today are such that they require variable pressure blows, or are so large they need more pressure to shape them than can be delivered by the gravity forging machine. For these forgings, the STEAM AND AIR DROP HAMMER, Fig. 16-21, has been developed. Steam or air pressure is used to drive the upper die assembly against the metal blank in the lower die. The operator is able to control the amount of pressure and the distance of the drop. This enables the force of the blow to be varied for blocking, shaping, and finishing as required for the job being done.

DIES are made from specially hardened high strength steel. In addition to the cavity which forms the finished forging (part of it in each die) there may be additional cavities included to shape the piece gradually, Fig. 16-22. To assure complete filling of the die, the forging blank is purposely increased in volume. The surplus metal forms a FLASH at the parting line of the dies and must be removed. This operation is called TRIMMING.

PRESS FORGING

PRESS FORGING, Fig. 16-23, also known as PRESSING, NO—DRAFT FORGING, or PRECISION FORGING, is a variation of conventional forging in that the metal is shaped by the gradual application

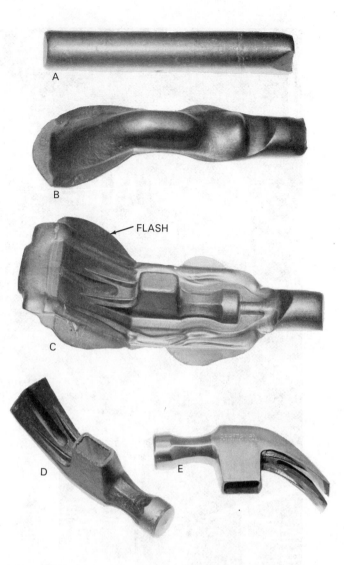

Fig. 16-22. Sequence followed in forging a hammer head. A—Piece of high carbon steel sheared to length. B—After heating the blank is forged to rough shape. C—Further heating and forging brings the blank to this shape. Note the flashing. The opening for the handle is partially made in the underside. D—The handle opening is completed and the flashing has been trimmed (removed). E—The completed hammer head. The forging has been heat-treated and polished.

of pressure rather than by impact. It is sometimes used with drop forging to bring the work to final size when a smooth finish and close tolerances are specified. This is expensive compared with conventional forging because the process is slow, requires costly precision dies, and has a relatively long development time. But the techniques often reduce, or eliminate, machining requirements.

Most press forging is done for the aerospace industries, Fig. 16-24.

ROLL FORGING

ROLLING and UPSETTING are two forging techniques often used together to produce such

Fig. 16-21. This 35,000 lb. steam hammer is being used to forge an aircraft engine crankcase.

Fig. 16-23. Two giant forging presses for making aluminum forgings. A 50,000 ton press is in the foreground and a 35,000 ton press can be seen in the background. (Aluminum Company of America)

products as auto and truck axles.

Rolls of the desired shape reduce short thick metal sections into long slender sections. See Fig. 16-25. Upsetting may be employed to complete the shaping operation. Since only a portion of the stock can be upset without buckling, several passes may have to be made in the dies to produce the required shape. See Fig. 16-26.

INTERMITTENT ROLLING, Fig. 16-27, is a forging technique that is often used to form metal rod into sections suitable for drop forging or pressing.

Fig. 16-24. This aircraft wing spar is a 23 ft. long press forging.   (Aluminum Company of America)

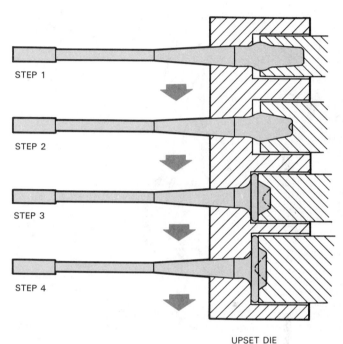

STEP 1

STEP 2

STEP 3

STEP 4

UPSET DIE

Fig. 16-26. Upsetting operations 1, 2, 3, and 4 at right show how a compact car axle is made.

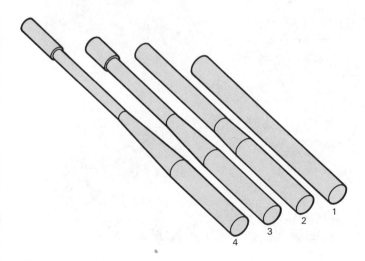

Fig. 16-25. In roll forging, a roll of the desired shape reduces a short thick metal section 1 into long slender sections 2, 3, and 4. Most auto and truck axles are made this way.

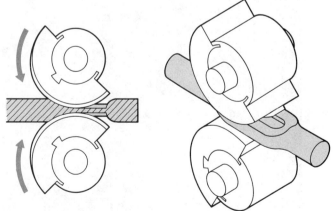

Fig. 16-27. Intermittent rolling is a forging technique that is often used to form metal rod into sections suitable for drop forging or pressing.

In CROSS FORGING, Fig. 16-28, metal is passed between two rolls, each containing a wedge that gradually shapes the stock. Only simple parts of axial symmetry can be formed.

COLD FORMING

COLD FORMING, also known as COLD HEADING and CHIPLESS MACHINING, Fig. 16-29, is a forging technique that uses a series of dies to replace

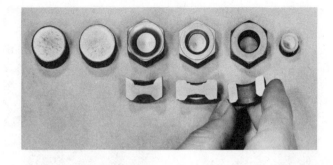

Fig. 16-30. Many fasteners are made by cold forming. Here the steps in making a hexagonal nut are illustrated. The small slug of metal to the upper right is the only waste. (National Machinery Company)

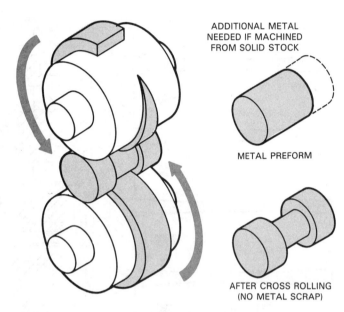

Fig. 16-28. In cross forging metal is passed between two rolls, each containing a wedge that gradually shapes the stock.

ADDITIONAL METAL NEEDED IF MACHINED FROM SOLID STOCK

METAL PREFORM

AFTER CROSS ROLLING (NO METAL SCRAP)

the conventional cutting tools of the lathe, drill press, and milling machine. The dies shape the metal and accuracy can be held to tolerances of 0.002 in. (0.05 mm). No chips are produced and scrap is kept to a minimum, Fig. 16-30.

The process is an economical and efficient way to make bolts, nuts, and other fasteners, Fig. 16-31. Almost all automotive spark plug bases are made this way.

Most metals can be cold formed. However, the ease by which metals like stainless steel, copper, and nickel alloys can be shaped depends on the design of the part being formed.

Metal up to 1/2 in. (12.7 mm) diameter used in cold form is referred to as WIRE. Larger material, up to 1 1/2 in. (38.1 mm), is used in ROD form.

There are five basic operations performed by

Fig. 16-29. In cold forming (often called chipless machining) a series of dies replace the usual cutting tools. The work is transferred from station to station to permit the various operations to be performed. Scrap is eliminated or kept to a minimum. Here a nut is being shaped. (National Machinery Company)

machines designed for the cold forming process, Fig. 16-32. Combinations and variations of these basic operations permit highly complex shapes to be formed.

The sequence of steps needed to produce bolts by this forging technique is shown in Fig. 16-33.

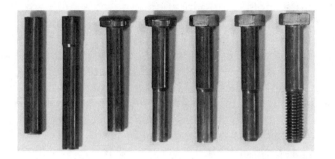

Fig. 16-31. The steps in forming a machine bolt. Note there is no waste.

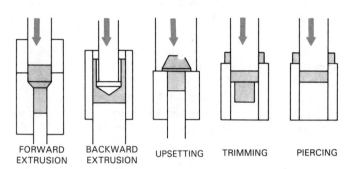

FORWARD EXTRUSION BACKWARD EXTRUSION UPSETTING TRIMMING PIERCING

Fig. 16-32. The five basic operations performed by machines designed for the cold forming process.

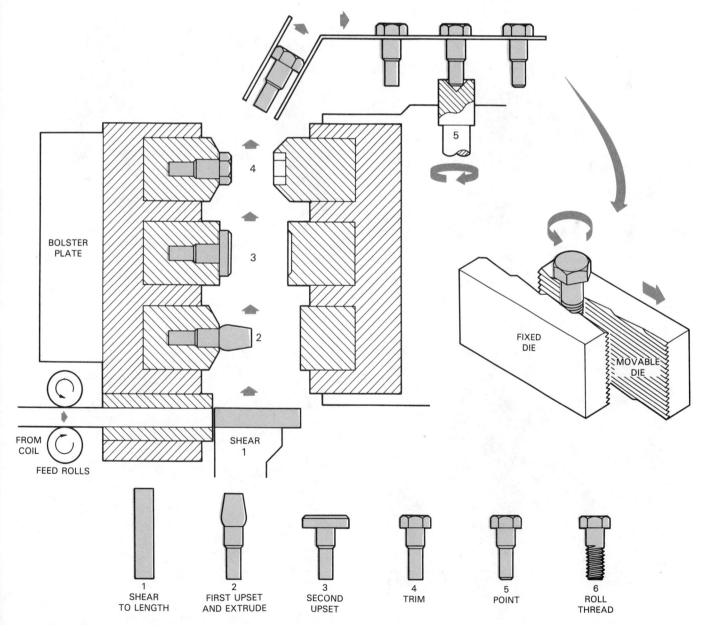

BOLSTER PLATE

5

FIXED DIE

MOVABLE DIE

4

3

2

SHEAR 1

FROM COIL

FEED ROLLS

1 SHEAR TO LENGTH

2 FIRST UPSET AND EXTRUDE

3 SECOND UPSET

4 TRIM

5 POINT

6 ROLL THREAD

Fig. 16-33. Heavy arrows and number indicate the sequence involved in producing bolts by chipless machining.

INTRAFORM

INTRAFORM (Cincinnati Milacron Trademark) is a SWAGING process. Swaging is a form of forging in which metal is formed by a series of rapid hammerlike blows. Intraform is a development of chipless machining that makes it possible to form profiles on the inside diameter(s) of cylindrical pieces that would be extremely difficult and expensive to produce by other means.

In this process a piece of hollow cylindrical stock is placed over a steel mandrel, Fig. 16-34, and is squeezed by rapidly pulsating dies, Fig. 16-35. At the completion of the operation, the profile of the mandrel has been produced on the inside diameter of the part, Fig. 16-36. Stock diameter has also been reduced. As Fig. 16-37 shows, fixed rolls cause the four dies to pulsate rapidly around the outside diameter of the work. The tops of the cams are shaped to permit a smooth continuous squeezing action of the dies. And even though the work is being squeezed by the dies more than 1000 times per minute, noise and vibration are not a problem. A cross section of the Intraform machine is shown in Fig. 16-38.

This technique has proven to be a practical way to produce rifle barrels. Predrilled steel blanks are fed into the machine which forms the chamber and rifling. In addition to improving the surface finish of the bore, the operation also improves the physical characteristics of the metal.

A typical Intraform sequence is shown in Fig. 16-39, Fig. 16-40, and Fig. 16-41.

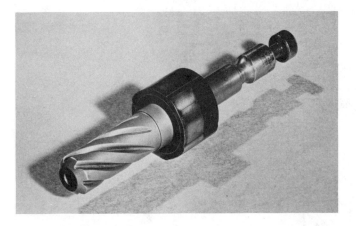

Fig. 16-34. Two-piece Intraform mandrel used in the production of automotive starter clutch housing. (Cincinnati Milacron)

Fig. 16-36. Clutch housing and sectioned part showing helical spline and cam clutch profile which was formed in one operation, at a production rate of 220 parts per hour.

Fig. 16-35. Dies used in the production of automotive starter clutch housing.

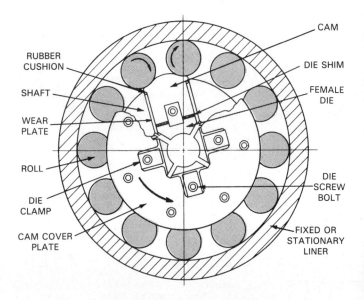

RUBBER CUSHION

SHAFT

WEAR PLATE

ROLL

DIE CLAMP

CAM COVER PLATE

CAM

DIE SHIM

FEMALE DIE

DIE SCREW BOLT

FIXED OR STATIONARY LINER

Fig. 16-37. A drawing of the die head of the Intraform machine. It is in the open position.

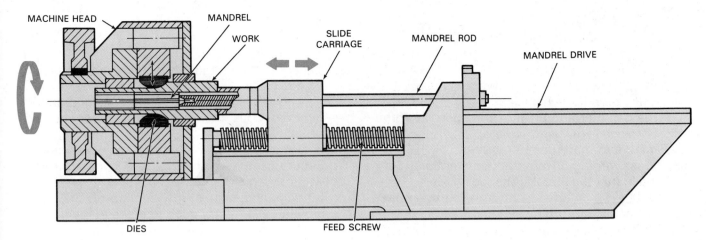

Fig. 16-38. A cross-sectional view of the Intraform machine.

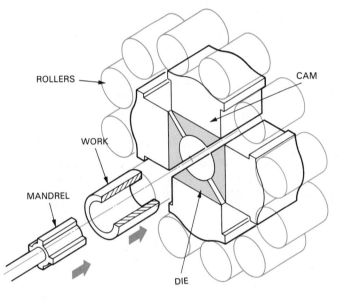

Fig. 16-39. Work ready to be formed by Intraform process.

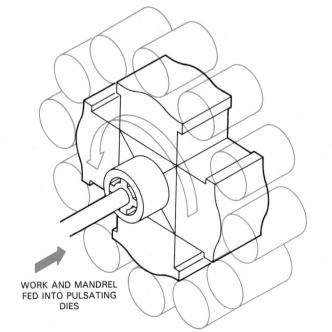

Fig. 16-40. Work and mandrel between Intraform dies. Contact with rotating dies causes freewheeling work (and mandrel) to revolve at about 80 percent of die rpm. Work feeds over mandrel.

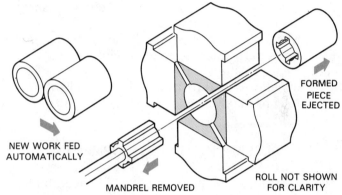

Fig. 16-41. When the operation is completed the mandrel is retracted. The next piece feeds into position and the formed piece is ejected.

TEST YOUR KNOWLEDGE, Unit 16

Please do not write in the text. Place your answers on a separate sheet of paper.

1. Describe the forging process.
2. The forge is used to _____. It may be _____ or _____ fired.
3. Make a sketch of an anvil. Label the parts.
4. For best forging conditions, mild steel should be heated to a _____.
5. Of what use are tongs in forging?
6. What is the recommended procedure for safely lighting a gas-fired forge?
7. Drawing out a piece of metal means:
   a. It has been shortened.
   b. It has been lengthened.
   c. It has been bulged or enlarged.
   d. None of the above.
8. Upsetting means:
   a. The opposite of drawing out.
   b. It has been stretched or lengthened.
   c. It has been forged to a circular shape.
   d. None of the above.

Forging 229

9. Forging _____ the physical characteristics of most metals.
10. In open die forging, the work is _____.
11. In the drop forge technique _____ replace the hammer and anvil of the open die forge.
12. Forgings are used where _____ and minimum material are required.
13. Press forging differs from conventional forging in that the metal is shaped by the _____ _____ rather than by impact.
14. Describe roll forging.
15. Cold forming is also known as _____ heading and _____ machining. It is a forging technique where a series of _____ replace conventional cutting tools.
16. This process is called _____ machining because _____ are produced and scrap is kept to a minimum.
17. Make a sketch showing the five basic operations performed in cold forming.
18. Describe the INTRAFORM process.
19. Intraform has proven to be an excellent way to produce certain automotive parts and _____.

RESEARCH AND DEVELOPMENT

1. What does the term ''plasticity'' mean as applied to the forging process?
2. Experiment with the forging process by making a cold chisel.
   a. How does the metal work if forged cold?
   b. How does the metal work when heated properly?
   c. What happens if the metal is overheated?
3. Secure sample of forgings and compare them with castings. Contact a company that produces forgings and request information on the techniques the industry uses to make etched cross sections of forged pieces to show grain structure and grain flow.
4. Make a poster or chart with an automobile as the theme. Around the illustration list the various auto parts that are made by forging. Run colored twine or cord from the part name to the location where it is used.
5. Secure samples of small forgings made from brass, aluminum, and steel. Locate and mark the die parting lines. Why are they located where they are?
6. Secure samples of work produced by cold forming. Mount the samples on a display panel with an explanation of the chipless machining process used to make them.
7. Prepare a display that illustrates the five basic cold forming processes.

Unit 17

SOLDERING AND BRAZING

Soldering is a method of joining metals with a nonferrous metal filler without having to heat them to a point where the base metals melt, Fig. 17-1. It is carried out at temperatures lower than 800 °F (427 °C).

As the strength of solder is relatively low, a well designed soldered joint should employ a lock seam or fold.

SOLDERING CONDITIONS

Before two metals can be joined by soldering, several conditions must be met:
1. The correct solder alloy must be used.
2. The proper flux must be applied.

3. An adequate source of heat must be available.
4. The surfaces to be soldered must be clean.

SOLDER

Solders are tin-lead alloys. A 50-50 alloy, that is, 50 percent tin and 50 percent lead (tin is always the first figure mentioned) is most commonly used. It melts at about 420 °F (215 °C). A 60-40 solder is suited for electrical work. A higher percentage of tin results in a lower melting temperature alloy.

Solder is available in solid wire, acid or resin core wire, and bar form, Fig. 17-2.

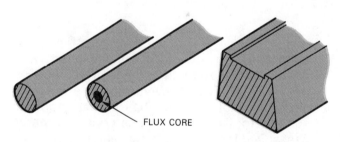

FLUX CORE

Fig. 17-2. Solder is available in solid wire, acid or resin core wire, and bar form.

FLUXES

All metals oxidize to some extent when exposed to the atmosphere. This film of tarnish or rust must be eliminated before the solder will adhere to the work surface.

A chemical mixture called FLUX is applied to the joint to remove the oxides, prevent further oxides from forming while the metal is heated to soldering temperature, and to lower the surface tension of the molten solder, enabling it to cover the area and to alloy with the work.

Fluxes fall into two categories: CORROSIVE and

Fig. 17-1. A technician is soldering a few of the hundreds of connections in this circuit board. Much skill is required. Otherwise, a solder "bridge" might be produced between two connections and a short circuit would result. The circuit board could be damaged and require expensive and time-consuming repairs.   (Bell Telephone Laboratories)

NONCORROSIVE. Corrosive fluxes (acid) are more effective for some purposes. After soldering, however, the residue encourages oxidation that may cause the eventual failure of the soldered joint. Joints soldered using corrosive fluxes should be cleaned with hot water after soldering.

Resin is a noncorrosive flux that works best on tin plate, solder coated surfaces, brass, and tin.

Aluminum can be soldered when a flux specifically designed for this material is used. Regular fluxes will not work.

It is advisable to use commercially prepared fluxes because of their consistent results rather than trying to prepare them in the shop.

SOLDERING DEVICES

There are many ways of applying heat to the metal surface:
1. SOLDERING COPPER, Fig. 17-3. A soldering copper is a square or octagonal shaped piece of

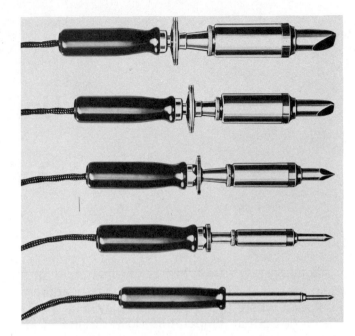

Fig. 17-4. Electric soldering coppers are available in a wide range of sizes. (American Electrical Heater Co.)

Fig. 17-3. A soldering copper of the type that must be heated by external means.

copper with a four-sided tapered point. It is heated by a blowtorch or a gas fired SOLDERING FURNACE, and is available in a range of sizes or weights. A one-half pound copper is suitable for light work. A one-pound copper is best suited for most work. Soldering coppers are usually purchased in pairs—one heats while the other is in use.
2. ELECTRIC SOLDERING COPPER, Fig. 17-4. This type is preferred if current is available, because it maintains a uniform heat. A 200-watt electric copper is suitable for most sheet metal work. The electric gun, Fig. 17-5, is used mostly for electric/electronic work.
3. GAS TORCH, Fig. 17-6. This self-contained heating unit makes it possible to solder directly without using the usual soldering copper.

CLEANLINESS

A dirty or oxidized surface cannot be soldered. Oily or greasy surfaces should be cleaned with a liquid cleaner. Oxidized surfaces are cleaned with abrasive cloth until they are bright.

Fig. 17-5. A soldering gun.

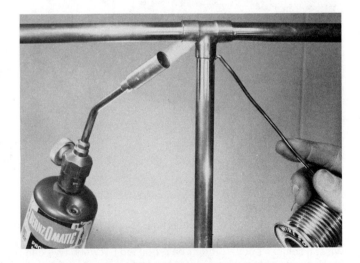

Fig. 17-6. The gas torch makes it possible to solder directly with heat. (Bernz-O-Matic Corp.)

HOW TO TIN A SOLDERING COPPER

A soldering copper is tinned or coated with solder, so molten solder will adhere to it. This makes the handling of the solder easier. See Fig. 17-7.

Clean the copper tip with a file, if it is badly oxidized and pitted. Heat it until it will melt solder freely and do one of the following:

1. Rub the tip on a sal-ammoniac block on which a few drops of solder have been dropped, Fig. 17-8. This will clean the tip and cause the solder to adhere.
2. Apply flux cored solder to the point.

Remove the excess solder by wiping the tip with a clean cloth.

Fig. 17-7. A properly tinned soldering copper.

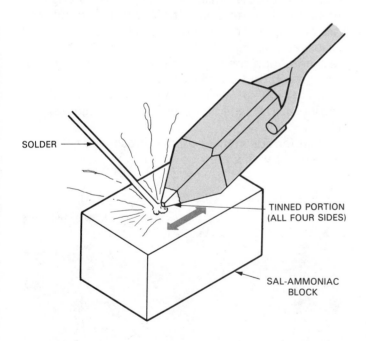

Fig. 17-8. Tinning a soldering copper on a sal-ammoniac block. This should only be done in a well-ventilated area.

HOW TO SOLDER A LAP JOINT

1. Clean the area to be soldered, apply flux, and place the pieces to be soldered on a piece of insulation sheet, Fig. 17-9, A.
2. Clean, heat, and tin the soldering copper, Never let is become red hot.
3. Hold the seam together and tack it with small amounts of solder at several points across the joint, Fig. 17-9, B. Apply the solder directly in front of the soldering copper tip rather than on it.

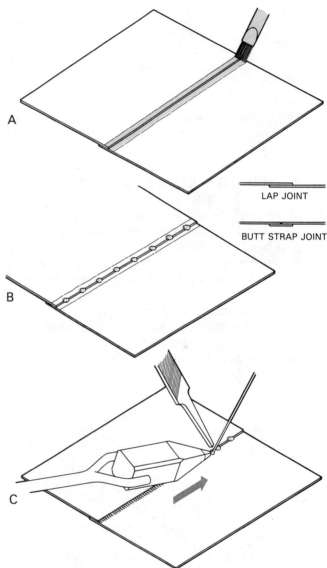

Fig. 17-9. Soldering lap and butt strap joints. A—Apply flux. B—Tack the joint with drops of solder. C—Use a metal object, such as a file tang, to hold the joint together until the solder hardens.

4. Return to the starting point. With the copper flat on the work, Fig. 17-10, and with the seam pressed together with a file tang, start moving the copper slowly toward the far end of the joint as soon as the solder melts and begins to flow,

Fig. 17-9, C. As the copper advances, follow it with the file tang as soon as the solder hardens.

5. Clean the seam with hot water and neutralize any corrosive flux residue by brushing on a thin mixture of baking soda and water. This only needs to be done if the acid flux is used.

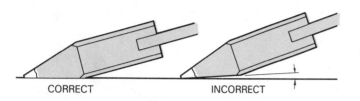

Fig. 17-10. The correct and incorrect way to use a soldering copper on a joint.

HOW TO SOLDER A SEAM JOINT

1. Make the seamed joint desired, Fig. 17-11.
2. Clean and prepare the area to be soldered as previously described.
3. Apply drops of solder along the edge of the seam. Whenever possible, solder seam joints on the inside.
4. Place the copper flat on the seam until the solder begins to melt and flow into the joint, then draw the copper along the seam slowly so the solder will flow into the joint, Fig. 17-12.

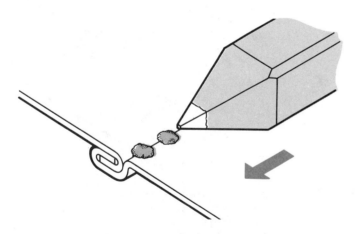

Fig. 17-11. A typical seamed joint.

HOW TO SWEAT SOLDER A JOINT

Sweat soldering is done when two or more pieces must be assembled and no solder is to be seen after assembly.

1. Clean the surfaces and apply flux. Each surface is then coated with a thin layer or coating of solder.
2. Clip the prepared pieces together and apply heat until the solder melts and joins the pieces together.

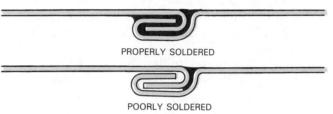

Fig. 17-12. The solder flows through a properly soldered joint.

HARD SOLDERING

In hard soldering or silver brazing, alloys are used which melt at a much higher temperature than soft solder, and a stronger joint is produced. In silver brazing, the temperatures needed range between 800 and 1400 °F (426 to 760 °C). More heat is required than can be furnished by the conventional soldering copper. While various types of torches are available for different fuel combinations ox-yacetylene, city or natural gas, and air may be used for silver brazing (the torch and fuel combination depends upon the size of the pieces to be joined), the familiar self-contained torch and gas cylinder unit, Fig. 17-13, will handle most small jobs. Silver brazing is well suited for production techniques, Fig. 17-14.

Most ferrous metals, copper, brass, and silver can be joined by this method.

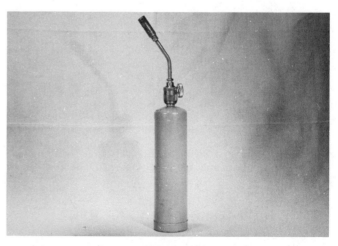

Fig. 17-13. The gas torch is a self-contained unit.

Fig. 17-14. Hard soldering is well suited for production work. Here, cooling fans are being assembled to their hubs by this method, on a production line. (Handy & Harman)

SOLDERS

Hard or silver solder is available in many alloy combinations. It is commonly designated by three grades:

1. EASY FLOW (flow point up to 1300 °F or 704 °C) is used when only one joint is required.

2. MEDIUM (flow point to 1360 °F or 738 °C) is used to solder the first joint when two joints must be made. Easy flow is used for the second joint.

3. HARD (flow point to 1460 °F or 793 °C) makes the best joint. Care must be taken when using the alloys in the upper temperature ranges to join sterling silver because the flow point is very close to its melting point.

In addition to the many alloys, silver solder is also available in a large range of forms and sizes.

FLUXES

Fluxes are needed to clean the surfaces to be joined because the brazing alloy cannot wet or flow over dirty or oxidized areas. A mixture of borax thinned to a heavy paste with water makes a suitable flux. However, a commercially prepared flux usually gives more consistent results.

Fluxing should be done just prior to brazing; otherwise, it will dry and flake or be knocked off in handling.

HOW TO SILVER BRAZE

Silver brazing is a relatively simple process. Strong joints are obtained by following six steps. Each is important and none should be overlooked or eliminated.

1. GOOD FIT AND PROPER CLEARANCE, Fig. 17-15. Thin films make the highest strength

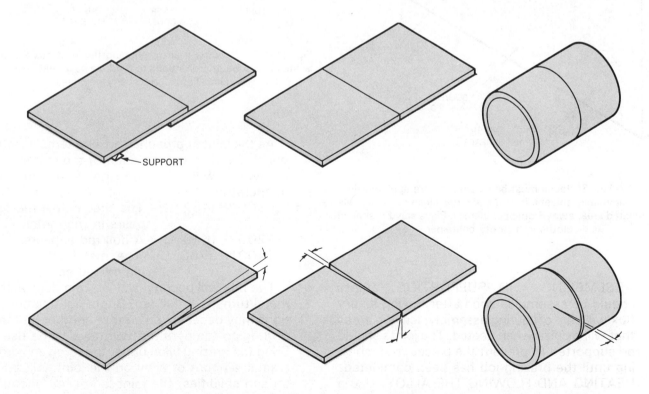

Fig. 17-15. The top row shows good joint design. The bottom row shows poor joint design.

joints. A clearance of 0.001 to 0.003 in. (.025 to .076 mm) provides the necessary capillary action to flow a thin film of alloy throughout the joint.

2. CLEAN METAL, Fig. 17-16. The metal surfaces to be joined must be cleaned. This may be done mechanically with emery cloth, steel wool, or a fine file, or chemically by pickling. Oil and grease may be removed with a suitable solvent. Clean the pieces just prior to brazing time.

3. PROPER FLUXING, Fig. 17-17. A good flux is essential because it protects the metals from oxidation while the joint is being heated, dissolves any existing oxides, and assists the flow of the brazing alloy. Apply the flux evenly to all surfaces to be joined, and to the brazing alloy. This should be applied just prior to brazing.

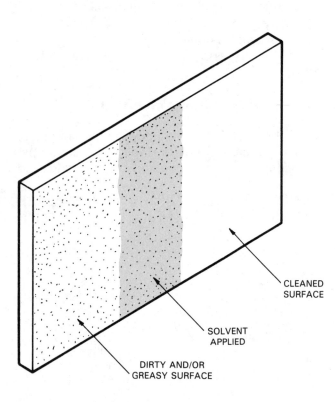

Fig. 17-16. Surfaces must be cleaned before applying flux. If a flammable solvent is used, do the cleaning in a well-ventilated area, away from open flames. Place solvent-soaked cloths in a safety container.

4. ASSEMBLING AND SUPPORTING. Joints should be assembled soon after fluxing as dry flux will chip off during assembly, leaving areas that will oxidize when heated. The joints should be supported to prevent the pieces from shifting until the brazing job has been completed.

5. HEATING AND FLOWING THE ALLOY. Use a neutral to reducing flame, to apply the heat, Fig.

17-18. Heat the joint to slightly above the flow point of the brazing alloy by keeping the torch in motion to apply a uniform heat, Fig. 17-19. Large surfaces to be joined should be heated well away from the joint. If a heavy section is to be joined to a lighter section, concentrate the heat on the heavy section.

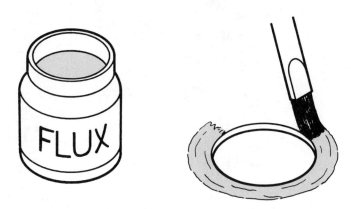

Fig. 17-17. The joint must be properly fluxed. Be sure the flux is distributed evenly over the joint.

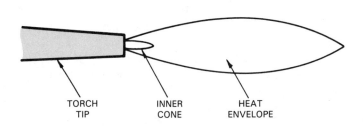

Fig. 17-18. Use a neutral to reducing flame. It has a sharp white inner cone of proportions to produce best heat. The surrounding flames are nearly colorless.

As the joint approaches brazing temperature, watch the flux and the color of the metal. The following will give an indication of the temperature:

900°F (482°C)—The first visible red appears in the metal.
1200°F (649°C)—A dull red appears.
1400°F (760°C)—The metal takes on a cherry red color.

The flux will become a clear, thin fluid as the metal turns to a dull red. Bright lighting conditions may deceive you so that another method of judging temperature will have to be used. Bring the brazing alloy under the torch and drop a small amount of alloy on the joint. If it balls up and solidifies, the joint is not hot enough. When the proper temperature has been reached, the brazing alloy will flow into the joint by capillary action.

6. FINAL CLEANING. All surfaces must be cleaned after brazing too. Some fluxes can be removed with hot water. If a large quantity of oxides have been dissolved in the flux, its removal becomes more difficult and a small amount of acid may have to be added to the water, or the contaminated flux will have to be removed by mechanical means.

Use slightly more brazing alloy than is necessary to fill the joint. It may be applied to the joint as a preform or small pieces placed along the joint in the flux.

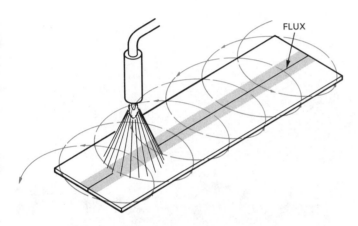

Fig. 17-19. Avoid hot spots. Keep the torch in motion. Bring both parts of joint to brazing heat at the same time.

HOW TO SILVER BRAZE MORE THAN ONE JOINT ON THE SAME PIECE

It is often necessary to silver braze several joints on the same piece. The first joint is made with high temperature brazing alloy and the remainder with lower temperature alloys. If only one alloy is available, the first joint is made and then covered with flux. This will help to keep it from melting when the remaining joints are brazed. The flux, plus the fact that it requires 15 to 20° higher temperature to remelt a silver brazed joint, prevents it from coming apart when the other joints are made.

SAFETY

1. Use care when storing the soldering copper after use. Improper storage can result in serious burns or a fire.
2. Wash your hands thoroughly after using soft solder.
3. Protect your eyes from splattering solder and do not get flux in your eyes.
4. Have cuts and burns treated promptly.
5. Tin the soldering copper in a well-ventilated area.
6. Do not touch joints that have just been soldered.
7. Because of the temperatures reached and the composition of silver brazing alloys, good ventilation is a must. The fumes are poisonous and should be removed at the point of origin.
8. Use care when handling objects that have just been brazed.
9. Wear goggles when cleaning surfaces with an acid solution or with a wire brush.
10. Pour acid into the water slowly, never water into the acid, when preparing the solution.
11. Double check to be certain that all gas valves have been turned off after completing the job.

TEST YOUR KNOWLEDGE, Unit 17

Please do not write in the text. Place your answers on a separate piece of paper.

1. Soldering is a method of:
   a. Joining metals by fusing the base metals.
   b. Joining the metals with a nonferrous metal filler.
   c. Joining metals that are similar to welding.
   d. None of the above.
2. List four requirements for a satisfactory soldered joint:
   a. _____.
   b. _____.
   c. _____.
   d. _____.
3. Soldered seams should employ a lock seam or a fold in its design because _____.
4. _____ is always the first figure mentioned when the solder alloys are mentioned.
5. _____-_____ solder is most commonly used.
6. Flux is used to _____.
7. _____ and _____ are the two categories of fluxes used for soft soldering.
8. Joints soldered when using a _____ flux must be washed with hot water to remove the flux residue.
9. Silver brazing resembles _____ more closely than _____.
10. List the three grades of silver brazing alloys.
    a. _____.
    b. _____.
    c. _____.
11. What are three uses of a flux in silver brazing?
    a. _____.
    b. _____.
    c. _____.
12. Six steps must be followed if a solid joint is to result by silver brazing. List them in their

proper sequence:

a. _____.

b. _____.

c. _____.

d. _____.

e. _____.

f. _____.

RESEARCH AND DEVELOPMENT

1. Make up samples of well-made and poorly-made seams or joints by the soft soldering method. Mount them on a display panel and label to indicate what constitutes a good solder joint and a poorly made joint.

2. Secure samples of commercially made products assembled by the soft solder technique. Display them in such a way to permit the solder seams to be seen and compared.

3. Visit local industries that produce objects that are assembled with soft solder. Prepare a short report on the methods used, and how they vary from those used in the school shop.

4. Demonstrate the correct method to silver braze a joint.

5. Prepare a display panel that illustrates properly and improperly made silver brazed joints.

Semiskilled worker performs brazing operation to assemble manufactured parts into complete unit. (Volkswagen of America, Inc.)

Unit 18

WELDING

WELDING is the process of joining metals by heating them to a suitable temperature where they will melt and fuse together. This may be done with or without the application of pressure, and with or without the use of filler metal of a similar composition and melting point as the base metal. Welding is a very important facet of modern fabricating techniques, Fig. 18-1.

There are about eighty welding processes classified by the American Welding Society (AWS), Fig. 18-2. And with the discovery of new alloys, applications, and requirements by industry additional welding processes are added on a regular basis.

It is not possible to cover the entire field of welding in a book of this type. Therefore, only the

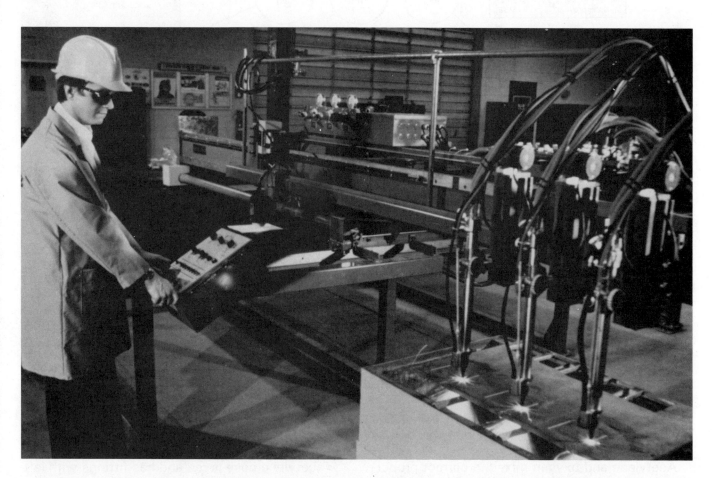

Fig. 18-1. This oxy-fuel multicutting head is operated from the console in front of the operator. An electronic scanner moves over a line or silhouette tracing, providing torch movement to make the desired cuts. It can also be equipped with pre-programmed shapes for which it is only necessary to key in the dimensions. (Linde Div., Union Carbide)

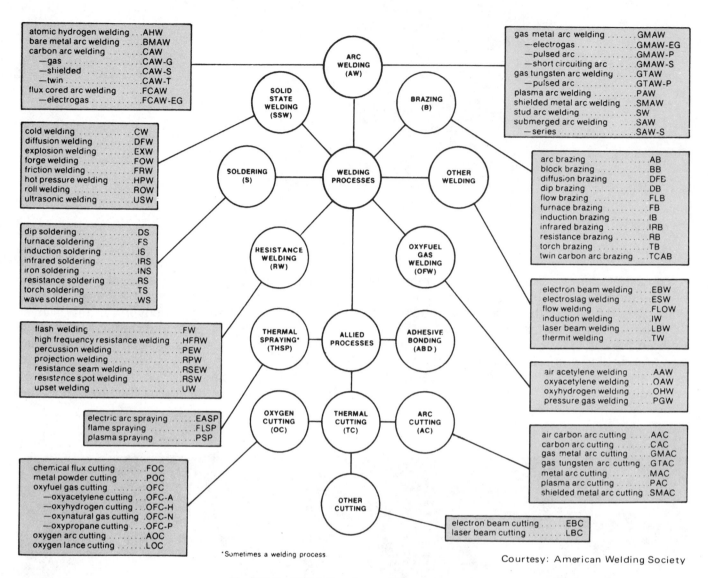

Fig. 18-2. Chart showing welding processes.

*Sometimes a welding process

Courtesy: American Welding Society

more important processes will be included. To aid your study of welding, the unit has been divided into three parts:

1. Gas welding.
2. Simple electric arc and resistance welding.
3. Other welding processes.

GAS WELDING

GAS WELDING includes a group of welding processes that make use of burning gases, such as acetylene or hydrogen mixed with oxygen, to produce the required heat needed for the metal to melt and fuse. Filler material of a similar composition and melting temperature as the base metal may or may not be used.

Acetylene and oxygen mixed in correct proportions are most commonly used for gas welding in the school shop. They burn with an extremely hot flame (6300°F or 3 482°C); more than ample for

doing an adequate job of joining most weldable metals.

GAS WELDING EQUIPMENT

Basically, OXYACETYLENE welding equipment, Fig. 18-3, consists of:

1. A source of supply for the two gases (gas cylinders), Fig. 18-4.
2. A mechanism for reducing the pressure and controlling the gases as they come from the cylinder (oxygen regulator and acetylene regulator).
3. A method for transferring the gases to the point of use (oxygen hose and acetylene hose—for easy identification, the oxygen hose is green and has fittings with right hand threads and the acetylene hose is red and has fittings with left hand threads).
4. A device to mix and control the gases in proper proportion when welding (welding torch).

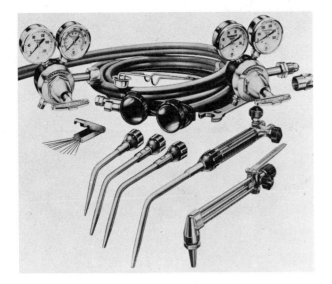

Fig. 18-3. A typical oxyacetylene welding outfit.
(Marquette Mfg. Co.)

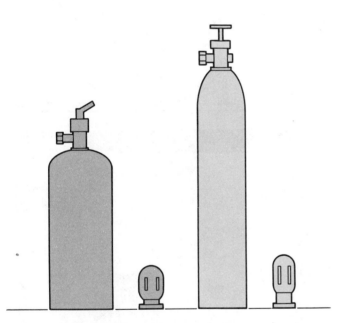

Fig. 18-4. Gas cylinders. On the left is an acetylene cylinder.
On the right is an oxygen cylinder.

In addition to the above, a wrench that fits the various connections (PLIERS ARE NEVER USED), a spark lighter, Fig. 18-5, for lighting the torch, and a pair of suitable goggles are needed.

Torches are manufactured in a variety of sizes with a wide range of tip diameters. The basic elements of a typical welding torch are shown in Fig. 18-6.

CARE OF GAS WELDING EQUIPMENT

Gas welding equipment is very rugged but certain precautions must be taken for safe operation.

Fig. 18-5. A spark or friction lighter should be used to light the torch. Never light the torch with a match or cigarette lighter.
(Linde Div., Union Carbide)

REGULATORS

1. Clean cylinder valve outlets with a CLEAN, DRY cloth. Blow dust from the outlet by opening the valve before connecting the regulator. This is known as "cracking" the valve.
2. Release the regulator adjusting screw before opening the cylinder valve.
3. Prevent the high pressure gases in the cylinder from surging (suddenly increasing in pressure) by opening the cylinder valves slowly.
4. Check gauges regularly to assure correct readings.
5. Turn the adjusting screw slowly to prevent the regulator from being damaged by a sudden surge of high pressure gas.
6. Always use the correct size wrench on the fittings. Avoid forcing the threaded fitting.
7. NEVER use oil or grease on a regulator or fitting. Use a lubricant specified by the manufacturer.
8. Use soapy water free of oils and greases to check for suspected leaks.
9. Have all equipment repaired by trained persons. Use only factory approved parts.

TORCHES

1. Keep all oil and grease away from torches.
2. NEVER clamp a torch in a vise. The internal passages may be damaged, causing the gases to escape.
3. If a needle valve does not shut off when tightened in a normal nammer, DO NOT force it. Blow foreign matter from the valve seat. If this cannot be done, remove the stem assembly (close the regulator valve before attempting this) and wipe the seat clean with a lint-free cloth. Reassemble the unit.
4. Check the torch carefully before you use it.

SAFETY PRECAUTIONS WHEN GAS WELDING

1. Wear suitable goggles when welding, Fig. 18-7. The lenses are made in different degrees of density. Select the lenses that are best suited for you.
2. NEVER LIGHT A TORCH WITH A MATCH. Use a spark lighter.

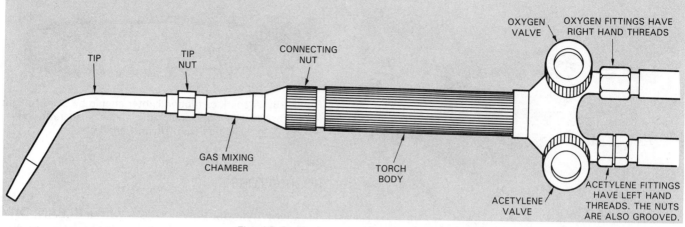

Fig. 18-6. Basic parts of a gas torch.

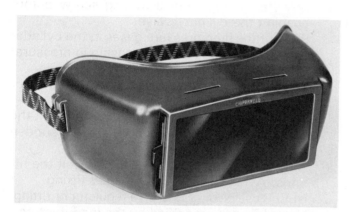

Fig. 18-7. Welding requires special goggles with tinted lenses. Do not wear goggles designed for gas welding when arc welding.

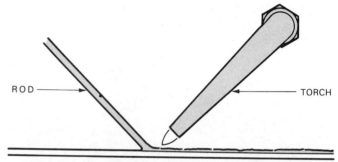

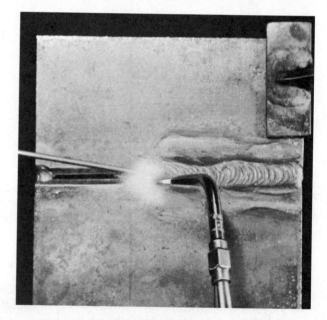

Fig. 18-8. Adding filler rod to the weld. (Linde Div., Union Carbide)

3. Do not allow anyone to watch you weld unless they wear suitable goggles.
4. It is only necessary to turn off the torch if you are going to reposition the work. However, the entire unit should be turned off if the welding job is completed. Carefully hang up the torch.
5. NEVER light the torch with both valves open.
6. For added protection, wear welder's gloves, leather apron, and sleeves when welding. AVOID WEARING CANVAS SHOES.
7. NEVER attempt to blow dirt off your clothing with gas pressure. The clothing will become saturated with oxygen and/or acetylene and will literally explode if a spark happens to come in contact with it.
8. Be sure there are no oily rags or other flammable materials in the area where you are welding.

GAS WELDING RODS

Often metal from filler rod is added to a joint during welding, Fig. 18-8, to build it up and make it as strong as the base metal. A steel filler rod having a very low carbon content will prove satisfactory for most gas welding operations on ferrous metal in the school shop. This rod is available in a number of sizes (diameters) and is copper plated to prevent rusting.

The following rod sizes are recommended for oxy-acetylene welding:

Metal Thickness	Rod Diameter
18 gauge	1/16 in.
16 gauge	1/16 to 3/32 in.
10 gauge	3/32 to 1/8 in.
1/8 in.	3/32 to 1/8 in.
3/18 in.	1/8 to 5/32 in.
1/4 in. and up	3/16 to 1/4 in.

Cast-iron filler rod is a high grade cast rod with a square cross section. To produce a satisfactory joint, it (the joint) must be clean and free of all dirt, grease, and oxidation. A flux must be used with this rod.

Brazing rod must be of high quality and purity to obtain good results. It is made of brass or bronze. Bronze filler rod is preferred because it has superior strength. A flux must also be used with this rod.

Brazing rod and fluxes for joining some aluminum alloys are available. However, as aluminum gives no warning by change of color prior to melting, extreme care must be taken when it is brazed. For best results, carefully follow the instructions furnished by the rod and flux manufacturer.

FLUXES

FLUXES must be used on most nonferrous and cast-iron welds. Flux cleans the metal, prevents oxidation and other forms of corrosion, and promotes a better weld. Unless the metal is free of all oxides, it is difficult to make a good weld. A flux should not be used as a substitute for cleaning the base metal during joint preparation.

Borax can be used as a brazing flux; however, commercial fluxes are superior and should ordinarily be employed. Aluminum and cast-iron welds require fluxes made especially for these metals.

PREPARING AND ADJUSTING THE EQUIPMENT AND LIGHTING THE TORCH

A careful study should be made of the manufacturer's recommended operating procedures furnished with the welding equipment. If this is not available, the following should be observed:

1. Carefully check the equipment. If it must be assembled, ask your instructor to demonstrate how this should be done.
2. Select the proper tip size for the job to be done. The tips are usually made of copper because its high thermal conductivity reduces the danger of it burning up at high temperatures. Use the guide furnished with the torch to determine the tip best suited. If necessary, clean the tip with a TIP CLEANER, Fig. 18-9. NEVER clean the tip with a piece of wire. Attach the tip to the torch.

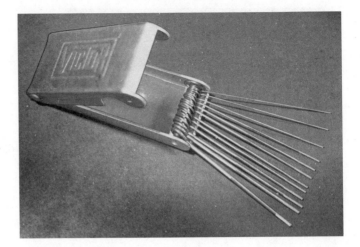

Fig. 18-9. Torch tip cleaners. Wire and small nails should never be used to clean torch tips!

3. Turn the adjusting screws on both regulators out until they are loose.
4. Open the oxygen cylinder VERY SLOWLY until the high pressure gauge shows its maximum rating, then continue to turn the valve until it seats against the top of the valve cylinder. The valve has a double seat and turning it all of the way out prevents oxygen leakage.
5. Secure the proper size wrench and SLOWLY open the acetylene cylinder valve 1 to 1 1/2 turns—NEVER MORE. It is good practice to stand to one side of the regulator valves when the cylinder valves are opened.
6. Open the oxygen valve on the torch about one turn and turn in the adjusting screw on the regulator until the low pressure indicates the correct pressure for the tip being used. Turn off the oxygen valve on the torch.
7. Repeat the sequence for acetylene.
8. Open the acetylene valve on the torch about 1/4 turn. Permit the gas to flow long enough to blow any air in the unit out before igniting the torch with a spark lighter. Hold the torch away from the cylinders and pointed away from the body, Fig. 18-10.
9. Adjust the acetylene valve on the torch until the flame jumps away from the tip slightly. Open and adjust the oxygen valve on the torch until you get a NEUTRAL FLAME, Fig. 18-11. This flame is best for most welding. An excess of acetylene produces a CARBURIZING FLAME, Fig. 18-12. A sharp "hissing" sound indicates there is an excess of oxygen, and an OXIDIZING FLAME, Fig. 18-13, is the result.
10. If the torch is to be idle for only a few minutes, it is only necessary to turn off the torch valves. However, if the job is completed and the torch is not to be used for some time, it is best that

Fig. 18-10. When lighting the torch, hold it away from the cylinders and pointed away from the body. (Linde Div., Union Carbide)

Fig. 18-11. A neutral flame is obtained by burning an approximately one-to-one mixture of acetylene and oxygen. The pale blue core of the flame is known as the inner cone. The oxygen required for combustion of the carbon monoxide and hydrogen in the outer envelope of the flame is supplied from the air.

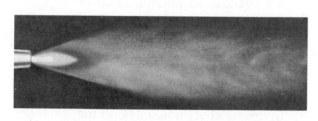

Fig. 18-12. The carburizing flame results when the one-to-one mixture has an excess amount of acetylene.

Fig. 18-13. The oxidizing flame is the result of too much oxygen in the mixture. The whole flame will be smaller, and hotter, than either the neutral flame or the carburizing flame because the combustible gases will not have to search as far to find the necessary oxygen.

the unit be shut down completely. The proper way for doing this is as follows:

a. Close the valves on the torch. The acetylene is closed first to prevent a slight backfire or "pop." It will also prevent the carbon smudge that burning acetylene makes.

b. Close the cylinder valves tightly.

c. Open the valves on the torch to release any gas in the hose and regulator.

d. When all gauges read zero, turn the adjusting screws on both of the regulators all of the way out.

e. Close the torch valves and store the torch in a suitable place. Avoid hanging the torch and hoses over the regulators. Their weight may damage the regulators.

MAKING A GAS WELD

After the proper tip has been installed on the torch, a welding table is made ready, Fig. 18-14. The table shown is steel with a fire brick top which is not affected by the high welding temperatures. If this is the first attempt at gas welding, a careful study should be made of the various welding joints and how the torch is handled to make them.

TYPES OF WELDING JOINTS

Joint preparation is of paramount importance before a sound weld can be made. The type of

Fig. 18-14. Gas welding table. (Marquette Mfg. Co.)

preparation is dependent upon the thickness of the metal to be welded and the type of joint required. In addition, rust, scale, and other impurities must be removed from the base metal.

In general, there are five basic types of joints. They are common to both gas and arc welding.

BUTT JOINT

The BUTT JOINT, Fig. 18-15, is the most common of the welded joints. Metals up to 1/8 in. (3.0 mm) thick can be welded from one side. Metals up to 3/8 in. (9.0 mm) should be welded from both sides. Heavier plate must be beveled before welding will secure a solid joint.

TEE JOINT

The TEE JOINT, Fig. 18-16, is frequently used. Joint preparation is similar to that used for the butt joint.

LAP JOINT

The LAP JOINT, Fig. 18-17, consists of lapping a section of metal over the section to which it is to be welded. It is important that the pieces fit together tightly and that the weld is made on a flat surface.

EDGE JOINT

Welding the EDGE JOINT, Fig. 18-18, differs somewhat from making other joints in that it is not necessary to use filler rod. The base metal serves as filler material.

CORNER JOINT

The open CORNER JOINT, Fig. 18-19, is employed when welding heavier plate. For additional strength, a light bead is often added to the inside.

In general, welding without the use of filler rod is not considered good welding technique. Maximum strength is not always achieved because the thickness of the metal is reduced along the weld.

To weld with filler rod, bring the torch to the point to be welded and melt a small ''puddle'' on the surface of the work. Bring the filler rod close to the torch and as it becomes white hot, dip it into the molten puddle. Do not heat the rod directly and allow the molten metal to fall into the molten puddle. And enough filler rod material to create a slight crown on the joint.

Expansion and contraction of the base metal during welding must be taken into consideration and allowance must be made for them. Otherwise, the piece will twist out of shape as it cools. Fig. 18-20 illustrates two ways of allowing for contraction as the metal cools.

Fig. 18-15. Butt joint.

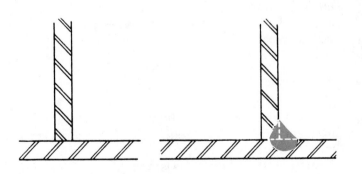

Fig. 18-16. Tee joint.

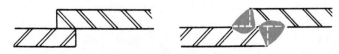

Fig. 18-17. Lap joint.

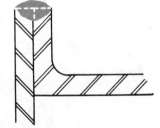

Fig. 18-18. Edge joint.

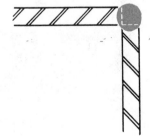

Fig. 18-19. Corner joint.

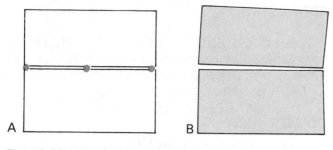

Fig. 18-20. Welded joints will become distorted if allowances are not made for metal contraction as the weld cools. A—Tack weld the joint at intervals. B—Position the work so that one end of the proposed weld is slightly wider than the other end (where weld starts).

TORCH WELDING

FOREHAND WELDING is used for joining thin metal. The torch and filler rod are positioned as shown in Fig. 18-21. The flame is in the direction the weld is progressing.

BACKHAND WELDING, Fig. 18-22, is employed for joining heavier sections. The torch is held at an

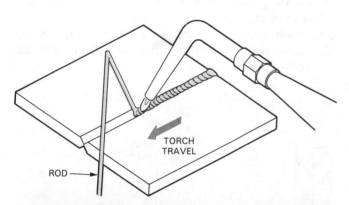

Fig. 18-21. With a forehand weld, the welding action progresses from right to left. The flame is between the completed weld and the welding rod. (Linde Div., Union Carbide)

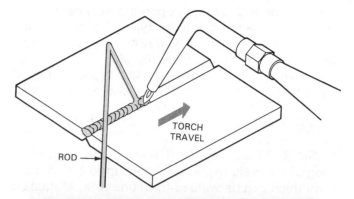

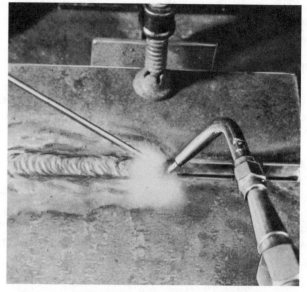

Fig. 18-22. In the backhand technique, the weld progresses from left to right. The welding rod is between the completed weld and the torch flame.

angle of 30 to 45 degrees with the flame being directed back over the portion that has been welded. This permits the weld to cool more slowly, helping to relieve the stresses that develop in the metal during welding.

PUDDLING

It is suggested that a student welding for the first time should practice "puddling." The puddle is the molten spot that is produced by the torch flame. It spans the metal sections being welded causing them to fuse. This is basic for both gas and arc welding.

As the puddle forms, and the filler metal is added, make a circular or oscillating motion with the torch, Fig. 18-23. Whatever motion is used, be careful not to allow the inner cone of the flame to go outside the puddle perimeter. Fig. 18-24 illustrates some of the problems usually encountered by the novice welder.

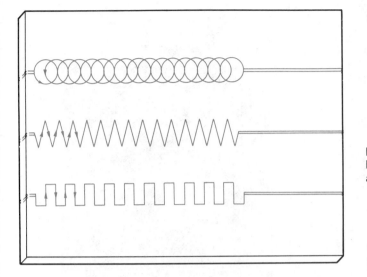

Fig. 18-23. Torch movement recommended for a satisfactory weld.

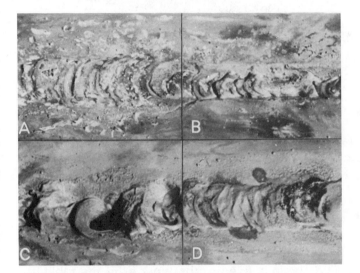

Fig. 18-24. In these four views are shown: A—An oxidized weld. B—Poor fusion and lack of reinforcement because insufficient heat was used. C—Holes burned through the plate because too much heat was employed. D—The appearance of a satisfactory weld. (Linde Div., Union Carbide)

BRAZING OR BRONZE WELDING

This welding technique is widely utilized for repair work. The resulting joints, if properly made, are almost as strong as a conventional welded joint. However, they are quicker and less expensive to make, Fig. 18-25. Bronze filler rod is preferred to brass because it makes a stronger joint.

It is essential that the surfaces to be joined are clean. Clamp the pieces into position and heat them. If one section is heavier than the other, apply more heat to it. As the metal heats up, use care to pre-

Fig. 18-25. Shown is a properly deposited layer of bronze. During bronze-welding the blowpipe and rod should be held at angles of about 45 degrees to the plate surface, with the flame at the forward end of the puddle.

vent burning through. Heat the filler rod and stick it into the flux. The fluxed end is held slightly ahead of the torch. As the proper welding temperature is reached, allow the rod to melt and flow onto the base metal. Avoid melting the rod directly with the torch. Be careful not to overheat the resulting joint.

ARC WELDING

ARC WELDING is a joining technique that makes use of an electric current to produce the heat needed to cause the metals to melt and fuse together, Fig. 18-26. Filler metal in the form of an ELECTRODE, Fig. 18-27, may be added to the joint.

Today, there are few industries or businesses that do not depend upon arc welding in some way.

ARC WELDING EQUIPMENT AND ACCESSORIES

Like most other manufacturing equipment, arc welders are available in a large range of sizes (ratings). Arc welders are rated according to their current output. Most of those used in the average school shop range from 100 to 250 amperes.

Welding machines are of two basic types: those that provide DIRECT WELDING CURRENT (DC), Fig.

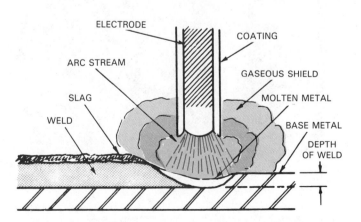

Fig. 18-26. Close-up showing electric welding procedure.

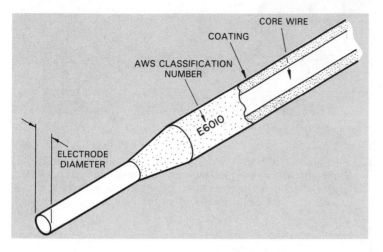

Fig. 18-27. Electrode used in arc welding.

Fig. 18-29. Combination AC/DC welder used by many schools. (Miller Electric Mfg. Co.)

18-28, and those that provide ALTERNATING WELDING CURRENT (AC). Also available are COMBINATION WELDERS, Fig. 18-29, that produce both AC and DC welding current.

The DC welding machine has some advantages over the AC welders. It is better for welding sheet metal, and a wider variety of electrodes are made for DC welding. Power output can be controlled more precisely, and gasoline powered models permit the welders to be used where there are no power lines.

Safe and efficient welding procedures require the use of many accessories. NO welding should be attempted unless the equipment is in first-class condition.

Arc welding requires the use of TWO CABLES to carry the current through a complete circuit. Size and length of the cables is determined by the capacity of the machine. One cable is attached to an ELECTRODE HOLDER, Fig. 18-30. This holds the electrode during the welding operation. The second cable is attached to a GROUND CLAMP, Fig. 18-31. The clamp is fixed to the work or, if the table has a cast iron top, to the welding table.

A HEAD SHIELD, Fig. 18-32, protects the face and eyes of the operator from the rays of the electric arc and spatter of molten metal. NEVER ATTEMPT TO ARC WELD UNLESS A SHIELD IS USED. The rays can cause serious and often permanent eye damage.

GAUNTLET TYPE GLOVES, a LEATHER APRON,

Fig. 18-28. DC welding machine. It is compact and portable. (Multiquip Inc.)

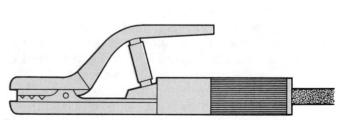

Fig. 18-30. Electrode holder.

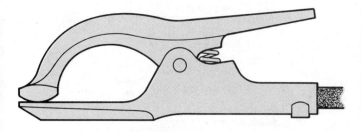

Fig. 18-31. One type of ground clamp.

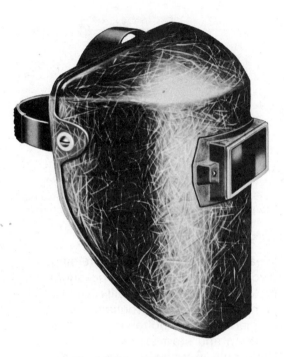

Fig. 18-32. Head shield.

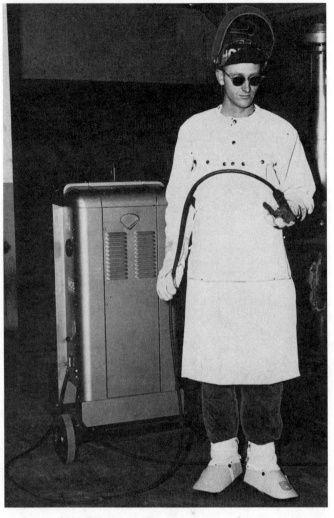

Fig. 18-33. Wear clothing designed for welding. This includes a head shield (with safety glasses underneath), leather jacket, gloves, and fire resistant coveralls. Tennis shoes should never be worn when arc welding.

and SLEEVES should be worn for additional protection, Fig. 18-33. A WIRE BRUSH and CHIPPING HAMMER, Fig. 18-34, are needed to remove slag and to clean the weld bead. Be sure to wear goggles when chipping and wire brushing. TONGS or pliers should be available to handle hot metal. A WELDING TABLE, Fig. 18-35, will prove helpful for practice and small job welding. An assortment of clamps, punches, and small tools will help to make the job easier.

ELECTRODES

ELECTRODES are metal rods covered with a baked flux coating. Rods are used to support the welding arc and to provide filler metal to the joint. The flux melts under the high temperatures and cleans the oxides from the base metal. It also acts as insulation, slowing down the cooling rate of the joint. This helps relieve internal strains which develop from sudden changes of temperature.

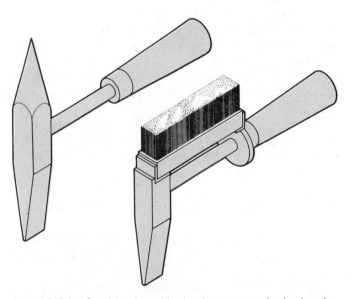

Fig. 18-34. Combination chipping hammer and wire brush.

Fig. 18-35. One type of arc welding table. The curtain should be closed to protect nearby workers from the arc.

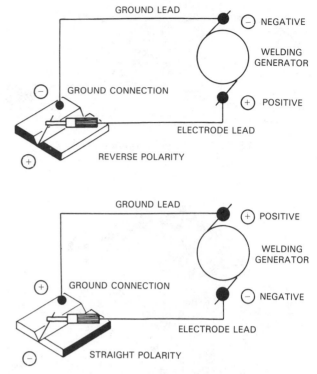

Fig. 18-36. Two methods of setting up a DC welder to take advantage of desirable electrode characteristics.

When using a DC welder, it is necessary to know the correct terminal (pole) of the machine to attach the electrode cable. The current flow on the DC welder flows constantly in one direction, or has a definite polarity. Electrodes are designed to take advantage of this condition, Fig. 18-36. When the electrode is POSITIVE (+), the arc is forceful and digs into the base metal for deep penetration. When the electrode is NEGATIVE (−), the arc is not as forceful, but the electrode metal is deposited about a third faster.

The electrode polarity in DC welding is determined by the flux coating. A specific polarity must be used for some electrodes while others can be used with either polarity. Polarity instructions are given on the electrode container.

Store electrodes where they will be dry. Moisture destroys the desirable characteristics of the flux coating.

A uniform system of classifying electrodes has been established by the American Welding Society. Fig. 18-37 lists the most commonly used mild steel electrodes for general welding.

SAFETY PRECAUTIONS FOR ARC WELDING

1. NEVER arc weld or watch arc welding without using a protective shield. Gas welding goggles or sun glasses are not satisfactory!
2. Wear safety goggles when chipping slag or cleaning welds.
3. Wear suitable clothing for welding.
4. Avoid wearing athletic type shoes when arc welding. Serious burns will result from stepping on hot weld spatter. Trousers with cuffs are also dangerous since molten weld spatter can fall into them and start a fire.
5. Weld only in well-ventilated areas.
6. Treat any cuts or burns promptly.
7. Do not weld where solvents or paint fumes may collect. Remove all flammable materials from the welding area.
8. Wear goggles under the shield for additional protection. The tinted glass in the shield may not be safety glass.
9. Do not weld containers until you can determine whether they contained flammable liquids at one time. If they do, get them steam cleaned or fill them with water before welding.

PREPARING TO ARC WELD

Check the machine to be sure that all connections are tight and clean. As the heat of the arc is determined by the amount of the current (amperes) used, it is suggested that you set the machine to the middle of the recommended range for the type of electrode used. Make a few trial beads and raise or lower the setting until you get a satisfactory weld; one that does not burn through and gives sufficient penetration, Fig. 18-38.

AWS NO.	WELDING CURRENT	END (E) SECONDARY (S) COLOR MARKING	WELDING POSITION	PENETRATION AND CHARACTERISTICS	APPLICATION
E-6010	DC, reverse polarity	None	All	Deep penetration; thin slag, easy to remove; forceful arc.	Building construction, pipe lines, pressure tanks, bridges, ship building, storage tanks, machinery frames.
E-6011	AC or DC, reverse polarity	Blue (S)	All	Deep penetration; thin slag, easy to remove; forceful arc.	Same as E-6010. For use on AC welding current, not all are usable with limited-input welders.
E-6012	DC straight polarity or AC	White (S)	All	Medium penetration; heavy slag; soft arc.	Work with poor fit-up, high speed welding, light gauge welding, build-up.
E-6013	AC or DC, straight polarity	Brown (S)	All	Medium to shallow penetration; light slag, easy to remove; soft arc.	Mild steel repair, sheet metal, auto bodies, general farm welding and repair with limited-input welders.
E-6014	AC or DC	Brown (S)	All	Iron powder coating; medium to shallow penetration; drag technique; exceptionally easy to operate; little spatter; heavy slag almost self-removing.	High speed welding, for ease of operation in all general welding. This is an E-6013 electrode with iron powder added to the coating.
E-6016	DC reverse polarity or AC	Orange (S)	All	Medium to deep penetration; forceful arc; medium to heavy slag.	Higher carbon steels, alloy steels, armor plate, auto bumpers. Not usable with limited-input welders.

Fig. 18-37. Commonly used mild steel electrodes for general welding.

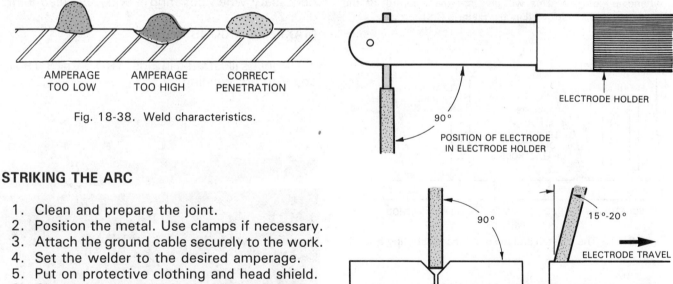

AMPERAGE TOO LOW   AMPERAGE TOO HIGH   CORRECT PENETRATION

Fig. 18-38. Weld characteristics.

ELECTRODE HOLDER

90° POSITION OF ELECTRODE IN ELECTRODE HOLDER

90°   15°-20° ELECTRODE TRAVEL

Fig. 18-39. Electrode position when running a flat weld.

STRIKING THE ARC

1. Clean and prepare the joint.
2. Position the metal. Use clamps if necessary.
3. Attach the ground cable securely to the work.
4. Set the welder to the desired amperage.
5. Put on protective clothing and head shield.
6. Clamp the electrode in the electrode holder. It should be at a 90 degree angle to the jaws, Fig. 18-39.
7. Keep the electrode holder clear of the work area and turn the machine on.
8. Grasp the electrode holder with a comfortable grip. Use two hands whenever possible, Fig. 18-40. Lower the electrode to about 1 in. (25.0 mm) above the base metal. Lean the electrode at a 15 to 20 degree angle from the vertical in the direction of travel.
9. Lower your head shield and strike the arc.

While the SCRATCH or TAP method may be used, Fig. 18-41, the scratch method is recommended. The electrode is scratched over the face of the base metal as you would strike a match. As the arc starts, lift the electrode 1/8 in. (3.2 mm) and maintain the arc. Keep the electrode moving while starting the arc or

Fig. 18-40. Grasp the electrode holder with two hands whenever possible. This will give improved control of the holder. (Lincoln Electric Co.)

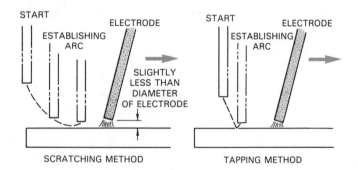

Fig. 18-41. The scratch and tap methods for starting a weld.

it will "freeze" (stick) to the base metal.

10. Once the arc is established, it is important that the correct arc length be maintained. Hold a short arc, 1/16 to 1/8 in. (1.5 to 3.0 mm). As the electrode burns down, keep feeding it to the work to maintain the correct arc length.

11. Maintaining correct welding speed is important. Watch the puddle of molten metal directly behind the arc. Do not watch the arc. The appearance of the puddle and the ridge where the molten metal has solidified, Fig. 18-42, in-

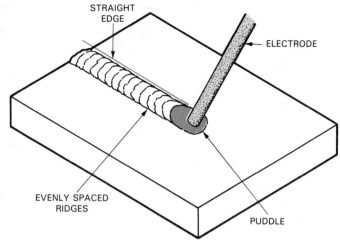

Fig. 18-42. The correct welding speed is indicated by the looks of the puddle and ridge of the bead.

dicates correct welding speed. The ridge should be about 3/8 in. (9.0 mm) behind the electrode. Most beginners weld too rapidly, resulting in a shallow, uneven bead. Fig. 18-43, shows the various types of beads.

For general welding, it is not necessary to move the electrode in any direction but a straight one, at an even pace. A weaving motion, Fig. 18-44, is necessary when covering a wide, beveled joint.

MAKING VARIOUS WELDS

The joints illustrated in Figs. 18-15 to 18-19 also apply to arc welding.

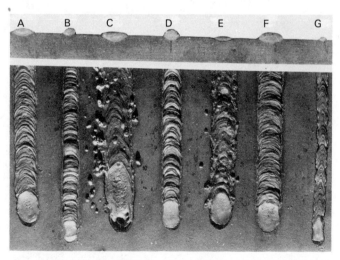

Fig. 18-43. Characteristics of welds made under various conditions. The conditions are accentuated to illustrate differences. A—Current, voltage, and speed normal. B—Current too low. C—Current too high. D—Arc length too short. E—Arc length too long. F—Speed too slow. G—Speed too high. (Lincoln Electric Co.)

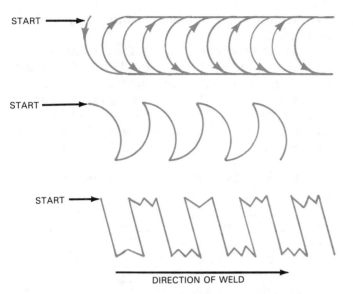

Fig. 18-44. Recommended electrode travel when covering wide, beveled joint.

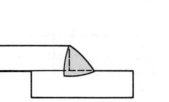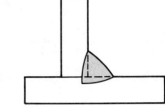

Fig. 18-46. Fillet weld.

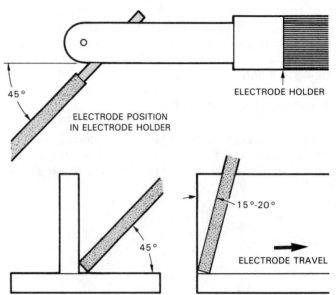

Fig. 18-47. Electrode position when making a fillet weld.

When making a butt joint, place the two metal sections side-by-side with a 1/16 in. (1.5 mm) space between them (1/8 in. [3.0 mm] for heavy plate). Tack the plates at both ends to prevent them from pulling apart as they are welded, Fig. 18-45. Take care to distribute the weld evenly on both sections.

FILLET WELDS, Fig. 18-46, are made by holding electrodes in the electrode holder at a 45 degree angle to the jaws, Fig. 18-47.

Welds must penetrate close to 100 percent; otherwise, they will be weaker than the base metal, Fig. 18-48. It may be necessary to bevel the joint edges for the best penetration in heavier sections, Fig. 18-49.

ARC WELDING ALUMINUM WITH A CARBON ARC TORCH

Aluminum and other nonferrous metals like copper and brass can be electric welded almost as easily

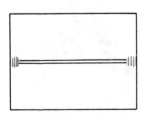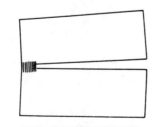

TACKED BUTT JOINT

WELD STARTED WITHOUT TACKING BOTH ENDS. NOTE THE DISTORTION.

Fig. 18-45. Tack plates to be joined at both ends to prevent them from pulling apart as they are welded.

Fig. 18-48. Welds must penetrate close to 100 percent or they will be weaker than the base metal.

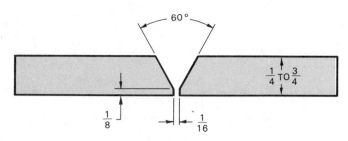

Fig. 18-49. Joint preparation for welding heavy sections.

as ferrous metals. About the only apparatus needed, in addition to an AC welding machine and its normal related equipment, is an arc torch, Fig. 18-50, and electrodes developed for the metal being welded.

TORCH ADJUSTMENTS

In using a carbon arc torch, the distance between the carbons and the work controls the amount of heat going into the work. Fig. 18-51 indicates car-

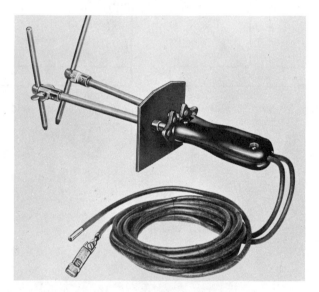

Fig. 18-50. Carbon arc torch.   (Lincoln Electric Co.)

RECOMMENDED CURRENT AND CARBONS

Thickness of base metal	Approximate current setting	Carbon Diameter
1/16 in.	50 - 60 amps.	1/4 in.
1/8 in.	70 - 80 amps.	5/16 in.
1/4 in.	90 - 100 amps.	3/8 in.
over 1/4 in.	110 - 125 amps.	3/8 in.

Fig. 18-51. Table of recommended currents and carbon diameters for carbon arc torch applications. (Lincoln Electric Co.)

bon diameter and amperage setting for various metal thicknesses.

Extend the carbons 2 to 2 1/2 in. (51.0 to 63.5 mm) beyond the torch jaws, Fig. 18-52. Adjust arc length (distance between carbons) as often as necessary to keep the arc going smoothly and to concentrate the flame in a small cone. As the carbons burn away, adjust the arc by manipulating the carbons with the thumb control on the torch handle.

SAFETY PRECAUTIONS WHEN CARBON ARC WELDING

The rays of the carbon arc torch are just as dangerous as those generated during conventional arc welding. A head shield and protective clothing are required!

Always turn the welder off when adjusting carbons. This will prevent arcing should they touch adjustment. The resulting flash can cause serious burns or damage your eyes.

JOINT PREPARATION

The thickness of the metal being welded will determine how the joint must be prepared, Fig. 18-53. It is recommended that all welds be made in the horizontal downhand position, even though this may require rotating the pieces.

MAKING THE WELD

The following sequence is recommended for welding aluminum and copper alloys.
1. Set the welder to the current recommended in Fig. 18-51. An AC welder is preferred (a DC machine may be used but the carbons will be consumed faster).
2. Use a 1/8 in. (3.2 mm) diameter electrode as filler rod. It should be the same type of metal

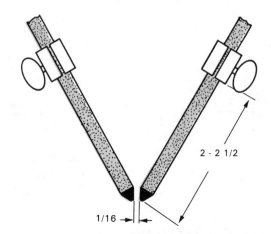

Fig. 18-52. Carbon adjustment.

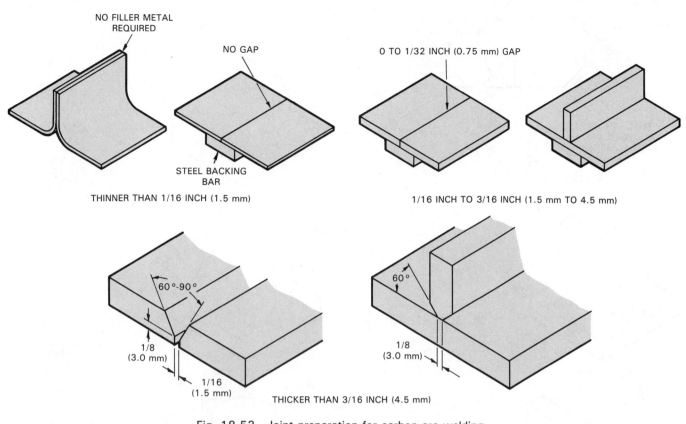

Fig. 18-53. Joint preparation for carbon arc welding.

as the metal being welded. Hold it in the left hand.

3. Ignite the torch by bringing the carbons together. Make adjustments until the arc is going smoothly.
4. Keep the torch parallel to the joint as shown in Fig. 18-54. Observe the welding process by looking between the carbons.
5. Preheat the joint by running the flame 3 to 4 in. (75.0 to 100.0 mm) up and down the joint.
6. Begin the weld by moving the torch to the start of the joint.
7. Place the tip of the electrode in the arc. If the coating melts off and flows into the joint easily, the metal is hot enough and ready for welding. Let the filler metal melt and fuse into the joint.
8. Move the torch arc slowly along the joint adding filler metal into the puddle as needed.

WELDING SYMBOLS

The American Welding Society has developed a series of symbols to give the welder specific welding instructions. The symbols, Fig. 18-55, are included on drawings where assemblies require some sort of welding.

OTHER WELDING PROCESSES

All areas of welding have made significant advances in recent years. The use of "exotic" metals for aerospace and nuclear applications has resulted in improved equipment and the development of new welding techniques and processes.

TIG AND MIG WELDING

TIG (Tungsten Inert Gas) welding, Fig. 18-56, is a gas shielded arc welding technique that uses a

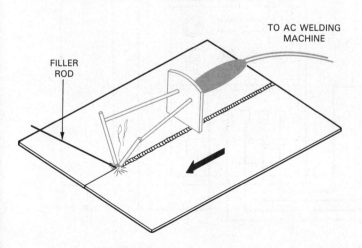

Fig. 18-54. Keep the torch parallel to the joint.

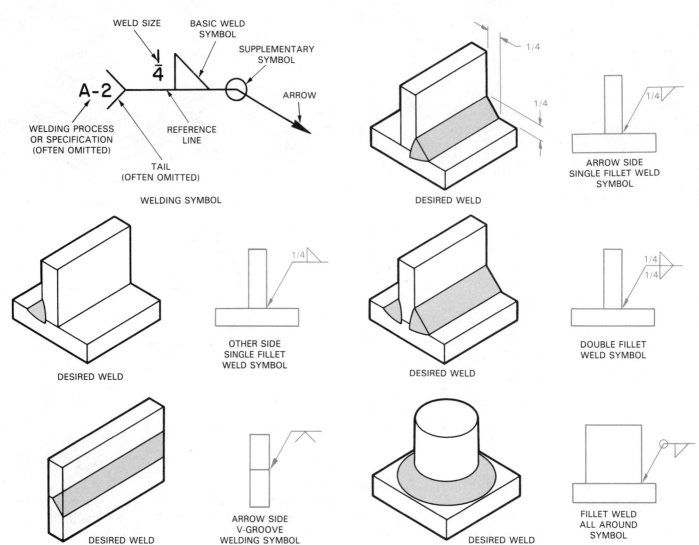

Fig. 18-55. Typical welding symbols and their meanings.

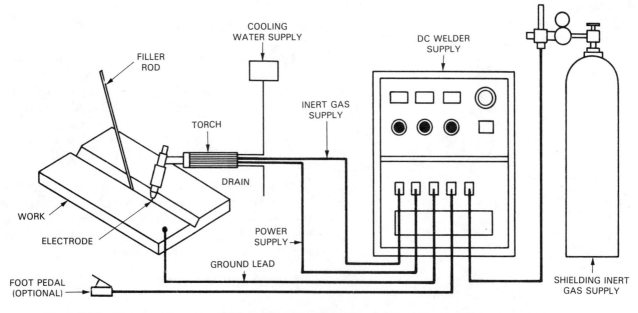

Fig. 18-56. Tungsten Inert Gas (TIG) welding is a gas shielded arc welding technique done with a permanent electrode (electrode is not consumed in welding process).

permanent electrode (the electrode is NOT consumed or melted in the welding process). The electrode, arc, and molten pool of weld metal are protected from atmospheric contamination by a stream of inert gas (helium or argon). The gas is directed to the weld area by a tube that surrounds the electrode.

MIG (Metal Inert Gas) welding, Fig. 18-57, is similar to TIG welding in that the weld area is also protected from atmospheric contamination by a stream of inert gas. In MIG welding, however, the electrode melts and contributes filler metal to the joint.

SUBMERGED ARC WELDING

SUBMERGED ARC WELDING, Fig. 18-58, is an arc welding technique that does NOT produce smoke, arc rays, radiant heat, or spatter. The consumable, bare metal electrode is shielded by a blanket of flux that covers the weld area.

To weld, the operator fills the flux cone, points the gun into the joint, allows a pile of flux to accumulate and then strikes an arc under the flux. See Fig. 18-59. Once the arc is struck, the electrode automatically feeds into the arc as the gun is moved over the joint.

STUD WELDING

STUD WELDING, Fig. 18-60, is another arc welding process. Fusion is produced by an electric arc between the metal stud, or similar part, and the work surface. The work is heated until the surfaces to be joined together reach the proper temperature. Then they are brought together under pressure. Shielding gas or flux may or may not be used.

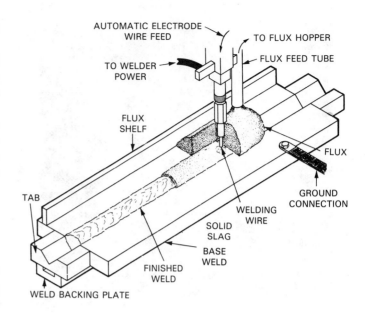

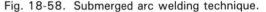

Fig. 18-58. Submerged arc welding technique.

RESISTANCE WELDING

RESISTANCE WELDING refers to a group of welding techniques that utilizes pressure, electric current, electrical resistance of the work, and the resulting heat to join metal sections. An electric circuit is produced by the welding device and the work.

SPOT WELDING

SPOT WELDING, Fig. 18-61, is the best known of the resistance welding techniques. It is widely

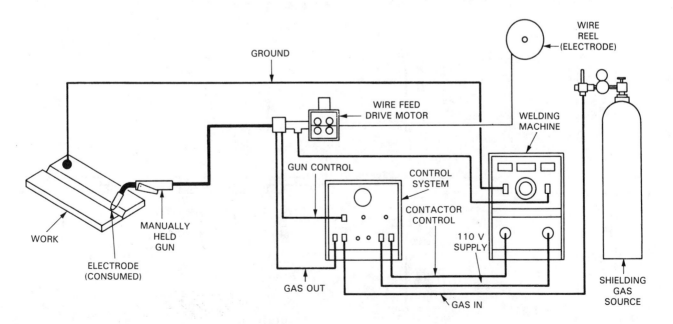

Fig. 18-57. Metal Inert Gas (MIG) welding is a gas shielded arc welding technique using an electrode that is consumed and contributes filler metal to the joint.

Fig. 18-59. Preparing to weld by the submerged arc process. (Lincoln Electric Co.)

used because it saves time and weight and is adaptable to robotic production techniques, Fig. 18-62. The welds can be made quickly and do not require the addition of filler metal. The welds are made directly between the metal parts being joined.

Spot welding, whether done by a portable unit, Fig. 18-63, a larger, manually controlled unit, Fig. 18-64, or an automated unit fitted to a computer controlled robotic unit, Fig. 18-65, depends upon four definite time stages in the welding cycle:
1. Squeeze time (application of electrode force).
2. Weld time (time electric current flows).

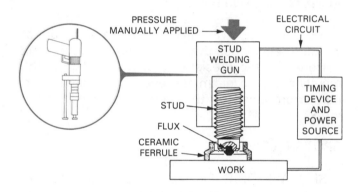

Fig. 18-60. Stud welding is an arc welding technique that welds a metal stud or similar part to another metal surface.

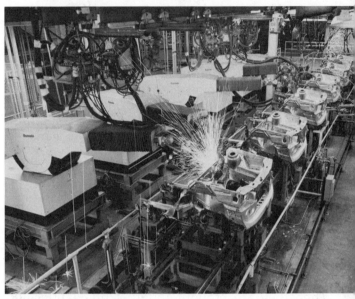

Fig. 18-62. Spot welding is readily adaptable to robotic production techniques. (Ford Motor Co.)

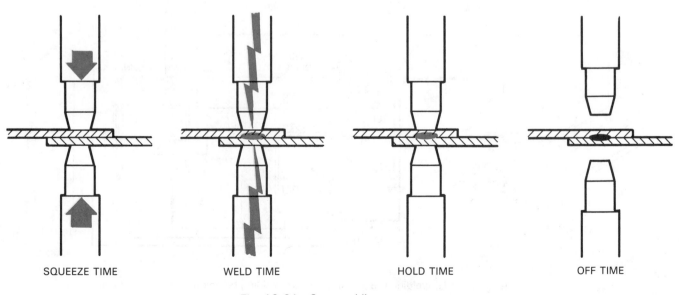

SQUEEZE TIME   WELD TIME   HOLD TIME   OFF TIME

Fig. 18-61. Spot welding sequence.

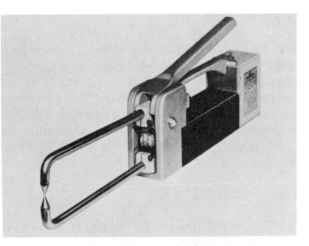

Fig. 18-63. Portable spot welding unit.
(Miller Electric Mfg. Co.)

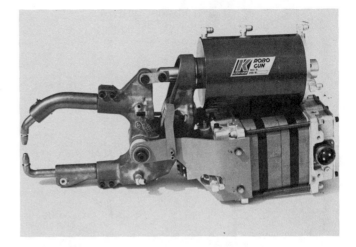

Fig. 18-65. Spot weld unit designed for use on robot.
(Milco)

Fig. 18-64. Manually controlled spot welding unit.
(Taylor-Winfield)

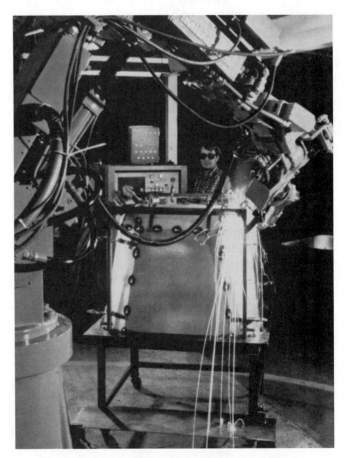

Fig. 18-66. Computer controlled robotic welding unit can produce resistance welds of extremely high quality.
(Cincinnati Milacron)

3. Hold time (forging time).
4. Off time (release of electrode).

The cycles are regulated by controls on the spot welding device. Tables for calculating the exact time of each stage for different types and thicknesses of metal are furnished with each machine.

Resistance welding, done properly, produces welds of extremely high quality. See Fig. 18-66.

SEAM WELDING

SEAM WELDING, Fig. 18-67, is a resistance welding process where fusion is produced by the

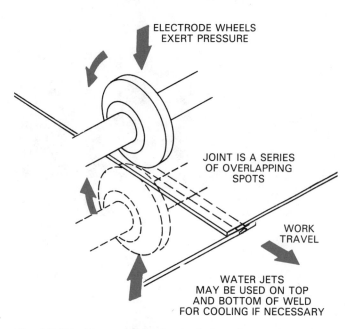

Fig. 18-67. Seam welding is a technique that produces a progressive series of overlapping spot welds along the joint.

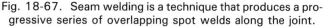

heat obtained from resistance of electric current flow through the work sections. The sections are held together under pressure by circular electrodes. The resulting weld is a series of overlapping spot welds progressively made along the joint by rotating the electrodes.

PROJECTION WELDING

PROJECTION WELDING, Fig. 18-68, is also a resistance welding technique. Heat is produced by the flow of electric current through work parts held under pressure by the electrodes. The welds are localized at predetermined points by the design of the parts to be welded.

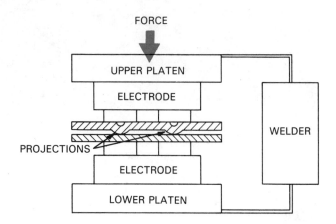

Fig. 18-68. Projection welding uses heat produced by flow of electric current through work parts held under pressure by the electrodes.

FLASH WELDING

In FLASH WELDING, Fig. 18-69, fusion is produced simultaneously over the entire surface areas of touching parts. Heat for the process is obtained from resistance to electric current flow between the two surfaces. AFTER the heating is substantially completed, pressure is applied. Flashing is accomplished by the ejection of molten metal from the joint.

UPSET WELDING

UPSET WELDING, Fig. 18-70, is a resistance welding technique very similar to flash welding. The pieces to be joined, however, are first butted together under pressure, THEN current is allowed to flow through the abutting pieces until the joint is heated to the fusion point. Pressure is continued after the power is turned off. This causes an upsetting (bulging) action at the point where fusion occurs.

NEW WELDING PROCESSES

While many of the following welding techniques have been known for some time, their development for industrial applications is fairly recent.

ELECTRON BEAM WELDING

The ELECTRON BEAM WELDING process, Fig. 18-71, makes use of fast-moving electrons to supply the energy to melt and fuse the parts being

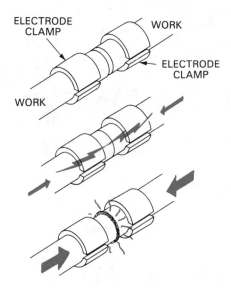

Fig. 18-69. In flash welding, fusion is produced simultaneously over the entire area of the abutting surfaces. Necessary heat is obtained from resistance to electric current between the two surfaces and by application of pressure after heating.

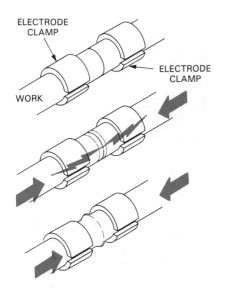

Fig. 18-70. Upset welding is very similar to flash welding. However, pieces to be joined are first butted together under pressure, then current is allowed to flow through the abutting parts until the joint is heated to the fusion point.

joined. Welds must be made in a vacuum which practically eliminates weld contamination by atmospheric gases, Fig. 18-72.

The electron beam is capable of melting any known metal, Fig. 18-73. Work is enclosed in a vacuum chamber and an electron gun directs electrons onto the work. The electron beam is further focused by an electromagnetic lens located at the base of the column. When properly focused, the fast moving electrons supply the energy to melt and fuse the metal sections together.

INERTIA WELDING

INERTIA WELDING, Fig. 18-74, is one of the simplest, newest, and most unique welding techniques. The process utilizes frictional heat and pressure to produce full strength welds in a matter of seconds, Fig. 18-75.

The parts to be joined are often bar or tubular in shape. However, flat plates or formed shapes also can be joined as long as the INTERFACE (surfaces forming joint) is generally circular.

ULTRASONIC WELDING

ULTRASONIC WELDING, Figs. 18-76 and 18-77, is a process for joining metals without using solders, fluxes, or filler metals and usually without the

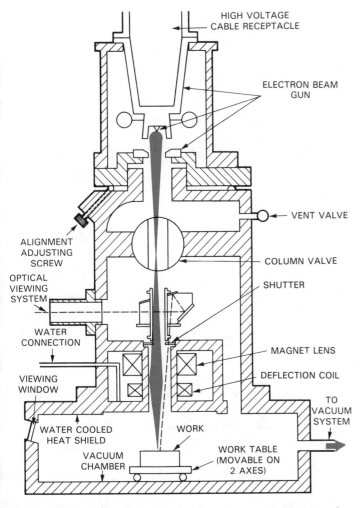

Fig. 18-71. Electron beam welding process makes use of a beam of fast moving electrons to supply energy for the melting and fusion of base metals. Weld must be made in a vacuum.

Fig. 18-72. Shown is the ''clam shell' chamber, electron beam welder, and controls. The chamber is closed and a vacuum created before welding process can begin. This unit is one of the largest in the world.
(Grumman Aerospace Corp.)

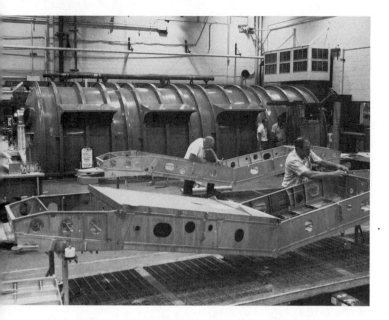

Fig. 18-73. Titanium F-14 aircraft wing center sections after they have been electron beam welded. The clam shell vacuum chamber (it can accommodate work up to 12 x 26 ft. [3.66 x 7.93 m]), can be seen in the background. (Grumman Aerospace Corp.)

Fig. 18-75. Inertia welding requires that the joint face of at least one part being welded be round or nearly so. Note the neat, clean joint on this sample inertia weld.

Fig. 18-74. In inertia welding, the flywheel, chuck, and one of the pieces to be welded are accelerated to a preset speed. Upon reaching required speed, the drive is disengaged and the rotating part is thrust against the stationary part. Energy in flywheel is discharged into interface (joint) and weld is produced. (Caterpillar Tractor Co.)

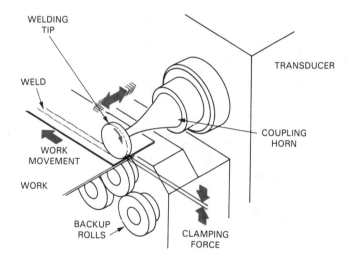

Fig. 18-76. Ultrasonic welding is a process of joining metals without the use of solders, fluxes, or filler metals and usually without the application of external heat. Ultrasonic energy is utilized to make strong metallurgical bond.

application of external heat. The metals being joined are clamped lightly between SONOTRODES (welding tips), and ULTRASONIC ENERGY (sound waves or vibrations above 20,000 hertz or cycles per second). This ultrasonic energy is introduced for a short time, usually 1 to 3 seconds. A strong

metallurgical bond is produced. There is little or no external deformation which is characteristic of pressure welding. Nor are there heat affected zones like those found in resistance welding.

COLD PRESSURE WELDING

Pressure alone is used to join the two metals in COLD WELDING. See Fig. 18-78. The process, however, involves more than pressure. Special tools

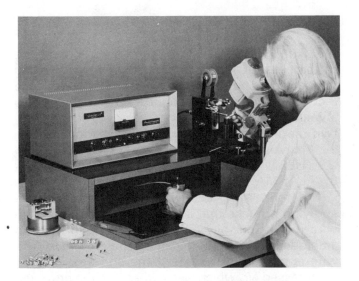

Fig. 18-77. Ultrasonic welding production machine for welding subminiature electronic devices. The machine includes a micropositioner and illuminated microscope. (Sonoweld Inc.)

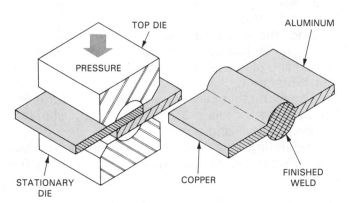

Fig. 18-78. Pressure alone is used to join two metal surfaces in cold or pressure welding. Dissimilar metals can be joined with this technique.

must be developed to produce the deformation required to direct this flow of metal into a true weld.

Cold welding is especially adaptable to some aluminum alloys. However, other dissimilar, but relatively soft, metals such as aluminum and copper can be joined by this process. Silver, lead, and nickel also can be cold welded. Another advantage is that thin metal sheet can be readily bonded to thick sections.

LASER WELDING

LASER is the abbreviation for Light Amplification by Stimulated Emission of Radiation. The laser produces a narrow and intense beam of coherent monochromatic light (light of one color or of a single wavelength) that can be focused onto an area only

a few microns (millionth part of a meter) in diameter. See Fig. 18-79.

LASER BEAM WELDING vaporizes the work at its point of focus. Molten metal surrounds the point of vaporization when the beam is moved along the weld path. A vacuum is not required, as with electron beam welding.

MICRO WELDING

Technology has made it possible to fit 10,000 transistors on a chip only 0.025 in. thick and 0.20 in. square (0.64 mm thick and 5.08 mm square). MICRO WELDING, Fig. 18-80 was developed to attach leads to these microcircuits (called CHIPS) so

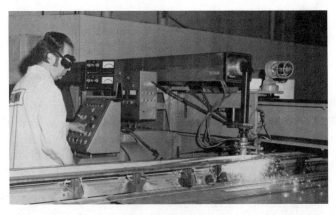

Fig. 18-79. In laser welding, a light beam (narrow and intense beam of monochromatic light) is focused on and used to vaporize the pieces being welded. Molten metal surrounds the point of vaporization when beam is moved along the joint to make the weld. (Grumman Aerospace Corp.)

Fig. 18-80. This machine spends less than 30 seconds to "stitch" forty .0015 in. (0.04 mm) gold threads between the microcircuit and the larger external leads. (Delco Electronics Div., General Motors Corp.)

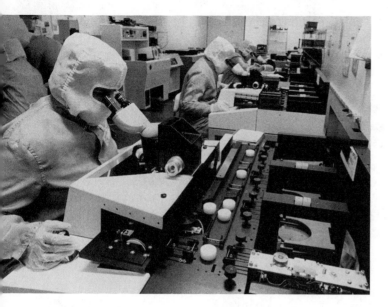

Fig. 18-81. Microwelding must be done in a dust-free environment to prevent damage to the microcircuits. (Delco Electronics Div., General Motors Corp.)

they can be used. The first stage attaches (called STITCHING) 0.0015 in. (0.04 mm) gold wire to the chip and to heavier leads. This is done in a dust-free room, Fig. 18-81. A micro welding machine can attach 40 wires in 15 seconds. Very little heat is produced in making the welds. Otherwise, the chips would be ruined.

After checking each weld, chips are enclosed in protective covers.

FLAME SPRAYING

FLAME SPRAYING is the term used to describe the process in which a metal is brought to its melting temperature and sprayed onto a surface to produce a coating. The AWS recognizes the technique as a welding process although it is never used to join two metal sections. These processes include:
1. METALLIZING.
2. THERMO SPRAY.
3. PLASMA FLAME.

The term METALLIZING describes the flame-spraying process that involves the use of metal in wire form. Specially made wire is drawn through a unique spray gun by a pair of powered rolls. The wire is melted in the gas flame and atomized by compressed air, which also carries it to the previously prepared work surface, Fig. 18-82. Upon striking the surface the particles interlock or mesh to produce a coating of the desired metal. Receiving surfaces must be cleaned and roughened before spraying, or the metal will not bond to it. Theoretically, there is no limit to the thickness that can be built up by flame spraying.

Since the air blast also keeps the sprayed surface cool, the technique can be used to spray metal on wood and plastic either for decorative purposes or for protection.

Any metal that can be drawn into wire form can be sprayed by this process. Fig. 18-83 shows a modern metallizing gun.

Metallizing has been used to apply protective, corrosion-resistant coatings of zinc and aluminum

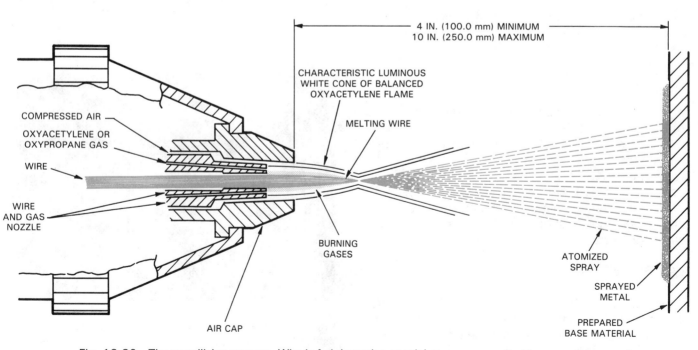

Fig. 18-82. The metallizing process. Wire is fed through a special spray gun, melted by a gas flame, and atomized and sprayed onto the work by compressed air.

Fig. 18-83. Metallizing gun applying stainless steel onto a roll surface. (Metco Inc.)

Fig. 18-85. METCO Type 5P-II ThermoSpray Gun uses metal and ceramic materials in powder form and an oxy-fuel gas flame to apply coatings. (Metco Inc.)

to steel surfaces, to build up worn bearings and shafts that might otherwise have to be discarded, and to repair machine parts.

The term THERMO SPRAY is used to describe the flame spraying equipment that involves the application of metals, and other materials that cannot be drawn into wire. They are used in powder form. See Fig. 18-84 and Fig. 18-85.

These special alloys and materials are ideal for hard surfacing critical areas that must operate under severe conditions. High temperature refractory materials which are also chemically inert can be sprayed.

In the PLASMA FLAME SPRAY PROCESS the spray gun utilizes an electric arc that is contained within a water-cooled jacket, Fig. 18-86. An inert gas, passed through the arc, is ''excited'' to temperatures up to 30,000°F (16 649°C). In general, most inorganic materials that can be melted without decomposition can be applied, Fig. 18-87.

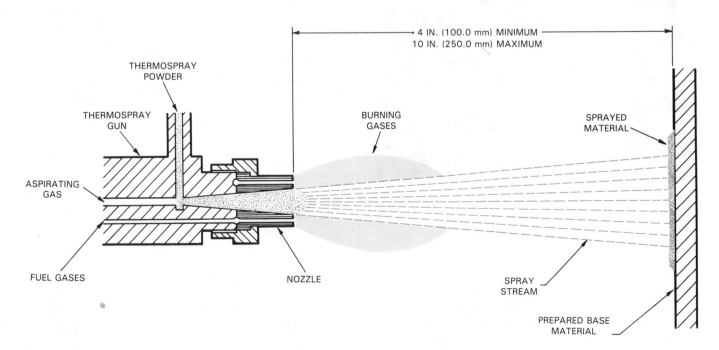

Fig. 18-84. A diagram of the thermo spray process and how it operates.

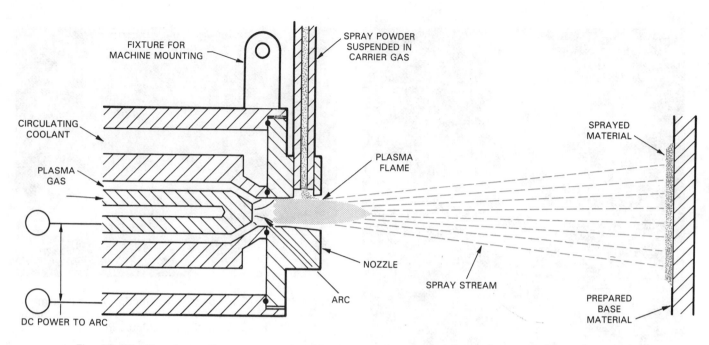

Fig. 18-86. The plasma flame process, capable of temperatures up to 30,000 °F (16 649 °C) can spray any material that will melt without decomposing.

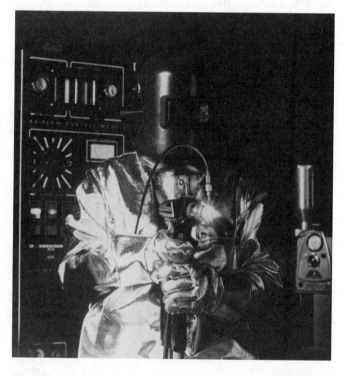

Fig. 18-87. Preparing to use the plasma flame process. Note how the operator is dressed for protection against the high heats generated. (Metco Inc.)

Application of this process includes the spraying of rocket nozzles and nose cones with high melting point materials. Jet engine turbine blades are often given a protective coating by the plasma flame process.

TEST YOUR KNOWLEDGE, Unit 18

Please do not write in the text. Place your answers on a separate sheet of paper.

1. Welding is a method of joining metals by heating to a suitable temperature to cause them to _____.
2. When gas welding, filler metal (welding rod) _____ added.
3. Gas welding includes a group of welding processes that _____.
4. Oxyacetylene welding equipment consists of:
   a. _____ (stores the gases).
   b. _____ (regulates and controls gas flow).
   c. _____ (carries the gases to the point of use).
   d. _____ (mixes and controls the gases when welding).
5. The acetylene hose is colored _____.
6. The oxygen hose is colored _____.
7. The torch is lit with a _____, never with a _____.
8. Gas welding rod is frequently copper plated to prevent it from _____.
9. Brazing rod is made of _____ or _____.
10. Flux is needed when brazing to _____ _____.
11. The torch may be held in one of two different positions: _____, usually used when joining thin metal, and _____, for joining heavier sections.

12. List the five basic types of weld joints. Draw a sketch of each.
13. Arc welding makes use of an _____ to produce the necessary welding temperature.
14. A head shield must be worn to protect the eyes and face from _____.
15. Electrodes are: (List the correct answer or answers.)
    a. Metal rods.
    b. Copper plated metal rods.
    c. Metal rods with a baked on flux.
    d. All of the above.
    e. None of the above.
16. How can you maintain correct welding speed?
17. List the equipment needed for arc welding.
18. Make a sketch showing how two metal sections must be prepared to prevent them from pulling apart as they are welded.
19. Why are welding symbols used?
20. Make a sketch of an arrow side fillet weld.
21. Why should athletic type shoes and trousers with cuffs be avoided when arc welding?

Match each of the following terms with the correct statement listed below by placing the appropriate letter in the blank next to each term.

22. ____ TIG and MIG.
23. ____ Resistance welding.
24. ____ Electron beam welding.
25. ____ MIG.
26. ____ TIG.
27. ____ Inertia welding.
28. ____ Submerged arc welding.
29. ____ Stud welding.
30. ____ Micro welding.
31. ____ Projection welding.
32. ____ Flash welding.
33. ____ Upset welding.
34. ____ Ultrasonic welding.
35. ____ Cold pressure welding.
36. ____ Laser welding.
37. ____ Flame spraying.

a. Used to stitch fine wire to microcircuits.
b. A process that uses frictional heat and pressure to produce a weld in seconds.
c. Uses light amplification by stimulated emission of radiation to make welds.
d. Pressure alone is used in this welding process.
e. Sound wave or vibrations above 20,000 hertz or cycles per second are employed to make a strong metallurgical bond.
f. Fast moving electrons supply the energy to melt and fuse the parts being joined.
g. With this technique the parts to be welded are butted together under pressure and then electric current is allowed to flow through the abutting parts.
h. Term used to describe any process where a metal is brought to its melting point and sprayed onto a surface to produce a coating.
i. After heat from an electric current passing through two abutting surfaces has reached suitable temperature, pressure is applied to join the molten surfaces.
j. A form of resistance welding. The welds are localized at predetermined points by the design of the parts to be welded.
k. An arc welding technique that produces no smoke, arc rays, radiant heat, or spatter.
l. Shields the weld and arc with a stream of inert gases.
m. The filler rod forms the electrode.
n. The electrode is not consumed.
o. A group of welding processes that uses pressure, an electric current, the resistance of the work, and the resulting heat to join the parts.
p. Fusion is produced by an electric arc between a metal stud, or similar part, and the other metal surface.

RESEARCH AND DEVELOPMENT

1. Secure samples of welded and brazed joints and mount them on a display panel. Label the samples according to the process used to make them.
2. Prepare samples of the five basic joints by gas welding.
3. Prepare samples of the five basic joints by arc welding.
4. Make a teaching aid that shows the appearance of gas welds made:
    a. With excessive heat.
    b. With insufficient heat.
    c. Satisfactorily.
5. Contact a local industry that makes use of welding in its manufacturing cycle. Request information on how they check the quality of the welds.
6. Secure or make a weld fillet gauge and demonstrate its use to the class.
7. Secure additional information on stud welding, electric slag welding, plasma arc welding, and laser welding.
8. Invite a professional welder to the school shop to demonstrate the safe and proper way to gas weld and electric arc weld.
9. Thermoplastics such as Plexiglas® and Lucite® can be joined using a technique similar to inertia welding. Secure the necessary plastic and demonstrate the inertia welding process.
10. Demonstrate the flame spray process to the class. Use the following techniques.
    a. Roughen a piece of steel or aluminum rod in the lathe.
    b. Spray it with aluminum paint from a spray

can until a 1/32 in. (0.8 mm) thick covering has been built up. When thoroughly dry, machine it until the shaft runs true.

CAUTION: Take the necessary precautions not to breathe the paint fumes. Also, cover the lathe to protect it from overspray.

11. Make a large poster showing the American Welding Society approved welding symbols.

Welding in its many modern forms is a very important facet of fabricating techniques.

Unit 19

HEAT TREATMENT OF METALS

HEAT TREATMENT includes a number of processes. They all involve the controlled heating and cooling of a metal, or an alloy, for the purpose of obtaining certain desirable changes in its physical characteristics such as toughness, hardness, and resistance to shock, Fig. 19-1.

Fig. 19-1. Heat-treating can greatly improve the physical characteristics of many metals. (Grumman Aerospace Corp.)

Fig. 19-2. Shown in the cryogenic quenching area in a modern heat-treating facility. The characteristics of several aluminum alloys and some space age metals are greatly improved by heating them to a predetermined temperature and quickly cooling (quenching) in liquid nitrogen at about −300 °F (−185 °C). (Grumman Aerospace Corp.)

Similar techniques can be employed to ANNEAL (soften) metals to make them easier to machine, or to CASE HARDEN (produce a hard exterior surface) steel for better resistance to wear.

Steel and its alloys are hardenable. Aluminum, magnesium, copper, beryllium, and titanium are also capable of being heat-treated.

Heat treatment is done by heating the metal to a predetermined temperature, then QUENCHING (cooling rapidly) in water, brine, oil, liquid nitrogen, or blasts of cold air, Fig. 19-2. Because the desired qualities do not always prevail after quenching, the material may have to be reheated to a lower temperature, followed by another cooling cycle to develop the proper degree of hardness and toughness.

The heat treatment of metals may be divided into two major categories. One deals with FERROUS metals, the other with NONFERROUS metals. Because each area is so broad, it is beyond the scope of this text to include more than basic information on all types of heat treatment of steel.

TYPES OF HEAT TREATMENT

In describing the heat treatment of carbon steel, it must be remembered that the carbon content of the metal is crucial. This carbon content is important because it will determine what can be done to improve a particular part, and how the improving will be done.

Changes in the physical characteristics of steel and its alloys can be affected by six basic types of heat treatment.

STRESS RELIEVING

STRESS RELIEVING is done to reduce stress that has developed in parts which have been cold worked, machined, or welded. The parts are heated to 1100 to 1200°F (590 to 650°C), held at this temperature for one hour per inch (25.4 mm) of thickness, and then slowly cooled.

ANNEALING

ANNEALING, Fig. 19-3, is the process of reducing the hardness of a metal to make it easier to machine or work. The metal is heated to above its normal hardening temperature (the time it is to be held at this temperature depends upon the shape and thickness of the piece). After that time it is allowed to cool slowly in some insulating material, such as ashes or vermiculite.

NORMALIZING is a process closely related to annealing.

CASE HARDENING

Low carbon steel cannot be hardened to any great degree by conventional heat treatment. However, a hard shell can be put on the surface, Fig. 19-4, by heating the piece to a red heat and introducing small quantities of carbon or nitrogen to its surface. This can be done by one of the following methods:

1. PACK METHOD, Fig. 19-5. Often referred to as CARBURIZING, the part is buried in a container of carbonaceous material and placed in a furnace for 15 minutes to one hour (depending upon the depth of the case required). The part is quenched upon removal from the furnace.

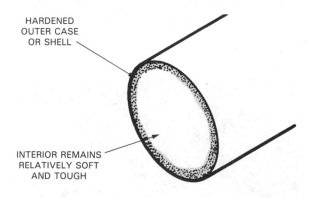

HARDENED
OUTER CASE
OR SHELL

INTERIOR REMAINS
RELATIVELY SOFT
AND TOUGH

Fig. 19-4.   Cross section of a case-hardened piece. The interior of the rod remains relatively soft and tough.

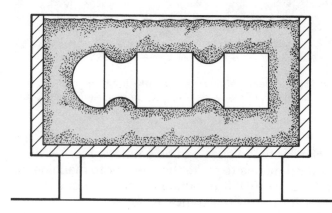

Fig. 19-5.   Part packed in container of carbonaceous material, ready to be case hardened.

Fig. 19-3.   Annealing machine parts in a hydrogen atmosphere. The hydrogen atmosphere prevents the formation of scale and surface defects that sometime develop during heat treatment. (Lindberg Steel Treating Co.)

2. LIQUID-SALT METHOD, Fig. 19-6. This technique is also known as CYANIDING and involves heating the part in a molten cyanide salt bath

and then quenching. The immersion period is usually less than one hour.

3. GAS METHOD, Fig. 19-7. NITRIDING is another term for this technique. It involves placing the parts in a special airtight heating chamber where ammonia gas is introduced at high temperature and decomposes into nitrogen and hydrogen. The nitrogen enters the steel to form nitrides which give an extreme hardness to the metal's surface.

Fig. 19-6. Operator removing hardened die block from cyanide salt pot.   (Master Lock Company)

Fig. 19-7. Loading a multi-zone carbo-nitriding furnace with padlock shackles.   (Master Lock Company)

SURFACE HARDENING

SURFACE HARDENING, Fig. 19-8, is the process that permits the surface of high carbon and alloy steels to be hardened without affecting the internal structure of the metal. FLAME HARDENING and INDUCTION HARDENING are used to attain these characteristics. Flame hardening involves the rapid heating of the surface with the flame of a gas torch, and then quenching the heated surface. Induction hardening makes use of a high frequency electrical current to heat the metal. It is done very rapidly and is ideal for production hardening.

Fig. 19-8. A railroad rail being flame hardened.

HARDENING

HARDENING, Fig. 19-9, is a technique normally employed to obtain optimum physical qualities in steel. It is accomplished by heating the part to a predetermined temperature for a specified length of time. The temperature at which steel will harden is called the CRITICAL TEMPERATURE and may range from 1400 to 2400 °F (860 to 1316 °C), depending upon the alloy and carbon content. After heating, the part is quenched in water, brine, oil, or with a blast of cold air. Water or brine is used to quench plain carbon steel. Oil is usually used to quench alloy steel. Blasts of cold air are used for the high alloy steels.

Quenching leaves the steel hard and brittle. It may fracture if exposed to a sudden change in temperature. For most purposes, this brittleness and hardness must be reduced by a TEMPERING or DRAWING OPERATION, Fig. 19-10. This involved heating the piece to below critical temperature (300

Fig. 19-9. Molds for plastic bowling pins being placed in a furnace for hardening.   (Lindberg Steel Treating Co.)

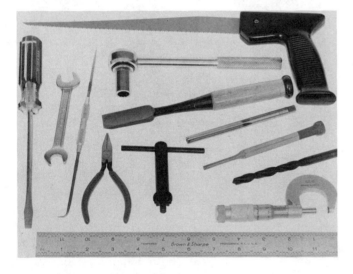

Fig. 19-10. Without the tempering operation these tools would be too brittle for use.

to 1300°F or 150 to 700°C), and allowing it to cool in still air. With the internal stresses released, toughness and impact resistance increases. However, there is a decrease in hardness and strength.

FURNACES

Heat-treating furnaces are fired by electricity, gas, or oil. The ELECTRIC FURNACE, Fig. 19-11, is

Fig. 19-11. Electric furnace of the type often found in school shops and labs.   (Lindberg, Div. Solar Industries)

found in many school shops because it is quiet, requires no venting, heats to temperature rapidly, and the temperature can be controlled with accuracy.

There are two types of gas fired furnaces: the BOX or MUFFLE type, Fig. 19-12, right, and the POT type, Fig. 19-12, left. A PYROMETER, Fig. 19-13, must be used for measuring temperature. Industry employs many variations of these furnaces. Some may be several stories high. Others can be sealed and flooded with inert gases (gases that do not oxidize and affect the metal), or sealed and vacuum drawn to avoid atmospheric gases from contaminating the metal during heat treatment, Fig. 19-14.

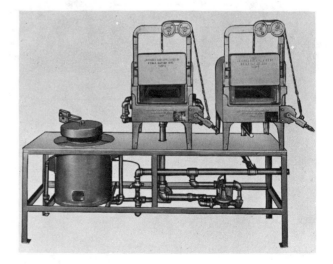

Fig. 19-12. Unit of two muffle furnaces and a pot type heat treating furnace.   (Johnson Gas Appliance Co.)

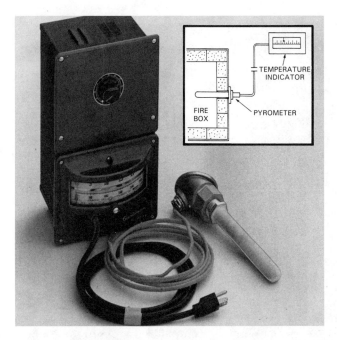

Fig. 19-13. Pyrometer for measuring furnace temperature. Inset shows a cross section of unit in place.

Fig. 19-14. Opening vacuum furnace to remove heat treated machine parts. (Master Lock Company)

Oxidation is avoided in school shop heat-treating operations by wrapping the part being heat-treated in stainless steel foil, Fig. 19-15.

HOW TO HARDEN CARBON TOOL STEEL

The exact critical temperature and quenching procedure for various kinds of steel will be found on information sheets furnished by steel manufacturers and in machinist's handbooks.

Accurate temperatures are obtained by utilizing a pyrometer. This instrument accurately measures furnace temperature. On electric furnaces the pyrometer can be set to the desired temperature and can maintain that temperature once it is reached.

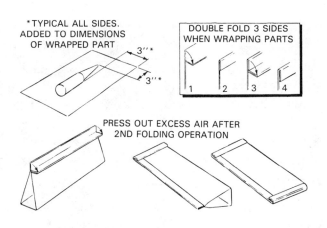

Fig. 19-15. Procedure for wrapping parts to be heat treated in stainless steel foil as protection against oxidation and decarburization. (Lindberg, Div. Solar Industries)

If the furnace is not equipped with such a device it will become necessary to judge the temperature by the color of the steel as it heats up. See Fig. 19-16.

The following procedure is recommended when hardening steel.
1. Bring the furnace to the desired temperature. If it is a gas furnace, light it according to the manufacturer's instructions.
   CAUTION: When lighting a gas furnace, stand to one side and do not look into the fire box. When the gas has ignited, adjust the air and gas valves for the best combination.
2. Heat the metal to its critical temperature. Avoid directly placing the metal being heat-treated in the gas flames. Place it in a section of iron pipe as shown in Fig. 19-17. Allow it to "soak" at this temperature until it is heated uniformly throughout.
3. Preheat the tong jaws and remove the piece from the furnace. CAUTION: Dress properly for this operation, Fig. 19-18. The metal is very hot and serious burns can result from relatively minor accidents.
4. Quench the piece in water, brine, or oil depending upon the type of steel used. Water quenching causes very rapid cooling. This creates strains and may cause cracks to form in those steels not designed for water hardening. Only certain steels may be quenched in water. Oil cools the metal more slowly and so fewer stresses develop.
   CAUTION: Quench oil hardening steels in a well-ventilated area only. Avoid inhaling any fumes. Steels are usually classified as WATER HARDENING or OIL HARDENING, according to the technique recommended for use with them. The quenching technique is critical. To secure an even hardness throughout the piece, long slender parts are dipped straight down into the

Heat Treatment of Metals 273

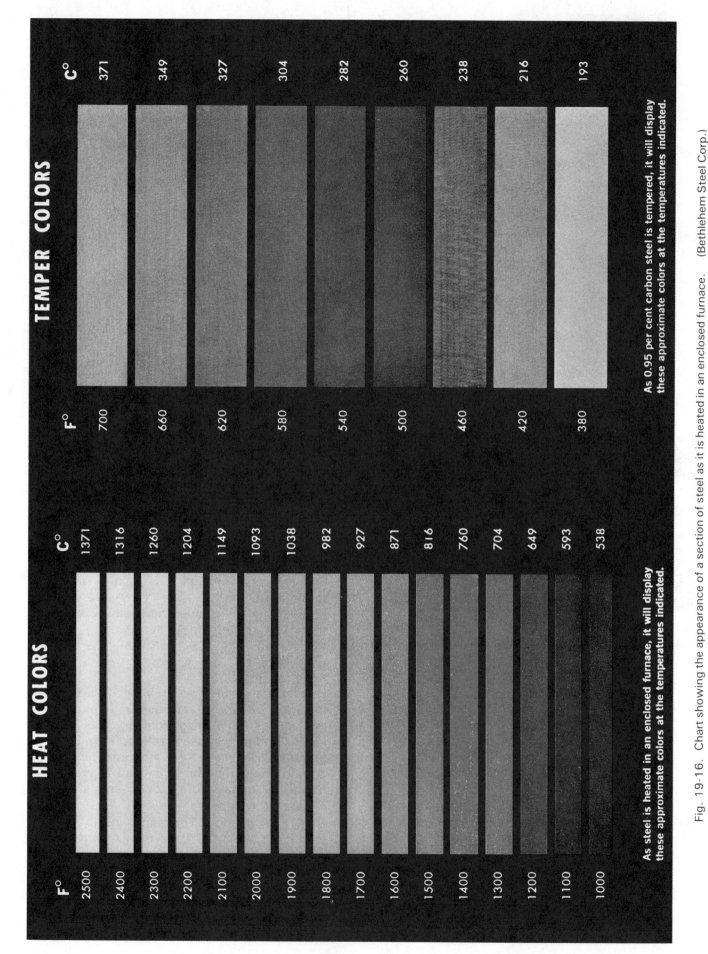

TEMPER COLORS

C°		F°
371		700
349		660
327		620
304		580
282		540
260		500
238		460
216		420
193		380

As 0.95 per cent carbon steel is tempered, it will display these approximate colors at the temperatures indicated.

HEAT COLORS

C°	F°
1371	2500
1316	2400
1260	2300
1204	2200
1149	2100
1093	2000
1038	1900
982	1800
927	1700
871	1600
816	1500
760	1400
704	1300
649	1200
593	1100
538	1000

As steel is heated in an enclosed furnace, it will display these approximate colors at the temperatures indicated.

Fig. 19-16.   Chart showing the appearance of a section of steel as it is heated in an enclosed furnace.   (Bethlehem Steel Corp.)

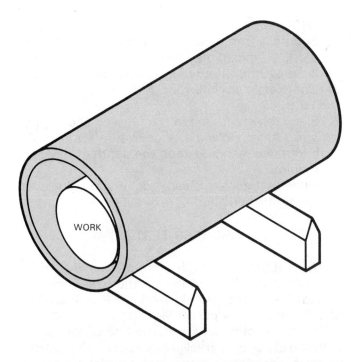

Fig. 19-17. Work being heat treated must be protected from the direct flames in a gas furnace by inserting it in a section of pipe. Elevate the unit from the furnace floor to permit uniform heating.

Fig. 19-18. Tong jaws should be preheated before removing a heated part from the furnace. Note how the operator is dressed and how clean the area is around the furnace. (McEnglevan Heat Treating & Mfg. Co.)

quenching medium with an UP and DOWN motion. Avoid a circular motion as this may cause uneven cooling and the part will warp. Other pieces may be moved around in such a manner to permit quick and even cooling.

Steel that has been hardened properly will be "glass hard" and too brittle for much use. Hardness may be checked by trying to file the surface of the work. A file will not cut the surface if the piece has been hardened properly. DO NOT USE A NEW FILE FOR TESTING.

HOW TO TEMPER CARBON STEEL

Tempering should immediately follow hardening since the "glass hard" steel may crack if exposed to sudden changes in temperature. Tempering should be done as follows.
1. Polish the hardened piece with abrasive cloth.
2. Reheat to the correct temperature. Use the color scale as a guide if a pyrometer is not available. When the proper color has been attained, quench the piece in oil.
3. Small tools are best tempered by placing them on a steel plate that has been fired to a red heat. Have the point of the tool extending beyond the edge of the plate, Fig. 19-19. Watch the temper color as the piece heats up. Quench when the proper color reaches the tool point.

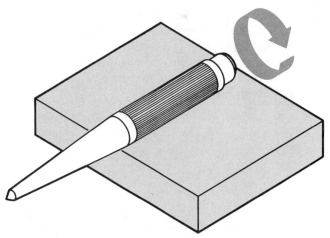

Fig. 19-19. Use a heated steel plate when tempering small tools. Have the point of the tool extend beyond the edge of the plate.

HOW TO CASE HARDEN LOW CARBON STEEL

Of the several case-hardening techniques the simplest technique, requiring a minimum of equipment, is CARBURIZING using a nonpoisonous commercial compound such as KASENIT. CYANIDING

Heat Treatment of Metals 275

There are two methods recommended for using Kasenit.

METHOD #1

1. Bring the furnace to temperature.
2. Bring the work to a bright red, 1650 to 1700 °F (900 to 930 °C), Fig. 19-20. Use a pyrometer to monitor the temperature.

Fig. 19-20. A pyrometer should be used to maintain the recommended heat. To what temperature has this furnace been heated?

3. Dip, roll, or sprinkle the Kasenit on the piece, Fig. 19-21. The powder will melt and adhere to the surface forming a shell.
4. Reheat to a bright red and hold at this temperature for a few minutes.
5. Quench in cold water.

METHOD #2

1. Secure a container large enough to hold the work. A tin can may be used if care is taken to burn off the tin coating before use.
2. Completely cover the job with Kasenit. See Fig. 19-5.
3. Place the entire unit in the furnace and heat to a red heat. Hold the temperature for 5 to 30 minutes depending upon the depth of the case required.
4. Quench the job in clean, cool water using DRY tongs for handling.

HARDNESS TESTING

HARDNESS TESTING is a process used to make certain the metal is brought to the best condition of heat treatment, or cold work, or a combination of the two, for its particular use.

The more commonly used method is concerned with the distance a steel ball or special shaped diamond penetrates into the metal under a specific load. BRINELL and ROCKWELL testing machines, known as INDENTATION HARDNESS TESTERS, Fig. 19-22, are utilized. The HARDNESS NUMBER indicates the degree of hardness of the material.

BRINELL HARDNESS TESTER

The Brinell Hardness Tester, Fig. 19-23, makes use of a steel ball which is forced into the material. A given load is applied for 30 seconds, and upon removing the load, the diameter of the impression produced is measured with a microscope containing a graduated scale. The microscope reading is compared with a table that gives the hardness number. The narrower the indentation, the harder the metal and the higher the hardness number.

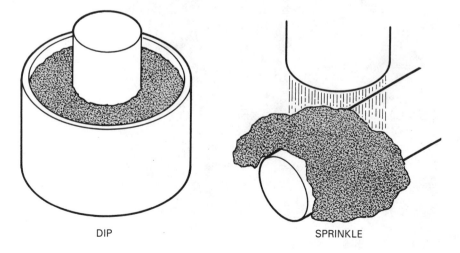

ROLL   DIP   SPRINKLE

Fig. 19-21. Dip, roll, or sprinkle Kasenit (or other commercial case-hardened compound) on the work to be case hardened, until a shell has been formed.

Fig. 19-22. Technician checking Rockwell hardness of heat treated parts. (Master Lock Company)

Fig. 19-24. Rockwell Hardness Tester. (Wilson Mechanical Instrument Div.)

Fig. 19-23. Brinell Hardness Tester. (Detroit Testing Machine Co.)

ROCKWELL HARDNESS TESTER

The Rockwell Hardness Tester, Fig. 19-24, employs a steel ball and a diamond penetrator to measure the degree of hardness. The diamond penetrator is used for testing all heat-treated steel, while the ball is utilized for other materials. A light load is applied to the ball or diamond (cone shaped), after which the dial gauge on the machine is set to zero. A major load is added and removed. The dial gauge then directly indicates the Rockwell hardness.

SHORE SCLEROSCOPE

A hardness tester that operates on a different principle is known as the Shore Scleroscope, Fig. 19-25. A diamond faced hammer is dropped within a glass tube onto the surface of the metal being tested. The height of the rebound indicates the degree of hardness. This tester does not mar the surface tested and can be used to test the hardness of very large pieces.

SAFETY

1. Heat-treating involves metal heated to very high temperatures. Handle it with the appropriate tools.
2. Wear goggles and the proper protective clothing—gloves, apron, etc. Never wear clothing that is greasy or oil soaked.
3. Avoid looking at the furnace flame unless you are wearing tinted goggles.
4. Do not try to light a gas furnace until you have been instructed in its operation. If you are not sure how it is to be done, ask for additional instruction.

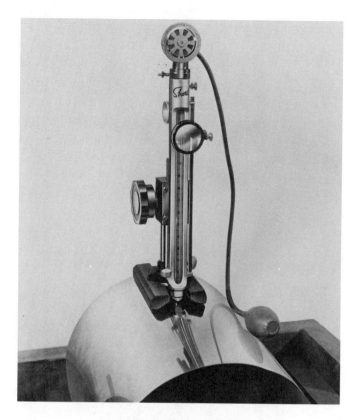

Fig. 19-25. The Shore Scleroscope.
(Shore Instrument & Mfg. Co.)

5. Avoid working in poorly ventilated areas.
6. Use only commercially prepared, nonpoisonous case-hardening compounds.
7. Avoid standing over the quenching bath when immersing work.
8. After quenching, place the work in a cleared area until it is thoroughly cooled.

TEST YOUR KNOWLEDGE, Unit 19

Please do not write in the text. Place your answers on a separate sheet of paper.

1. Heat treatment of metal includes a number of processes. They all involve _____ _____.
2. The heat-treating process that reduces the hardness of a metal, making it easier to machine is called _____.
3. How is the above usually done?
4. Case hardening means that the metal has been:
   a. Properly tempered.
   b. Only the exterior shell has been hardened.
   c. Softened.
   d. All of the above.
   e. None of the above.
5. Tempering a piece of hardened steel makes it:
   a. Brittle.
   b. Tough.
   c. Soft.
   d. All of the above.
   e. None of the above.
6. Why is tempering done?
7. Name the three quenching mediums usually employed to cool metal during heat treating.
8. For accurate temperature control in a heat-treating furnace, a _____ should be used. It measures the temperature.
9. There are two case-hardening techniques. Briefly describe each.
10. List the three kinds of hardness testers.

RESEARCH AND DEVELOPMENT

1. Secure materials that have been heat treated using the various techniques. Mount them on a panel for observation and comparison of uses.
2. The METCALF Experiment is a simple way to show the grain structure of heat-treated metal and the effect of heat on steel. How is it performed? Perform the experiment and mount the pieces that show the results for observation.
3. Secure pieces of heat-treated nonferrous metals from industrial sources. How do their uses compare with the uses of the heat-treated steel on the first display panel?
4. Prepare a metallic specimen that has been heat-treated, for observation under a microscope. Do the same to an identical piece of steel cut from the same piece of stock, which has not been heat-treated. Examine both under a microscope. What differences can be noted? What conclusions can be drawn?
5. Demonstrate the proper way to case harden low carbon steel by carburizing. Use Kasenit as the source of carbon.
6. Demonstrate the proper way to temper a hardened piece of tool steel.

Unit 20

METAL FINISHES

The surface treatment of metals as these materials come from the mill or foundry is not suitable for many applications. Additional finishing operations must be performed on them. Finishes for metals, and the methods used to apply them, play an important part in the metalworking industry.

Finishes are applied for:

1. APPEARANCE. More important than often realized, appearance affects product salability. The product is much more attractive with a proper finish than when the metal is left unfinished. An automobile would be drab if left unpainted, Fig. 20-1.
2. PROTECTION. All metals are affected to some degree by contaminants in the atmosphere and by abrasion. For example, metal sheet is often embossed or textured, Fig. 20-2, to reduce reflected light so that surface defects (scratches

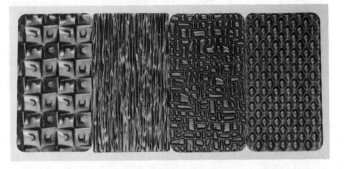

Fig. 20-2. A few examples of embossed and textured metal sheet. These surfaces do not show surface defects such as scratches and small dents.

and small dents that occur during the product's use) are "hidden" within the irregularities of the surface treatment.

3. IDENTIFICATION. This makes the product stand out over its competition or for safety reasons. Finishes are also applied to make the product blend into the surroundings, Fig. 20-3.
4. COST REDUCTION. An expensive metal can be coated onto a less expensive metal (or other material) and the finished part will be less costly than if it were made from the higher priced metal. The part will retain the properties of the more costly metal. Silver and gold, for example, are often applied to steel to improve electrical, wear, and heat distribution properties.

TYPES OF FINISHES

Metal finishing techniques fall into several groups. Finishes that can be applied to aluminum, for example, are shown in Fig. 20-4. Some finishes are coated onto the metal. Enamel, lacquer, porcelain, and many types of plastic are applied in this way. Through another process called ANODIZING, the finish is made part of the aluminum surface.

Fig. 20-1. An automobile would be quite drab if a color finish were not applied. Automotive finishes are planned in the design stage as can be seen in this study of an advanced two-passenger sports car.   (General Motors Corp.)

Fig. 20-3. A computer designed camouflage pattern for an aircraft that will be used in desert areas. It has been developed to make the aircraft blend into the surroundings, both in the air and on the ground. (Evans & Sutherland)

Other finishes are applied by sticking vinyl sheet or decals on the metal surface. Removing some metal with an abrasive (polishing, satin finishing, buffing, etc.) is another technique employed to change the texture of a metal surface.

Regardless of the type applied, the metal's surface must be clean of any oxidation, dirt, oil, and grease. Oxidation may be removed mechanically or chemically. Oil and grease are removed with solvents.

HAND POLISHING WITH ABRASIVES

An ABRASIVE is commonly thought of as any hard substance that can be used to wear away another material. The substance, grain size, backing material, and the manner the abrasive is bonded to the backing material determines the performance and efficiency of the abrasive.

ABRASIVE MATERIALS

EMERY is a natural abrasive. It is black in color and cuts slowly, with a tendency to polish.

ALUMINUM OXIDE has replaced emery as an abrasive when large quantities of metal must be removed. It is a manufactured abrasive that works best on high carbon and alloy steels. Aluminum oxide, when designed for use on metal, has a grain shape that is not as sharp as that made for use in woodworking.

SILICON CARBIDE is the hardest and sharpest of the synthetic (manufactured) abrasives. It is ideal for "sanding" metals like cast iron, bronze, and aluminum.

Silicon carbide is greenish black in color. It is superior to aluminum oxide in its ability to cut fast under light pressure.

CROCUS may be synthetic or natural iron oxide. It is bright red in color, very soft, and used for cleaning and polishing when a minimum of stock is to be removed.

GRAIN SIZE

The table in Fig. 20-5 shows a comparison of grain size and indicates how the various abrasives are graded.

COATED ABRASIVES

A coated abrasive is cloth or paper with abrasive grains cemented to one surface. Because of its flexibility, cloth is used as a backing material for coated abrasives used in metalworking. It is available in 9 in. x 11 in. (228.6 mm x 279.4 mm) sheets, or in rolls starting at 1/2 in. (12.7 mm) in width, and is called ABRASIVE CLOTH.

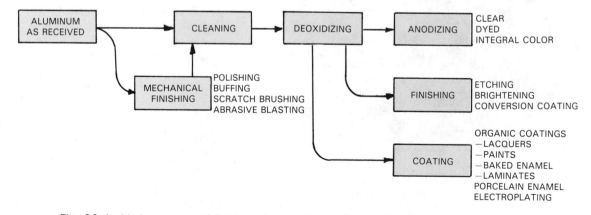

Fig. 20-4. Various types of finishes that can be applied to aluminum.

TECHNICAL GRADES		SIMPLIFIED GRADES	OTHER GRADES
Mesh	Aluminum Oxide Silicon Carbide	Emery	Emery Polishing
600			4/0
			3/0
500			2/0
400	10/0		0
360			
320	9/0		1/2
280	8/0		
240	7/0		1 G
220	6/0		2
180	5/0		3
150	4/0	Fine	
120	3/0		
100	2/0	Medium	
80	0	Coarse	
60	1/2		
50	1	Extra Coarse	
40	1 1/2		
36	2		
30	2 1/2		
24	3		
20	3 1/2		
16	4		
12	4 1/2		

Fig. 20-5. Abrasive Comparative Grading Chart. (Coated Abrasive Manufacturers' Institute)

USING ABRASIVE CLOTH

1. Abrasive cloth is quite expensive. Use only what you need. Tear the correct amount from the sheet or roll.
2. Do not throw away used abrasive cloth unless it is completely worthless. Used cloth is excellent for polishing.
3. If the piece has been filed properly, only a fine-grain cloth will be needed to polish the surface. However, if scratches are deep, start the polishing operation by using a coarse-grain cloth first. Change to a medium-grain cloth next and finally a fine-grain abrasive. A few drops of oil will speed the operation. For a high polish, leave the oil on the surface after the scratches have been removed. Reverse the cloth and rub the cloth, or smooth backing, over the work.
4. Abrasive cloth must be supported to work efficiently. To get this support, wrap it around a block of wood or a file, Fig. 20-6. Apply pressure and rub the abrasive back and forth in a straight line; if possible, parallel to the long edge of the work.
5. DO NOT USE ABRASIVES ON MACHINED SURFACES.

SAFETY PRECAUTIONS WHEN HAND POLISHING WITH ABRASIVES

1. Avoid rubbing your fingers or hand over polished surfaces or surfaces yet to be polished. Burrs on the edges of the metal can cause painful cuts.
2. Wash your hands thoroughly after polishing operations.
3. Treat ALL cuts immediately, no matter how small.
4. Place all oily rags in a closed metal container. Never put them in the pocket of your apron/shop coat or in a locker.
5. Wipe up any oil dropped on the floor during polishing operations.

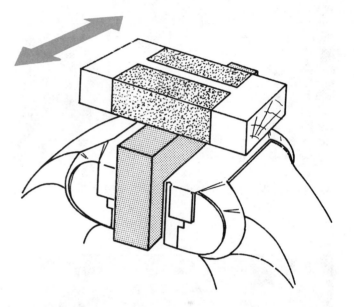

Fig. 20-6. Abrasive cloth should be supported with a block of wood or a file. Avoid supporting it with your fingers.

MECHANICAL FINISHES

Mechanical finishes are most frequently applied to aluminum, copper base alloys, stainless steel, and precious metals. They include three processes.

BUFFING, Fig. 20-7, is the brightest mechanical finish. A smooth, bright finish is produced by two or more buffing operations with progressively softer buffs and/or finer abrasive compounds. Care must be taken not to overheat the metal. Quality of a buffed surface depends upon the skill of the operator. Copper base alloys should be protected with a clear lacquer or plastic to preserve the highly reflective surface.

WIRE BRUSHING (also called SATIN FINISHING and SCRATCH-BRUSHING), Fig. 20-8, produces a smooth satin sheen. Smoothness depends on wire size of the wheel; the thinner the wire, the smoother the surface. Wheel brushes made with a combination wire and fiber are often employed for burr removal in addition to surface finishing, Fig. 20-9.

SANDBLASTING yields a matte finish. It is

accomplished by spraying the work surface with a fine abrasive driven by compressed air.

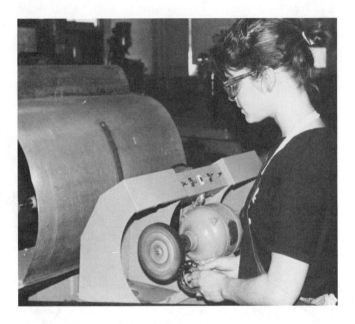

Fig. 20-7. Buffing is one way to produce a bright mechanical finish.

Fig. 20-8. Applying a satin finish to stainless steel with a wire brush. (Osborn Mfg. Co.)

METAL COATINGS

Metal coatings, with the exception of electroplating and sputtering, are primarily applied to steel. They adhere to the surface of the steel tightly enough to offer protection from corrosion. Following are the more commonly used techniques.

HOT DIPPING, Fig. 20-10. The coating is applied by dipping the steel in molten aluminum, zinc, lead,

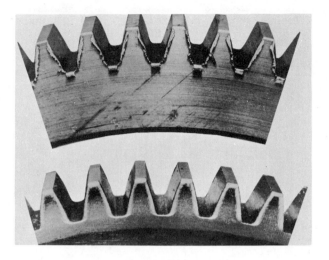

Fig. 20-9. Top. Gear with burrs. Bottom. Gear after burrs are removed with a wire brush. (Osborn Mfg. Co.)

Fig. 20-10. Hot dipping steel pipe in molten zinc to apply a protective finish. (American Hot Dip Galvanized Assoc., Inc.)

tin, or a lead-tin alloy. GALVANIZED STEEL is an example of hot dipping (the steel is dipped in molten zinc).

ELECTROPLATING, Fig. 20-11. A coating of one

metal is deposited on the surface of another metal (or plastic) through the action of an electric current, Fig. 20-12. Practically any metal can be employed as the coating. Coating thickness can be controlled and, unlike most other metal coating techniques, electroplating can deposit wear resistant surfaces as well as add a finish to make the product more attractive in appearance.

Fig. 20-11. Silver plating—Forks rotate in plating tank containing cyanide solution and bars of pure silver. Amount of electric current and length of time pieces remain in tank determines amount of silver that will be deposited on each piece. (International Silver Co.)

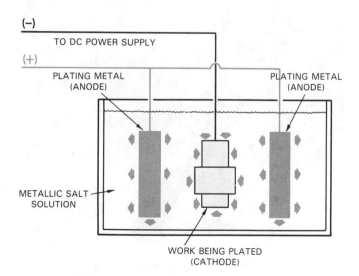

Fig. 20-12. Basic electroplating process.

FLAME SPRAYING. Metal wire or powder is heated to its melting point and sprayed by air pressure onto the work surface. Upon striking the surface, the particles interlock or mesh to produce a coating of the desired metal. This process is explained in more detail in Unit 18.

SPUTTERING, Fig. 20-13, is a technique that makes it possible to coat almost anything with a thin film of almost any material. That is, metals can be coated on metals, metals on plastics, ceramics on metals, etc. The operation is performed in a vacuum. High voltage electricity is used to excite argon gas. The gas ions bombard the surface of the target (source of the coating). The gas ions striking the target cause atomic size particles to be ejected from its surface. The target-ejected particles are deposited on the material being coated.

If you have ever constructed a plastic model automobile, the chromed parts were coated by the sputtering technique.

Fig. 20-13. The metal coating (chrome) was applied to the plastic parts of these model vehicles by sputtering. The same technique is also used to apply the plating to full size auto parts. With sputtering there are no dangerous by-products that must be disposed of, as with electroplating.

ORGANIC COATINGS

A wide range of finishes fall into this category. Paints, varnishes, lacquers, enamels, the various plastic-base materials and epoxies in both clear and pigmented (color) formulas are the most common. With the exception of the epoxies, they set by the evaporation of their solvents. This may be accomplished by air drying or baking. Epoxies require the addition of a hardener or catalyst to set.

A primer is often required to secure a satisfactory bond between the metal and the finish. Some types of castings may require a filler to smooth out the rough cast surface.

Organic coatings are applied in the following ways.

BRUSHING. At one time, this was the only way

of applying finishes.

SPRAYING. The finish is atomized and carried to the work surface by air pressure. Small pressurized spray cans, Fig. 20-14, offered in a wide range of colors, are available. Spraying is easily adapted to mass-production techniques, Fig. 20-15.

Fig. 20-14. Natural and synthetic finishes, offered in a wide range of colors, are available in individual pressurized spray cans. Before using, carefully read the instructions on the container.

Fig. 20-15. Robot painting is used by the automotive industry. Robot movement is controlled by computer.   (Chrysler Corp.)

ROLLER COATING. This can be used only on flat surfaces. It is a low-cost technique that can be mechanized.

DIPPING. The part is dipped into the finish, Fig. 20-16, removed, and allowed to dry. Dipping is widely used today by the auto industry to apply body primer and rust proofing. The coating is dried by warm air.

FLOW COATING. The part is flooded with the finish and allowed to drain while held in an atmosphere saturated with solvent vapor. Drying is then delayed until draining is complete.

Fig. 20-16. Electrically charged particles of paint evenly coat and protect all bare surfaces of this van body as it is submerged in this tank containing tens of thousands of gallons of primer. (Chrysler Corp.)

INORGANIC COATINGS

Several well-known finishing materials fall into this category.

VITREOUS OR PORCELAIN ENAMEL. These are glass coatings that are fused to sheet or cast surfaces. They form an extremely hard coating that is smooth and easy to clean, Fig. 20-17. Available in many colors, they can be applied to metals that remain solid at the firing (melting) temperatures of the

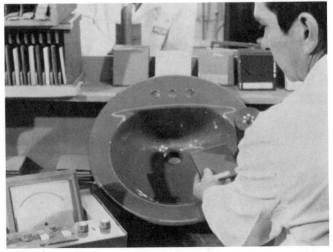

Fig. 20-17. Vitreous or porcelain enamel is a glass coating fused to sheet or cast surfaces. It is an extremely hard coating that is smooth and easy to clean.   (Eljer Plumbingware)

coating. The finish is applied as a powder, Fig. 20-18, or as a thin slurry known as "slip." After drying, it is fired to about 1500 °F (815 °C) until it fuses to the metal surface, Fig. 20-19. Most kitchen and bathroom fixtures are protected with porcelain enamel.

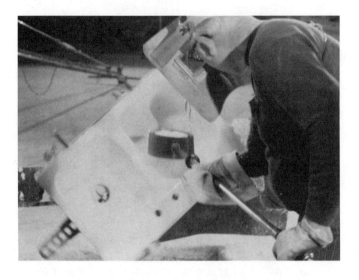

Fig. 20-18. Porcelain is applied as a powder, called "frit," or as a thin slurry known as "slip." (Eljer Plumbingware)

Fig. 20-19. After drying, the unit is fired at 1500 °F (815 °C) until the porcelain has fused to the metal surface. (Eljer Plumbingware)

ANODIZING

ANODIZING is an electrochemical process in which the oxide film on aluminum is thickened by passing an electric current through certain acid electrolytes with the aluminum as the anode, Fig. 20-20.

Color can be added to the anodized surface, Fig.

20-21. Color depth depends upon the anodizing method employed. In HARD-COLOR ANODIZING the coloring material is spread through the anodic film.

BRIGHTENING

The surface smoothness and reflectance of aluminum can be improved by certain chemical and electrochemical processes. The term used to describe these processes is called BRIGHTENING. It finds many applications in the manufacture of reflectors, jewelry, appliance trim, and automotive trim. The surface must be protected with a thin coat of lacquer to preserve the bright finish.

FILM COAT

Steel and aluminum sheet are available with a vinyl film covering that can be cut, shaped, formed, and joined like other types of metal sheet. They are made in various colors, textures, and wood grained finishes.

OTHER FINISHES

The finishes in this group offer the least protection and durability. For this reason they are seldom used by industry.

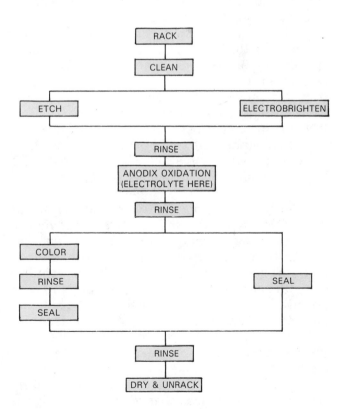

Fig. 20-20. Sequence of operations followed when anodizing aluminum.

Fig. 20-21. These aluminum tumblers have been color anodized.

Fig. 20-22. Polishing and buffing head of the type found in school industrial arts facilities. (Rockwell Mfg. Co., Power Tool Div.)

WAXING. A coating of paste wax is applied to the metal surface that has been warmed slightly. Polishing is done with a soft cloth after the metal has cooled.

HEATING. The steel is heated until the desired temper color appears. It is then plunged into cool water. The surface must be protected with wax, clear lacquer, or plastic spray.

METAL BUFFING

BUFFING should not be attempted until ALL tool marks and major scratches have been removed with abrasive cloth. After the surface has been prepared, select a buffing compound and wheel that will produce the surface required. For example, aluminum should be buffed with buffing compounds specifically developed for the metal. The compounds include both the lubricant and abrasive (tripoli, crystalline silica, Vienna lime, etc.) in stick form. Buffing wheels should operate at 7000 to 8000 surface feet per minute (a 10 in. diameter wheel would operate at 2500 to 3000 rpm).

Mount the wheels to a polishing lathe, Fig. 20-22. Use a separate wheel for each step of the polishing operation.

Buffing is usually done in two operations. A hard wheel is charged with the abrasive. This wheel is made of many layers of cotton, flannel, felt, canvas, or leather sewn together to make the wheel face stiff but with some "give." The lubricant that holds the abrasive melts when the polishing compound stick is held against the wheel. The softened lubricant and abrasive adhere to the wheel face. The abrasive-buffing wheel combination then removes the scratches formed on the metal by the abrasive cloth.

A fine abrasive belt is preferred for industrial applications. There is less chance of overheating the metal and causing a buildup of the abrasive. The belt also provides a larger polishing area.

Final polishing is done with a loose wheel (made of many layers of flannel, sewn or glued only at the center) and a polishing compound. This compound consists of a soft abrasive, such as rouge or whiting, and a lubricant of tallow or grease that holds the compound in bar form. The lubricant also causes the abrasive to adhere to the wheel. Polishing speed is about half the speed used to remove scratches caused by the abrasive cloth.

One of the fundamental polishing and buffing techniques is the correct position of the work. Polishing is best done when the work is held BELOW the centerline of the wheel, Fig. 20-23, A.

When considerable stock must be removed, best results can be obtained by pulling the work against the rotation of the wheel, Fig. 20-23, B. It is also safer because the hands are being pulled AWAY from the wheel.

Final polish is obtained by making light downward passes on the wheel, Fig. 20-23, C.

Remove buffing and polishing residue from the metal with warm soapy water or a solvent. Dry with a soft cloth.

METAL FINISHING SAFETY

1. Read instructions on the finish container AND FOLLOW THEM.
2. Wash your hands after applying a finish or after using chemicals and/or solvents to clean the work.
3. Examine the work for rough edges and burrs BEFORE attempting to clean it. Remove any that are found.
4. Apply finishes in a well-ventilated area.
5. Keep open flames and sparks away from areas

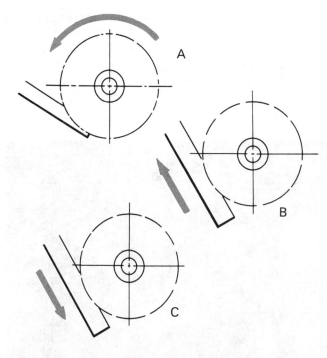

Fig. 20-23. Recommended positions of work when polishing on a buffing head. A—Hold work below the centerline of the wheel. B—When a large amount of stock must be removed, pull the work against the rotation of the wheel. C—Final polish is obtained by making light downward passes on the wheel.

where finishes are to be applied or solvents used.

6. Use an approved filter mask when spraying finishes.

7. Wear goggles and protect your clothing when applying finishes.

8. Clean up any spilled finishing material and/or solvent.

9. Dispose of used waste or wiping cloths by placing them in an approved steel safety container.

10. Should you get any solvent, finish, or cleaning chemical in your eyes flood them with large quantities of clean, cool, running water for at least 10 minutes, then seek IMMEDIATE medical attention.

TEST YOUR KNOWLEDGE, Unit 20

Please do not write in the text. Place your answers on a separate sheet of paper.

1. An abrasive is: (List the correct answer or answers.)
   a. A hard substance.
   b. Any hard, sharp substance that can be used to wear away another material.
   c. Used to polish metal.
   d. All of the above.
   e. None of the above.

2. List three manufactured abrasives.

3. Abrasive cloth must be _____ to work efficiently.

4. Finishes are applied for what four reasons? Give an example of each.

5. Metal is often embossed (design stamped into the metal's surface) to: (List the correct answer or answers.)
   a. Make inexpensive metals look more costly.
   b. Lower manufacturing costs.
   c. Hide scratches and small dents.
   d. All of the above.
   e. None of the above.

6. Buffing produces a _____ finish on metal.

7. Wire brushing produces a _____ sheen on metal.

8. Galvanized steel sheet is steel that has been hot dipped in _____.

9. Before any finish can be applied, the surface of the metal must be:
   a. Cut to size.
   b. Made wear resistant.
   c. Thoroughly cleaned.
   d. Electroplated.
   e. Purchased.
   f. Machined.

10. Name five methods used to apply paints and varnishes.

11. Porcelain enamel is a _____ coating that is fused to the metal.

12. List three organic type finishes.

13. Buffing should not be attempted until _____ _____.

14. The lubricant and abrasive are often combined in buffing compound. Why?

15. Describe how to buff metal.

16. List at least four safety factors that should be observed when applying finishes to metal.

RESEARCH AND DEVELOPMENT

1. Develop and construct displays that show:
   a. Samples of various types of abrasive cloth.
   b. Metal samples in various stages of hand polishing with abrasive cloth. Spray them with lacquer or acrylic plastic to prevent rust.

2. Devise an experiment that will determine what abrasive materials are best for aluminum, brass, steel, cast iron, and tool steel. The investigation should include the quantity of material removed within a specified period of time; surface finish of the polished work; clogging of the abrasive cloth; and, the effect lubricating oil has on the quality of the surface finish. Abrasives of similar grade value must be used if the test is to be valid.

3. Visit a local body and fender repair shop and observe how an auto body is prepared for the finish, how the finish is applied and what is done

to complete the job. Make a report to your class on what you saw.

4. Secure samples of metal finished by wire brushing, buffing, sandblasting, etc. Label and mount them on a display panel.

5. Contact your science teacher for equipment needed to demonstrate electroplating to the class.

6. Demonstrate hot dipping to the class. Use a lead-tin alloy (solder).

Finishes for metals take many forms, ranging from chemical, pigmented, and plastic coatings to the degree of smoothness of the metal's surface. This precision surface grinder is capable of producing a mirror-like surface on metal.   (DoALL Company)

Unit 21

GRINDING

GRINDING, Figs. 21-1 and 21-2, is the operation that removes material by rotating an abrasive wheel or belt against the work. It is usually used for sharpening tools, removing material too hard to be machined by other techniques, cleaning the parting line(s) from castings and forgings, or when fine surface finishes and close tolerances are required.

ABRASIVE BELT GRINDERS

ABRASIVE BELT GRINDING MACHINES, Fig. 21-3, are heavy-duty versions of the belt and disc sanders used in woodworking. A wide variety of abrasive belts permit these machine tools to be employed for grinding to a line, deburring, contouring, and sharpening tools.

BENCH AND PEDESTAL GRINDER

The familiar bench and pedestal grinders are the simplest and most widely used grinding machines.

The grinding done on them is called OFFHAND GRINDING. This is work that does not require great accuracy in size or shape, and is held in the hands and manipulated until it is ground to the desired shape.

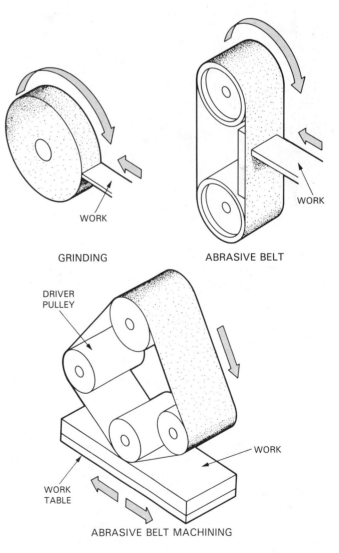

Fig. 21-2. How typical grinding machines operate.

Fig. 21-1. Grinding is the operation that removes material by rotating an abrasive wheel or belt against the workpiece. This grinding operation is being performed on a cylindrical grinder. The guards have been removed and the coolant fluid turned off for a better view of the operation. (Cincinnati Milacron)

Fig. 21-3. Abrasive belt grinding machines. The machine to the right has a flexible belt and adapts to three-dimensional contours. (Rockwell International, Power Tool Div.)

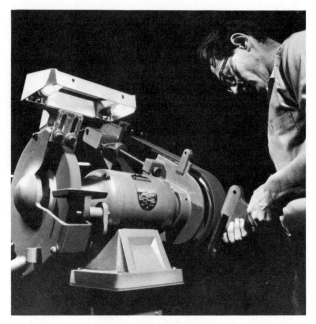

Fig. 21-5. Pedestal grinder. (South Bend Lathe Inc.)

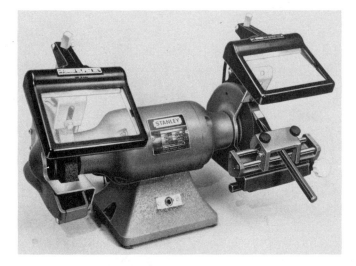

Fig. 21-4. Bench grinder. Never operate a bench or pedestal grinder unless all guards are in place and in sound condition. Wear safety glasses! (Stanley Tools)

Fig. 21-6. Pedestal grinder with a built-in coolant system. (Hammond Machinery Builders Inc.)

The bench grinder, Fig. 21-4, is a grinder that is fitted to a bench or table. The grinding wheels mount directly onto the motor shaft; one is coarse for roughing, and the other is fine for finish grinding.

The pedestal grinder is usually larger than the bench grinder, and is equipped with a base (pedestal) that is fastened to the floor. The DRY TYPE, Fig. 21-5, has no provisions for cooling the work during grinding other than a water container into which the tool may be dipped. In the WET TYPE, Fig. 21-6, a coolant system is built into the grinder and keeps the wheels constantly flooded with fluid. The coolant washes away particles of loose abrasive and metal and keeps the work cool.

Bench and pedestal grinders can be dangerous if not used properly. They must never be used unless fitted with guards and safety glass EYE SHIELDS, Fig. 21-7. Even then, it is advisable to wear goggles. A TOOL REST is provided to support the work while grinding. It is recommended that the rests be adjusted to within 1/16 in. (1.5 mm) of the wheels. This will prevent work from being wedged between the rest and the wheel, Fig. 21-8. Turn the wheel by hand after adjusting the rest to be sure there is sufficient clearance.

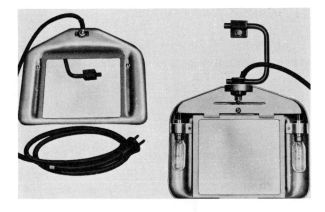

Fig. 21-7. Eye shields for bench and pedestal grinders.

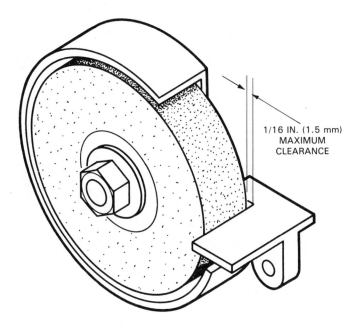

1/16 IN. (1.5 mm)
MAXIMUM
CLEARANCE

Fig. 21-8. A properly spaced tool rest.

Grinding wheels can be another source of danger and should be examined frequently for eccentricity and soundness. A new wheel can be tested by suspending it on a string or wire and tapping the side of the wheel with a light metal rod. A solid wheel will give off a clear ringing sound. A wheel which does not give off such a sound must be assumed to be cracked and should be destroyed. Under no condition should it be used. Because it is not possible to check the wheels by this manner each time the grinder is used, it is considered safe practice to never stand in front of a grinder when it is first turned on.

The wheel must also run true and be balanced on the shaft. A WHEEL DRESSER, Fig. 21-9, should be used to bring abrasive wheels back to round and remove the glaze. The dresser is supported on the

Fig. 21-9. A mechanical wheel dresser.
(Black and Decker Co.)

tool rest and is held firmly against the wheel with both hands, Fig. 21-10. It is moved back and forth across the surface.

Maximum efficiency can be secured from the grinder if the following recommendations are observed.

1. Use the face of the wheel, never the sides.
2. Move the work back and forth across the face of the wheel. Even wear will result, preventing the wheel from becoming grooved.
3. Keep the wheel dressed and the tool rests properly adjusted.
4. Soft metals like aluminum, brass, and copper tend to load (clog) the abrasive wheel. If the grinder is to be used primarily for tool grinding, it is suggested that another grinder be secured for grinding soft metals, castings, and weldments.

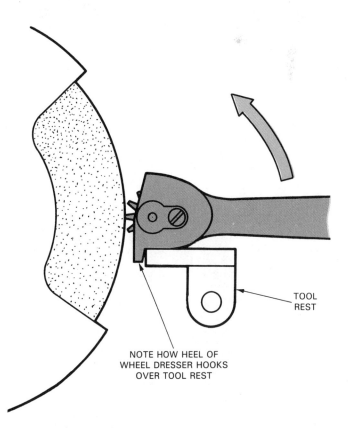

TOOL
REST

NOTE HOW HEEL OF
WHEEL DRESSER HOOKS
OVER TOOL REST

Fig. 21-10. Using a wheel dresser.

FLEXIBLE SHAFT HAND GRINDERS

Flexible shaft hand grinders, Fig. 21-11, do many grinding jobs from light deburring and polishing to light milling operations. They are used extensively on jobs such as finishing dies, Fig. 21-12.

PRECISION GRINDING

Precision grinding is a way to economically remove excess material and to finish hardened steel parts to very accurate sizes with extremely fine surface finishes. Tolerances as close as 1/100,000 in. (.00025 mm) are possible using modern grinding techniques.

Precision grinding includes many specialized methods of grinding. However, for general classification, it may be divided into the following six methods.

Fig. 21-11. Finishing a machine part with a rotary type hand grinder. The tool is fitted with a flexible shaft.   (Dumore Co.)

Fig. 21-12. A reciprocating type hand grinder polishing a die casting mold. The abrasive stone can be replaced with various shaped files and hones.   (Diamond Tool Div., Engis Corp.)

CYLINDRICAL GRINDING

In cylindrical grinding, the work is mounted between centers and rotates while in contact with the grinding wheel, Fig. 21-13. Straight, taper, and form grinding can be done by this method. There are two variations of cylindrical grinding.

1. TRAVERSE GRINDING, Fig. 21-14. The revolving piece moves past the rotating grinding wheel. A fixed amount of metal is removed on each pass of the work. Traverse grinding permits work that is wider than the face of the grinding wheel to be ground.

Fig. 21-13. A close-up of a cylindrical grinding operation. (Cincinnati Milling Machine Co.)

Fig. 21-14. In traverse grinding, the work moves past the revolving grinding wheel.   (Landis Tool Co.)

2. PLUNGE GRINDING, Fig. 21-15. The work rotates while in contact with the grinding wheel but does not reciprocate past it, because the wheel is the same width as the area being ground. The infeed of the grinding wheel is continuous rather than intermittent.

CENTERLESS GRINDING

With centerless grinding, Fig. 21-16, it is not necessary to support the work between centers as it is rotated against the grinding wheel. Instead, the piece is positioned on a work support blade and is fed automatically between a regulating or feed wheel which causes the work to rotate, and the grinding wheel which does the cutting. Through feed is obtained by setting the regulating wheel at a slight angle.

There are three variations of centerless grinding.

1. THROUGH FEED GRINDING. Only simple cylindrical shapes can be produced by this method. The work is fed continuously by hand, or from a feed hopper, into the gap between the grinding wheel and the regulating wheel. The pieces drop off the work support blade when the grinding operation is completed. See Fig. 21-17.
2. INFEED GRINDING, Fig. 21-18. With this technique, the work is fed into the wheel gap until it reaches a stop. When the grinding operation is complete the work is ejected. The diameter of the work is controlled by the width of the gap between the regulating wheel and the grinding wheel. Infeed grinding is ideally suited for grinding work with a shoulder.
3. END FEED GRINDING, Fig. 21-19. End feed grinding is used for grinding spheres and short tapers. Both wheels are dressed to the required shape and the work is fed in from the side of the wheel to an end stop. The finished pieces are automatically ejected.

Centerless grinding is done when relatively large quantities of the same part are required. The production rate is high and the costs are low because there is no need to drill center holes nor to mount the work in a holding device.

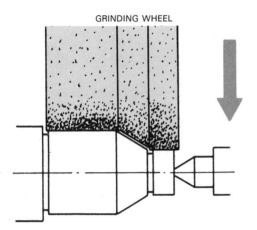

Fig. 21-15. Plunge grinding — the grinding wheel is fed into the rotating work. Since the work is no wider than the grinding wheel, it is not necessary for it to be given a reciprocating motion.

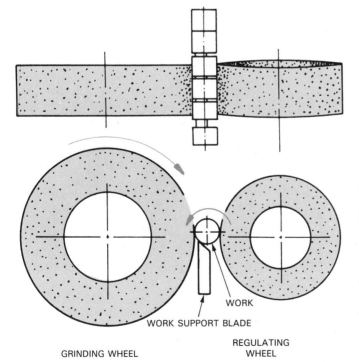

Fig. 21-16. How centerless grinding works.

Fig. 21-17. Drill press column being finished on centerless grinding machine. (Clausing)

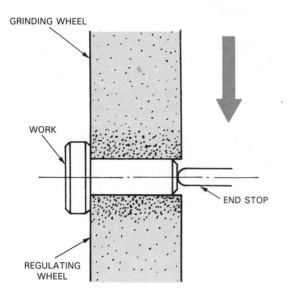

Fig. 21-18. Infeed centerless grinding.

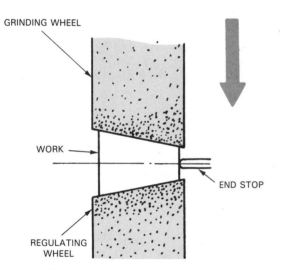

Fig. 21-19. End feed centerless grinding.

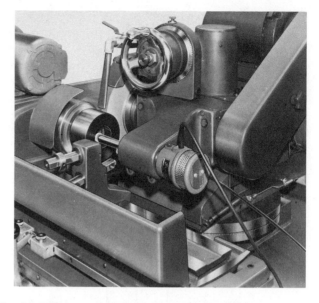

Fig. 21-20. Internal grinding operation being done on universal grinding machine. (Landis Tool Co.)

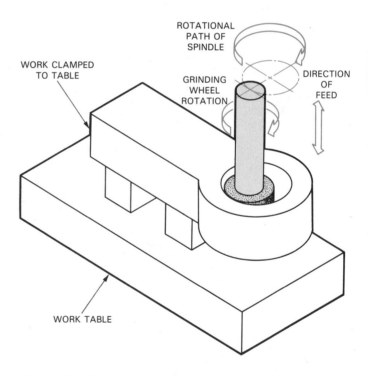

Fig. 21-21. Internal grinding of shapes too large to be rotated.

INTERNAL GRINDING

Internal grinding, Fig. 21-20, is done to secure a fine surface finish and accuracy on internal diameters. The work is held in a chuck and rotated. The revolving grinding wheel moves in and out of the hole during the grinding operation. A special internal grinding machine is used to finish holes in pieces too large to be rotated, Fig. 21-21. The hole diameter is controlled by regulating the diameter of the circle in which the grinding head moves.

TOOL AND CUTTER GRINDING

Milling cutters, taps, and reamers represent a considerable investment in the inventory of the average machine shop. Since much of their period of

usefulness and efficiency depends on the keenness of their cutting edges, it is important that they be sharpened at the first sign of dullness. The setup of a grinding machine is shown in Fig. 21-22.

FORM GRINDING

In form grinding, Fig. 21-23, the grinding wheel is shaped to produce the required design on the

Fig. 21-22. Machine setup for sharpening a milling cutter. Before grinding, operator will put on goggles. (Norton Co.)

work. Thread grinding is an example of form grinding. A form (at top of illustration) is used to guide the cemented diamond particle wheel as it trues the wheel which grinds the required thread shape. The grinding machine compensates for any material removed from the grinding wheel.

SURFACE GRINDING

Flat surfaces are ground on a surface grinder. There are two basic types of surface grinding machines.

1. PLANER TYPE, Fig. 21-24. This machine makes use of a reciprocating motion to move the work table back and forth under the grinding wheel. Three variations of planer type surface grinding are illustrated in Fig. 21-25.
2. ROTARY TYPE SURFACE GRINDER, Fig. 21-26. The machines in this category have circular work tables which revolve under the rotating grinding wheel. Two variations of this technique are shown in Fig. 21-27.

In a planer type surface grinder the reciprocating table movement can be controlled manually or by means of a mechanical or hydraulic drive. A manually operated machine is shown in Fig. 21-28. A machine operated by automatic power feed is illustrated in Fig. 21-29.

Much of the work done on a surface grinder is held in position by a MAGNETIC CHUCK, Fig.

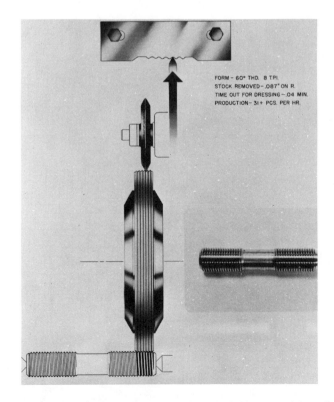

FORM - 60° THD. 8 T.P.I.
STOCK REMOVED - .087" ON R.
TIME OUT FOR DRESSING - .04 MIN.
PRODUCTION - 31+ PCS. PER HR.

Fig. 21-23. Form grinding precision threads on a special stud. (Jones & Lamson Machine Co.)

Fig. 21-24. Planer type surface grinder machines flat surfaces.

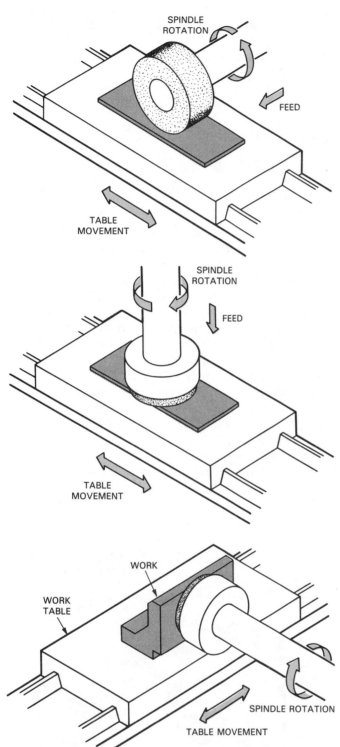

Fig. 21-26. The rotary type surface grinder. (Clausing Corp.)

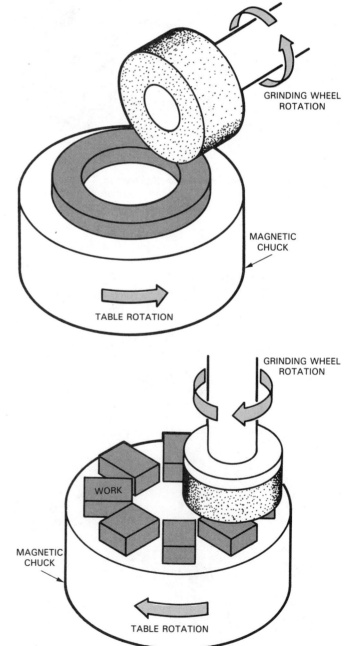

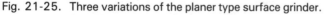

Fig. 21-25. Three variations of the planer type surface grinder.

21-30. This holds the work by exerting magnetic force. Nonmagnetic materials can be ground by bracing with steel blocks or parallels to prevent them from sliding. The MAGNETIC CHUCK, Fig. 21-31, makes use of a permanent magnet, eliminating all cords and any danger of the electrical connection being broken accidentally, permitting the work to fly off.

Fig. 21-27. Two variations of the rotary type surface grinder.

Fig. 21-28. Manually operated surface grinder. This machine is found in many school shops.
(Harig Products, Bridgeport Machine Div. of Textron, Inc.)

Fig. 21-29. Surface grinder fitted with hydraulic power feeds. The panel on the right portion of the machine base contains the switches to activate the power feeds. The panel at upper right contains digital readouts of table and wheel movements (feed).
(Harig Products, Bridgeport Machine Div. of Textron, Inc.)

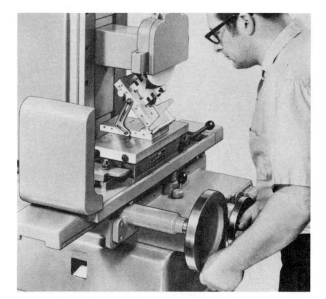

Fig. 21-30. Magnetic chuck being used to hold an angle plate to position work for grinding. (Clausing)

Fig. 21-31. Magnetic chuck with a permanent type magnet.
(O.S. Walker Co., Inc.)

The ELECTROMAGNETIC CHUCK, Fig. 21-32, makes use of an electric current to create the magnetic field.

Frequently, work mounted on a magnetic chuck becomes magnetized and must be demagnetized before it can be used. A DEMAGNETIZER, shown in Fig. 21-33, may be used to neutralize the piece.

Work can also be held on surface grinders by using a universal vise with index centers, Fig. 21-34, or clamping it directly to the table, Fig. 21-35.

GRINDING WHEELS

The grinding wheel, with its thousands of abrasive grains, Fig. 21-36, might be compared

Fig. 21-32. Magnetic chuck which uses electric current to create magnetic field.

Fig. 21-33. A demagnetizer. (L-W Chuck Co.)

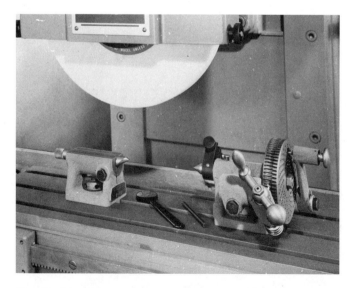

Fig. 21-34. Centers and an indexing head are used when the shape of the work permits. The indexing head is used in much the same manner as the dividing head in milling.

Fig. 21-35. Work bolted directly to the table for grinding. (Brown & Sharpe Mfg. Co.)

Fig. 21-36. Close-up of abrasive grains that make up a typical grinding wheel, magnified about 50 times. (Cincinnati Milling Machine Co.)

with a many toothed milling cutter since each of the abrasive grains is actually a cutting tooth.

As the wheel cuts, the chips dull the abrasive grains and wear and cut away the bonding material (the material that holds the abrasive particles together). The ideal grinding wheel, of course, would be one in which the bonding medium wears away slowly enough to get maximum use from the individual abrasive grains, yet rapidly enough to permit the dulled particles to drop off and expose sharp new particles. Because so many factors govern the efficiency of the grinding wheel, the wheel eventually dulls and must be dressed with a DIAMOND DRESSING TOOL, Fig. 21-37. Failure to dress the wheels of a precision grinding machine in time will result in the faces becoming loaded or glazed so they will not cut freely, Fig. 21-38.

Only manufactured abrasives are suitable for modern high speed grinding wheels. The properties and the spacing of the abrasive grains and the composition of the bonding medium can be controlled to obtain the desired grinding performance.

To aid in duplicating grinding performance, a standard system of marking grinding wheels was adopted by the Abrasive Industry. Five factors were considered.

1. ABRASIVE TYPE—manufactured abrasives fall into two main groups. Letter symbols are used to identify them.
    A—Aluminum Oxide
    C—Silicon Carbide

Fig. 21-37. Diamond tool being used to dress grinding wheel. (Clausing)

A prefix number is used to designate a particular type of aluminum oxide or silicon carbide abrasive.
2. GRAIN SIZE—indicated by a number usually ranging from 10 (coarse) to 600 (fine).
3. GRADE—the strength of the bond holding the wheel together ranging from A to Z (soft to hard).
4. STRUCTURE—the grain spacing or the manner in which the abrasive grains are distributed throughout the wheel. It is numbered 1 to 12. The higher the number the ''more open'' the structure (wider grain spacing).
5. BOND—the material that holds the abrasive grains together. Five types are used.
    V—Vitrified. Carefully selected clays mixed with the abrasive particles are fired until the clay becomes molten and fuses to the abrasive grains.
    B—Resinoin (synthetic resins).
    R—Rubber.
    E—Shellac.
    S—Silicates.

Most grinding wheels are made with a vitrified bonding medium.

The acceptance and adoption of the grinding wheel marking system has guaranteed, to a reasonable degree, duplication of grinding performance. The standard system for marking grinding wheels is given in Fig. 21-39.

GRINDING WHEEL SHAPES

Grinding wheels are made in nine standard shapes, Fig. 21-40, and while twelve basic face shapes are generally available, Fig. 21-41, the shape may be changed to suit the job. Wheels used for internal grinding are available in a large selection of shapes and sizes.

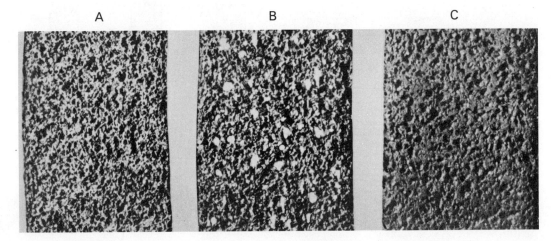

Fig. 21-38. Grinding wheels in various conditions. A—Properly dressed. B—Loaded. C—Glazed. (Norton Co.)

32A46-H8VBE

(Sometimes omitted)

ABRASIVE
Alundum = A
19 Alundum = 19A
23 Alundum = 23A
32 Alundum = 32A
38 Alundum = 38A
44 Alundum = 44A
57 Alundum = 57A
75 Alundum = 75A
37 Crystolon = 37C
39 Crystolon = 39C

GRIT SIZE

Coarse	Medium	Fine	Very Fine
10	30	70	220
12	36	80	240
14		90	280
16	46	100	320
20	54	120	400
24	60	150	500
		180	600

GRADE

Soft	Medium	Hard
A E	I M	Q Y
B F	J N	R W
C G	K O	S X
D H	L P	T Y
		U Z

STRUCTURE

The structure number of a wheel refers to the relative spacing of the grains of abrasive; the larger the number, the wider the grain spacing.

BOND TYPE

V = Vitrified
S = Silicate
B = Resinoid
R = Rubber
E = Shellac

NORTON SYMBOL

Letter or numeral or both to designate a variation or modification of bond or other characteristic of the wheel. Typical symbols are "P," "G," "BE."

Fig. 21-39. Standard system for marking grinding wheels.

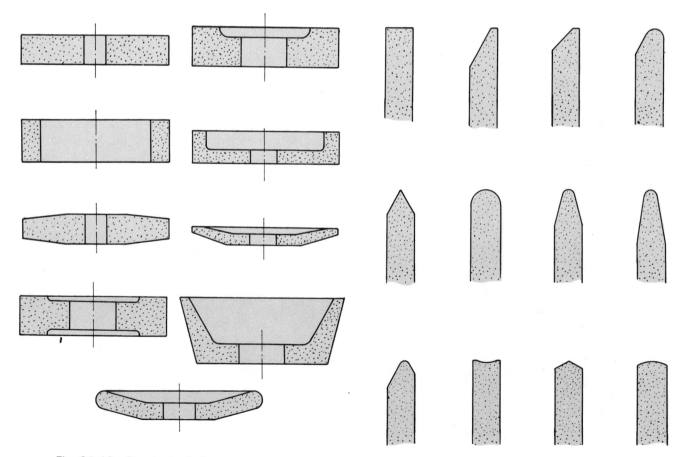

Fig. 21-40. Standard grinding wheel shapes.

Fig. 21-41. Standard shapes of grinding wheel faces.

HOW TO MOUNT THE GRINDING WHEEL

Select a grinding wheel recommended for the material to be ground. Check it for soundness and mount it on the spindle. It is essential that it be mounted properly or excessive strains will develop in it, causing it to shatter during the grinding operation. Fig. 21-42 illustrates a properly mounted wheel.

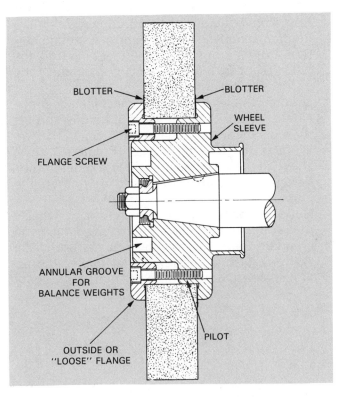

BLOTTER

BLOTTER

WHEEL SLEEVE

FLANGE SCREW

ANNULAR GROOVE FOR BALANCE WEIGHTS

OUTSIDE OR "LOOSE" FLANGE

PILOT

Fig. 21-42. A properly mounted grinding wheel.
(Norton Co.)

SAFETY

1. Always wear goggles or an eye shield when performing any grinding operation.
2. Never put a wheel on the grinder before checking it for soundness. Destroy wheels that are not sound.
3. Because it is not always possible to check the wheel on the grinder each time you use it, stand to the side of the machine when it is first turned on and until it reaches operating speed. This will keep you clear of flying pieces if the wheel shatters.
4. Do not attempt to use a grinder unless the wheel guards are in place and securely fastened.
5. If the grinding operation is to be performed dry, do not forget to hook up the exhaust attach-ment before starting.
6. Check the machine thoroughly before using it. Lubricate it according to the manufacturer's specifications.
7. Keep your hands clear of the rotating grinding wheel. It is a cutting tool and can cause serious injuries.
8. Make sure that the tool rest is properly adjusted, but never adjust it while the machine is running.
9. Never force work against the grinding wheel.
10. Always stop the machine before making measurements or adjustments.
11. Make sure that the wheel is clear of the work before starting the machine.
12. If a magnetic chuck is used, make sure that it is holding the work solidly before starting to grind.
13. If an automatic feed is to be used, run the work through one cycle by hand to be sure that there is adequate clearance and that the dogs are adjusted properly.
14. Keep all tools clear of the work table.
15. Do not permit the wheel to become too badly glazed or loaded before dressing it.
16. Never operate a grinding wheel at speeds higher than that recommended by the manufacturer.
17. Remove your watch before using a magnetic chuck to prevent the watch from becoming magnetized.

TEST YOUR KNOWLEDGE, Unit 21

Please do not write in the text. Place your answers on a separate sheet of paper.
1. Grinding is the operation that _____ _____.
2. How does an abrasive belt grinding machine differ from the bench and pedestal grinder?
3. The bench and pedestal grinder are used to do _____ grinding.
4. This grinding technique is so named because:
   a. It can only be used on external work.
   b. The work is too hard to be machined by other means.
   c. The work is manipulated with the fingers until the desired shape is obtained.
   d. None of the above.
5. Name the two types of pedestal grinders.
6. The tool rest should be about _____ in. away from the grinding wheel for safety. This prevents the work from _____.
7. Grinding wheel soundness can be checked by _____.
8. As this cannot be done each time, it is recommended that the operator _____ when first turning on the machine.

9. _____ grinding mounts the work between centers and rotates it while it is in contact with the grinding wheel.

10. With _____ grinding it is not necessary to support the work between centers since it is rotated against the grinding wheel.

11. The surface grinder is used to grind _____ surfaces.

12. Much surface grinder work is held on a _____.

13. One disadvantage in using a magnetic chuck is that the work may become _____.

14. Prepare a sketch showing the operating principle of the surface grinder.

15. The _____ might be compared to a many-toothed milling cutter.

16. The ideal grinding wheel will:
    a. Wear away as the abrasive particles become dull.
    b. Wear away at a predetermined rate.
    c. Wear away slowly to save money.
    d. None of the above.

17. List the five factors that are the distinguishing characteristics of a grinding wheel.

18. Grinding wheels on many types of grinding machines are trued with _____.

19. Make a sketch showing standard grinding wheel shapes.

20. A solid grinding wheel will give a _____ when struck with a metal rod.

21. Modern high speed grinding wheels are made only from _____ abrasives.

22. What two conditions will prevent a grinding wheel from cutting freely?

RESEARCH AND DEVELOPMENT

1. Abrasive machining is a relatively new machining technique. What is it and how does it differ from conventional precision grinding?

2. Prepare samples that show how a ground surface differs from a surface machined on the lathe, shaper, vertical milling machine, and horizontal milling machine.

3. Secure samples of products machined by precision grinding. Examine them carefully and list their distinguishing characteristics.

4. What is the MOHS SCALE? Prepare a chart showing the common abrasives in order of their hardness. Secure samples to mount on the chart.

5. How are natural sandstone grinding wheels made? Secure sample of natural sandstone and compare them with samples of the artificially manufactured abrasives. What makes the artificial abrasive superior to the natural product?

Unit 22

DRILLS AND DRILLING MACHINES

The drill press, as shown in Fig. 22-1, probably is the best known of the machine tools. A machine tool is a power-driven machine that holds or supports the workpiece and a cutting instrument or tool, and brings them together so that the material is drilled, cut, shaved, or ground.

While a drill press can be used for many different machining operations such as reaming, counterboring, and spotfacing, it is primarily used for cutting round holes. It operates by rotating a cutting tool, or drill, against the material with sufficient pressure to cause the drill to penetrate the material, Fig. 22-2.

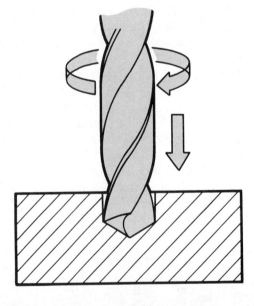

Fig. 22-2. How a drill works.

The size of the drill press is determined by the largest diameter of a circular piece that can be drilled on center, Fig. 22-3. A 14 in. (356.0 mm) drill press can drill to the center of a 14 in. diameter piece. The centerline of the drill is 7 in. (178.0 mm) from the column.

DRILLS

Common drills are known as TWIST DRILLS because most of them are made by forging or milling rough flutes, and then twisting to a spiral configuration. After twisting, the drills are milled to the

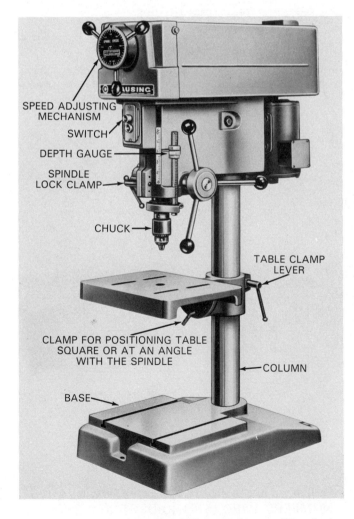

SPEED ADJUSTING MECHANISM

SWITCH

DEPTH GAUGE

SPINDLE LOCK CLAMP

CHUCK

TABLE CLAMP LEVER

CLAMP FOR POSITIONING TABLE SQUARE OR AT AN ANGLE WITH THE SPINDLE

COLUMN

BASE

Fig. 22-1. A bench model drilling machine.   (Clausing)

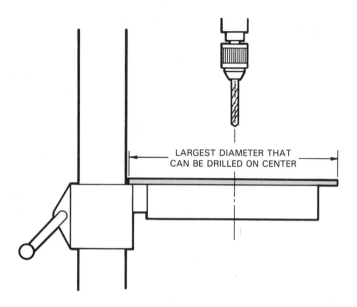

Fig. 22-3. How a drill press size is determined.

desired size, Fig. 22-4, and heat treated.

Drills are made of HIGH SPEED STEEL (HS or HSS) or CARBON STEEL. High speed steel drills can be operated at much higher cutting speeds without danger of burning up.

TYPES OF DRILLS

Industry uses special drills to improve the accuracy of the drilled hole, to speed production, and to improve drilling efficiency. The STRAIGHT FLUTE DRILL, Fig. 22-5, is designed for cutting brass and other soft metals. The OIL HOLE DRILL, Fig. 22-6, has coolant holes through its body to permit fluid

Fig. 22-4. Milling the flutes on a large diameter drill. (Chicago-Latrobe)

or air to be forced to the point as a coolant, or to eject chips from the hole while it is being drilled. THREE and FOUR FLUTE CORE DRILLS, Fig. 22-7, are used to enlarge core holes in castings. Special STEP DRILLS, Fig. 22-8, permit the elimination of one or more drilling operations in production work.

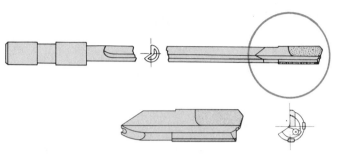

Fig. 22-5. The straight flute drill. The tip (circled) is shown in larger scale. The shaded portion is tungsten carbide. The large section does the cutting, the smaller sections act as wear surfaces.

Fig. 22-6. The oil hole drill. Cutting fluid is forced through the coolant holes. The cutting fluid not only keeps the cutting edges of the tool cool but also forces the chips from the hole.

Fig. 22-7. The multi-flute core drill.

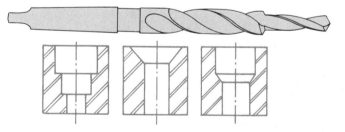

Fig. 22-8. A step drill.

DRILL SIZE

Drill sizes are expressed by the following series. NUMBERS—#80 to #1 (0.0135 to 0.2280 in. diameters).

LETTERS—A to Z (0.234 to 0.413 in. diameters).
INCHES AND FRACTIONS THEREOF—1/64 to 3 1/2 in. diameters.
METRIC—3.0 mm to 76.0 mm diameters.

The drill size chart, Fig., 22-9, will give an idea of this vast array of drill sizes.

HOW TO MEASURE DRILLS

Most drills, with the exception of small number drills, have the diameter stamped on the shank. These figures frequently become obliterated with use and it is almost impossible to determine the drill

Inch	Mm.	Wire Gage	Decimals of an Inch
		80	.0135
		79	.0145
1/64			.0156
	.4		.0157
		78	.0160
		77	.0180
	.5		.0197
		76	.0200
		75	.0210
	.55		.0217
		74	.0225
	.6		.0236
		73	.0240
		72	.0250
	.65		.0256
		71	.0260
	.7		.0276
		70	.0280
		69	.0293
	.75		.0295
		68	.0310
1/32			.0313
	.8		.0315
		67	.0320
		66	.0330
	.85		.0335
		65	.0350
	.9		.0354
		64	.0360
		63	.0370
	.95		.0374
		62	.0380
		61	.0390
	1		.0394
		60	.0400
		59	.0410
	1.05		.0413
		58	.0420
		57	.0430
	1.1		.0433
	1.15		.0453
		56	.0465

Inch	Mm.	Wire Gage	Decimals of an Inch
3/64			.0469
	1.2		.0472
	1.25		.0492
	1.3		.0512
		55	.0520
	1.35		.0531
		54	.0550
	1.4		.0551
	1.45		.0571
	1.5		.0591
		53	.0595
	1.55		.0610
1/16			.0625
	1.6		.0630
		52	.0635
	1.65		.0650
	1.7		.0669
		51	.0670
	1.75		.0689
		50	.0700
	1.8		.0709
	1.85		.0728
		49	.0730
	1.9		.0748
		48	.0760
	1.95		.0768
5/64			.0781
		47	.0785
	2		.0787
	2.05		.0807
		46	.0810
		45	.0820
	2.1		.0827
	2.15		.0846
		44	.0860
	2.2		.0866
	2.25		.0886
		43	.0890
	2.3		.0906
	2.35		.0925
		42	.0935

Inch	Mm.	Wire Gage	Decimals of an Inch
3/32			.0938
	2.4		.0945
		41	.0960
	2.45		.0966
		40	.0980
	2.5		.0984
		39	.0995
		38	.1015
	2.6		.1024
		37	.1040
	2.7		.1063
		36	.1065
	2.75		.1083
7/64			.1094
		35	.1100
	2.8		.1102
		34	.1110
		33	.1130
	2.9		.1142
		32	.1160
	3		.1181
		31	.1200
	3.1		.1220
1/8			.1250
	3.2		.1260
	3.25		.1280
		30	.1285
	3.3		.1299
	3.4		.1339
		29	.1360
	3.5		.1378
		28	.1405
9/64			.1406
	3.6		.1417
		27	.1440
	3.7		.1457
		26	.1470
	3.75		.1476
		25	.1495
	3.8		.1496
		24	.1520
	3.9		.1535
		23	.1540

Inch	Mm.	Wire Gage	Decimals of an Inch
5/32			.1563
		22	.1570
	4		.1575
		21	.1590
		20	.1610
	4.1		.1614
	4.2		.1654
		19	.1660
	4.25		.1673
	4.3		.1693
		18	.1695
11/64			.1719
		17	.1730
	4.4		.1732
		16	.1770
	4.5		.1772
		15	.1800
	4.6		.1811
		14	.1820
		13	.1850
	4.7		.1850
	4.75		.1870
3/16			.1875
	4.8		.1890
		12	.1890
		11	.1910
	4.9		.1929
		10	.1935
		9	.1960
	5		.1969
		8	.1990
	5.1		.2008
		7	.2010
13/64			.2031
		6	.2040
	5.2		.2047
		5	.2055
	5.25		.2067
	5.3		.2087
		4	.2090
	5.4		.2126
		3	.2130
	5.5		.2165
7/32			.2188
	5.6		.2205
		2	.2210
	5.7		.2244
	5.75		.2264
		1	.2280
	5.8		.2283

Fig. 22-9. Decimal and metric equivalents of drill sizes. (Continued).

Inch	Mm.	Letter Sizes	Decimals of an Inch
	5.9		.2323
		A	.2340
15/64			.2344
	6		.2362
		B	.2380
	6.1		.2402
		C	.2420
	6.2		.2441
		D	.2460
	6.25		.2461
	6.3		.2480
1/4		E	.2500
	6.4		.2520
	6.5		.2559
		F	.2570
	6.6		.2598
		G	.2610
	6.7		.2638
17/64			.2656
	6.75		.2657
		H	.2660
	6.8		.2677
	6.9		.2717
		I	.2720
	7		.2756
		J	.2770
	7.1		.2795
		K	.2810
9/32			.2812
	7.2		.2835
	7.25		.2854
	7.3		.2874
		L	.2900
	7.4		.2913
		M	.2950
	7.5		.2953
19/64			.2969
	7.6		.2992
		N	.3020
	7.7		.3031
	7.75		.3051
	7.8		.3071
	7.9		.3110
5/16			.3125
	8		.3150
		O	.3160
	8.1		.3189
	8.2		.3228
		P	.3230
	8.25		.3248
	8.3		.3268
21/64			.3281
	8.4		.3307
		Q	.3320
	8.5		.3346
	8.6		.3386
		R	.3390
	8.7		.3425
11/32			.3438
	8.75		.3345
	8.8		.3465
		S	.3480
	8.9		.3504
	9		.3543
		T	.3580
	9.1		.3583
23/64			.3594
	9.2		.3622
	9.25		.3642
	9.3		.3661
		U	.3680
	9.4		.3701
	9.5		.3740
3/8			.3750
		V	.3770
	9.6		.3780
	9.7		.3819
	9.75		.3839
	9.8		.3858
		W	.3860
	9.9		.3898
25/64			.3906
	10		.3937
		X	39.70
		Y	.4040
13/32			.4063
		Z	.4130
	10.5		.4134
27/64			.4219
	11		.4331
7/16			.4375
	11.5		.4528
29/64			.4531
15/32			.4688
	12		.4724
31/64			.4844
	12.5		.4921
1/2			.5000
	13		.5118
33/64			.5156
17/32			.5313
	13.5		.5315
35/64			.5469
	14		.5512
9/16			.5625
	14.5		.5709
37/64			.5781
	15		.5906
19/32			.5938
39/64			.6094
	15.5		.6102
5/8			.6250
	16		.6299
41/64			.6406
	16.5		.6496
21/32			.6563
	17		.6693
43/64			.6719
11/16			.6875
	17.5		.6890
45/64			.7031
	18		.7087
23/32			.7188
	18.5		.7283
47/64			.7344
	19		.7480
3/4			.7500
49/64			.7656
	19.5		.7677
25/32			.7812
	20		.7874
51/64			.7969
	20.5		.8071
13/16			.8125
	21		.8268
53/64			.8281
27/32			.8438
	21.5		.8465
55/64			.8594
	22		.8661
7/8			.8750
	22.5		.8858
57/64			.8906
	23		.9055
29/32			.9063
59/64			.9219
	23.5		.9252
15/16			.9375
	24		.9449
61/64			.9531
	24.5		.9646
31/32			.9688
	25		.9843
63/64			.9844
1			1.0000
	25.5		1.0039
1 1/64			1.0156
	26		1.0236
1 1/32			1.0313
	26.5		1.0433
1 3/64			1.0469
1 1/16			1.0625
	27		1.0630
1 5/64			1.0781
	27.5		1.0827
1 3/32			1.0938
	28		1.1024
1 7/64			1.1094
	28.5		1.1220
1 1/8			1.1250
1 9/64			1.1406
	29		1.1417
1 5/32			1.1562
	29.5		1.1614
1 11/64			1.1719
	30		1.1811
1 3/16			1.1875
	30.5		1.2008
1 13/64			1.2031
1 7/32			1.2188
	31		1.2205
1 15/64			1.2344
	31.5		1.2402
1 1/4			1.2500
	32		1.2598
1 17/64			1.2656
	32.5		1.2795
1 9/32			1.2813
1 19/64			1.2969
	33		1.2992
1 5/16			1.3125
	33.5		1.3189
1 21/64			1.3281
	34		1.3386
1 11/32			1.3438
	34.5		1.3583
1 23/64			1.3594
1 3/8			1.3750
	35		1.3780
1 25/64			1.3906
	35.5		1.3976
1 13/32			1.4063
	36		1.4173
1 27/64			1.4219
	36.5		1.4370

Fig. 22-9. (Continued). Decimal and metric equivalents of drill sizes.

diameter without measuring. When a micrometer is used for measuring, the measurement is made across the drill margins. However, if the drill is worn, the measurement is made on the shank at the end of the flute, Fig. 22-10. The diameter can also be checked with a DRILL GAUGE, Fig. 22-11. Drill gauges are made for various drill series; however, 1/2 in. drills are the largest that can be checked by

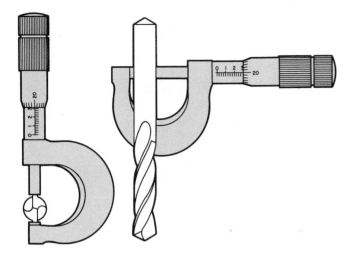

Fig. 22-10. Measuring drill diameters with a micrometer.

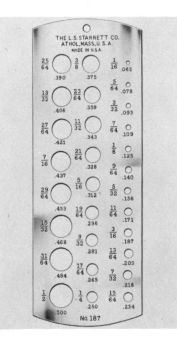

Fig. 22-11. Drill gauge for measuring fractional size drills. Similar gauges are available for measuring letter size, number size, and metric size drills.

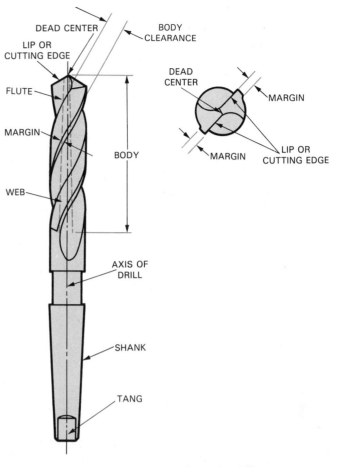

Fig. 22-12. Parts of a twist drill.

this method in the fractional series. New drills are checked at the points; worn drills at the end of the flutes.

ALWAYS CHECK THE DRILL'S DIAMETER BEFORE USING.

PARTS OF THE DRILL

The twist drill has been scientifically designed to produce an efficient cutting tool. It is composed of three principal parts, Fig. 22-12.

1. The POINT which is the cone-shaped end that does the cutting. The point consists of the following.

   a. DEAD CENTER. The sharp edge at the extreme tip of the drill. This should always be in the exact center of the drill AXIS.

   b. LIPS. The cutting edges of the drill.

   c. HEEL. The portion of the point back from the lips or cutting edge.

   d. LIP CLEARANCE. The amount the surface of the point is relieved back from the lips.

2. Twist drills are made with SHANKS that are either STRAIGHT or TAPERED, Fig. 22-13. Straight shank drills are used with a chuck. Taper shank drills have self-holding tapers (No. 1 to No. 5 Morse taper) that fit directly into the drill press spindle. Found on the taper shank is the TANG. This fits into a slot in the spindle, sleeve, or socket and assists the shank in driving the tool. The tang also offers a means of separating the taper from the holding device.

3. The BODY is the portion between the point and the shank. The body consists of the following.

   a. FLUTES. Two or more spiral grooves that run the length of the drill body. The flutes do four things.

     1. Help form the cutting edge of the drill point.

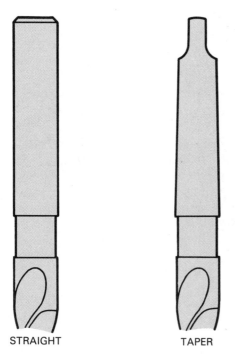

STRAIGHT   TAPER

Fig. 22-13. Types of drill shanks.

2. Curl the chip tightly within itself for easier removal.
3. Form channels through which the chips can escape the hole being drilled.
4. Allow the lubricant and coolant to get down to the cutting edge.

b. MARGIN. The narrow strip extending back the entire length of the flute. It is the full diameter of the drill.

c. BODY CLEARANCE. The part of the drill body that has been reduced in order to cut down friction between the drill and the wall of the hole.

d. WEB. The metal column that separates the flutes. It gradually increases in thickness toward the shank to give added strength.

HOW TO HOLD DRILLS IN DRILL PRESS

A drill is held in place by one of the following methods.
1. CHUCK. For drills with straight shanks, Fig. 22-14.
2. TAPERED OPENING IN THE DRILL PRESS SPINDLE. For drills with tapered shanks, Fig. 22-15. Drill chucks with tapered shanks make it possible to use straight shank drills with the drill press is fitted with a taper spindle opening.

When a chuck is used, the drill should be inserted and the chuck jaws tightened by hand. After a quick flip of the switch to determine that the drill is centered and running true, tighten the chuck with

Fig. 22-14. A typical drill chuck.

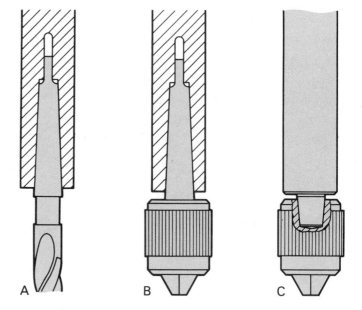

A   B   C

Fig. 22-15. Drill press spindle with tapered opening. A and B—Taper shank tools used in a drill press spindle with a tapered opening. C—Solid spindle with a short taper that only fits a drill chuck. The chuck is attached permanently to the spindle.

A CHUCK KEY. ALWAYS REMOVE THE KEY BEFORE TURNING ON THE MACHINE.

Taper shank drills should be wiped clean before inserting the shank into the spindle. Nicks in the shank can be removed with an oilstone. If this is not done, the shank will not seat properly.

Most drill press spindles are made with No. 2 or No. 3 Morse tapers. A drill with a taper shank smaller than the spindle taper must have its shank enlarged by fitting it with a SLEEVE, Fig. 22-16. Drills with shanks larger than the opening in the spindle can often be used by fitting a SOCKET, Fig.

22-17. The taper opening in the socket is larger than the taper on the shank.

Sleeves, sockets, and taper shank drills are separated with a DRIFT, Fig. 22-18. To use the drift insert it in the slit with the round edge up, Fig. 22-19. A sharp rap with a lead hammer will cause the separation. NEVER use a file tang in place of a drift. It will damage the drill shank and machine spindle.

Hold the drill when removing it from the spindle to prevent it from falling to the floor. Falling may damage the drill point, and if the drill is large enough, injure your foot.

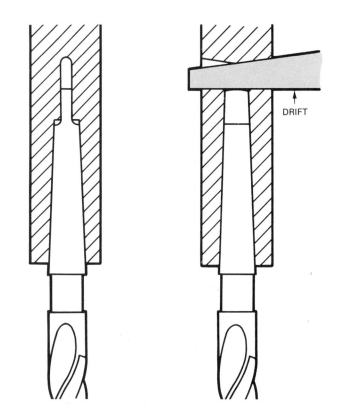

Fig. 22-19. Removing a taper shank tool from a drill spindle with a drift.

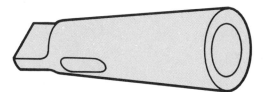

Fig. 22-16. Drill sleeve.

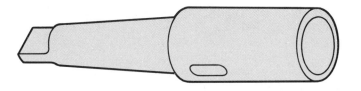

Fig. 22-17. Drill socket.

VISES

Vises, Fig. 22-20, are widely used to hold work of regular size and shape. For best results the vise must be bolted to the drill table. A piece of wood or flat stock placed under the work will protect the vise when the drill breaks through the work. Parallels are often used for this purpose; however, because they are hardened, care must be taken to

Fig. 22-20. Top. A swivel vise. The base is designed to permit the vise to swivel through 180°. Bottom. Quick-acting vise. (L-W Chuck Co.)

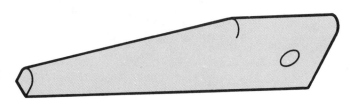

Fig. 22-18. Drift.

WORK HOLDING DEVICES

Work must be clamped solidly to the drilling machine. When improperly clamped it will spring and move, causing drill damage or breakage. Serious injury can result from work that becomes loose and spins about. To facilitate the process of holding work, the machinist has the following devices at his disposal.

prevent the drill from making contact with them. Seat the work on the parallels by tightening the vise and tapping on the work with a mallet. Loose parallels indicate that the work is not seated properly.

The ANGULAR VISE, Fig. 22-21, permits angular drilling without tilting the drill press table.

V-BLOCKS

V-blocks, Fig. 22-22, support round work for drilling. These are made in many sizes. Some are fitted with clamps to hold the work. The larger sizes must be clamped with the work, Fig. 22-23.

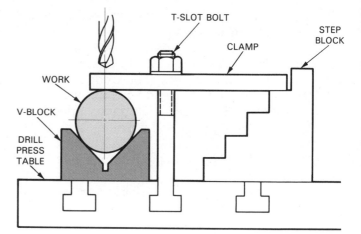

Fig. 22-23. One way of clamping work in V-block, to the drill press table.

Fig. 22-21. An angular vise can be adjusted through 90° to permit drilling on an angle without having to tilt the entire vise. It also has a swivel base.

T-BOLTS

T-bolts, Fig. 22-24, fit in the slots of the drill press table and fasten the work or clamping devices to the machine. A washer should always be used between the nut and the holding device. For convenience, have an assortment of different length T-bolts available. To reduce the chance of a setup working loose, place the bolt as close to the work as possible, Fig. 22-25.

Fig. 22-24. A few of the many types of T-bolts available.

STRAP CLAMPS

Strap clamps, Fig. 22-26, make the clamping operation easier if a good assortment is available. The elongated slot permits some adjustment without removing the nut. The U-strap clamp is used when the clamp must bridge the work. It can straddle the drill and not interfere with the drilling operation. The small round piece that projects from the finger clamp permits the use of small holes or openings in the work to be used for clamping. Use

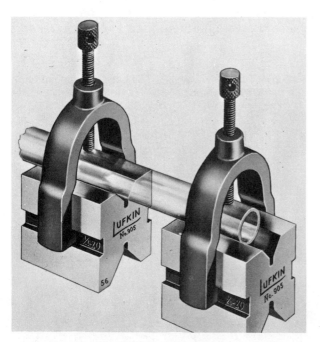

Fig. 22-22. A set of V-blocks.   (Lufkin Rule Co.)

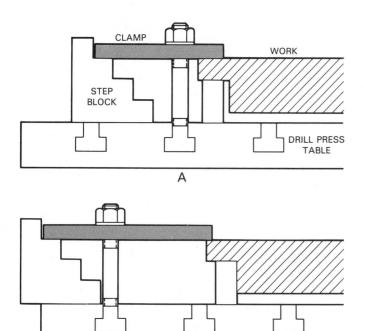

Fig. 22-25. Examples of clamping techniques. A—Correct clamping technique. Note that the clamp is parallel to the work. Clamp slippage can be reduced by placing a piece of paper between the work and the clamp. B—Incorrect clamping technique. The T-bolt is too far from the work. This allows the clamp to spring under pressure.

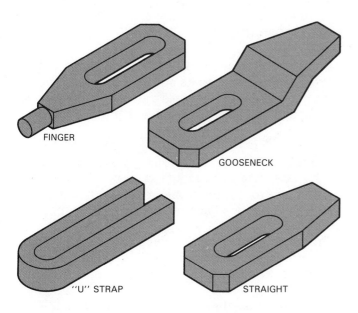

Fig. 22-26. Strap clamps.

a strip of copper to protect a machined surface that must be clamped.

STEP BLOCKS

The step block, Fig. 22-27, supports the strap clamp opposite the work. The steps allow the ad-

justments necessary to keep the strap level, Fig. 22-25.

ANGLE PLATE

The angle plate, Fig. 22-28, is used when the work must be clamped to a support. The angle plate is then bolted to the machine table.

DRILL JIG

A drill jig, Fig. 22-29, is used when holes must be drilled in a number of identical pieces. It is a clamping device that supports and locks the piece in the proper position and with the use of bushings, guides the drill to the correct location. This makes it unnecessary to lay out each individual piece for drilling. Quantity production requires the use of jigs.

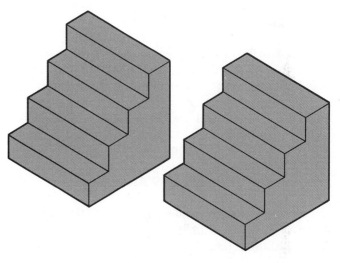

Fig. 22-27. Step block.

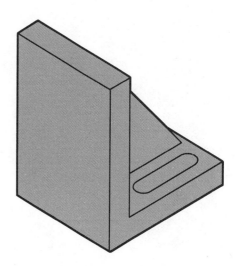

Fig. 22-28. Angle plate.

Fig. 22-29. A typical jig for holding small parts for drilling. Eight holes are drilled at a time.

PARALLELS

Parallels, Fig. 22-30, can be made from standard steel shapes or from special steel that is heat-treated. The heat-treated steel is then ground to size. These are helpful for raising work in the vise so that the drilling can be better observed. Parallels must be located so that the drill does not come in contact with them when the drill breaks through.

CUTTING SPEEDS AND FEEDS

The speed that the drill rotates (CUTTING SPEED) and the distance that it is fed into the work with each revolution (FEED) are important considerations

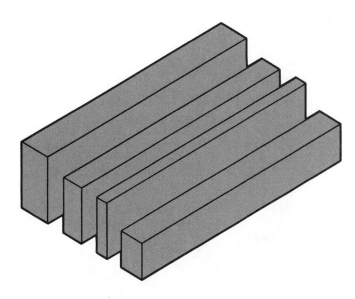

Fig. 22-30. Steel parallels.

because they govern the time required to produce the hole.

Drill cutting speed, also known as PERIPHERAL SPEED, does NOT refer to the REVOLUTIONS PER MINUTE (RPM) of the drill, but rather to the distance the cutting edge travels, at its circumference, per minute.

FEED

Contrary to popular belief, the spiral of the drill flutes DOES NOT cause the drill to pull itself into the work piece. Constant pressure must be applied and maintained to advance the drill point at a given rate. This advance is called FEED and is measured in decimal fractions of an inch.

Because so many variables affect results, there can be no hard and fast rule for determining EXACT cutting speeds and feeds for a given material. For this reason the drill speed and feed table, Fig. 22-31, indicates only recommended speeds and feeds. The feed cannot be controlled accurately on a hand fed drill press so the machinist must become aware of the characteristics (such as uniform chips) that indicate whether the drill is being fed at the correct rate. A feed that is too light will cause the drill to scrape, "chatter," and dull rapidly. Chipped cutting edges, drill breakage, and the drill heating up despite the application of coolant usually indicates that the feed is too great.

SPEED CONVERSION

A problem arises in setting the drill press to the correct speed because its speed is given in revolutions per minute (RPM), while the recommended drill cutting speed (CS) is given in feet per minute (FPM).

The simple formula $RPM = \dfrac{CS}{0.250\ D}$ will determine the RPM to operate any diameter drill (D) at any specified cutting speed.

Solve the following problem, using the information in the drill speed and feed table and the formula for determining RPM.

Problem: At what RPM must a drill press operate when drilling aluminum with a 1/2 in. diameter high speed steel drill?

Solution:
1. A glance at the speed and feed chart, Fig. 22-31, lists the recommended cutting speed for aluminum as 250 FPM.
2. Convert the drill diameter (1/2 in.) to a decimal fraction (0.500).
3. Set down the formula.
$$RPM = \frac{CS}{0.250\ D}$$
4. Substitute and solve.
$$RPM = \frac{250}{0.250 \times 0.500} = \frac{250}{0.125} = 2000\ RPM$$

MATERIAL	CUTTING FLUID	SPEED FEET PER MINUTE	FEEDS PER REVOLUTION Over .040 Diameter**				
			Under 1/8	1/8 to 1/4	1/4 to 1/2	1/2 to 1	Over 1
Aluminum & Aluminum Alloys	Sol. Oil, Ker. & Lard Oil, Lt. Oil	200-300	.0015	.003	.006	.010	.012
Aluminum & Bronze	Sol. Oil, Ker. & Lard Oil, Lt. Oil	50-100	.0015	.003	.006	.010	.012
Brass, Free Machining	Dry, Sol. Oil, Ker. & Lard Oil, Lt. Min. Oil	150-300	.0025	.005	.010	.020	.025
Bronze, Common	Dry, Sol. Oil, Lard Oil, Min. Oil	200-250	.0025	.005	.010	.020	.025
Bronze, Soft and Medium Hard	Min. Oil with 5%–15% Lard Oil	70-300	.0025	.005	.010	.020	.025
Bronze, Phosphor, 1/2 hard	Dry, Sol. Oil, Lard Oil, Min. Oil	110-180	.0015	.003	.006	.010	.012
Bronze, Phosphor, Soft	Dry, Sol. Oil, Lard Oil, Min. Oil	200-250	.0025	.005	.010	.020	.025
Cast Iron, Soft	Dry or Airjet	100-150	.0025	.005	.010	.020	.025
Cast Iron, Medium	Dry or Airjet	70-120	.0015	.003	.006	.010	.012
Cast Iron, Hard	Dry or Airjet	30-100	.001	.002	.003	.005	.006
*Cast Iron, Chilled	Dry or Airjet	10-25	.001	.002	.003	.005	.006
*Cast Steel	Soluble Oil, Sulphurized Oil. Min. Oil	30-60	.001	.002	.003	.005	.006
Copper	Dry, Soluble Oil, Lard Oil, Min. Oil	70-300	.001	.002	.003	.005	.006
Magnesium & Magnesium Alloys	Mineral Seal Oil	200-400	.0025	.005	.010	.020	.025
Manganese Copper, 30% Mn.	Soluble Oil, Sulphurized Oil	10-25	.001	.002	.003	.005	.006
Malleable Iron	Dry, Soluble Oil, Soda Water, Min. Oil	60-100	.0025	.005	.010	.020	.025
Monel Metal	Sol. Oil, Sulphurized Oil, Lard Oil	30-50	.0015	.003	.006	.010	.012
Nickel, Pure	Sulphurized Oil	60-100	.001	.002	.003	.005	.006
Nickel, Steel 3-1/2%	Sulphurized Oil	40-80	.001	.002	.003	.005	.006
Plastics, Thermosetting	Dry or Airjet	100-300	.0015	.003	.006	.010	.012
Plastics, Thermoplastic	Soluble Oil, Soapy Water	100-300	.0015	.003	.006	.010	.012
Rubber, Hard	Dry or Airjet	100-300	.001	.002	.003	.005	.006
Spring Steel	Soluble Oil, Sulphurized Oil	10-25	.001	.002	.003	.005	.006
Stainless Steel, Free Mach'g.	Soluble Oil, Sulphurized Oil	60-100	.0025	.005	.010	.020	.025
Stainless Steel, Tough Mach'g.	Soluble Oil, Sulphurized Oil	20-27	.0025	.005	.010	.020	.025
Steel, Free Machin'g SAE 1100	Soluble Oil, Sulphurized Oil	70-120	.0015	.003	.006	.010	.012
Steel, SAE-AISI, 1000-1025	Soluble Oil, Sulphurized Oil	60-100	.0015	.003	.006	.010	.012
Steel, .30-.60% CARB., SAE 1000-9000							
Annealed 150-225 Brinn.	Soluble Oil, Sulphurized Oil	50-70	.0015	.003	.006	.010	.012
Heat Treated 225-283 Brinn.	Sulphurized Oil	30-60	.0025	.005	.010	.020	.025
Steel, Tool Hi. Car. & Hi. Speed	Sulphurized Oil	25-50	.0025	.005	.010	.020	.025
Titanium	Highly Activated Sulphurized Oil	15-20	.0025	.005	.010	.020	.025
Zinc, Alloy	Soluble Oil, Kerosene & Lard Oil	200-250	.0015	.003	.006	.010	.012

*Use Specially Constructed Heavy Duty Drills
**For drill under .040, feeds should be adjusted to produce chips and not powder with ability to dispose of same without packing.

Fig. 22-31. Drill speed and feed table. (Chicago-Latrobe)

DRILL PRESS SPEED CONTROL MECHANISMS

With some drill presses it is possible to dial the desired RPM, Fig. 22-32. However, on most conventional drilling machines it is not possible to set the machine at the exact speed, so the machinist must settle for a speed nearest the desired RPM. The number of speed settings is limited by the number of pulleys in the drive mechanism, Fig. 22-33. An engraved metal chart showing spindle speeds is attached to many machines. If not available, information on spindle speeds can be found in the operator's manual, or they can be calculated if the motor speed and pulley diameters are known.

CUTTING COMPOUNDS

Drilling at the recommended cutting speeds and feeds generates considerable heat at the cutting point. This heat must be dissipated as fast as it is generated or it will destroy the temper of the drill and cause it to dull rapidly.

Cutting compounds, usually oils, are applied to absorb the heat. These fluids not only cool the cutting tool but also act as a lubricant to reduce friction at the cutting edges, and to minimize the tendency of the chips to become welded to the lips. They improve the finish and aid in the rapid removal of chips from the hole.

Animal oils (lard oil), mineral oils (kerosene), and

Fig. 22-32. Split pulley speed control mechanism. The machine must be running when spindle speed is changed by dialing. (Clausing)

soluble oils make excellent cutting compounds. A soluble oil is made from an oily paste or concentrate that mixes readily with water.

Cutting fluids should be applied liberally as too little does no good. They cannot be used when drilling cast iron or other brittle material because they tend to cause the chips to pack and glaze the opening. Compressed air is used to cool the drill when working these materials.

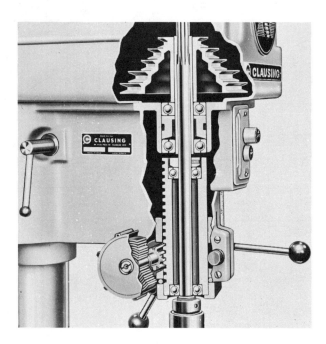

Fig. 22-33. Step pulley speed control. The belt is tranferred to different pulley ratios to change spindle speed. (Clausing)

SHARPENING DRILLS

A drill becomes dull with use and must be resharpened. Continued use of a dull drill may result in its breakage or may cause it to burn up as it is forced into the metal. Improper sharpening will cause the same difficulties.

Remove the entire point if it is badly worn or if the margins are burned or worn off near the point. If, by accident, the drill becomes overheated during grinding, DO NOT plunge it into water to cool. Allow it to cool in still air. The shock of sudden cooling may cause it to crack.

Three factors must be considered when repointing a drill:

1. LIP CLEARANCE, Fig. 22-34. The two cutting edges or lips are comparable to chisels. To cut effectively, the heel must be relieved. Without this clearance it would be impossible for the lips to cut. If there is too much clearance, cutting edges are weakened. Too little clearance results

in the drill point merely rubbing without penetrating. Gradually increase lip clearance toward the center until the line across dead center stands at an angle of 120 to 135 degrees with the cutting edge, Fig. 22-35.

2. LENGTH AND ANGLE OF LIPS, Fig. 22-34. The material to be drilled determines the proper point angle. The angles, in relation to the axis, must be the same—59 degrees has been found satisfactory for most metals. If the angles are unequal only one lip will cut and the hole will be oversize, Fig. 22-36.

3. THE PROPER LOCATION OF THE DEAD CENTER, Fig. 22-37. Equal angles but lips of different lengths will result in oversize holes. The resulting ''wobble'' places tremendous pressures on the drill press spindle and bearings.

A combination of both faults can result in a broken drill and, if the drill is very large, permanent damage to the drilling machine. The hole produced, Fig. 22-38, will be oversize and often out-of-round.

The web of the drill increases in thickness toward the shank, Fig. 22-39. When the drill has been shortened by repeated grindings, the web must be

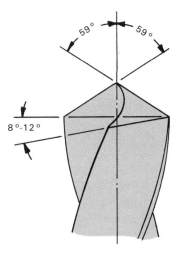

Fig. 22-34. Lip clearance on a drill.

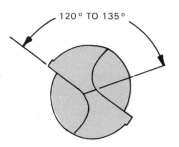

Fig. 22-35. Angle of the dead center.

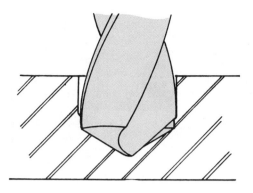

Fig. 22-36. Unequal drill point angles.

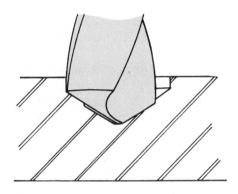

Fig. 22-37. Drill point ground off center.

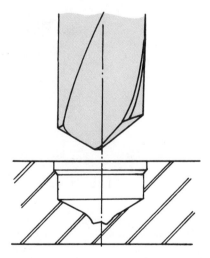

Fig. 22-38. A drill point with unequal point angles and with the drill point sharpened off center.

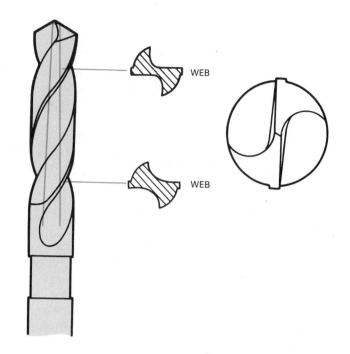

Fig. 22-39. The web of a drill, and how the drill point is relieved by grinding.

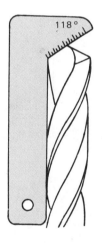

Fig. 22-40. Using a drill point gauge.

thinned to minimize the pressures required to make the drill penetrate the material. The thinning must be done equally to both sides of the web. Care must be taken to insure that the web is centered.

The DRILL POINT GAUGE, Fig. 22-40, is the tool most frequently used to check the drill point during the sharpening operation.

HOW TO SHARPEN A DRILL

Use a coarse wheel for roughing out the drill point if much metal must be ground away. Complete the operation on a fine wheel.

Many hand sharpening techniques have been developed. The following are recommended.
1. Grasp the drill shank with the right hand and the rest of the drill with the left hand.
2. Place the fingers of the left hand that are supporting the drill on the grinder tool rest. The tool rest should be slightly below center (about 1 in. [25.0 mm] on a 7 in. [175.0 mm] wheel).
3. Stand so the centerline of the drill will be at a 59 degree angle in relation to the centerline of

the wheel, Fig. 22-41. Lightly touch the drill lip to the wheel in approximately a horizontal position.

4. Use the left hand as a pivot point and slowly lower the shank with the right hand. Increase pressure as the heel is reached to insure proper clearance.

5. Repeat the operation on each lip until the drill is sharpened. DO NOT QUENCH HIGH SPEED STEEL DRILLS IN WATER TO COOL. LET THEM COOL IN CALM AIR.

6. Check the drill tip frequently with the drill point gauge to assure a correctly sharpened drill.

Secure a drill that is properly sharpened and run through the motions of sharpening it. When you have acquired sufficient skill, sharpen a dull drill. To test, drill a hole in soft metal and observe the chip formation. When properly sharpened, the chips will come out of the flutes in curled spirals of equal length. The tightness of the chip spiral is governed by the RAKE ANGLE, Fig. 22-42.

The standard drill point has a tendency to stick in the hole when it is used to drill brass. When brass is to be drilled, the drill should be sharpened as shown in Fig. 22-43.

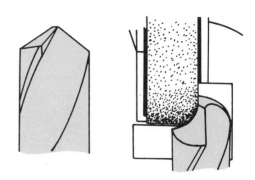

Fig. 22-43. Modified rake angle for drilling brass.

DRILL GRINDING ATTACHMENTS

A DRILL SHARPENING MACHINE is shown in Fig. 22-44.

An attachment for conventional tool grinders is shown in Fig. 22-45. In the machine shop, where a high degree of hole accuracy is required and a large amount of sharpening is to be done, a machine or attachment is a must.

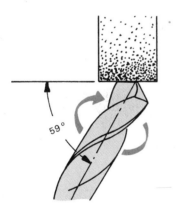

Fig. 22-41. The correct position of the drill at the start of the grinding operation. This is a top view of the grinder.

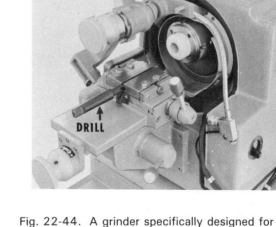

Fig. 22-44. A grinder specifically designed for sharpening drills. (Cincinnati Lathe and Tool Co.)

DRILLING HOLES

Accurate drilling is dependent on observing a few simple rules.

1. Carefully study the drawing to determine the hole location. Lay out the position and mark the intersecting lines with a prick punch.

2. Secure the necessary equipment. Check drill(s) for size.

3. Mount the work solidly on the machine, Fig. 22-46. DO NOT ATTEMPT TO HOLD THE

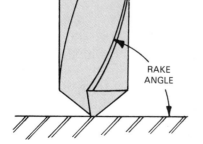

Fig. 22-42. Rake angle of the drill for ordinary work.

WORK BY HAND. It may be whipped out of your hand, causing what is known as a MERRY-GO-ROUND. This development can cause very serious injuries.

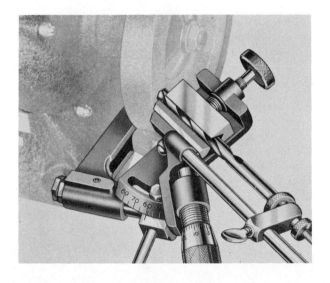

Fig. 22-45. A drill sharpening attachment mounted on a conventional bench grinder. (Clausing)

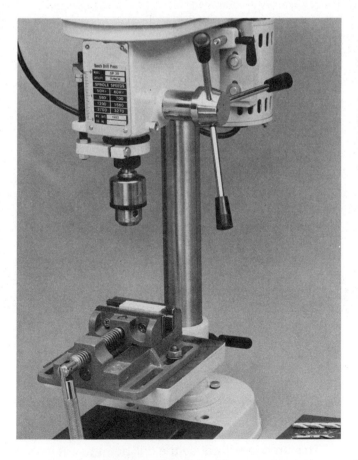

Fig. 22-46. Secure all necessary equipment and mount the work solidly in a vise or on the drill table.

4. Insert a WIGGLER or CENTER FINDER, Fig. 22-47, in the drill chuck. Turn on the power and center the wiggler point with your fingers. Position the work until the revolving centered wiggler point does not "wiggle" when it is removed from the punched location. If there is point movement when it is withdrawn, the work is not positioned properly. Additional alignment will be necessary.
5. Remove the wiggler and insert a center drill hand tight, Fig. 22-48. Check to be sure it runs true. If it does, tighten the chuck with a chuck key. REMOVE THE KEY BEFORE STARTING THE MACHINE.

Fig. 22-47. It is difficult to align the drill with the centerlines by eye. To assist in this operation, use the center finder or "wiggler."

6. After center drilling, replace the tool with the required drill, Fig. 22-49. Hand tighten it in the chuck and turn the machine on. If it does not run true, the drill may be bent or placed in the chuck off center. Also check to be sure it will drill to the required depth.
7. Calculate the correct cutting speed and adjust the machine to operate as closely as possible to this speed.
8. Turn on the power, apply cutting fluid liberally, and start the cut. Even pressure on the feed handle will keep the drill cutting freely.
9. Watch for the following signs that indicate a

poorly cutting drill:

   a. A dull drill will squeak and overheat. Chips will be rough and blue, and cause the machine to slow down. Small drills will break.

   b. Infrequently, a chip will get under the dead center and act as a bearing preventing the drill from cutting. Remove by raising and lowering the drill several times.

   c. Chips packed in the flutes cause the drill to bind and slow the machine or cause the drill to break. Remove the drill from the hole and clean it with a brush that has been dipped in cutting fluid. DO NOT USE CUTTING FLUID WHEN CUTTING CAST IRON.

Fig. 22-49. After checking the drill size, complete the drilling operation.

Fig. 22-48. Center drilling will assure that the drill will make the hole where specified.

10. Clear chips and apply cutting fluid as needed.

11. The most critical time of the drilling operation occurs when the drill starts to break through the work. Ease up on feed pressure at this point to prevent the drill from digging in.

12. Remove the drill from the hole and turn off the power. DO NOT TRY TO STOP THE CHUCK BY HAND. Clear the chips with a brush (NOT YOUR HAND). Unclamp the work and use a file to remove all burrs.

13. Clean chips and cutting fluid from the machine. Wipe it down with a soft cloth. Return equipment to storage.

Observe extreme care in positioning the piece for drilling. A poorly planned setup may permit the drill to cut into the vise or drill table as it comes through the work.

When a hole must be located precisely, additional precautions must be taken to insure that the hole is drilled where it should be. This is especially true of larger drills.

After the center point has been determined, a series of PROOF CIRCLES are scribed, Fig. 22-50, A. They will be reference points to check whether the drill remains on center as it starts to penetrate the material.

Even when work is properly centered, the drill may drift from center when the hole is started. Various factors can cause this—hard spots in the metal, an improperly sharpened drill, work not clamped tightly, etc. The drill cannot be brought back on center by simply moving the work, as it will follow the original hole.

The condition, Fig. 22-50, B, must be corrected before the full diameter of the drill starts to cut. The tool is brought back on center by using a round nose cape chisel to cut a groove on the side of the hole towards where the drill must be drawn, Fig. 22-50, C. This groove will cause the drill point to cut in that direction. Repeat the sequence until the hole is again concentric with the proof circles, Fig. 22-50, D.

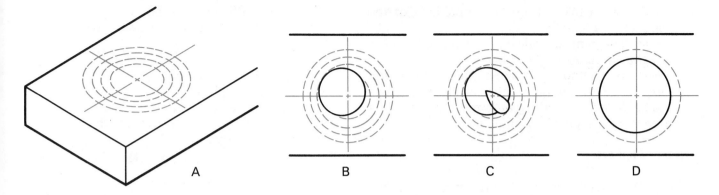

Fig. 22-50. Bringing a drill back on center. A—The proof circles. B—The drill off center (exaggerated). C—Groove cut to bring drill back on center. D—The drill back on center. This operation will only work if the drill has not started to cut to its full diameter.

DRILLING LARGER HOLES

Drills larger than 1/2 in. (12.5 mm) diameter require considerable power and pressure to get started. Even then they may run off center. The pressure can be greatly reduced, and hole accuracy improved, by first drilling a PILOT or LEAD HOLE, Fig. 22-51. The small hole permits pressure to come directly on the cutting edges of the large drill causing it to cut easier and faster.

The diameter of the pilot hole should be as large as, or slightly larger than, the width of the dead center.

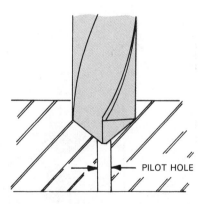

Fig. 22-51. The pilot or lead hole.

DRILLING ROUND STOCK

Holes are more difficult to drill in the curved surface of round stock. Many difficulties can be eliminated by holding the round material in a V-block, Fig. 22-21. The V-block can be clamped directly on the table, Fig. 22-22, or held in a vise.

It is a simple matter to center round stock in a V-block.

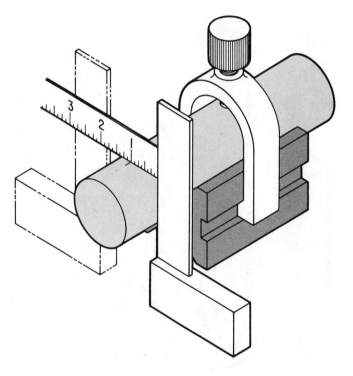

Fig. 22-52. Centering round stock in a V-block for drilling.

1. Locate the position of the hole on the stock. Prick punch the intersection of the layout lines. Place the stock in a V-block. Make certain that the hole, if it is to go through the piece, will clear the V-block. Also be sure there is ample clearance between the clamp and the drill chuck.
2. To align the hole for drilling through the exact center, place the work and V-block on the drill press table, or on a surface plate. Rotate the punch mark until it is upright. Place a steel square on the flat surface with the blade against the round stock as shown in Fig. 22-52. Measure from the blade to the punch mark, and rotate the stock until the measurement is the

same when taken from both positions of the square.

3. From this point, the drilling sequence is identical to that previously described.

It may be desirable to make a drill jig, as shown in Fig. 22-53, if a large number of identical parts are to be drilled. The drill jig automatically positions and centers the piece for drilling.

BLIND HOLES

A BLIND HOLE is a hole that is not drilled all the way through the work. Hole depth is measured by the distance the full diameter goes into the work, Fig. 22-54. Using a drill press fitted with a DEPTH

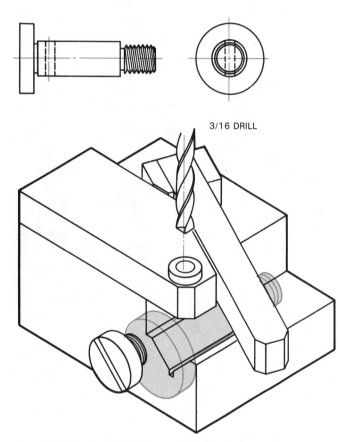

3/16 DRILL

Fig. 22-53. A drill jig. The arm lifts to allow easy insertion and removal of the bolt being drilled.

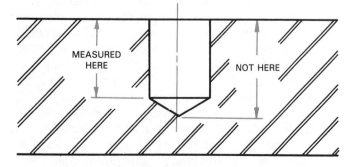

MEASURED HERE

NOT HERE

Fig. 22-54. Measuring the depth of a blind hole.

STOP or GAUGE, Fig. 22-55, is the most rapid means of securing the proper depth when drilling blind holes.

OTHER DRILL PRESS OPERATIONS

The drill press is used to perform many operations other than drilling. As with drilling, they require a thorough knowledge of the machine and the cutting tools.

REAMING

REAMING is the operation that produces holes that are extremely accurate and have an exceptionally fine finish.

Machine reamers are made in a variety of sizes and styles. They are usually manufactured from high speed steel. Following are descriptions of a few of the more common machine reamers.

JOBBER'S REAMER

The JOBBER'S REAMER, Fig. 22-56, is identical to a hand reamer except that the shank is designed for machine operation.

CHUCKING REAMER

The CHUCKING REAMER, Fig. 22-57, is manufactured with straight and taper shanks. It is similar

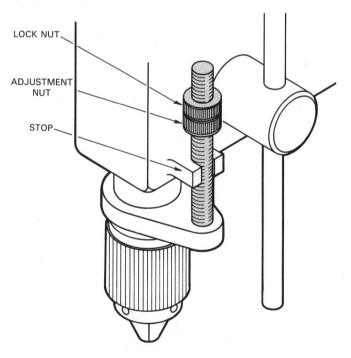

LOCK NUT

ADJUSTMENT NUT

STOP

Fig. 22-55. Depth gauge attachment fitted to most drill presses.

to the jobber's reamer but the flutes are shorter and deeper. It is available with straight or spiral flutes.

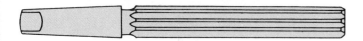

Fig. 22-56. A jobber's reamer.

Fig. 22-57. A chucking reamer.

ROSE CHUCKING REAMER

A ROSE CHUCKING REAMER, Fig. 22-58, is designed to cut on its end. The flutes provide chip clearance and are ground to act only as guides. This reamer is best suited when considerable metal must be removed and quality of finish is not critical.

EXPANSION CHUCKING REAMER

The EXPANSION CHUCKING REAMER, Fig. 22-59, which has straight flutes, is available with either a straight or taper shank. Slots are cut in the body to permit the reamer to expand when the adjusting screw in the end is tightened.

SHELL REAMER

A SHELL REAMER, Fig. 22-60, is mounted on a special arbor that can be used with several reamer sizes. The reamer may have straight or spiral flutes and is also made in the rose style. The arbor shank may be straight or taper. The hole in the reamer is tapered to fit the arbor which is fitted with drive lugs.

Fig. 22-58. A rose chucking reamer.

Fig. 22-59. One type of expansion chucking reamer.

Fig. 22-60. A shell reamer and its arbor.

HOW TO USE MACHINE REAMERS

Reamers are precision tools. The quality of finish and the accuracy of the reamed hole will depend upon how the tool is used.
1. Mount the work solidly.
2. Allow enough material in the drilled hole to permit the reamer to cut rather than burnish. The following allowances are recommended:
   a. To 1/4 in. (6.3 mm) diameter allow 0.010 in. (0.25 mm).
   b. 1/4 to 1/2 in. (6.3 to 12.5 mm) allow 0.015 in. (0.38 mm).
   c. 1/2 to 1.0 in. (12.5 to 25.0 mm) allow 0.020 in. (0.5 mm).
   d. 1.0 to 1.5 in. (25.0 to 38.0 mm) allow 0.025 in. (0.6 mm).
3. Use sharp reamers.
4. The cutting speed for a high speed steel reamer should be about two-thirds that of a similar size drill.
5. The feed should be as much as possible while giving a good finish and accurate hole size.
6. Carefully check reamer diameter before use. If the hole diameter is critical, drill and ream a hole in a piece of similar material to check tool accuracy.
7. When not in use, reamers should be stored in separate containers or storage compartments. This will minimize the danger of chipping or dulling the cutting edges.
8. Use an ample supply of cutting fluid.
9. Remove the reamer from the hole before stopping the machine.

COUNTERSINKING

COUNTERSINKING, Fig. 22-61, is the operation that cuts a chamfer in a hole to permit a flat-headed fastener to be inserted with the head flush with the surface, Fig. 22-62. The tool used is called a COUNTERSINK, Fig. 22-63. It is available with cutting edge angles of 60, 82, 90, 100, 110, and 120 degree included angles. Countersinks may also be employed for deburring holes.

HOW TO USE A COUNTERSINK

1. The cutting speed should be about one-half that recommended for a similar size drill. This will

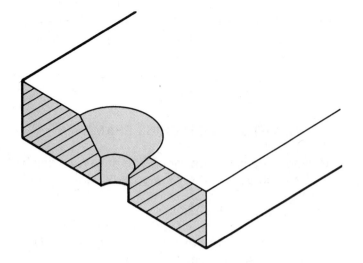

Fig. 22-61. Cross section of a hole that has been countersunk

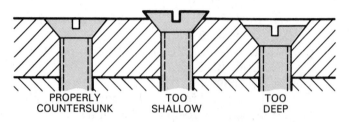

PROPERLY COUNTERSUNK　　TOO SHALLOW　　TOO DEEP

Fig. 22-62. Correctly and incorrectly countersunk holes. The countersunk angle must match the fastener head angle.

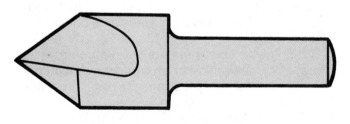

Fig. 22-63. The countersink tool.

minimize the possibility of "chatter."
2. Feed the tool into the work until the chamfer is large enough for the fastener head to be flush.
3. Use the depth stop on the drill press if a number of similar holes must be countersunk.

COUNTERBORING

The heads of fillister and socket head screws are usually set below the work surface. A COUNTER-BORE, Fig. 22-64, is used to enlarge the hole to proper depth and machine the square shoulder on the hole bottom to secure maximum clamping action from the fastener.

The tool has a guide, called a PILOT, which keeps it positioned correctly in the hole.

Solid counterbores are available. However, counterbores with interchangeable pilots and cutters are commonly used, Fig. 22-65. They can be changed easily from one size cutter or pilot to another size. A drop of oil on the pilot will prevent it from binding in the hole.

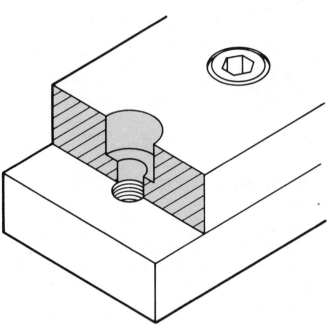

Fig. 22-64. A sectional view of a hole that has been drilled and counterbored to receive a socket head cap screw.

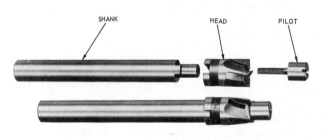

SHANK　　HEAD　　PILOT

Fig. 22-65. A straight shank interchangeable counterbore.

SPOTFACING

SPOTFACING, Fig. 22-66, is the term applied when a circular spot is machined on a rough surface to furnish a bearing surface for the head of a bolt or nut. A counterbore may be employed for spotfacing, although a special tool manufactured for inverted spotfacing is available.

TAPPING

TAPPING may be done by hand on the drill press.
1. Drill a hole of the correct size.

2. With the work still clamped in the machine, insert a small 60° center in the chuck. The center will hold the tap in a vertical position.

3. Carefully place the center point in the center hole of the tap.

4. Feed the tap into the work by holding down the feed handle and turning the tap with a tap wrench.

SAFETY NOTE: NEVER INSERT A TAP IN A DRILL PRESS CHUCK AND ATTEMPT TO USE POWER TO CUT THE THREADS. THE TAP WILL SHATTER AS SOON AS POWER IS APPLIED.

Tapping can be done with power through the use of a TAPPING ATTACHMENT, Fig. 22-67. This device fits the standard drill press and has reducing gears that slows the tap to about one-third drill press speed. (A table with the attachment provides recommended spindle speeds for tapping.) A clutch arrangement drives the tap until it reaches the predetermined depth, at which time the tap stops rotation. Raising the feed handle causes the tap to reverse direction and back out of the hole.

POLISHING, GRINDING, AND BORING

POLISHING, GRINDING, and BORING can be done with limited success on a standard drill press. However, the machine does not always have the necessary rigidity or means to make fine depth adjustments to do these as well as they can be done on more specialized equipment.

INDUSTRIAL APPLICATIONS

Specialized drilling machines enable industry to drill holes as small as 1/10,000 (0.0001) in. (0.0025 mm) in diameter, to as large as 3 1/2 in. in diameter.

The machine that drills these small holes (so small that 25 holes could be drilled in the diameter of a human hair, Fig. 22-68), is called an ULTRASENSITIVE MICROSCOPIC PRECISION DRILLING MACHINE, Fig. 22-69. However, laser drilling machines and electron beam drilling machines are replacing this precision technique of drilling (cutting) these small diameter holes.

The RADIAL DRILL PRESS, Fig. 22-70, is at the other end of the drilling machine scale. This machine

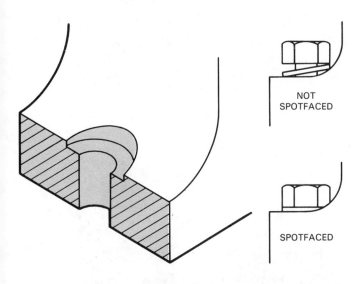

Fig. 22-66. Sectional view of a casting with a mounting hole that has been spotfaced. Smaller drawings show a side view of the casting before and after spotfacing. Note the bolt cannot be drawn down tightly until the mounting hole is spotfaced.

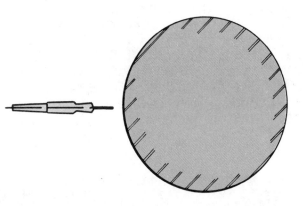

Fig. 22-68. A micro drill (left) compared with a human hair.

Fig. 22-69. A skilled operator using a micro drilling machine. The drilling operation is so small that a microscope must be used to see what is being done.   (National Jet Co.)

Fig. 22-67. Tapping attachment that fits to the drill press spindle.   (Ettco Tool & Machine Co.)

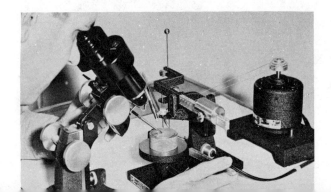

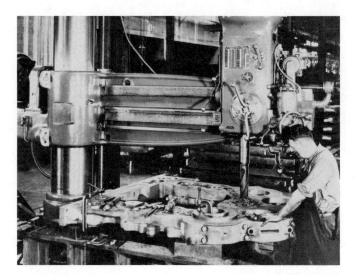

Fig. 22-70. A radial drill press.

Fig. 22-72. Portable electric drill. It is manufactured in a large range of sizes and types. Some are battery powered. (Stanley Tool Co.)

can handle very large work. The drill head is mounted in such a manner that it can be moved back and forth on an arm that extends from the massive machine column. The arm can be moved up and down and pivoted on the column.

Often a large pit is located along one side of this machine to permit the positioning of large, odd-shaped work. The pit is covered when not in use. It is not uncommon to drill holes 3 1/2 in. in diameter with this machine.

In between these two extremes are many types of drilling machines. The ELECTRIC HAND DRILL, the HIGH SPEED SENSITIVE DRILL PRESS, TAPE CONTROLLED TURRET HEAD, and DEEP HOLE DRILLING MACHINES, the GANG and MULTIPLE SPINDLE and familiar FLOOR and BENCH DRILLING MACHINES are pictured in Fig. 22-71 through Fig. 22-77.

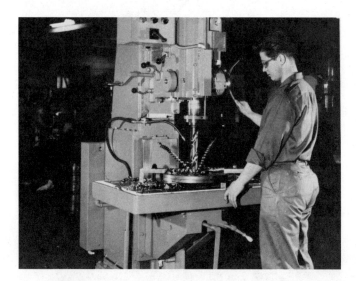

Fig. 22-71. Heavy duty conventional drill press.

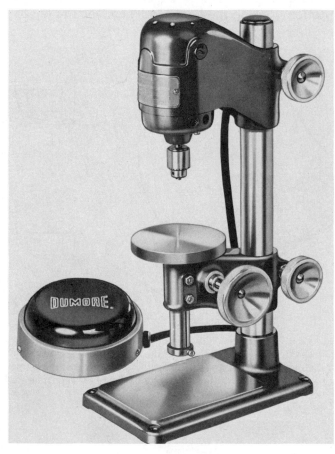

Fig. 22-73. High speed sensitive drill press.   (Dumore Co.)

Some drilling machines are designed for special applications. What is perhaps the largest drilling machine ever constructed is shown in Fig. 22-78. This 2 1/2 story tall machine precisely drills and mills 39 mounting pads that locate and support the exterior body panels of the Pontiac Fiero. The drilling/milling is done simultaneously with a tolerance

Fig. 22-74. Specially designed portable drill. It is set up here to drill a tire mold. (Firestone Tire & Rubber Co.)

Fig. 22-76. Gang of four drilling machines. Each machine is fitted with a different cutting tool. Work held in a drill jig moves from position to position as each operation is performed. (Clausing)

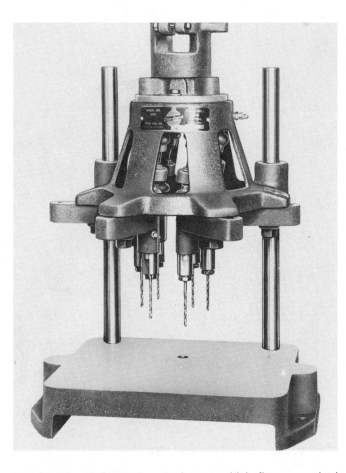

Fig. 22-75. Multispindle attachment which fits a standard drilling machine and enables the machine to drill several holes at one time. (Ettco Tool & Machine Co.)

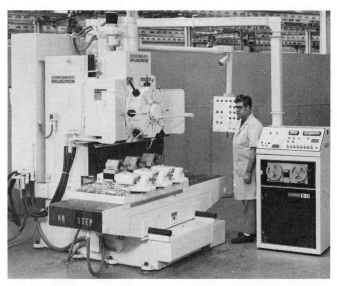

Fig. 22-77. Computer controlled machining center set up for drilling operations. No drill jigs are necessary as the parts are positioned electronically. (Cincinnati Milacron)

of 1.0 to 1.5 mm (0.039 to 0.059 in.). Sensors tell the operator when a tool breaks or dulls, or when they begin to dull. The machine is completely automated.

ROBOTIC DRILLING MACHINES, Fig. 22-79, are the latest in drilling technology. To put the machine to work, the operator notifies a minicomputer which has available parts programs on a disk. Next the operator loads the part onto the work station, which has been fitted with the required fixtures.

When the operator notifies the master computer that the part is ready for drilling, the robot, equipped

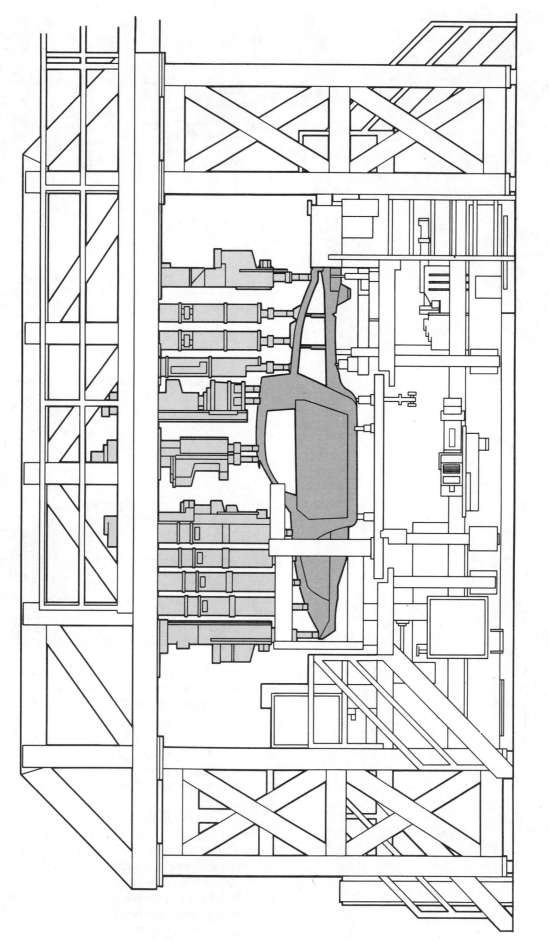

Fig. 22-78. One of the largest drilling/milling machines made stands 2 1/2 stories high. It simultaneously drills and mills 30 pads on the space frame chassis that supports and positions the external plastic body panels on the Pontiac Fiero. It performs this operation in less than a minute.

with the correct tool, moves along the track to a starting position at the work station.

The robot moves through the prescribed drilling operations, changing tools as needed, and upon completing the job, moves to the next position in the work cell to begin another production sequence.

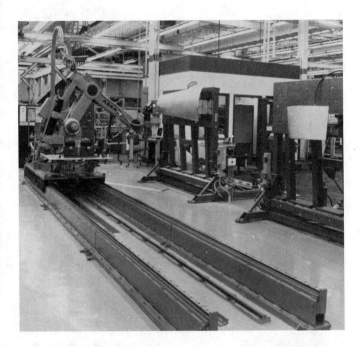

Fig. 22-79. Robot in automated routing and drilling cell moves between work station on rails. The use of the track for traversing motion simplified the programming required to keep the tools normal to the work. (Grumman Aerospace Corp.)

DRILL PRESS SAFETY

1. Remove neckties and tuck in loose clothing so there is no chance of them becoming tangled in the rotating drill.
2. Check out the machine. Are all guards in place? Switches work? Does the machine operate properly? Are the tools sharpened properly for the material being worked?
3. Clamp the work solidly. Do not hold it with your hands. A merry-go-round can inflict serious and painful injuries.
4. Wear goggles.
5. Place a piece of wood under drills being removed from the machine. Small drills are damaged in dropping and the larger tools can injure you if they fall on your foot.
6. Use sharp tools.
7. Clean chips from the work with a brush, not your hands.
8. Treat cuts and scratches immediately.
9. Always remove the key from the chuck before turning on the power.

10. Let the drill spindle stop of its own accord after the power has been turned off. Do not try to stop it with your hand.
11. Wipe up all cutting fluid that spills on the floor.
12. Never clean the tapered opening in the spindle while the machine is operating.
13. After using the drill, wipe it clean of chips and cutting fluid with a piece of cotton waste. Do not use your hands.
14. Place all oily and dirty waste in a closed container when the job is finished.

TEST YOUR KNOWLEDGE, Unit 22

Please do not write in the text. Place your answers on a separate sheet of paper.

1. Drill press size is determined by:
   a. The largest drill that will fit the machine.
   b. The largest piece of work that will fit on the drill table.
   c. The largest diameter work piece that can be drilled on center.
   d. None of the above.
   e. All of the above.
2. A drill made from _____ can be operated at higher speeds than a drill made from carbon steel.
3. Drill sizes are expressed by the following series:
   a. _____.
   b. _____.
   c. _____.
   d. _____.
4. List two commonly used methods of measuring drills if the drill size is worn from the shank.
5. What are the two different types of drill shanks?
6. _____ shank drills are used with a chuck.
7. _____ shank drills fit directly into the drill press spindle.
8. _____ are the spiral grooves that run the length of the drill body.
9. They are used to:
   a. Help form the cutting edge of the drill point.
   b. Curl the chips for easier removal.
   c. Form channels through which the chips can escape from the hole.
   d. None of the above.
   e. All of the above.
10. Tapered drill shanks too small to fit directly into the drill press spindle can be enlarged to fit properly by fitting them with a _____.
11. The item described above is removed from the drill shank with a _____. It is never removed with a file tang.
12. The material from which the drill is made must be taken into consideration when _____ _____.

13. Explain briefly what use is made of a drill socket.
14. "Chatter" causes a drill to _____ _____.
15. Explain why it is necessary for constant pressure to be applied and maintained on the drill while it is cutting.
16. Cutting fluids are used to:
    a. Cool the drill.
    b. Improve the finish of the drilled hole.
    c. Aid in the rapid removal of chips.
    d. None of the above.
    e. All of the above.
17. Continued use of a dull drill may result in it _____ _____.
18. The three factors that must be considered when repointing a drill are:
    a. _____.
    b. _____.
    c. _____.
19. When the cutting lips of the drill are uneven in length, the drill will:
    a. Drill a hole larger than the drill size.
    b. Drill a hole smaller than the drill size.
    c. Drill a hole the same size as the drill size.
    d. None of the above.
    e. All of the above.
20. When sharpening the drill, a coarse grinding wheel is used because it cuts faster. True or False?
21. The _____ should be used frequently during grinding to assure a correctly sharpened drill.
22. The included angle of a point sharpened for general drilling is _____ degrees.
23. The _____ is very useful for centering work for drilling.
24. _____ cutting fluid is required when drilling cast iron.
25. Large drills require considerable power and pressure to get them started. They also have a tendency to drift off center. These conditions can be improved by first drilling a _____. This hole should be as large as, or slightly larger than, the width of the _____ of the drill point.
26. A blind hole goes _____ through the work.
27. The depth of a drilled hole can be regulated by adjusting the _____.
28. How does a reamed hole differ from a drilled hole?
29. The _____ reamer is almost identical to the hand reamer except that the shank has been designed for machine use.
30. The _____ reamer is ideal for finishing holes that must be a few thousandths over standard size.
31. A reamed hole must first be drilled slightly _____ than the finished hole size.
32. _____ is the operation that cuts a chamfer in a hole to permit it to receive a flat head screw.
33. The _____ is used to prepare a hole to receive a fillister or socket head screw.
34. _____ is the operation that machines a circular spot on a rough surface for the head of a bolt or nut.

RESEARCH AND DEVELOPMENT

1. Make a large drawing of a twist drill as a teaching aid. Label the various parts.
2. Prepare a research paper on early drilling devices. Include sketches.
3. Make a series of tape recordings that indicate how drills in various conditions of sharpness sound while drilling.
4. Develop a research problem to investigate the effects of cutting compounds in drilling. This may be accomplished by recording the sounds of the tool drilling when different cutting fluids are used, or when no cutting fluids are used. It may be shown visually by clamping two pieces of metal together and drilling at different points along the joint. Be sure the metal and drill are clean before starting the next hole.
5. Prepare a teaching aid that will show samples of a drilled hole, reamed hole, countersinking, counterboring, and spotfacing.
6. Borrow drill jigs from a local industry. Explain their use.
7. Make a drawing that shows the parts of a chucking reamer. Label the various parts.
8. Demonstrate one of the following lessons.
    a. Centering round stock in V-block.
    b. Properly using a wiggler.
    c. Sharpening a twist drill.
    d. Clamping work correctly on the drill press table.
9. Make a series of safety posters on the use of the drill press.

Unit 23

POWER SAWING

There are three principal types of metal-cutting power saws. One has a reciprocating (back and forth) cutting action, Fig. 23-1. It uses a blade similar to the one in a hand hacksaw, only larger and heavier. Another type has a continuous or band-type blade, Fig. 23-2. The third type employs a circular blade or abrasive wheel, Figs. 23-14 and 23-15.

Fig. 23-1. A bench model reciprocating type power hacksaw. (Covel Mfg. Co.)

Fig. 23-2. Band-type metal cutting saw. (Kalamazoo Tank & Silo Co.)

RECIPROCATING POWER HACKSAW

Reciprocating power hacksaws are manufactured in many sizes. The blade cuts only on the back stroke, Fig. 23-3. A cam lifts the blade on the forward stroke to prevent the blade from rubbing across the metal.

HOW TO SELECT THE BLADE

As in the use of a hand hacksaw, proper blade selection is important. The three-tooth rule (at least three teeth in contact with the work) still applies, Fig. 23-4. Large pieces and soft materials require coarse teeth, while small or thin work and hard materials demand a fine tooth blade. For best cutting action, apply heavy feed pressure on soft materials and large work, and light pressure on hard materials and small work.

Blades are manufactured in two main types, FLEXIBLE BACK and ALL-HARD. The choice depends upon the use. Flexible back blades should be used where safety requirements demand a shatterproof blade or for cutting odd-shaped work that

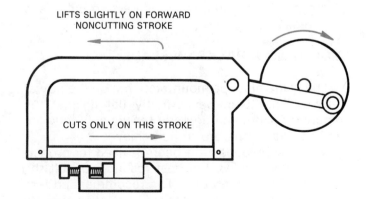

Fig. 23-3. Reciprocating power hacksaws cut on the back stroke. A cam lifts the blade from the metal on the noncutting forward stroke.

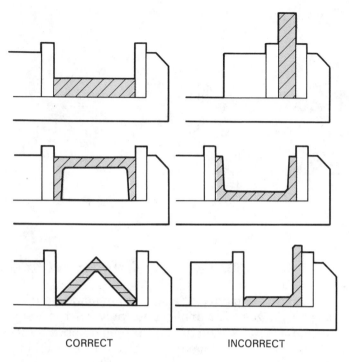

CORRECT   INCORRECT

Fig. 23-4. Recommended ways to hold sharp cornered work for cutting. A carefully planned setup will assure that at least three teeth on the blade will be cutting most of the time, greatly extending blade life.

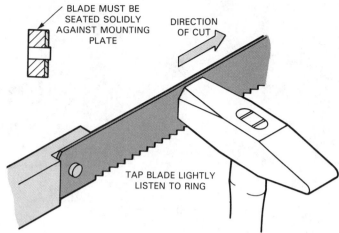

Fig. 23-5. Adjusting the blade on a reciprocating type power hacksaw. Be sure it is perfectly flat against the mounting plate before tensioning. Tighten the blade until a low toned musical ring is heard when the blade is lightly tapped with a small hammer.

cannot be mounted firmly on the machine. For the majority of sawing jobs, the all-hard blade is first choice for straight accurate cutting under a variety of conditions.

Blades are made from tungsten and molybdenum steel with carbide teeth on alloy steel backs. The following rule-of-thumb can be followed for selecting the correct blade:

    4-tooth blade (4 teeth per inch) for cutting large sections or readily machined materials.

    6-tooth blade for cutting harder alloys and miscellaneous cutting.

    10- and 14-tooth blades are used on the majority of light duty machines where work is limited to small sections and moderate to light feed pressures.

MOUNTING A HACKSAW BLADE

The blade must be mounted to cut on the power stroke, Fig. 23-5, be perfectly flat against the mounting plate, and properly tensioned if long life and accurate cuts are to be achieved.

Many techniques have been devised for properly mounting blades. For best results, consult the manufacturer's literature. The recommended tension can be secured with the aid of a torque wrench. If this information is not available, tighten the blade until a low toned musical ring is heard when the blade is tapped lightly. A tone too high in pitch in-

dicates that the blade is too tight. A dull thud indicates the blade is too loose.

CUTTING

Measure off the distance to be cut. Mark the stock and firmly mount the work on the saw. If several sections of the same size are to be cut, use a STOP GAUGE, Fig. 23-6. Use ample supplies of coolant if the machine is designed to use it.

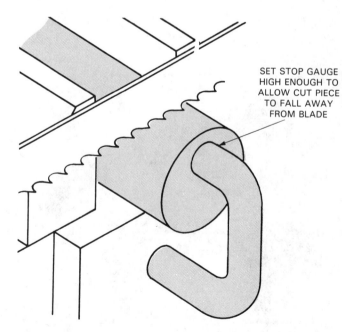

Fig. 23-6. The stop gauge is employed when several pieces of the same length metal must be cut. Adjust it high enough to permit the work to fall free when it has been cut through.

HORIZONTAL BAND SAW

The band saw, Fig. 23-7, offers three advantages over the hacksaw:

1. FASTER. The long blade moves in only one direction, and being continuous, can be run at much higher speeds as the blade rapidly dissipates the heat generated in cutting.
2. PRECISION. The blade can be guided more accurately than the blade on a reciprocating type saw. It also can utilize a thinner blade for a given piece of material. It is common practice to cut directly on the line when band sawing.
3. LITTLE WASTE. The small cross section of the band saw blade makes smaller and fewer chips for a given length or thickness of material.

HOW TO SELECT BLADE

Band saw blades are made with the teeth RAKER SET or WAVY SET, Fig. 23-8. The raker set is preferred for general use. The blade pattern determines the efficiency of the blade in various materials.

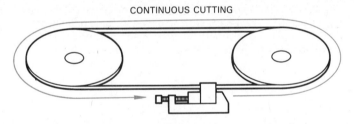

CONTINUOUS CUTTING

Fig. 23-7. The band-type power saw offers three advantages over the reciprocating power hacksaw: it is faster, more precise, and it produces little waste.

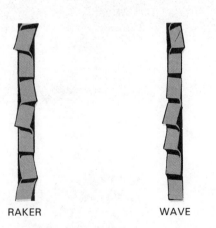

RAKER   WAVE

Fig. 23-8. Saw blade teeth are commonly made with the teeth raker set or wavy set. The raker set teeth are preferred for general use and for cutting large solid sections or thick plate.   (Capewell Mfg. Co.)

The STANDARD TOOTH is best for cutting most ferrous metals. The SKIP TOOTH blade pattern is best suited for cutting aluminum, magnesium, copper, and soft brass. The HOOK TOOTH is recommended for most nonferrous metallic materials. See Fig. 23-9.

HOW TO INSTALL BLADE

The blade must be installed carefully, if the saw is to work efficiently. The blade guides should be adjusted to permit the blade to cut true and square with the work table. Follow the manufacturer's instructions for adjusting blade tension. Improper blade tension will ruin the blade and can cause early failure of the wheel bearings.

VERTICAL BAND SAW

A VERTICAL BAND SAW is shown in Fig. 23-10. With this type of saw, finish and accuracy can be held to within 0.010 to 0.015 in. (0.25 to 0.38 mm), Fig. 23-11. This accuracy eliminates or minimizes many secondary machining operations. Finishing operations can be performed with file and finishing bands, Fig. 23-12. Abrasive and brittle materials, and even the hardest steels can be cut rapidly and economically on the band saw by substituting a diamond-edge blade for the conventional blade.

The vertical band saw is manufactured in a wide range of sizes, and has been adapted to do many kinds of BAND MACHINING. The machine illustrated in Fig. 23-13, has been fitted with a closed

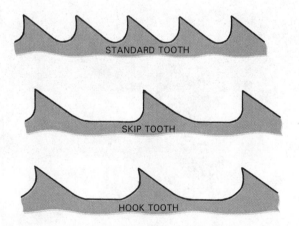

STANDARD TOOTH

SKIP TOOTH

HOOK TOOTH

Fig. 23-9. Standard tooth blades, with their well rounded gullets, are usually best for most ferrous materials, hard bronzes, and brasses. Skip tooth blades provide for more gullet and better chip clearance without weakening the blade body. They are best for aluminum, copper, magnesium, and soft brasses. Hook tooth blades offer two advantages over the skip tooth blade: the blade design allows it to feed easier, and its chip breaker design prevents gumming up.

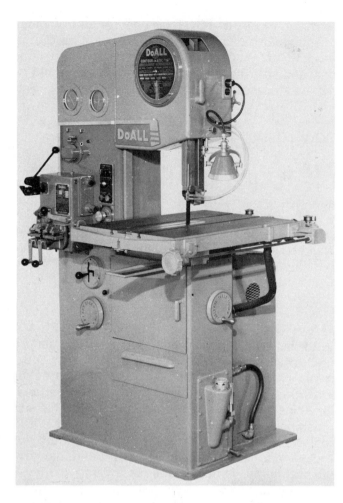

Fig. 23-10. The vertical band saw for metal machining. (DoALL Co.)

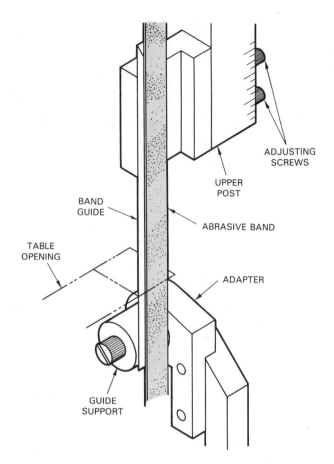

Fig. 23-12. Polishing and filing can be done on a band machine by replacing the saw band with an adhesive band or a file band. An abrasive band is shown. Guides used with the blade must be replaced with guides that support the abrasive band or file band.

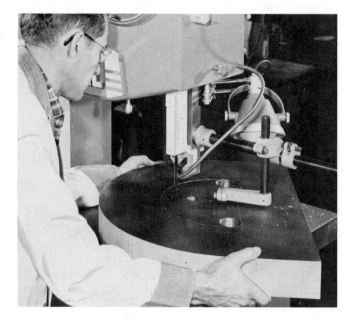

Fig. 23-11. Close-up showing how precision internal cuts can be made on a band saw. The blade is threaded through holes drilled in the piece, welded, and maneuvered along the prescribed line. (DoALL Co.)

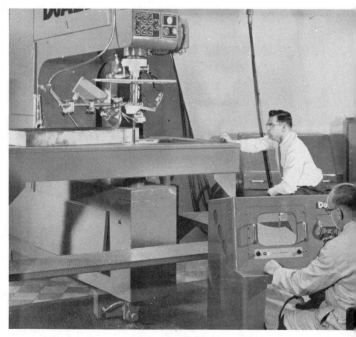

Fig. 23-13. A band-type machine fitted with a closed circuit TV and a remote control console. (DoALL Co.)

circuit TV and a remote control console to permit the operator to safely perform hazardous or dangerous work. For example, this procedure has been used for cutting radioactive materials.

CIRCULAR TYPE METAL-CUTTING SAWS

Metal-cutting circular saws find limited but specialized use in industry. They are primarily production machines and are divided into three classes:

1. ABRASIVE CUTOFF SAW. This saw cuts material by means of a rapidly revolving, thin abrasive wheel, Fig. 23-14. Most materials (glass, ceramics, and a long list of metals) can be cut to close tolerances. Hardened steel does not have to be annealed to be cut. Abrasive cutting can be done dry or wet. Wet abrasive cutting, while not quite as rapid as dry cutting, produces a finer surface finish and permits cutting to closer tolerances.

2. COLD CIRCULAR SAW. This type machine utilizes a circular toothed blade, Fig. 23-15. The blade is capable of producing very accurate cuts with a finish that is comparable to that produced by milling. The larger machines are able to rapidly cut metal sections up to 27 in. (686.0 mm) in diameter.

3. FRICTION SAW. The blade of this machine may or may not have teeth. The saw operates at very high speed—20 to 25,000 surface feet per minute—and actually burns and/or melts its way through the metal. If teeth are on the blade, their primary use is to carry oxygen to the cut. These machines are widely used in steel mills to cut billets while they are still hot.

Fig. 23-15. An automated cold circular saw used for cutting metal. (Motch & Merryweather Machinery Co.)

SAFETY

1. Wear safety glasses and dress appropriately—no loose clothing, no jewelry, etc.
2. Get help when cutting heavy material.
3. Clean oil and grease from the floor around the saw area.
4. Burrs on cut pieces are sharp. Handle cut pieces with care until the burrs can be removed.
5. Do not remove chips while the machine is running. After the saw has stopped, clean them away with a brush. NEVER REMOVE CHIPS WITH YOUR HAND OR COMPRESSED AIR!
6. Follow the manufacturer's instructions for tensioning the blade. Too much tension could cause the blade to shatter.
7. Keep your hands clear of the moving blade.
8. Stop the machine before making adjustments.
9. Avoid operating the saw unless all guards and safety features are in place.
10. Have all cuts and scratches, no matter how minor, treated promptly.

TEST YOUR KNOWLEDGE, Unit 23

Please do not write in the text. Place your answers on a separate sheet of paper.

1. The continuous blade power saw is also known as a _____.
2. The three-tooth rule for sawing means:
   a. That the blade teeth are in good condition.
   b. The blade should be adjusted frequently so that three consecutive teeth are always in good condition.
   c. At least three teeth are in contact with the work at all times during the cutting sequence.
   d. None of the above.

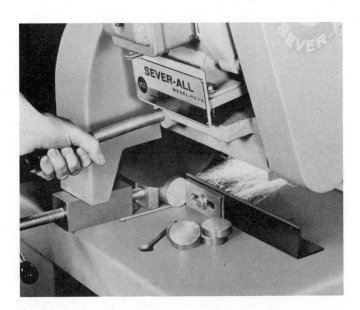

Fig. 23-14. Dry type abrasive cutoff saw.
(Allison-Campbell Div., American Chain and Cable Co.)

3. If manufacturer's instructions for tensioning a hacksaw blade are not available, what other method can be used to tension the blade?
4. List three advantages the continuous blade saw offers over the hacksaw.
5. The _____ allows finish and accuracy to within 0.010 to 0.015 in. (0.25 to 0.38 mm).
6. Describe the three classes of metal-cutting circular saws.

RESEARCH AND DEVELOPMENT

1. The abrasive cutoff wheel is also used to cut metal. How does its operation differ from conventional sawing? Make a display panel that shows photographs or drawings of a cutoff machine, a sample of the abrasive wheel it uses, and samples of materials for which it is better suited than the conventional saw.
2. Prepare models of the following blade types from suitable sheet aluminum. Secure samples and mount in hardwood blocks in such a manner that the tooth configuration can be observed with a magnifying glass.
   a. Raker and wavy set teeth.
   b. Standard tooth blade.
   c. Skip tooth blade.
   d. Hook tooth blade.
3. If the power hacksaw in your shop has seen considerable service, contact the manufacturer for a service manual and parts list. If time permits, and the machine can be spared, recondition it and paint it according to "color dynamics" specifications.
4. Design and produce a power saw safety poster.

Unit 24

METAL LATHE

A LATHE is a machine tool in which the work is held and rotated, while being shaped by a cutting tool that is fed against the work. See Figs. 24-1 and 24-2.

LATHE SIZE

Lathe size is determined by the SWING and BED LENGTH, Fig. 24-3. The swing indicates the largest diameter that can be turned. Bed length is the entire length of the ways (flat or V-shaped bearing surface that aligns and guides movable part of machine), and should not be mistaken for the maximum length of metal that can be turned.

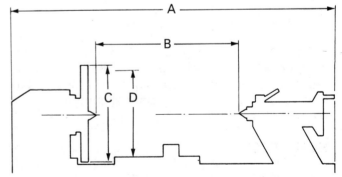

Fig. 24-2. The operating principle of the lathe.

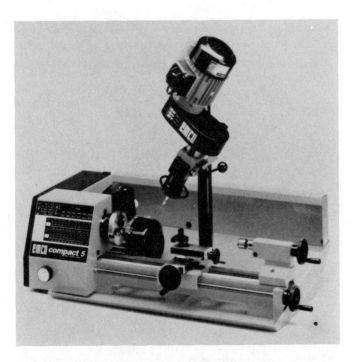

Fig. 24-1. Machine tools like this combination lathe/drill, press/vertical milling machine can be found in increasing numbers in school, home, and experimental shops. (Emco Maier Corp.)

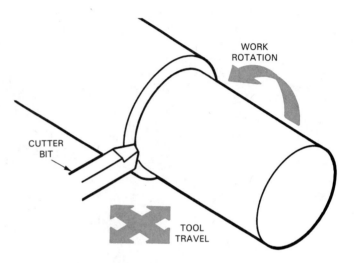

Fig. 24-3. Study how a lathe is measured. A—Length of bed. B—Distance between centers. C—Diameter of work that can be turned over the ways. D—Diameter of work that can be turned over the cross slide.

MAJOR PARTS OF A LATHE

Each of the lathe parts, Fig. 24-4, fall into one of three functional divisions:

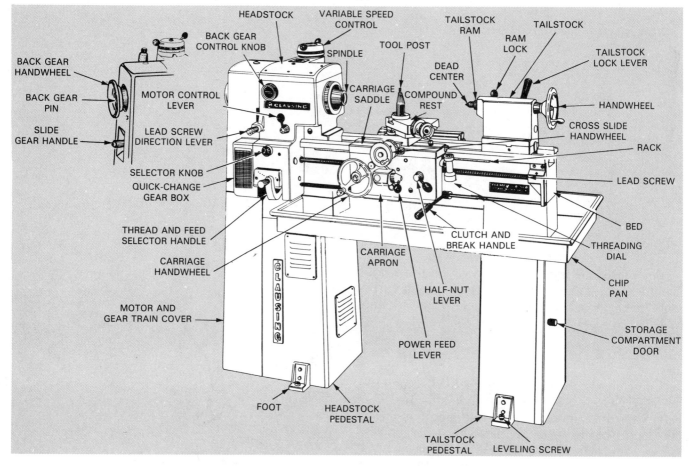

Fig. 24-4. The engine lathe and its major parts. (Clausing)

1. DRIVING THE LATHE.
2. HOLDING AND ROTATING THE WORK.
3. HOLDING AND MOVING THE CUTTING TOOL.

LATHE BED

The LATHE BED, Fig. 24-5, is the foundation or base on which the other parts of the lathe are fitted. Carefully machined ways on top of the bed support and provide for precise alignment of the headstock and tailstock.

HEADSTOCK

The HEADSTOCK, Figs. 24-6 and 24-7, contains the SPINDLE to which the various work holding attachments are fitted. The spindle is hollow with the front end tapered internally to receive tools and attachments with taper shanks. The opening permits long stock to be turned and allows a KNOCKOUT BAR, Fig. 24-8, to be used to remove taper shank tools.

The spindle is usually fitted with one of two standardized taper spindle noses, or with a threaded spindle nose, Figs. 24-9, 24-10, and 24-11.

Also found in the headstock is the SPEED CON-

Fig. 24-5. The lathe bed is the foundation of the machine.

TROL MECHANISM. Power supplied by an electric motor is transmitted to the spindle by a series of belts or a gear train. Spindle speed is controlled by using various pulley combinations or by changing the gear ratio.

Slower speeds are obtained on belt driven lathes

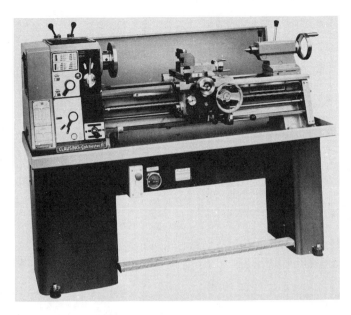

Fig. 24-6. The headstock of this lathe, in addition to containing the spindle and back gears, also has the speed control, quick-change gear box, switch, etc. (Clausing)

Fig. 24-9. Cam-lock type spindle nose. (Clausing)

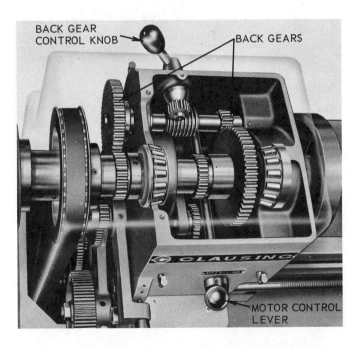

BACK GEAR CONTROL KNOB

BACK GEARS

MOTOR CONTROL LEVER

Fig. 24-7. Headstock interior of a modern lathe.

Fig. 24-10. Long taper key spindle nose. (Clausing)

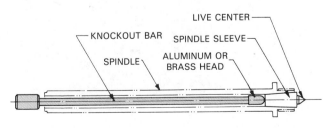

LIVE CENTER
KNOCKOUT BAR
SPINDLE SLEEVE
SPINDLE
ALUMINUM OR BRASS HEAD

Fig. 24-8. The knockout bar is used to tap taper shank lathe accessories from the spindle.

Fig. 24-11. Threaded type spindle nose. (South Bend Lathe, Inc.)

by engaging the BACK GEARS, Fig. 24-12. The large gear (BULL GEAR) is keyed to the spindle and is locked to the pulley with the BULL GEAR LOCK PIN. The back gears can be engaged by disconnecting the bull gear from the drive pulley. This is done by releasing the bull gear lock pin.

SAFETY NOTE: DO NOT ENGAGE THE BACK GEARS WHILE THE SPINDLE IS ROTATING.

TAILSTOCK

The TAILSTOCK, Fig. 24-13, can be adjusted alone the lathe ways to accommodate work of different lengths. It mounts the dead center that supports the outer end of the work. It also can be fitted with cutting tools for drilling, reaming, and threading. The tailstock is clamped to the ways by tightening the CLAMPBOLT NUT or LEVER. The ram or spindle is positioned by rotating the HANDWHEEL and locked in place with the RAM LOCK.

CARRIAGE

The CARRIAGE, Fig. 24-14, includes the SADDLE, APRON, CROSS SLIDE, LONGITUDINAL FEED AND SCREW CUTTING MECHANISM, COMPOUND REST, and TOOL POST. The cutting tool is supported and controlled by the carriage which is moved along the ways by hand or by power feed. A power feed mechanism is located in the apron. A friction clutch controls longitudinal and cross power feeds. Half-nuts are engaged for thread cutting.

FEED MECHANISM

The FEED MECHANISM, Fig. 24-15, transmits power through a train of gears to the QUICK-

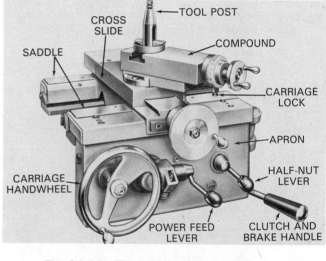

Fig. 24-14. The lathe carriage.   (Clausing)

Fig. 24-12. Back geared headstock. Guards have been removed for visibility.

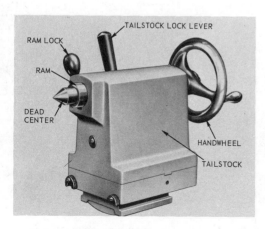

Fig. 24-13. The tailstock.   (Clausing)

Fig. 24-15. The feed mechanism.
(Sheldon Machine Co., Inc.)

CHANGE GEAR BOX, which in turn regulates the distance of tool travel per revolution of the spindle. The feed mechanism also contains gears for reversing tool travel. Lettering on the INDEX PLATE, Fig. 24-16, tells how to position the levers for various thread cutting and feed combinations.

The LEAD SCREW, Fig. 24-17, transmits the power to the carriage through a gearing and clutch arrangement in the apron. The FEED CHANGE LEVERS on the apron, Fig. 24-18, control the operation of power feeds and, when placed in neutral, permit the half-nuts to be engaged for threading operations.

GENERAL LATHE SAFETY

The following precautions should be observed at all times when working with the lathe. Study them carefully.

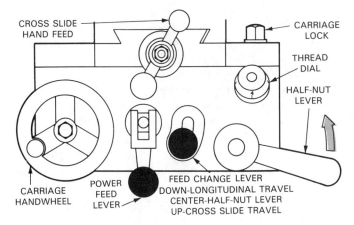

Fig. 24-18. Feed change levers on the apron control the operation of power feed. The half-nut is engaged only for thread cutting.

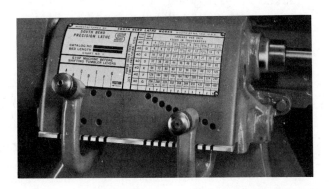

Fig. 24-16. The index plate.   (South Bend Lathe, Inc.)

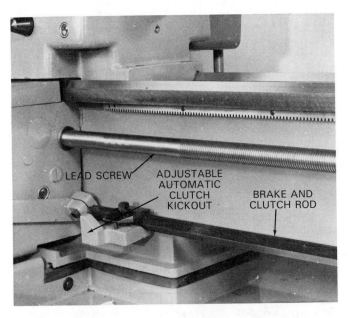

Fig. 24-17. The lead screw.   (Clausing)

1. Do not attempt to operate the lathe until you have been supervised on it and are thoroughly familiar with its operation.
2. Dress appropriately. Remove your necktie, sweater, wristwatch, and rings. Wear an apron or a properly fitted shop coat. Safety goggles are a must.
3. Clamp all work solidly. Use the correct size tool or work holding device for the job. Get help if you must use heavy chucks or attachments.
4. Check your work frequently when it is being machined between centers. The work expands as it heats up and could damage the tail center if it overheats.
5. Replace all guards before starting to work. The guards should only be removed to make adjustments, and then only with the power turned off at the main electrical panel to prevent the machine from being turned on accidentally. Replace the guards immediately after the adjustments have been made.
6. Return all unnecessary tools to the proper storage area. Remove all other tools from the immediate work area.
7. Turn the chuck or faceplate by hand to be sure there is no binding or danger of the work striking any part of the lathe.
8. Stop the machine before making adjustments or measurements.
9. Remember that the chips are razor sharp. Do not attempt to remove chips with your fingers. Stop the machine and use pliers to remove them.
10. Support all work solidly. Do not permit small diameter work to project too far from the chuck without support from the tailstock center.
11. Be careful not to run the cutting tool into the chuck or dog. Check out any readjustment of work or tool to be sure there is ample clearance

between the tool and the chuck or dog, when the tool has been moved left to the farthest point that will be machined.

12. Do not use cotton waste or rags to wipe grease or oil from the work surface unless the machine is stopped. Keep brushes used for cleaning and applying coolant, clear of work when knurling.

13. If work must be removed from the lathe, or repositioned in the chuck, always move the cutting tool clear of the work or reverse it in the tool post to prevent it from cutting you accidentally.

14. Do not talk to anyone, or permit anyone to horseplay near the machine while you are operating it. You are the only one who should turn the machine on or off, or make adjustments to the lathe during operation.

15. Never attempt to run the chuck on or off the spindle by using power. It is also a dangerous practice to stop the lathe by reversing its direction of rotation.

16. You should always be aware of the direction and speed of the carriage or cross-feed before engaging automatic feed.

17. Never leave the key in the chuck. Make it a habit never to let go of the key until it is out of the chuck and clear of the work area.

18. Tools must not be placed on the lathe ways. Use a tool board or place them on the lathe tray, Fig. 24-19.

19. Do not wrap the cord around your hands when cleaning the lead screw. Grip it lightly between the fingers so if it catches on the screw it will slip safely out of your hand.

20. Never use a file without a handle.

21. Stop the machine immediately if some odd noise or vibration develops while you are operating it. If you cannot find what is causing the trouble, inform your instructor. Under no condition should the machine be operated until the trouble has been found and corrected.

22. Remove all burrs and sharp edges from the piece before removing it from the lathe.

23. Plan your work thoroughly before starting. Have all of the tools that will be needed at hand before beginning.

24. Be careful when you clean the machine. As stated before, chips and shavings are sharp and will cause serious cuts if you attempt to remove them with your hands. Use a cleaning brush, NOT A DUST BRUSH, for the job. NEVER USE THE AIR HOSE. The flying chips may injure someone. Use pliers to remove stringy chips.

PREPARING THE LATHE FOR OPERATION

1. Clean and lubricate the lathe as recommended by the manufacturer.
2. Turn the spindle by hand to be sure it is not locked in back gear, Fig. 24-20. Set the drive mechanism to the desired speed and feed.
3. All guards must be in position.
4. Move the carriage along the ways, Fig. 24-21. There should be no binding.
5. Inspect the cross-feed and compound rest slides. Adjust the gibs if there is play (looseness), Fig. 24-22. Avoid excessive compound overhang, Fig. 24-23.
6. Inspect the tailstock if it is to be used for any portion of your work. Check it for alignment, Fig. 24-24. Use a ball bearing or smooth dead center.
7. Mount the proper working holding attachment

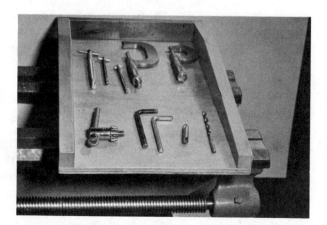

Fig. 24-19. A lathe board will keep tools within easy reach.

Fig. 24-20. Be sure the machine is not locked in back gear. Be sure power is off and if possible, belt tension released before checking.

Fig. 24-21. The carriage should be checked for binding by moving it along the ways. Correct any binding before attempting to use the lathe. (Clausing)

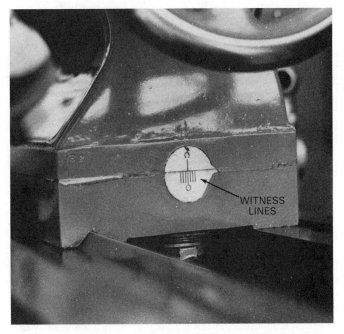

Fig. 24-24. Witness lines on the tailstock indicate whether the tailstock is aligned with the headstock.

Fig. 24-22. If there is too much play in the unit, adjust the gibs according to the instructions in the manufacturer's handbook. (Clausing)

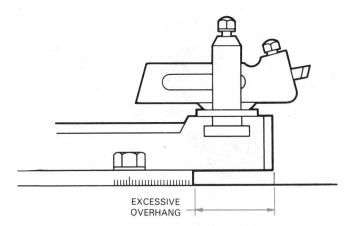

Fig. 24-23. Excessive compound rest overhang usually causes tool "chatter" that results in a poorly machined surface.

(chuck, faceplate, collet, etc.) on the headstock spindle. After cleaning the spindle and work holding device, apply a light coating of lubricating oil to the threads or contact surfaces.

8. Sharpen the cutter bit. Clamp it in the appropriate tool holder and mount it in the tool post.

CLEANING THE LATHE

A lathe must be cleaned after each work session. Remove chips with a brush, not your hands. Wipe all painted surfaces with a soft cloth. To complete the job, move the tailstock to the extreme right and, with a soft cloth, wipe the remaining oil, chips, and dirt from the machined surfaces. DO NOT USE COMPRESSED AIR TO REMOVE CHIPS. The flying chips are dangerous.

The lead screw needs an occasional cleaning too. This is done by adjusting the lathe to rotate the lead at a slow speed and using a section of cord as shown in Fig. 24-25. Permit the cord to feed along the threads. Do not wrap the cord around your hand. The cord might catch on the lead screw and cause serious injury.

LATHE CUTTING TOOLS
AND TOOL HOLDERS

Before a machinist can operate a lathe effectively he or she must have a good understanding of cutting tools and how these should be sharpened to machine various materials.

Metal Lathe 341

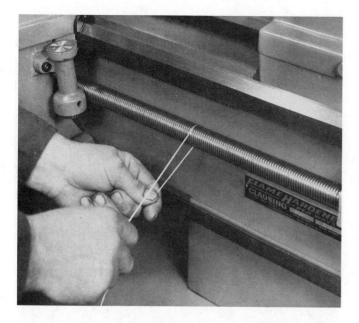

Fig. 24-25. Cleaning the lead screw with a piece of cord. (Clausing)

CUTTING TOOLS

Carbon steel tool cutter bits have been almost entirely replaced by high speed steel (HSS) bits. These are, in all probability, the type of cutting tools you will be using.

LATHE TOOL HOLDERS

In use, a cutter bit is inserted in a TOOL HOLDER, Figs. 24-26 through 24-28, and tightened down with a setscrew. The tool holders are made in STRAIGHT, RIGHT-HAND, and LEFT-HAND

Fig. 24-26. Straight tool holder. (J.H. Williams & Co.)

Fig. 24-27. Right-hand tool holder. (J.H. Williams & Co.)

Fig. 24-28. Left-hand tool holder. (J.H. Williams & Co.)

SHAPES. To differentiate between a right and left-hand tool holder, hold the head of the holder in your hand and note the direction the shank points. The right-hand tool holder points to the right, the left-hand tool holder to the left.

On some lathes a turret type tool holder is used, Fig. 24-29.

CUTTING TOOL SHAPES

Parts of a cutter bit are shown in Fig. 24-30. Most cutter bits are ground to cut in one direction only. Some cutting tools for general turning are shown in Fig. 24-31. To get satisfactory results from a metal lathe, the tool bit must have a keen, properly shaped cutting edge. The shape to grind the bit depends on the class of work (roughing or finishing) and upon the metal to be cut.

LEFT-CUT AND RIGHT-CUT ROUGHING TOOLS

The left-cut roughing tool, Fig. 24-32, A, cuts most efficiently when it travels from left to right.

Fig. 24-29. A turret type toolholder. Four cutter bits are fixed in the holder and can be brought into cutting position by loosening the lock (handle) and pivoting the desired cutter bit into cutting position and locking it in place. (ENCO Mfg. Co.)

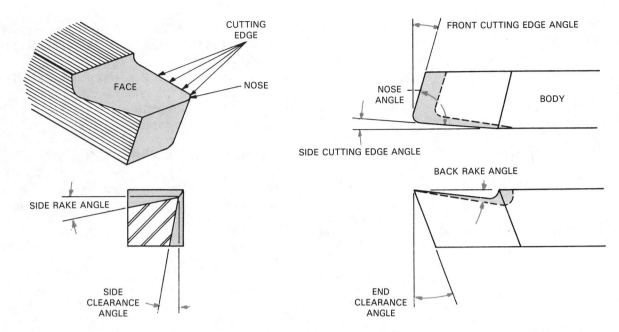

Fig. 24-30. The cutter bit and its parts.

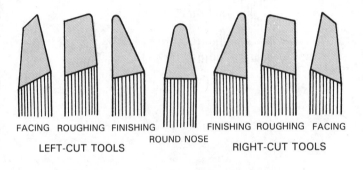

Fig. 24-31. Standard cutting tool shapes.

The right-cut roughing tool, Fig. 24-32, B, operates just the opposite.

The tool shape, straight cutting edge with a small rounded nose, permits deep cuts at heavier feeds. The slight side relief angle provides ample support to the cutting edges.

FINISHING TOOL

The finishing tool, Fig. 24-33, has a nose that is more rounded, Such a tool will produce a smooth finish, if the cutting edge is honed with a fine

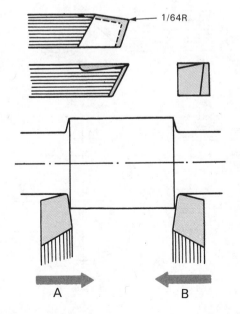

Fig. 24-32. Roughing tool. A—Left-cut. B—Right-cut.

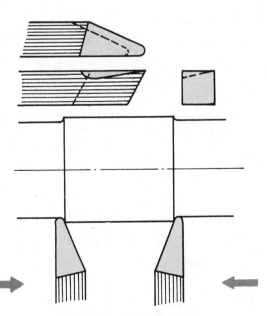

Fig. 24-33. Finishing tool.

oilstone after grinding. A light cut with fine feed is used with this tool.

FACING TOOL

The facing tool, Fig. 24-34, is ground to prevent interference with the tailstock center. The tool point is set at a slight angle to the work face with the point leading slightly.

ROUND NOSE TOOL

The round nose tool, Fig. 24-35, is designed for lighter turning and is ground flat on the face (without back or side rake) to permit cutting in either direction. A slight variation with a negative rake ground on the face is excellent for machining brass, Fig. 24-36.

Aluminum requires a different tool shape, Fig. 24-37, from those previously described. The tool is set slightly above center to reduce any tendency to chatter (vibrate rapidly).

HOW TO SHARPEN THE CUTTER BIT

When first attempting to grind a cutter bit, it may be desirable to use chalk and draw the shape of the

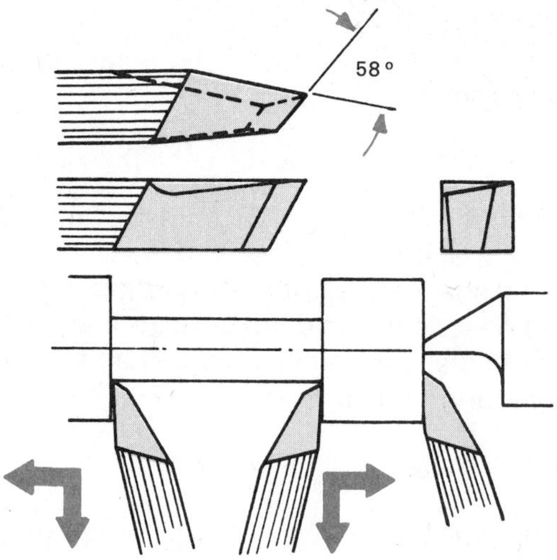

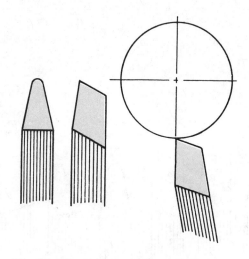

Fig. 24-36. Round nose tool for brass.

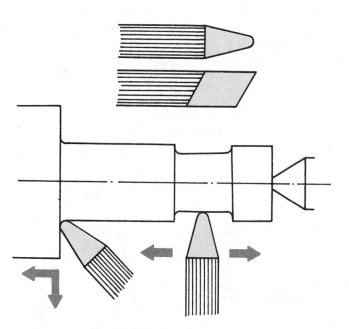

Fig. 24-34. Facing tool.

Fig. 24-35. Round nose tool.

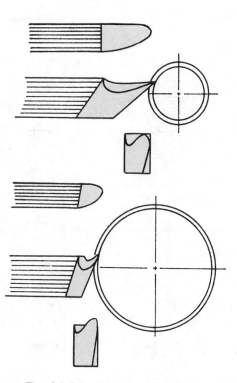

Fig. 24-37. Tools for aluminum.

desired point on the front portion of the blank, Fig. 24-38. In grinding, the chalk lines serve as a guide.

Fig. 24-39 shows the grinding sequence. Side clearance, top clearance, and end relief may be checked with a CLEARANCE AND CUTTING ANGLE GAUGE, Fig. 24-40.

CUTTING SPEEDS, FEEDS, AND DEPTH OF CUT

The term CUTTING SPEED indicates the distance in feet per minute the work moves past the cutting tool. Measuring is done on the circumference of the work.

To explain this differently, if a lathe were to cut one long chip, the length of that chip in feet cut in one minute would be the cutting speed of the lathe. Feed is the distance the cutter moves lengthwise along the lathe bed during one revolution of the work.

The specifications on the SPEED AND FEED CHART, Fig. 24-41, are intended for use with high speed steel cutter bits. These can be increased 50 percent if a coolant is used and another 300 to 400 percent if a tungsten carbide cutting tool is used.

HOW TO CALCULATE CUTTING SPEEDS

Cutting speeds (CS) are given in feet per minute (FPM), while the work speed is given in revolutions per minute (RPM); thus, the peripheral speed of the work (CS) must be converted to RPM in order to determine the lathe speed required. The following formula can be used:

$$RPM = \frac{CS \times 4}{D}$$

Where: RPM = Revolutions per minute.
CS = Cutting speed of the particular metal being turned, in feet per minute.
D = Diameter of the work in inches.

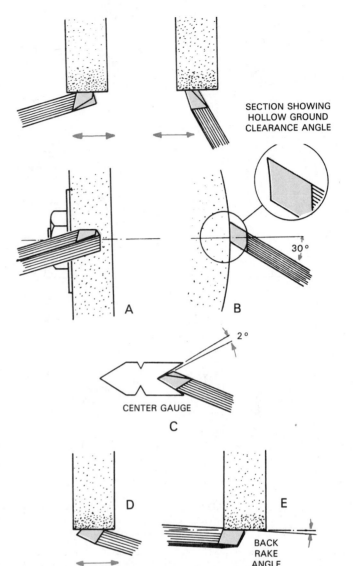

Fig. 24-39. Cutter bit grinding sequence. A and B—Grinding side and front of cutter bit to shape. Note how cutter bit is held against wheel so side clearance is ground in automatically. Keep moving bit across face of wheel and use care so the bit does not burn. C—Using a center gauge (fish tail) to check clearance angle. D—Finishing tip shape. E—How to hold cutter bit when grinding in top clearance.

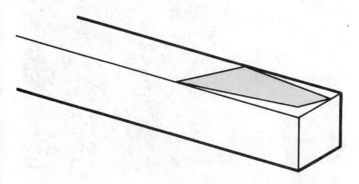

Fig. 24-38. Laid out cutter bit blank can make sharpening easier.

EXAMPLE: What spindle speed is required to finish turn 4 inch diameter aluminum alloy?

$$RPM = \frac{CS \times 4}{D} \qquad CS = 1000 \ FPM \ for \ finish \ turning$$

$$RPM = \frac{1000 \times 4}{4} \qquad D = 4 \ in.$$

$$= 1000$$

Adjust the speed control mechanism to a speed as close to this figure as possible.

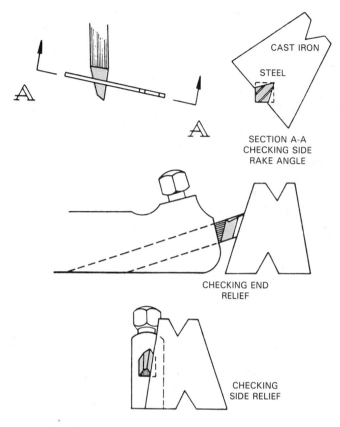

Fig. 24-40. The cutter bit gauge and how it is used.

MATERIAL TO BE CUT	ROUGHING CUT 0.01 to 0.020 in. 0.25 to 0.50 mm Feed		FINISHING CUT 0.001 to 0.020 in. 0.050 to 0.24 mm Feed	
	ft/min	m/min	ft/min	m/min
Cast Iron	70	20	120	36
Steel				
Low Carbon	130	40	160	56
Med Carbon	90	27	100	30
High Carbon	50	15	65	20
Tool Steel				
(annealed)	50	15	65	20
Brass—Yellow	160	56	220	67
Bronze	90	27	100	30
Aluminum*	600	183	1000	300

The speeds for rough turning are offered as a starting point. It should be all the machine and work will withstand. The finishing feed depends upon the finish quality desired.

*The speeds for turning aluminum will vary greatly according to the alloy being machined. The softer alloys can be turned at speeds upwards of 1600 ft/min (488 m/min) roughing to 3500 ft/min (106 m/min) finishing. High silicon alloys require a lower cutting speed.

Fig. 24-41. Suggested cutting speeds and feeds for turning using high speed steel tools.

ROUGHING CUTS

Roughing cuts are taken to reduce the work quickly to approximate size. The work is left 1/32 in. oversize for the finishing operation. As the finish of the roughing cut is not important, the highest speed and coarsest feed, consistent with safety and accuracy, should be used.

FINISHING CUTS

The finish cut brings the work to the required diameter and surface finish. A sharp tool, used at high speed and fine feed, is used.

DEPTH OF CUT

Depth of cut is the distance the cutter is fed into the work. Desired depth can be set accurately with a MICROMETER DIAL, Fig. 24-42, on both cross slide and compound rests. They are usually graduated in 0.001 in. (0.025 mm). On some lathes the dial is direct reading and, if fed in one graduation, will reduce work diameter 0.001 in. (0.025 mm). However, on other lathes the same movement will move the cutter in 0.001 in. (0.025 mm) and will remove 0.002 in. (0.05 mm) of material, Fig. 24-43. CHECK YOUR LATHE.

WORK HOLDING ATTACHMENTS

The work is machined while supported by one of the following methods.
1. Between centers, Fig. 24-44.
2. Held in a chuck, Fig. 24-45.
3. Held in a collet, Fig. 24-46.
4. Bolted to faceplate, Fig. 24-47.

Fig. 24-42. Combination English/metric graduated feed dials on the cross slide and compound handwheels.

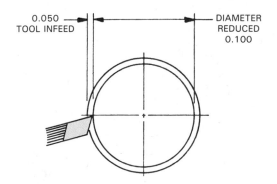

Fig. 24-43. How material is removed on each cut.

Fig. 24-44. Machining work mounted between centers.

Fig. 24-45. Turning work held in a 3-jaw universal chuck.

Fig. 24-46. Turning work held in a collet chuck. (The Jacobs Mfg. Co.)

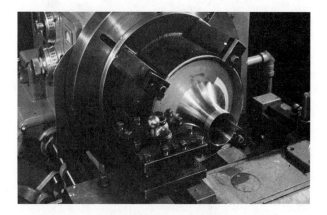

Fig. 24-47. Work mounted to a faceplate for boring. (National Machine Tool Builders Assoc.)

Fig. 24-48. Lathe faceplates.

TURNING BETWEEN CENTERS

Considerable lathe work is done between centers. For this operation, a faceplate, Fig. 24-48, is threaded to the spindle nose and a SLEEVE and LIVE CENTER, Fig. 24-49, is inserted in the headstock spindle. A dead center is placed in the tailstock. The ends of the stock are drilled to fit the centers. The stock is connected to the faceplate with a DOG. Three types of lathe dogs are pictured in Figs. 24-50 through 24-52.

DRILLING CENTER HOLES

Before work can be turned between centers, it is necessary to locate and drill a center hole in each end of the stock. Fig. 24-53 illustrates several methods of locating the center of the stock.

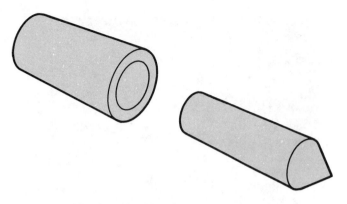

Fig. 24-49. Sleeve and head center.

Fig. 24-50. Bent tail standard lathe dog.
(Armstrong Bros. Tool Co.)

Fig. 24-51. Bent tail safety dog. (Armstrong Bros. Tool Co.)

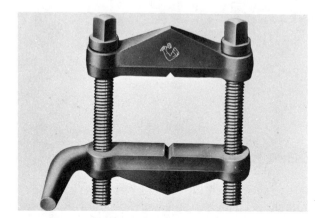

Fig. 24-52. Clamp type lathe dog. (Armstrong Bros. Tool Co.)

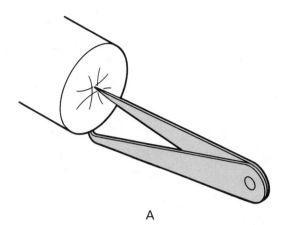

A

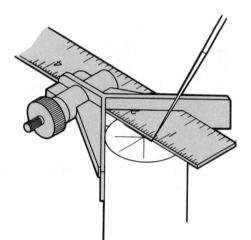

B

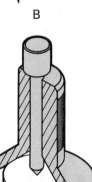

C

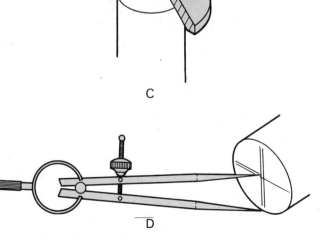

D

Fig. 24-53. Several ways to locate the center of round stock.
A—With hermaphrodite caliper. B—With center head and rule
of combination set. C—With bell center punch. D—With
dividers.

Center holes are drilled with a COMBINATION DRILL AND COUNTERSINK, Fig. 24-54. They provide a reservoir for a lubricant. The center hole may be drilled on the drill press, on the lathe with the work centered in a chuck, or supported on the dead center with the center drill mounted in the headstock. See Fig. 24-55.

CHECKING ALIGNMENT OF LATHE CENTERS

Accurate work requires centers that run true and in precise alignment. If the live center does not run true, the diameters will be eccentric, Fig. 24-56, as the piece must be reversed to machine the entire length.

A tapered piece will result if the centers are not aligned.

Fig. 24-54. Plain type combination drill and countersink. (Standard Tool Co.)

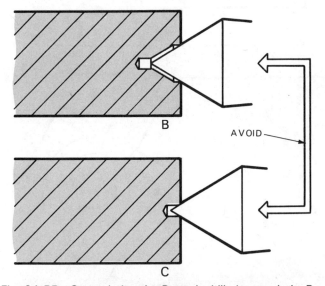

Fig. 24-55. Center holes. A—Properly drilled center hole. B—Hole drilled too deep, center rides on lip of hole. Groove will wear on the dead center. C—Hole not drilled deep enough. Not enough support, center point will burn off.

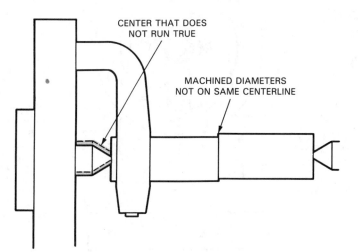

Fig. 24-56. Eccentric diameters will result if the live center does not run true and the piece must be reversed in the dog so the stock can be machined its entire length.

Approximate alignment can be determined by:
1. Bringing the centers together and checking them visually, Fig. 24-57.
2. Checking the alignment of the two lines on the back of the tailstock, Fig. 24-58.

Extremely accurate machining requires a more precise method of checking center alignment. A test piece is machined and "miked" at several points along its length. If the piece tapers, the tailstock should be adjusted until the diameter is the same the entire length. Use the adjusting screws on the base of the tailstock.

Make the adjustments gradually. A common mistake is to move the setscrews too far and overshoot the mark.

HOW TO MOUNT WORK BETWEEN CENTERS

Clamp a lathe dog on one end of the work. Place lubricant (white lead and oil, white lead, graphite and oil, or a commercial center lubricant) in the

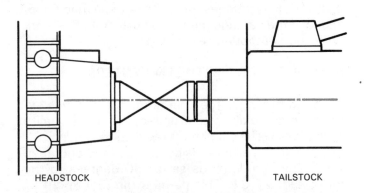

Fig. 24-57. Checking center alignment by bringing the center points together.

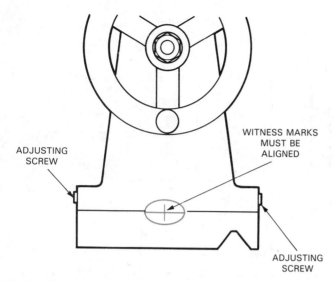

Fig. 24-58. Alignment of centers can be determined by checking witness marks on tailstock.

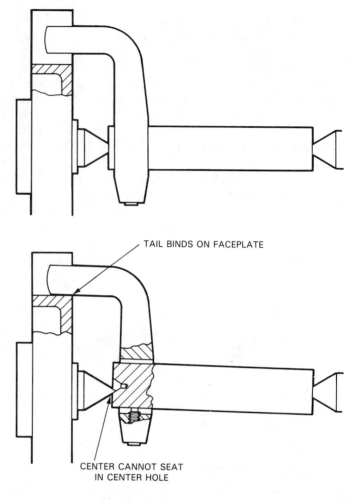

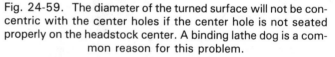

Fig. 24-59. The diameter of the turned surface will not be concentric with the center holes if the center hole is not seated properly on the headstock center. A binding lathe dog is a common reason for this problem.

center hole. Fit the work on the centers and adjust the tail center until the work is snug on the centers. Check the adjustment from time to time during the machining operation as the heat generated causes the piece to expand.

Be sure that the dog tail does not bind on the faceplate slot, Fig. 24-59.

FACING STOCK HELD BETWEEN CENTERS

Facing is the operation of machining the end of the stock square and reducing it to a specific length.

There are times when considerable material must be removed. In normal practice, the work is left longer than finished size and the center holes are drilled deeper for better support during rough turning. The stock is faced to length before starting the finishing operation.

A right-cut facing tool is used. The point of the tool permits a slight clearance between the work face and the center. A half center may be used for the facing operation. With the compound rest set at 30 degrees, Fig. 24-60, bring the cutting tool up until it just touches the surface to be machined, and lock the carriage. Feed the cutter into the work with the compound rest.

ROUGH TURNING BETWEEN CENTERS

Rough turning is the operation that removes excess metal rapidly with little regard for the quality of the finish. The diameter is reduced to within 1/32 in. of required size by using coarse feed and deep cuts. The compound is set at 30 degrees to the work, Fig. 24-61. This permits the tool to cut as close as possible to the left end of the work without the dog striking the compound rest.

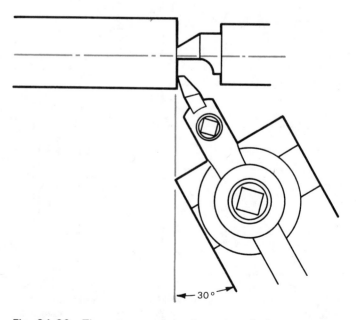

Fig. 24-60. The compound setting when facing stock to length.

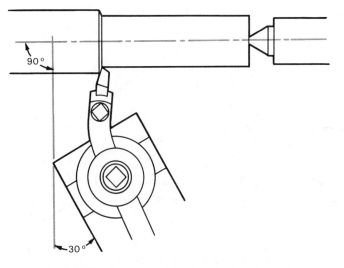

Fig. 24-61. Compound setting for rough turning.

Check before starting the machine to determine how far the carriage can be moved to the left without danger of the dog striking the compound rest.

Use a left-hand tool holder to support the cutter bit. Position the tool post as far to the left in the compound rest T-slot as possible. When mounting the tool holder, do not permit too much overhang, Fig. 24-62. The cutting edge of the tool should be

about 1/16 in. (1.59 mm) above center for each inch of diameter.

It is also important to have the tool holder in the correct position in the tool post. This is especially true when making heavy cuts. The side pressures that develop sometimes cause the tool holder to turn in the tool post. If not positioned correctly, the cutting tool will be forced still deeper in the work, Fig. 24-63. The correct position permits the tool to swing away from the work, Fig. 24-64.

Apply lubricant to the center hole on each cut. A heavy-duty BALL BEARING CENTER (the center revolves in the unit) is ideal for rough turning, Fig. 24-65.

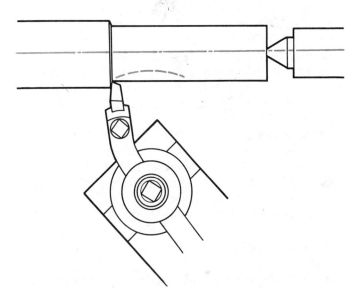

Fig. 24-63. An incorrectly positioned tool will cut deeper and deeper into the work if it slips in the tool post.

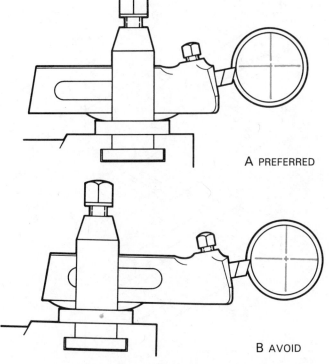

Fig. 24-62. Mounting the tool holder. A—Tool holder and cutter bit in the proper position. B—Too much overhang. Tool will "chatter" and produce a machined surface that is rough.

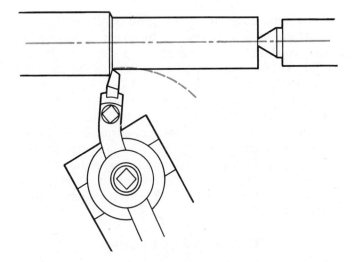

Fig. 24-64. A correctly positioned tool will swing clear of the work if the tool holder slips in the tool post.

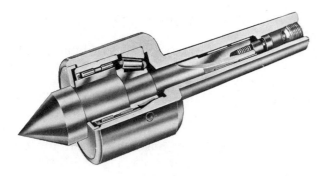

Fig. 24-65. A heavy-duty ball bearing center.

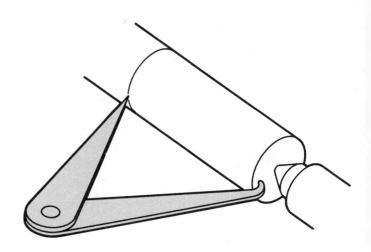

Fig. 24-66. Locating reference points on the work with a hermaphrodite caliper.

FINISH TURNING

A right-cut finishing tool is used for finish machining. Adjust the lathe for a faster spindle speed and a finer cut. Feed the cutting tool into the work until a very light cut is being made and engage the power feed. After a sufficient distance has been machined, disengage the power feed and stop the lathe. UNDER NO CONDITION SHOULD THE LATHE BE REVERSED TO STOP IT. Do not interfere with the cross slide setting. Measure the machined diameter with a micrometer. Calculate the additional material that must be removed to bring the piece down to size. Move the cutting tool clear of the right end of the work and feed it in ONE-HALF the amount that must still be removed. Make another cut about 1/2 in. (12.7 mm) wide, and remeasure. If to size, complete the cut; if not, reposition the cutter.

If the piece must be reversed to machine its entire length, protect the section under the lathe dog setscrew by inserting a piece of soft aluminum or copper sheet.

TURNING TO A SHOULDER

It is often necessary to machine several different diameters on a single piece of stock. Locate the points to which the different diameters are to be cut by scribing them with a hermaphrodite caliper set to the specified size, Fig. 24-66.

The machining is done as previously described with the exception of machining the SHOULDER— the point where the diameters change. One of the shoulders illustrated in Fig. 24-67 will be specified.

A right-cut facing tool is used to make the square and angular type shoulder. A round nose tool, ground to the proper radius, is used to machine the filleted shoulder.

TURNING WITH CHUCKS

CHUCKS are the most rapid method of mounting work for turning. Operations such as drilling, ream-

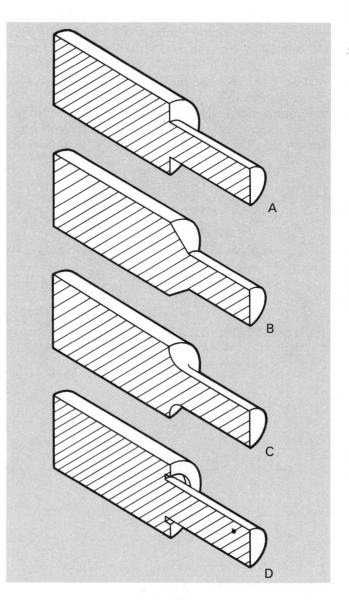

Fig. 24-67. Four kinds of shoulders. A—Square. B—Angular. C—Filleted. D—Undercut.

ing, boring, and internal threading can be done to work held in a chuck. Additional support can be secured by supporting the free end of work with the tailstock center, Fig. 24-68.

The chucks most commonly used are:
1. 3-jaw universal chuck.
2. 4-jaw independent chuck.
3. Jacobs chuck.
4. Draw-in collet chuck.

3-JAW UNIVERSAL CHUCK

The 3-JAW UNIVERSAL CHUCK, Fig. 24-69, permits all jaws to operate simultaneously. This automatically centers round or hexagonal shaped stock to within a few thousandths of an inch.

Two sets of jaws are normally provided with each universal chuck. They permit a wide variety of work to be mounted, Fig. 24-70. Avoid gripping work near the front of the jaws, Fig. 24-71.

4-JAW INDEPENDENT CHUCK

As each jaw of a 4-JAW INDEPENDENT CHUCK, Fig. 24-72, can operate individually, irregular

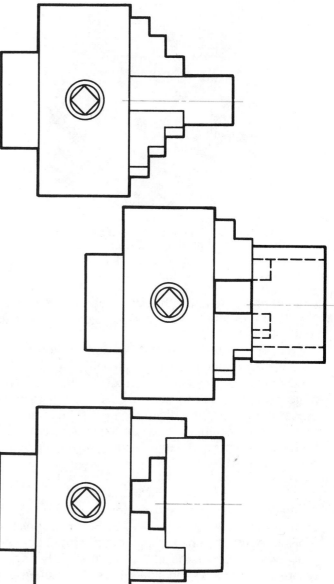

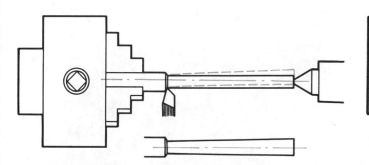

Fig. 24-68. If not properly supported by the tailstock center, small diameter work will spring away from the cutting tool and will be machined at a slight taper.

Fig. 24-70. Methods of holding work in a 3-jaw universal chuck.

Fig. 24-69. The 3-jaw universal chuck.   (L.W. Chuck Co.)

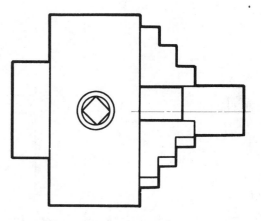

Fig. 24-71. Avoid gripping work near the front of the jaws. It could fly out and cause injuries.

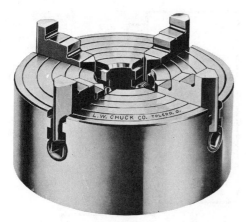

Fig. 24-72. The 4-jaw independent chuck.
(L.W. Chuck Co.)

Fig. 24-74. Centering work in a 4-jaw chuck using a dial
indicator.

shaped castings and other work can be centered. The jaws can also be reversed to hold different size work, Fig. 24-73.

The most accurate method of centering work in this type of chuck is with a DIAL INDICATOR, Fig. 24-74. Center the work approximately, using the rings on the chuck face as a guide. Bring to final adjustment using the dial indicator. (The indicator needle does not fluctuate when the chuck is rotated by hand.) Tighten all jaws securely after the work has been centered.

SAFETY NOTE: REMOVE THE CHUCK KEY BEFORE STARTING THE MACHINE.

Chalk can also be used to position the work on approximate center, Fig. 24-75. Rotate the work while bringing the chalk into contact with it. Loosen the jaws opposite the chalk mark slightly. Then tighten the jaws on the side where the chalk mark is located. Continue the operation until the work is centered. A cutter bit may be used if the work is oversize enough.

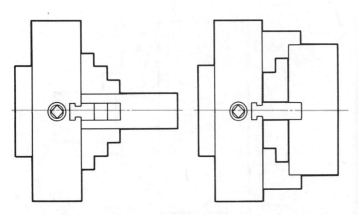

Fig. 24-73. The reversing feature of the jaws in the 4-jaw independent chuck makes it possible to turn work having extreme differences in diameter without difficulty.

Fig. 24-75. Using chalk to position work on approximate center.

JACOBS CHUCK

The JACOBS CHUCK, Fig. 24-76, can be used to hold small diameter and short work for turning. A standard drill chuck can be employed if fitted with a sleeve. Wipe the shank clean before inserting the chuck and sleeve.

DRAW-IN COLLET CHUCK

A DRAW-IN COLLET CHUCK, Fig. 24-77, is another work holding device for the lathe. The standard collet has a circular hole for round stock, but collets for holding square, hexagonal, and octagonal material are available. Their chief advantage lies in their ability to center work automatically and maintain accuracy with hard usage, Fig. 24-78.

A collet chuck that utilizes steel segments bonded to rubber is shown in Fig. 24-79. An advantage of this chuck is that each collet has a range of 0.100 in. (2.5 mm), rather than being a single size like steel collets.

HOW TO MOUNT CHUCKS

Chuck accuracy is affected if it is not installed on the spindle nose correctly. Remove the center and sleeve (if they had been left in the spindle) by holding the spindle with one hand and lightly tapping them loose with the other hand, using a knockout bar. Carefully wipe the spindle clean of chips and dirt. Apply a few drops of lubricating oil. If the chuck uses a threaded mount, clean the threads with a SPRING CLEANER, Fig. 24-80.

On the tapered key spindle nose, rotate the spindle until the key is in the up position. Slide the chuck on the taper and tighten the threaded ring with a spanner wrench. Pins on the cam-lock spindle chuck are fitted into place and locked.

Fig. 24-76. Turning small diameter work in a Jacobs chuck.

Fig. 24-78. A collet chuck in use.

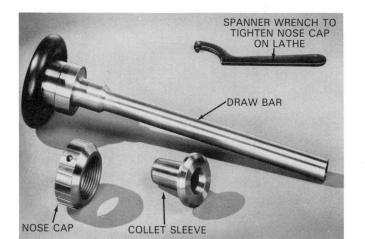

Fig. 24-77. The units that make up a collet chuck. (South Bend Lathe, Inc.)

Fig. 24-79. The Rubber-Flex collet chuck in use. (The Jacobs Mfg. Co.)

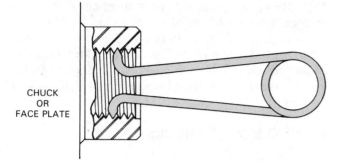

Fig. 24-80. A spring cleaner for cleaning threads in chucks that mount on threaded spindles.

Fitting a chuck onto a threaded spindle nose requires a different technique. Hold the chuck against the spindle nose with the right hand and turn the spindle with the left hand. Screw the chuck on until if fits firmly against the shoulder. DO NOT SPIN IT ON OR USE POWER. RELEASE BELT TENSION IF POSSIBLE, TO ELIMINATE ANY CHANCE OF POWER BEING TRANSFERRED ACCIDENTLY TO THE SPINDLE.

Place a board on the ways under the chuck for protection of your hands and the machine ways, Fig. 24-81.

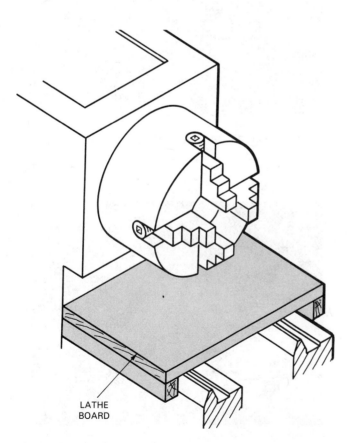

Fig. 24-81. A board placed under a chuck when mounting or removing it will protect your hand should you drop the chuck.

REMOVING A CHUCK FROM A THREADED SPINDLE

There are several accepted method for removing chucks from a threaded spindle. The first step in all methods is the placement of a wooden cradle across the ways beneath the chuck, Fig. 24-82. Then one of the following techniques is employed.

1. Lock the spindle in back gear and use a chuck key to apply leverage.
2. Place an adjustable wrench of a suitable size on one jaw, Fig. 24-83. Grasp the drive pulley with one hand or lock the spindle in back gear, and apply pressure to the wrench.
3. If neither of the first two methods work, place a block of wood between the back lathe way and a chuck jaw. Engage the back gear and give the drive pulley a quick backward turn. When

Fig. 24-82. A wooden cradle placed under a chuck will make removing it from a threaded spindle safer and easier.

Fig. 24-83. An adjustable wrench fitted to one of the jaws may be used to loosen a chuck fitted to a threaded spindle.

using this technique, secure help from your instructor.

HOW TO FACE STOCK HELD IN A CHUCK

A facing cutting tool held in a straight tool holder is normally employed to face stock held in a chuck. The tool is set up as shown in Fig. 24-84. Move the carriage into position and lock it to the ways.

A facing cut can be made in either direction; the tool may be started in the center and fed out, or the reverse may be done. The usual practice is to start from the center and feed out. If the material is over 1 1/2 in. (38.0 mm) in diameter, automatic feed may be employed.

If the facing tool is on exact center, a smooth surface will result from the cut. A rounded "nubbin" will be formed if the tool is above center. A "nubbin" with a square shoulder indicates the cutting tool is below center. Reset the tool and repeat the operation if either is obtained.

PLAIN TURNING AND TURNING TO A SHOULDER

Work mounted in a chuck is machined in the same manner as it is machined between centers. To prevent springing while being machined, long work should be center drilled and supported with the tailstock center.

PARTING OPERATIONS

PARTING is the operation of cutting off material after machining, Fig. 24-85. This is one of the most difficult jobs performed on a lathe.

The cutting tool, Fig. 24-86, must be ground with the correct clearance (front, side, and end). It is held

Fig. 24-85. Parting is one of the most difficult jobs performed on the lathe.

Fig. 24-86. Concave rake ground into top of parting tool.

in a STRAIGHT or OFFSET TOOL HOLDER, Fig. 24-87.

The blade is set at exactly 90 degrees to the work surface, Fig. 24-88. The cutting edge is set on center when cutting off stock 1 in. (25.0 mm) or less in diameter and 1/16 in. (1.5 mm) above center for each additional inch (25.0 mm) in diameter. The tool must be lowered as the diameter is reduced, unless the center of the piece has been drilled out.

Spindle speed is about one-third the speed used for conventional turning. Use ample supplies of

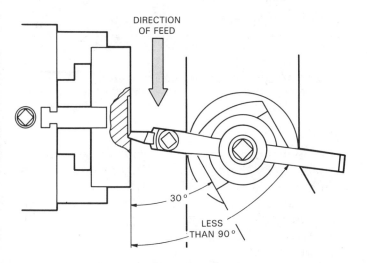

Fig. 24-84. The tool and tool holder in the correct position for facing.

DIRECTION OF FEED

30°

LESS THAN 90°

Fig. 24-87. Parting tool holders.   (Armstrong Bros. Tool Co.)

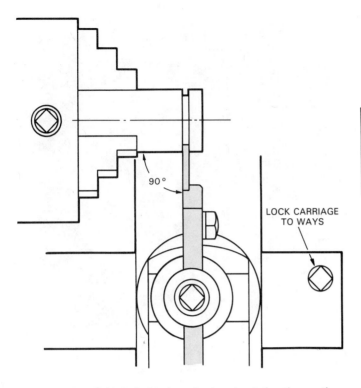

Fig. 24-88. Work is held close in the chuck for the parting operation, the parting tool blade is set at a 90° angle to the cut, and the carriage is locked to the ways.

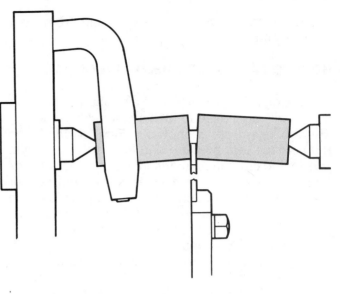

Fig. 24-89. Work cannot be parted safely while being held between centers.

coolant. Whenever possible, hold the work close in the chuck.

SAFETY NOTE: DO NOT CUT OFF WORK HELD BETWEEN CENTERS. IT CANNOT BE DONE SAFELY, Fig. 24-89.

HOW TO TURN A TAPER

There are four generally accepted methods for machining tapers on the lathe. Each has its advantages and disadvantages.
1. Using the compound rest.
2. Offsetting the tailstock.
3. Using the taper attachment already fitted to the lathes.
4. Using a cutting tool ground to the desired taper.

COMPOUND REST METHOD

The COMPOUND REST method of turning tapers, Fig. 24-90, is the easiest of the group. It can be used to cut internal and external tapers, Fig. 24-91. However, the length of the taper is limited by compound rest movement. The base of the compound rest is graduated in degrees.

OFFSET TAILSTOCK METHOD

The OFFSET TAILSTOCK method, Fig. 24-92, is also known as the TAILSTOCK SETOVER method.

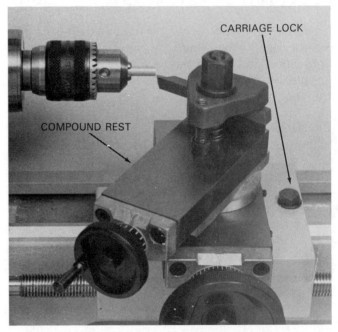

Fig. 24-90. Getting ready to cut a taper using a compound rest. Make sure there is clearance between the compound and the chuck. Tighten carriage lock before cutting taper.

Any job that can be machined between centers can be tapered by this technique. Only external tapers can be turned.

The lathe tailstock is constructed in two main parts permitting the part mounting the center to be moved off center, Fig. 24-93. This is accomplished by loosening the anchor bolt that locks the tailstock to the lathe ways. There are adjusting screws on each side of the tailstock base.

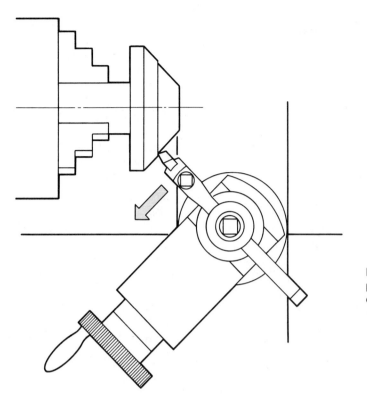

Fig. 24-91. Turning a taper using the compound rest.

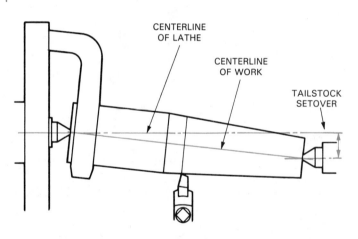

Fig. 24-92. Machining a taper by the offset tailstock technique.

CALCULATING SETOVER

Offset tailstock taper turning is not a precise art and requires some trial and error adjustments to produce an accurate piece. The approximate setover can be calculated when certain basic information is known.

The offset must be calculated for each job because the work length plays an important part in the calculations. When the length varies, different tapers will result with the same tailstock setover, Fig. 24-94.

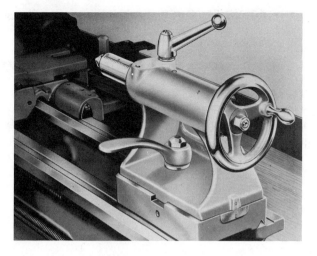

Fig. 24-93. The tailstock on most lathes is constructed in two parts permitting the section mounting the center to be moved off center. Distance off center can be checked by the spacing of the witness lines. (Rockwell International)

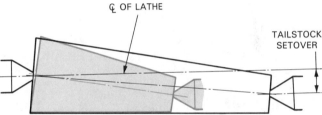

Fig. 24-94. Note how the length of the work causes the taper to vary even though the tailstock offset remains the same.

The following terms are used when calculating tailstock setover, Fig. 24-95.

TPI = Taper per inch
TPF = Taper per foot
TPmm = Taper per millimeter
D = Diameter at large end of work
d = Diameter at small end of work
l = Length of taper
L = Total length of work

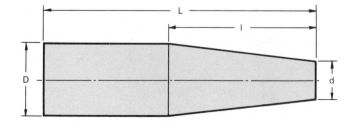

Fig. 24-95. Basic taper information. D = Diameter at large end of taper. d = Diameter at small end of taper. l = Length of taper. L = Total length of piece.

CALCULATING SETOVER, TAPER PER INCH GIVEN

Information needed: TPI = Taper per inch
L = Total length of work

FORMULA USED: Offset $= \dfrac{L \times TPI}{2}$

EXAMPLE: What will be the setover for the following job?
TPI = 0.050 in.
L = 8.000 in.

Offset $= \dfrac{L \times TPI}{2} = \dfrac{8.000 \times 0.050}{2}$
$= 0.200$ in.

CALCULATING SETOVER, TAPER PER FOOT GIVEN

When the taper per foot (TPF) is known, it must first be converted to taper per inch (TPI). The formula shown takes this into account:

Offset $= \dfrac{TPF \times L}{24}$

CALCULATING SETOVER, TAPER PER MILLIMETER GIVEN

FORMULA USED: Offset $= \dfrac{L \ (\text{in mm}) \times TPmm}{2}$

CALCULATING SETOVER, DIMENSIONS OF TAPERED SECTION GIVEN: TPF, TPI, TPmm NOT GIVEN

Quite often plans do not specify TPF, TPI, or TPmm but do give other pertinent information. If inch dimensions are given in fractions, they must be converted to decimals.

FORMULA USED: Offset $= \dfrac{L \times (D-d)}{2 \times l}$

EXAMPLE: D = 1 1/4 in.
d = 7/8 in.
l = 3.000 in.
L = 9.000 in.

Offset $= \dfrac{L \times (D-d)}{2 \times l} \quad \dfrac{9.000 \times (1.250 - 0.875)}{2 \times 3.000}$

$= \dfrac{9.000 \times 0.375}{6} = 0.562$ in.

EXAMPLE: D = 30.0 mm
d = 20.0 mm
l = 75.0 mm
L = 225.0 mm

Offset $= \dfrac{L \times (D-d)}{2 \times l} \quad \dfrac{225.0 \times (30.0 - 20.0)}{2 \times 75.0}$

$= \dfrac{225.0 \times 10.0}{150.0} = 15.0$ mm

MEASURING TAILSTOCK SETOVER

When an ample tolerance is allowed ($\pm$ 1/64 in. or 0.4 mm) the setover can be measured with a rule, Fig. 24-96.

More accurate work requires extra care in making the tailstock setover. This can be done using the compound rest and a strip of paper. See Fig. 24-97. The compound must be manipulated to remove all play. A tool holder is reversed in the tool post. It is fed against the tailstock spindle until it just touches the paper strip. The compound is then backed out the required setover distance. Adjusting screws in the tailstock are moved until the spindle is brought out to again just contact the paper strip.

A dial indicator, Fig. 24-98, may also be used to accurately measure tailstock setover.

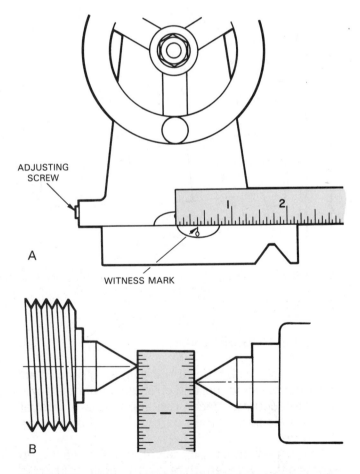

Fig. 24-96. Using a rule to measure tailstock setover. A—Measuring distance between witness marks on base of the tailstock. B—Using center points to determine amount of tailstock setover.

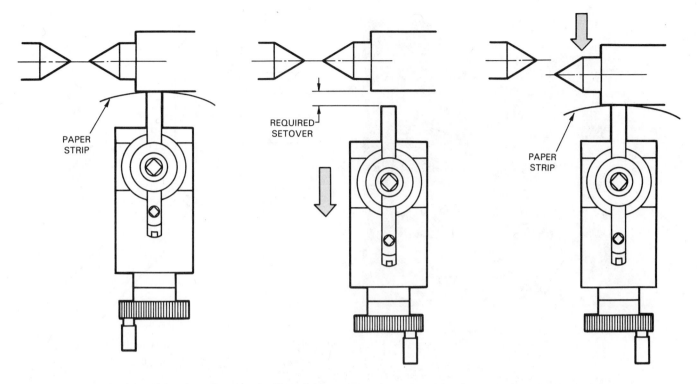

Fig. 24-97. Using the micrometer collar of the compound rest to make the setover measurement.

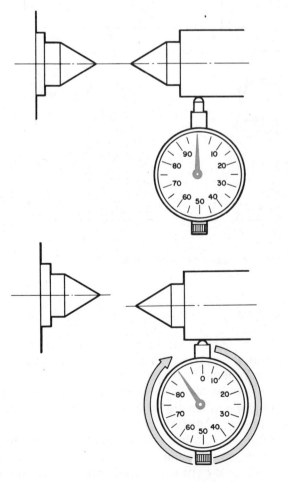

Fig. 24-98. Using a dial indicator to measure the amount of setover.

TAPER ATTACHMENT METHOD

A TAPER ATTACHMENT, Fig. 24-99, is a guide that can be attached to most metal cutting lathes. It provides an accurate way to cut tapers and offers some advantage over the other methods. Internal and external tapers are both possible. Work can be held by conventional means—chuck, between centers, collet chuck, etc. Once the attachment is set, the same taper can be machined on any length material. The lathe does not have to be altered in any manner. It can be employed for straight turning by simply locking out the device. No realigning is necessary to reengage the taper attachment.

TAPER TURNING WITH A SQUARE NOSE TOOL

This method is limited to the production of very short tapers, Fig. 24-100. The cutter is ground with a square nose and is set to the correct angle with a protractor head and rule of a combination set. Be sure the tool is set on exact center.

MEASURING TAPERS

Two methods for testing taper accuracy are the comparison method using taper plug and ring gauges, or taking a direct measurement of the taper. This method will be explained.

A surface plate, steel parallels, and sections of drill rod are required. The tapered section is placed

Fig. 24-99. Lathe fitted with telescopic taper attachment. (Clausing)

Fig. 24-100. Turning a short taper with a square nose tool.

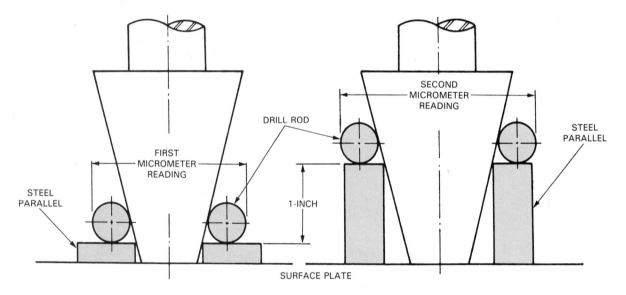

Fig. 24-101. Measuring a taper using parallels, drill rod, micrometers, and a surface plate.

on the surface plate, and two steel parallels or gauge blocks of the same height are placed on opposite sides of taper. Two sections of drill rod with the same diameter are placed on the blocks. Fig. 24-101. Distance across rods is measured with a micrometer.

The second reading is made 1, 3, or 6 in. above the first measurement. The difference is converted to required information.

HOW TO DRILL AND REAM ON THE LATHE

Operations other than turning can be performed on a lathe.

DRILLING

The usual method for drilling is to hold the work in a chuck and mount the drill in the tailstock spindle. For holes less than 1/2 in. (12.5 mm), the drill is held in a Jacobs chuck, Fig. 24-102. Larger drills with taper shanks are fitted directly into the tailstock spindle, Fig. 24-103.

Drills with taper shanks too large to fit the tailstock spindle can be held with a dog, with the tailstock center pressed into the center hole in the drill shank, Fig. 24-104, A. Otherwise, a commercial drill holder may be used. This is shown

Fig. 24-102. Drilling with a straight shank drill held in a Jacobs chuck.

Fig. 24-103. Drills larger than 1/2 in. (12.7 mm) in diameter are usually fitted with a self-holding taper that fits into the tailstock spindle.

in Fig. 24-104, B.

SAFETY NOTE: The two previous drilling techniques should not be attempted until considerable experience in lathe operation has been acquired.

Greater accuracy requires an exactly centered starting point for the drill. A starting point made with a center drill is adequate for most drilling jobs.

Holes over 1/2 in. (12.5 mm) in diameter should not be drilled until a pilot hole has been made. The drill employed for this purpose should have a diameter slightly larger than the dead center of the larger drill's tip. Ample clearance must be provided in the back, to permit the drill to break through without striking the chuck.

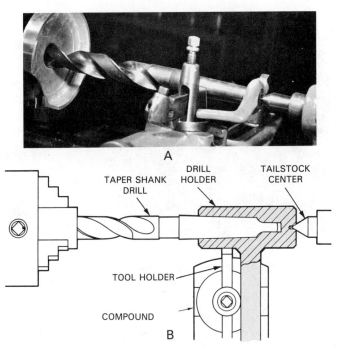

Fig. 24-104. Methods for drilling when the taper shanks are too large to fit the tailstock. A—The lathe dog, with its tail supported by the compound, prevents it from revolving during the drilling operation. B—Using a commercial drill holder for drills too large to fit the tailstock.

REAMING

A hole is reamed when a high degree of accuracy in diameter and finish are required, Fig. 24-105. The hole is first drilled allowing sufficient stock for reaming. Do not apply power if a hand reamer is used, Fig. 24-106. Use regular hand reaming techniques. However, feed the reamer into the hole with the tailstock handwheel. Use ample supplies of the proper cutting fluid.

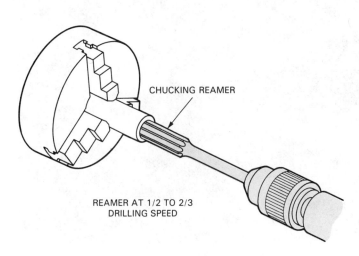

Fig. 24-105. Using a chucking reamer mounted in a Jacobs chuck.

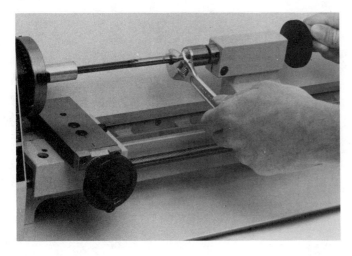

Fig. 24-106. Do not use power when using a hand reamer on the lathe.

HOW TO BORE ON A LATHE

BORING, Fig. 24-107, is an internal machining operation where a single-point cutting tool is used to enlarge a hole. Boring is done to enlarge a hole to exact size when a drill or reamer of the proper size is not available. Its main purpose, however, is to produce a hole that is exactly concentric with the outside diameter of the work.

The size of the hole to be bored determines the type and size of boring bar to be used, Fig. 24-108. Always employ the largest bar possible as this gives maximum support to the tool. The bar should extend from the holder only far enough to permit the tool to cut to the proper depth, Fig. 24-109.

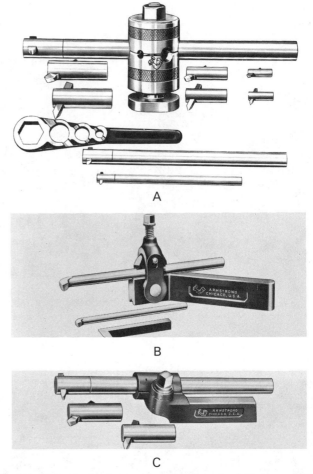

A

B

C

Fig. 24-108. Boring bars and tool holders. A—Interchangeable type boring bar permits the machinist to use the stiffest bar for the job. The body replaces the lathe tool post. B—Boring tool holder for light work. C—Boring tool holder and bar with interchangeable end caps. (Armstrong Bros. Tool Co.)

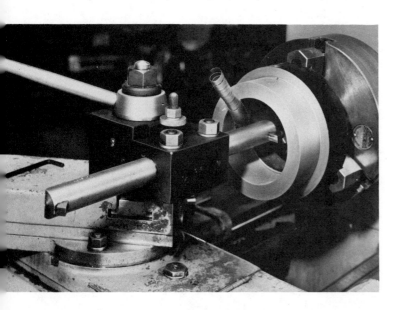

Fig. 24-107. Boring (machining internal surfaces on the lathe). (Clausing)

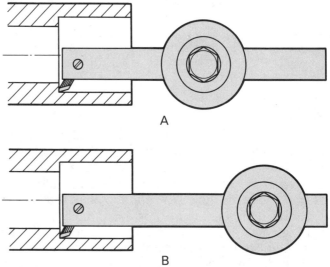

A

B

Fig. 24-109. Keep the cutting tool as close to the tool post as possible for maximum support. A—Properly positioned boring bar. B—Boring bar projects too far from the tool post. Vibration and "chatter" will produce a roughly machined surface.

Set the tool on center, or slightly below, with the boring bar parallel with tool travel. Check for adequate clearance when the tool is at maximum depth in the hole. Make your cuts in much the same manner as you would for external cutting.

CUTTING SCREW THREADS ON A LATHE

SCREW THREADS are utilized for many purposes, including:
1. Making adjustments.
2. Assembling parts.
3. Transmitting motion.
4. Applying pressure.
5. Making measurements.
   Can you name an example for each of these uses?

SCREW THREAD FORMS

The first machine cut threads were square, but since that time many different thread forms have been developed—American National (Unified), sharp "V", acme, and square, to name a few. Each thread form has a particular use and formula for calculating its shape and size. See Figs. 24-110 through 24-113.

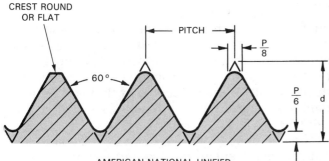

AMERICAN NATIONAL UNIFIED

Fig. 24-110. Unified thread form. It is interchangeable with American National Threads. N = Number of threads per inch; P = Pitch = $\frac{1}{N}$; d = Depth of thread = $\frac{0.866}{N}$.

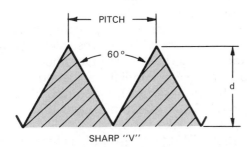

SHARP "V"

Fig. 24-111. Sharp "V" thread form. N = Number of threads per inch; P = Pitch = $\frac{1}{N}$; d = Depth of thread = $\frac{0.866}{N}$.

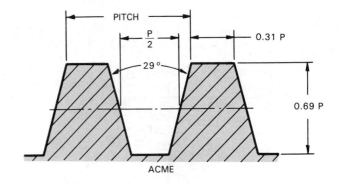

ACME

Fig. 24-112. Acme thread form. N = Number of threads per inch; P = Pitch = $\frac{1}{N}$; Depth of thread = $\frac{P}{2}$ + 0.010; Flat = $\frac{0.3707}{P}$; Root = $\frac{0.3707}{P}$; = 0.0052.

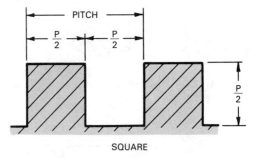

SQUARE

Fig. 24-113. Square thread form. N = Number of threads per inch; P = Pitch = $\frac{1}{N}$; Depth of thread = $\frac{P}{2}$; Flat or space = $\frac{P}{2}$.

THREAD TERMINOLOGY

Various parts of the thread have been given specific names, Fig. 24-114. PITCH is the distance from one point on a thread to the corresponding point on the next thread. LEAD is the distance a nut or threaded section will travel in one full revolution. On a single thread, the pitch and lead are the same. Double thread screws have a lead twice the pitch.

CUTTING SHARP "V" THREADS ON THE LATHE

Sharpen the cutting tool to the correct shape including the proper clearances. Grind the top flat with no side or back rake, Fig. 24-115. A CENTER GAUGE (also called a "FISH TAIL"), Fig. 24-116, is used for grinding and setting the tool on the work.

The work is set up in much the same manner as for straight turning. If held between centers, the centers must be precisely aligned and must run true. Many machinists leave the stock slightly oversize and make a light truing cut to bring the material to size before cutting the threads.

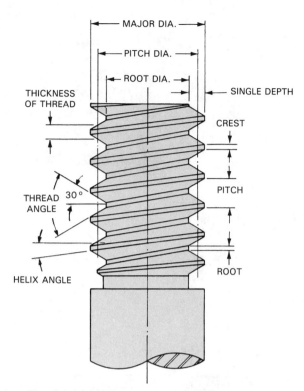

Fig. 24-114. The parts of the screw thread.

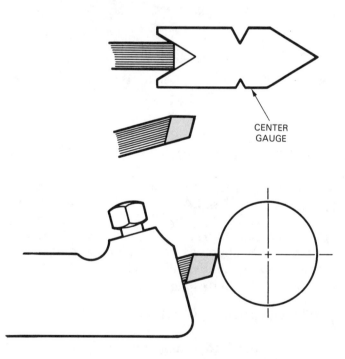

Fig. 24-115. A cutting tool properly ground for machining sharp "V" screw threads. The tool is set on center as shown.

A groove is frequently cut at the point where the thread terminates. It is cut equal to the width and depth of a thread, Fig. 24-117.

After making the proper gear and apron adjustments for the number of threads per inch (or

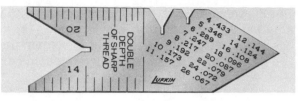

Fig. 24-116. A center gauge or "fish tail." (The Lufkin Tool Co.)

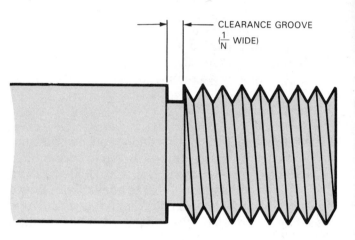

Fig. 24-117. Terminating a screw thread.

pitch for metric threads) to be cut, pivot the compound rest 29 degrees to the right, Fig. 24-118, and set the threading tool in the tool post. It is essential that the tool be set on center and at a 90 degree angle to the centerline of the work. This is done by using the center gauge as shown in Fig. 24-119.

The compound rest is set at a 29° angle to permit the tool to shear the chip better than if it were fed in straight, Fig. 24-120.

Since the tool must be removed from the work after each cut and repositioned before the next cut can be started, a THREAD CUTTING STOP, Fig. 24-121, may be used. After the point of the tool is set so that it just touches the work, the stop is locked to the saddle dovetail, with the adjusting screw just bearing on the stop.

After a cutting pass has been made, move the tool back from the work with the cross slide handwheel. Move the carriage back to start another cut and feed the tool into the work until the adjusting screw again bears on the stop. Turn the compound rest handwheel in 0.002 in. (0.05 mm) and the tool will be in position to make the next cut.

A THREAD DIAL, Fig. 24-122, is fitted to the carriage of many lathes. It meshes with the lead screw and is used to indicate when to engage the half-nuts to permit the cutting tool to follow in the original

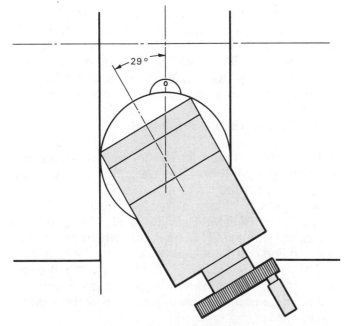

Fig. 24-118. The compound set-up for machining right-hand external threads.

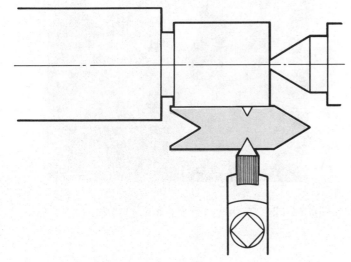

Fig. 24-119. Using a center gauge to position the tool for machining threads.

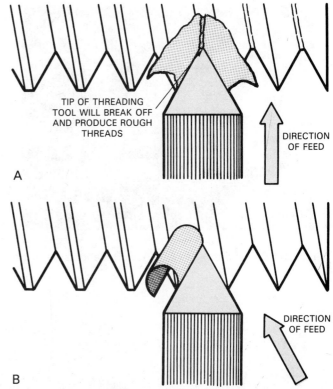

Fig. 24-120. The cutting action of the tool. A—Fed straight in. Note that both edges are cutting and the weakest part of the tool (the point) is doing the most work. B—Fed in at a 29° angle. Note that only one edge is cutting and the cutting load is distributed across that edge evenly.

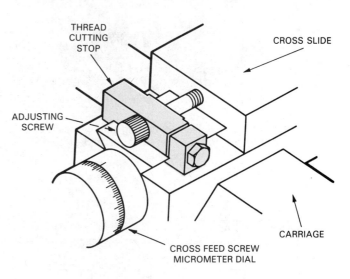

Fig. 24-121. The thread cutting stop.

cut, Fig. 24-123. The thread dial eliminates the necessity of reversing the spindle rotation in order to bring the tool back to the starting point after each cut.

MAKING THE CUT

Set the spindle speed to about one-quarter of that used for conventional turning. Feed the tool in until it touches the work. The work must be revolving or you will damage the cutter bit point. Then move the tool to the right until it clears the work.

Adjust the thread cutting stop screw.

Turn on the power and engage the half-nuts when indicated by the thread dial. This cut will be a check to see whether the machine has been set to cut the desired number of threads per inch, Fig. 24-124.

Fig. 24-122. The thread dial. (South Bend Lathe, Inc.)

CHASING DIAL

Fig. 24-123. This thread dial for cutting metric threads allows the split or half-nut to be released at the end of each cut. (Clausing)

When this checks out, additional cuts of 0.005 in. (0.10 mm) additions are made until the thread is almost to size. The last few cuts should be no more than 0.002 in. (0.05 mm) deep.

A liberal application of lard oil or cutting oil before each cut will aid in producing a smooth finish.

HOW TO MEASURE THREADS

Measure the thread at frequent intervals during the machining operation. Probably the easiest way to check the thread is to fit it to a nut of the proper size. However, closer tolerance threads require the use of a THREAD MICROMETER, Fig. 24-125. This gives the true PITCH DIAMETER which is equal to the outside diameter less the depth of one thread.

The THREE-WIRE METHOD of measuring threads, Fig. 24-126, has proved quite satisfactory. A micrometer measurement is made over three wires

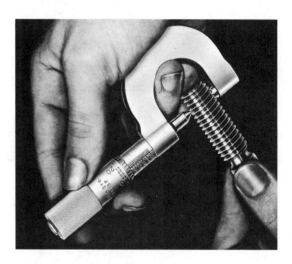

Fig. 24-125. A thread micrometer. (L.S. Starrett Co.)

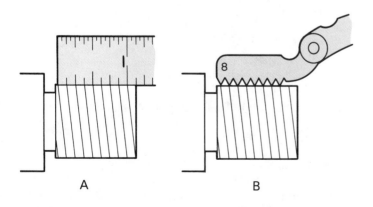

Fig. 24-124. Checking the pitch after the first light cut has been made. A—With a rule. B—With a screw pitch gauge.

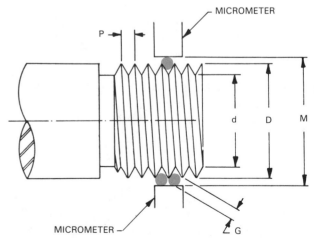

Fig. 24-126. The three-wire method of measuring screw threads.

of a specified diameter that are fitted into the threads. The formula, Fig. 24-127, is used to calculate the correct measurements over the wire and wire diameter.

HOW TO CUT LEFT-HAND THREADS

Left-hand threads are cut in basically the same manner as right-hand threads. The major difference involves pivoting the compound rest to the left and changing lead screw rotation so that the carriage will travel towards the tailstock.

HOW TO CUT AN INTERNAL THREAD

INTERNAL THREADS, Fig. 24-128, are made with a conventional boring bar and a cutting tool sharpened to thread shape.

A hole is drilled and bored (if necessary) to the correct size for the minor diameter. A recess is machined with a square nose tool at the point where the thread terminates, Fig. 24-129. The recess diameter is equal to the major diameter of the desired thread.

Pivot the compound rest 29 degrees to the LEFT for cutting RIGHT-HAND internal threads. Mount the tool on center with a center gauge, Fig. 24-130. Machine as you would external threads.

When cutting internal threads remember that tool feed and removal from the cut are exactly the reverse of those used when cutting external threads.

$$M = D + 3G - \frac{1.5155}{N}$$

Where: M = Measurement over the wires
   D = Major diameter of thread
   d = Minor diameter of thread
   G = Diameter of wires
   $P = \text{Pitch} = \frac{1}{N}$

   N = Number of threads per inch

The smallest wire size that may be used for a given thread—
$$G = \frac{0.560}{N}$$

The largest wire size that can be used for a given thread—
$$G = \frac{0.900}{N}$$

The three-wire formula will work only if "G" is no larger or smaller than the sizes determined above. Any wire diameter between the two extremes may be used. All wires must be the same diameter.

Fig. 24-127. The three-wire thread measuring formula.

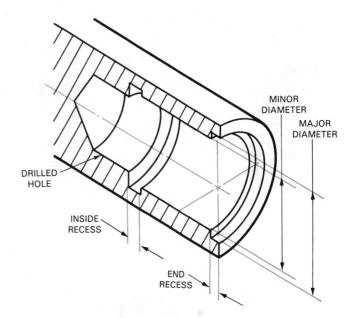

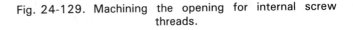

Fig. 24-129. Machining the opening for internal screw threads.

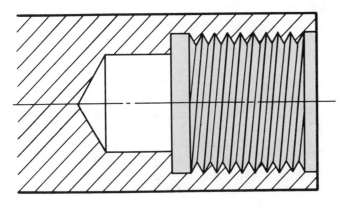

Fig. 24-128. Internal screw threads.

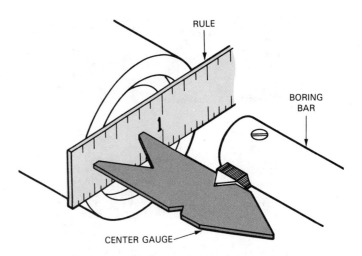

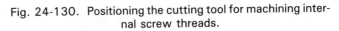

Fig. 24-130. Positioning the cutting tool for machining internal screw threads.

KNURLING

KNURLING, Fig. 24-131, is the process that forms horizontal or diamond-shaped serrations on the circumference of the work to provide a gripping surface. It is done with a KNURLING TOOL that is mounted in the lathe tool post, Fig. 24-132. The knurl pattern is raised by rolling the knurls against the metal to raise the surface. STRAIGHT and DIAMOND PATTERN KNURLS, Fig. 24-133, can be produced in coarse, medium, and fine pitch.

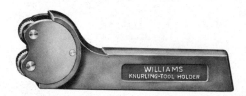

Fig. 24-131. The knurling operation.

Fig. 24-132. Knurling tool.   (J.H. Williams & Co.)

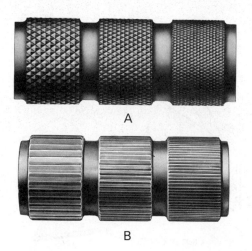

A

B

Fig. 24-133. Knurl patterns. A—Diamond knurl pattern in coarse, medium, and fine patterns. B—Straight knurl pattern in coarse, medium, and fine patterns.   (J.H. Williams & Co.)

HOW TO USE A KNURLING TOOL

The knurling tool must be set up correctly. Otherwise, the knurls will not track properly and will dull rapidly. Use this procedure:
1. Mark off the section to be knurled.
2. Adjust the lathe to a slow back gear speed and a fairly rapid feed.
3. Place the knurling tool in the tool post and set it up to the work. Both wheels must bear evenly with the wheel faces parallel with the work surface.
4. Start the lathe and force the knurls slowly into the work surface until a pattern begins to form. Engage the automatic feed and let the tool move across the work. When it reaches the proper position, stop the machine but do not disengage the feed. Reverse spindle rotation and permit the tool to move back to the starting point. Repeat the operation until a satisfactory knurl has been formed. Flood the surface with cutting fluid during the operation.

FILING AND POLISHING ON A LATHE

Lathe filing is done to remove burrs, improve the surface finish by removing tool marks, round off sharp edges, and finish off slight irregularities on tapers. However, filing should only be done as a last resort. A properly set up lathe and a sharp cutting tool will make filing unnecessary.

When filing is used to finish a job, stock diameter should be left oversize by 0.002 to 0.003 in. (0.05 to 0.07 mm).

HOW TO FILE ON A LATHE

When filing work on a lathe, avoid holding the file stationary but move it constantly across the work. If held in one position, the file will "load" and score the work surface.

An ordinary mill file will produce satisfactory results, but a LONG ANGLE LATHE FILE, Fig. 24-134, produces superior results without chatter. Operate the lathe at a high spindle speed and use long even strokes. Release filing pressure on the return stroke.

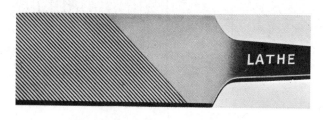

Fig. 24-134. Long angle lathe file.

FILE SAFETY

1. Move the carriage out of the way and remove the tool post.
2. There are two ways to hold the tool for lathe filing. In the RIGHT-HAND METHOD, Fig. 24-135, the file handle is held in the right hand, putting the left hand over the revolving chuck or dog. The LEFT-HAND METHOD, Fig. 24-136, involves holding the handle in the left hand and is the recommended procedure.
3. Remove rings and wrist watch, and roll up your sleeves.
4. Avoid touching the work while it is revolving.

HOW TO POLISH ON A LATHE

Polishing is the operation that produces a fine finish on the work. Again remember, polishing IS NOT a substitute for a properly set up lathe and a sharp cutting tool.

A strip of abrasive cloth, suitable for the material to be polished, is cut to length. It can be grasped between the fingers and held across the work, Fig. 24-137. If more pressure is required, mount the abrasive cloth on a strip of wood or a file, Fig. 24-138. Use a high spindle speed.

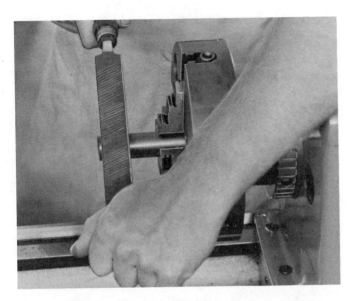

Fig. 24-135. Right-hand method of filing on the lathe. Note how the left hand and arm must be over the revolving chuck.

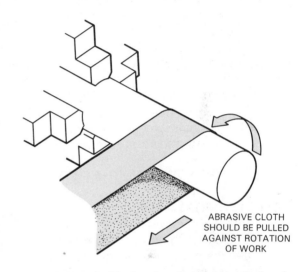

ABRASIVE CLOTH SHOULD BE PULLED AGAINST ROTATION OF WORK

Fig. 24-137. Polishing with abrasive cloth held by the hands. Keep them clear of the revolving chuck or dog.

Fig. 24-136. Left-hand method of filing on the lathe. How does this technique differ from the right-hand method?

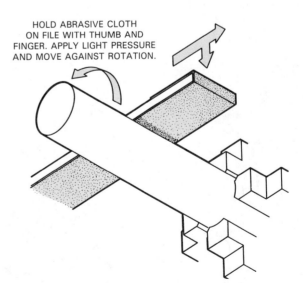

HOLD ABRASIVE CLOTH ON FILE WITH THUMB AND FINGER. APPLY LIGHT PRESSURE AND MOVE AGAINST ROTATION.

Fig. 24-138. More pressure can be applied if the cloth is supported by a file or block of wood.

Metal Lathe 371

The finer the abrasive the finer the resulting finish. A few drops of machine oil on the abrasive will improve the finish. For the final polish, reverse the abrasive cloth so the cloth backing is in contact with the work.

Clean the lathe thoroughly after polishing. Any abrasive chips left from the cloth can cause rapid wear of the machine's moving parts.

HOW TO USE LATHE MANDRELS

It is sometimes necessary to machine the outside diameter of a part concentric with a hole that has been previously bored or reamed. This is a simple operation if the material can be held in the lathe by conventional means. There are times, however, when the part cannot be gripped satisfactorily to permit accurate machining. In such cases, the work is mounted on a MANDREL and turned between centers, Fig. 24-139.

A mandrel is a cylindrical piece of hardened steel that has been machined with a very slight taper. The ARBOR PRESS, Fig. 24-140, is used to press the mandrel into the work. It is also employed to remove the mandrel after machining.

An arbor press is excellent for straightening bent shafts, pressing parts together, etc.

GRINDING ON THE LATHE

The TOOL POST GRINDER, Fig. 24-141, permits both internal and external grinding on a lathe. With a few simple attachments, the lathe can be utilized to sharpen reamers and milling cutters in addition to grinding shafts and trueing lathe centers.

It is important that the lathe be protected with cloth or canvas during the grinding operation to safeguard the machine from the resulting abrasive dust and grit, Fig. 24-142.

Fig. 24-140. The arbor press. It is made in many sizes. (Dake Corp.)

Fig. 24-141. Tool post grinder finishing shaft mounted between centers.   (Clausing)

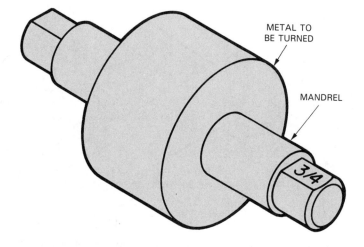

Fig. 24-139. A lathe mandrel.

METAL TO BE TURNED

MANDREL

3/4

Fig. 24-142. Face grinding on the lathe. The protective cloth was removed to take the photo.

MILLING ON THE LATHE

Many small shops are not equipped with a milling machine. Therefore, lathe manufacturers have devised attachments that permit milling operations to be performed on the lathe, Fig. 24-143.

The milling cutters are mounted on an arbor or fitted to the headstock spindle. The cut is controlled by carriage and cross slide movements.

Some lathes are fitted with a vertical milling head. The compound is removed from the cross slide and the vise or other work holding devices are mounted in its place. See Fig. 24-144.

INDUSTRIAL APPLICATIONS

When a part to be manufactured requires several turning, drilling, facing, reaming, and threading operations, and the quantity needed is sufficient, variations of the basic lathe are employed.

For limited production runs, 100 to 5000 pieces, a MANUALLY-OPERATED TURRET LATHE, Figs. 24-145 and 24-146, is generally used. This type of lathe is equipped with a six-sided tool holder called a TURRET, to which a number of different cutting tools are fitted. Stops control the length of tool travel and rotate the turret to bring the next cutting tool into position automatically. A cross slide unit is used for turning, facing, forming, and cut-off operations.

Fig. 24-143. Milling on the lathe.

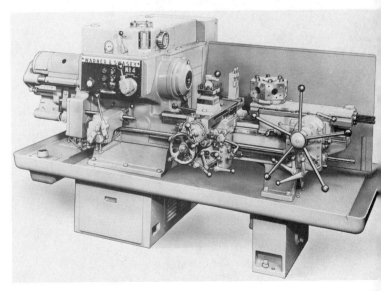

Fig. 24-145. Manually-operated turret lathe.   (Clausing)

Fig. 24-144. Lathe fitted with milling/drilling head. Work holding devices are mounted on the cross slide.

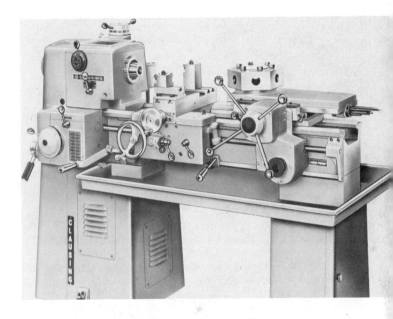

Fig. 24-146. Larger more versatile model of the turret lathe. (The Warner & Swasey Co.)

Metal Lathe   373

The SCREW MACHINE, Fig. 24-147, another variation of the lathe, was developed for the high speed production of large number of identical turned parts. These machines have been designed to perform the maximum number of operations, either simultaneously or in rapid sequence.

Work too large or too heavy to be machined in a horizontal position, can be machined on a VERTICAL BORING MACHINE, Fig. 24-148. These huge machines, known as BORING MILLS, are capable of turning and boring work with diameters up to 40 ft. (12 m).

Computer controlled TURNING CENTERS, Fig. 24-149, are designed to go from blueprint to program to tape to finished machined part in the shortest possible time. Universal models of the turning center are capable of performing internal machining operations: boring, threading, profiling, grooving, drilling, and reaming as well as external machining operations.

Conventional metalworking lathes are manufactured in a large range of sizes from the tiny jeweler's lathe to large machines that turn forming rolls for the steel industry, Fig. 24-150.

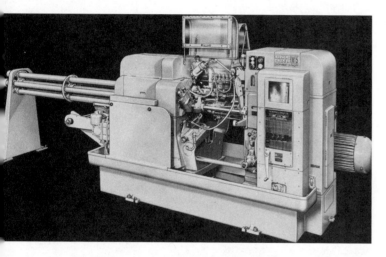

Fig. 24-147. Multiple spindle automatic screw machine for precision high speed production. (The Warner & Swasey Co.)

Fig. 24-149. One of the most sophisticated lathes made, the computer-controlled turning center. (Cincinnati Milacron)

Fig. 24-148. A typical boring mill. Note that the work is mounted horizontally. (The G.A. Gray Co.)

Fig. 24-150. Some idea of the size of the large modern lathe can be gained by comparing it with the machinist in the photo.

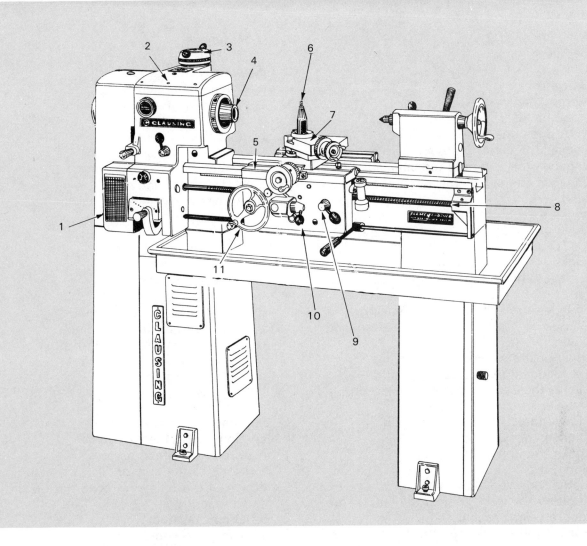

TEST YOUR KNOWLEDGE, Unit 24

Please do not write in the text. Place your answers on a separate sheet of paper.

Refer to the numbered illustration to answer the following questions.

1. If item #1 is changed, the cutting tool will (assume that power is being transmitted through the gear box):
   a. Cut deeper.
   b. Move faster or slower.
   c. Cut better.
   d. Move faster or slower if the carriage is engaged to the lead screw.
   e. None of the above.

2. Item #3 does one of the following:
   a. Reduces or increases motor speed.
   b. Increases power to the spindle.
   c. Puts tension on the belt.
   d. Changes spindle speed.
   e. None of the above.

3. Item #8 transmits power from the quick change gear box to the:
   a. Tailstock.
   b. Headstock.
   c. Spindle.
   d. Back gears.
   e. None of the above.

4. Item #4:
   a. Is removed with a hammer.
   b. Supports the work.
   c. Is lubricated each day.
   d. Makes the centers line up.
   e. None of the above.

5. Item #2 is known as the:
   a. Chuck holder.
   b. Work holder.
   c. Headstock.
   d. Gear box.
   e. None of the above.

6. Item #7 is called the:
   a. Apron.
   b. Carriage.
   c. Cross-feed.
   d. Compound rest.
   e. None of the above.

7. Item #6 is called a:
   a. Tool post assembly.
   b. Tool post ring.
   c. Tool post wedge.
   d. Tool holder adjuster.
   e. None of the above.

8. Item #5 is called the:
   a. Saddle.
   b. Guide.
   c. Carriage.
   d. Apron.
   e. None of the above.
9. Item #9 does one of the following:
   a. Causes the cutter bit to move in and out.
   b. Engages the half-nuts for threading.
   c. Engages the clutch for automatic power feed.
   d. Locks the unit to the ways.
   e. None of the above.
10. Item #10 does one of the following:
    a. Locks the unit to the ways.
    b. Engages the clutch for automatic power feed.
    c. Engages the half-nuts for threading.
    d. Causes the cutter bit to move up and down.
    e. None of the above.
11. Item #11 does one of the following:
    a. Moves the entire unit right and left on the ways.
    b. Moves the cutter bit in and out.
    c. Engages the unit for threading.
    d. Locks the unit to the ways.
    e. None of the above.
12. The lathe removes material by:
    a. Rotating the work against the cutter; the tool remains stationary.
    b. Rotating the cutter against the work; the work moves against the cutter.
    c. Rotating the work against the cutter; the tool travels or feeds into or across it.
    d. Rotating the cutter as it feeds into the work; the work remains stationary.
    e. None of the above.
13. To remove 0.028 in.(0.71 mm) from the diameter of a piece being turned on the lathe, feed the cutter into the work:
    a. 0.0007 ot 0.0014 in. depending upon the lathe.
    b. 0.007 or 0.014 in. depending upon the lathe.
    c. 0.070 or 0.140 in. depending upon the lathe.
    d. 0.0014 or 0.0028 in. depending upon the lathe.
    e. None of the above.
14. When setting up a lathe to turn material:
    a. Cut the material to the correct size.
    b. Carefully check over and lubricate it.
    c. Plug it in.
    d. Make sure that it is clean.
    e. None of the above.
15. The compound on the lathe can be used to cut:
    a. A hole.
    b. A taper.
    c. Threads.
    d. A ring.
    e. None of the above.
16. The 4-jaw lathe chuck is called:
    a. An independent chuck.
    b. A universal chuck.
    c. A Jacobs chuck.
    d. A metal chuck.
    e. None of the above.
17. The 3-jaw lathe chuck is called:
    a. An independent chuck.
    b. A universal chuck.
    c. A Jacobs chuck.
    d. A metal chuck.
    e. None of the above.
18. Item #10 engages:
    a. The automatic power feed.
    b. The half-nuts for threading.
    c. The automatic power cross-feed.
    d. Locks the unit to the ways.
    e. None of the above.
19. Item #8 is the:
    a. Lead screw.
    b. Lengthwise feed screw.
    c. Compound feed screw.
    d. Cross-slide feed screw.
    e. None of the above.
20. Which of the following does not belong:
    a. Compound.
    b. Offset tailstock.
    c. Taper attachment.
    d. Cross-slide.
    e. All of the above.
21. The _____ guides the carriage when it is moved.
22. Name four ways to hold work in the lathe.
23. What three chucks may be used to hold work for turning?
24. The chuck is fitted to the headstock _____.
25. List four methods used to cut tapers on the lathe.

Match each of the following terms with the correct statement listed below by placing the appropriate letter in the blank next to each term.

26. ____ Ways.
27. ____ Tool post.   32. ____ Dead center.
28. ____ Tool post   33. ____ Apron.
         wedge.   34. ____ 4-jaw chuck.
29. ____ Lead screw.   35. ____ 3-jaw chuck.
30. ____ Knurl.   36. ____ Lead.
31. ____ Center gauge.   37. ____ Boring tool.

   a. Supports the tool holder.
   b. The distance a thread advances in one turn.
   c. Used to position the threading tool for the sharp ''V'' thread.
   d. Positions the tool holder by permitting it

to be raised or lowered in the tool post.

    e. Transmits power from the quick change gear box to the carriage.

    f. The tailstock center.

    g. Universal chuck.

    h. Guides the carriage.

    i. For internal machining.

    j. Independent chuck.

    k. The carriage front.

    l. A diamond or straight pattern pressed into the surface of the work piece.

38. Calculate the correct rpm for machining the following materials. Round your answer off to the nearest 50 rpm.

    a. Aluminum: 3 1/2 in. in diameter.

    b. Mild steel: 1 1/4 in. in diameter.

    c. Tool steel: 2 3/8 in. in diameter.

39. Using the three-wire method for measuring screw threads, calculate the correct measurement over the wires for the following threads. Use the wire size given in the problem.

    a. 1/2-20NF (wire size 0.032 in.)

    b. 1/4-20NC (wire size 0.032 in.)

    c. 3/8-16NC (wire size 0.045 in.)

    d. 7/16-14NC (wire size 0.060 in.)

40. Using the formulas previously presented, find the tailstock setover when the following information is known:

a.	Taper per in.	= 0.008 in.
	Length of piece	= 7.250 in.
b.	Large diameter	= 2.000 in.
	Small diameter	= 1.000 in.
	Length of taper	= 3.000 in.
	Length of piece	= 9.000 in.
c.	Taper per foot	= 0.123 in.
	Length of piece	= 6.330 in.
d.	Large diameter	= 1.000 in.
	Small diameter	= 0.075 in.
	Length of taper	= 2.000 in.
	Length of piece	= 8.000 in.
e.	Large diameter	= 65.0 mm
	Small diameter	= 32.5 mm
	Length of taper	= 125.0 mm
	Length of piece	= 250.0 mm

RESEARCH AND DEVELOPMENT

1. Demonstrate milling on the lathe.
2. Plan and produce a series of 35mm color slides showing how to prepare the lathe for turning.
3. Make a model of a tree lathe.
4. Make wooden models of the seven basic cutting tool shapes. They should be cut-away models to permit easy viewing of the various clearance angles.
5. Prepare a comparison test using carbon steel, high speed and cemented carbide cutting tools. Make the tests on mild steel (annealed), tool steel (heat treated), and aluminum. Use the recommended cutting speeds and feeds and make a graph that will show the time needed by the various tools to perform an identical machining operation.
6. Prepare models of the sharp "V," acme, and square thread forms.
7. Make a series of six posters on lathe safety.
8. Make an appointment with a skilled machinist. Ask him for the shortcuts and unusual techniques he uses when operating the lathe. Evaluate the techniques for safety, good work habits, time saved, and adaptability to the school shop.
9. Invite the manager of the state or federal employment agency in your area to discuss work opportunities in metalworking in your community.
10. Make arrangements to tour a plant that uses automatic screw machines and turret lathes in manufacturing their products. Write a paper describing these machines in action.
11. Prepare a paper, with illustrations if possible, on how the first screw threads were made. What does the term "chasing" mean in reference to first threads cut on a metalworking lathe?
12. Demonstrate the proper method of machining screw threads. Illustrate how tool can be repositioned and how to use the three-wire thread measuring technique to measure threads.

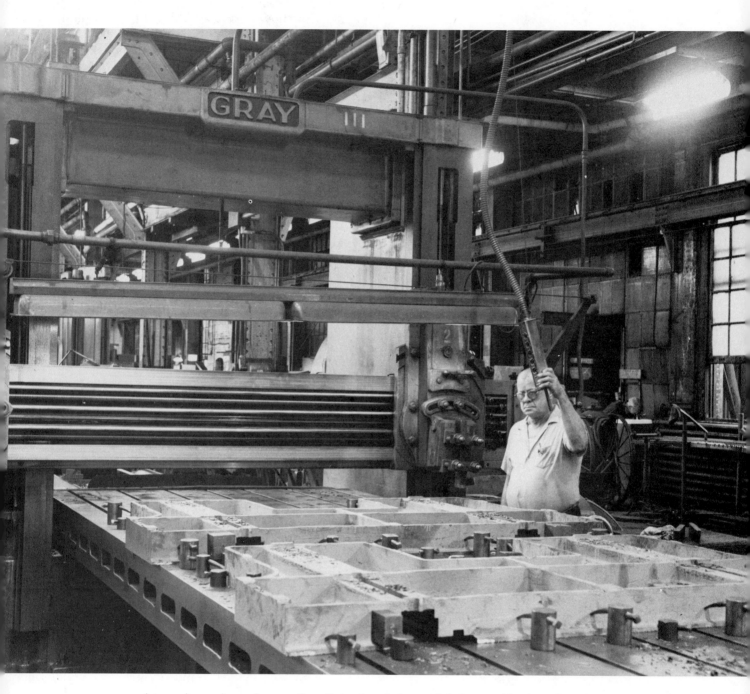

Large planer shown in operation. Note size of the work being machined. (G.A. Gray Co.)

Unit 25

PLANING MACHINES

PLANING MACHINES are designed to machine horizontal, vertical, or angular planed flat surfaces. These planing machines are classified into the following categories.

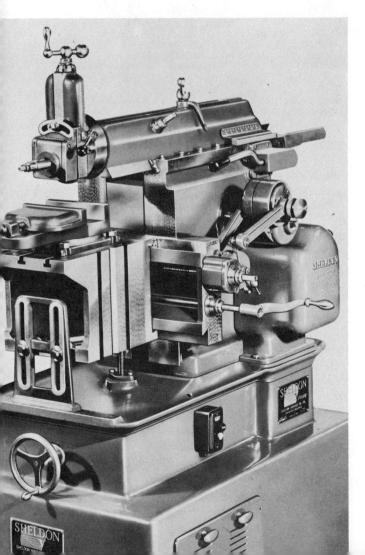

Fig. 25-1. The shaper.   (Sheldon Machine Co., Inc.)

SHAPER

The SHAPER, Fig. 25-1, is too slow for modern production techniques. Most of the work formerly done by it is now done faster and more economically on milling and broaching machines. However, to better understand the operation of other types of planing machines some knowledge of the shaper is desirable.

On the shaper, the work is stationary and the cutting tool moves against it, Fig. 25-2. The work is usually held in a vise, Fig. 25-3.

If there is a shaper in your shop, do not attempt to operate it until you are thoroughly familiar with its operation.

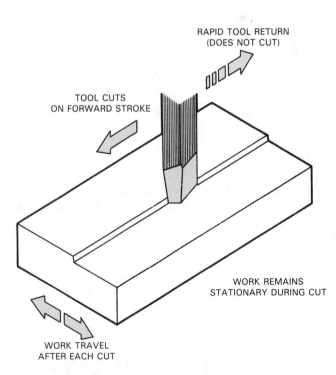

RAPID TOOL RETURN
(DOES NOT CUT)

TOOL CUTS
ON FORWARD STROKE

WORK REMAINS
STATIONARY DURING CUT

WORK TRAVEL
AFTER EACH CUT

Fig. 25-2. Diagram showing how the shaper operates. The work is stationary and the cutting tool moves against it.

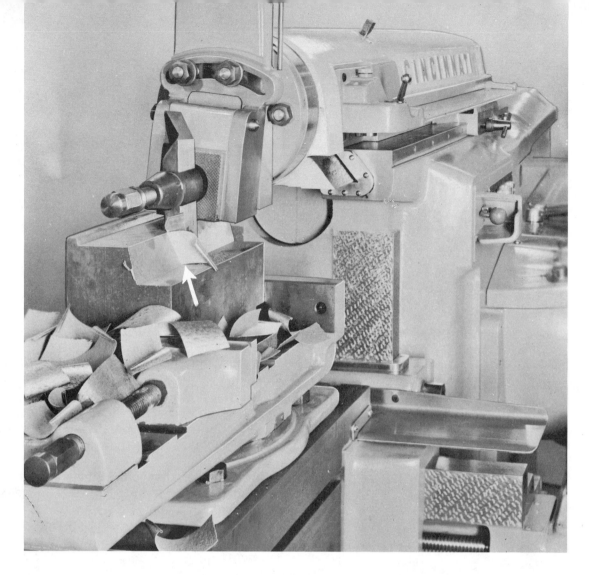

Fig. 25-3. With the work held in a vise, the shaper is making a cut that is 2 in. (51 mm) deep and 1/32 in. (0.8 mm) thick. (Cincinnati Shaper Co.)

As with any machine tool, carefully examine the shaper to be sure it is in safe operating condition. The machine should be lubricated according to the manufacturer's lubrication chart.

SHAPER SIZE

Shaper size is determined by the maximum length of material that the tool can machine in one setup. A 7 in. shaper has a stroke (the distance the tool travels) that is sufficient to machine a surface 7 in. long.

MOUNTING WORK

The position of the vise is an important consideration when using a shaper. It should be positioned so the machining can be done in the shortest possible time. Assuming that the cutter is making the same number of strokes per minute, the setup shown in Fig. 25-4, A, will permit the work to be

machined in about a third of the time needed to machine the work if setup as shown in Fig. 25-4, B.

Avoid excessive tool and slide overhang, Fig. 25-5. The resulting ''chatter'' will cause a rough finish.

The cutting stroke of the machine should be adjusted to work as shown in Fig. 25-6. Make the adjustments as recommended by the tool's manufacturer.

CUTTING SPEED AND FEED

The speed is the number of cutting strokes the ram makes per minute. The feed is the distance the work travels or moves after each cutting stroke. Generally the following should be observed:
1. The harder the metal or the deeper the cut the slower the cutting speed.
2. The softer the metal or the lighter the cut the faster the cutting speed.
3. Coarse feed, deep cut, and slow cutting speed

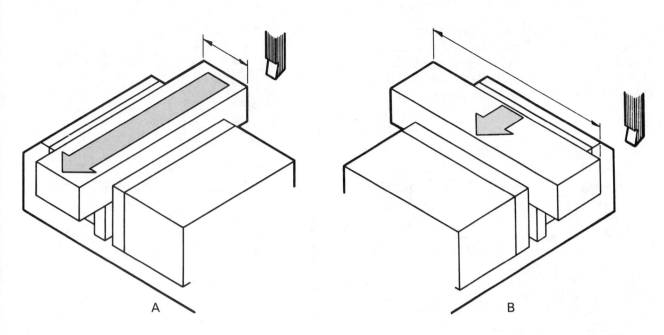

Fig. 25-4. Position the work in the vise to machine in the shortest amount of time. A—Proper setup. B—This setup will take approximately one-third longer than the other setup.

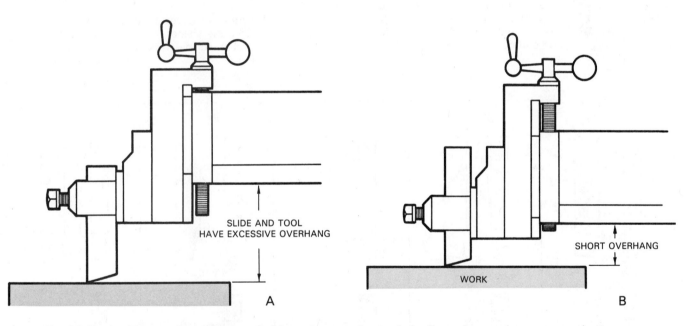

SLIDE AND TOOL
HAVE EXCESSIVE OVERHANG

SHORT OVERHANG

WORK

Fig. 25-5. Avoid excessive overhang of slide and   or cutting tool. A—Excessive overhang causes chatter, producing a rough finish. B—Keep the slide up and a short grip on the tool for rigidity.

for the roughing cut.

4. Fine feed, light cut, and fast cutting speed for the finishing cut.

The shape of the cutting tool is determined by the material being machined and the degree of finish desired. The tool shapes shown in Fig. 25-7 are recommended for mild steel.

SLOTTER

The chief difference between the SLOTTER and the shaper is the direction of the cutting action, Fig. 25-8. The slotting machine is classified as a vertical shaper. It is used to cut slots, to cut keyways (both internal and external), and to machine internal and external gears. See Fig. 25-9.

PLANER

The PLANER, Fig. 25-10, differs from the shaper in that the work travels back and forth while the cutter remains stationary, Fig. 25-11. A planer is used to handle work that is too large or impractical to be machined on a milling machine. Planers are in themselves large pieces of equipment. Some must handle and machine surfaces up to 20 ft. (6.1 m) wide and often twice as long!

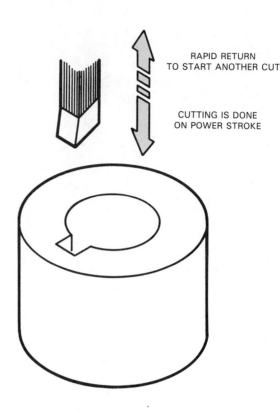

RAPID RETURN TO START ANOTHER CUT

CUTTING IS DONE ON POWER STROKE

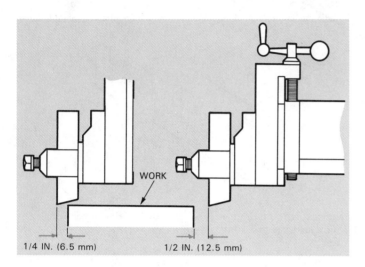

Fig. 25-6. The 1/4 in. (6.5 mm) allowance at the end of the stroke gives ample chip clearance, while the 1/2 in. (12.5 mm) allowance permits the cutter to drop back in position for the next cutting stroke.

Fig. 25-8. Diagram of the slotter operation (vertical shaper). The slotter, unlike the shaper, moves vertically rather than horizontally and the work is held stationary.

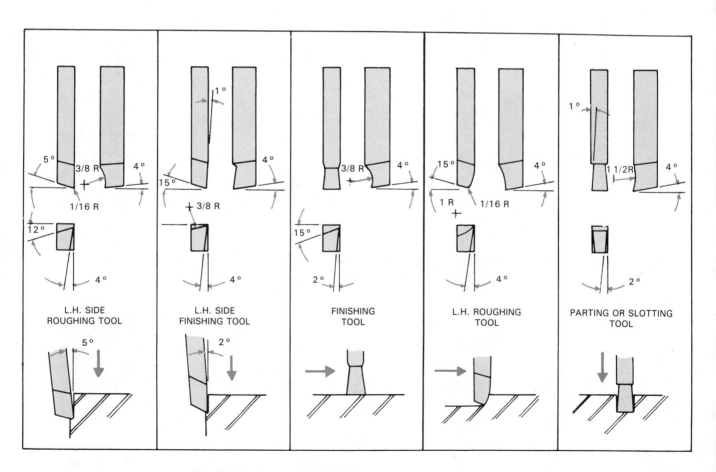

Fig. 25-7. Cutting tool shapes recommended for mild steel.

Fig. 25-9. Job being done on a slotter. The tool head has limited angular movement.

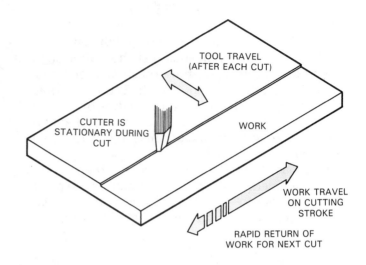

Fig. 25-11. Diagram showing how the planer works. The tool remain stationary while the work moves against it.

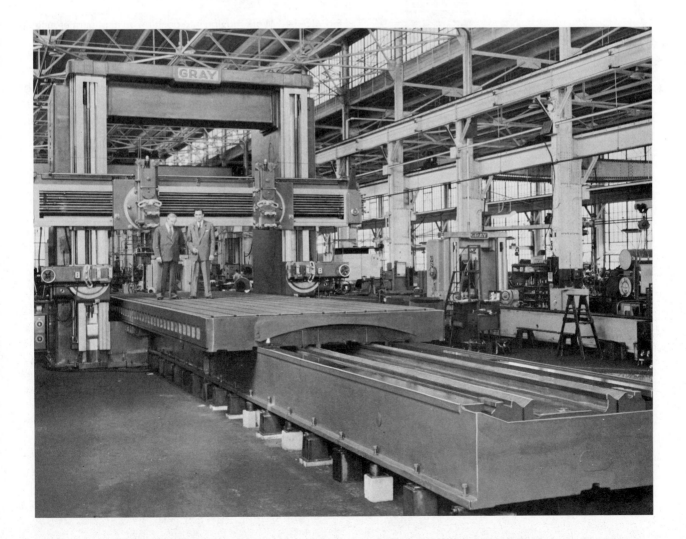

Fig. 25-10. A 144 in. by 126 in. by 40 ft. (3.66 m by 3.20 m by 12.2 m) double housing planer (two cutting heads). The two people add perspective to the machine's size.   (G.A. Gray Co.)

BROACHES

BROACHING is similar to shaping, but instead of a single cutting tool advancing slightly after each stroke across the work, the broach is a long tool with many teeth. See Fig. 25-12. Each tooth has a cutting edge that is a few thousandths of an inch higher than the one before. The cutting edges increase in size until the exact finished size required is reached, Fig. 25-13.

The broach is pushed or pulled over the surface to be machined, Fig. 25-14, and can be used for internal machining—keyways, splines, and irregular shaped openings (like the slots that hold the turbine

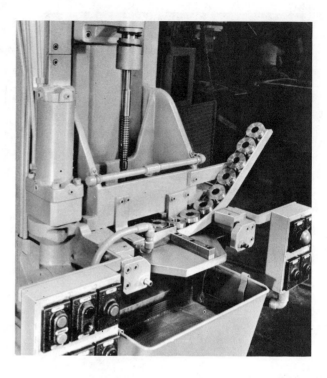

Fig. 25-14. Work moving into position on a modern broaching machine. (Sinstrand Corp.)

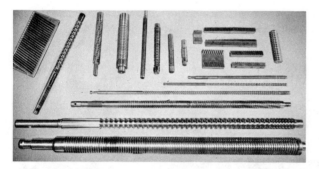

Fig. 25-12. A selection of broaching cutters. Note the many teeth on each cutter.

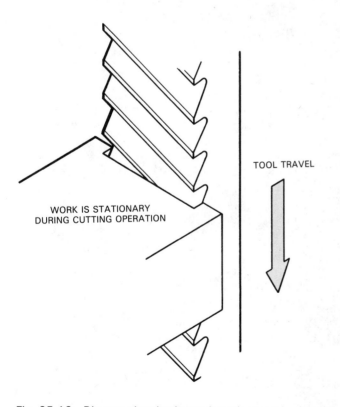

TOOL TRAVEL

WORK IS STATIONARY DURING CUTTING OPERATION

Fig. 25-13. Diagram showing how a broach operates. A multi-tooth cutter moves against the work. The operation may be on a vertical or horizontal plane.

blades in a jet engine). The broach is also used for facing automobile engine blocks and heads. The technique is an economical way of doing certain finish machining operations.

SHAPER SAFETY

1. Be sure you understand the operation of the machine thoroughly before you attempt to operate it.
2. Getting caught between the work and the tool is one of the most common injuries occurring around the shaper. Don't let this happen to you. Turn off the power before you attempt to make any adjustments in this area of the machine.
3. Wear goggles to protect your eyes from flying chips.
4. Keep out of the line of the stroke of the shaper if it is throwing chips. The chips are hot and while they will not cause serious burns, they can cause extreme discomfort.
5. Use a brush to remove accumulated chips and shavings. It will greatly diminish the danger of getting caught between the tool and the work, and will likewise diminish the chance of receiving a serious cut from the sharp chips.
6. Handle the cutter bit with care. If it will cut hard steel you can be sure it can also cut you.
7. Making a cut too deep or not firmly clamping work in a vise can cause the work to drop to the floor, possibly resulting in a serious foot injury.

TEST YOUR KNOWLEDGE, Unit 25

Please do not write in the text. Place your answers on a separate sheet of paper.

1. The cutting tool on the shaper:
   a. Is stationary and the work moves against it.
   b. Moves across the work which is stationary.
   c. Is pulled or pushed across the work.
   d. All of the above.
   e. None of the above.
2. The cutting tool on the planer:
   a. Is stationary and the work moves against it.
   b. Moves across the work which is stationary.
   c. Is pulled or pushed across the work.
   d. All of the above.
   e. None of the above.
3. Planing machines are used to machine _____ surfaces.
4. Shaper size is determined by _____.
5. Prepare a sketch showing the proper way to position work for machining on the shaper.
6. How does the slotter differ from the shaper?
7. How do the teeth on a broach differ from cutting tools used on other planing machines?
8. The cutting tools on the broach:
   a. Is stationary and the work moves against it.
   b. Moves across the work which is stationary.
   c. Is pulled or pushed across the work.
   d. All of the above.
   e. None of the above.

RESEARCH AND DEVELOPMENT

1. Make a display panel that shows the operating principles of the four types of planing machines.
2. Prepare a display of photos, drawings, or magazine illustrations showing the four types of planing machines.

Large, 2-spindle, 3-axis milling machines shaping Boeing 727 upper wing skins. (Grumman Aerospace Corp.)

Unit 26

MILLING MACHINES

With the exception of the lathe, the MILLING MACHINE, Fig. 26-1, is the most versatile machine tool used in the machining of metal. In MILLING, metal is removed by a rotating multi-toothed cutter that is fed into the work, Fig. 26-2.

TYPES OF MILLING MACHINES

It is difficult to classify the various categories of the milling machine because their designs tend to merge with one another. However, for practical purposes, milling machines may be classified into two large families:
1. Fixed bed type.
2. Column and knee type.

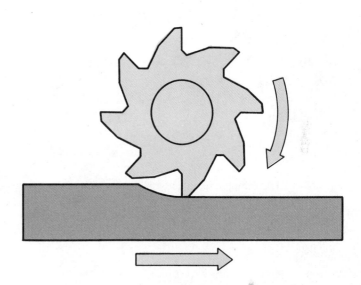

Fig. 26-2. How the milling machine works.

FIXED BED TYPE MILLING MACHINE

The FIXED BED MILLING MACHINE, Fig. 26-3, is a production type machine. Its table is mounted at a fixed height and is restricted to longitudinal (back and forth) movement. Vertical (up and down) and traverse (in and out) movements are obtained by cutter head movements.

COLUMN AND KNEE TYPE MILLING MACHINE

The COLUMN AND KNEE TYPE MILLING MACHINE, Fig. 26-4, is so named because the parts that provide movement to the work consist of a COLUMN that supports and guides the KNEE in vertical movement. The KNEE supports the mechanism for obtaining cross, traverse, and longitudinal table movements. There are three kinds of column and knee type milling machines:
1. Plain milling machine. ⎫
2. Universal milling machine. ⎬ Horizontal spindle
3. Vertical spindle milling machine.

Fig. 26-1. The computer numerical controlled milling machine (CNC) is the latest in technology. It is equipped with automatic tool changing and offers milling, drilling, boring, and reaming capabilities. It is easily programmed for machining a single part or for assembly line work.   (Cincinnati Milacron)

PLAIN MILLING MACHINE

The work table of the PLAIN MILLING MACHINE, Fig. 26-5, has three movements: VERTICAL, CROSS, and LONGITUDINAL, Fig. 26-6. The cutter spindle projects horizontally from the column.

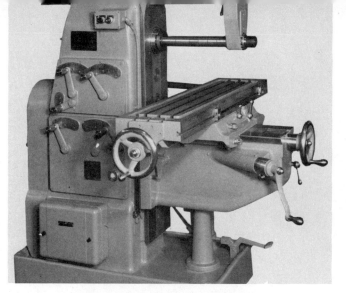

Fig. 26-5. Plain milling machine. (Greaves Machine Tool Div., J.A. Fay & Egan Co.)

Fig. 26-3. The Simplex fixed bed milling machine makes use of one cutting head. (Kearney & Trecker Corp.)

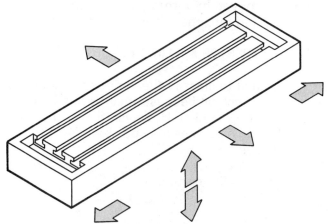

Fig. 26-6. Table movements of the plain milling machine.

UNIVERSAL MILLING MACHINE

The UNIVERSAL MILLING MACHINE, Fig. 26-7, is similar to the plain milling machine but the table has a fourth movement. On this type of machine, the table can be swiveled on the saddle through an angle of 45 degrees or more, Fig. 26-8. This makes it possible to produce spiral gears, spiral splines, and similar work, Fig. 26-9.

VERTICAL SPINDLE MILLING MACHINE

A VERTICAL SPINDLE MILLING MACHINE, Fig. 26-10, differs from the plain and universal machines by having the cutter spindle in a vertical position, at a right angle to the top of the worktable. The cutter head can be raised and lowered by hand or power feed and, on many models, pivoted for angular cuts.

COLUMN

COLUMN

KNEE

VERTICAL

KNEE

HORIZONTAL

Fig. 26-4. Column and knee type milling machines. (Cincinnati Milacron)

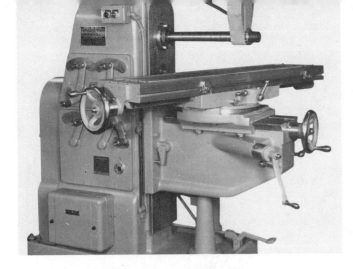

Fig. 26-7. The universal milling machine.
(Greaves Machine Tool Div., J.A. Fay & Egan Co.)

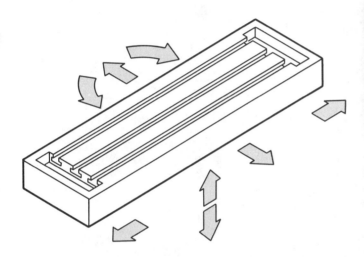

Fig. 26-8. Table movements of the universal milling machine.

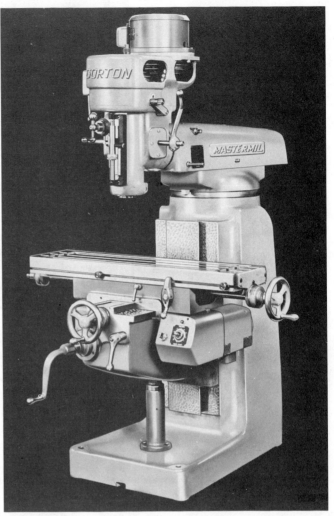

Fig. 26-10. The vertical milling machine.
(George Gorton Machine Co.)

Fig. 26-9. Note how the table is swiveled at an angle to the cutting tool. This feature makes it possible to machine spiral gears like the one shown.

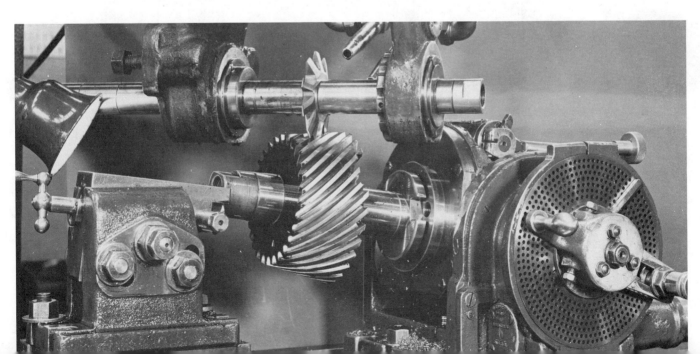

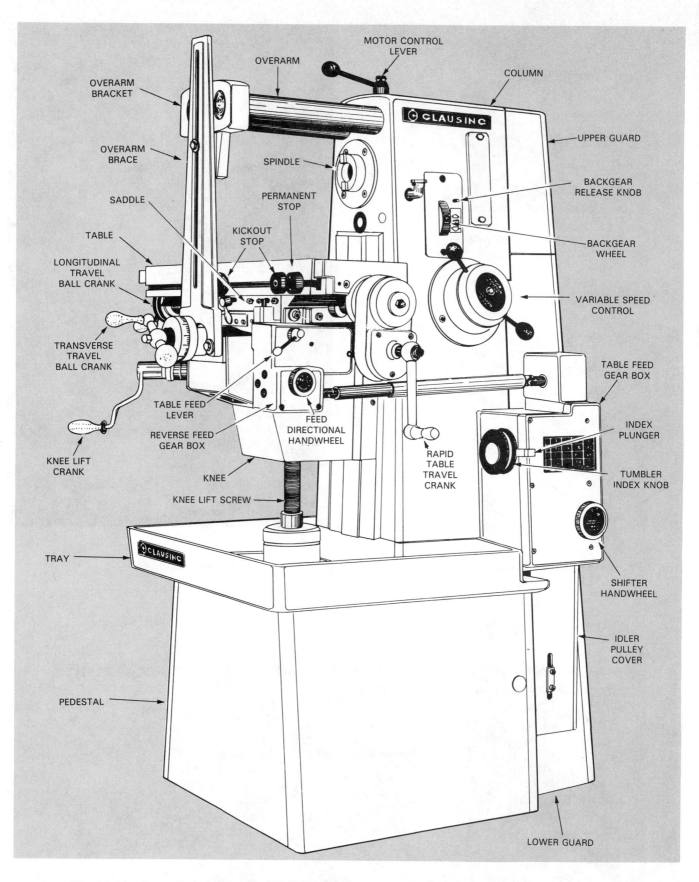

Fig. 26-11. An example of a bench mill. This particular model is mounted on a metal stand. (Clausing)

METHODS OF CONTROL

The method used to control table movement is another way of classifying milling machines, and all machine tools in general. Basically there are four methods of control:

1. MANUAL—All movements are made by hand lever control.
2. SEMI-AUTOMATIC—Movements are controlled by hand and/or power feeds.
3. FULLY AUTOMATIC—A complex hydraulic feed arrangement follows two or three dimensional templates to guide the cutters automatically, or specifications are programmed on punch cards, magnetic tape, or perforated tape which guides the cutters through the required machining operations.
4. COMPUTERIZED (CNC)—Machining coordinates are entered into a master computer or computer on the machine using a special programming language. Computer instructions electronically guide the cutters through the machining sequence.

Machines used in the school shop are ordinarily manual or semi-automatic. Smaller machines like the BENCH MILL, Fig. 26-11, have only longitudinal table movement fitted with power feed. Other movements are controlled manually.

MILLING OPERATIONS

There are two main categories of milling operations:

1. FACE MILLING—The surface being machined is parallel with the face of the cutter, Fig. 26-12. Large flat surfaces are machined by this method.

Fig. 26-12. Face milling. (Lovejoy Tool Co., Inc.)

2. PERIPHERAL MILLING—The surface being machined is parallel with the periphery of the cutter, Fig. 26-13.

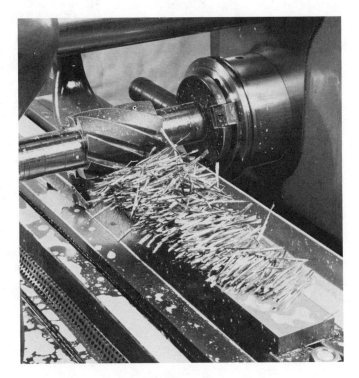

Fig. 26-13. Peripheral milling.

MILLING CUTTERS

MILLING CUTTERS, Fig. 26-14, cannot be readily or economically ground for a particular job as can a lathe cutter bit. Therefore, they are made in a large number of stock shapes, sizes, and kinds to meet many requirements.

TYPES OF MILLING CUTTERS

Milling cutters are manufactured in two general types:

1. SOLID CUTTER—The shank and body are made in one piece, Fig. 26-15.
2. INSERTED TOOTH CUTTER—The teeth are made of special cutting material and are brazed or clamped in place, Fig. 26-16. Badly worn or broken teeth can be replaced.

HOW CUTTERS ARE CLASSIFIED

Cutters are frequently classified by the method used to mount them in the machine:

1. ARBOR CUTTERS—There is a suitable hole for mounting on an arbor, Fig. 26-17.
2. SHANK CUTTERS—They have either a straight

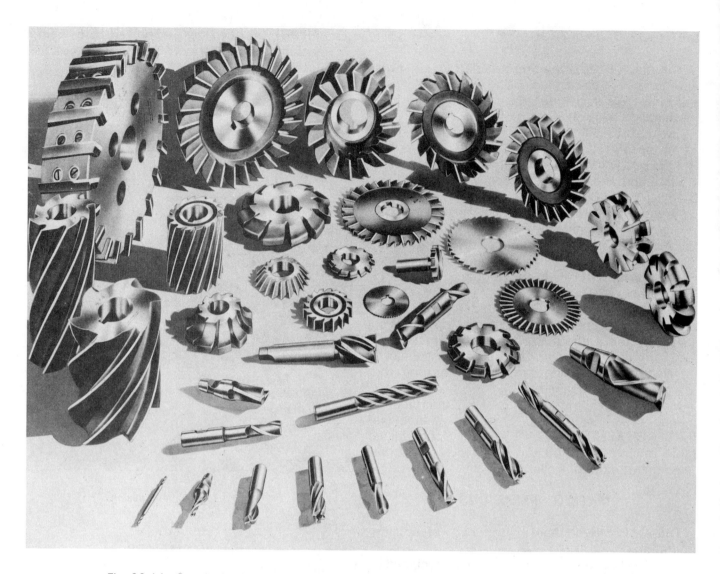

Fig. 26-14. Standard milling cutters. Study this Unit, then identify as many cutters as possible.
(Brown & Sharpe Mfg. Co.)

Fig. 26-15. With the exception of the cutter in the back row, these are solid milling cutters. How many can you identify?
(Brown & Sharpe Mfg. Co.)

Fig. 26-16. Inserted tooth cutters. The cutting edges are made of tungsten carbide and are brazed to the cutting tool body. They are easily replaced when they wear out because the entire cutter does not have to be discarded.
(Brown & Sharpe Mfg. Co.)

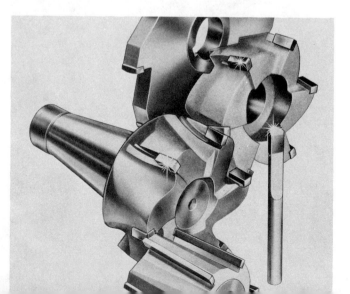

Fig. 26-17. An arbor cutter.

Fig. 26-19. A facing cutter. The cutting edges are cam-locked into place and can be easily replaced if broken or worn out. (Brown & Sharpe Mfg. Co.)

or taper shank, Fig. 26-18. Shank cutters are held in the machine by a sleeve or collet.
3. FACING CUTTERS—Cutters that can be mounted directly to the spindle nose of the machine, or on a stub arbor, Fig. 26-19.

TYPES AND USES OF MILLING CUTTERS

Following are the more commonly used milling cutters and the work to which they are best suited.

PLAIN MILLING CUTTER

PLAIN MILLING CUTTERS are cylindrical with teeth located around the circumference. Plain cutters less than 3/4 in. (19.0 mm) wide are made with straight teeth. Wider plain cutters, called SLAB CUTTERS, are made with helical teeth.
1. LIGHT-DUTY PLAIN MILLING CUTTER—Used chiefly for light slabbing cuts and cutting shallow slots, Fig. 26-20.
2. HEAVY-DUTY PLAIN MILLING CUTTER— Recommended for heavy cuts when considerable metal must be removed, Fig. 26-21.

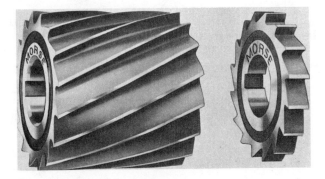

Fig. 26-20. Light-duty plain milling cutters.

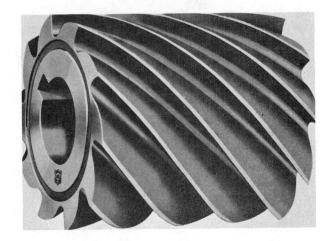

Fig. 26-21. Heavy-duty plain milling cutter.

Fig. 26-18. Shank cutters.

3. HELICAL PLAIN MILLING CUTTER—Can be operated at a higher speed than other plain cutters and produces an exceptionally smooth finish, Fig. 26-22. They cut with a shearing action.

Milling Machines 393

Fig. 26-22. Helical plain milling cutter.   (Morse Cutting Tools)

SIDE MILLING CUTTERS

SIDE MILLING CUTTERS have cutting edges on their circumference and on one or both sides.
1. PLAIN SIDE MILLING CUTTER—Used for side milling, straddle milling, and slotting, Fig. 26-23.
2. STAGGERED TOOTH SIDE MILLING CUTTER— Has alternate right-hand and left-hand helical teeth. Ideal for deep slotting operations, Fig. 26-24.

Fig. 26-23. Plain side milling cutter.

ANGLE CUTTERS

ANGLE CUTTERS differ from other cutters in that the cutting edges are neither parallel, nor at right angles to the cutter axis.
1. SINGLE ANGLE CUTTER—Suitable for cutting dovetails, ratchet wheels, etc. Made in both right-hand or left-hand cut, with included angles

of 45 or 60 degrees, Fig. 26-25.
2. DOUBLE ANGLE CUTTER—Used for milling threads, notches, serrations, and similar work. Manufactured with included angles of 45, 60, and 90 degrees, Fig. 26-26.

Fig. 26-24. Staggered tooth side milling cutter.

Fig. 26-25. Single angle milling cutter.

Fig. 26-26. Double angle milling cutter.

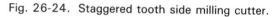

METAL SLITTING SAWS

METAL SLITTING SAWS are thin milling cutters that resemble circular saw blades used in woodworking. They are used for narrow slotting and cut-off operations.

1. PLAIN ANGLE SLITTING SAW—This is essentially a thin plain milling cutter and is employed for ordinary slotting and cut-off operations, Fig. 26-27.
2. SIDE CHIP CLEARANCE SLITTING SAW—This type of cutter is especially suited, because of ample chip clearance, for deep slotting and sawing, Fig. 26-28.

Fig. 26-27. Plain metal slitting saw.

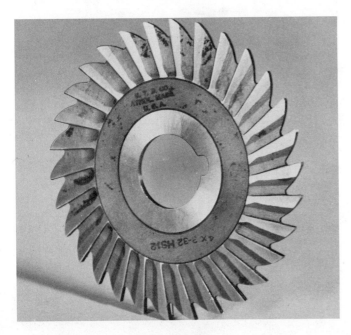

Fig. 26-28. Side chip clearance slitting saw.

END MILLS

END MILLS are designed for milling slots, keyways, pockets, and similar work, Fig. 26-29, where ordinary arbor type milling cutters will not work. Solid end mills may have straight or helical flutes, Fig. 26-30, and straight or taper shanks, Fig. 26-31. Straight shank end mills are made in single

Fig. 26-29. An end mill. The cutting fluid cools the cutter, preventing chips from sticking or fusing to the tool, and also helps flush chips away from the cutting area.
(Cincinnati Milacron)

Fig. 26-30. Left. Straight flute end mill (inserted tooth type). Right. Helical fluted end mill.

and double end styles, Fig. 26-32. A cut with a depth equal to one-half the cutter diameter can generally be taken in solid stock.

1. TWO FLUTE END MILL—Can be fed into the work like a drill, Fig. 26-33.
2. MULTI-FLUTE END MILL—It has a longer cutting life and produces a better finish than a two

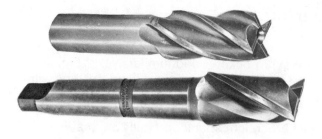

Fig. 26-31. Top. Straight shank end mill. Bottom. Taper shank end mill.

Fig. 26-32. Most solid end mills are made in single and double end styles.

Fig. 26-33. Two flute end mill.

Fig. 26-35. Shell end mill. They are made with right-hand cut, right-hand helix or left-hand cut, left-hand helix. (Greaves Machine Tool Div., J.A. Fay & Egan Co.)

FACE MILLING CUTTERS

FACE MILLS, Fig. 26-36, are intended for machining large flat surfaces parallel to the face of the cutter. The teeth are designed to make the roughing and finishing cuts in one operation. Because of their cost, most face milling cutters have inserted cutting edges.

The FLY CUTTER, Fig. 26-37, is a single cutting tool face mill.

FORMED MILLING CUTTERS

FORMED MILLING CUTTERS are designed to accurately duplicate a required contour. A wide range

flute end mill when run at the same speed, Fig. 26-34.

3. SHELL END MILL—Has teeth similar to the multi-flute end mill but is mounted on a stub arbor. It is designed for face and end milling, Fig. 26-35.

Fig. 26-34. Multi-fluted end mills.

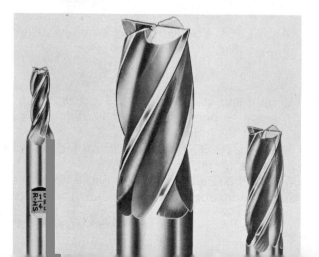

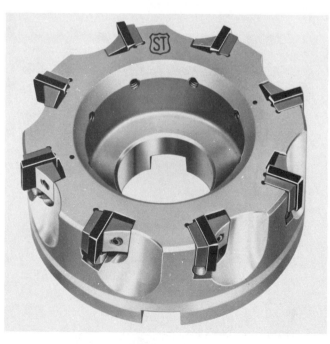

Fig. 26-36. Face mill. (Standard Tool Co.)

Fig. 26-37. Fly cutter. This type milling cutter is a single cutting tool face mill.

of shapes can be machined with standard form cutters available. Included in this cutter class are the CONCAVE CUTTER, Fig. 26-38, CONVEX CUTTER, Fig. 26-39, CORNER ROUNDING CUTTER, Fig. 26-40, and the GEAR CUTTER, Fig. 26-41.

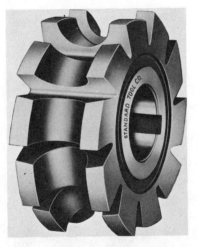

Fig. 26-38. Concave cutter.

Fig. 26-39. Convex cutter.   (Standard Tool Co.)

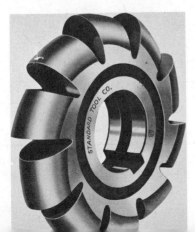

Fig. 26-40. Corner rounding cutter. It is available as left- and right-hand cut.

Fig. 26-41. Gear cutter.   (Standard Tool Co.)

MISCELLANEOUS MILLING CUTTERS

This category includes cutters that do not fit into any of the previously mentioned groups:
1. T-SLOT MILLING CUTTER—These have cutting edges on the circumference and both sides, and are used to mill the bottom of T-slots after the slot has been cut with a side cutter, Fig. 26-42.
2. WOODRUFF KEYSEAT CUTTER—Used to mill the circular keyway required for Woodruff keys, Fig. 26-43.
3. DOVETAIL CUTTER—This machines dovetail type ways in the same manner as the T-slot cutter, Fig. 26-44.

METHODS OF CUTTING

There are two distinct methods of milling operations:

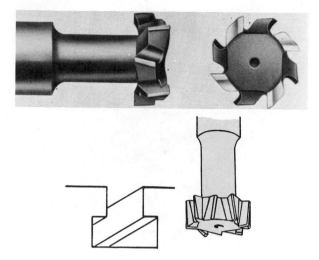

Fig. 26-42. T-slot milling cutter. (Morse Cutting Tools)

Fig. 26-43. Woodruff keyseat cutter. (Standard Tool Co.)

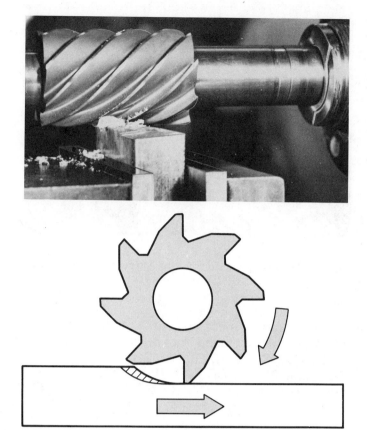

Fig. 26-45. Conventional milling.

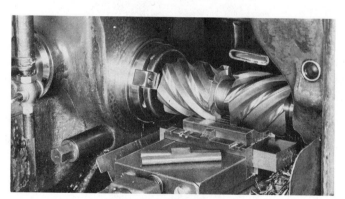

Fig. 26-44. Dovetail cutter. (Brown & Sharpe Mfg. Co.)

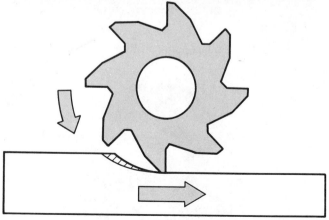

1. CONVENTIONAL or UP-MILLING, Fig. 26-45. The work is fed into the rotation of the cutter. The chip is at minimum thickness at the start of the cut, and is so slight that the cutter has a tendency to slide until sufficient pressure is built up to make it bite into the work.

2. CLIMB or DOWN MILLING, Fig. 26-46. The work moves in the same direction as the rotation of the cutter. Full engagement of each tooth is instant. The sliding action of conventional milling is eliminated resulting in a better surface finish and longer tool life.

Climb milling is not recommended on light milling machines because lack of rigidity and light support offsets any advantages of the technique.

Fig. 26-46. Climb milling.

CARE OF MILLING CUTTERS

Milling cutters are very expensive and are easily ruined if care is not taken in their use and storage. These precautions are recommended:

1. Support the cutter properly and hold the work rigid.
2. Use the correct cutting speed and feed.
3. Use an ample supply of cutting fluid.
4. Use the correct cutter for the job.
5. Store cutters in individual compartments or on wooden pegs, Fig. 26-47.
6. Clean cutters before storing.
7. Never hammer a cutter on the arbor, Fig. 26-48. Instead, examine the arbor for burrs or nicks if the cutter does not slip on easily.
8. Place a board under an end mill when removing it from a vertical milling machine. This will prevent damage to the cutting edges if it is accidently dropped, Fig. 26-49.
9. Use sharp cutters.
10. Before starting the first cut make sure the cutter is rotating in the proper direction.

HOLDING AND DRIVING CUTTERS

The most common method of holding and driving milling cutters is the ARBOR. Arbors are made in a number of sizes and styles. In addition to arbors made with SELF-HOLDING TAPERS for use on small hand milling machines, Fig. 26-50, there are three other arbor styles in general use:

1. STYLE A, Fig. 26-51. It is fitted with a small pilot that runs in a bronze bearing in the arbor support.

Fig. 26-48. Never hammer a cutter on the arbor.

Fig. 26-47. Suggestions for storing cutters. Cutters should be stored so they cannot come in contact with other cutters.

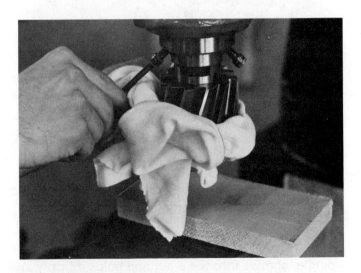

Fig. 26-49. When removing or placing a cutter on the vertical milling machine, protect your hand with a heavy cloth and place a board under the cutter.

Fig. 26-50. Arbor with self-holding taper. A draw-in bar also should be used with this type of arbor.

Fig. 26-51. Style A arbor.

2. STYLE B, Fig. 26-52. This arbor is characterized by the large bearing that can be positioned to any location on the arbor to localize support.
3. STYLE C, Fig. 26-53. Used to hold smaller sizes of shell end mills and face mills that cannot be bolted directly to the spindle nose.

It is advisable to use the shortest arbor possible that permits adequate clearance between the arbor support and the work.

Fig. 26-52. Style B arbor.

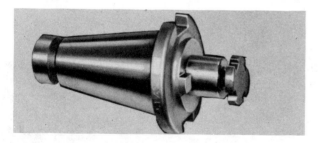

Fig. 26-53. Style C arbor.

SPACING COLLARS are used to position a cutter on the arbor. They are made in a variety of thicknesses and permit the accurate spacing of two or more cutters for gang or straddle milling.

A DRAW-IN BAR, Fig. 26-54, fitted through the spindle, screws into the arbor and holds it firmly in the spindle. DRIVE KEYS on the spindle nose, Fig. 26-55, fit into corresponding slots in the arbor flange to provide positive (nonslip) drive.

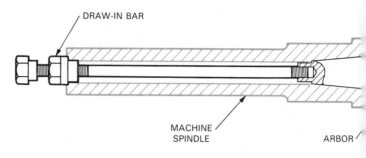

Fig. 26-54. Draw-in bar. Avoid operating a milling machine if the arbor is not held in place with a draw-in bar.

Fig. 26-55. Spindle drive keys.   (Kearney & Trecker Corp.)

ADAPTERS, Fig. 26-56, permit a wide variety of milling cutter types and sizes to be mounted on the machine spindle.

SPRING COLLETS, Fig. 26-57, accommodate straight shank end mills and drills. Most collets are designed for use with a COLLET HOLDER.

Fig. 26-56. Two of the many types of milling adapters. The adapter on the left permits an end mill to be used. The adapter on the right permits an arbor cutter to be used on a vertical milling machine.

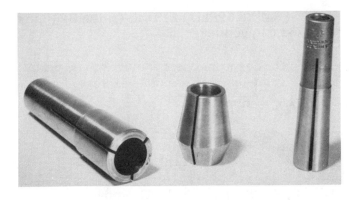

Fig. 26-57. Spring collets to hold straight shank cutters and other devices in a milling machine.

CARE OF CUTTER HOLDING AND DRIVING DEVICES

To maintain accuracy during the machining operation it is necessary to prevent damage to the cutter holding and driving devices.

1. Keep the arbor taper free of nicks.
2. Clean and lubricate the bearing sleeve and arbor support bearing before use.
3. Clean the spacing collars before placing them on an arbor. Otherwise, cutter run-out will occur.
4. Store arbors separately and in a vertical position.
5. NEVER loosen or tighten an arbor nut unless the arbor support is locked in place, Fig. 26-58. Use a wrench of the correct type and size, Fig. 26-59.
6. Do not tighten an arbor nut by striking the wrench with a hammer or mallet. This may crack the nut or distort the threads.
7. To remove an arbor or adapter from the machine:

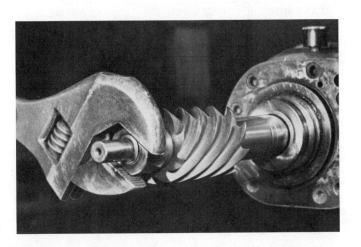

Fig. 26-58. Tightening or loosening the arbor nut without the arbor support in place will spring the arbor.

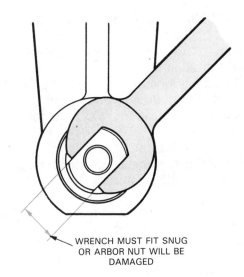

WRENCH MUST FIT SNUG OR ARBOR NUT WILL BE DAMAGED

Fig. 26-59. Use a wrench of the correct type and size.

a. Loosen the nut on the draw-in bar a few turns. Do not remove it from the arbor completely.
b. Tap the draw-in bar head with a lead hammer to loosen the arbor from the spindle.
c. Hold the loosened arbor with one hand and unscrew the draw-in with the other.
d. Remove the arbor from the spindle. Clean and store it.

CUTTING SPEEDS AND FEEDS

The time required to complete a milling operation and the quality of the machined surface is almost completely governed by the cutting speed and feed of the cutter.

CUTTING SPEED

CUTTING SPEED refers to the distance (measured in feet or meters) a point (tooth) on the circumference of the cutter moves in one minute. It is expressed in FEET PER MINUTE (FPM) or METERS PER MINUTE (MPM) and is directly dependent on the REVOLUTIONS PER MINUTE (RPM) of the cutter.

FEED

FEED is the rate at which the work moves into the cutter. It is given in FEED PER TOOTH PER REVOLUTION (FTR). The selection of the proper feed is probably the most difficult thing for the machinist to determine. In view of the many variables—width of cut, depth of cut, machine condition, cutter sharpness, etc.—feed should be as coarse as possible and consistent with the desired finish.

CALCULATING CUTTING SPEEDS AND FEEDS

Considering the previously mentioned variables, the speeds listed in Fig. 26-60, and feeds listed in Fig. 26-61, are suggested. The usual procedure is to start with the midrange figure and increase or reduce speeds until the most satisfactory setting is obtained.

Refer to the rules for determining speeds and feeds, Fig. 26-62, to calculate the cutting speed and feed for specific materials.

EXAMPLE

PROBLEM: Determine the proper speed and feed for a 6 in. diameter side cutter (HSS) with 16 teeth, milling aluminum.

INFORMATION AVAILABLE:

Recommended cutting speed for
aluminum (midpoint on range) . . . . . 750 FPM
Recommended feed per tooth
(midpoint on range) . . . . 0.015 in.
Cutter diameter . . . . 6 in.
Number of teeth on cutter 16

TO DETERMINE SPEED SETTING (cutter RPM) the following is given (Fig. 26-62):

RULE: Divide the feet per minute (FPM) by the circumference of the cutter, expressed in feet.

FORMULA: $RPM = \dfrac{FPM \times 12}{\pi D}$

$= \dfrac{750 \times 12}{3.14 \times 6} = \dfrac{9000}{18.84}$

$= \dfrac{1500}{3.14} = 478*$

TO DETERMINE FEED SETTING (feed in inches per minute = F)

RULE: Multiply feed per tooth per revolution by number of teeth on cutter and by speed (RPM).

FORMULA: $F = FTR \times T \times RPM$
$= 0.015 \times 16 \times 478 = 117*$

*The speeds and feeds are only approximate. Set machine to closest setting.

MATERIAL	HIGH SPEED STEEL CUTTER		CARBIDE CUTTER	
	FEET PER MINUTE	METERS PER MINUTE*	FEET PER MINUTE	METERS PER MINUTE*
Aluminum	550-1000	170-300	2200-4000	670-1200
Brass	250- 650	75-200	1000-2600	300- 800
Low Carbon Steel	100- 325	30-100	400-1300	120- 400
Free Cutting Steel	150- 250	45- 75	600-1000	180- 300
Alloy Steel	70- 175	20- 50	280- 700	85- 210
Cast Iron	45- 60	15- 20	180- 240	55- 75

Reduce speeds for hard materials, abrasive materials, deep cuts, and high alloy materials. Increase speeds for soft materials, better finishes, light cuts, frail work, and setups. Start at midpoint on the range and increase or decrease speed until best results are obtained.
*Figures rounded off.

Fig. 26-60. Recommended cutting speeds for milling. Speed is given in surface feet per minute (SPM) and in surface meters per minute (MPM).

TYPE OF CUTTER	MATERIAL				
	ALUMINUM	BRASS	CAST IRON	FREE CUTTING STEEL	ALLOY STEEL
End mill	0.009 (0.22) 0.022 (0.55)	0.007 (0.18) 0.015 (0.38)	0.004 (0.10) 0.009 (0.22)	0.005 (0.13) 0.010 (0.25)	0.003 (0.08) 0.007 (0.18)
Face mill	0.016 (0.40) 0.040 (1.02)	0.012 (0.30) 0.030 (0.75)	0.007 (0.18) 0.018 (0.45)	0.008 (0.20) 0.020 (0.50)	0.005 (0.13) 0.012 (0.30)
Shell end mill	0.012 (0.30) 0.030 (0.75)	0.010 (0.25) 0.022 (0.55)	0.005 (0.13) 0.013 (0.33)	0.007 (0.18) 0.015 (0.38)	0.004 (0.10) 0.009 (0.22)
Slab mill	0.008 (0.20) 0.017 (0.43)	0.006 (0.15) 0.012 (0.30)	0.003 (0.08) 0.007 (0.18)	0.004 (0.10) 0.008 (0.20)	0.001 (0.03) 0.004 (0.10)
Side cutter	0.010 (0.25) 0.020 (0.50)	0.008 (0.20) 0.016 (0.40)	0.004 (0.10) 0.010 (0.25)	0.005 (0.13) 0.011 (0.28)	0.003 (0.08) 0.007 (0.18)
Saw	0.006 (0.15) 0.010 (0.25)	0.004 (0.10) 0.007 (0.18)	0.001 (0.03) 0.003 (0.08)	0.003 (0.08) 0.005 (0.13)	0.001 (0.03) 0.003 (0.08)

Increase or decrease feed until the desired surface finish is obtained.
Feeds may be increased 100 percent or more depending upon the rigidity of the machine and the power available, if carbide tipped cutters are used.

Fig. 26-61. Recommended feed in inches per tooth and millimeters per tooth for high speed steel cutters.

TO FIND	HAVING	RULE	FORMULA
Speed of cutter in feet per minute (FPM)	Diameter of cutter and revolutions per minute	Diameter of cutter (in inches) multiplied by 3.1416 (π) multiplied by revolutions per minute, divided by 12	$FPM = \dfrac{\pi D \times RPM}{12}$
Speed of cutter in meters per minute	Diameter of cutter and revolutions per minute	Diameter of cutter multiplied by 3.1416 (π) multiplied by revolutions per minute, divided by 1000	$MPM = \dfrac{D(mm) \times \pi \times RPM}{1000}$
Revolutions per minute (RPM)	Feet per minute and diameter of cutter	Feet per minute, multiplied by 12, divided by circumference of cutter (πD)	$RPM = \dfrac{FPM \times 12}{\pi D}$
Revolutions per minute (RPM)	Meters per minute and diameter of cutter in millimeters (mm)	Meters per minute multipled by 1000, divided by the circumference of cutter (πD)	$RPM = \dfrac{MPM \times 1000}{\pi D}$
Feed per revolution (FR)	Feed per minute and revolutions per minute	Feed per minute, divided by revolutions per minute	$FR = \dfrac{F}{RPM}$
Feed per tooth per revolution (FTR)	Feed per minute and number of teeth in cutter	Feed per minute (in inches or millimeters) divided by number of teeth in cutter $\times$ revolutions per minute	$FTR = \dfrac{F}{T \times RPM}$
Feed per minute (F)	Feed per tooth per revolution, number of teeth in cutter, and RPM	Feed per tooth per revolutions multiplied by number of teeth in cutter, multiplied by revolutions per minute	$F = FTR \times T \times RPM$
Feed per minute (F)	Feed per revolution and revolutions per minute	Feed per revolution multiplied by revolutions per minute	$F = FR \times RPM$
Number of teeth per minute (TM)	Number of teeth in cutter and revolutions per minute	Number of teeth in cutter multiplied by revolutions per minute	$TM = T \times RPM$

RPM = Revolutions per minute	TM = Teeth per minute
T = Teeth in cutter	F = Feed per minute
D = Diameter of cutter	FR = Feed per revolution
π = 3.1416 (pi)	FTR = Feed per tooth per revolution
FRM = Speed of cutter in feet per minute	MPM = Speed of cutter in meters per minute

Fig. 26-62. Rules for determining speed and feed.

CUTTING FLUIDS

CUTTING FLUIDS serve many purposes. They carry away the heat generated during the machining operation, act as a lubricant to prevent chips from sticking or fusing to the cutter teeth, and flush away chips. The lubricating qualities also influence the quality of the finish of the machined surface. See Fig. 26-63.

WORK HOLDING ATTACHMENTS

One of the more important milling machine features is its adaptability to large numbers of work holding attachments; this in turn increases the usefulness of the machine.

VISE

The VISE is probably the most widely used method of holding work for milling. The jaws are hardened and ground for accuracy and wear. It is keyed to the milling table with LUGS.

A FLANGED VISE, Fig. 26-64, has slotted flanges for fastening the vise to the worktable. The slots

Aluminum and its Alloys	Kerosene, kerosene and lard oil, soluble oil
Plastics	Dry
Brass, Soft	Dry, soluble oil, kerosene and lard oil
Bronze, High Tensile	Soluble oil, lard oil, mineral oil, dry
Cast Iron	Dry, air jet, soluble oil
Copper	Soluble oil, dry, mineral lard oil, kerosene
Magnesium	Low viscosity neutral oils
Malleable Iron	Dry, soda water
Monel Metal	Lard oil, soluble oil
Slate	Dry
Steel, Forging	Soluble oil, sulphurized oil, mineral lard oil
Steel, Manganese	Soluble oil, sulphurized oil, mineral lard oil
Steel, Soft	Soluble oil, mineral lard oil, sulphurized oil, lard oil
Steel, Stainless	Sulphurized mineral oil, soluble oil
Steel, Tool	Soluble oil, mineral lard oil, sulphurized oil
Wrought Iron	Soluble oil, mineral lard oil, sulphurized oil

Fig. 26-63. Recommended cutting fluids for various materials.

Fig. 26-64. Flanged vise.

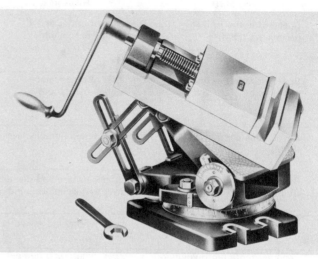

Fig. 26-66. Two styles of universal vises.

permit the vise to be mounted parallel or at right angles to the spindle.

The body of a SWIVEL VISE, Fig. 26-65, is similar to the flanged vise but is fitted with a circular base, graduated in degrees. This permits the vise to be pivoted on a horizontal plane and locked at any angle to the spindle.

The TOOLMAKER'S UNIVERSAL VISE, Fig. 26-66, permits compound or double angles to be machined without complex or multiple setups.

A ROTARY TABLE, Fig. 26-67, can perform a variety of operations such as cutting segments of circles, circular slots, locating angularly spaced holes or slots, cutting irregular shaped slots, etc. A dividing attachment can be fitted in place of the handwheel.

An INDEX TABLE, Fig. 26-68, permits the rapid positioning of the material for angular work.

The DIVIDING HEAD is one of the more important attachments for the milling machine. Its main function is to divide the circumference of a circular piece into equally spaced divisions. This makes the dividing head indispensable when milling gear teeth, cutting splines, and spacing holes on a circle. It also

Fig. 26-67. A rotary table being used to produce machine parts.   (Greaves Machine Tool Div., J.A. Fay & Egan Co.)

makes possible the milling of squares, hexagons, octagons, etc., when needed.

The dividing head consists of two parts, a dividing unit and a footstock, Fig. 26-69. The work may be mounted between centers, held in a chuck, or clamped in a collet.

Fig. 26-65. Swivel vise.   (Wilton Tool Mfg. Co.)

Fig. 26-68. Indexing table.

The standard ratio for a dividing head is five turns of the index crank for one complete revolution of the spindle (5:1); or 40 turns of the index crank for one revolution of the spindle (40:1).

The ratio between the index crank turns and spindle revolution, plus the index place with its series of equally spaced hole circles, makes it possible to divide the circumference of circular work into the required number of equal spaces.

For example, if 10 teeth were to be cut in a gear, it would require 1/10 of 40 turns (assuming the dividing head has a 40:1 ratio), or four full turns of the index crank for each tooth.

For 28 teeth, the number of crank turns would be 1/28 of 40, or 1 12/28 of 40, or in lowest terms, 1 3/7 turns of the index crank for each tooth.

This is where the holes in the index plate come into use: they allow fractional turns to be made accurately. On one such plate the circles have 46, 47, 49, 51, 53, 54, and 57 holes. In this situation, 49 is divisible by 7; then 3/7 of 49 or 21 holes on the 49 hole circle. It is not necessary to count 21 holes each time the work is repositioned after a tooth is cut. The two arms, called index fingers, are loosened. One is positioned until it touches the pin in the index crank; the other is moved clockwise until the arms are 21 holes apart (DO NOT COUNT THE HOLE THE PIN IS IN).

To index, rotate the crank one complete revolution, plus the section taken up by the index fingers. Drop the pin into the hole at this position and lock the dividing head. Move the index fingers in the

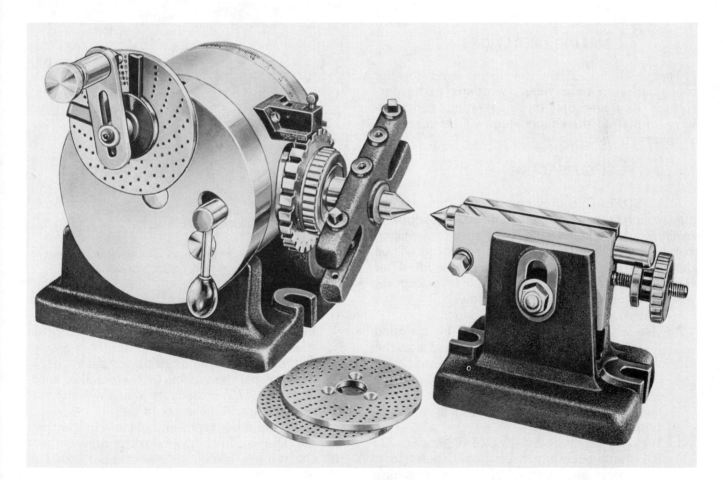

Fig. 26-69. Dividing head and footstock. (L-W Chuck Co.)

same direction as crank rotation to catch up with the plunger. Repeat the operation after each cut, Fig. 26-70.

The dividing head can be elevated for cutting bevel gears.

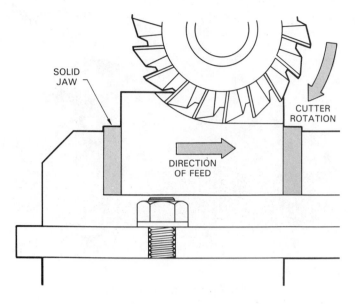

Fig. 26-71. The solid jaw of the vise should be in this position whenever the setup permits.

Fig. 26-70. Cutting a gear on the milling machine. Work is being held in a three-jaw universal chuck. Many machinists make a light cut at each tooth position to check whether the dividing head has been set up properly.

MILLING OPERATIONS

The versatility of the milling machine permits many different machining operations to be performed. However, only those operations commonly performed in the school shop will be described in this text.

MILLING FLAT SURFACES

FLAT SURFACES may be milled with a plain or slab milling cutter mounted on an arbor (peripheral milling), and an inserted tooth or shell face milling cutter (face milling). The method employed will be determined by the size and shape of the work. After the method has been decided, the following sequence of operations is to be followed:

1. Check and lubricate the machine.
2. Use a vise if the work cannot be clamped directly to the table. Clean the base and the worktable, and bolt the vise to the machine. Locate it as close to the column as the work shape will allow. When possible, pivot the vise so the solid jaw supports the work against cutting pressure, Fig. 26-71.
3. Align the vise with a dial indicator, Fig. 26-72, if extreme accuracy is required. Otherwise, a square can be used, Fig. 26-73, or a machine arbor, Fig. 26-74.

Fig. 26-72. The use of a dial indicator permits extreme accuracy in aligning a vise on the machine.

4. Place parallels in the vise with the work on them. Tighten the jaws and tap the work onto the parallels. Paper strips will aid in checking whether the work is on the parallels solidly, Fig. 26-75. Protect the vise jaws with soft metal strips if the work is rough.
5. Wipe the arbor taper and place it in the spindle. Draw it in tightly with the draw-in bar.
6. Use the smallest cutter diameter possible, Fig. 26-76. It should be large enough, however, to provide adequate clearance, Fig. 26-77.

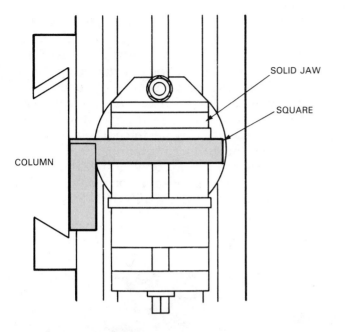

Fig. 26-73. Aligning a vise at right angles to the table with a machinist's square.

SOLID JAW

SQUARE

COLUMN

Fig. 26-75. Seating work on parallels. Note the two strips of paper. You will know the work is solidly on the parallels if the paper strips cannot be removed.

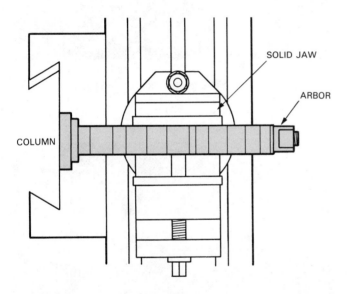

SOLID JAW

ARBOR

COLUMN

Fig. 26-74. The arbor can also be used to align the vise.

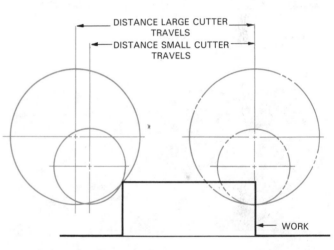

DISTANCE LARGE CUTTER TRAVELS

DISTANCE SMALL CUTTER TRAVELS

WORK

Fig. 26-76. A small diameter cutter is more efficient than a large diameter cutter because it travels less distance while doing the same amount of work.

PROTECT YOUR HANDS FROM THE CUTTER TEETH WITH A SECTION OF CLOTH WHEN MOUNTING THE CUTTER, Fig. 26-78.

7. Place the cutter on the arbor and key it to the shaft. If a helical slab is used, mount it so the cutting pressure forces it towards the column, Fig. 26-79.

8. Swing the arbor support into place and tighten the arbor nut.

9. Adjust the machine to the proper cutting speed and feed.

10. Turn on the machine, then check cutter rotation and direction of power feed. If this is

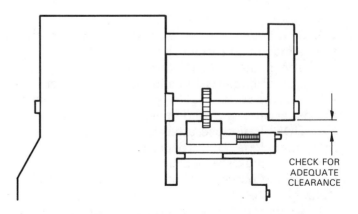

CHECK FOR ADEQUATE CLEARANCE

Fig. 26-77. Use the smallest cutter diameter possible, but be certain it is large enough for adequate clearance.

satisfactory, loosen all worktable and knee locks, and position the work under the rotating cutter until it just touches the work surface. Set the micrometer dial to "0." Back the work away from the rotating cutter and raise the table the required distance. Make the cut and apply ample cutting fluid.

Fig. 26-78. Protect your hand when handling a cutter.

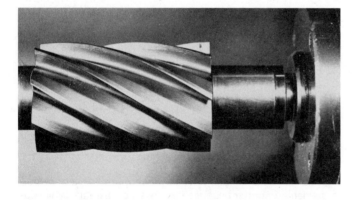

Fig. 26-79. Mount helical cutters so cutting pressure will force the cutter towards the spindle.

Should additional material have to be removed from a machined surface, it will be best to position the cutter in the following manner. Hold a long, narrow strip of paper with its loose end between the work and the cutter, Fig. 26-80. Raise the table until the paper strip is pulled lightly from your fingers. CAUTION: Pay close attention when using alignment technique. Use a paper strip long enough to keep your fingers well clear of the rotating cutter. Release the paper as soon as you feel the cutter "grabbing" at it.

After the cutter has been positioned, it is only necessary to move the cutter clear of the work and raise the table the required distance.

11. Tighten all locks (except longitudinal) and feed the work into the cutter. As soon as cutting starts, turn on the coolant and power feed. Do not stop the work during the machining operation. This practice causes a slight depression to be made in the machined surface, Fig. 26-81. CAUTION: Do not attempt to feel the machined surface while the cut is in progress or while the cutter is rotating.

12. Complete the cut. Stop the cutter. Return the work to the starting position. NEVER FEED THE WORK BACK UNDER THE ROTATING CUTTER.

Fig. 26-80. Setting the cutter using a long strip of paper.

Fig. 26-81. A slight depression will be made in the machined surface if the feed is stopped during the cut.

13. Following these directions exactly, make the number of cuts necessary to bring the machined surface to size.

SQUARING STOCK

A definite sequence of operations must be followed to machine several surfaces of a piece square with one another.

The sequence is very similar to that just explained:

1. Machine the first surface, Fig. 26-82, A. Remove burrs and place the first machined surface against the fixed vise jaw. Insert a length of soft metal rod between the work and the movable jaw if necessary, Fig. 26-82, B.
2. Machine the second surface.
3. Remove burrs and reposition the work as shown in Fig. 26-82, C, then machine the third surface. This side must be machined to the specified dimension. Take a light cut and mike for thickness. The difference between this measurement and the required thickness is the amount of material that must be removed.

4. Repeat the above operation to machine the fourth size, Fig. 26-82, D.
5. If the piece is short enough, the ends may be machined by placing it in a vertical position. Otherwise, it may be machined with a side mill as shown in Fig. 26-83.

FACE MILLING

FACE MILLING makes use of a cutter that machines a surface at right angles to the spindle axis and parallel to the face of the cutting tool.

1. Select a cutter that is 3/4 to 1 in. (19.05 to 25.4 mm) larger in diameter than the width of the surface to be machined.
2. The work should project about 1 in. (25.4 mm) beyond the edge of the worktable to provide ample clearance. Mount it to the work table or in a suitable holding device.
3. Adjust the machine for correct speed and feed.

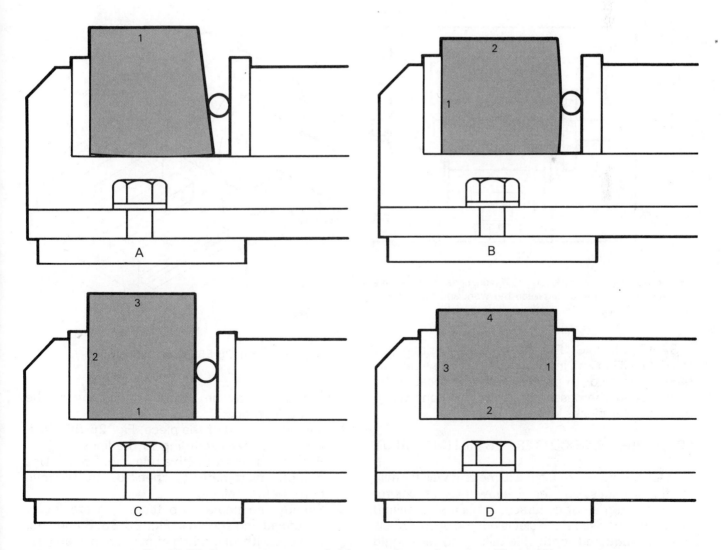

Fig. 26-82. Sequence recommended for squaring work on the milling machine.

4. Slowly feed the cutter until it starts to remove metal.
5. Use an adequate supply of cutting fluid.
6. Upon completion of the cut, stop the cutter and return the work to the starting position for additional cutting if needed.
7. Make the finishing cut and tear down the setup. Use a brush to remove chips and cutting fluid. DO NOT USE YOUR HAND OR COMPRESSED AIR.

SIDE MILLING

SIDE MILLING refers to any milling operation that utilizes side milling cutters. When the cutters are used in pairs to machine two opposite sides of a job at the same time, the setup is called STRADDLE MILLING, Fig. 26-84.

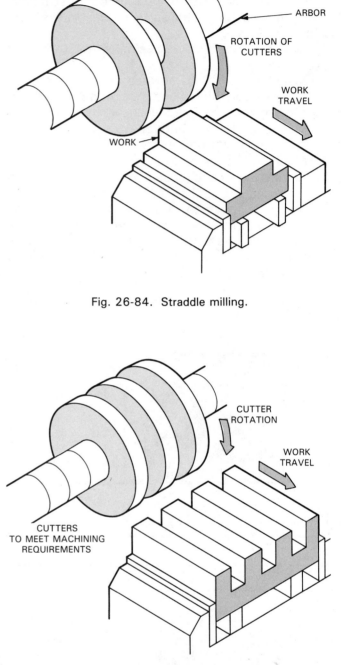

Fig. 26-84. Straddle milling.

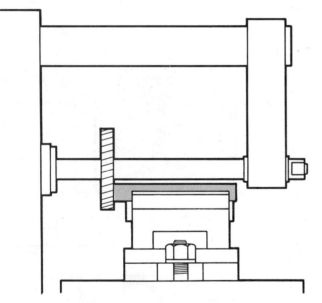

Fig. 26-83. One method of squaring work ends. Be sure there is adequate clearance between the work and the arbor.

GANG MILLING, Fig. 26-85, is a variation of straddle milling and involves mounting several cutters on the arbor to permit several surfaces to be machined in one pass. Gang milling is done when many similar pieces must be made.

LOCATING A SIDE CUTTER FOR MILLING A SLOT

Machine setup is much the same as it was for milling flat surfaces. Use the vise jaw if tolerances require this degree of accuracy. A plain side milling cutter may be used if the slot is not too deep. Otherwise, a staggered tooth side milling cutter should be used.

Fig. 26-85. Gang milling.

The cutter may be positioned by one of the following methods:
1. Lay out the end of the piece, Fig. 26-86. Position the cutter according to the lines.
2. Position the cutter with a rule, Fig. 26-87. Use a depth micrometer to check depth. Remove burrs before miking.
3. Employ the paper strip technique previously described and shown in Fig. 26-88. Remember to work with long strips of paper and keep your fingers clear of the rotating cutter.

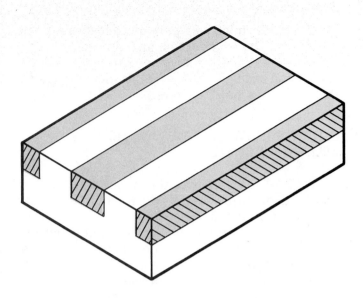

Fig. 26-86. Work laid out for milling.

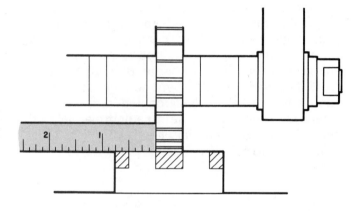

Fig. 26-87. Positioning the cutter with the aid of a steel rule.

ter. An oval shaped cut will result, and the location of the cut will be perfectly centered. Position the cutter on the oval, Fig. 26-90.

3. The previously mentioned paper strip technique may also be used to locate the cutter precisely, Fig. 26-91. After the cutter has been brought

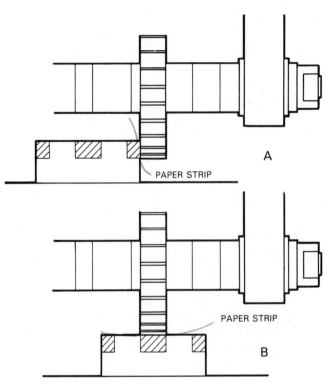

A

PAPER STRIP

B

PAPER STRIP

Fig. 26-88. Positioning the cutter. A—Using a paper strip. B—Using a paper strip to position for depth.

LOCATING A SIDE CUTTER FOR MILLING A SLOT AT THE CENTER OF ROUND STOCK

There are many situations that require keyways for the standard square key to be cut in round stock. The keyway must be exactly on center if it is to be in alignment with the keyway in the mating part.

After the machine has been set up, cutter mounted in a vise, between centers, in a V-block or in a fixture, precise centering of the cutter may be accomplished by one of the following methods:

1. Center the cutter visually on the work. With a steel square and a rule, adjust the table until both sides measure the same, Fig. 26-89. A depth micrometer may be used in place of the rule for more accurate positioning.

2. Short pieces cannot always be centered by the above method. For situations of this type, the work is positioned under and lightly brought into contact with the rotating cutter. Traverse (in-out) feed is used to pass the work under the cut-

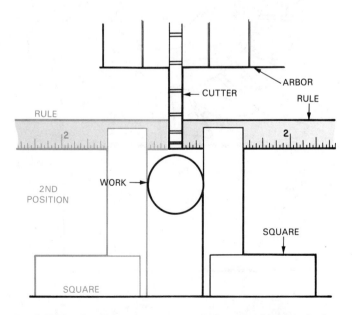

ARBOR

CUTTER

RULE

RULE

2ND POSITION

WORK

SQUARE

SQUARE

Fig. 26-89. Centering a cutter on round stock with a steel rule and machinist's square.

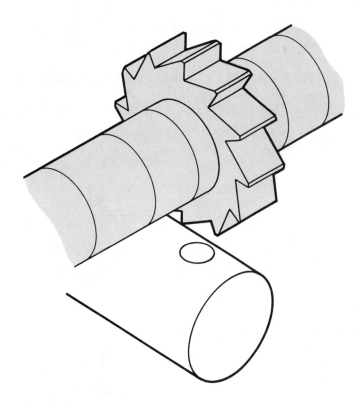

Fig. 26-90. Positioning a cutter on center using an oval made in the work with the cutter as a guide.

up against the stock, the table must be lowered for the cutter to clear the top of the work. Move the cutter in one-half the diameter plus one-half

the cutter thickness plus the thickness of the paper. The same technique is employed to center a Woodruff keyseat cutter, Fig. 26-92.

Lock the saddle to prevent table movement after the cutter has been centered.

SLITTING (HOW TO SAW ON THE MILLING MACHINE)

SLITTING or SAWING thin stock into various widths, Fig. 26-93, is a fairly common operation performed on a milling machine.

A slitting saw of the smallest diameter which will permit adequate clearance should be used. It must be keyed to the arbor and the key should pass into the spacers on either side of the cutter.

If the section is narrow enough, clamp the metal in a vise, Fig. 26-94. It must be well-supported with parallels. Do not permit the parallels to project out into the path of the cutter.

Long strips must be clamped to the worktable. The clamp shown in Fig. 26-95, is made from a section of angle iron. The work is aligned with the column face and must be located to permit the saw to make the cut over the center of a table slot, Fig. 26-96. A piece of paper between the work and the table will prevent work slippage during the slitting operation. The cutter is set to a depth equal to the thickness of the material plus 1/16 in. (1.5 mm). USE A SHARP SAW.

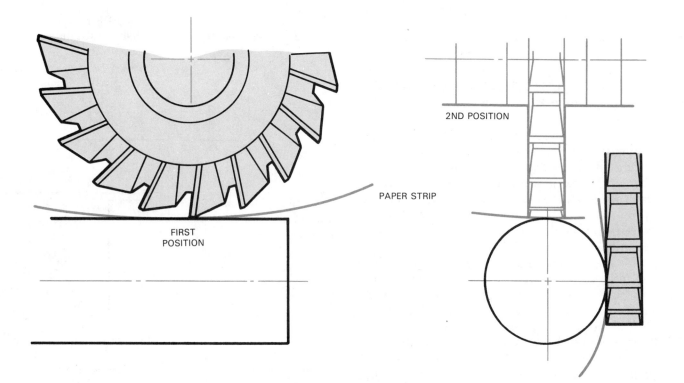

FIRST POSITION

2ND POSITION

PAPER STRIP

Fig. 26-91. Using a paper strip to position the cutter on round stock.

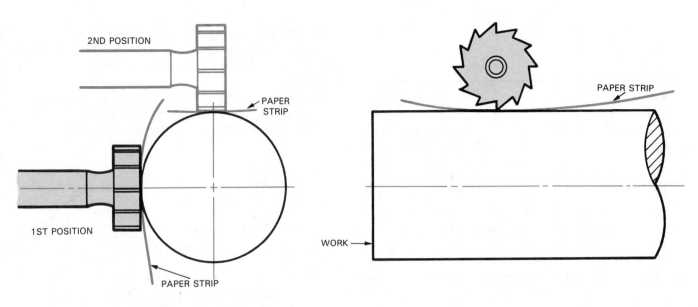

Fig. 26-92. The paper strip technique can also be used to center a Woodruff keyseat cutter.

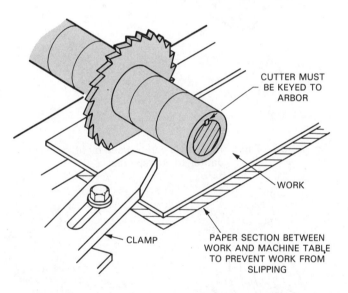

CUTTER MUST BE KEYED TO ARBOR

WORK

CLAMP

PAPER SECTION BETWEEN WORK AND MACHINE TABLE TO PREVENT WORK FROM SLIPPING

Fig. 26-93. A slitting saw can be employed to cut sheet and plate into strips.

SLOTTING

SLOTTING, Fig. 26-97, is very similar to slitting except the cut is made only part way through the work. The slots in the heads of screws were made by this technique.

HOW TO DRILL AND BORE ON A MILLING MACHINE

The toolmaker often finds it necessary to produce precision holes in jigs, fixtures, and machine parts. The milling machine offers a convenient way to drill and bore holes in precise alignment with one another.

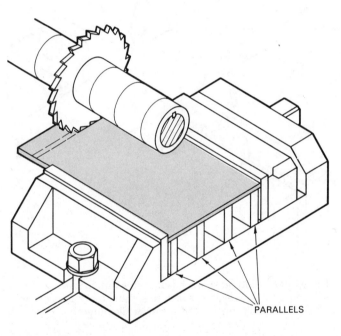

PARALLELS

Fig. 26-94. Slitting work held in a vise. Be sure the parallels do not project out into the path of the cutter.

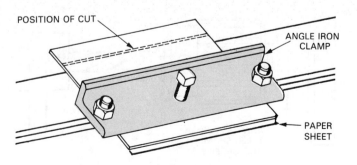

POSITION OF CUT

ANGLE IRON CLAMP

PAPER SHEET

Fig. 26-95. A table clamp made from angle iron.

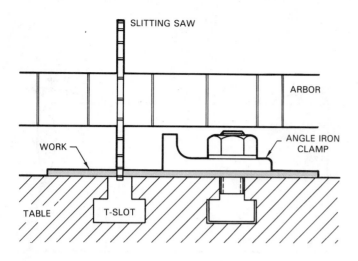

Fig. 26-96. Position the work so the cut will be made over a T-slot.

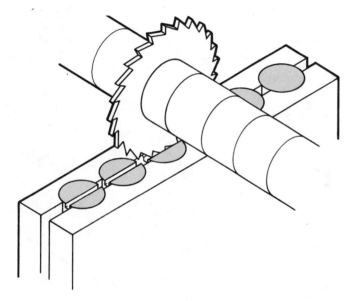

Fig. 26-97. Slotting screw heads with a slitting saw. A special slotting saw is available which has many more teeth than a slitting saw of a similar diameter.

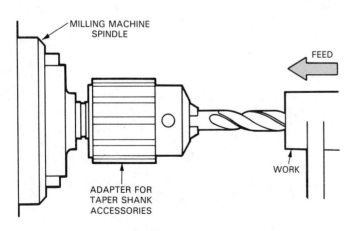

Fig. 26-98. Drilling on a horizontal mill.

Small drills are held in a standard Jacobs chuck mounted in the machine spindle, Fig. 26-98. Taper shank drills are held in a sleeve or adapter, Fig. 26-99.

BORING is done with a single point cutting tool fitted in a BORING HEAD, Fig. 26-100. The boring tool is held in the spindle by a collet adapter.

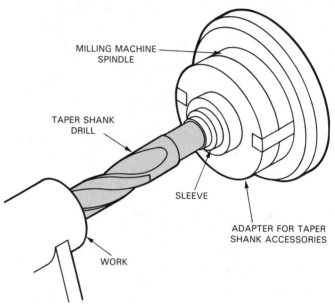

Fig. 26-99. Taper shank drills can be used by fitting a special adapter to the spindle.

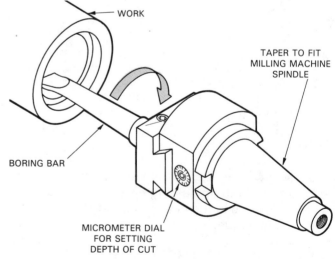

Fig. 26-100. Boring permits large holes to be machined to close tolerances.

A WIGGLER, Fig. 26-101, will aid in aligning the machine if holes are to be drilled prior to reaming or boring. A DIAL INDICATOR, must be used to realign existing holes for boring, Fig. 26-102.

THE VERTICAL MILLING MACHINE

The VERTICAL MILLING MACHINE, Fig. 26-103, is a highly versatile machine tool for milling, drilling, reaming, and boring. It differs from the conventional mill in that the spindle is normally in a vertical position. The SPINDLE HEAD, Fig. 26-104, swivels 90 degrees left or right for angular work, Fig. 26-105. The ram on which it is mounted can be adjusted in and out and, on many vertical mills, revolves 180 degrees to a horizontal plane. Both type swivels are graduated with a Vernier scale to assure accurate angular settings, Fig. 26-106.

Fig. 26-101. Locating the position of a hole with a "wiggler."

Fig. 26-102. A dial indicator permits an existing hole to be realigned accurately for additional machining.

Fig. 26-103. Vertical milling machine.   (Cincinnati Milacron)

Fig. 26-104. Spindle head assembly. A—Spindle draw-in bar. B—Spindle feed lever. C—Spindle stop-brake lever. D—Micrometer spindle feed crank. E—Micrometer depth stop. F—Spindle. G—Spindle clamping lever. H—Feed clutch lever. I—Spindle power down-feed engagement lever. J—Swivel adjustment bolt. K—Spindle feed rate lever. L—Infinitely variable down-feed unit. M—Directional power feed lever. N—Motor. (George Gorton Machine Co.)

Fig. 26-105. Note the range of angular settings possible with this vertical milling machine spindle head.   (Clausing)

Fig. 26-106. The Vernier scale on this machine permits the spindle head to be positioned to an angular setting with extreme accuracy. (South Bend Lathe, Inc.)

CUTTERS FOR THE VERTICAL MILLING MACHINE

Although adapters are available that permit side and angular cutters to be used on a vertical milling machine, Fig. 26-107, face mills and end mills are the normally used cutters.

Taper shank end mills too small to fit directly into the spindle are fitted into a sleeve for mounting, Fig. 26-108, A. Taper shanks that are large enough are mounted directly into the spindle, Fig. 26-108, B. Straight shank end mills are held in collet chucks, Fig. 26-108, C, or in an adapter, Fig. 26-108, D. Small drills and reamers are held in a Jacobs chuck.

Fig. 26-107. Adapter which permits arbor-type cutters to be used on a vertical milling machine.

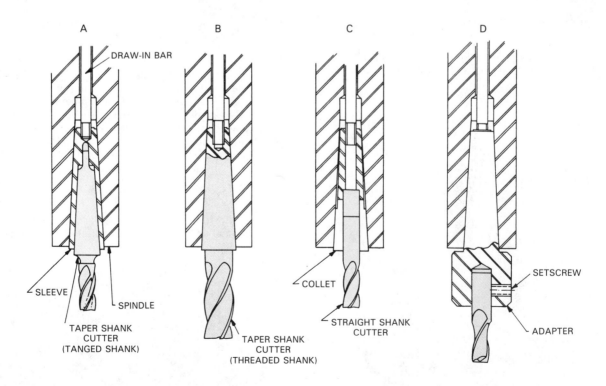

Fig. 26-108. Four of the more common methods for mounting end mills in a vertical milling machine. A—Fitted in a sleeve. B—Mounted directly. C—Fitted in a collet chuck. D—Fitted in an adapter.

HOW TO MACHINE ANGULAR SURFACES

Angular surfaces (bevels, chamfers, and tapers) can be milled by tilting the spindle head, Fig. 26-109, at the required angle, by setting the work at an angle in the vise, Fig. 26-110, or by using a universal vise, Fig. 26-111.

Fig. 26-111. Angular cut being made on work held in a universal vise. With this setup compound angles (angles on two planes) are easily cut.

Fig. 26-109. Cutting an angular surface with the spindle head set at the desired angle. (Clausing)

Work held at an angle in the vise for machining must be set up with a protractor, fitted with a spirit level, Fig. 26-112, or with a surface gauge, Fig. 26-113.

Fig. 26-110. Cutting an angular surface by positioning the work at the desired angle.

Fig. 26-112. The work can be set at the desired angle with the aid of a protractor head.

HOW TO MILL A SLOT OR KEYWAY

Keyways and slots can be cut with end mills. The work is clamped in the vise and a cutter equal in diameter to the width of the cut is selected. A two-flute end mill is necessary if a blind keyway must

With the pivoted spindle head assembly, it is essential that the vise be aligned with a dial indicator. Make a layout of the required angle on the work and clamp it in the milling vise. Position the cutter and machine to the line.

Fig. 26-113. Positioning angular work with a surface gauge.

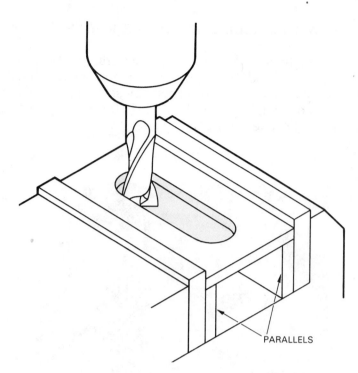

Fig. 26-115. Milling an internal opening with an end mill.

be cut, Fig. 26-114. Otherwise, a four-flute mill will be satisfactory.

The end mill is centered in the same manner as a side milling cutter would be for the same operation.

HOW TO MACHINE AN INTERNAL OPENING

Internal openings, Fig. 26-115, are easily machined on a vertical mill. If the cutter must start the opening, a two-fluted end mill will be required. It can be fed directly into the metal like a drill.

When the slot is wider than the cutter diameter, it is important that the proper direction of feed, in relation to cutter rotation, be observed. THE DIRECTION OF FEED IS ALWAYS AGAINST CUTTER ROTATION, Fig. 26-116.

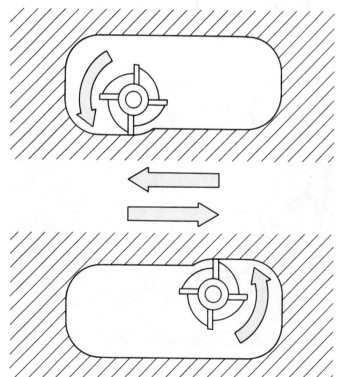

Fig. 26-116. Feed direction is always against cutter rotation.

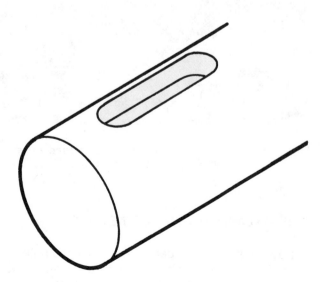

Fig. 26-114. Blind slot.

HOW TO MACHINE MULTI-LEVEL SURFACES

Milling multi-level surfaces, Fig. 26-117, is probably the easiest of the milling operations. A layout

Fig. 26-117. Machining multi-level surfaces.

of the various levels is made on the surface of the work. Cuts are made until the layout lines are reached. For accuracy, the depth of the cut must be checked with a micrometer and table adjustments made accordingly.

HOW TO DRILL AND BORE ON A VERTICAL MILLING MACHINE

Holes may be located for drilling, reaming, and boring to very close tolerances on the vertical mill. After the first hole is located with a wiggler, Fig. 26-118, or EDGE FINDER, Fig. 26-119, and

Fig. 26-118. After the first hole is aligned with a "wiggler," positions of additional holes are located by using the micrometer dials on the table movement screws.

machined, it is possible to locate the remaining holes by using the micrometer feed dials on the table movement screws.

Boring, Fig. 26-120, permits holes of any diameter to be machined accurately with fine surface finishes. A single point tool is fitted to the boring head, which is in turn mounted in the spindle. Hole diameter is controlled by off-setting the tool point from center. The adjustment screw is graduated for direct reading.

CARE OF THE MILLING MACHINE

Many of the problems encountered in the operation of a milling machine will not occur if careful thought is given to pre-planning the job:

1. Check and lubricate the machine with the recommended lubricants.
2. Clean the machine thoroughly after each job. Use a brush to remove chips, Fig. 26-121. Never use your hands or compressed air. Stop the machine before attempting to do any cleaning.
3. Keep the machine clear of tools.
4. Check each setup for adequate clearance, Fig. 26-122.
5. Clean the spindle opening and arbor taper before inserting the arbor.
6. Never force a cutter on an arbor.
7. No attempt should be made to loosen or tighten the arbor nut without proper arbor support. Make it a habit of tightening the nut as the last step in a setup, and loosening it as the first step in the teardown.
8. Use a wrench of the correct size and type to

tighten the arbor nut.

9. Never use a dull cutter.
10. Check the machine to determine whether it is level. This should be done at regular intervals.
11. Speed and feed changes should be made according to the manufacturer's recommendations and specifications.
12. Never operate a machine until all guards are in place.
13. Check the level and condition of the cutting fluid if the reservoir is built into the machine. Change it when it becomes contaminated.
14. Do not operate the machine until you are sure that everything is in satisfactory working condition. Ask for help if you are not sure how an operation should be performed.
15. Some milling accessories are heavy. Get help carrying and moving them.

INDUSTRIAL APPLICATIONS

The milling machines used by industry operate on the same basic principle as those in the school shop. However, it is possible to program many industrial machines by the use of automatic feeds and a series of trip dogs, through an automatic machining cycle. Many of the newest machines are computer-controlled. Figs. 26-123 through 26-128 illustrate a number of machine types now found in industry.

SAFETY

1. Do not attempt to operate the machine until you are thoroughly familiar with it. When in doubt, ask for assistance.
2. Wear appropriate clothing and goggles.
3. Get help to move any heavy attachment like

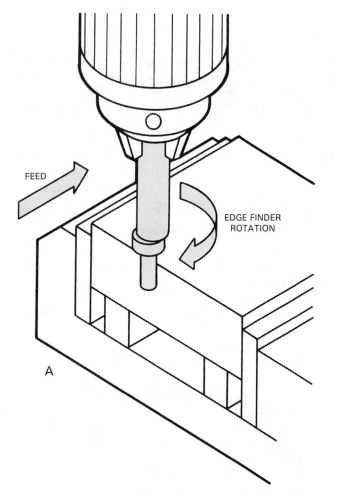

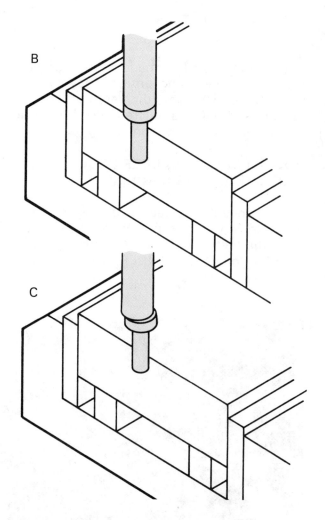

Fig. 26-119. The EDGE FINDER is a precision positioning tool that makes it possible to locate the edge of a work piece in relation to the center of the spindle (as close as 0.0002 in.). A—With the spindle rotating at a moderate speed, and with the tip of the edge finder as shown, slowly feed the tip of the tool against the work. B—The tip of the edge finder will gradually become centered with the shank. C—When the tip becomes exactly centered the tip will abruptly jump sideways about 1/32 in. (0.8 mm). Stop table immediately when this occurs. The center of the spindle will be exactly one half the tip diameter away from the edge of the work. Set the micrometer dial to "O" and, with the edge finder clear of the work, move the table longitudinally the required distance PLUS one half tip diameter. The same procedure is followed to get the traverse measurement.

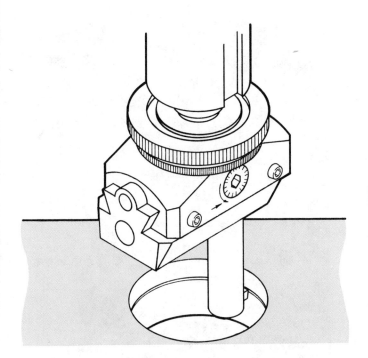

Fig. 26-120. Boring on the vertical mill produces a very accurately sized hole.

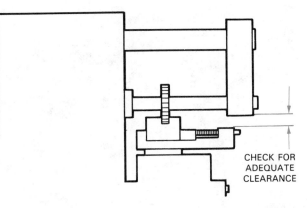

Fig. 26-122. Check for adequate clearance before starting the cut.

Fig. 26-121. Use a brush to remove metal chips, never your hands.

Fig. 26-123. A vertical milling machine fitted with a hydraulic tracer unit. The tracer finger, fitted into the hydraulically actuated tracer unit, is to the right. The cutter on the left duplicates the movement of the tracer finger. (Bridgeport Machines, Div. of Textrons Inc.)

the vise, dividing head, rotary table, etc.

4. Never handle a cutter with bare hands. Use a piece of heavy cloth for protection.
5. Use a small brush to remove chips—NEVER BRUSH WITH YOUR HAND.
6. Stop the machine before attempting to remove chips.
7. Never reach over or near the rotating cutter.
8. Make sure the holding device is mounted solidly to the table, and the work held firmly. Spring or vibration can cause thin cutters like the slitting saw to jam and shatter.
9. Do not talk to anyone while operating the

machine, nor allow anyone to turn on your machine for you.
10. No adjustments should be made while the cutter is rotating. Stop it before making measurements, removing chips, etc.
11. Keep the floor around the machine clear of chips. Wipe up spilled cutting fluid at once.

Fig. 26-124. Vertical 5-Axis CNC (Computer Numerical Control) milling machine. In addition to longitudinal, traverse, and vertical movements, the spindle head also tilts on two angular planes. (Cincinnati Milacron)

Fig. 26-125. A 3-Axis stringer mill (designed to machine wing skins of aircraft) has four cutter heads, and a work table 80 x 866 in. (approx. 2.0 x 22.0 m). It is the only machine of its kind. (Avco Corp.)

12. Be thoroughly familiar with the STOP lever.
13. Treat any small cuts and skin punctures immediately. Report any injury, even though minor, to your instructor.
14. Do not permit your work clothes to become saturated with oil and cutting fluids. Greasy clothing is a fire hazard.
15. Put all oily rags used to wipe down the machine in a metal container that can be closed tightly.
16. Do not fool around while operating the mill. Keep your mind on your job and be ready for any emergency.

Fig. 26-126. The back head of a solid propellant rocket chamber is contoured on a template controlled three-dimensional milling machine. The template, located at the top of the work table, guides the cutting tool. Three-dimensional milling eliminates much milling that would otherwise be necessary. (Avco Corp., Lycoming Div.)

Fig. 26-127. Duplex type fixed bed milling machine utilizes two cutting heads. On this particular machine, one cutting head is face milling while the other cutting head is fitted with an end mill.

Fig. 26-128. Another type of fixed bed milling machine. Machine movement is controlled by a computer to the left of the machine. Tools (in foreground) must be changed by the machinist. (Portage Machine Co.)

TEST YOUR KNOWLEDGE, Unit 26

Please do not write in the text. Place your answers on a separate sheet of paper.

1. The _____ and _____ are the two basic milling machine families.
2. The worktable has three movements: _____, _____, and _____.
3. The vertical milling machine is best suited for operations done with an _____ and a _____ cutter.
4. What are the two basic types of milling cutters?
5. Cutters are also classified by the method used to mount them in the machine. List them.
6. The slab milling cutter is a member of the _____ milling cutter family.
7. The _____ fluted end mill is used when the cutter must be fed into the work like a twist drill.
8. Make a sketch showing the difference between conventional milling and climb milling.
9. In general, the _____ arbor suitable for the job should be used.
10. The _____ goes through the spindle and helps to hold the arbor in the spindle.
11. The base on the _____ vise permits the vise to be pivoted to any desired angle.
12. Cutting fluids have three functions:
    a. _____.
    b. _____.
    c. _____.
13. The dividing head is used to:
    a. Locate the center of round stock.
    b. Divide the circumference of a workpiece into any number of equal parts.
    c. Locate hole positions for drilling.
    d. None of the above.
14. Gang milling means:
    a. Several cutters are used to do the job.
    b. One or more cutters straddle the job.
    c. Two or more cutters cut at the same time.
    d. None of the above.
15. Explain how to center a side cutter on round stock for the purpose of machining a keyway. Use the paper strip technique.
16. The _____ is the most accurate tool to be used to align a vise.
17. Milling cutters should be handled with _____ to prevent hand injuries.
18. Blind or closed keyways are made with a _____ end mill.
19. Small drills and reamers are held in a _____ in the vertical milling machine.
20. List two ways of machining a bevel, chamfer, or taper on a vertical milling machine.
21. Calculate the cutting speed (RPM) of a 6 in. diameter side mill (HSS) to machine aluminum.
22. Calculate the cutting speed (RPM) of a 1 in. diameter end mill (HSS) to machine mild steel.
23. The _____ tooth side milling cutter is used to machine deep slots.
24. The _____ is used for cutoff operations.
25. End mills are available with _____ and _____ shanks.
26. An _____ is used to support a slab milling cutter.
27. Flat surfaces are machined with _____ or _____ tooth _____ milling cutter.
28. Accurate holes may be machined on a vertical milling machine with the aid of a _____ head.
29. Chips are removed from the machine with _____, never your _____.
30. Stop the milling machine before _____ or attempting to _____.
31. Get help when moving _____.
32. Make sure that the work holding device is mounted _____ to the machine.

RESEARCH AND DEVELOPMENT

1. The milling machine and its inventor, Eli Whitney, played an important part in early attempts at mass production. Prepare a term paper on Whitney's project of producing 10,000 muskets, with interchangeable parts, for the federal government in 1798, and how it lead to the invention of the milling machine.
2. Make a series of 35mm slides illustrating the safety precautions that must be followed when

operating the milling machine.

3. Cutting fluids play an important part in any machining operation. Secure samples of cutting fluids used by local industries. Conduct a series of experiments to show the quality of surfaces machined dry and with the various cutting compounds. Your experiment should show the best cutting fluid for use with steel, aluminum, and brass.

4. Contact a shop that uses milling machines and secure cutters that have been ruined. Make a panel to display them along with an explanation of how they were ruined.

5. Demonstrate the proper way to center a cutter to mahcine a keyway in a shaft. Use the paper strip technique.

6. Milling machines were the first automated machines. Do a research project on automated milling machines. Secure samples of the perforated tapes and punch cards used to control them, and some small products made on a tape programmed machine.

Machining a mold section for a plastic model airplane. Milling machine doing work is fitted with a universal tracer unit. Tracer finger (arrow 1) is moved across the wing pattern and a tiny cutter (arrow 2) duplicates the movement of the tracer finger, but in a smaller scale. Mold is machined in an aluminum block and, after polishing, will be fitted with other mold sections and placed in a plastic injection molding machine to produce the familiar plastic parts you find in a model airplane kit. (Bill Hannan, Williams Bros. Inc.)

Unit 27

METAL SPINNING

METAL SPINNING is a method of working metal sheet into three-dimensional shapes, Fig. 27-1. It involves, in its simplest form, rotating a metal disc with a forming block (chuck) made to the dimensions specified for the INSIDE of the desired object. As the lathe rotates the metal disc and forming block, pressure is applied and the metal is gradually worked around the form until it assumes its size and shape, Figs. 27-2 to 27-5.

The pressure is applied by a simple lever consisting of a forming tool, Fig. 27-6. The spinner (person doing the work) rests the forming tool on a tool rest and begins to apply pressure at the center of the disc. The disc responds by starting to form itself over the chuck.

Most metals can be spun. However, aluminum, copper, brass, pewter, and silver are best suited for spinning in the school shop. They must be in an annealed state and may have to be annealed from time

Fig. 27-2. Sheet metal disc and forming block (chuck) revolving on a spinning lathe. (Phoenix Products Co.)

Fig. 27-1. A selection of student-made objects spun from pewter. Only the holders on the candlesticks were not spun.

Fig. 27-3. With pressure applied, the disc begins to assume the shape of the forming chuck.

Metal Spinning   425

Fig. 27-4. As the metal disc begins to assume the final shape it may have to be removed and annealed (softened) before it can be completed.

Fig. 27-5. The finished product; in this case it is part of a lighting fixture.

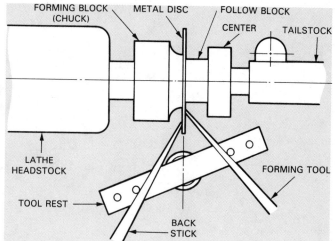

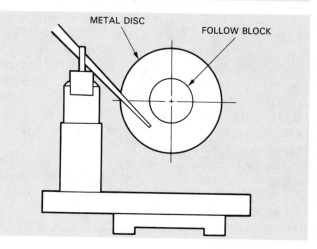

Fig. 27-6. A typical spinning setup for hand operation. Pressure is applied with the forming tool. The back stick supports the disc and prevents it from buckling.

to time as they become workhardened during the spinning operation.

SPINNING EQUIPMENT

Any lathe with heavy-duty head spindle bearings and an adequate speed range can be used for spinning. For best results, the tailstock should be fitted with a ball bearing center, Fig. 27-7. The conventional tool rest or tool post is replaced by a tool rest fitted with movable steel pins, Fig. 27-8. The pins act as fulcrum points for applying pressure to the spinning tools.

TOOLS

Spinning tools may be made from hickory hammer handles (18 to 24 in. or 450 to 600 mm long) or commercially made from steel, Fig. 27-9.

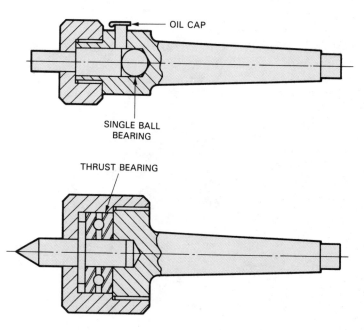

Fig. 27-7. Ball bearing tailstock centers usually found on spinning lathes.

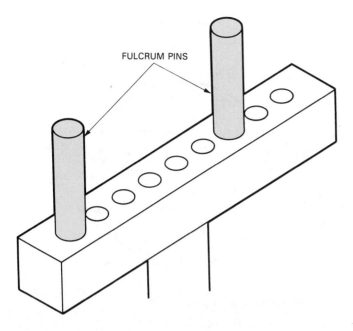

FULCRUM PINS

Fig. 27-8. Tool rest used for spinning. The fulcrum pins are movable to different positions on the rest.

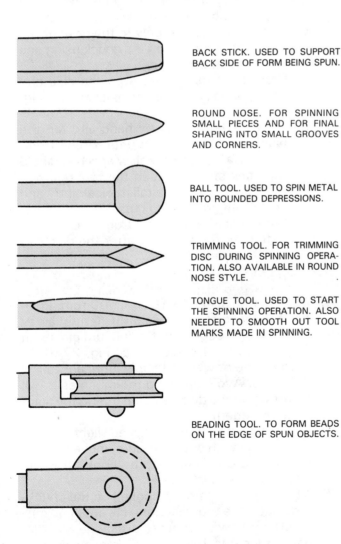

BACK STICK. USED TO SUPPORT BACK SIDE OF FORM BEING SPUN.

ROUND NOSE. FOR SPINNING SMALL PIECES AND FOR FINAL SHAPING INTO SMALL GROOVES AND CORNERS.

BALL TOOL. USED TO SPIN METAL INTO ROUNDED DEPRESSIONS.

TRIMMING TOOL. FOR TRIMMING DISC DURING SPINNING OPERATION. ALSO AVAILABLE IN ROUND NOSE STYLE.

TONGUE TOOL. USED TO START THE SPINNING OPERATION. ALSO NEEDED TO SMOOTH OUT TOOL MARKS MADE IN SPINNING.

BEADING TOOL. TO FORM BEADS ON THE EDGE OF SPUN OBJECTS.

Fig. 27-9. Spinning tools.

CHUCKS

Chucks are the forms over which the metal disc is shaped. Most are made from birch, cherry, or maple woods. Metal chucks are used if great accuracy or long production runs are required. The SOLID CHUCK, Fig. 27-10, is used for spinning simple forms while the SEGMENTED CHUCK, Fig. 27-11, must be used for more complex shapes like the tankard in Fig. 27-12. The chuck is made in segments that are disassembled after the form has been spun. A STARTING CHUCK, Fig. 27-13, is employed for initial shaping of the metal after which it is fitted on the segmented chuck. A JOINED CHUCK, Fig. 27-14, is required when spinning a bulged form like the teapot, Fig. 27-15. The form spun on the joined chuck cannot be made on a segmented chuck. After spinning, the form is cut at its largest diameter, the chuck sections removed, and the metal sections are fused or soldered back together.

FOLLOW BLOCK

The FOLLOW BLOCK, Fig. 27-16, is a wooden block that fits over the tailstock center and applies the pressure needed to hold the metal disc on the chuck.

LUBRICANT

A lubricant such as yellow bar soap or beeswax is applied to the metal disc to prevent the forming tool from galling (damaging) the surface of the metal during the spinning operation.

HOW TO SPIN A SIMPLE FORM

1. Secure or turn a chuck of the desired shape.
2. Cut a metal disc to size. Disc diameter can be

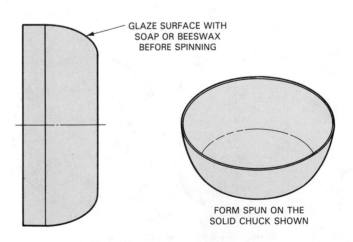

GLAZE SURFACE WITH SOAP OR BEESWAX BEFORE SPINNING

FORM SPUN ON THE SOLID CHUCK SHOWN

Fig. 27-10. Simple solid chuck.

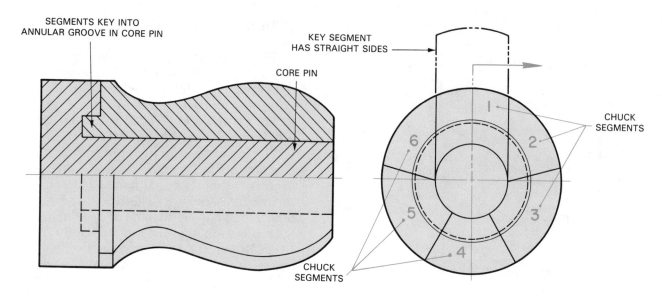

Fig. 27-11. Segmented chuck used for spinning a tankard.

Fig. 27-12. A silver tankard made by the spinning process.
(Henry J. Kauffman)

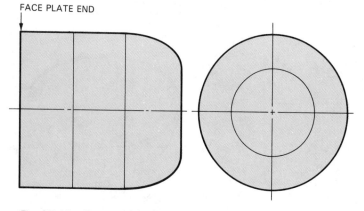

Fig. 27-13. Starting chuck for spinning objects such as the tankard
and teapot.

determined as shown in Fig. 27-17.

3. Insert the disc between the chuck and follow block. Turn up the tailstock until the follow block holds the disc snugly to the base of the chuck. Center the disc on the chuck using one of the following methods:

   a. Draw a series of circles on the disc and position the circles on the follow block, Fig. 27-18.

   b. Turn the lathe over by hand and tap the blank on the high side until it runs true.

   c. Run the lathe at a very slow speed and hold the back stick between the tool rest and the disc. Loosen the tailstock slightly and apply light pressure to the edge of the rotatating disc until it runs true, Fig. 27-19. Retighten the tailstock after the disc has been centered.

   SAFETY NOTE: Do not stand directly behind the revolving disc while it is being centered.

4. Adjust lathe speed to 1000-1500 rpm. Position the tool rest about 2 in. (50.0 mm) away from the disc edge with the fulcrum pin about 1 in. (25.0 mm) in front. See Fig. 27-20.

5. Turn on the power and apply lubricant to the disc face. Avoid applying too much as it will fly off when the disc heats up during the spinning operation.

6. Use a round nose tool positioned slightly below center, and with body pressure, move the tool nose down and to the left to "hook" the disc on the chuck, Fig. 27-21.

7. After the disc has been hooked on the chuck, reposition the tool rest until it is about 1/2 in. (10.0 mm) away from the disc edge and trim until it runs true. Use a file to remove any burrs formed during the trimming operation.

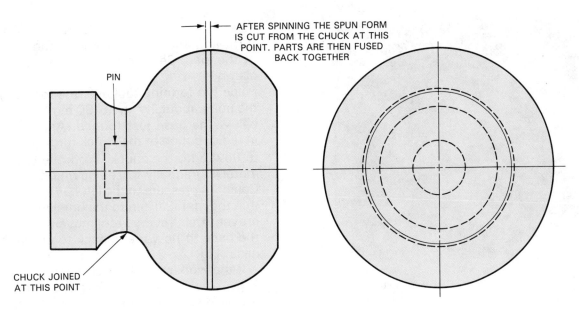

Fig. 27-14. Joined chuck for spinning a teapot.

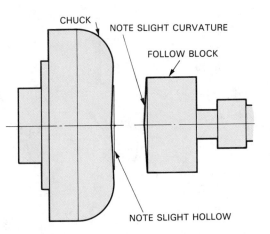

Fig. 27-15. The body of this pewter teapot made by the author was spun on a joined chuck.

Fig. 27-16. Follow block. The slight curvature on the chuck and follow block help hold the disc to the chuck.

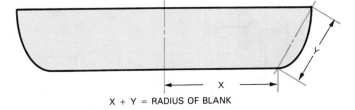

X + Y = RADIUS OF BLANK

Fig. 27-17. How to determine disc size.

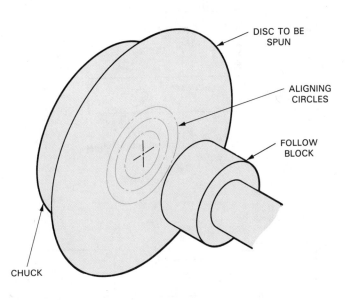

Fig. 27-18. Centering a disc using aligning circles.

SAFETY NOTE: Keep your hands clear of the rotating disc at all times.

8. Move the tool rest back far enough to permit the forming tool to have room to move freely.

Metal Spinning 429

Fig. 27-19. Centering a disc with a back stick. (Stieff Silver Co.)

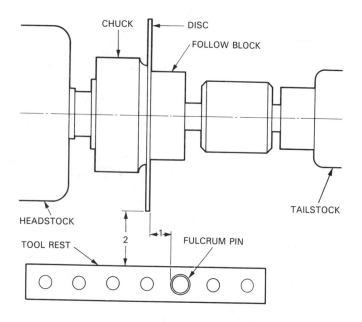

Fig. 27-20. Typical spinning setup.

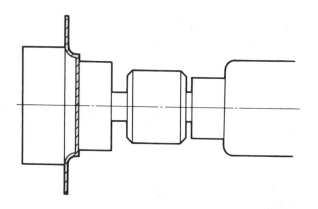

Fig. 27-21. A disc "hooked" on the chuck.

Insert one pin about 1 1/2 in. (40.0 mm) in front and another the same distance in back of the disc. Be sure the tool rest is securely clamped.

9. Place the forming tool over the tool rest with the point about 1/4 in. (6.50 mm) outside and below the base just formed. Apply pressure in the direction of the chuck forcing the metal to flow onto the chuck. Work the tool so the metal is gradually forced down on the chuck. Constant pressure to the left has a tendency to thin the metal, often to the breaking point. To prevent this, reverse tool movement towards the base to flow metal back to normal thickness, Fig. 27-22.

If the work starts to buckle or wrinkle on the edge, place the back stick against the left side of the disc and force the metal to pass between the back tool and the forming tool, Fig. 27-23. Work too buckled to be straightened by this method must be removed from the chuck and flattened with a mallet. Force metal tightly on the chuck and move the forming tool back and forth along the surface to remove ridges and distribute metal evenly, Fig. 27-24.

10. Trim the edge if needed. Remove any burr that may have formed. Remove all traces of the lubricant with a cloth and a solvent or soap and water.

11. Increase lathe speed. Polish the work with fine steel wool (3/0) or aluminum oxide cloth (300). Buff if a high polish is desired.

FORMING A BEAD ON THE EDGE OF A SPUN SHAPE

The edge of a spun piece is often turned back to form a BEAD, Fig. 27-25. This operation can be performed with a beading tool as shown in Fig. 27-26, or it may be done with conventional spinning tools and a back stick as shown in Fig. 27-27.

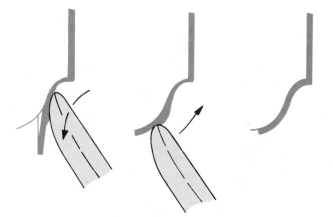

Fig. 27-22. Reverse tool travel to keep metal thickness uniform and to prevent the disc from tearing.

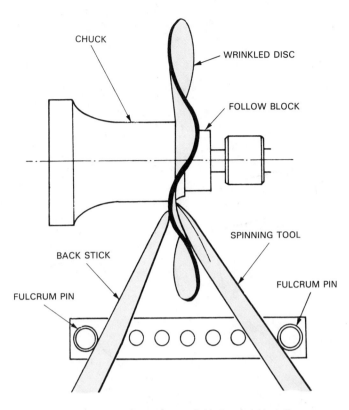

Fig. 27-23. Straightening a wrinkled or buckled disc.

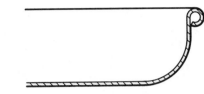

Fig. 27-25. A bead that was spun on a simple form.

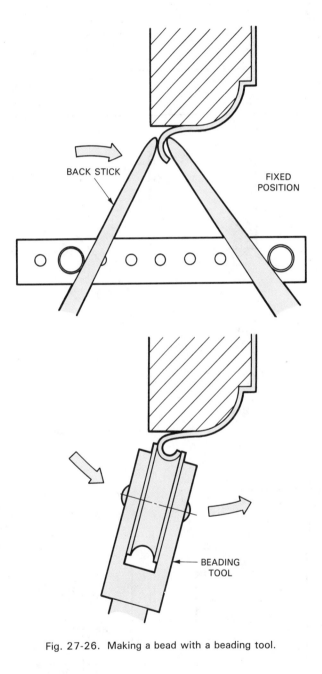

BACK STICK

FIXED POSITION

BEADING TOOL

Fig. 27-26. Making a bead with a beading tool.

Fig. 27-24. Spinning a tankard body by conventional spinning techniques. A segmented chuck is used. (Stieff Silver Co.)

SPINNING DEEP FORMS

Objects that are rather tall with straight sides, Fig. 27-28, require a slightly different spinning technique to maintain uniform metal thickness along their entire length.

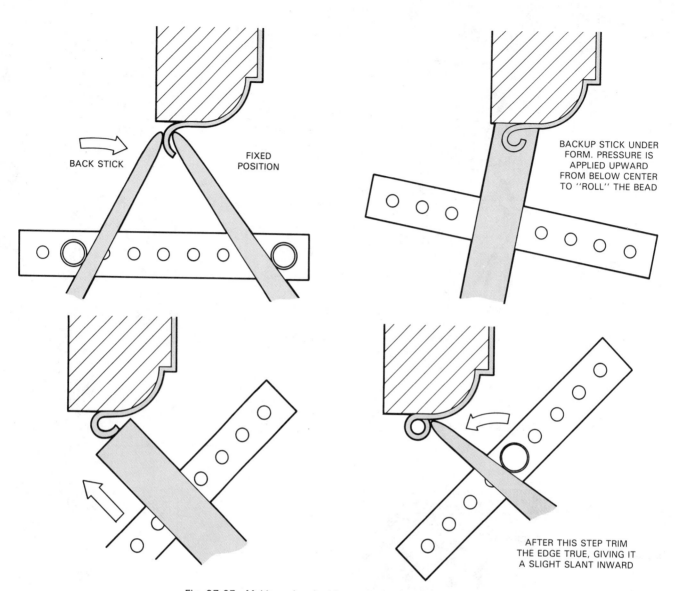

BACK STICK FIXED POSITION

BACKUP STICK UNDER FORM. PRESSURE IS APPLIED UPWARD FROM BELOW CENTER TO "ROLL" THE BEAD

AFTER THIS STEP TRIM THE EDGE TRUE, GIVING IT A SLIGHT SLANT INWARD

Fig. 27-27. Making a bead with conventional spinning tools.

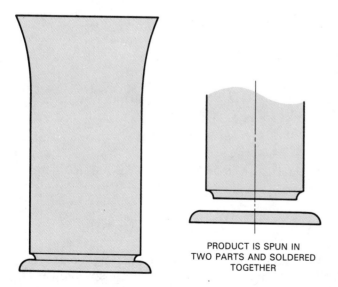

PRODUCT IS SPUN IN TWO PARTS AND SOLDERED TOGETHER

Fig. 27-28. Tall form. Made in two parts, the base is soldered to the body.

The constant application of pressure often causes the metal to tear before it can be worked down on the chuck. This can often be avoided if a BREAKDOWN CHUCK, Fig. 27-29, is used first. This chuck has a base that is the same diameter and shape as the final chuck. The steps in spinning a deep form are shown in Fig. 27-30.

INDUSTRIAL APPLICATIONS

Modern spinning practices have gained wide acceptance as a method of forming metal sheet and plate into shapes that cannot be done physically or economically by stamping or drawing.

The size and thickness (gauge) of metal spun manually is limited only by the skilled spinner's muscle power. The desire to increase power to spin larger and thicker diameters has lead to the development of the COMPOUND LEVER TOOL, Fig. 27-31.

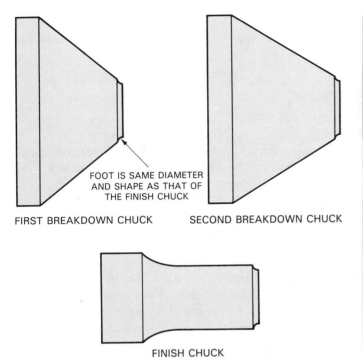

Fig. 27-29. Examples of breakdown chucks and finish chuck for spinning a tall form.

FIRST BREAKDOWN CHUCK

SECOND BREAKDOWN CHUCK

FOOT IS SAME DIAMETER AND SHAPE AS THAT OF THE FINISH CHUCK

FINISH CHUCK

Fig. 27-31. A compound tool multiplies the spinner's muscle power for large, heavy work. (Phoenix Products Co.)

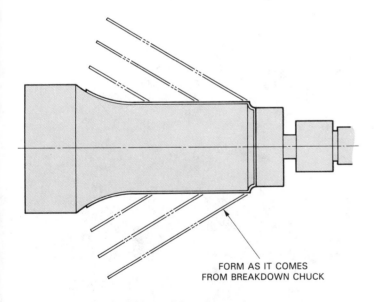

FORM AS IT COMES FROM BREAKDOWN CHUCK

Fig. 27-30. A tall form is spun in steps.

Fig. 27-32. Hydraulic spinning setup with built-in "feel."

This tool resembles a large nutcracker with a steel roller near the fulcrum. The tool pivots on a lever and permits changes of fulcrum to give the operator maximum leverage in forming heavy metal sections.

Although the manual methods are still used when the operation is economical and efficient, they are not adequate for most industrial needs. Today, thanks to lathes with tremendous power and hydraulically driven forming tools, Fig. 27-32,

manual movement can be duplicated. In addition, the machine also allows the operator to "feel" so the metal thickness can be controlled on the most intricate forms. They are so powerful that diameters of up to 200 in. (5080.0 mm) and thickness over 2 in. (50.0 mm) can be spun to close tolerances.

For certain kinds of conical shapes, automatic machinery, Fig. 27-33, has been developed. These machines are capable of spinning heavy sections

Metal Spinning 433

Fig. 27-33. Conical shapes being spun on an automatic spinning machine.

of "exotic" metals in large quantities and to close tolerances.

ADVANTAGES OF SPINNING

Spinning has many advantages over other types of metal forming:
1. The forms over which the metal is spun can be made quickly and inexpensively of wood. They cost only a fraction of the amount needed to make tools and dies for other metalworking processes.
2. The forms can be made in days, and in some instances hours, compared to weeks and months when tools and dies have to be made.
3. Working the metal cold improves its physical characteristics.
4. Spinning is ideal for pilot production or product development. As an example, experimental scientific rocket nose sections can be made for a few hundred dollars instead of the several thousand dollars the next most economical method of metal forming would have cost. Changes are made quickly and easily as requirements change.

USES FOR SPUN OBJECTS

Many inexpensive novelty items such as ash trays, flower pots, and lamp shades are made by spinning. However, the majority of the items spun are used as components of major products such as radar units, jet engines, tank trucks, air conditioning units, and heating plants. The process is also

employed to produce some of the finer things of life . . . goblets, tableware, silver, and pewter hollowware, Fig. 27-34.

SHEAR SPINNING

SHEAR SPINNING is a metalworking technique that is similar to conventional spinning in outward appearance only. It is actually a cold extrusion process wherein the parts are shaped by rollers that exert tremendous pressures on a rotating starting blank or preform, and displace the metal parallel to the centerline of the workpiece.

The metal is taken from the thickness of the blank, whereas in spinning the metal is taken from the diameter of the blank. See Fig. 27-35. Instead of displacing the metal as in the shear spinning technique, spinning folds the metal over and places it on or close to the spinning form.

The process, Fig. 27-36, known commercially as FLOTURN and HYDROSPIN, is well adapted for manufacturing parts for aircraft and missiles, Figs. 27-37 and 27-38. Shear spinning has made it feasible to shape a single metal disc part that formerly had to be welded of several pieces. The tolerances that can be attained make it possible to eliminate unwanted weight. Fine surface finishes that require

Fig. 27-34. A teapot made by the spinning process. (Henry J. Kauffman)

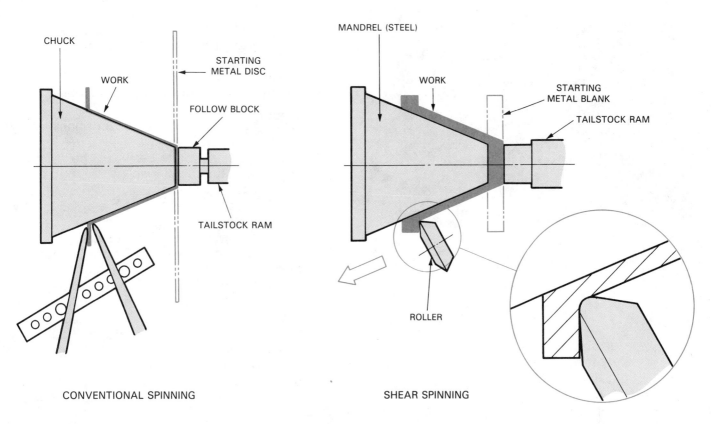

CONVENTIONAL SPINNING

SHEAR SPINNING

Fig. 27-35. Note how conventional spinning and shear spinning differ.

Fig. 27-36. A 42 by 50 in. (1067 by 1270 mm) shear spinning machine producing the head for a rocket motor case. When completely formed it will be 13 1/2 in. (343 mm) deep and 40 in. (1016 mm) in diameter.   (Meta-Dynamics Div., Cincinnati Milacron Inc.)

Fig. 27-37. Using the shear spinning technique to shape a section for a modern aircraft.   (Lodge & Chipley Co.)

little or no additional work can be obtained.

Templates are needed to guide the rollers and maintain the proper relationship between the tool and mandrel. They make it possible to hold tolerances as close as 0.005 in. (0.13 mm) on diameters.

Preforms, workpieces that have been partially shaped by forging, machining, or one of the other metalworking techniques, are often used for increased economy.

Fig. 27-38. Modern aircraft with jet engines utilize many parts made by the shear spinning process. (USAF Thunderbirds)

SPINNING SAFETY

1. Wear eye protection.
2. Beware of sharp, pointed metal edges when cutting the metal disc from stock and when getting it ready for spinning.
3. Check the spinning lathe to be certain it is in safe operating condition.
4. Be sure the tool post and tool rest are securely tightened.
5. With a file, remove all burrs formed during the trimming operation.
6. Make certain the spinning tools are solidly attached to their handles.
7. Never stand in line with the disc when drilling and centering.
8. Always double-check the condition of the follow block on the disc. Remember to retighten the tailstock after the disc has been centered.
9. Use care when handling a disc that has been annealed. It may still be hot enough to burn you. Use tongs or pliers, or wear heavy gloves.
10. Do not attempt to do spinning unless you have been instructed properly. Be certain about what must be done and how to do it. Get help from your instructor when you are unsure of a procedure.

TEST YOUR KNOWLEDGE, Unit 27

Please do not write in the text. Place your answers on a separate sheet of paper.

1. Metal spinning is a method of working metal sheet into _____ shapes.
2. The forming tool is positioned on a _____

3. The metal disc may have to be annealed because _____ during the spinning operation.
4. When a piece of metal is annealed it is _____.
5. The _____ chuck is used for spinning simple shapes.
6. The _____ fits between the tailstock center and the metal disc.
7. A lubricant is used to _____.
8. _____ and _____ are frequently used as lubricants in spinning.
9. When is a segmented chuck used in spinning?
10. List three safety precautions that should be observed when spinning metal.
11. Modern spinning practices have gained wide acceptance as a method of forming metal sheet into _____.
12. List several advantages that metal spinning has to offer.
13. How does shear spinning differ from conventional spinning?
14. Shear spinning is a metalworking technique that is:
    a. Similar to spinning.
    b. Accomplished by using great pressures applied by rollers to displace the metal over the form.
    c. Accomplished by folding the metal back over the form with tremendous pressures.
    d. None of the above.

RESEARCH AND DEVELOPMENT

1. Develop a spinning unit for your school shop if there is not one already in operation.
2. Prepare a display board showing the steps in spinning a simple coaster. Demonstrate to the class how you went about spinning it.
3. Secure samples of objects that were produced by spinning. Select novelty items, items used in the home or by industry, and an item spun in pewter or silver.
4. Contact a firm that does spinning and ask what the term "spinning on air" means.
5. Present a motion picture on spinning to the class.
6. Prepare a series of slides on the spinning process. Emphasize the safety aspects.
7. Design a project that must be spun on a segmented chuck. Make the chuck and other necessary tools to spin the job. Prepare a display that will show the step-by-step procedures you followed to produce the item.

Unit 28

COLD FORMING METAL SHEET

STAMPING is the term used for many press forming operations, Fig. 28-1. The process can be divided into two separate operations: CUTTING and FORMING. On many jobs both operations, although separate and distinct, can be done on the same machine with only minor modifications.

CUTTING OPERATIONS

CUTTING is the process where the metal is cut or sheared by tool action. Two cutting techniques have been developed for volume production.

Fig. 28-2. Powered shears cut sheet metal to the desired shape and size. (Volkswagen of America, Inc.)

Fig. 28-1. Many parts of the modern automobile are made by stamping. Tolerances as close as 1.0 mm permit the precise fit of the various components that make up the frame and body. (Pontiac Div., General Motors Corp.)

SHEARING

SHEARING, Figs. 28-2 and 28-3, is employed to bring sheet and plate stock to a specified size or shape. Straight edges are cut on SQUARING SHEARS. Subsequent forming operations may follow shearing.

Fig. 28-3. Straight shearing of polished stainless steel sheet. Felt placed under the hold-down protects the finished surface. (Allegheny Ludlum Steel Corp.)

BLANKING AND PIERCING

BLANKING and PIERCING, Fig. 28-4, involves cutting flat sheet metal to the shape and size of the finished part, Fig. 28-5. The holes and openings of various shapes are cut with PUNCHES and DIES, Fig. 28-6.

Fig. 28-5. Blanking, the first operation in making spoons and forks, produces a blank from which the fork or spoon will be cut after it has been rolled to thickness.
(International Silver Co.)

FORMING OPERATIONS

FORMING is a process in which flat metal blanks are formed into three-dimensional shapes. The technique is often called DRAWING. A press and die are required. A few of the more widely used forming techniques are draw press, Guerin process, Marform process, Hydroforming, bulging, stretch forming, bending, and roll forming.

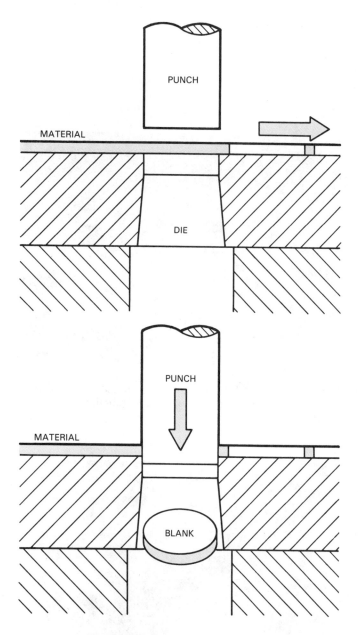

Fig. 28-4. The blanking operation.

PROGRESSIVE DIES are often used in this operation. Each stage in making the part cuts a portion of the blank, but leaves small connections so the metal section can be transferred to the next stage, Fig. 28-7. The main parts of the blanking and piercing setup include the punch, die, and stripper plate. The punch is attached to the ram of the press.

Fig. 28-6. Flat rolled blanks are fed to a machine that punches out the piece close to its final shape. The safety device on the operator's right hand stops the machine from operating when the blank is being placed into position.
(International Silver Co.)

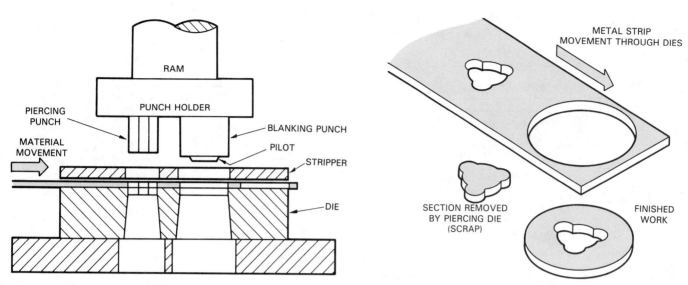

Fig. 28-7. Simple progressive die punching operation. As the internal opening of the part is pierced in one section of the metal strip, the finished part is punched out at another station.

DRAW PRESS

The DRAW PRESS operation, Fig. 28-8, is the shaping performed on either mechanical or hydraulic presses that employ a matched punch and die set, Fig. 28-9.

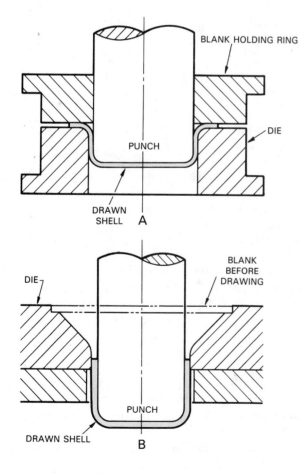

Fig. 28-8. The drawing process.

Fig. 28-9. A draw press.   (Niagara Machine and Tool Works)

GUERIN PROCESS

The GUERIN PROCESS, Figs. 28-10 and 28-11, is employed for forming shallow parts in rubber dies rather than metal dies. Several thin rubber mats are

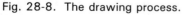

Cold Forming Metal Sheet   439

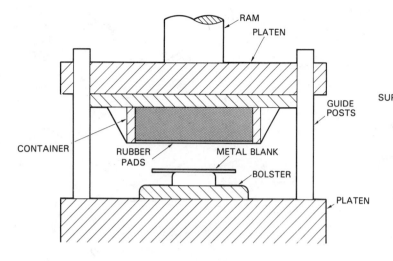

Fig. 28-10. A diagram of the Guerin process. The rubber pad forms the female part of the die.

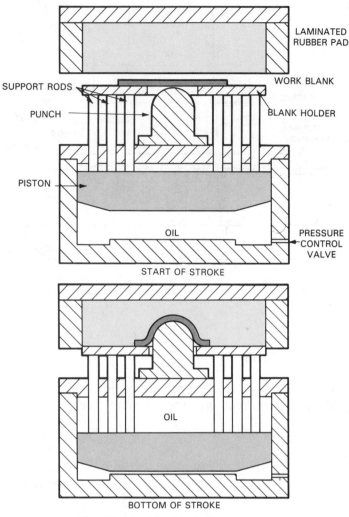

START OF STROKE

BOTTOM OF STROKE

Fig. 28-12. The Marform process.

Fig. 28-11. Press used to form metal by the Guerin process.

mounted in a container attached to the press ram. The rubber mats compress as the ram is lowered, forcing the metal blank to assume the shape of the form block.

MARFORM PROCESS

MARFORM, Fig. 28-12, is similar to the Guerin process but is used for deep drawing. The rubber pad is forced down against a flat blank which rests on a support. As downward pressure mounts, the support is slowly lowered forcing the metal blank to take the shape of the die.

The Marform process is a development of the Martin Marietta Company.

HYDROFORMING

HYDROFORMING, Fig. 28-13, differs from the Guerin and Marform processes in that a rubber diaphragm, backed up by hydraulic pressure, replaces the solid rubber mats and pads. Deeper draws can be made by this process and only two parts, the punch and the draw ring, are needed for the tool. The Hydroform process, a product of Cincinnati Milacron, is outlined in Fig. 28-14.

BULGING

BULGING, Fig. 28-15, is sometimes referred to as entrapped rubber forming. It is used in the manufacture of many products, Fig. 28-16.

STRETCH FORMING

STRETCH FORMING, Fig. 28-17, is a technique

Fig. 28-13. Production type Hydroform machine. This can be quickly converted to a conventional press. (Cincinnati-Milacron)

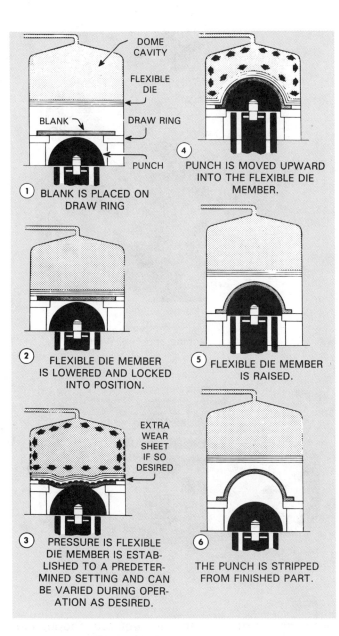

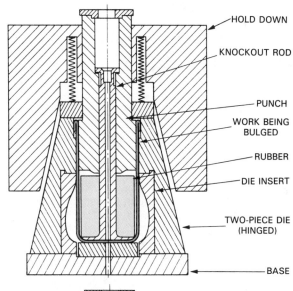

Fig. 28-15. The bulging or entrapped rubber forming process.

Fig. 28-16. Hub caps produced by the bulging process.

in which a metal blank is gripped on opposite edges with clamps, then lightly pulled, forcing the metal to wrap around a form block of the desired shape. The piece is trimmed to final shape after the forming operation is completed.

When stretch forming was first devised, the operator had to continually adjust the machine and check the fit of the part to the die. Innovative, computer-controlled machines now do the work of nine older machines and all produced parts are uniform, Fig. 28-18.

Fig. 28-14. A diagram of the Hydroform process. (Allegheny Ludlum Steel Corp.)

DOME CAVITY

FLEXIBLE DIE

BLANK

DRAW RING

PUNCH

① BLANK IS PLACED ON DRAW RING

② FLEXIBLE DIE MEMBER IS LOWERED AND LOCKED INTO POSITION.

③ PRESSURE IS FLEXIBLE DIE MEMBER IS ESTABLISHED TO A PREDETERMINED SETTING AND CAN BE VARIED DURING OPERATION AS DESIRED.

EXTRA WEAR SHEET IF SO DESIRED

④ PUNCH IS MOVED UPWARD INTO THE FLEXIBLE DIE MEMBER.

⑤ FLEXIBLE DIE MEMBER IS RAISED.

⑥ THE PUNCH IS STRIPPED FROM FINISHED PART.

HOLD DOWN

KNOCKOUT ROD

PUNCH

WORK BEING BULGED

RUBBER

DIE INSERT

TWO-PIECE DIE (HINGED)

BASE

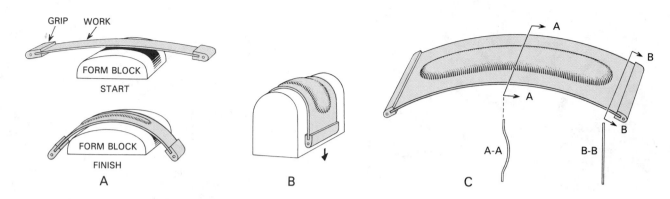

Fig. 28-17. The stretch forming process. A—Relative position of the work. Form block and clamps at the start and finish of a typical stretch forming operation produce a raised rib. B—Typical shape produced by stretch forming over a form block. C—A stretch formed shape is similar to the bottom of a canoe. The section will be riveted or welded to other sections to make the canoe.   (Allegheny Ludlum Steel Corp.)

Fig. 28-18. On this computerized machine the operator makes the first piece. All machine movements made during this initial production are recorded on a tape cassette. Subsequent parts are then made by directions given from the tape. (Grumman Aerospace Corp.)

Fig. 28-19. Forming brake. (Niagara Machine and Tool Works)

Fig. 28-20. Forming rolls.

BENDING

BENDING is the operation in which the surface area of the work is not appreciably changed. Types of conventional bending machines include the BRAKE, Fig. 28-19, FORMING ROLLS, Fig. 28-20, and TUBE BENDERS, Fig. 28-21. Several of the bending operations that can be performed on a brake are shown in Fig. 28-22.

ROLL FORMING

ROLL FORMING, Fig. 28-23, shapes a flat metal strip by passing it through a series of rollers, gradually forming it to the required shape, Fig. 28-24. The process is extremely rapid and almost any shape is possible, Fig. 28-25.

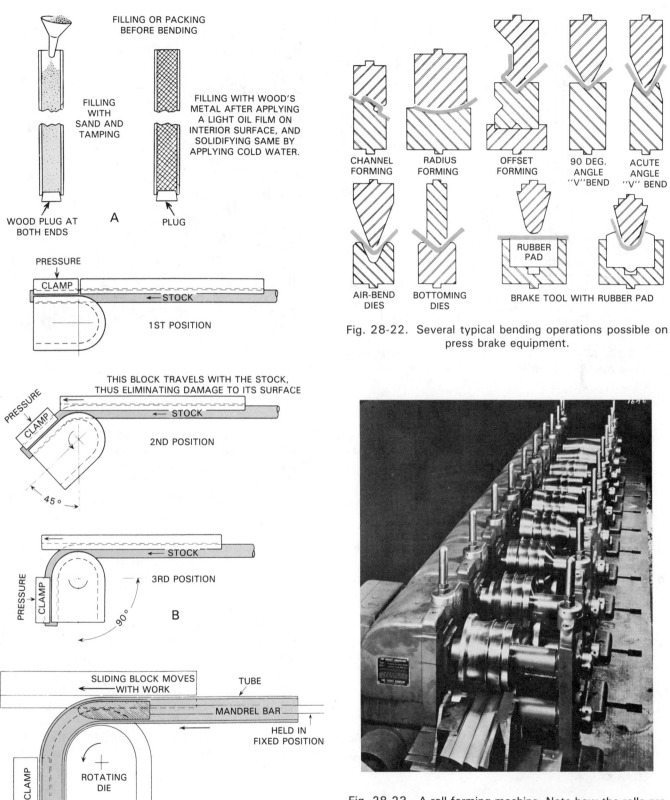

FILLING OR PACKING
BEFORE BENDING

FILLING
WITH
SAND AND
TAMPING

FILLING WITH WOOD'S
METAL AFTER APPLYING
A LIGHT OIL FILM ON
INTERIOR SURFACE, AND
SOLIDIFYING SAME BY
APPLYING COLD WATER.

WOOD PLUG AT
BOTH ENDS

A

PLUG

PRESSURE

CLAMP

STOCK

1ST POSITION

THIS BLOCK TRAVELS WITH THE STOCK,
THUS ELIMINATING DAMAGE TO ITS SURFACE

PRESSURE

CLAMP

STOCK

2ND POSITION

45°

STOCK

PRESSURE

CLAMP

3RD POSITION

90°

B

SLIDING BLOCK MOVES
WITH WORK

TUBE

MANDREL BAR

HELD IN
FIXED POSITION

CLAMP

ROTATING
DIE

C

Fig. 28-21. A diagram of the rotating die tube bending technique. A—Preparing the tube for bending. The filler material
prevents the tube from collapsing during the bending operation. B—Steps in bending a tube. C—It is not necessary to fill
the tube before bending if a reinforcing mandrel is used.
(Allegheny Ludlum Steel Corp.)

CHANNEL
FORMING

RADIUS
FORMING

OFFSET
FORMING

90 DEG.
ANGLE
"V" BEND

ACUTE
ANGLE
"V" BEND

AIR-BEND
DIES

BOTTOMING
DIES

RUBBER
PAD

BRAKE TOOL WITH RUBBER PAD

Fig. 28-22. Several typical bending operations possible on
press brake equipment.

Fig. 28-23. A roll forming machine. Note how the rolls progressively shape the metal sheet.   (Yoder Co.)

TEST YOUR KNOWLEDGE, Unit 28

Please do not write in the text. Place your
answers on a separate sheet of paper.
1. Shearing is a cutting operation that _____.

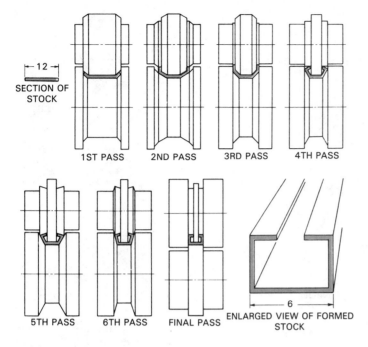

Fig. 28-24. Sequence followed for roll forming channel. Rolls are in a machine similar to the one shown in Fig. 28-23.

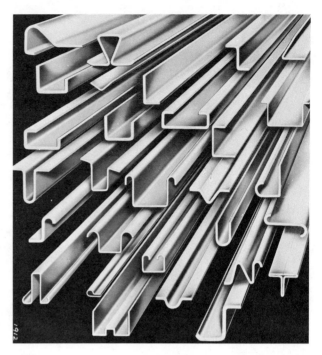

Fig. 28-25. Typical shapes made by the roll forming technique. (Yoder Co.)

2. Blanking and piercing:
   a. Cuts straight edges.
   b. Cuts flat sheet metal to the shape and size of the finished part, including cutting holes and other shape openings.
   c. Is an operation also knows as drawing.
   d. All of the above.
   e. None of the above.
3. In the forming process flat metal blanks are _____.
4. Briefly describe each of the following forming techniques:
   a. Draw press.
   b. Guerin process.
   c. Marform process.
   d. Hydroforming.
   e. Bulging.
5. Describe the stretch forming process.
6. What is roll forming?

RESEARCH AND DEVELOPMENT

1. Design a simple blanking die for use in making tool checks.

2. Secure samples of progressive die products from a local manufacturer. Get sections showing the various stages of the operation.
3. Secure samples of the drawing process at various stages of the draw. Mount them on a panel in proper sequence.
4. Develop a simple design (a small tray, coaster, etc.) and produce it by the Guerin process. Use an arbor press for pressure. If this is not suitable, design a hydraulic press that makes use of a hydraulic auto jack.
5. Use the same equipment and demonstrate the bulging process.
6. Design simple equipment to demonstrate stretch forming, use offset printing plates or heavy gauge aluminum foil for material. Produce a wing section for a model airplane.
7. Make the equipment to demonstrate tube bending. Use hardwood dies.
8. Secure samples of products made by the various cold forming processes. Mount them according to family: cutting or forming.

Unit 29

EXTRUSION PROCESSES

There are two extrusion processes used to shape metal. They are HYDRAULIC EXTRUSION and IMPACT EXTRUSION.

Hydraulic extrusion is used to manufacture irregular shapes, both solid and hollow, that cannot be made economically by any other process because of their design, Fig. 29-1. The second method which is known as impact extrusion, was used originally to form collapsible tubes—toothpaste, shaving cream, etc.—from tin and other soft metals. Today this process has been developed to such a point that items weighing up to 100 lbs. (45.0 kg) can be formed.

Hydraulic extrusion of metal may be compared to the squeezing of frosting from a tube when decorating a cake. The frosting (as it comes from the tube) assumes the shape of the nozzle on the end of the tube. In hydraulic extrusion, metal is substituted for the frosting. A press actuated by hydraulic pressure is used in place of the tube and a die is employed to shape the metal. See Figs. 29-2 and 29-3.

The metal, known as an ingot or billet, is heated to a plastic (but not molten) state and is inserted in the press. Tremendous pressures are exerted on the metal and it is literally squeezed through the die, Fig. 29-4. After forming, the piece is cut to length and straightened. Some alloys require heat treatment to develop their maximum strength.

The extrusion process is an economical method

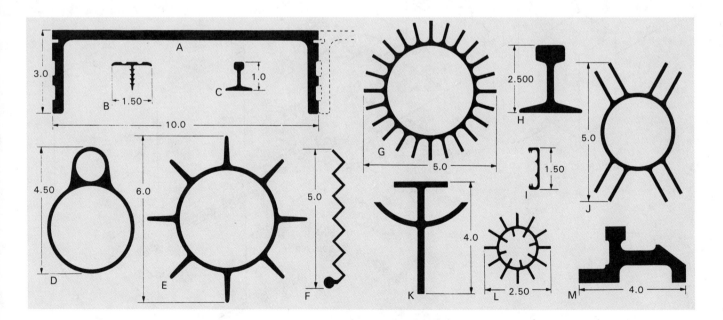

Fig. 29-1. The wide scope of extrusion applications is illustrated by this group of aluminum sections. A—Diving board. B—Table edge trim molding. C—Rail for miniature railroad. D—Milk bottle warmer. E—Heat exchanger. F—Window jalousy section. G—Shape for pencil vending machine. H—Mine track rail. I—Price tag holder for grocery store shelves. J—Hinge section for clothes drier. K—Drip catcher for roofs of textile mills. L—Heat exchanger. M—Track rail for woolen mill.   (Reynolds Metals Co.)

Fig. 29-2. A large extrusion press. Notice how it compares in size to the operator. (Reynolds Metals Co.)

of producing complex shapes.

The size of the extruded shape is limited by the press capacity. A press recently put into operation

Fig. 29-3. An extrusion die. Fitted into extrusion presses, dies shape aluminum and other metals into a wide variety of cross sections.

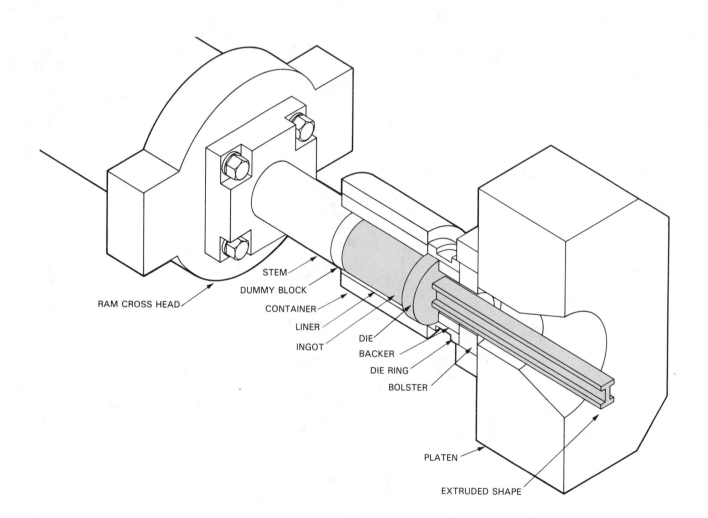

RAM CROSS HEAD
STEM
DUMMY BLOCK
CONTAINER
LINER
INGOT
DIE
BACKER
DIE RING
BOLSTER
PLATEN
EXTRUDED SHAPE

Fig. 29-4. A sectional view of an extrusion press showing the metal (billet) being extruded in the shape of a channel.

by the Air Force has made it possible to shape sections that will fit into a 24 inch circle, have a cross section areas up to 75 square inches, and weigh 25 lbs. per foot. Fig. 29-5, illustrates how sections wider than 24 inches can be made.

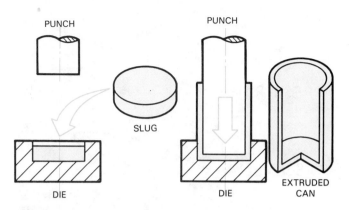

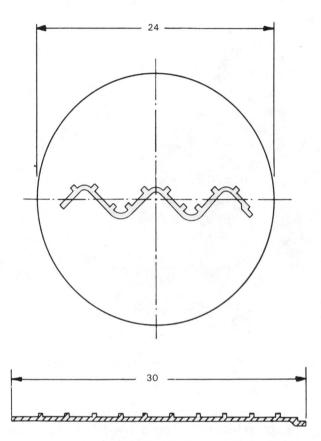

Fig. 29-5. Sections larger than the diameter of the die can be made by flattening the section after extrusion, as shown in the lower drawing. A floor section for a trailer truck is shown.

Extruded shapes are widely used in bus, truck, and trailer body construction, aircraft and missile work, machine parts, bridge rails, storm windows, store fronts, and other architectural applications.

The impact extrusion process, Fig. 29-6, was introduced to the United States shortly after World War I. The process makes it possible to produce parts that can be round, square, oval, or a combination of these shapes. The part can be solid or hollow, and can vary in size from a thimble to an item several feet high and up to a foot in diameter, Fig. 29-7.

The process can be described as the making of a part by placing a disc or slug of metal into a die cavity and applying pressure with a punch, Fig. 29-8. The pressure (cycle occurs in 1/50 to 1/100 of a second) causes the metal to ''squirt'' up the side of the punch. The wall thickness is determined by the clearance between the punch and the die.

Fig. 29-6. A diagram of the impact extrusion process. A slug is placed in the die and pressure is applied. The cycle occurs in 1/50 to 1/100 of a second.

Fig. 29-7. A sampling of the large variety of sizes and shapes that can be formed by the impact extrusion process.

TEST YOUR KNOWLEDGE, Unit 29

Please do not write in the text. Place your answers on a separate sheet of paper.
1. In the extrusion process, metal is heated to the plastic stage and literally _____ through a die of the required shape.
2. The size of the extrusion is governed by the _____ of the extrusion press.
3. What extrusion process was originally used to produce toothpaste tubes?
4. In the impact extrusion process a disc or slug of metal is placed into a die cavity. When pressure is applied, the metal:
   a. Squirts up the side of the punch.
   b. Is punched to shape.
   c. Is forced into a mold.
   d. None of the above.

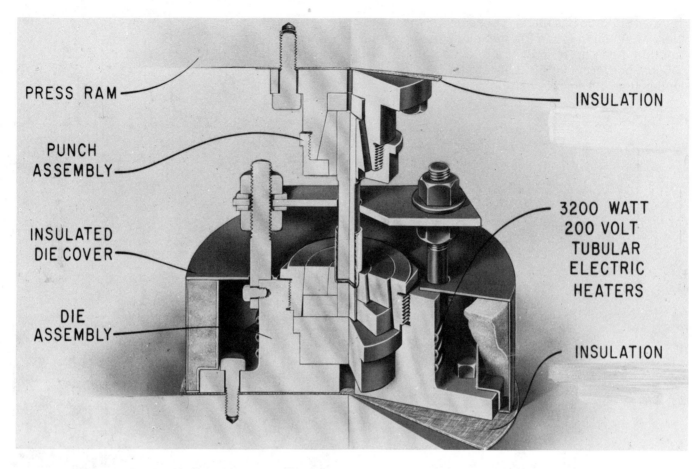

PRESS RAM

PUNCH ASSEMBLY

INSULATED DIE COVER

DIE ASSEMBLY

INSULATION

3200 WATT 200 VOLT TUBULAR ELECTRIC HEATERS

INSULATION

Fig. 29-8. Close-up of a die assembly for impact extrusion. (Dow Chemical Co.)

RESEARCH AND DEVELOPMENT

1. Demonstrate the hydraulic extrusion process by using a tube of toothpaste as the press and supply of material. Cut different shaped openings in several caps to vary the cross section of the extruded material. The demonstration can also be performed with a cake frosting tube and plaster of Paris.

2. Develop a simple method to demonstrate the impact extrusion process. Modeling clay may be used in place of the metal slug.

3. Design a display that illustrates samples of metal formed by the extrusion processes. Use thin cross sections.

4. Make transparencies of the extrusion processes for use on the overhead projector.

The extrusion process is employed to make the molding and trim on many automobiles. Complex shaped cross sections can be made quickly and economically.   (Pontiac Motor Div., GMC)

THE POWDER METALLURGY PROCESSES

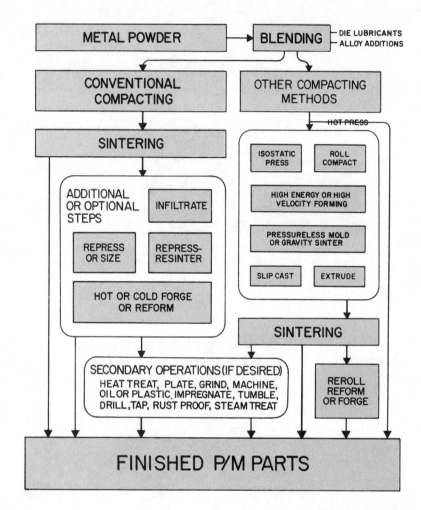

SINTERING — Sintering is a solid state phenomenon in which powdered metal particles become metallurgically bonded below the melting point of the metal. No adhesives or cements are used.

INFILTRATION — Pores of P/M parts are filled with a lower melting point metal such as copper base alloy. When the part is sintered, the infiltrant material melts and penetrates into the P/M part by capillary action.

COINING AND SIZING — Basically, this operation involves repressing sintered parts in a die similar to the original compacting die.

IMPREGNATION — The pores of the P/M part are filled with a lubricant or other non-metallic such as plastic resin. This may be done by means of a vacuum or by soaking. The part then becomes self-lubricating or pressure-tight if resin is used.

Unit 30

POWDER METALLURGY
(Sintering)

The technique of fabricating parts from metal powders usually known as POWDER METALLURGY or P/M, Figs. 30-1 and 30-2, was developed in the late twenties in the automotive industry. While the process is relatively unknown to the average person it is widely used by industry for applications such as:

1. Self-lubricating bearings and bearing materials.
2. Precision finished machine parts, gears, cams, ratchets, etc., with tolerances as close as ±.0005 in. (.0127 mm).
3. Permanent metal filters.
4. Fabricating materials that are very difficult to work by other methods:
   a. Tough cutting tools (tungsten carbide).
   b. Supermagnets (aluminum-nickel alloys—alnico).

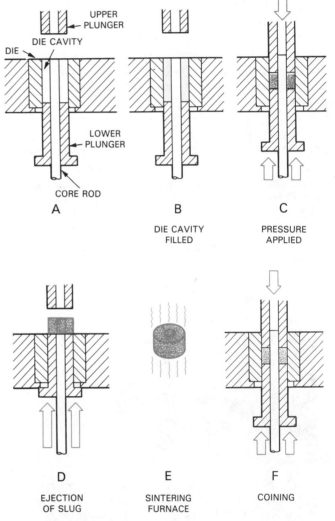

A

DIE CAVITY
FILLED
B

PRESSURE
APPLIED
C

D
EJECTION
OF SLUG

E
SINTERING
FURNACE

F
COINING

Fig. 30-2. Steps in fabricating an article by the powder metallurgy process: A—Cross section of die and die cavity. Depth of cavity is determined by thickness of required part, and amount of pressure that will be applied. B—Die cavity is filled with proper metal powder mixture. C—Pressure as high as 50 tons per square inch is applied. D—Briquette is pushed from the die cavity. E—Pieces are then passed through a sintering furnace to convert them into a strong useful product. F—Some pieces can be used as they come from the furnace. Others may require a coining or sizing operation to bring them to exact size and to improve their surface finish.

Fig. 30-1. Powder metallurgy (P/M) parts are produced by mixing carefully selected metal powders, compacting them at room temperature in a precision die, then heating (sintering) the resulting shapes to complete the metallurgical bond between the powder particles. (Metal Powder Industries Federation)

c. Mixtures of metals and ceramics for jet and missile applications that require the heat resistance of ceramics and the heat transfer qualities of metals and special cutting tools (ceramets).

d. High density counterweights for missile instruments that require maximum weight concentrated in a minimum space.

The first phase in the manufacture of powder metal products is the careful mixing of high purity metal powders, Fig. 30-3. The powders are carefully weighed and thoroughly mixed into a blend of correct proportions. Many materials—iron, steel, stainless steel, brass, bronze, nickel, chromium, and combinations of these metals and nonmetals, can be used for P/M products.

The powder blend is then fed into a precision die with a cavity that is the shape, and several times deeper than the thickness, of the desired piece. It is compressed by a lower and upper punch, Fig. 30-4. Pressures applied range from 15 to 50 tons per square inch. This portion of the operation is known as BRIQUETTING.

The piece, as ejected from the die, appears to be solid metal: however, it is quite brittle and fragile and will crumble if not handled carefully, Fig. 30-5.

To transform the briquette or "green compact" into a strong, useful unit, it must be "sintered" at 1500 to 2300 °F (815 to 1260 °C) for 30 minutes to 2 hours, depending upon the metals. This is done in a carefully controlled atmosphere furnace. See Fig. 30-6.

Fig. 30-4. Powder is compacted at pressures up to 50 tons per square inch. (Burgess-Norton Mfg. Co.)

Fig. 30-5. A close-up of the briquetting press showing "green compacts" moving to the furnace. (Delco Moraine, Div. of General Motors Corp.)

Fig. 30-3. Metal powder is blended to meet the physical requirements of the part. (Burgess-Norton Mfg. Co.)

Many parts can be used as they come from the furnace, Fig. 30-7. Because of shrinkage and distortion caused by the heating operation, the pieces may be subject to a sizing, coining, or forging operation, Fig. 30-8. This consists of pressing the sintered pieces into accurate dies to obtain precision

Fig. 30-6. The compacted P/M shape is sintered in a controlled atmosphere furnace.

Fig. 30-7. The finished pieces emerging from the sintering furnace. They may be used as is, or they may require additional operations to make them usable.

Fig. 30-8. Hot forging takes place in closed dies with the compact at red heat. (Burgess-Norton Mfg. Co.)

finish dimensions, Fig. 30-9, higher densities, and smoother surface finishes.

When the part is to be forged, it must be reheated just prior to the forging operation, Fig. 30-10.

The tool cost is moderate and the process is best suited to quantity production. If production quantities exceed several thousand units, the finished piece can frequently be produced at less than the cost of rough sand castings.

Powder metal parts can be drilled, tapped, plated, heat-treated, machined, and ground, Fig. 30-11.

Fig. 30-9. Gauging finished P/M parts to determine whether they meet design specifications. (Burgess-Norton Mfg. Co.)

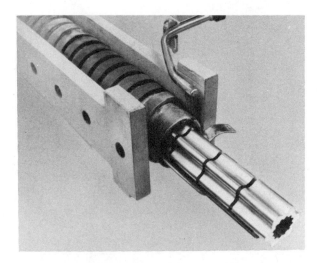

Fig. 30-10. Induction heating brings the P/M compact rapidly up to hot forging temperature. After forging, sintering is complete. (Burgess-Norton Mfg. Co.)

Powder Metallurgy (Sintering) 453

Fig. 30-11. Flat lapping (a grinding operation) to generate a micro finish is being performed on these gear faces. (Burgess-Norton Mfg. Co.)

TEST YOUR KNOWLEDGE, Unit 30

Please do not write in the text. Place your answers on a separate sheet of paper.

1. The technique of fabricating parts from metal powders is known as sintering or _____ _____.
2. The process is used to make:
   a. Self-lubricating bearings.
   b. Precision finished machine parts.
   c. Permanent metal filters.
   d. All of the above.
   e. None of the above.
3. List the steps in making an object by the sintering process.
4. Metal parts made from powder metals can be:
   a. Machined.
   b. Tapped.
   c. Heat-treated.
   d. All of the above.
   e. None of the above.

RESEARCH AND DEVELOPMENT

1. Secure a bearing and a filter made by the sintering process. (The filters on the fuel lines of some automobiles are made by this process. Such a filter has the ability to separate water from gasoline.) Examine the filter under a microscope. Make a sketch, with exaggerated detail and reproduce it. Distribute the copies to the class.
2. Contact a firm that makes metal products by the sintering process and request samples of the various sintering stages. Prepare a display panel using these samples for the class bulletin board.

Unit 31

NONTRADITIONAL MACHINING TECHNIQUES

The metalworking industry is responsible for cutting, shaping, and fabricating both metals and nonmetals. Since the range of materials is so broad, with additional ones being developed rapidly, new and different metalworking techniques have been devised. A few of these recently devised systems which differ from the traditional chip removal methods of the lathe, drill press, milling machine, grinder, and saw are described in this unit.

WATER-JET CUTTING

The advent of composites caused new problems for the metalworking areas that had to fabricate them. Most composite structures are made of ''lay-ups'' (several layers of the fabric-like materials) bonded together into three-dimensional shapes. The many sections that made the lay-ups had to be accurately cut to outline shape, Fig. 31-1. However,

Fig. 31-1. After being cut to outline shape by a computer-driven water jet (or laser) each layer of boron/epoxy material is transferred to a forming mold. Here the wing skins for the X-29 experimental aircraft are shown in the mold.   (Grumman Aerospace Corp.)

the nature of the composites quickly dulled conventional cutting tools.

WATER-JET CUTTING did the job quickly and accurately. Computer controlled, the technique uses a 55,000 psi (pounds per square inch) water jet, Fig. 31-2, to cut complex shapes from composites, thin metal sheet, and plastics with minimal waste. Tolerances can be held to ±.0004 (0.010 mm). No heat is produced to damage the material and there is little particulate (fragments) generated.

CHEMICAL MACHINING

CHEMICAL MACHINING is a refinement of one of the techniques used by the printing industry to make printing cuts and plates. Chemicals, usually in an aqueous (water) solution, etch away selected portions of the material to produce an accurately contoured part.

Chemical machining falls into two classifications:
1. CHEMICAL MILLING.
2. CHEMICAL BLANKING.

Fig. 31-2. Operating from an overhead gantry, this 6-axis robot can cut complex shapes from a sheet of raw material using a water jet.   (GCA/Industrial Systems Group)

CHEMICAL MILLING

CHEMICAL MILLING, CHEM-MILLING, or CONTOUR ETCHING is a recognized and accepted technique for controlled removal of metals by chemical action rather than by conventional machine milling.

This process is used to remove metal to exacting tolerances, on parts that are shaped in such a manner that conventional machining methods would be extremely difficult, Fig. 31-3. However, chemical milling is not recommended for castings and forgings.

Chemical milling is not a rival to conventional milling. Both processes should be considered complimentary. Basically, it is a process in which the part is immersed in an etchant (usually a strong alkaline solution) where the resulting chemical action removes the unwanted metal. Immersion time must be carefully controlled. Areas that are not to be subjected to etching must be protected by materials (called ''masks'') which do not react to the etching solution.

The principal steps in chem-milling are shown in Figs. 31-4 to 31-9.

CHEMICAL BLANKING

CHEMICAL BLANKING, CHEM-BLANKING, PHOTO CHEMICAL MACHINING, or PHOTO-ETCHING is a variation of chemical milling. The process involves total removal of metal from certain areas by chemical action. Chem-blanking is used by the aerospace and electronics industries to produce

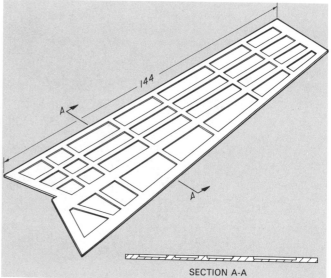

Fig. 31-3. Chemical milling is used to remove metal to close tolerances, on parts shaped in a unique manner.

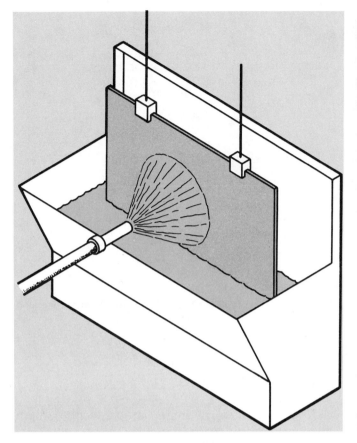

Fig. 31-4. Cleaning includes the removal of all grease and dirt that might affect the etching process.

Fig. 31-6. While scribing and stripping, a template is placed over the entire part, then the areas to be exposed are circumscribed and the masking material stripped away. (Grumman Aerospace Corp.)

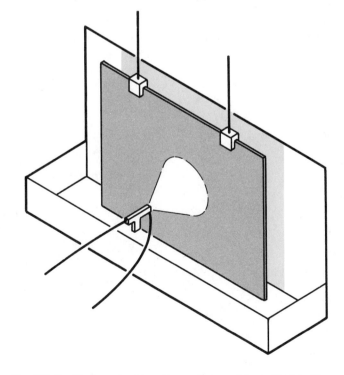

Fig. 31-5. During masking the entire part is coated with a masking material, applied by brushing, dipping, spraying, or roller coating.

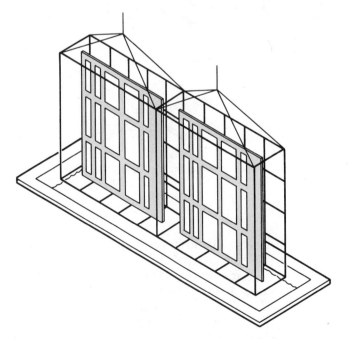

Fig. 31-7. Etching is the process of the parts being racked and lowered into the etchant for the milling operation.

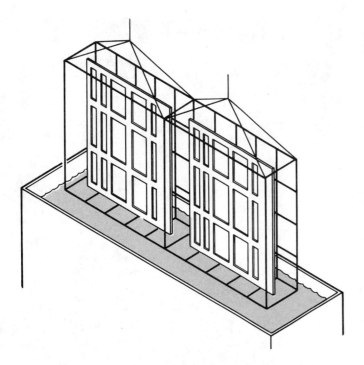

Fig. 31-8. After rinsing, in the rinsing and solvent strip phase the parts are lowered into the solvent tank which releases the maskant bond and the residue of the maskant is stripped from the part.

Fig. 31-9. Inspection includes measuring the accuracy of the chemical milling etch with the aid of an ultrasound thickness gauge.

small, intricate, ultrathin parts, Fig. 31-10.

Metal foil as thin as 0.00008 in. (0.002 mm) (a cigarette paper is 0.001 in. [0.025 mm] thick) can be worked by chem-blanking. This ultrathin metal must be laminated to a plastic backing to protect the part from damage during shipping.

The process is not recommended for metals thicker than 0.090 in. (3.00 mm). However, almost any metal can be worked.

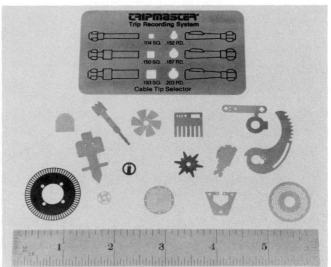

Fig. 31-10. A sampling of parts made by chemical blanking. (Microphoto, Inc.)

STEPS IN THE PROCESS

There are several major steps in the chem-blanking technique:

1. A master drawing is made of the part, Fig. 31-11. Depending upon the tolerances that must be met, it may be drawn 50 times the size of the required part.
2. The drawing is reduced photographically. This produces a film or glass master that is the exact size of the required part. Since many identical parts must be made, a multiple negative,

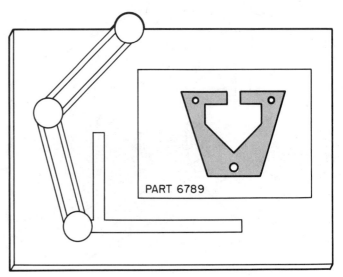

Fig. 31-11. The master drawing may be up to 50 times the size of the required part, depending on the tolerances that must be met.   (Microphoto, Inc.)

containing several images, is produced on a photorepeating machine, Fig. 31-12.

3. Metal sheet is thoroughly cleaned and coated with a photosensitive resist. The multiple image negative is contact printed on its surface. After exposure, the images are developed. The resist in unexposed areas is dissolved during the developing process and will expose bare metal, Fig. 31-13.

4. The processed metal sheet is placed in a spray etcher. Etching removes all metal not protected by the resist coating, Fig. 31-14.

5. After etching, the photo resist is removed with solvents. Visual inspection of the parts assures strict adherence to specifications, Fig. 31-15.

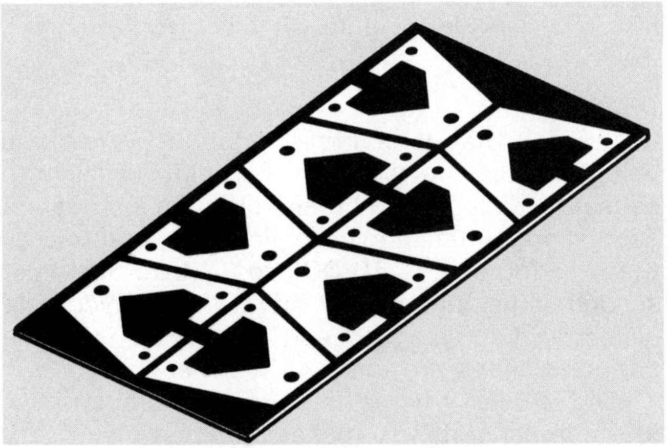

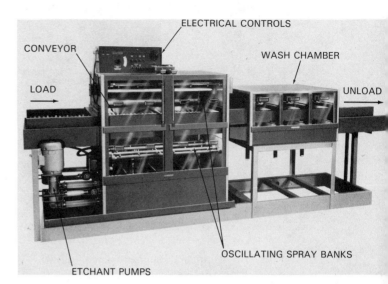

Fig. 31-14. Continuous spray etching machine. The processed metal sheet is placed in the etcher; all metal not protected by the resist coating is removed during the etching process. (Chemcut)

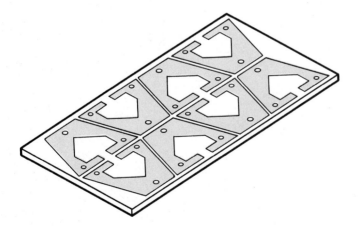

Fig. 31-12. The master drawing is photographically reduced to required size. Since many parts must be made, it is more economical to etch several at a time. (Microphoto, Inc.)

Fig. 31-15. Visually inspecting a microchip section that was chem-blanked. It will become part of the electronic control module of an automotive emission/fuel control system. (Delco Electronics, Div. of General Motors Corp.)

ELECTRICAL DISCHARGE MACHINING (EDM)

ELECTRICAL DISCHARGE MACHINING (EDM) is a process in which metals that are difficult or impossible to machine by traditional machining processes can be machined, Fig. 31-16. Metal can be machined in a heat-treated condition, eliminating the warpage and distortion that frequently occurs during the heat-treating process. Superhard metals, that previously could not be worked, are readily "cut" to tolerances as small as 0.0005 in. (0.013 mm) with very fine surface finishes.

Fig. 31-13. The metal sheet, with a photosensitive coating, has the image of the part contact printed on its surface using the multiple part negative. During development, the photosensitive material in the unexposed areas is dissolved, exposing bare metal. (Microphoto, Inc.)

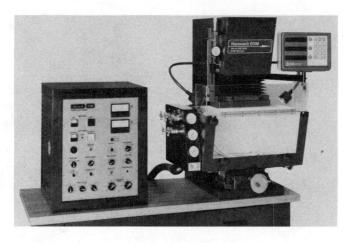

Fig. 31-16. An electrical discharge machine (EDM).
(Hansvedt Industries, Inc.)

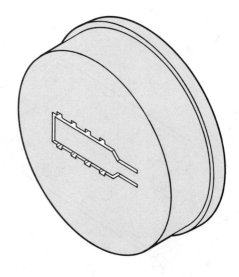

Fig. 31-18. An EDM electrode must be an exact reversal or mirror image of the cut to be made.

HOW EDM WORKS

Almost everyone is familiar with the sparking and arcing that occurs when an electrical switch is turned on or off. The "pitting" or "burning" that occurs on the switch contacts is the basis of electrical discharge machining.

An electrical discharge unit, Fig. 31-17, is composed of a power supply to provide DC current and act as a method to control voltage and frequency; an electrode of the proper configuration, Fig. 31-18; a servomechanism to accurately control electrode movement so the correct distance between it and the work can be maintained as the machining is done; and a coolant, usually a light oil, that forms a dielectric barrier between the electrode and the work at the arc gap.

The servomechanism maintains a very thin gap (about 0.001 in. or 0.025 mm) between the electrode and the work. These are submerged in a fluid

(dielectric) that is a non-conductor. When the voltage across the gap reaches a point sufficient to cause the dielectric to break down, an arc occurs. Each spark erodes a minute piece of metal, but as the sparking occurs 20,000 to 30,000 times per second, large quantities of metal are removed. The dielectric fluid also flushes the particles from the gap, and keeps the tool and work cool.

EDM is used where the physical characteristics of the metal or its use makes it impossible or very expensive to machine by conventional methods. See Fig. 31-19.

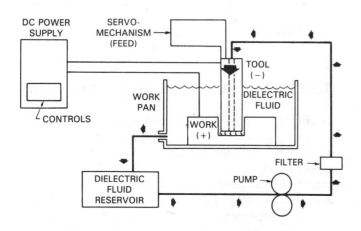

Fig. 31-17. A diagram showing the principle used by the EDM process.

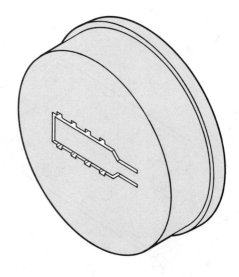

Fig. 31-19. Die blanks, like this extrusion die used for producing storm window sections, can be machined by EDM while in the heat-treated stage. The job can be done quickly, with no possibility of the die warping, and at a considerable saving over traditional machining techniques.

ELECTRO CHEMICAL MACHINING (ECM)

ELECTRO CHEMICAL MACHINING (more commonly known as ECM) might be classified as electroplating in reverse. As in electroplating, the process requires DC electricity and a suitable electrolyte (an electrically conductive fluid); however, the metal is removed from the work rather than being deposited, Fig. 31-20.

A stream of electrolyte, usually common salt (NaCl) mixed with water, is pumped at high pressure through a gap between the positively (+) charged work and the negatively (−) charged shaped tool called the electrode. The current passing through the gap removes metal from the work by electrolysis, duplicating in reverse the shape of the electrode as it is advanced into the material. In some applications, tolerances as close as 0.0004 in. (0.010 mm) can be maintained.

Metal is removed rapidly and difficult shapes can be machined easily, Fig. 31-21. The work is not touched by the tool, there is no friction, no heat, no sparking, and no tool wear. The machined surface is burr free and in some instances, highly polished. Machine operation, Fig. 31-22, is most unique as the only sound heard is the rush of liquid, Fig. 31-23.

Fig. 31-21. Complex shapes like the blades on this titanium turbine wheel can be machined at the rate of 1/4 in. (6.35 mm) a minute. Two wheels are machined simultaneously.

Fig. 31-20. Vertical ECM machine. The size of the work enclosure and fixed open height impose limits on the size of the work and fixtures that can be accommodated under the ram. (ANOCUT Engineering Co.)

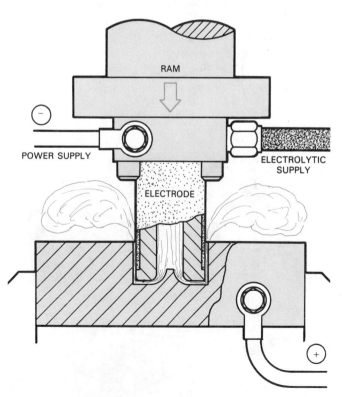

Fig. 31-22. How electro chemical machining (ECM) process works.

Fig. 31-23. The rush of the electrolyte fluid is the only noise heard when ECM is being done.

ELECTRON BEAM MACHINING

The development of the ELECTRON BEAM CUTTER-WELDER MACHINE TOOL, Fig. 31-24, is the direct result of the special needs of the atomic energy, electronics, and aerospace industries. In some aspects, electron beam machining is the most precise and versatile of the nontraditional machining techniques. Any known metal or nonmetal can be cut by this process.

Fig. 31-24. Electron beam welder.
(Hamilton Standard Div., United Technologies)

EB cutting action can be controlled so precisely that it is possible to drill holes as small as 0.0002 in. (0.005 mm) in diameter, Fig. 31-25, and machine slots with widths of only 0.0005 in. (0.013 mm). Cut geometry (shape) is controlled by movement of the worktable in the vacuum chamber and by using the deflection coil to bend the beam of electrons to the desired cutting path, Fig. 31-26. Hole diameter is controlled by the amount of power applied and length of cutting time.

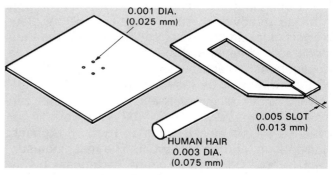

Fig. 31-25. Size of work done by the electron beam (EB) technique. The parts machined and the human hair are drawn to the same scale.

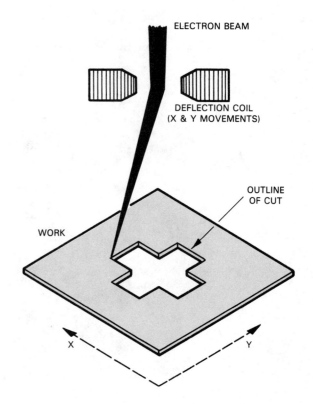

Fig. 31-26. The path of the cut is controlled by deflecting the electron beam or by movement of the worktable. The work must be done in a vacuum.

The EB machine is similar in some respects to a television set. In the TV, a heated tungsten filament emits a beam of electrons. The beam is concentrated by an electron focusing system into a small diameter beam that is moved so rapidly by a deflection system that a picture is produced on a fluorescent screen (TV tube).

The EB machine tool makes use of a beam that is several times more intense than the one used to produce a television picture. Controls similar to those on the TV set are used to focus and adjust the electron beam for useful work. It is basically a source of thermal energy. The beam of electrons can be focused to a very sharp point. Cutting is achieved by alternately heating and cooling the area to be cut. This must be done carefully so the material at the point of focus is heated high enough to vaporize it, yet not cause the surrounding area to melt. This is done by a pulsing technique. The beam is on for only a few milliseconds and is extinguished for a considerably longer time. Temperature of 12,000°F (6649°C) can be achieved at the focal point of the beam.

LASER MACHINING

The LASER produces a narrow and intense beam of light that can be focused optically onto an area only a few microns in diameter. Depending upon the initial energy source used to activate the laser, it is possible to instantly create temperatures up to 75,000°F (41 649°C) at the point of focus, Fig. 31-27. No known material can withstand such heat.

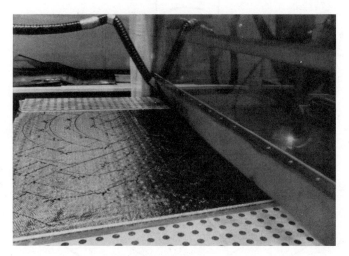

Fig. 31-27. This N/C controlled laser is cutting graphite composite aircraft sections with great accuracy. The laser cut outline is smooth with no burrs or rough edges. The transparent shield allows operators to observe the cutting operation while protecting their eyes from the intense light of the laser.
(Grumman Aerospace Corp.)

When used for machining and cutting, the energy output of the laser is not continuous, but rather, operates at 1 to 5 cycles per second. The cycle can be controlled manually or electronically. The laser operates on the principle shown in Fig. 31-28.

As the intense light of the laser can easily damage or destroy the operator's vision if viewed, closed circuit TV is usually employed as a means of assuring technician safety. Television cannot transmit laser light, but only an electrical signal that can be controlled.

ULTRASONIC MACHINING

ULTRASONIC MACHINING (also known as IMPACT MACHINING and SLURRY MACHINING) is based on the science of silent sound. The average person can hear sounds that vibrate between 20 to 20,000 cycles per second. Below 20 cycles per second, sound waves are known as INFRASONIC. Above 20,000 cycle per second, sound waves are known as ULTRASONIC. Industrial applications utilize energy up to 100,000 cycles per second. In addition to machining, ultrasonics are employed in welding, in quality control, and for cleaning purposes.

Ultrasonic waves are created by passing an electric current (usually 60 cycle AC) into a suitable generator (transducer) that changes the electrical energy to mechanical energy. In ultrasonic machining, the energy is applied directly to the cutting tool, Fig. 31-29.

Machining is done by a shaped cutting tool that oscillates about 25,000 times per second. It pounds a slurry of fine abrasive particles against the work. The tool stroke at the vibrating end is only 0.003 in. (0.076 mm), Fig. 31-30. The tool does not touch the work. No heat is generated, eliminating any possibility of the work becoming distorted.

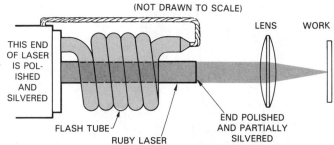

(NOT DRAWN TO SCALE)

THIS END OF LASER IS POLISHED AND SILVERED

LENS   WORK

FLASH TUBE   RUBY LASER   END POLISHED AND PARTIALLY SILVERED

Fig. 31-28. The ruby laser is one type of laser device used by industry. In one technique, the helical flash tube produces an intense flash of light. After the chromium atoms in the ruby laser are pumped by the flash to a higher energy level, they are reflected back and forth between the mirrors and grow in intensity. At a critical point an intense red beam flashes out of the partially silvered end of the crystal and is focused onto the work.

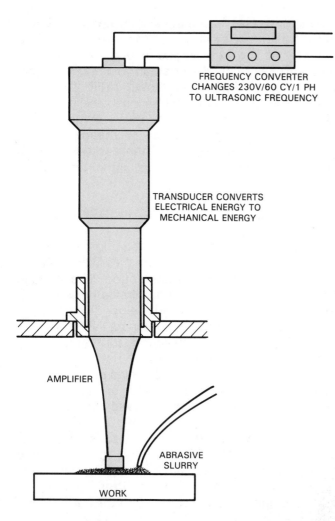

FREQUENCY CONVERTER
CHANGES 230V/60 CY/1 PH
TO ULTRASONIC FREQUENCY

TRANSDUCER CONVERTS
ELECTRICAL ENERGY TO
MECHANICAL ENERGY

AMPLIFIER

ABRASIVE
SLURRY

WORK

Fig. 31-29. Ultrasonic machining setup.

Minute particles of the work are chipped away to produce the shape desired. The machined section is a mirror image of the cutting tool, Fig. 31-31.

The solid funnel-shaped horn must be used to amplify and transmit the vibrations because the ultrasonic vibrations coming directly from the transducer do not produce enough motion to provide the required tool movement.

The process is slow and the surface finish is dependent on the grit size of the abrasive used. One inch (25.4 mm) is about the deepest cut possible with existing equipment. Tolerances of 0.001 in. (0.025 mm) can be maintained on hole size and geometry in most materials. Equipment cost is moderate and the training period for machine operators is short and does not require special skills.

HIGH ENERGY RATE FORMING (HERF)

The introduction of super-tough alloys and the need for shaping thin, brittle metals has been responsible for developing new ways to do the work. These new techniques are known as HIGH ENERGY RATE FORMING or HERF. The metal is shaped in microseconds with pressure generated by the sudden application of large amounts of energy. The great pressurs needed are generated by detonating explosives, releasing compressed

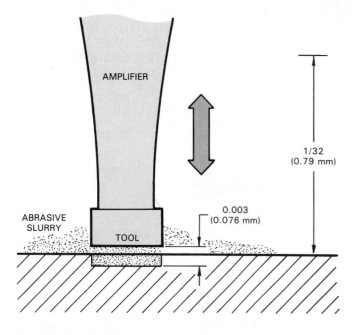

AMPLIFIER

1/32
(0.79 mm)

0.003
(0.076 mm)

ABRASIVE
SLURRY

TOOL

Fig. 31-30. Tool motion in ultrasonic (impact) machining is slight—only 0.003 in. (0.076 mm). (The 1/32 in. [0.79 mm] is for reference purposes only.)

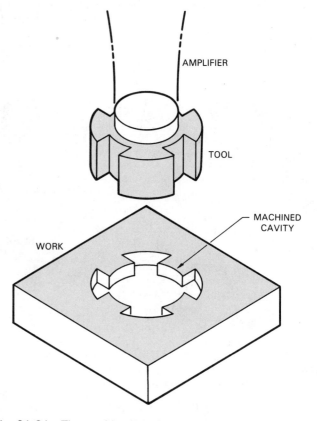

AMPLIFIER

TOOL

MACHINED
CAVITY

WORK

Fig. 31-31. The machined section is a mirror image of the tool.

gases, or discharging powerful electrical sparks or electromagnetic force.

EXPLOSIVE FORMING

The sheer size of some aerospace and marine components (up to 144 in. by 230 in. by 1 in. thick or 3657 mm by 5842 mm by 25.4 mm thick) makes it impossible to form them on existing presses. The presses are either too small or not powerful enough to shape the high strength alloys.

EXPLOSIVE FORMING uses a high energy pressure pulse of very short duration to do the work.

The pressure pulse can be generated by a chemical explosive or electrical discharge in a fluid to force the metal being formed against the walls of the die, Fig. 31-32. The fluid has the effect of rounding off the pressure pulse generated by the detonation.

One advantage of explosive forming is the greatly reduced lead required. (Lead is the time needed to get the part into production and produce the first piece.) For example, when the San Francisco Bay Naval Shipyard was constructing SEALAB II, two 144 in. (3657 mm) diameter dished heads made from 1 in. (25.4 mm) thick steel were needed to cap the vessel ends, Fig. 31-33. The parts could

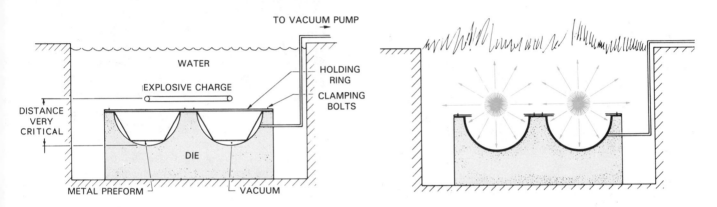

Fig. 31-32. This diagram illustrates the principle of the explosive forming process. Fifty cents worth of explosives, in some applications, will do the work of a press that costs hundreds of thousands of dollars.

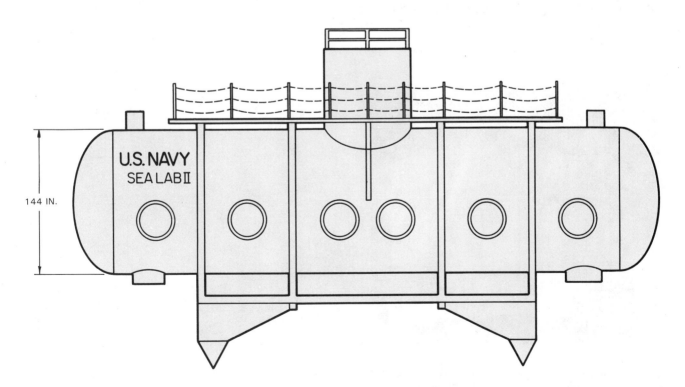

Fig. 31-33. Domes used to cap the ends of SEALAB II were shaped using explosive forming. Since no tank large enough was available to hold the die and blank, engineers used San Francisco Bay to contain the explosion.

have been spun but would require six months for delivery. Work could not be held up for that length of time so in less than a week the shipyard engineers constructed a die of concrete faced with an epoxy/glass fiber laminate. It was calculated that 100 lbs. of explosive would be required. Since there was no tank large enough to hold them, the 60 ton die and workpiece was moved to San Francisco Bay and lowered to a depth of 30 ft. After detonation, the parts were examined and found to be within 1/16 in. (1.6 mm) of being circular and no more than 1/4 in. (6.4 mm) off at any point in the desired shape.

Quite often the preform, or metal section to be shaped, can be fabricated by welding to a shape predetermined by the contours of the finished piece, Fig. 31-34. It is then placed in the die, the tank is filled with water, and an explosive form is suspended above the preform.

A large ring, clamped over the outer edge of the work, assures the necessary seal for drawing a vacuum in the die. If a vacuum could not be drawn below the part, the compressed air that would result below the work would cause the part to spring back and it would not assume the shape of the die, Fig. 31-35.

The distance between the explosive and the preform is of critical importance. If it is too close, the pressure pulse could perforate the metal; too far away, the preform would not be forced against the die.

A surge of electrical energy can also be employed to produce the high energy pressure pulse in much the same way as a chemical explosive, Fig. 31-36.

Fig. 31-35. Once resembling a cake pan, the exploded metal is now doughnut shaped. Shaped by the die underneath, metal clamps around the die edge secured a holding ring which assured the tight seal necessary for drawing a vacuum into the die during the explosion. (Martin Marietta)

Fig. 31-34. Welding the preform of a torus (doughnut) shaped tank for explosive forming. Formed by conventional techniques, it would require 40 sections rather than 12 and would need 60 percent more weld footage. (Martin Marietta)

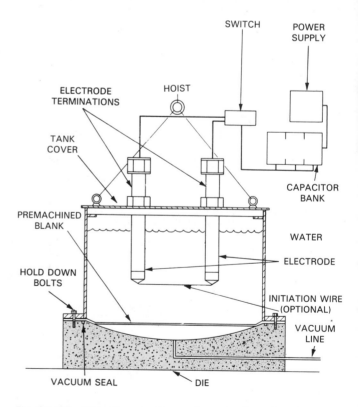

Fig. 31-36. This diagram shows the setup for using electrical energy as a source of power. (NASA)

The electrical energy is stored in devices, called capacitor banks, until needed.

The controlled discharge of this electrical energy across a gap between two electrodes or across an exploding bridge wire submerged in water produces a high energy shock wave. This wave radiates out from the electrodes and forces the metal part against the die face.

When electrical energy is utilized to produce the energy pulse, the process is also known as ELECTROHYDRAULIC FORMING.

MAGNETIC FORMING

MAGNETIC FORMING, also known as ELECTROMAGNETIC FORMING or MAGNETIC PULSE FORMING, uses an insulated induction coil either wrapped around or placed within the work, depending on whether the metal is to be squeezed inward or bulged outward, Figs. 31-37 through 31-40. The coil is shaped to produce the desired contours in the work.

As very high momentary currents are passed through the coil, an intense magnetic field is developed that causes the work to collapse, compress, shrink, or expand depending on the design and placement of the coil, Fig. 31-41.

The power source is basically the same as that used for electrohydraulic forming—a capacitor bank. The spark gap is replaced by a coil. Energy is obtained by capacitor discharge through the coil.

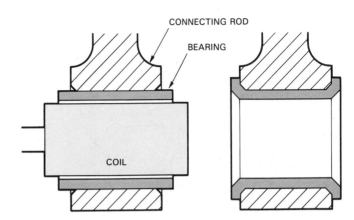

Fig. 31-38. Utilizing magnetic pulse forming to expand a bearing sleeve into a connecting rod.

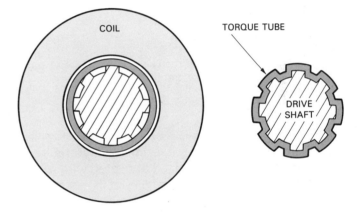

Fig. 31-39. Compressing a torque tube on an automotive drive shaft.

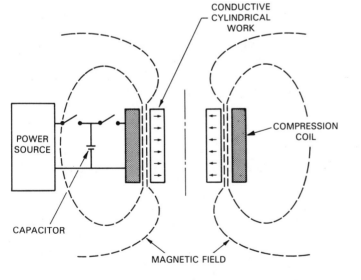

Fig. 31-37. How magnetic pulse metal forming works. A heavy magnetic field is produced by discharging a capacitor through a coil in a period of microseconds. During the brief impulse, eddy currents in the work restrict the magnetic field to the surface of the work, creating a uniform force to form the metal. The process can be used directly on highly conductive metals. Low conductive metals can be shaped by using aluminum (highly conductive) between the work and the coils.

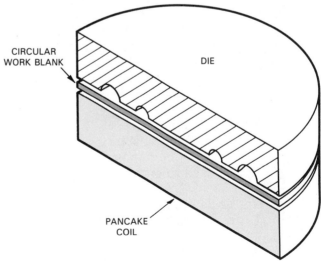

Fig. 31-40. Flat forming applications (forcing sheet metal into a die) requires a pancake coil to provide uniform magnetic pressure.

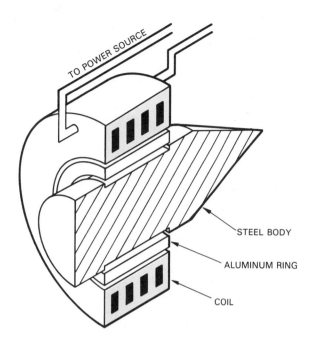

Fig. 31-41. A magnetic field can also be employed to shrink or squeeze parts together.

Highly conductive metals can be formed easily. Nonconductive or low-conductivity materials can be formed if they are wrapped or coated with a high-conductivity auxilary material that is usually removed after forming.

TEST YOUR KNOWLEDGE, Unit 31

Please do not write in the text. Place your answers on a separate sheet of paper.
1. Briefly describe water-jet cutting.
2. Chemical machining is the process that:
   a. Removes metal by immersing in a fluid; the fluid is heated to remove the metal.
   b. Requires an acid be poured over the metal to etch away the metal that is not needed.
   c. Removes metal with an etchant rather than by conventional machining.
   d. All of the above.
   e. None of the above.
3. The immersion time must be _____ or too much metal will be removed.
4. A mask is used to protect the portion of the job that is:
   a. Not to be etched.
   b. To be etched.
   c. To be cleaned.
   d. All of the above.
   e. None of the above.
5. List the four steps in the chem-blanking technique.

Match each word or phrase in the left column with the correct sentence in the right column.
6. ____ Electrical discharge machining.
7. ____ Electro chemical machining.
8. ____ Electron beam machining.
9. ____ Laser machining.
10. ____ Ultrasonic.
11. ____ Infrasonic.
12. ____ Impact machining.
13. ____ High energy rate forming.

   a. Sound waves below 20 cycles per second.
   b. Uses an intense beam of light to cut material.
   c. Sound waves above 20,000 cycles per second.
   d. Focused electron beam vaporizes the material at the cutting point.
   e. An electric spark is used to erode the metal.
   f. Electroplating in reverse.
   g. Ultrasonic sound pounds a slurry of fine abrasive particles against the work.
   h. Metal shaped in microseconds by pressure wave generated by chemical explosives, powerful electric sparks, or electromagnetic force.

14. Briefly describe the electrical discharge machining technique.
15. In electro chemical machining how does the shape of the tool affect the shape of the cut?
16. Beside the high heat generated, from what other danger must the operator of a laser machining tool be protected?
17. Prepare a sketch of the explosive forming technique, using chemical explosives.
18. Why is the placement of the explosive important in explosive forming?
19. HERF stands for _____.
20. What is unique about magnetic forming?

RESEARCH AND DEVELOPMENT

1. Examine technical publications for information on water-jet cutting. Prepare a report on your findings.
2. Prepare a series of transparencies for use with an overhead projector, showing the chemical milling sequence.
3. Secure information on chemical blanking from technical magazines and prepare a short paper on the latest developments in this area. Make drawings of several parts made by this process.
4. Develop and construct equipment to do chemi-

cal milling in the school shop. Prepare a technical paper with photographs. Submit it to a professional industrial education magazine.

5. Secure samples of superhard and/or fragile metals—carbide cutting tools, stainless steel, or aluminum honeycomb, for example. Try to work them with conventional hand cutting tools. Prepare a report on your success or failure in working these materials.

6. Some of the larger tool and metalworking machinery supply houses have demonstration models of electrical discharge machining units. Contact such firms and try to borrow samples of metals worked by the technique along with the electrodes used.

7. Research a paper on EB machining and welding techniques. Include the history of its development and how the atomic energy, electronics, and aerospace industries utilize the unique characteristics of the electron beam machine.

8. Illustrate the operating principle of the laser.

9. Research the history of the laser. Include some of the other applications in which it is used.

10. Demonstrate how ultrasonic sound waves can be measured. Borrow a transducer and oscilloscope from the science department.

11. Gather information on other uses of ultrasonics and prepare a bulletin board display around the information.

12. Design and construct an impact machining device. Demonstrate it on various materials. Prepare an evaluation of your work.

13. Explosives are used in other facets of metalworking such as cutting, shearing, and punching metal; joining, welding, and cladding; forming powder metal parts; and improving metallurgical properties of metals. Research these applications and write a paper about them.

14. Trace the history of explosive forming. Begin in 1888 when C.E. Monroe inscribed metal engraving using this technique.

15. Secure information on various HERF techniques from trade journals and from companies using HERF. Make this material into a bulletin board display.

The partnership of technology and skill of a craftworker results in precision wax tooling. This is the first step—and a critical one—in the manufacture of castings which meet exacting quality control standards.

Unit 32

QUALITY CONTROL

The primary purpose of QUALITY CONTROL is to seek out potential product defects before they can cause damage and to prevent their occurrence in the manufacturing process, Fig. 32-1.

Quality control can be divided into two classifications:

1. DESTRUCTIVE TESTING. The part is destroyed during the test period.
2. NONDESTRUCTIVE TESTING. This testing procedure does not destroy or damage the product or part. It can be used for the purpose for which it was originally intended.

DESTRUCTIVE TESTING

DESTRUCTIVE TESTING is a costly, time consuming, unreliable testing technique. It is an indirect process whereby the test specimen is selected at random from a given number of pieces and, statistically at least, indicates the characteristics of the undestroyed and untested remaining pieces. This method is used only when absolutely necessary. An example would be the controlled crashing of automobiles to determine, theoretically, whether drivers and front-seat passengers would

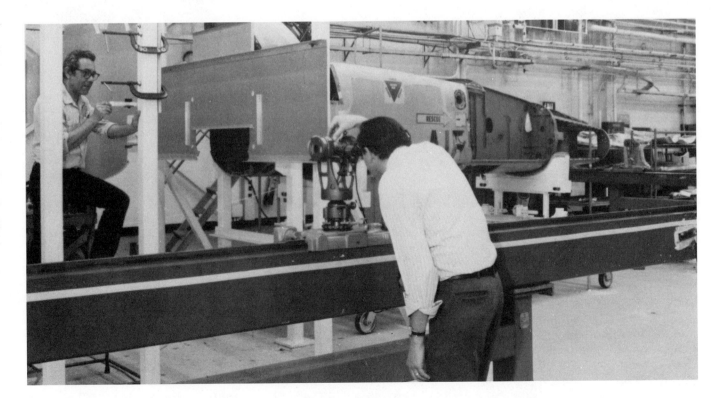

Fig. 32-1. The eventual goal of quality control is not to detect imperfect parts and discard them, but to prevent them from ever being made. The nose section of this aircraft was made in California and is being prepared for attachment to the engine and tail sections that were made in Long Island, New York. Quality control assured a proper fit. (Grumman Aerospace Corp.)

survive a similar type of accident. The test vehicle is destroyed and cannot be used again.

NONDESTRUCTIVE TESTING

NONDESTRUCTIVE TESTING programs are well adapted to electronic and aerospace vehicles where the performance of each of the thousands of parts is critical. Each piece can be tested and compared for its conformity to specifications.

METHODS OF NONDESTRUCTIVE TESTING

You are familiar with many methods of non-destructive testing; measuring, weighing, and visual conventional measuring tools cannot be used to give accurate measurements. Tools have been devised that measure electronically and check thousands of individual reference points on the object against specifications, Fig. 32-2.

Precise visual inspection can be done with an optical comparator, Fig. 32-3. An enlarged image of the part being inspected is projected on a screen where it is superimposed upon an accurate drawing overlay of the part. Variations as small as 0.0005 in. (0.013 mm) will be noted by a skilled operator.

Quality control can also be assured by statistical means. This is done by measuring a number of parts in a production run, Fig. 32-4. This is a carefully

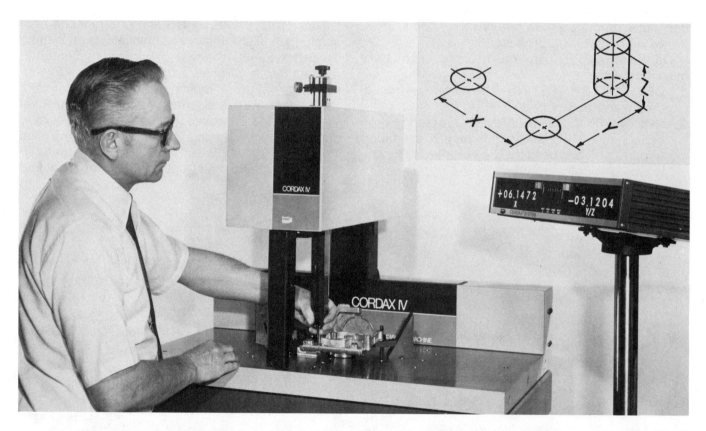

Fig. 32-2. Small, direct-reading measuring devices, like the Bendix CORDAX IV Measuring Machine, bring advanced measurement technology within the scope of the small shop. Measurements can be made in two or three planes (X, Y, and Z) without error. Measurements are shown up to 0.0002 in. (0.005 mm). English to metric conversion is accomplished with the push of a button. (Bendix, Automation & Measurement Div.)

observation. This simple type of quality control is satisfactory for many products, but for others it leaves much to be desired. Industry has developed many testing techniques to eliminate these shortcomings.

MEASURING

The shape of some products is so complex that worked out mathematical approach to quality control. If there is a wide variation in the accuracy of the part being inspected it will be necessary to increase the inspection rate to include all of the units manufactured.

Special measuring fixtures, Fig. 32-5, are employed when large numbers of the product must be checked for accuracy and it must be done rapidly.

Fig. 32-3. Checking the hole location on the plate lamination of an automatic lock body assembly, using a Shadograph with a part overlay transparency. (Master Lock Co.)

Fig. 32-5. Checking the shape of a turbine blade for a jet engine with a Guillotine type gauge. (Westinghouse Electric Corp.)

RADIOGRAPHIC (X RAY) INSPECTION

Inspection by radiography has become a routine step in the acceptance of critical parts and materials, Fig. 32-6. The technique involves the use of X rays and gamma radiation (highly energetic, penetrating radiation found in certain radioactive elements)

Fig. 32-4. Performing frequency distribution on plate lamination thickness, using a digimatic micrometer and a digimatic mini-processor. (Master Lock Co.)

Fig. 32-6. This laser alignment device is used with an X-ray generator to precisely locate X-ray radiation on an electron beam welded titanium structure. Highly accurate alignment is required due to the very narrow heat affected zone characteristics of EB welds. (Grumman Aerospace Corp.)

projected through the object being inspected, onto a film, Fig. 32-7. The developed film has an image of the internal structure of the part or assembly.

Many kinds of peripheral (outside circumference) inspection operations can be performed because of the omnidirectional (all directions) characteristics of radiation, Fig. 32-8.

Extreme care must be taken when using radiographic inspection techniques because of the harmful effects prolonged exposure to radiation has on the human body.

ducting sound.

With this technique, sound waves in the millions of cycles per second frequency (the human ear can only hear sound waves in the 20 to 20,000 cycles per second range) are transmitted through the material and flaws, which reflect the sound beam, and are detected on an oscilloscope, Fig. 32-10.

The high frequency sound needed for ultrasonic testing is produced by a piezoelectric transducer (electricity produced by pressure on a nonconducting crystal) which is electrically pulsed, Fig. 32-11, and then vibrates at its own natural frequency. For

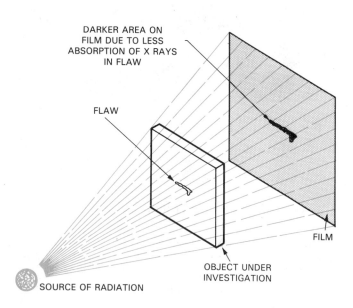

Fig. 32-7. How radiographic inspection works.

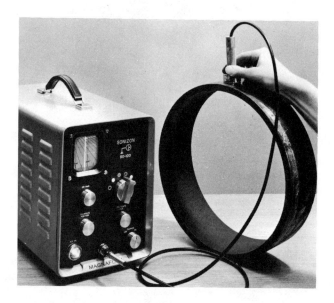

Fig. 32-9. The ultrasonic testing device is often called a "one arm micrometer." It makes thickness measurements as quickly as the probe can be moved over the surface, then reports findings on a direct reading scale on the face of the cathode ray tube. (Magnaflux Corp.)

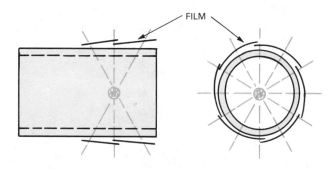

Fig. 32-8. Technique used to inspect cylindrical objects by radiographic means.

ULTRASONIC TESTING

ULTRASONIC TESTING techniques utilize sound waves above the audible range to detect cracks and flaws in a product, or to measure its thickness, Fig. 32-9. It is possible to do nondestructive testing on almost any kind of material that is capable of con-

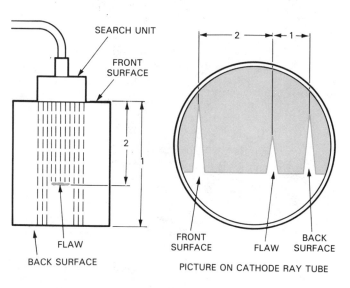

Fig. 32-10. Detecting and locating a flaw in a test piece.

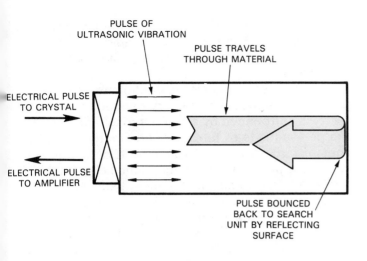

Fig. 32-11. How sound waves are employed to locate flaws in material.

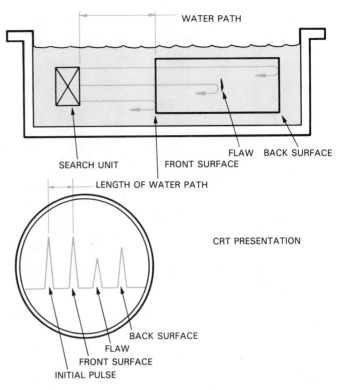

Fig. 32-13. Immersion type ultrasonic testing. Note the extra "pip" on the CRT.

best results, the transducer must be coupled to the piece being tested by a liquid coupling such as a film of oil, glycerine, or water, or by immersing both the test piece and transducer in water, Figs. 32-12 and 32-13.

There is no size limitation on work that can be tested by ultrasonic techniques, Fig. 32-14.

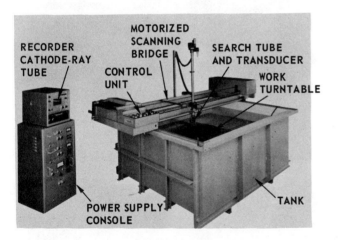

Fig. 32-12. Complete automatic ultrasonic immersion testing system.   (The Budd Co., Instrument Div.)

FLUORESCENT PENETRANT INSPECTION

The theory of FLUORESCENT PENETRANT IN-SPECTION, Fig. 32-15, is based on capillary action. The penetrant solution is applied to the surface of the part being inspected by dipping, spraying, or brushing. Capillary action literally pulls the solution into the defect. The surface is rinsed clean, and before or after drying, a wet or dry developer is applied. This acts like a blotter, and draws the

penetrant back to the surface.

When inspected under black light, any defects glow with fluorescent brilliance, marking the defect.

SPOTCHECK (Trademark: Magnaflux Corp.)

SPOTCHECK, Fig. 32-16, is another of the penetrant type inspection techniques. It is easy to use, economical, and does not require a black light to bring out the flaws. Application is similar to that described for the fluorescent type penetrant. The specimen is coated with a red liquid dye which

Fig. 32-14. Ultrasonic testing of a large gear blank reveals subsurface flaws.   (Philadelphia Gear Corp.)

Fig. 32-15. Three ways to inspect a kingpin of a truck front axle. Left—Under visual inspection, the part is apparently sound, and safe for service. Center—Inspection with Magnaflux reveals dangerous cracks caused during the grinding operations. Right—Treated with a fluorescent penetrant testing material and photographed under black light, the same cracks are revealed. (Magnaflux Corp.)

magnetized. It is sometimes called magnetic particle inspection. The technique is rapid, but shows only serious defects, not scratches or minor visual defects.

The magnetic particle inspection technique is based on the theory that every conductor of electricity is surrounded by a circular magnetic field. If the part is made of ferromagnetic material, these lines of force will, to a large extent, be contained within the piece. A circular magnetic field, if not interrupted, has no poles. However, because a flaw or other imperfection present in the part is oriented to cut through these lines of magnetic force, poles will form at each edge of the flaw. These poles will hold the finely divided magnetic particles, thus outlining the flaw. The limitations of this technique are apparent when the flaw is parallel to the line of

soaks into the surface crack or flaw. The liquid is washed off and the part dried. A developer is then dusted or sprayed on the part. Flaws and cracks show up red against the white background of the developer.

MAGNAFLUX (Trademark: Magnaflux Corp.)

MAGNAFLUX, Fig. 32-17, is a method of non-destructive testing used on materials that can be

Fig. 32-17. Magnafluxing a large crankshaft to determine whether any flaws have developed during use.

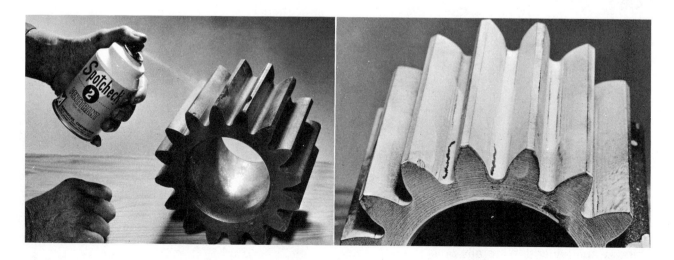

Fig. 32-16. With the Spotcheck penetrant inspection technique, the part being inspected is cleaned of grease and dirt, then sprayed with the penetrant. After the part is dry, the developer is applied, and the part is inspected for flaws. Flaws not seen before the part was treated, are now visible to the naked eye. (Magnaflux Corp.)

magnetic force. The flaw will not interrupt the force, so no indication of it will appear when the magnetic particles are applied, Fig. 32-18.

A magnetic field is introduced into the part and fine particles of iron are blown (dry method) or flowed in liquid suspension (wet method) over the part. Because the flaw will disturb or distort the magnetic field, it will have different magnetic properties than the surrounding material. Many of the iron particles will be attracted to the area and form a definite indication of the flaw, (its exact location, shape, and extent) Fig. 32-19.

tronically, Fig. 32-21, with a PROFILOMETER.

Because of the versatility of the computer, many new quality control techniques will be developed as the need arises. The computer will also make 100 percent inspection possible. This will not be done so imperfect parts will be detected and discarded but to prevent them from ever being made.

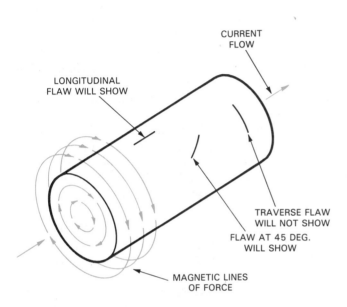

Fig. 32-18. The theory, scope, and limitations of the magnetic particle inspection procedure.   (Magnaflux Corp.)

Fig. 32-20. Checking the surface finish on a machined part to determine whether it meets specifications. The device used is a surface roughness comparative standard.   (Surf-Chek)

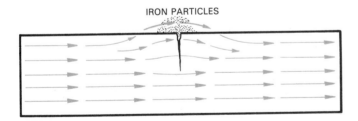

Fig. 32-19. The crack in a steel bar makes a magnetic field outside of the part to hold the iron particles, and build up an indication of the flaw.

OTHER QUALITY CONTROL TECHNIQUES

In addition to the quality control techniques described, industry makes wide use of highly specialized testing devices. For example, the quality of the machined surface may be highly critical. The surface finish is inspected visually using a comparative type checking unit, Fig. 32-20, or elec-

Fig. 32-21. Surface roughness can be checked electronically using a profilometer.   (Clevite Corp.)

Quality Control 477

TEST YOUR KNOWLEDGE, Unit 32

Please do not write in the text. Place your answers on a separate sheet of paper.

1. Quality control falls into two basic classifications. Name and explain each.
2. List three familiar forms of nondestructive testing.
3. Quality control is important because:
   a. It is inexpensive.
   b. It is quickly and easily accomplished.
   c. It guarantees that the parts being manufactured maintain predetermined standards and specifications.
   d. All of the above.
   e. None of the above.
4. Radiographic inspection makes use of:
   a. Accurately made measuring fixtures.
   b. A high frequency sound beam.
   c. X rays.
   d. All of the above.
   e. None of the above.
5. Ultrasonic inspection makes use of:
   a. Accurately made measuring fixtures.
   b. High frequency sound beam.
   c. X rays.
   d. All of the above.
   e. None of the above.
6. A profilometer makes use of:
   a. Accurately made measuring fixtures.
   b. High frequency sound beam.
   c. X rays.
   d. All of the above.
   e. None of the above.
7. Describe the fluorescent penetrant inspection process.
8. How does fluorescent penetrant inspection differ from the Spotcheck inspection technique?
9. Briefly describe the Magnaflux inspection technique.

RESEARCH AND DEVELOPMENT

1. Devise a quality control system for your school shop.
2. Ask for a demonstration of the Magnaflux technique the next time you take a field trip to a plant that uses the system.
3. Select a machine part and examine it carefully. What points on this piece come under the quality control system in the plant that made it? What points must be checked against specifications if the piece is to be interchangeable with similar pieces?
4. Design a project and develop simple measuring fixtures to check it against the plans.
5. Have a plant in your area demonstrate the Rockwell or Brinell hardness testing methods.
6. The penetrants described in the text are simple and easy to use. Their cost is within reach of many shop budgets. Carefully analyze the needs of your shop, and present your analysis to the instructor with a request that the penetrants be purchased.
7. Show a film on quality control. Preview it before showing it and prepare an outline on the more significant parts.

Unit 33

AUTOMATION

AUTOMATION is a technique or system for operating a mechanical device by highly automatic means. Controls are activated electronically, hydraulically, mechanically, pneumatically, or in combination, and they are often computer controlled. Human intervention is reduced to an absolute minimum.

AUTOMATION is a way of production that utilizes a machine or group of machines to automatically perform one or more of the five basic manufacturing processes:
1. Making.
2. Inspection.
3. Assembly.
4. Testing.
5. Packaging.

The computer integrated with specially designed machines, Fig. 33-1, has revolutionized automation

Fig. 33-1. This group of machines, called a palletized cell, combines general purpose machine tools, using a common pallet designed to hold the parts for machining. Each machine has a microcomputer. Note how the work moves from station to station. (Kearney & Trecker Corp.)

technology while improving product quality and reducing manufacturing costs. Two of the latest techniques are known as FMS (Flexible Manufacturing Systems), Fig. 33-2, and CIM (Computer Integrated Manufacturing). Both systems consist of several machine tools fed by automated handling equipment and robots, Fig. 33-3, under the directions of a computer-based controller. Each step in the manufacturing process is linked with the succeeding one, Fig. 33-4. An assortment of products can be made simultaneously. Reprogramming for design changes or for new products can be done quickly.

Every part is inspected, Fig. 33-5, using computer-controlled devices. The measuring sensors, often using lasers, are sensitive enough to detect tool wear as it occurs and compensate for it automatically. Machine tool malfunction and tool breakage can also be identified and corrective steps taken.

Fig. 33-2. Flexible manufacturing system (FMS) consists of several machine tools, fed by automated materials handling equipment and robots, all under the direction and control of a central computer. The parts move from station to station on the carts shown in the foreground.
(Kearney & Trecker Corp.)

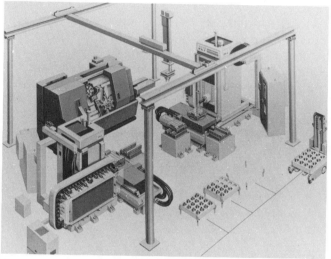

Fig. 33-4. With the FMS each step in the manufacturing process is linked with the succeeding one. There is an automated flow of raw material, total machining of the part across the machines, and then the removal of the finished part.
(Kearney & Trecker Corp.)

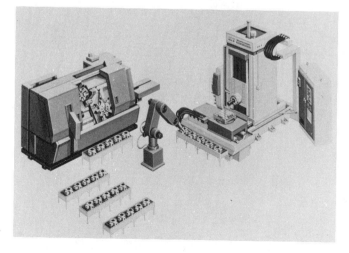

Fig. 33-3. This robot, or automated cell, consists of several machines with robotics material handling. The cell becomes a fully automatic process through the application of robotics, power clamping of parts, special tools, and other forms of automation.   (Kearney & Trecker Corp.)

Fig. 33-5. Lasers scan front end, door frames, and tail assembly to an accuracy of 3.0 mm (about 1/9 in.). Inspection is done to prevent imperfect parts from ever being made.
(Pontiac Div., General Motors Corp.)

AN INTRODUCTION TO NUMERICAL CONTROL

In machining, when cutting operations are to be performed on conventional machine tools the machinist studies the print, then mounts and positions the work for machining. This is done by moving one or more of the machine's lead or feed screws. After selecting the proper cutting speed and feed, the cutter is fed into the material and MANUALLY guided through the various machining operations that will produce the part specified on the drawing.

With NUMERICAL CONTROL, or N/C, Fig. 33-6, all of the machine movements are controlled electronically by electric motors called SERVOS. The servos are connected to the lead and feed screws

are controlled by the same set of instructions or program, Fig. 33-7.

Since the N/C program must instruct the servos in what direction the work and/or tool must move, there has to be some way to define this movement. The CARTESIAN COORDINATE SYSTEM, Fig. 33-8, is the basis for all N/C programming. Program coordinates in either metric or inch units specify the destination of a particular movement. With it, the AXIS OF MOVEMENT (X, Y, or Z) and the direction of movement (+ or −) can be identified. (To determine whether the move is positive (+) or negative (−) the program is written as though the tool, rather than the work, is doing the moving.)

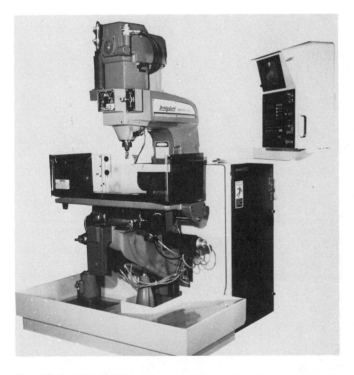

Fig. 33-6. This CNC vertical milling machine has two levels of programming; the first level can be done while manually running the first part. The machining coordinates are entered and recorded in memory, using the manual data input panel. The next part is machined automatically. The machinist needs no programming experience. A high level programming language is also embedded in the unit for use by experienced programmers or for programs already developed.
(Bridgeport Machines A Division of Textron, Inc.)

Fig. 33-7. Automatic tool changes are also controlled by the program on some machine tools like this machining center. Note the tools contained in the magazine on the side of the machine. (Mazak Corp.)

of the machine. They provide the power that positions the work and feeds the cutter. Instructions from a punched tape, magnetic tape, or directly from a computer, control electronic impulses that tell the servos when to start, in what direction to move, and how far they are to move. Feed rate, cutter speed and, on some N/C machines, tool changes

Spindle motion is assigned the Z axis. This means that for a drill press or vertical milling machine, for example, the Z axis is vertical. For such machines as a lathe or horizontal milling machine, the Z axis will be horizontal. See Fig. 33-9.

Tool positioning may be INCREMENTAL or ABSOLUTE, Fig. 33-10. With incremental positioning,

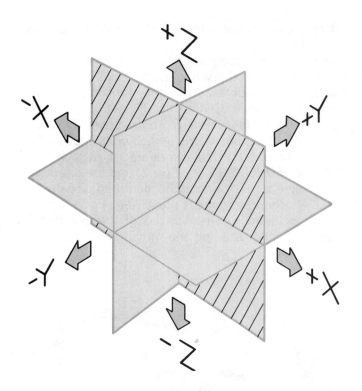

Fig. 33-8. The Cartesian coordinate system is the basis of all N/C programming.

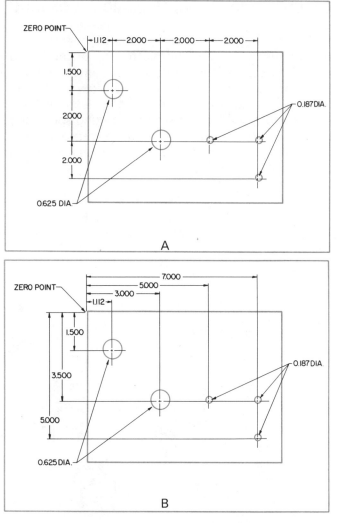

Fig. 33-10. Tool positioning. A—Incremental measuring. In this system, each set of coordinates has as its point of origin the last point established. B—Absolute measuring. In this system, all coordinates are measured from a fixed point (zero point) of origin.

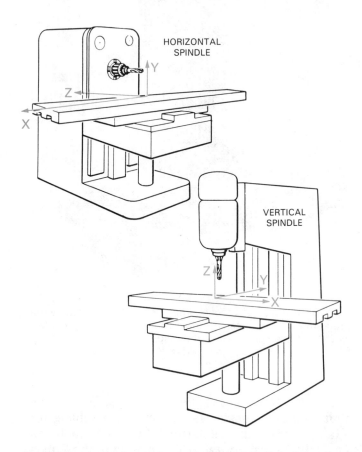

Fig. 33-9. Axes of machine tool movement. Spindle motion is assigned the Z axis. Note how it differs between the machine with the horizontal spindle and the machine with the vertical spindle. (IBM)

each tool movement is made with reference to the prior or last tool position. Absolute positioning measures all tool movement from a fixed point, origin, or zero point. Many N/C MACHINE CONTROL UNITS (MCU) accept incremental and/or absolute date input. (INPUT, in this case, is the dimensional information required to position the cutting tool.)

There are two basic N/C systems:
1. Point-to-point.
2. Contour or continuous path.

POINT-TO-POINT SYSTEM

The POINT-TO-POINT SYSTEM is usually used for drilling, punching, spot welding, and straight line milling. It is the simpler of the two systems. Unless it adversely affects accuracy, tool movement from

Point A to Point B does not have to follow a specific path, Fig. 33-11. This is because the tool is performing no productive work (except in straight line milling) until it gets to Point B. No computer is needed for point-to-point programming.

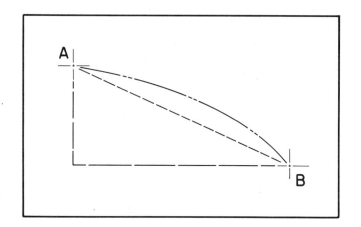

Fig. 33-11. In point-to-point N/C systems there is no concern what path is taken when the tool moves from Point A to Point B.

CONTOUR OR CONTINUOUS PATH SYSTEM

The path the cutting tool takes as well as the location to which it is to move can be specified with the CONTOUR OR CONTINUOUS PATH SYSTEM, Fig. 33-12, as the tool is continuously cutting as

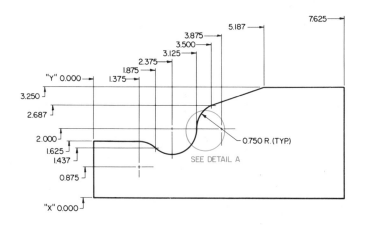

Fig. 33-12. Contour or continuous path system. The machine slides must be moved certain distances at the same rate of speed and at the same time, and in specific directions. When planning these movements, the coordinate positions of all points where changes in direction occur must be known. For example, the point where two different curves become tangent to each other is shown. By adding a Z axis, three-dimensional machining is possible.

it moves along the programmed path (this can be on 1, 2, or 3 axes simultaneously). Each movement is monitored and adjusted through a feed-back mechanism to the machine control unit (MCU), in order to maintain the correct direction of movement and the proper cutting speed and feed.

Cutter size and other machining variables must be taken into consideration when programming the cutter path.

Because of the many thousands of coordinate points needed, a computer is mandatory for preparing a program to machine two- and three-dimensional shapes as the tool paths must describe the entire surface of the object. In a way, contour or continuous path machining might be described as a very sophisticated (complex or intricate) form of point-to-point machining because tool movement is only in a straight line. However, the straight line distances are so short (0.0005 in. or 0.013 mm) and blend so well that they appear to be a continuous, smooth cut, Fig. 33-13.

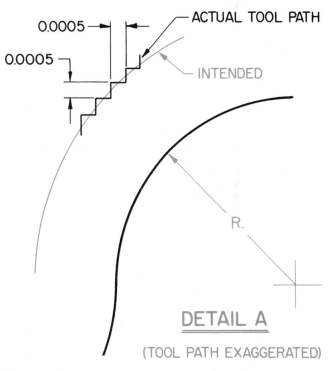

Fig. 33-13. In contour or continuous path machining the cutter movement is actually in a straight line. However, the increment of each movement is so small (0.0005 in. or 0.013 mm) and the curvature of the cutter blended so well that they appear to be a continuous, smooth cut.

Very complex parts can be produced economically in small numbers, without the need for expensive jigs, fixtures, and templates by the contour or continuous path system. On some N/C machine tools, mirror image parts (right-hand and left-hand units) can be machined using the same program, Fig. 33-14.

PROGRAMMING N/C MACHINES

An N/C machining program is a sequence of instructions that "tells" the machine what operations to perform, and where on the material they are to be done. A program is also referred to as SOFTWARE.

Each line of an N/C program is called a BLOCK. It consists of a sequence number, preparatory codes for setting up the machine at this stage, Fig. 33-15,

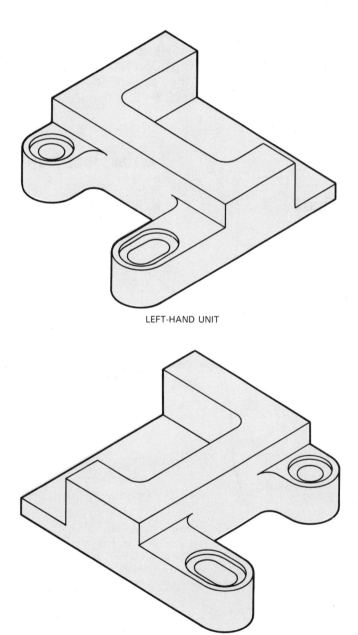

LEFT-HAND UNIT

RIGHT-HAND UNIT

Fig. 33-14. On some N/C machine tools, mirror image parts can be machined using the same program.

PREPARATORY FUNCTIONS (G-CODES)*	
CODE	FUNCTION
G00	Rapid traverse (slides move only at rapid traverse speed).
G01	Linear interpolation (slides move at right angles and/or at programmed angles).
G02	Circular interpolation CW (tool follows a quarter part of circumference in a clockwise direction).
G03	Circular interpolation CCW (tool follows a quarter part of circumference in a counterclockwise direction).
G04	Dwell (timed delay of established duration. Length is expressed in X or F word).
G33	Thread cutting.
G70	Inch programming.
G71	Metric programming.
G81	Drill.
G90	Absolute coordinates.
G91	Incremental coordinates.

*G-CODES may vary on different N/C machines.

MISCELLANEOUS FUNCTIONS (M-CODES)*	
CODE	FUNCTION
M00	Stop machine until operator restart.
M02	End of program.
M03	Start spindle—CW.
M04	Start spindle—CCW.
M05	Stop spindle.
M06	Tool change.
M07	Coolant on.
M09	Coolant off.
M30	End program and rewind tape.
M52	Advance spindle.
M53	Retract spindle.
M56	Tool inhibit.

*M-CODES may vary on different N/C machines.

Fig. 33-15. Example of codes of N/C preparatory and miscellaneous functions.

the coordinates for the destination of the tool, and additional commands such as feed rate to be used during the movement.

N/C equipment can be programmed:
1. Manually.
2. Computer-assisted.

MANUAL PROGRAMMING

Point-to-point N/C programming can be done manually by anyone who can interpret engineering drawings and has a working knowledge of machine tool operations, Fig. 33-16.

A program is developed by converting each machining sequence and machine function into a coded block of information that the MCU (machine control unit) can understand, Fig. 33-17. The code consists of ALPHANUMERIC DATA (letters,

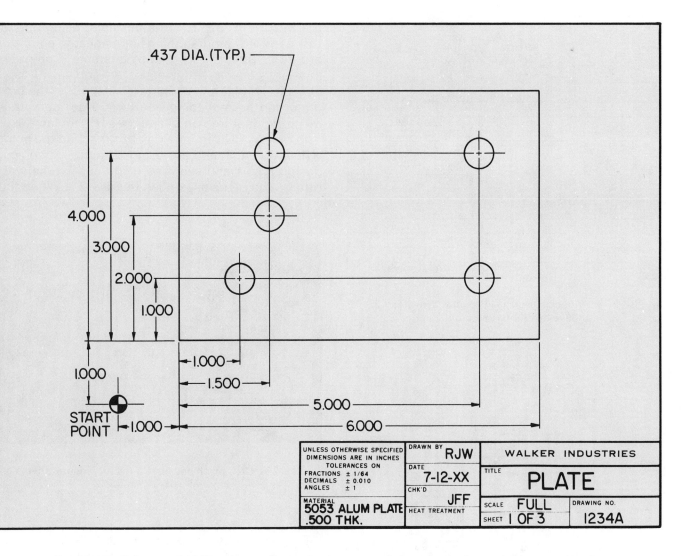

.437 DIA.(TYP.)

4.000

3.000

2.000

1.000

1.000

START
POINT

1.000

1.000

1.500

5.000

6.000

UNLESS OTHERWISE SPECIFIED DIMENSIONS ARE IN INCHES TOLERANCES ON FRACTIONS ± 1/64 DECIMALS ± 0.010 ANGLES ± 1	DRAWN BY RJW	WALKER INDUSTRIES	
	DATE 7-12-XX	TITLE PLATE	
	CHK'D JFF		
MATERIAL 5053 ALUM PLATE .500 THK.	HEAT TREATMENT	SCALE FULL	DRAWING NO. 1234A
		SHEET 1 OF 3	

Fig. 33-16. Point-to-point N/C programming can be done manually by anyone who can interpret engineering drawings and has a working knowledge of machine tool operations.

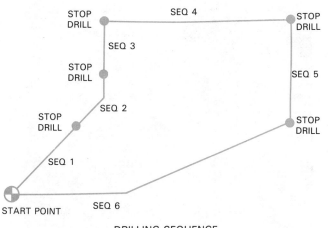

STOP DRILL   SEQ 4   STOP DRILL

SEQ 3

STOP DRILL

SEQ 2

STOP DRILL

SEQ 5

SEQ 1

STOP DRILL

START POINT   SEQ 6

DRILLING SEQUENCE

Fig. 33-17. The machining operations must be converted into individual coded blocks of information that the machine control unit (MCU) can understand. This is the planned drilling sequence for the part shown in Fig. 33-16.

numbers, punctuation marks, and special characters). Each identifies a different machine function.

Each block of information is a line on the PROCESS SHEET or PROGRAM MANUSCRIPT, Fig. 33-18, and is identified by a sequence number. Included in the information are the coordinate dimensions (X, Y, or Z movement) or location where the operation (drilling, punching, spot welding, etc.) is to take place, along with miscellaneous functions (spindle on, spindle off, tool change, etc.)

Every block of information must be separated with an END OF BLOCK (EOB) code. An END OF PROGRAM code completes the program. A final EOB code rewinds the tape. It will then be ready to repeat the machining cycle.

The coded information is punched into a paper or mylar tape, Fig. 33-19 on a TAPE PUNCH MACHINE. After proofing for omissions and errors, the tape is released to the production area for use.

PART NO. 1234A		MACHINE 2-AXIS DRILLING WITH FIXED FEED RATE		REMARKS SET POINT (0,0) M56 IS TOOL INHIBIT					
PART NAME PLATE								
TAPE NO. 1234A		TOOLING 7/16 DIA. DRILL						
DATE 7-12-XX PAGE I OF I				PROCESSOR JFF		APPROVED LJ		
N	G	X	Y	Z	F	EOB	M	INSTRUCTIONS
000	90					EOB		7/16 DIA. DRILL
00						EOB		SET DEPTH STOP
0		0	0			EOB	03	
I		2000	2000			EOB	07	
2		2500	4000			EOB		
3		2500	4000			EOB		
4		6000	4000			EOB		
5		6000	2000			EOB		
6		0	0			EOB	0956	
7						EOB	05	
8						EOB	30	CHANGE PART

Fig. 33-18. Information given on the print shown in Fig. 33-16 is developed into this program.

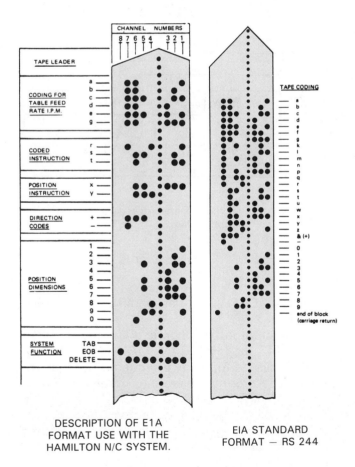

DESCRIPTION OF E1A FORMAT USE WITH THE HAMILTON N/C SYSTEM.

EIA STANDARD FORMAT — RS 244

Fig. 33-19. Tape code.

COMPUTER-ASSISTED N/C PROGRAMMING

The latest in machine technology has a computer-assisted numerical control system (CNC) designed around a microcomputer that is an integral part of the MCU, Fig. 33-20. It is possible, using one of the many N/C programming languages, to enter the program directly into the system. Computer memory capacity is given as an equivalent tape capacity in feet and/or meters. After use, the program can be moved to another, larger computer memory, or stored on a tape cassette for later use.

In reality, CNC technology has reached the point where an engineer can, using computer graphics, design a part and see how it fits and works with other parts in the assembly, Fig. 33-21. When the

Fig. 33-20. CNC machines have a microcomputer that is an integral part of the MCU.

Fig. 33-21. CAD/CAM (Computer Aided Design/Computer Aided Manufacturing), through the use of computer graphics, enables the engineer to design a part and see how it will function with other parts in the assembly. (Evans & Sutherland)

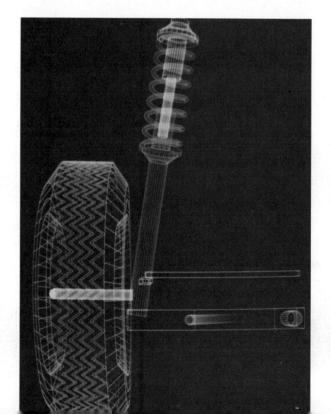

design has been confirmed, the computer can be instructed to analyze the geometry of the part and calculate the tool paths that will be required to make it. The tool paths generated on the computer screen are translated into a detailed sequence of commands for an appropriate CNC machine tool to follow in making it.

The computer generated instructions are stored in a central master computer for direct transfer to the CNC machine tool for parts manufacturing, or stored for future use on magnetic tape (similar to an audio tape cassette) or a magnetic disk. However, before being released for production, the program is verified by machining a sample part from some inexpensive material like plastic or wax.

The system that makes all of this possible is called CAD/CAM (Computer Aided Design/Computer Aided Manufacturing), Fig. 33-22.

The data can also be used to produce hard copy documentation of the part (detail drawings) and to determine how it fits into the overall assembly (assembly drawings), Fig. 33-23.

N/C AND CNC IN THE SCHOOL SHOP/LAB

Many N/C and CNC machine tools have been developed for industrial education classes, Figs.

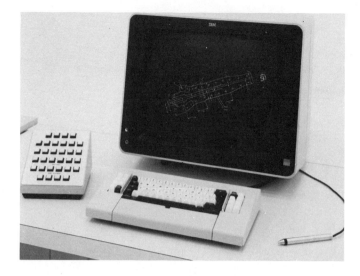

Fig. 33-22. The computer makes CAD/CAM possible. (IBM)

33-24 and 33-25. The complexity of the work they are capable of performing is limited by machine size and computer memory capacity.

When using these machines, students are able to develop programs, introduce the program to the machine computer, and see the resulting finished part within a reasonable time.

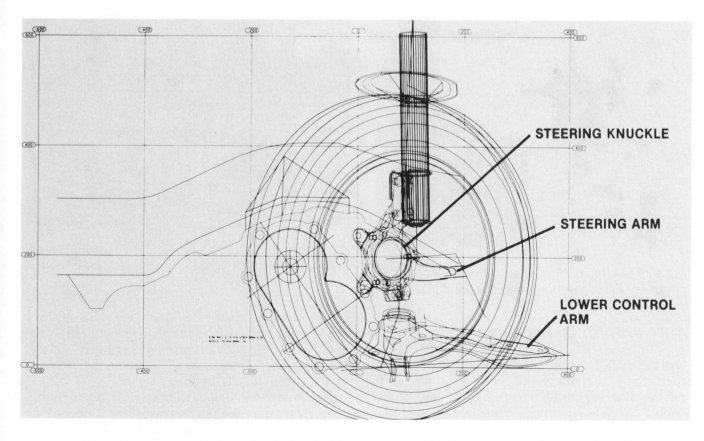

STEERING KNUCKLE

STEERING ARM

LOWER CONTROL ARM

Fig. 33-23. Computer data on the design of a part can be turned into hard copy in the form of detail and assembly drawings. (Chrysler Corp.)

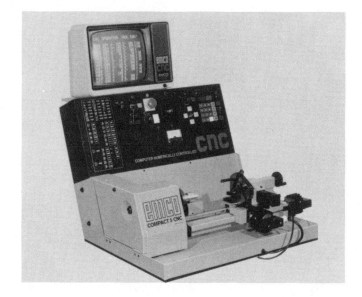

Fig. 33-24. CNC lathe designed for school shop/lab use. (Emco Maier)

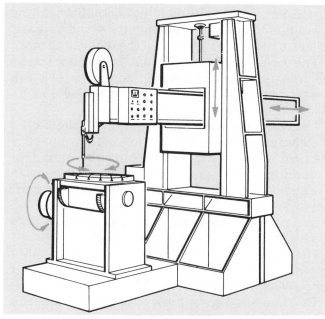

Fig. 33-26. Drawing of a welding machine showing the four axes of controlled movement.

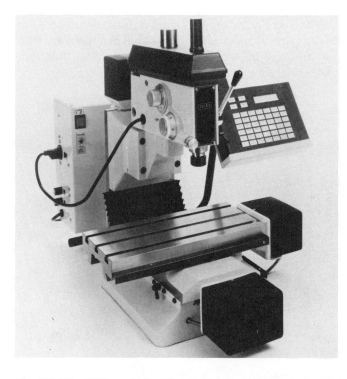

Fig. 33-25. CNC vertical milling/drilling machine designed for school shop/lab and industrial use. (Dyna Electronics Inc.)

Fig. 33-27. Photo of a welding machine of slightly different design. Note the built-in microcomputer and screen used to visually check the program. (Sciaky)

OTHER N/C AND CNC APPLICATIONS

N/C and CNC systems have been adapted to a broad range of metalworking related equipment. Spot welding, Figs. 33-26 and 33-27, riveting, and punching were among the first machines to use N/C as they are basically point-to-point operations.

Multi-operational equipment like that used to machine automobile engine blocks are computer-

controlled. The machine shown in Fig. 33-28, has the rough casting loaded into one end, tranfers them from station-to-station through several machining operations, and unloads the finished block automatically at the other end.

Automated sytems have been adapted to operations other than the removal of metal. Robots load machine tools and remove the machined parts, Fig. 33-29, and spray paint auto bodies. See Fig. 20-15. Some are even capable of selecting and position-

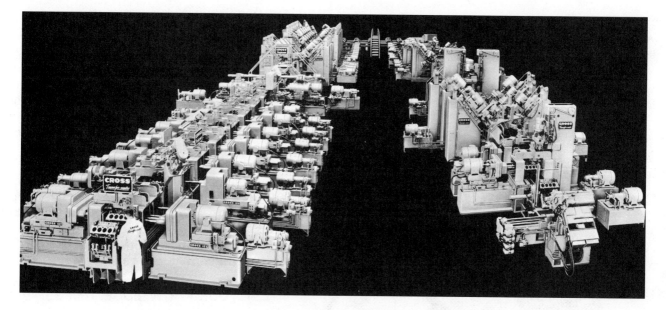

Fig. 33-28. A large machine tool employed to machine automobile engine blocks. At any one time, 104 blocks are having some machining operation performed on them. The machine is almost two city blocks long and performs 555 operations; including 265 drilling, 6 milling, 56 reaming, 101 countersinking, 106 tapping, and 133 inspection operations. It produces 100 pieces per hour. (Cross Co.)

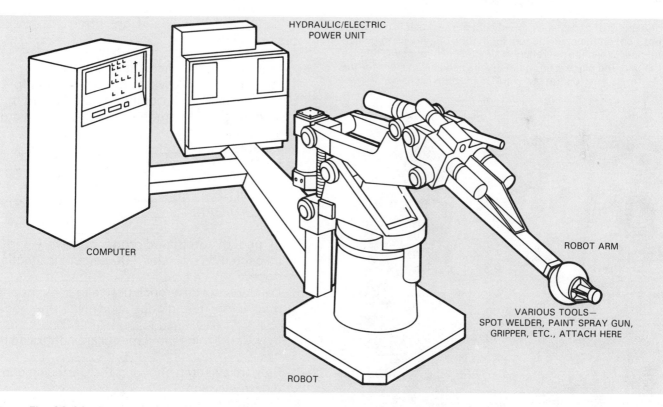

Fig. 33-29. Robots can be programmed to do many types of jobs—spot welding, paint spraying, drilling, inspection, etc. Most of the jobs they perform are too hazardous for human operators.

ing specifically shaped parts for machining, Fig. 33-30. A laser is employed to ''see'' and define the part outline so the correct parts will be selected.

Coordinates for machining auto body dies (steel blocks used to shape sheet metal) can be ''lifted'' from handmade clay and wood models, Fig. 33-31. The coordinates are stored in the computer memory and mathematically define the vehicle surface. This

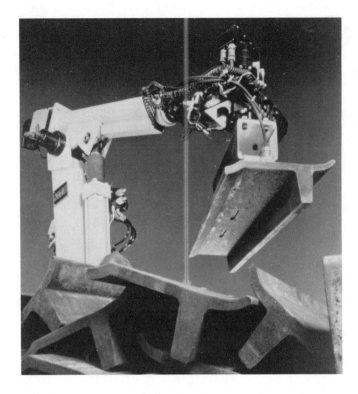

Fig. 33-30. Some robots can be programmed to see with the use of lasers. They define the shape of parts, pick them out of a group of parts, and properly orient them (set in a definite position) on the machine tool for cutting operations to be performed. When the operation is complete, the robot will remove the part and place it on the materials handling system for the next operation. (MTS Systems Corp.)

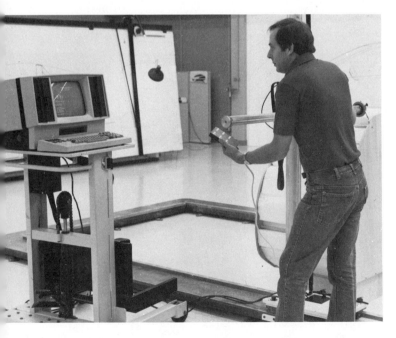

Fig. 33-31. An engineer is shown digitizing coordinates of an automotive design concept. The coordinates are automatically stored in the computer memory and are used to mathematically define the vehicle surface. This information is then utilized for engineering and manufacturing purposes. (Advanced Concept Center, General Motors Corp.)

information is used to control the cutting tools when the body dies are made.

Only time will tell what impact automation will have on our society. Some workers, mostly semiskilled and unskilled, will lose their jobs much like the home artisan of the Industrial Revolution, and the carriage maker, blacksmith, buggy whip manufacturer, and feed dealer when Henry Ford started to mass-produce the automobile. These developments were condemned during their introduction just as automation and robotics are condemned today. They eventually employed, directly or indirectly, many more people than the number of workers they originally replaced. Better jobs (but requiring better education), with higher pay, and improved working conditions were created.

TEST YOUR KNOWLEDGE, Unit 33

Please do not write in the text. Place your answers on a separate sheet of paper.
1. What is automation? _____
   _____.
2. The controls on automated machines are activated _____, _____, _____, or in _____, and are often _____ controlled.
3. List the five basic manufacturing processes that automated machines can perform.
4. What do the following acronyms stand for in they relation to automation? (An acronym is a word formed from the initial letters of words in a phrase.)
   a. FMS—_____ _____ _____
   b. CIM—_____ _____ _____
   c. N/C—_____ _____
   d. CNC—_____ _____ _____
   e. CAD/CAM—_____ _____ _____/
      _____ _____ _____
5. In modern automated production every part is inspected. Why is this 100 percent inspection done? _____.
6. Describe the difference between conventional machining techniques and N/C methods.
   _____.
7. In N/C, machine movements are controlled by
   _____.
8. Prepare a sketch showing the Cartesian coordinate system.
9. Prepare two similar sketches. Show incremental dimensioning on the first sketch and absolute dimensioning on the second sketch.
10. List the two basic N/C systems.
11. Using sketches, show how the two N/C systems differ.
12. Which of the two methods require the use of a computer? Why?
13. List several uses made of N/C machines.

RESEARCH AND DEVELOPMENT

1. Review several up-to-date technical magazines that have articles on N/C, CNC, robotics, etc. Prepare a brief outline of each article to use as a basis of discussion.
2. The advent of automation is frequently thought of as the second Industrial Revolution. Prepare a research paper on the first Industrial Revolution with emphasis on wages, and working and living conditions.
3. Arrange to visit a plant that uses automated machinery. If visiting an automated plant is not possible, show an instructional tape that illustrates automation.
4. Prepare an oral book report on a book about automation. Include a discussion period.
5. Develop a simple machine that will illustrate how automation works.
6. If your shop/lab is fortunate enough to have an N/C machine tool, ask your teacher to assign a problem. Prepare a program for the problem, proof it, and follow it through to the finished machined part.

Numerically controlled band machine has "X" and "Y" table movement. The controller has circular interpolation (can cut circular and elliptical shapes) and both manual and tape data input.   (DoALL Company)

GLOSSARY OF TERMS

A

ABRASIVE: A material that penetrates and cuts a material softer than itself. It may be natural (emery, corundum, and diamonds) or synthetic (silicon carbide, aluminum oxide).

ABSOLUTE SYSTEM: System in which all coordinates are measured from a fixed point of origin (specified reference point).

ACCESS: The ability to obtain data from and/or place it in the memory of a computer.

ACCURATE: Made within the tolerance allowed.

ACME THREAD: Similar in form to the square thread in that the top and bottom of the thread is flat, but the sides have a 29 degree included angle. The Acme thread is used for feed and adjusting screws on machine tools.

ACUTE ANGLE: An angle of less than 90 degrees.

ADDENDUM: That portion of the gear tooth that projects above or outside of the pitch circle.

ALIGN: Adjusting to given points.

ALLOWANCE: The limits permitted for satisfactory performance of the machined parts.

ALLOY: A mixture of two or more metals fused or melted together to form a new metal.

ALPHANUMERIC: Consisting of letters, punctuation marks, numbers, and special characters.

ANALOG: A representation of numeric quantities using continuously changing physical qualities as a reference.

ANGLE PLATE: A precisely made tool of cast iron, steel, or granite that is used to hold work in a vertical position for layout or machining. Faces are at right angles (90 degrees) and may have slotted openings for easier mounting of the work or clamping to the machine tool table.

ANNEALING: The process of heating metal to a given temperature, then cooling it slowly to remove stresses and induce softness. The exact temperature and the period the temperature is held depends upon the composition of the metal being annealed.

ANODIZING: A process for applying an oxide coating to aluminum. It is done electrolytically in an acid solution with equipment similar to that used for electroplating. The technique can be varied to produce a light colored, porous coating that can be dyed in a variety of colors to a harder and nonporous coating for protection against corrosion.

APRON: A covering plate or casting that encloses and protects a mechanism. The portion of the lathe carriage that contains the gears, clutches, and levers for moving the carriage by hand and power feed.

ARBOR: A shaft or spindle for holding cutting tools.

ARTIFICIAL INTELLIGENCE: Computer techniques that mimic certain functions associated with human intelligence.

ASSEMBLY: A unit fitted together from manufactured parts. A machine tool may include several assemblies.

AUTOMATICALLY PROGRAMMED TOOLS (APT): They provide for five axes of motion by machine tools.

AUTOMATION: An industrial technique whereby mechanical labor and mechanical control are substituted for human labor and human control. Basically an extension and a refinement of mass-production.

AXIS: The centerline, real or imaginary, passing through an object about which it could rotate. A point of reference.

B

BACK GEARS: Gears fitted to belt-driven machine tools to increase the number of spindle speeds. Used to slow the spindle speed of the lathe for cutting threads, knurling, and for making heavy roughing cuts.

BACKLASH: Lost motion (play) in moving parts, such as the thread in a nut or in the teeth of meshing gears.

BED: One of the principle parts of a machine tool. It contains ways or bearing surfaces that support and guide the work or cutting tool.

BERYLLIUM: A metal that weighs almost 80 percent less than steel, yet offers virtually equal strength characteristics. It is easy to machine but is brittle. Used in missiles and aircraft where weight is critical and in nuclear reactors. One of the ''exotic'' metals.

BEVEL: The angle formed by a line or a surface that is not at right angles to another line or surface.

BLANKING: A stamping operation in which a die is used to shear or cut a desired shape from flat sheets or strips of metal.

BLOWHOLE: A hole produced in a casting when gases are trapped during the pouring operation.

BINARY: A numbering system utilizing a base of two.

BINARY DIGIT: A digit in the binary scale of notation. This digit can only be zero or one. It is equivalent to a ''yes'' condition or a ''no'' condition.

BIT: An abbreviation of ''binary digit.'' Also, a single character of language employing exactly two distinct characters.

BLOCK: A section of tape considered a unit, and separated from other such units by an ''End of Block'' (EOB) character. In a punched tape, it consists of rows of punched holes that collectively provide complete information for a unit of cutting operation.

BRAZING: Joining metals by the fusion of nonferrous alloys that have melting temperatures above 800 °F (427 °C) but lower than the metals being joined.

BRITTLENESS: The characteristics that cause metal to break easily. In some respects the opposite of toughness.

BUFFING: The process of bringing out the luster of metal. Buffing is accomplished by using cloth wheels (usually cotton or muslin disks sewed together), and a tripoli compound. Proper wheel speed depends on the size of the wheel.

BURNISHING: The process of finishing a metal surface by compressing its surface, often done by tumbling the work with steel balls.

BURR: The sharp edge remaining on the metal after cutting, stamping, or machining. The burr can be dangerous if not removed.

BUSHING: A bearing for a revolving shaft. A hardened steel tube used on jigs to guide drills and reamers.

C

CAM: A rotating or sliding element that, because of the curvature of its driving surface, imparts complicated motions to the followers or driven elements of the machine tool.

CARBURIZING: A process that introduces carbon to the surface of steel by heating the metal below its melting temperature in contact with carbonaceous solids, liquids, or gases. It is held at that temperature for a predetermined time, after which the piece is quenched.

CASE HARDENING: A process of surface hardening iron base alloys so that the surface layer or case is made substantially harder than the interior or core. Typical case-hardening processes are carburizing, cyaniding, and nitriding.

CASTING: An object made by pouring molten metal into a mold.

CAT HEAD: A sleeve or collar which fits over out-of-round or irregular shaped work permitting it to be supported in a steady rest. The work is centered in the cat head by using the adjusting screws located around its circumference.

CENTER, DEAD: A stationary center.

CENTERLINE: A line used to indicate an axis of a symmetrical part. The centerline consists of a series of long and short dashes.

CENTER, LIVE: A rotating center.

CENTRIFUGAL CASTING: A casting technique in which the mold is rotated during pouring and solidification of the metal. It produces a casting with certain desirable characteristics.

CERMETS: A combination of ceramics and metals that is finding increased use for high temperature applications. Resistance to high temperatures and wear indicates great promise as a super high-speed cutting tool.

CHARACTER: One of a set of marks or events which may be combined to express information in a program. The characters normally used in N/C include the decimal digits from 0 to 9, directional signs, and special characters such as Tab, End of Block, and Rewind Stop.

CHASER: A thread cutting tool that fits into a die head and is used on a turret lathe or screw machine. Usually a hardened steel plate with several teeth of the correct pitch cut into it. Three or four chasers are used in a die head.

CHASING THREADS: Cutting threads on a machine tool.

CHATTER: Vibrations caused by the cutting tool springing away from the work. It produces small ridges on the machined surface.

CHEMICAL MILLING: Controlled removal of metal with chemicals rather than with conventional machining methods.

CHIP: A metal shaving removed by cutting action of a tool. Also an integrated circuit etched on a tiny piece of silicon or germanium.

CHIP BREAKER: A small groove ground on the top of the cutting tool, near the cutting edge, to break the chips into small sections.

CHUCK: A device to hold work or cutting tools on a machine tool.

CIRCULAR INTERPOLATION: A mode of contouring control which uses information contained in a single block to produce an arc of a circle.

CIRCULAR PITCH: The distance from the center of one gear tooth to the center of the next tooth measured on the pitch circle.

CLEARANCE: The distance by which one object clears another object.

CLIMB MILLING: Feeding work into the milling cutter in the same direction it rotates.

CLOCKWISE: From left to right in a circular motion; the direction clock hands move.

CLOSED LOOP SYSTEM: A system in which the output is fed back for comparison with the input.

COINING: The process that impresses the image or characters of the die and punch onto a plain metal surface.

COLD HEADING: An operation in which metal is worked cold.

COLOR HARDEN: A hardening technique usually done for appearance only.

COLOR TEMPER: Using the color range steel passes through when heated to determine the proper degree of hardness.

COMMAND: A pulse, signal, or set of signals commanding a specific performance.

COMPUTER AIDED DESIGN (CAD): A system which uses a computer to create and/or modify a design.

COMPUTER AIDED MANUFACTURING (CAM): A system which uses a computer in the control of a manufacturing process.

COMPUTER GRAPHICS: Graphs, charts, and/or drawings generated by a computer. They are displayed on a video screen or printed by a plotter or printer.

COMPUTER NUMERICAL CONTROL (CNC): Use of a dedicated computer to control some aspects of a numerically controlled machine tool.

CONCAVE SURFACE: A curved depression in the surface of an object.

CONCENTRIC: Having a common center.

CONE PULLEY: A one piece pulley having two or more diameters.

CONTINUOUS CASTING: A casting technique in which the ingot is continuously solidified while it is being poured. The length of the casting is not determined by mold dimensions.

CONTINUOUS PATH: A type of N/C machine in which rate and direction of relative movement of machine members are under continuous control.

CONTOUR: The outline of an object.

CONVENTIONAL: Not original. Customary or traditional.

CONVEX SURFACE: A rounded surface on an object

COOLANT: A fluid or gas used to cool the cutting edge of a tool. It prevents the tool from burning up during the machining operation.

COORDINATES: The position or relationship of points on planes; usually refers to Cartesian Coordinate System in which the three basic axes are designated X, Y, and Z.

CORE: A body of sand or other material that is formed to a desired shape and placed in a mold to produce a cavity or opening in a casting.

COUNTERBORE: Enlarging a hole to a given depth and diameter.

COUNTERCLOCKWISE: From right to left in a circular motion.

COUNTERSINK: Chamfering a hole to receive a flat head screw.

CUTTER PATH: The path described by the center of a cutter throughout a program.

CUTTING FLUID: A liquid used to cool and lubricate the cutting tool to improve the quality of the surface finish.

CYANIDING: A process of case-hardening a ferrous alloy by heating in molten cyanide causing the metal to absorb carbon.

CYCLE: A set of operations completely performed in a predetermined order.

D

DECARBURIZING: The process of removing carbon from metals.

DEDENDUM: The portion of the gear tooth between the pitch circle and the root circle; equal to the addendum plus the clearance.

DEMAGNETIZING: The removel of magnetism from a piece held in a magnet chuck.

DIE: A tool used to cut external threads. Also, a tool used to impart a desired shape to a piece of metal.

DIE CASTING: A method of casting metal under pressure by injecting it into the metal dies of a die casting machine.

DIE CAVITY: A hollow space inside a die where metal solidifies to form a casting.

DIE CHASERS: See CHASER.

DIE STOCK: The handle for holding a threading die.

DIVIDING HEAD: A machine tool attachment for accurate spacing of holes, slots, gear teeth, and flutes. When geared to the table lead screw it can be used to machine spirals.

DOG: A projecting piece on the side of a machine tool worktable used to trip the automatic feed mechanism off, or for reverse travel.

DOG, LATHE: A device for clamping work so that it can be machined between centers.

DRAFT: The clearance on a pattern that allows easy withdrawal of the pattern from the mold.

DRIFT: A tapered piece of flat steel used to separate tapered shank tools from sleeves, sockets, or machine tool spindles.

DRILLING: Cutting round holes by use of a cutting

tool sharpened on its point.

DRILL ROD: A carbon steel rod accurately and smoothly ground to size. Available in a large range of sizes.

DRIVE FIT: Using force or pressure to fit two pieces together. One of several classes of fits.

DROP FORGING: A forming operation, usually done under impact, that compresses the metal in dies designed to produce the desired shape.

DUCTILITY: The property of a metal that permits permanent deformation by hammering, rolling, and drawing without breaking or facturing.

E

ECCENTRIC: Not on a common center. A device that converts rotary motion into a reciprocating (back and forth) motion.

ELECTROPLATING: A plating process accomplished by passing an electric current from an anode (usually made of the plating material) to the work, through an electrolyte containing salts of the plating metal in solution.

EMERY: A natural abrasive.

END OF BLOCK (EOB): A symbol or indicator that defines the end of one block of data. When preparing machine control tapes, it is the typewriter function of the carriage return.

EXPANSION FIT: The reverse of shrink fit. The piece to be fitted is placed in liquid nitrogen or dry ice until it shrinks enough to fit into the mating piece. Interference develops between the fitted pieces as the cooled piece expands.

EZY-OUT: A tool for removing broken bolts and studs from a hole. It is made in several sizes.

F

FACE: To make a flat surface by machining.

FACEPLATE: A circular plate that fits to the headstock spindle and drives or carries work to be machined.

FATIGUE: The tendency for metal to break or fracture under repeated or fluctuating stresses.

FEED FUNCTION: The relative motion between the cutting tool and the work other than the motion that provides the power for removing material from the work. Also, the units such as inches per minute, mm per minute, inches per revolution, or mm per revolution.

FERROUS: Family of metals in which iron is the major ingredient.

FILLET: The curved surface that connects two surfaces that form an angle.

FIT: The clearance or interference between two mating parts. There are several classes of fits.

FIXTURE: A device for holding work in a machine tool not guiding the cutting tool.

FLAME HARDEN: A method of surface hardening steel by rapidly heating the surface with the flame of an oxyacetylene torch, then quenching.

FLASH: A thin fin of metal formed at the parting line of a forging or casting, where a small portion of metal is forced out between the edges of the die.

FLASK: A wooden or metal form consisting of a cope (the top portion) and a drag (the bottom portion) used to hold the sand that forms the mold.

FLOTURN PROCESS: Another term for shear spinning.

FLUORESCENT PENETRANT INSPECTION: A nondestructive testing technique in which an oil base penetrant is sprayed on the work and drawn into every crack and flaw. The surface is rinsed with solvent to remove excess penetrant. After developing, the surface is viewed under a black light. Defects glow with fluorescent brilliance.

FLUTE: A groove machined in a cutting tool to facilitate easy chip removal and to permit cutting fluid to reach the cutting point.

FLUX: The fusible material used in bracing and welding to dissolve and facilitate removal of oxides and other undesirable substances.

FLY CUTTER: A single point tool fitted in an arbor. Inexpensive to make but relatively inefficient because only one point does the cutting.

FORCE FIT: The interference between the two mating parts is sufficient to require force to press the piece together. The parts are considered permanently assembled.

FORGE: To form metal with heat and/or pressure.

FORMAT: A systematic arrangement of data. As applied to tape, the rules defining the position of the bits; as applied to programs, the rules defining the structure of the information.

FORMING: The operation necessary to shape metal to a desired form. The change does not intentionally change the thickness of the metal.

FREE FIT: Used when tolerances are liberal. Clearance is sufficient to permit a shaft to run freely without binding or overheating when properly lubricated.

G

GANG MILLING: Using two or more milling cutters to machine several surfaces at one time.

GATE: The point where molten metals enters the mold cavity.

GAUGE: A tool used for checking metal parts to determine whether they are made within specified limits.

GEARS: Wheels with teeth that transmit rotary motion from one shaft to another shaft without slippage.

GIB: A wedge-shaped strip that can be adjusted to

maintain a proper fit of movable surfaces of a machine tool.

GRADUATE: To divide into equal parts by engraving or cutting lines or graduations into the metal.

GRADUATIONS: The lines that indicate points of measurement on measuring tools and machine dials.

GUERIN PROCESS: A method of forming metal sheet in which the metal is forced to conform to the shape of a male die by the application of force to a confined rubber pad.

H

HALF-NUTS: The mechanism that locks the lathe carriage to the lead screw for the purpose of cutting threads.

HARDENING: The heating and quenching of certain iron-base alloys for the purpose of producing a hardness superior to that of the untreated material.

HARDNESS TESTING: Techniques used to determine the degree of hardness of heat-treated material.

HARDWARE: The electronic, mechanical, and electrical components which, when assembled, make up a complete computer system.

HEAT TREATMENT: The careful application of a combination of heating and cooling cycles to a metal or alloy in the solid state, to bring about certain desirable conditions such as hardness and toughness.

HELICAL GEARS: Gears with the teeth cut at some angle other than at right angles to the gear face, permitting two or more teeth to be engaged at all times. Their operation is smoother and not as noisy as the operation of spur gears.

HELIX: The path a point generates at it advances at a fixed rate on the surface of a cylinder, such as screw threads or the flutes on a twist drill.

HIGH ENERGY RATE FORMING (HERF): A metal forming technique involving the release of a source of high energy such as explosives, electrical, or pneumatic-mechanical materials.

HOB: A special type gear cutter designed to cut gear teeth on a continuous basis.

HOBBING: Cutting gear teeth with a hob. The gear blank and hob rotate together as in mesh during the cutting operation.

HONING: An expensive process used to produce an extremely fine surface finish on an object after the grinding operation and to permit a closer fit on critical parts. Abrasive blocks are forced against the work surface under very light spring pressure in a rotary motion, and at the same time moved back and forth while the area is flooded with cutting fluid.

HYDROFORM: A method of forming parts in rubber under accurately controlled fluid pressure. The metal is formed over a movable male die in a flexible diaphragm.

HYDROSPIN: Another name for shear spinning.

I

ID: Abbreviation for inside diameter.

IDLER GEAR: A gear or gears placed between two other gears to transfer motion from one to the other without changing the direction of rotation or the ratio between the gears.

INCREMENTAL COORDINATES: Coordinates measured from the preceding value in a sequence of values. Each move is referenced to the prior coordinate.

INDEPENDENT CHUCK: A chuck in which each jaw can be moved independently of the other jaws.

INDEXING: The term used to describe the correct spacing of holes, slots, etc., on the periphery of a cylindrical piece by the use of a dividing or indexing head.

INDICATOR: A sensitive instrument capable of measuring slight variations when testing the trueness of work, machines, or machine attachments.

INPUT: Transfer of information into the control system.

INSERTED TOOTH CUTTER: A milling cutter with teeth that can be replaced rather than the entire cutter when the teeth become damaged or worn.

INSPECTION: The measuring and checking of finished parts to determine whether they have been made to specifications.

INTERCHANGEABLE: A part made to specific dimensions and tolerances, capable of being fitted in a mechanism in place of a similarly made part.

INVESTMENT CASTING: A process that involves making a wax, plastic, or frozen mercury pattern, surrounding it with a wet refractory material, melting or burning the pattern after the investment material has dried and set, and finally pouring metal (usually under air or centrifugal pressure) into the cavity.

J

JARNO TAPER: A standard taper of 0.600 in. (15.24 mm) per foot. Used on machine tools.

JIG: A device that holds the work in position, and positions and guides the cutting tool.

JO BLOCK: Precisely made steel blocks used by industry as a standard of measurement. They are made in a range of sizes and with a dimensional accuracy of ± 0.000002 (two millionths) inch, with a flatness and parallelism of ± 0.000003 (three millionths) inch.

KEY: A small piece of metal imbedded partially in the shaft and partially in the hub to prevent rotation of the gear or pulley on the shaft.

KEYWAY: The slot or recess in the shaft that holds the key.

KNEE: The unit that supports the saddle and table of column and knee type milling machines.

KNURLING: The operation that presses grooved, hardened steel wheels (knurls) into the surface of cylindrical work, rotating in the lathe, to produce rows of uniformly spaced serrations for a better grip or for decorative purposes.

LAND: Metal left between flutes or grooves in drills, reamers, taps, and other cutting tools.

LAPPING: The process of finishing surfaces with a very fine abrasive such as diamond dust or abrasive flours.

LARD OIL: A cutting made from animal fats. It is often mixed with mineral oils to improve the lubricating qualities.

LAY OUT: To locate and scribe points for machining and forming operations.

LEAD: The distance a nut will advance on a screw in one revolution.

LEADER: The blank tape that appears ahead of and after a section of coded tape.

LEAD SCREW: The long precision screw on the front of the lathe bed that is geared to the spindle to transmit motion to the carriage for thread cutting.

LONGITUDINAL MOVEMENT: Lengthwise movement.

MACHINABILITY: The characteristic of a material that describes the ease or difficulty of machining it.

MACHINABILITY INDEX: The table that indicates the degree of ease or difficulty of machining a material. It is based on the machining characteristics of a common steel (AISI B1112 = 100). Magnesium alloy (machinability index = 500 to 2000) is relatively easy to machine. Tool steel (machinability index = 34) is difficult to machine.

MACHINE CONTROL UNIT (MCU): Synonymous with numerical control system in its hardware form. Sometimes referred to as the director or controller.

MACHINE LANGUAGE: The set of symbols and characters, and the rules for combining them, which translates the instructions or information to be processed.

MACHINE TOOL: The name given to that class of machines which, taken as a group, can reproduce themselves.

MACHINIST: A person who is skilled in the use of machine tools and is capable of making complex machine setups.

MAGNAFLUX: A nondestructive inspection technique that makes use of a magnetic field and magnetic particles to locate flaws in materials.

MAGNAGLO: Like fluorescent penetrant inspection but for use on magnetic materials only.

MAGNETIC CHUCK: A device that uses magnetic fields to hold work for machining (grinding).

MAJOR DIAMETER: The largest diameter of a thread measured perpendicular to the axis.

MALLEABILITY: The property of metal that determines its ease in being shaped when subjected to mechanical working (forging, rolling, etc.).

MANDREL: A slightly tapered, hardened steel shaft that supports work that cannot be held by any other method for machining between centers.

MANUSCRIPT: A paper or chart that contains raw N/C data in a form suitable for translation to tape.

MARFORM: A drawing process that forms metal sheet by using a movable steel punch and a rubber headed ram.

MATCH PLATE: Production pattern equipment usually made of metal. It consists of a plate with matching halves of the pattern mounted on each side.

MEMORY: Information held by the machine language in electrical or magnetic form.

MESH: To engage gears to a working contact.

MILL: To remove metal with a rotating cutter on a milling machine.

MILLING MACHINE: A machine that removes metal from the work by means of a rotary cutter.

MINOR DIAMETER: The smallest diameter of a screw thread measured across the roots and perpendicular to the axis. Also known as the ''root diameter.''

MISCELLANEOUS FUNCTION: An on-off function of a machine such as spindle stop, coolant on, clamp, etc.

MITER GEARS: Right angle bevel gears having the same number of teeth. Used to transmit power through shafts at right angles to each other.

MORSE TAPER: A standard taper of approximately 5/8 in. (15.9 mm) per foot. Used on lathe centers, drill shanks, etc.

MUSIC WIRE: A carbon steel wire used to manufacture springs.

NC: Abbreviation for National Coarse series of screw threads.

N/C CODES: A somewhat standardized system of simple codes for controlling the action of machine tools.

NECKING: Machining a groove around a cylindrical shaft.

NF: Abbreviation for the National Fine series of screw threads.

NITRIDING: A case-hardening technique in which a ferrous alloy is heated in an atmosphere of ammonia or in contact with a nitrogenous material to produce surface hardness by the absorption of nitrogen. Quenching is not necessary.

NONFERROUS: Metals containing no iron.

NORMALIZING: A process in which ferrous alloys are heated to approximately 100°F (37.7°C) above the critical temperature range, then cooled slowly in still air at room temperature. This relieves stresses that may have developed during machining, welding, or forming operations.

NUMERICAL CONTROL (N/C): A method of controlling the actions of a machine by numbers. The numbers may be supplied by paper tape, magnetic tape, computer memory, or by other means.

NUMERICAL DATA: Data in which information is expressed by a set of numbers and/or symbols.

O

OBTUSE ANGLE: An angle of more than 90 degrees.

OD: Abbreviation for outside diameter.

OFF-CENTER: Eccentric, not accurate.

OIL HARDENING: Using a mineral oil as a quenching medium in the heat treatment of certain alloys.

OUT-OF-TRUE: Not on center, eccentric, out of alignment.

OUTPUT: Information sent from the control unit.

P

PART PROGRAM: A computer program that describes the operation to be performed by a machine tool.

PEENING: An operation that involves the mechanical working of metal with hammerlike blows.

PERMANENT MOLD: A mold ordinarily made of metal, used for the repeated production of similar castings.

PICKLING: A technique employed in the removal of stains and oxide scales from metal surfaces by immersion in acid baths.

PINION: The smaller of two mating gears.

PITCH: The distance from a point on one thread to a corresponding point on the next thread.

PITCH DIAMETER: The diameter of an imaginary cylinder that would pass through the threads at such points as to make the width of the thread and width of the space equal at the point where they are cut by the cylinder. It is equal to the major diameter of the thread minus the depth of one thread. In gearing it is the diameter of the pitch circle (an imaginary circle located at about midpoint on the teeth) where the teeth of both gears contact each other.

PLASTER MOLD CASTING: A casting process which uses plaster molds in place of sand molds. The castings produced in a plaster mold have a much better surface finish than those cast in sand. Used primarily with aluminum.

PRESS FIT: A class of fit where the interference between the mating parts is enough to require force to press the pieces together. The assembly is considered permanent.

PROGRAMMING: Preparing a detailed sequence of operating instructions for a particular machining operation.

PUNCH CARD: A card of prescribed size and weight capable of receiving coded instructions in the form of punched holes. These cards are handled mechanically, either by a reader that senses the punched codes electrically with wire brushes, or by metal fingers.

PYROMETER: A device for measuring high temperatures. Temperatures are determined by measuring the electric current generated in the thermocouple as it heats up.

Q

QUENCHING: The process of rapid cooling from an elevated temperature by contact with fluids or gases.

QUICK RETURN: The mechanism on some machine tools that can be engaged to return the worktable rapidly to its starting point during the noncutting cycle.

QUILL: The steel tube in the head of some machine tools that encloses the bearings and rotating spindle on which are mounted the cutting tools. It is geared to a handwheel and/or lever that is used to raise or lower the rotating cutting tool on the work surface. The quill can be locked in position.

R

RACK: A flat strip with teeth designed to mesh with teeth on a gear. Used to change rotary motion to reciprocating motion.

RAM: The part of the shaper that moves back and forth and carries the cutting tool.

RAPID TRAVERS: Used to bring the work on the milling table rapidly into cutting position, then quickly return the table to the starting position for the next cut.

READOUT: A numerical display of the actual position of a machine slide or tool.

REAM: To finish a drilled hole to exact size with a reamer.

REAMER: A cutting tool used to produce a smooth, accurate hole by removing a small amount of metal from a drilled hole.

RELIEF: An undercut of offset surface to provide clearance.

RIGHT ANGLE: An angle of 90 degrees.

RISER: A reservoir of molten metal provided to compensate for the contraction of cast metals as they solidify.

ROLLING: Forming and shaping metal by passing it through a series of driven rolls.

ROOT DIAMETER: The smallest of a thread (see MINOR DIAMETER).

ROTARY TABLE: A milling attachment that gives a rotary motion to the piece. It consists of a circular worktable rotated by a handwheel through a worm and worm gear. The hub of the handwheel is graduated in degrees, permitting precise spacing of holes, slots, grooves, etc., around the piece.

ROUGHING: The rapid removal of stock without regard for the quality of the surface finish.

ROW: A path perpendicular to the edge of an N/C tape, along which information may be stored by means of holes.

RUNNER: The channel of a gating system through which molten metal flows from the sprue to the casting and risers.

S

SAE: Society of Automotive Engineers.

SAFE EDGE: The edge of a file on which no teeth have been cut.

SANDBLAST: The process of cleaning castings and metals by blowing sand at them under very high air pressure.

SAND MOLD CASTING: A process which involves pouring molten metal into a cavity that has been formed in a sand mold.

SCALE: Surface oxidation that forms on metal from heating the metal in air.

SCRAPING: The process of removing an exceedingly small portion of the wearing surfaces of machinery by means of scrapers, in order to bring such surfaces to a precision fit and finish not attainable by ordinary filing techniques.

SCRIBE: To draw a line with a scriber or other sharp-pointed tool.

SEQUENCE NUMBER: A series of numerals, programmed on a tape and displayed as a readout. Normally used as a data-location reference.

SETOVER: The distance a lathe tailstock has been offset from the normal centerline of the machine.

Used in one method of taper turning.

SET UP: The positioning of the workpiece, attachments, and cutting tools on a machine tool.

SHEAR SPINNING: A process whereby a metal blank, which may be flat or preformed to some shape, is clamped between the tailstock of the shear spinning machine and a power driven spinning mandrel. The mandrel is the same shape and size as the inside of the finished part, and the metal is forced to flow onto the mandrel by action of the forming rollers.

SHIM: Pieces of sheet metal, available in many thicknesses, that are used between mating parts to provide the proper clearance.

SHRINK FIT: A fit in which the outer member is expanded by heating to permit insertion of the inner member. A tight fit is obtained as the cooling outer member shrinks. A very tight fit must be considered permanent.

SINE SPINNING: Another name for shear spinning.

SINTERING: Bonding metal powders that have been compacted by heating them to a predetermined temperature.

SOFTWARE: Instructions and programs that tell the computer what operations to perform.

SOLDERING: Joining metals by means of a nonferrous filler metal, without fusion of the base metals; normally carried out at temperatures lower than 800 °F (427 °C).

SPINNING: A process that involves making a sheet metal disk into a hollow shape by pressing a tool against the disk forcing it against a rotating form (chuck).

SPLINE: A series of grooves, cut lengthwise, around a shaft or hole.

SPOTFACE: A circular spot machine on the surface of a part to furnish a flat bearing surface for the head of a bolt or nut.

SPRUE HOLE: The opening in a mold into which the molten metal is poured.

SPUR GEAR: A gear having straight teeth cut parallel to the direction of rotation. The most commonly used gears.

STAKING: The joining of two parts by upsetting the metal at their junction.

STANDARD: An accepted base for a uniform system of measurement and quality.

STELLITE: An alloy of cobalt, chromium, and tungsten used to make high speed cutting tools.

STOPS: Projections on the side of the worktable used to disengage automatic power feed. Also known as a dog.

STRADDLE MILL: Using two or more milling cutters to perform several milling operations simultaneously.

STRAIGHTEDGE: A precision tool for checking the accuracy of flat surfaces.

STRAIN: A measure of the change in shape or size

of a body, compared to the original shape or size.

STRESS: The intensity of the internal forces at a point in a body.

STRETCH FORM: A process of forming parts and shapes with large curvatures by stretching the sheet over a form of the desired shape.

SUBROUTINE: A portion of the total N/C program, stored in the computer's memory, and available upon call to accomplish a particular operation.

SUPER FINISH: A surface finish where surface irregularities have been reduced to a few millionths of an inch to produce an exceptionally smooth and long-wearing surface.

SURFACE PLATE: A plate of iron or granite that has been ground, and sometimes lapped, to a smooth, flat surface. It is used to give a base for layout measurements and inspection.

SURFACE ROUGHNESS SCALE: A series of small plates visualizing the degree of roughness for a particular surface. They establish a standard, permitting a machinist or an inspector to compare specified finishes by sight and by touch.

T

TAB: A nonprinting, spacing action on typewriters and tape preparation devices. This code is necessary to the tab sequential format.

TAB SEQUENTIAL FORMAT: The means for identifying a word by the number of tab characters in the block preceding the word.

TANG: The flats or tongue machined on the end of tapered shanks. The tank fits into a slot in the mating part and prevents the taper from rotating in the mating part.

TANTALUM: A metal that is capable of withstanding temperatures in the 2500-4000 °F (1370-2200 °C) range. A metal finding more and more use in the space age.

TAP: The tool used to cut internal threads.

TAPE CONTROL: The control of N/C equipment by means of a 1 in. wide punched tape. Tapes are read by means of photoelectric cells or electrical contacts.

TAPE FEED: A device or mechanism that will feed tape to be read or punched.

TAPER: A piece that increases or decreases in size at a uniform rate to assume a wedge or conical shape.

TAPPING: The operation of producing internal threads with a tap and may be done by hand or machine. Also, the process of removing molten metal from a furnace.

TEMPERING: A sequence in heat-treating consisting of reheating a quench hardened or normalized part to a temperature below the transformation range, then holding it for a enough time to produce the desired properties.

TEMPLATE: A pattern or guide.

TENSILE STRENGTH: The maximum load a piece can support in tension without breaking or failing.

TENSION: The stress due to forces that tend to make a body longer.

THREAD: Cutting a screw thread.

THREAD ROLLING: A technique for applying a thread to a bolt or screw by rolling it between two grooved die plates (one of which is in motion) or between rotating circular rolls.

TITANIUM: A metal used for applications that must be lightweight, high strength, temperature and corrosion resistant. It weighs only about half as much as steel, yet is almost as strong as some commonly used steels.

TOLERANCE: The permissible deviation from a basic dimension.

TOOL CRIB: A room or area in a machine shop where tools and supplies are stored and dispensed as needed.

TOOL FUNCTION: A command identifying a tool and calling for its selection, either automatically or manually.

TOOLROOM: The area or department where tools, jigs, fixtures, and dies are manufactured.

TRAIN: A series of meshed gears.

TRANSDUCER: A device that converts energy from one form to another: electrical to mechanical, mechanical to hydraulic, etc.

TRANSLATION: The changing of information from one form to another.

TRUE: On center.

TUMBLER GEARS: Gears in a gear train that can be adjusted to reverse the direction of rotation of the driven gear.

U

UNIFIED THREADS: A series of screw threads that have been adopted by the United States, Canada, and Great Britain to attain interchangeability of certain screw threads. The revised standard provides greater strength, easier assembly, and longer tool life.

UNIVERSAL CHUCK: A chuck on which all jaws move simultaneously at a uniform rate in order to center round or hexagonal stock automatically.

V

V-BLOCK: Square or rectangular shaped steel blocks with a 90 degree V accurately machined through its center. It is provided with a clamp to hold round stock for drilling, milling, and laying out operations. The blocks come in pairs and are frequently hardened and ground for additional accuracy.

VENTS: Narrow openings in molds that permit the

escape of gases generated during pouring.

VERIFY: To check, usually with an automatic machine, one typing or recording of data against another in order to minimize human error in the data transcription.

VERTICAL MILLING ATTACHMENT: A mechanism that can be attached to some milling machines to convert tham into vertical milling machines.

V-WAYS: The raised portion on machine tool beds that act as bearing surfaces and guide, and align the movable portion of the machine that rides on them. They are shaped like an inverted V.

W

WAYS: The flat or V-shaped bearing surfaces on a machine that align and guide the movable part of the machine that rides on them.

WHEEL DRESSER: A device used to true the face of a grinding wheel.

WORK HARDNESS: The increase in hardness that develops in metal as a result of cold forming.

WORKING DRAWING: A drawing that gives the machinist the necessary information to make and assemble a mechanism.

WRINGING FIT: A fit that is practically metal to metal. It is selective rather than interchangeable, and requires a twisting motion to assemble.

X

X RAY: A nondestructive inspection technique that has become a routine step in the acceptance of parts and materials.

Z

ZYGLO: A fluorescent penetrant inspection technique for detecting flaws in nonmagnetic metals and solids.

ACKNOWLEDGEMENTS

While it would indeed be a pleasant task, it would be impossible for one person to develop the material included in a text of this nature by visiting the industries that use the many metalworking techniques and processes described and observing, studying, and taking photos first hand.

My sincere thanks to those who helped in the gathering of the necessary material, information, and photographs. Their cooperation was heartwarming.

We have endeavored to give credit where due. Any omission was purely accidental.

John R. Walker

USEFUL TABLES

METALS WE USE

SHAPES		LENGTH	HOW MEASURED	* HOW PURCHASED
	Sheet less than 1/4 in. thick	to 144 in.	Thickness x width, widths to 72 in.	Weight, foot, or piece
	Plate more than 1/4 in. thick	to 20 ft.	Thickness x width	Weight, foot, or piece
	Band	to 20 ft.	Thickness x width	Weight, or piece
	Rod	12 to 20 ft.	Diameter	Weight, foot, or piece
	Square	12 to 20 ft.	Width	Weight, foot, or piece
	Flats	Hot rolled 20–22 ft. Cold finished	Thickness x width	Weight, foot, or piece
	Hexagon	12 to 20 ft.	Distance across flats	Weight, foot, or piece
	Octagon	12 to 20 ft.	Distance across flats	Weight, foot, or piece
	Angle	Lengths to 40 ft.	Leg length x leg length x thickness of legs	Weight, foot, or piece
	Channel	Lengths to 60 ft.	Depth x web thickness x flange width	Weight, foot, or piece
	I–beam	Lengths to 60 ft.	Height x web thickness x flange width	Weight, foot, or piece

* Charge made for cutting to other than standard lengths.

PHYSICAL PROPERTIES OF METALS

METAL	SYMBOL	SPECIFIC GRAVITY	SPECIFIC HEAT	MELTING POINT*		LBS. PER CUBIC INCH
				DEG. C	DEG. F.	
Aluminum (Cast)	Al	2.56	.2185	658	1217	.0924
Aluminum (Rolled).	Al	2.71	–	–	–	.0978
Antimony	Sb	6.71	.051	630	1166	.2424
Bismuth	Bi	9.80	.031	271	520	.3540
Boron.	B	2.30	.3091	2300	4172	.0831
Brass.	–	8.51	.094	–	–	.3075
Cadmium.	Cd	8.60	.057	321	610	.3107
Calcium	Ca	1.57	.170	810	1490	.0567
Carbon.	C	2.22	.165	–	–	.0802
Chromium	Cr	6.80	.120	1510	2750	.2457
Cobalt	Co	8.50	.110	1490	2714	.3071
Copper.	Cu	8.89	.094	1083	1982	.3212
Columbium . . .	Cb	8.57	–	1950	3542	.3096
Gold	Au	19.32	.032	1063	1945	.6979
Iridium.	Ir	22.42	.033	2300	4170	.8099
Iron.	Fe	7.86	.110	1520	2768	.2634
Iron (Cast) . . .	Fe	7.218	.1298	1375	2507	.2605
Iron (Wrought) .	Fe	7.70	.1138	1500–1600	2732–2912	.2779
Lead	Pb	11.37	.031	327	621	.4108
Lithium	Li	.057	.941	186	367	.0213
Magnesium . . .	Mg	1.74	.250	651	1204	.0629
Manganese . . .	Mn	8.00	.120	1225	2237	.2890
Mercury	Hg	13.59	.032	38.7	37.7	.4909
Molybdenum. . .	Mo	10.2	.0647	2620	4748	.368
Monel Metal. . .	–	8.87	.127	1360	2480	.320
Nickel	Ni	8.80	.130	1452	2646	.319
Phosphorus . . .	P	1.82	.177	43	111.4	.0657
Platinum.	Pt	21.50	.033	1755	3191	.7767
Potassium. . . .	K	0.87	.170	62	144	.0314
Selenium.	Se	4.81	.084	220	428	.174
Silicon.	Si	2.40	.1762	1427	2600	.087
Silver.	Ag	10.53	.056	961	1761	.3805
Sodium.	Na	0.97	.290	97	207	.0350
Steel	–	7.858	.1175	1330–1378	2372–2532	.2839
Strontium	Sr	2.54	.074	–	–	.0918
Sulphur.	S	2.07	.175	115	235.4	.075
Tantalum	Ta	10.80	–	2850	5160	.3902
Tin	Sn	7.29	.056	232	450	.2634
Titanium.	Ti	5.3	.130	1900	3450	.1915
Tungsten	W	19.10	.033	3000	5432	.6900
Uranium	U	18.70	–	–	–	.6755
Vanadium	V	5.50	–	1730	3146	.1987
Zinc	Zn	7.19	.094	419	786	.2598

* Circular of the Bureau of Standards No. 35, Department of Commerce and Labor.

MACHINE SCREW AND CAP SCREW HEADS

	SIZE	A	B	C	D
FILLISTER HEAD	#8	.260	.141	.042	.060
	#10	.302	.164	.048	.072
	1/4	3/8	.205	.064	.087
	5/16	7/16	.242	.077	.102
	3/8	9/16	.300	.086	.125
	1/2	3/4	.394	.102	.168
	5/8	7/8	.500	.128	.215
	3/4	1	.590	.144	.258
	1	1 5/16	.774	.182	.352
FLAT HEAD	#8	.320	.092	.043	.037
	#10	.372	.107	.048	.044
	1/4	1/2	.146	.064	.063
	5/16	5/8	.183	.072	.078
	3/8	3/4	.220	.081	.095
	1/2	7/8	.220	.102	.090
	5/8	1 1/8	.293	.128	.125
	3/4	1 3/8	.366	.144	.153
ROUND HEAD	#8	.297	.113	.044	.067
	#10	.346	.130	.048	.073
	1/4	7/16	.1831	.064	.107
	5/16	9/16	.236	.072	.150
	3/8	5/8	.262	.081	.160
	1/2	13/16	.340	.102	.200
	5/8	1	.422	.128	.255
	3/4	1 1/4	.526	.144	.320
HEXAGON HEAD	1/4	.494	.170	7/16	
	5/16	.564	.215	1/2	
	3/8	.635	.246	9/16	
	1/2	.846	.333	3/4	
	5/8	1.058	.411	15/16	
	3/4	1.270	.490	1 1/8	
	7/8	1.482	.566	1 5/16	
	1	1.693	.640	1 1/2	
SOCKET HEAD	#8	.265	.164	1/8	
	#10	5/16	.190	5/32	
	1/4	3/8	1/4	3/16	
	5/16	7/16	5/16	7/32	
	3/8	9/16	3/8	5/16	
	7/16	5/8	7/16	5/16	
	1/2	3/4	1/2	3/8	
	5/8	7/8	5/8	1/2	
	3/4	1	3/4	9/16	
	7/8	1 1/8	7/8	9/16	
	1	1 5/16	1	5/8	

TAP DRILL SIZES

Probable Percentage of Full Thread Produced in Tapped Hole
Using Stock Sizes of Drill

Tap	Tap Drill	Decimal Equiv. of Tap Drill	Tap	Tap Drill	Decimal Equiv. of Tap Drill
0-80	56	.0465	8-32	29	.1360
	3/64	.0469		28	.1405
1-64	54	.0550	8-36	29	.1360
	53	.0595		28	.1405
1-72	53	.0595		9/64	.1406
	1/16	.0625	10-24	27	.1440
2-56	51	.0670		26	.1470
	50	.0700		25	.1495
	49	.0730		24	.1520
2-64	50	.0700		23	.1540
	49	.0730		5/32	.1563
3-48	48	.0760		22	.1570
	5/64	.0781	10-32	5/32	.1563
	47	.0785		22	.1570
	46	.0810		21	.1590
	45	.0820		20	.1610
3-56	46	.0810		19	.1660
	45	.0820	12-24	11/64	.1719
	44	.0860		17	.1730
4-40	44	.0860		16	.1770
	43	.0890		15	.1800
	42	.0935		14	.1820
	3/32	.0938	12-28	16	.1770
4-48	42	.0935		15	.1800
	3/32	.0938		14	.1820
	41	.0960		13	.1850
5-40	40	.0980		3/16	.1875
	39	.0995	1/4-20	9	.1960
	38	.1015		8	.1990
	37	.1040		7	.2010
5-44	38	.1015		13/64	.2031
	37	.1040		6	.2040
	36	.1065		5	.2055
6-32	37	.1040		4	.2090
	36	.1065	1/4-28	3	.2130
	7/64	.1094		7/32	.2188
	35	.1100		2	.2210
	34	.1110	5/16-18	F	.2570
	33	.1130		G	.2610
6-40	34	.1110		17/64	.2656
	33	.1130		H	.2660
	32	.1160			

(Standard Tool Co.)

TAP DRILL SIZES—Continued

Probable Percentage of Full Thread Produced in Tapped Hole
Using Stock Sizes of Drill

Tap	Tap Drill	Decimal Equiv. of Tap Drill
5/16-24	H	.2660
	I	.2720
	J	.2770
3/8-16	5/16	.3125
	O	.3160
	P	.3230
3/8-24	21/64	.3281
	Q	.3320
	R	.3390
7/16-14	T	.3580
	23/64	.3594
	U	.3680
	3/8	.3750
	V	.3770
7/16-20	W	.3860
	25/64	.3906
	X	.3970
1/2-13	27/64	.4219
	7/16	.4375
1/2-20	29/64	.4531
9/16-12	15/32	.4688
	31/64	.4844
9/16-18	1/2	.5000
	33/64	.5156
5/8-11	17/32	.5313
	35/64	.5469
5/8-18	9/16	.5625
	37/64	.5781
3/4-10	41/64	.6406
	21/32	.6563
3/4-16	11/16	.6875
7/8-9	49/64	.7656
	25/32	.7812
7/8-14	51/64	.7969
	13/16	.8125
1″-8	55/64	.8594
	7/8	.8750
	57/64	.8906
	29/32	.9063
1″-12	29/32	.9063
	59/64	.9219
	15/16	.9375

Tap	Tap Drill	Decimal Equiv. of Tap Drill
1″-14	59/64	.9219
	15/16	.9375
1 1/8-7	31/32	.9688
	63/64	.9844
	1″	1.0000
	1 1/64	1.0156
1 1/8-12	1 1/32	1.0313
	1 3/64	1.0469
1 1/4-7	1 3/32	1.0938
	1 7/64	1.1094
	1 1/8	1.1250
1 1/4-12	1 5/32	1.1563
	1 11/64	1.1719
1 3/8-6	1 3/16	1.1875
	1 13/64	1.2031
	1 7/32	1.2188
	1 15/64	1.2344
1 3/8-12	1 9/32	1.2813
	1 19/64	1.2969
1 1/2-6	1 5/16	1.3125
	1 21/64	1.3281
	1 11/32	1.3438
	1 23/64	1.3594
1 1/2-12	1 13/32	1.4063
	1 27/64	1.4219

Taper Pipe		Straight Pipe	
Thread	Drill	Thread	Drill
1/8-27	R	1/8-27	S
1/4-18	7/16	1/4-18	29/64
3/8-18	37/64	3/8-18	19/32
1/2-14	23/32	1/2-14	47/64
3/4-14	59/64	3/4-14	15/16
1-11 1/2	1 5/32	1-11 1/2	1 3/16
1 1/4-11 1/2	1 1/2	1 1/4-11 1/2	1 33/64
1 1/2-11 1/2	1 47/64	1 1/2-11 1/2	1 3/4
2-11 1/2	2 7/32	2-11 1/2	2 7/32
2 1/2-8	2 5/8	2 1/2-8	2 21/32
3-8	3 1/4	3-8	3 9/32
3 1/2-8	3 3/4	3 1/2-8	3 25/32
4-8	4 1/4	4-8	4 9/32

DECIMAL EQUIVALENTS OF PARTS OF AN INCH

Fraction	Decimal	Fraction	Decimal
1/64	0.015625	33/64	0.515625
1/32	0.03125	17/32	0.53125
3/64	0.046875	35/64	0.546875
1/16	0.0625	9/16	0.5625
5/64	0.078125	37/64	0.578125
3/32	0.09375	19/32	0.59375
7/64	0.109375	39/64	0.609375
1/8	0.125	5/8	0.625
9/64	0.140625	41/64	0.640625
5/32	0.15625	21/32	0.65625
11/64	0.171875	43/64	0.671875
3/16	0.1875	11/16	0.6875
13/64	0.203125	45/64	0.703125
7/32	0.21875	23/32	0.71875
15/64	0.234375	47/64	0.734375
1/4	0.25	3/4	0.75
17/64	0.265625	49/64	0.765625
9/32	0.28125	25/32	0.78125
19/64	0.296875	51/64	0.796875
5/16	0.3125	13/16	0.8125
21/64	0.328125	53/64	0.828125
11/32	0.34375	27/32	0.84375
23/64	0.359375	55/64	0.859375
3/8	0.375	7/8	0.875
25/64	0.390625	57/64	0.890625
13/32	0.40625	29.32	0.90625
27/64	0.421875	59/64	0.921875
7/16	0.4375	15/16	0.9375
29/64	0.453125	61/64	0.953125
15/32	0.46875	31/32	0.96875
31/64	0.484375	63/64	0.984375
1/2	0.500	1	1.000

DECIMAL EQUIVALENTS NUMBER SIZE DRILLS

No.	Size of Drill in Inches	No.	Size of Drill in Inches	No.	Size of Drill in Inches	No.	Size of Drill in Inches
1	.2280	21	.1590	41	.0960	61	.0390
2	.2210	22	.1570	42	.0935	62	.0380
3	.2130	23	.1540	43	.0890	63	.0370
4	.2090	24	.1520	44	.0860	64	.0360
5	.2055	25	.1495	45	.0820	65	.0350
6	.2040	26	.1470	46	.0810	66	.0330
7	.2010	27	.1440	47	.0785	67	.0320
8	.1990	28	.1405	48	.0760	68	.0310
9	.1960	29	.1360	49	.0730	69	.0292
10	.1935	30	.1285	50	.0700	70	.0280
11	.1910	31	.1200	51	.0670	71	.0260
12	.1890	32	.1160	52	.0635	72	.0250
13	.1850	33	.1130	53	.0595	73	.0240
14	.1820	34	.1110	54	.0550	74	.0225
15	.1800	35	.1100	55	.0520	75	.0210
16	.1770	36	.1065	56	.0465	76	.0200
17	.1730	37	.1040	57	.0430	77	.0180
18	.1695	38	.1015	58	.0420	78	.0160
19	.1660	39	.0995	59	.0410	79	.0145
20	.1610	40	.0980	60	.0400	80	.0135

LETTER SIZE DRILLS

Letter	Size	Letter	Size	Letter	Size
A	0.234	J	0.277	S	0.348
B	0.238	K	0.281	T	0.358
C	0.242	L	0.290	U	0.368
D	0.246	M	0.295	V	0.377
E	0.250	N	0.302	W	0.386
F	0.257	O	0.316	X	0.397
G	0.261	P	0.323	Y	0.404
H	0.266	Q	0.332	Z	0.413
I	0.272	R	0.339		

DRILL SIZES FOR TAPER PINS

Length of Pins	6/0	5/0	4/0	3/0	2/0	0	1	2	3	4	5	6	7	8	9	10
						TAPER PIN AND REAMER SIZE*										
*3/8	50	44	38	32	29	27	21	16	13/64	15/64						
*1/2	51	45	39	33	30	27	5/32	11/64	9	1						
*5/8	52	46	41	34	30	9/64	25	16	10	2						
*3/4	1/16	47	42	7/64	1/8	29	26	19	3/16	7/32	I	P				
*1		49	44	37	31	30	*9/64	20	14	3	H	O	W			
*1 1/4					32	*1/8	*29	*5/32	*16	4	G	5/16	V	29/64		
*1 1/2						*31	*30	*25	*11/64	*13/64	F	N	V	29/64		
*1 3/4						*33	*1/8	*26	*19	*8	E	N	U	29/64	35/64	
*2						*7/64	*31	*28	*21	*11	D	M	U	7/16	35/64	21/32
*2 1/4							*33	*29	*5/32	*3/16	C	M	23/64	7/16	35/64	21/32
*2 1/2						*37	*35	*30	*24	*14	*B	L	T	7/16	17/32	41/64
*2 3/4						*40			*26	*16	*1	9/32	S	27/64	17/32	41/64
*3						*42				*17	*2	J	11/32	27/64	17/32	41/64
*3 1/4										*19	*2	*I	R	27/64	33/64	5/8
*3 1/2											*3	*H	Q	Z	33/64	5/8
*3 3/4											*4	*G	*Q	Z	33/64	5/8
*4											*5	*F	*P	13/32	1/2	39/64
*4 1/4												*1/4	*O	Y	1/2	39/64
*4 1/2												*D	*O	X	1/2	39/64
*4 3/4												*C	*5/16	*25/64	31/64	19/32
*5												*B	*N	*W	31/64	19/32
*5 1/4															15/32	19/32
*5 1/2															*15/32	37/64
*5 3/4															*15/32	37/64
*6															*29/64	37/64

* Hole sizes too small to admit taper pin reamers of standard length. Special, extra length reamers are required for these cases.

TABLE OF CUTTING SPEEDS

MATERIAL	ROUGHING CUT	FINISHING CUT	THREADING
1/8 IN. DIAMETER			
Machine Steel and Bronze	2880 rpm	3200 rpm	1020 rpm
Cast Iron (Annealed)	1920	2560	800
Tool Steel	1600	2400	640
Brass	4800	6400	1600
Aluminum	6400	9600	1600
3/16 IN. DIAMETER			
Machine Steel and Bronze	2880	3200	1120
Tool Steel	1600	2400	640
Brass	4800	6400	1600
Aluminum	6400	9600	1600
1/4 IN. DIAMETER			
Machine Steel and Bronze	1440	1600	560
Tool Steel	800	1200	320
Brass	2400	3200	800
Aluminum	3200	4800	800
3/8 IN. DIAMETER			
Machine Steel and Bronze	960	1066	270
Tool Steel	540	800	220
Brass	1700	2100	530
Aluminum	2130	3200	540
1/2 IN. DIAMETER			
Machine Steel and Bronze	720	800	280
Tool Steel	400	600	160
Brass	1200	1600	400
Aluminum	1600	2400	400
5/8 IN. DIAMETER			
Machine Steel and Bronze	576	640	160
Tool Steel	320	480	200
Brass	960	1280	320
Aluminum	1280	1920	320
3/4 IN. DIAMETER			
Machine Steel and Bronze	500	550	176
Tool Steel	266	400	106
Brass	800	1066	266
Aluminum	1066	1600	266
1 IN. DIAMETER			
Machine Steel and Bronze	360	400	140
Tool Steel	200	300	80
Brass	600	800	200
Aluminum	800	1200	200
1 1/4 IN. DIAMETER			
Machine Steel	288	320	112
Tool Steel	160	240	64
Brass	480	640	160
Aluminum	640	960	160

MATERIAL	ROUGHING CUT	FINISHING CUT	THREADING
1 1/2 IN. DIAMETER			
Machine Steel and Bronze	240	270	67
Tool Steel	134	200	53
Brass	400	534	134
Aluminum	534	800	134
1 3/4 IN. DIAMETER			
Machine Steel and Bronze	205	230	80
Tool Steel	115	170	50
Brass	340	450	115
Aluminum	456	680	115
2 IN. DIAMETER			
Machine Steel	180	200	50
Tool Steel	100	150	40
Brass	300	400	100
Aluminum	400	600	100
2 1/2 IN. DIAMETER			
Machine Steel	141	160	56
Tool Steel	80	120	32
Brass	240	320	80
Aluminum	320	480	80
3 IN. DIAMETER			
Machine Steel	120	140	40
Tool Steel	65	100	40
Brass	200	270	65
Aluminum	270	400	65
3 1/2 IN. DIAMETER			
Machine Steel	103	115	40
Tool Steel	60	85	23
Brass	171	228	57
Aluminum	228	342	57
4 IN. DIAMETER			
Machine Steel	90	100	35
Tool Steel	50	75	20
Brass	150	200	50
Aluminum	200	300	50
4 1/2 IN. DIAMETER			
Machine Steel	80	90	31
Tool Steel	45	67	18
Brass	133	178	45
Aluminum	178	267	45
5 IN. DIAMETER			
Machine Steel	72	80	28
Tool Steel	40	58	16
Brass	120	160	40
Aluminum	160	240	40

**CONVERSION TABLE
METRIC TO ENGLISH**

WHEN YOU KNOW	MULTIPLY BY: * = Exact		TO FIND
	VERY ACCURATE	APPROXIMATE	
LENGTH			
millimetres	0.0393701	0.04	inches
centimetres	0.3937008	0.4	inches
metres	3.280840	3.3	feet
metres	1.093613	1.1	yards
kilometres	0.621371	0.6	miles
WEIGHT			
grains	0.00228571	0.0023	ounces
grams	0.03527396	0.035	ounces
kilograms	2.204623	2.2	pounds
tonnes	1.1023113	1.1	short tons
VOLUME			
millilitres	0.06667	0.2	teaspoons
millilitres	0.03381402	0.067	tablespoons
millilitres		0.03	fluid ounces
litres	61.02374	61.024	cubic inches
litres	2.113376	2.1	pints
litres	1.056688	1.06	quarts
litres	0.26417205	0.26	gallons
litres	0.03531467	0.035	cubic feet
cubic metres	61023.74	61023.7	cubic inches
cubic metres	35.31467	35.0	cubic feet
cubic metres	1.3079506	1.3	cubic yards
cubic metres	264.17205	264.0	gallons
AREA			
square centimetres	0.1550003	0.16	square inches
square centimetres	0.00107639	0.001	square feet
square metres	10.76391	10.8	square feet
square metres	1.195990	1.2	square yards
square kilometres		0.4	square miles
hectares	2.471054	2.5	acres
TEMPERATURE			
Celsius	*9/5 (then add 32)		Fahrenheit

**CONVERSION TABLE
ENGLISH TO METRIC**

WHEN YOU KNOW	MULTIPLY BY: * = Exact		TO FIND
	VERY ACCURATE	APPROXIMATE	
LENGTH			
inches	*25.4		millimetres
inches	*2.54		centimetres
feet	*0.3048		metres
feet	*30.48		centimetres
yards	*0.9144	0.9	metres
miles	*1.609344	1.6	kilometres
WEIGHT			
grains	15.43236	15.4	grams
ounces	*28.349523125	28.0	grams
ounces	*0.028349523125	.028	kilograms
pounds	*0.45359237	0.45	kilograms
short ton	*0.90718474	0.9	tonnes
VOLUME			
teaspoons		5.0	millilitres
tablespoons		15.0	millilitres
fluid ounces	29.57353	30.0	millilitres
cups		0.24	litres
pints	*0.473176473	0.47	litres
quarts	*0.946352946	0.95	litres
gallons	*3.785411784	3.8	litres
cubic inches	*0.016387064	0.02	litres
cubic feet	*0.028316846592	0.03	cubic metres
cubic yards	*0.764554857984	0.76	cubic metres
AREA			
square inches	*6.4516	6.5	square centimetres
square feet	*0.09290304	0.09	square metres
square yards	*0.83612736	0.8	square metres
square miles		2.6	square kilometres
acres	*0.4046564224	0.4	hectares
TEMPERATURE			
Fahrenheit	*5/9 (after subtracting 32)		Celsius

FEEDS AND SPEEDS FOR HIGH SPEED STEEL DRILLS, REAMERS, AND TAPS

Material	Brinell	Drills			Reamers		Taps — S.F.M.			
							Threads per Inch			
		S.F.M.	Point	Feed	S.F.M.	Feed	3-7½	8-15	16-24	25-Up
Aluminum	99–101	200–250	118°	M	150–160	M	50	100	150	200
Aluminum bronze	170–187	60	118°	M	40–45	M	12	25	45	60
Bakelite	....	80	60°–90°	M	50–60	M	50	100	150	200
Brass	192–202	200–250	118°	H	150–160	H	50	100	150	200
Bronze, common	166–183	200–250	118°	H	150–160	H	40	80	100	150
Bronze, phosphor, ½ hard	187–202	175–180	118°	M	130–140	M	25	40	50	80
Bronze, phosphor, soft	149–163	200–250	118°	H	150–160	H	40	80	100	150
Cast iron, soft	126	140–150	90°	H	100–110	H	30	60	90	140
Cast iron, medium soft	196	80–110	118°	M	50–65	M	25	40	50	80
Cast iron, hard	293–302	45–50	118°	L	·67–75	L	10	20	30	40
Cast iron, chilled*	402	15	150°	L	8–10	L	5	5	10	10
Cast steel	286–302	40–50*	118°	L	70–75	L	20	30	40	50
Celluloid	....	100	90°	M	75–80	M	50	100	150	200
Copper	80–85	70	100°	L	45–55	L	40	80	100	150
Drop forgings (steel)	170–196	60	118°	M	40–45	M	12	25	45	60
Duralumin	90–104	200	118°	M	150–160	M	50	100	150	200
Everdur	179–207	60	118°	L	40–45	L	20	30	40	50
Machinery steel	170–196	110	118°	H	67–75	H	35	50	60	85
Magnet steel, soft	241–302	35–40	118°	M	20–25	M	20	40	50	75
Magnet steel, hard*	321–512	15	150°	L	10	L	5	10	15	25
Manganese steel, 7–13%*	187–217	15	150°	L	10	L	15	20	25	30
Manganese copper, 30% Mn.*	134	15	150°	L	10–12	L	..	..	..	..
Malleable iron	112–126	85–90	118°	H	....	H	20	30	40	50
Mild steel, .20–.30 C	170–202	110–120	118°	H	75–85	H	40	55	70	90
Molybdenum steel	196–235	55	125°	M	35–45	M	20	30	35	45
Monel metal	149–170	50	118°	M	35–38	M	8	10	15	20
Nickel, pure*	187–202	75	118°	L	40	L	25	40	50	80
Nickel steel, 3½%	196–241	60	118°	L	40–45	L	8	10	15	20
Rubber, hard	....	100	60°–90°	L	70–80	L	50	100	150	200
Screw stock, C.R.	170–196	110	118°	H	75	H	20	30	40	50
Spring steel	402	20	150°	L	12–15	L	10	10	15	15
Stainless steel	146–149	50	118°	M	30	M	8	10	15	20
Stainless steel, C.R.*	460–477	20	118°	L	15	L	8	10	15	20
Steel, .40 to .50 C	170–196	80	118°	M	8–10	M	20	30	40	50
Tool, S.A.E., and Forging steel	149	75	118°	H	35–40	H	25	35	45	55
Tool, S.A.E., and Forging steel	241	50	125°	M	12	M	15	15	25	25
Tool, S.A.E., and Forging steel*	402	15	150°	L	10	L	8	10	15	20
Zinc alloy	112–126	200–250	118°	M	150–175	M	50	100	150	200

*Use specially constructed heavy duty drills.
Carbon Steel Tools should be run at speeds 40% to 50% of those recommended for High Speed.
Spiral Point Taps may be run at speeds 15% to 20% faster than regular Taps.

DRILL FEED PER REVOLUTION IN INCHES

REAMER FEED

Reference Symbol	Diameter of Drill — Inches					All Diameters
	Under ⅛	⅛ to ¼	¼ to ½	½ to 1	Over 1" Diameter	
L — Light	.001	.002	.003	.005	.006	Use a feed equal to two or three times that recommended for Drills.
M — Medium	.0015	.003	.006	.010	.012	
H — Heavy	.0025	.005	.010	.020	.025	

CONVERSION CHART INCH/mm

Drill No. or Letter		Inch	mm
		.001	0.0254
		.002	0.0508
		.003	0.0762
		.004	0.1016
		.005	0.1270
		.006	0.1524
		.007	0.1778
		.008	0.2032
		.009	0.2286
		.010	0.2540
		.011	0.2794
		.012	0.3048
		.013	0.3302
80	.0135	.014	0.3556
79	.0145	.015	0.3810
	1/64	.0156	0.3969
78		.016	0.4064
		.017	0.4318
77		.018	0.4572
		.019	0.4826
76		.020	0.5080
75		.021	0.5334
		.022	0.5588
74	.0225	.023	0.5842
73		.024	0.6096
72		.025	0.6350
71		.026	0.6604
		.027	0.6858
70		.028	0.7112
		.029	0.7366
69	.0292	.030	0.7620
68		.031	0.7874
	1/32	.0312	0.7937
67		.032	0.8128
66		.033	0.8382
		.034	0.8636
65		.035	0.8890
64		.036	0.9144
63		.037	0.9398
62		.038	0.9652
61		.039	0.9906
		.0394	1.0000
60		.040	1.0160
59		.041	1.0414
58		.042	1.0668
57		.043	1.0922
		.044	1.1176
		.045	1.1430
56	.0465	.046	1.1684
	3/64	.0469	1.1906
		.047	1.1938
		.048	1.2192
		.049	1.2446
		.050	1.2700
		.051	1.2954
55		.052	1.3208
		.053	1.3462
		.054	1.3716
54		.055	1.3970
		.056	1.4224
		.057	1.4478
		.058	1.4732
53	.0595	.059	1.4986
		.060	1.5240
		.061	1.5494
		.062	1.5748
	1/16	.0625	1.5875
52	.0635	.063	1.6002
		.064	1.6256
		.065	1.6510
		.066	1.6764
51		.067	1.7018
		.068	1.7272
		.069	1.7526
50		.070	1.7780
		.071	1.8034
		.072	1.8288
49		.073	1.8542
		.074	1.8796
		.075	1.9050
48		.076	1.9304
		.077	1.9558
47	.0785	.078	1.9812
	5/64	.0781	1.9844
		.0787	2.0000
		.079	2.0066
		.080	2.0320
46		.081	2.0574
45		.082	2.0828
		.083	2.1082
		.084	2.1336
		.085	2.1590
44		.086	2.1844
		.087	2.2098
		.088	2.2352
43		.089	2.2606
		.090	2.2860
		.091	2.3114
		.092	2.3368
42	.0935	.093	2.3622
	3/32	.0937	2.3812
		.094	2.3876
		.095	2.4130
41		.096	2.4384
		.097	2.4638
40		.098	2.4892
39	.0995	.099	2.5146
		.100	2.5400

Drill No. or Letter		Inch	mm
		.101	2.5654
38	.1015	.102	2.5908
		.103	2.6162
37		.104	2.6416
		.105	2.6670
36	.1065	.106	2.6924
		.107	2.7178
		.108	2.7432
		.109	2.7686
	7/64	.1094	2.7781
35		.110	2.7490
34		.111	2.8194
		.112	2.8448
33		.113	2.8702
		.114	2.8956
		.115	2.9210
32		.116	2.9464
		.117	2.9718
		.118	2.9972
		.1181	3.0000
		.119	3.0226
31		.120	3.0480
		.121	3.0734
		.122	3.0988
		.123	3.1242
		.124	3.1496
	1/8	.125	3.1750
		.126	3.2004
		.127	3.2258
		.128	3.2512
30	.1285	.129	3.2766
		.130	3.3020
		.131	3.3274
		.132	3.3528
		.133	3.3782
		.134	3.4036
		.135	3.4290
29		.136	3.4544
		.137	3.4798
		.138	3.5052
		.139	3.5306
28	.1405	.140	3.5560
	9/64	.1406	3.5719
		.141	3.5814
		.142	3.6068
		.143	3.6322
27		.144	3.6576
		.145	3.6830
		.146	3.7084
26		.147	3.7338
		.148	3.7592
25	.1495	.149	3.7846
		.150	3.8100
		.151	3.8354
24		.152	3.8608
		.153	3.8862
23		.154	3.9116
		.155	3.9370
		.156	3.9624
	5/32	.1562	3.9687
22		.157	3.9878
		.1575	4.0000
		.158	4.0132
21		.159	4.0386
		.160	4.0640
20		.161	4.0894
		.162	4.1148
		.163	4.1402
		.164	4.1656
		.165	4.1910
19		.166	4.2164
		.167	4.2418
		.168	4.2672
		.169	4.2926
18	.1635	.170	4.3180
		.171	4.3434
	11/64	.1719	4.3656
		.172	4.3688
17		.173	4.3942
		.174	4.4196
		.175	4.4450
		.176	4.4704
16		.177	4.4958
		.178	4.5212
		.179	4.5466
15		.180	4.5720
		.181	4.5974
14		.182	4.6228
		.183	4.6482
		.184	4.6736
13		.185	4.6990
		.186	4.7244
		.187	4.7498
	3/16	.1875	4.7625
		.188	4.7752
12		.189	4.8006
		.190	4.8260
11		.191	4.8514
		.192	4.8768
		.193	4.9022
10	.1935	.194	4.9276
		.195	4.9530
9		.196	4.9784
		.1969	5.0000
		.197	5.0038
		.198	5.0292
		.199	5.0546
8		.200	5.0800

Drill No. or Letter		Inch	mm
7		.201	5.1054
		.202	5.1308
		.203	5.1562
	13/64	.2031	5.1594
6		.204	5.1816
5	.2055	.205	5.2070
		.206	5.2324
		.207	5.2578
		.208	5.2832
4		.209	5.3086
		.210	5.3340
		.211	5.3594
		.212	5.3848
3		.213	5.4102
		.214	5.4356
		.215	5.4610
		.216	5.4864
		.217	5.5118
		.218	5.5372
	7/32	.2187	5.5562
		.219	5.5626
		.220	5.5880
2		.221	5.6134
		.222	5.6388
		.223	5.6642
		.224	5.6896
		.225	5.7150
		.226	5.7404
		.227	5.7658
1		.228	5.7912
		.229	5.8166
		.230	5.8410
		.231	5.8674
		.232	5.8928
		.233	5.9182
A		.234	5.9436
	15/64	.2344	5.9531
		.235	5.9690
		.236	5.9944
		.2362	6.0000
		.237	6.0198
B		.238	6.0452
		.239	6.0706
		.240	6.0960
		.241	6.1214
C		.242	6.1468
		.243	6.1722
		.244	6.1976
		.245	6.2230
D		.246	6.2484
		.247	6.2738
		.248	6.2992
		.249	6.3246
E	1/4	.250	6.3500
		.251	6.3754
		.252	6.4008
		.253	6.4262
		.254	6.4516
		.255	6.4770
		.256	6.5024
F		.257	6.5278
		.258	6.5532
		.259	6.5786
		.260	6.6040
G		.261	6.6294
		.262	6.6548
		.263	6.6802
		.264	6.7056
		.265	6.7310
	17/64	.2656	6.7469
H		.266	6.7564
		.267	6.7818
		.268	6.8072
		.269	6.8326
		.270	6.8580
		.271	6.8834
I		.272	6.9088
		.273	6.9342
		.274	6.9596
		.275	6.9850
		.2756	7.0000
		.276	7.0104
J		.277	7.0358
		.278	7.0612
		.279	7.0866
		.280	7.1120
K		.281	7.1374
	9/32	.2812	7.1437
		.282	7.1628
		.283	7.1882
		.284	7.2136
		.285	7.2390
		.286	7.2644
		.287	7.2898
		.288	7.3152
		.289	7.3406
L		.290	7.3660
		.291	7.3914
		.292	7.4168
		.293	7.4422
		.294	7.4676
M		.295	7.4930
		.296	7.5184
	19/64	.2969	7.5406
		.297	7.5438
		.298	7.5692
		.299	7.5946
		.300	7.6200

Drill No. or Letter		Inch	mm
		.301	7.6454
N		.302	7.6708
		.303	7.6962
		.304	7.7216
		.305	7.7470
		.306	7.7724
		.307	7.7978
		.308	7.8232
		.309	7.8486
		.310	7.8740
		.311	7.8994
		.312	7.9248
	5/16	.3125	7.9375
		.313	7.9502
		.314	7.9756
		.3150	8.0000
		.315	8.0010
O		.316	8.0264
		.317	8.0518
		.318	8.0772
		.319	8.1026
		.320	8.1280
		.321	8.1534
		.322	8.1788
P		.323	8.2042
		.324	8.2296
		.325	8.2550
		.326	8.2804
		.327	8.3058
		.328	8.3312
	21/64	.3281	8.3344
		.329	8.3566
		.330	8.3820
		.331	8.4074
Q		.332	8.4328
		.333	8.4582
		.334	8.4836
		.335	8.5090
		.336	8.5344
		.337	8.5598
		.338	8.5852
R		.339	8.6106
		.340	8.6360
		.341	8.6614
		.342	8.6868
		.343	8.7122
	11/32	.3437	8.7312
		.344	8.7376
		.345	8.7630
		.346	8.7884
		.347	8.8138
S		.348	8.8392
		.349	8.8646
		.350	8.8900
		.351	8.9154
		.352	8.9408
		.353	8.9662
		.354	8.9916
		.3543	9.0000
		.355	9.0170
		.356	9.0424
		.357	9.0678
T		.358	9.0932
		.359	9.1186
	23/64	.3594	9.1281
		.360	9.1440
		.361	9.1694
		.362	9.1948
		.363	9.2202
		.364	9.2456
		.365	9.2710
		.366	9.2964
		.367	9.3218
U		.368	9.3472
		.369	9.3726
		.370	9.3980
		.371	9.4234
		.372	9.4488
		.373	9.4742
		.374	9.4996
	3/8	.375	9.5250
		.376	9.5504
V		.377	9.5758
		.378	9.6012
		.379	9.6266
		.380	9.6520
		.381	9.6774
		.382	9.7028
		.383	9.7282
		.384	9.7536
		.385	9.7790
W		.386	9.8044
		.387	9.8298
		.388	9.8552
		.389	9.8806
		.390	9.9060
	25/64	.3906	9.9219
		.391	9.9314
		.392	9.9568
		.393	9.9822
		.3937	10.0000
		.394	10.0076
		.395	10.0330
		.396	10.0584
X		.397	10.0838
		.398	10.1092
		.399	10.1346
		.400	10.1600

Drill No. or Letter		Inch	mm
		.401	10.1854
		.402	10.2108
		.403	10.2362
Y		.404	10.2616
		.405	10.2870
		.406	10.3124
	13/32	.4062	10.3187
		.407	10.3378
		.408	10.3632
		.409	10.3886
		.410	10.4140
		.411	10.4394
		.412	10.4648
Z		.413	10.4902
		.414	10.5156
		.415	10.5410
		.416	10.5664
		.417	10.5918
		.418	10.6172
		.419	10.6426
		.420	10.6680
		.421	10.6934
	27/64	.4219	10.7156
		.422	10.7188
		.423	10.7442
		.424	10.7696
		.425	10.7950
		.426	10.8204
		.427	10.8458
		.428	10.8712
		.429	10.8966
		.430	10.9220
		.431	10.9474
		.432	10.9728
		.433	10.9982
		.4331	11.0000
		.434	11.0236
		.435	11.0490
		.436	11.0744
		.437	11.0998
	7/16	.4375	11.1125
		.438	11.1252
		.439	11.1506
		.440	11.1760
		.441	11.2014
		.442	11.2268
		.443	11.2522
		.444	11.2776
		.445	11.3030
		.446	11.3284
		.447	11.3538
		.448	11.3792
		.449	11.4046
		.450	11.4300
		.451	11.4554
		.452	11.4808
		.453	11.5062
	29/64	.4531	11.5094
		.454	11.5316
		.455	11.5570
		.456	11.5824
		.457	11.6078
		.458	11.6332
		.459	11.6586
		.460	11.6840
		.461	11.7094
		.462	11.7348
		.463	11.7602
		.464	11.7856
		.465	11.8110
		.466	11.8364
		.467	11.8618
		.468	11.8872
	15/32	.4687	11.9062
		.469	11.9126
		.470	11.9380
		.471	11.9634
		.472	11.9888
		.4724	12.0000
		.473	12.0142
		.474	12.0396
		.475	12.0650
		.476	12.0904
		.477	12.1158
		.478	12.1412
		.479	12.1666
		.480	12.1920
		.481	12.2174
		.482	12.2428
		.483	12.2682
		.484	12.2936
	31/64	.4844	12.3031
		.485	12.3190
		.486	12.3444
		.487	12.3698
		.488	12.3952
		.489	12.4206
		.490	12.4460
		.491	12.4714
		.492	12.4968
		.493	12.5222
		.494	12.5476
		.495	12.5730
		.496	12.5984
		.497	12.6238
		.498	12.6492
		.499	12.6746
	1/2	.500	12.7000

DIAMETER/THREAD PITCH COMPARISON

INCH SERIES			METRIC			
Size	Dia. (In.)	TPI	Size	Dia. (In.)	Pitch (mm)	TPI (Approx)
			M1.4	.055	.3 .2	85 127
#0	.060	80				
			M1.6	.063	.35 .2	74 127
#1	.073	64 72				
			M2	.079	.4 .25	64 101
#2	.086	56 64				
			M2.5	.098	.45 .35	56 74
#3	.099	48 56				
#4	.112	40 48				
			M3	.118	.5 .35	51 74
#5	.125	40 44				
#6	.138	32 40				
			M4	.157	.7 .5	36 51
#8	.164	32 36				
#10	.190	24 32				
			M5	.196	.8 .5	32 51
			M6	.236	1.0 .75	25 34
1/4	.250	20 28				
5/16	.312	18 24				
			M8	.315	1.25 1.0	20 25
3/8	.375	16 24				
			M10	.393	1.5 1.25	17 20
7/16	.437	14 20				
			M12	.472	1.75 1.25	14.5 20
1/2	.500	13 20				
			M14	.551	2 1.5	12.5 17
5/8	.625	11 18				
			M16	.630	2 1.5	12.5 17
			M18	.709	2.5 1.5	10 17
3/4	.750	10 16				
			M20	.787	2.5 1.5	10 17
			M22	.866	2.5 1.5	10 17
7/8	.875	9 14				
			M24	.945	3 2	8.5 12.5
1"	1.000	8 12				
			M27	1.063	3 2	8.5 12.5

ALUMINUM ASSOCIATION DESIGNATION SYSTEM

NUMBER GROUP	PRINCIPLE ALLOYING ELEMENT
1XXX	Aluminum—100% purity or greater
2XXX	Copper
3XXX	Manganese
4XXX	Silicon
5XXX	Magnesium
6XXX	Magnesium and silicon
7XXX	Zinc
8XXX	An element other than mentioned above
9XXX	Unassigned

The last two digits in this system indicate similar alloys before the present identification was adopted. For example, the alloy 5052 was formerly 52S, 7075 was known as 75S.

The letter "H," when used to designate temper, is followed by two numbers. For example, 3003-H14. The first digit following the "H" denotes the process used to produce the temper. The second number indicates the actual temper (degree of hardness):

- 2 1/4 hard (2/8)
- 4 1/2 hard (4/8)
- 6 3/4 hard (6/8)
- 8 Full hard (8/8)

STEEL CLASSIFICATION TABLES

TABLE I CARBON STEELS

Type	Carbon Content
Low	0.05 to approximately 0.30 percent carbon
Medium	0.30 to approximately 0.60 percent carbon
High	0.60 to approximately 0.95 percent carbon

TABLE II SAE-AISI CODE CLASSIFICATION (First digit)

The first number of the SAE-AISI Code Classification System frequently, but not always, indicates the basic type of steel. When carbon or alloy steel contains the letter "L" in the code, it contains from 0.15 to 0.35 percent led to improve machinability. These steels are also known as free-machining steel. The prefix "E" before the alloy steel designation indicates it is made only by electric furnace.

- 1 — Carbon
- 2 — Nickel
- 3 — Nickel-chrome
- 4 — Molybdenum
- 5 — Chromium
- 6 — Chromium-vanadium
- 7 — Tungsten
- 8 — Nickel-chromium-molybdenum
- 9 — Silicomanganese

COLOR CODES FOR MARKING STEELS

S.A.E. Number	Code Color	S.A.E. Number	Code Color	S.A.E. Number	Code Color	S.A.E. Number	Code Color
	CARBON STEELS	2115	Red and bronze	T1340	Orange and green	3450	Black and bronze
1010	White	2315	Red and blue	T1345	Orange and red	4820	Green and purple
1015	White	2320	Red and blue	T1350	Orange and red		CHROMIUM STEELS
X1015	White	2330	Red and white		NICKEL-CHROMIUM STEELS	5120	Black
1020	Brown	2335	Red and white	3115	Blue and black	5140	Black and white
X1020	Brown	2340	Red and green	3120	Blue and black	5150	Black and white
1025	Red	2345	Red and green	3125	Pink	52100	Black and brown
X1025	Red	2350	Red and aluminum	3130	Blue and green		CHROMIUM-VANADIUM STEELS
1030	Blue	2515	Red and black	3135	Blue and green	6115	White and brown
1035	Blue		MOLYBDENUM STEELS	3140	Blue and white	6120	White and brown
1040	Green	4130	Green and white	X3140	Blue and white	6125	White and aluminum
X1040	Green	X4130	Green and bronze	3145	Blue and white	6130	White and yellow
1045	Orange	4135	Green and yellow	3150	Blue and brown	6135	White and yellow
X1045	Orange	4140	Green and brown	3215	Blue and purple	6140	White and bronze
1050	Bronze	4150	Green and brown	3220	Blue and purple	6145	White and orange
1095	Aluminum	4340	Green and aluminum	3230	Blue and purple	6150	White and orange
	FREE CUTTING STEELS	4345	Green and aluminum	3240	Blue and aluminum	6195	White and purple
1112	Yellow	4615	Green and black	3245	Blue and aluminum		TUNGSTEN STEELS
X1112	Yellow	4620	Green and black	3250	Blue and bronze	71360	Brown and orange
1120	Yellow and brown	4640	Green and pink	3312	Orange and black	71660	Brown and bronze
X1314	Yellow and blue	4815	Green and purple	3325	Orange and black	7260	Brown and aluminum
X1315	Yellow and red	X1340	Yellow and black	3335	Blue and orange		SILICON-MANGANESE STEELS
X1335	Yellow and black		MANGANESE STEELS	3340	Blue and orange	9255	Bronze and aluminum
	NICKEL STEELS	T1330	Orange and green	3415	Blue and pink	9260	Bronze and aluminum
2015	Red and brown	T1335	Orange and green	3435	Orange and aluminum		

INDEX

DATE DUE

MAY 3 1 1995		
NOV 0 6 1998		
AUG 3 1 1999		
DEC 1 7 2001		